Lecture Notes in Computer Scie

Commenced Publication in 1973
Founding and Former Series Editors:
Gerhard Goos, Juris Hartmanis, and Jan van Leeuwen

Marcel Vinícius Medeiros Oliveira
Jim Woodcock (Eds.)

Formal Methods: Foundations and Applications

12th Brazilian Symposium on Formal Methods, SBMF 2009
Gramado, Brazil, August 19-21, 2009
Revised Selected Papers

 Springer

Volume Editors

Marcel Vinícius Medeiros Oliveira
Universidade Federal do Rio Grande do Norte
Departamento de Informática e Matemática Aplicada
Campus Universitário, Lagoa Nova, 59078-900 Natal, RN, Brazil
E-mail: marcel@dimap.ufrn.br

Jim Woodcock
University of York
Department of Computer Science
Heslington, York YO1 7BZ, UK
E-mail: jim@cs.york.ac.uk

Library of Congress Control Number: 2009938928

CR Subject Classification (1998): D.2.4, D.2, F.3, D.3, D.1, K.6, F.4

LNCS Sublibrary: SL 2 – Programming and Software Engineering

ISSN   0302-9743

ISBN   978-3-642-10451-0 Springer Berlin Heidelberg New York

springer.com

© Springer-Verlag Berlin Heidelberg 2009

Typesetting: Camera-ready by author, data conversion by Scientific Publishing Services, Chennai, India
Printed on acid-free paper   SPIN: 12793839   06/3180   5 4 3 2 1 0

Preface

This volume contains the papers presented at SBMF 2009: the Brazilian Symposium on Formal Methods, held during August 19–21, 2009 in Gramado, Rio Grande do Sul, Brazil. The SBMF programme included three invited talks given by Leonardo de Moura (Microsoft Research), Sebastian Uchitel (University of Buenos Aires and Imperial College London), and Daniel Kröning (University of Oxford).

The symposium was accompanied by two short courses:

- Introduction to Software Testing, given by Márcio Eduardo Delamaro (University of São Paulo)
- Formal Models for Automatic Test Case Generation, given by Patrícia Machado and Wilkerson Andrade (Federal University of Campina Grande)

This year, the SBMF symposium had a special section on the Grand Challenge in Verified Software, inspired by recent advances in theory and tool support. Work on the grand challenge started with the creation of a Verified Software Repository with two principal aims:

- To collect a set of verified software components
- To conduct a series of industrial-scale verification experiments with theoretical significance and impact on tool-support

This special session on the grand challenge was dedicated to two pilot projects currently underway:

- *The Flash File Store*. The challenge is to verify the correctness of a fault-tolerant, POSIX-compliant file store implemented on flash memory. Verification issues include dependability guarantees as well as software correctness. Levels of abstraction include requirements specification, software design, executable code, device drivers, and flash translation layers. The challenge was inspired by the requirements for forthcoming NASA space missions.
- *FreeRTOS*. The challenge is to verify the correctness of an open source real-time mini-kernel. FreeRTOS is designed for real-time performance with limited resources, and is accessible, efficient, and popular: it runs on 17 different architectures and is very widely used in many applications. There are over 5,000 downloads per month from SourceForge, making it the repository's 250th most downloaded code (out of 170,000 codes). FreeRTOS presents a significant verification challenge, in spite of it containing less than 2,500 lines of pointer-rich code.

Attendance at the session gave speakers and participants an opportunity to discuss the state of the art in software verification and to discuss open problems in need of solutions. In particular, it helped to contribute to an open agenda of research actions for the grand challenge. The papers in the session are of interest to theoreticians, tool builders, tool users, and industrial practitioners.

SBMF was co-located with SAST 2009, the Brazilian Workshop on Systematic and Automated Software Testing. There was a joint technical session on formal aspects of testing, and a joint panel on Academic and Industrial Research Directions in Software Verification.

SBMF was organized by the Instituto de Informática at the Federal University of Rio Grande do Sul (UFRGS) under the auspices of the Brazilian Computer Society (SBC). It was sponsored by the following organizations:

- CNPq, the Brazilian Scientific and Technological Research Council
- CAPES, the Brazilian Higher Education Funding Council
- Banrisul, the Rio Grande do Sul state bank
- The Governor of the State of Rio Grande do Sul
- Microsoft Research
- The Federal University of Rio Grande do Norte (UFRN)
- The University of York

The deliberations of the Programme Committee and the preparation of these proceedings were handled by EasyChair, which made our lives much easier.

September 2009   Marcel Vinícius Medeiros Oliveira
                                                    James Charles Paul Woodcock

Conference Organization

Programme Chairs

Marcel Oliveira and Jim Woodcock

Programme Committee

Aline Andrade
David Aspinall
Luis Barbosa
Roberto Bigonha
Michael Butler
Andrew Butterfield
Ana Cavalcanti
Andrea Corradini
Jim Davies
David Déharbe
Ewen Denney
Clare Dixon
Adolfo Duran
Jorge Figueiredo
Leo Freitas
Rohit Gheyi
Rolf Hennicker
Juliano Iyoda
Moonzoo Kim

Luis Lamb
Gerald Lüttgen
Patrícia Machado
Ana Melo
Anamaria Moreira
Álvaro Moreira
Arnaldo Moura
Alexandre Mota
David Naumann
Daltro Nunes
José Nuno Oliveira
Alberto Pardo
Alexandre Petrenko
Leila Ribeiro
Augusto Sampaio
Leila Silva
Adenilso Simão
Willem Visser
Heike Wehrheim

Steering Committee

Ana C. V. de Melo (USP)
Jim Woodcock (University of York)
Leila Ribeiro (UFRGS)
Marcel Oliveira (UFRN)
Patrícia Machado (UFCG)

Organizing Committee

Álvaro Freitas Moreira (Chair; UFRGS)
Cláudio Fuzitaki (UFRGS)

Fabiane Cristine Dillenburg (UFRGS)
Germano Caumo (UFRGS)
Luciana Foss (UFRGS)
Lucio Mauro Duarte (UFRGS)
Olinto E. David de Oliveira (UFRGS)

Table of Contents

Speeding Up Simulation of SystemC
Using Model Checking⋆

Nicolas Blanc[1] and Daniel Kroening[2]

[1] ETH Zurich, Switzerland
[2] Oxford University, Computing Laboratory, UK

Abstract. SystemC is a system-level modeling language that offers a
wide range of features to describe concurrent systems. The SystemC standard permits simulators to implement a deterministic thread scheduling
policy, which often hides concurrency-related design flaws. We present a
novel compiler for SystemC that integrates a formal race analysis based
on Model Checking techniques. The key insight to make the formal analysis scalable is to apply the Model Checker only to small partitions of
the model. Our compiler produces a simulator that uses the race analysis information at runtime to perform partial-order reduction, thereby
eliminating context switches that do not affect the result of the simulation. Experimental results show simulation speedups of one order of
magnitude and better.

1 Introduction

Time-to-market requirements have rushed the Electronic Design Automation
(EDA) industry towards design paradigms that require a very high level of abstraction. This high level of abstraction can shorten the design time by enabling
the creation of fast executable verification models. This way, bugs in the design can be discovered early in the design process. As part of this paradigm,
an abundance of C-like system design languages has emerged. A key feature is
joint modeling of both the hardware and software component of a system using a
language that is well-known to engineers. A promising candidate for an industry
standard is SystemC.

SystemC offers a wide range of language features such as hierarchical design
by means of a hierarchy of modules, arbitrary-width bit-vector types, and concurrency with related synchronization mechanisms. SystemC permits different
levels of abstraction, from a very high-level specification with big-step transactions down to the gate level. The execution model of SystemC is driven by *events*,
which start or resume processes. In addition to communication via shared variables, processes can exchange information through predefined communication
channels such as signals and FIFOs.

⋆ This paper is an extended version of a conference paper that appeared at ICCAD
2008 [1]. This research is supported by ETH research grant TH-21/05-1 and by the
Semiconductor Research Corporation (SRC) under contract no. 2006-TJ-1539.

M.V.M. Oliveira and J. Woodcock (Eds.): SBMF 2009, LNCS 5902, pp. 1–16, 2009.
ⓒ Springer-Verlag Berlin Heidelberg 2009

Technically, SystemC programs rely on a C++ template library. SystemC modules are therefore plain C++ classes, which are compiled and then linked to a runtime scheduler. This provides a simple yet efficient way to simulate the behavior of the system. Methods of a module may be designated as *threads* or *processes*. Interleaving between those threads is performed at pre-determined program locations, e.g., at the end of a thread or when the wait() method is called. When multiple threads are ready for execution, the ordering of the threads is nondeterministic. Nevertheless, the SystemC standard allows simulators to adopt a deterministic scheduling policy. Consequently, simulators can avoid problematic schedules, which often prevents the discovery of concurrency-related design flaws.

When describing synchronous circuits at the register transfer level, system designers can prevent races by restricting inter-process communication to deterministic communication channels such as *sc_signals*. However, the elimination of races from the high-level model is often not desirable: In practice, system designers often use constructs that yield races in order to model nondeterministic choices implicit in the design. In particular, models containing standard transaction-level modeling (TLM) interfaces are frequently subject to race phenomena. TLM designs usually consist of agents sharing communication resources and competing for access to them. An example is a FIFO with two clock domains: the races model the different orderings of the clock events that can arise.

Contribution. Due to the combinatorial explosion of process interleavings, testing methods for concurrent software alone are unlikely to detect bugs that depend on subtle interleavings. Therefore, we propose to employ formal methods to statically pre-compute thread-dependency relations and predicates that predict race conditions, and to use this information subsequently during the simulation run to prune the exploration of concurrent behaviors. There are two possible ways of exploiting the information:

1. In general, proving or refuting process independence requires precise static analysis. From a designer perspective, the statically computed dependency relations between the threads provide key insights into potential races.
2. The statically computed race conditions improve the performance of partial order reduction, which results in a greatly reduced number of interleavings. The remaining interleavings can then be explored exhaustively, which is a valuable validation aid.

We have implemented this technique in SCOOT [2], a novel research compiler for SystemC. The static computation of the race conditions relies on a Model Checker. The technique we propose is independent of the specific formal engine. We have performed our experiments using SATABS [3], a SAT-based Model Checker implementing predicate abstraction, and CBMC, a SAT-based bounded Model Checker. Our experimental results indicate that strong race conditions can be computed statically at reasonable cost, and result in a simulation speedup of a factor of ten or better.

Related Work

Concurrent threads with nondeterministic interleaving semantics may give rise to *races*. A data race is a special kind of race that occurs in a multi-threaded application when several processes enter a critical section simultaneously [4]. Flanagan and Freud use a formal type system to detect race-condition patterns in Java [5]. *Eraser* is a dynamic data-race detector for concurrent applications [6]. It uses binary rewriting techniques to monitor shared variables and to find failures of the locking discipline at runtime. Other tools, such as *RacerX* [7] and *Chord* [8], rely on classic pointer-analysis techniques to statically detect data races. Data races can also occur in SystemC if processes call synchronization routines while holding shared resources.

Model Checkers are frequently applied to the verification of concurrent applications, and SystemC programs are an instance; see [9] for a survey on software Model Checking. Vardi identifies formal verification of SystemC models as a research challenge [10]. Prior applications of formal analysis to SystemC or similar languages are indeed limited. We therefore briefly survey recent advances in the application of such tools to system-level software. *DDVerify* is a tool for the verification of Linux device drivers [11]. It places the modules into a concurrent environment and relies on SATABS for the verification. *KISS* is a tool for the static analysis of multi-threaded programs written in C [12]. It reduces the verification of a concurrent application to the verification of a sequential program with only one stack by bounding the number of context switches. The reduction never produces false alarms, but is only complete up to a specific number of context switches. *KISS* uses SLAM [13], a Model Checker based on *Predicate Abstraction* [14,15], to verify the sequential model.

Verisoft is a popular tool for the systematic exploration of the state space of concurrent applications [16] and could, in principle, be adapted to SystemC. The execution of processes is synchronized at *visible operations*, which are system calls monitored by the environment. *Verisoft* systematically explores the schedules of the processes without storing information about the visited states. Such a method is, therefore, referred to as a *state-less search*. *Verisoft*'s support for partial-order reduction relies exclusively on dynamic information to achieve the reduction. In a recent paper, Sen et al. propose a modified SystemC-Scheduler that aims to detect design flaws that depend on specific schedules [17]. The scheduler relies on dynamic information only, i.e., the information has to be computed during simulation, which incurs an additional run-time overhead. In contrast, SCOOT statically computes the conditions that guarantee independence of the transitions. The analysis is very precise, as it is based on a Model Checker, and SCOOT is therefore able to detect opportunities for partial-order reduction with little overhead during simulation.

Flanagan and Godefroid describe a state-less search technique with support for partial-order reduction [18]. Their method runs a program up to completion, recording information about inter-process communication. Subsequently, the trace is analyzed to detect alternative transitions that might lead to different behaviors. Alternative schedules are built using *happens-before* information, which defines a partial-order relation on all events of all processes in the system [19]. The procedure explores alternative schedules until all relevant traces are discovered. Helmstetter et al. present a partial-order reduction technique for SystemC [20]. Their approach relies on dynamic information and is similar to Flanagan and Godefroid's technique [18]. Their simulator starts with a random execution, and observes visible operations to detect dependency between the processes and to fork the execution. Our technique performs a powerful analysis statically that is able to discover partial-order reduction opportunities not detectable using only dynamic information.

Kundu et al. propose to compute read/write dependencies between SystemC processes using a path-sensitive static analysis [21]. At runtime, their simulator starts with a random execution and detects dependent transitions using static information. The novelty of our approach is to combine conventional static analysis with Model Checking to compute sufficient conditions over the global variables of the SystemC model that guarantee commutativity of the processes.

Wang et al. introduce the notion of *guarded independence* for pairs of transitions [22]. Their idea is to compute a condition (or guard) that holds in the states where two specific transitions are independent. Our contribution in this context is to compute these conditions for SystemC using a Model Checker.

2   Partial-Order Reduction for SystemC

In this section, we provide a brief introduction to the concurrency model of SystemC and describe the challenges of applying partial-order reduction in the context of SystemC.

2.1   An Overview of the Concurrency Model of SystemC

The dominating concurrency model for software permits asynchronous interleavings between threads, that is, running processes are preempted. SystemC is different as it is mainly designed for modeling synchronous systems. Its scheduler has a *co-operative multitasking* semantics, meaning that the execution of processes is serialized by explicit calls to a `wait()` method, and that threads are not preempted.

The SystemC scheduler tracks simulation time and *delta cycles*. The simulation time is a positive integer value (the clock). Delta cycles are used to stabilize the state of the system. A delta cycle consists of three phases: *evaluate*, *update*, and *notify*.

1. The evaluation phase selects a process from the set of runnable processes and triggers or resumes its execution. The process runs immediately up to the point where it returns or invokes the *wait* function. The evaluation phase is iterated until the set of runnable processes is empty. The SystemC standard allows simulators to choose any runnable process, as long as the policy is consistent between runs.

Program 1. A SystemC module with a race condition

```
SC_MODULE(m) {
    sc_clock clk;  int pressure;

    void guard() {
        if(pressure == PMAX)  pressure = PMAX-1;
    }

    void increment(){ pressure++; }

    SC_CTOR(m) {
        SC_METHOD(guard);  sensitive << clk;
        SC_METHOD(increment);  sensitive << clk;
    }
};
```

2. In order to simulate synchronous executions, processes can delay change-of-state effects by scheduling *update requests*. After the evaluation phase terminates, the kernel executes any pending update request. This is called the *update phase*. Signal assignments are typically implemented using the update mechanism. Therefore, signals keep their value for an entire evaluation phase.
3. Finally, during the *delta-notification phase*, the scheduler determines which processes are sensitive to events that have occurred, and adds all such processes to the set of runnable processes.

The scheduler executes delta cycles until the set of runnable processes is empty at the beginning of the evaluation phase. Subsequently, it updates the simulation time and notifies processes waiting for the time event.

2.2 A Motivating Example

Program 1 serves as running example and illustrates the need for a combination of Model Checking and partial-order reduction. The module m declares two processes *guard* and *increment*. The process *guard* watches the value of shared variable *pressure*, which shall not exceed the value $PMAX$ and is incremented by process *increment*. Both processes are sensitive to the clock signal *clk*. The semantics of the SystemC scheduler guarantees that a method process is executed without interruption up to the point where it returns. Thus, the scheduler has to choose either the scheduling sequence (*guard*; *increment*) or (*increment*; *guard*) each time the clock is updated. Consequently, the pressure can exceed the limit if its value reaches $PMAX$ and the process *increment* is triggered before *guard*. It is clear that the number of traces grows exponentially with the number of clock cycles. As a result, systematic exploration of all interleavings rapidly becomes unmanageable, and the bad behavior might go unnoticed.

A conventional static analysis can discover that *guard* reads the pressure and that *increment* modifies the pressure, concluding that the processes are indeed dependent and that all interleavings must be explored. Similarly, a conventional dynamic analysis would always detect a read/write dependency between *guard* and *increment*, forcing the simulator to execute all schedules. However, such analyses fail to detect that *guard* and *increment* are commutative in most cases. Our tool uses a Model Checker to compute the weakest predicate over the pre-state variables that guarantees the absence of races between the processes. In this example, it is easy to see that the execution of *increment* and *guard* is commutative if and only if

$$pressure \neq PMAX - 1 \quad \wedge \quad pressure \neq PMAX$$

holds. SCOOT generates a simulator for the systematic exploration of the state space that checks this condition at runtime to avoid exploring redundant schedules.

2.3   Background on Partial-Order Reduction

Partial-order reduction is a technique to explore the state space of concurrent systems in a way that preserves the soundness of the verification result [23,24,25]. The key idea is to exploit commutativity of transitions to obtain a subset of all possible interleavings from a state such that the reduced state graph retains a representative behavior for each behavior that is removed. SCOOT uses partial-order reduction to generate a simulator that explores only necessary interleavings. We briefly survey the standard definitions from the literature in this section [25].

The literature distinguishes between partial-order reduction based on *persistent sets* and reduction based on *sleep sets*. The two approaches are orthogonal and achieve better results when combined. Both techniques compute a subset of the runnable transitions for each visited state and restrict future exploration to transitions in this set.

We denote the set of states and the set of processes of a SystemC model by S and θ, respectively. We denote the set of enabled (runnable) processes (transitions) in a state s by $Enabled(s)$, i.e., $Enabled$ is a mapping from S to $\mathscr{P}(\theta)$. Processes are relations between states. We write $s \xrightarrow{\alpha} t$ to denote that the state changes from s to t by executing process α.

Definition 1. *[22] Two transitions α and β are guarded independent with respect to a guard $\phi \subseteq S$ if and only if for all $s \in \phi$ and $t \in S$ the following hold:*

1. $\alpha \in Enabled(s) \wedge s \xrightarrow{\alpha} t \Rightarrow$
   $\beta \in Enabled(s) \Leftrightarrow \beta \in Enabled(t)$
2. $\beta \in Enabled(s) \wedge s \xrightarrow{\beta} t \Rightarrow$
   $\alpha \in Enabled(s) \Leftrightarrow \alpha \in Enabled(t)$
3. $\alpha, \beta \in Enabled(s) \Rightarrow$
   $\langle s, t \rangle \in \alpha \circ \beta \Leftrightarrow \langle s, t \rangle \in \beta \circ \alpha$

The first two conditions guarantee that α and β cannot disable nor enable each other in s, while the third condition requires α and β to be commutative in s.

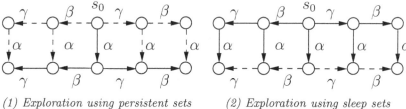

(1) *Exploration using persistent sets*   (2) *Exploration using sleep sets*

Fig. 1. Example of partial-order reduction using persistent sets (1) and sleep sets (2). The reduced state graph contains only the transitions depicted with solid lines.

SCOOT uses Model Checking to compute the condition ϕ. Transitions α and β are *independent in s* if and only if α, β are guarded independent with respect to the guard $\{s\}$ [25].

Definition 2. *[25] Let $D \subseteq \theta \times \theta$ be a symmetric and reflexive relation over the transitions of the system. The relation D is a valid dependency relation for θ if and only if $(\alpha, \beta) \notin D$ implies that α, β are independent in all reachable states.*

Similar to [21], SCOOT uses a data-flow analysis in order to compute an over-approximating dependency relation.

Definition 3. *[25] Let (S, S_0, θ) be a transition system, and $s_0 \in S$ denote one of its states. A set of transitions $T \subset Enabled(s_0)$ is persistent in s_0 if and only if for all $\beta \in T$ and all sub-traces $s_0 \xrightarrow{\alpha_0} s_1 \xrightarrow{\alpha_1} s_2...s_n \xrightarrow{\alpha_n} s_{n+1}$ obtained from transitions $\alpha_i \notin T$, β and α_i are independent in s_i.*

The Definition 3 is, thus, concerned about what can happen in the *future*. The persistent-set technique computes a persistent set of runnable transitions in each visited state and restricts the exploration to transitions in this set only. Persistent sets are typically computed using information from a preliminary static analysis.

Figure 1.1 illustrates the effects of the persistent-set technique. In state s_0, the exploration uses the persistent set $T = \{\alpha\}$ to avoid visiting some of the states. In contrast, the sleep-set technique maintains a set of runnable transitions that can be skipped during the exploration (the sleep set). The method is concerned with branching information from the *past*. Figure 1.2 shows a typical exploration using sleep sets. Unlike the previous approach, the sleep-set technique only reduces the number of explored transitions and has no effect on the number of explored states. The exploration backtracks early when the sleep set contains all runnable transitions.

3   Implementation

3.1   Overview of Scoot

Figure 2 shows an overview of SCOOT. We use an in-house C++ front-end to translate the SystemC source files into a control flow graph (CFG). The

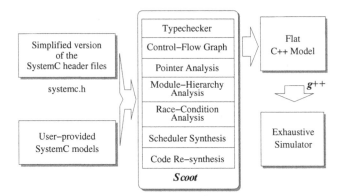

Fig. 2. Overview of SCOOT

front-end of SCOOT accepts a large subset of C++ including inheritance, over-loading, virtual functions, and many forms of templates.

SCOOT abstracts implementation details of the SystemC library by using simplified header files that declare only relevant aspects of the API and omit the actual implementation. Subsequently, SCOOT uses static analysis techniques to discover the module hierarchy, the sensitivity list of processes, and the port bindings. The next step is the computation of race conditions for each pair of processes, which is explained in Sec. 3.3. SCOOT then generates the code for the exhaustive simulator. Finally, SCOOT translates the CFG back to a flat C++ program, which no longer requires the SystemC library. We use $g++$ to compile the C++ file and to obtain an executable simulator.

We forbid dynamic creation of processes and dynamic modifications of sensitivity lists (*next_trigger* functions). The support for SystemC currently comprises static creation of processes, static sensitivity lists, waiting using sensitivity lists, waiting for a specific event, waiting for a certain amount of time, immediate notification, delta notification, time notification, and communication channels such as *sc_signals*, *sc_fifos*, and *tlm_fifos*. We have a broad support for the general features of C++; e.g., our support for STL container classes is described in [26].

3.2 A Scheduler with Partial-Order Reduction

Algorithm 1 is SCOOT's implementation of the evaluation phase. In contrast to the related work, *evaluation_phase* schedules runnable processes using information *statically* collected to reduce the number of interleavings explored. We are not aware of tools that compute equally strong conditions statically.

The evaluation phase terminates once the set of runnable processes is empty. The algorithm performs partial-order reduction using persistent sets and sleep sets, and is a variation of techniques presented by Godefroid [25]. On line 3, the procedure calls the function *runnable()* to check if the set of runnable processes is empty before proceeding to the next iteration.

Algorithm 1. Evaluation Phase: the commutativity condition checked by commutative(p_i, p_j) is a predicate over states computed statically at compile-time

---

```
       void evaluation_phase ()
2        Set sleeps := ∅;
         while (runnable ()≠∅ ) do
4            persistents := get_pers ();
             awakes := persistents \ sleeps;
6            if(awakes= ∅) then exit (0);
             Map next_sleeps; // Process −> Set
8            for all (Process pᵢ ∈ awakes) do
                 for all (Process pⱼ ∈ sleep) do
10                   if (commutative(pᵢ,pⱼ))
                         next_sleeps [pᵢ] := next_sleeps [pᵢ] ∪ {pⱼ};
12               end for
                 sleep := sleep∪ {pᵢ};
14           end for
             Process p := nondet_select (awakes);
16           run (p);
             sleeps := next_sleeps [p];
18       end while
```

At simulation time, the scheduler calls *get_pers* to compute the set *persistents* of persistent processes. The subsequent part of the algorithm uses the set *sleeps*, declared outside the main loop on line 2, to perform partial-order reduction. On line 5, the set *awakes* consists of the persistent processes *not* in *sleeps*. If the set of awaken processes is empty (line 6), then other traces are covering all subsequent behaviors, and therefore, the simulator stops the execution. Otherwise, the scheduler computes the sleep sets for the next iteration using the map *next_sleeps*, which maps processes to a set of processes (lines 7–14). One line 10, the call to *commutative* returns *true* if the processes p_i and p_j are commutative in the current state. The scheduler reduces the computation of conditional independence to the computation of commutativity conditions by considering that all the processes are always enabled – if $\rho \notin Enabled(s)$, then this is interpreted as $s \xrightarrow{\rho} s$. This way, two processes are independent in the current state if and only if they are commutative in this state. SCOOT relies on Model Checking to compute a conservative condition that guarantees commutativity of the processes in the current state; the details of this pre-computation are presented in the following subsection. In contrast, traditional approaches need to rely on either executing the processes to determine which transitions are independent in the current state, which adds overhead, or on an imprecise data-flow analysis.

Finally, in lines 15–17, the scheduling algorithm nondeterministically runs a process from *awakes* and computes the sleep set of the next iteration.

3.3   Computing the Process Commutativity Conditions

We present an iterative technique to compute the commutativity condition for a given pair of processes p_1 and p_2 based on formal analysis. The condition is checked during simulation by Alg. 1. In general, SystemC processes need not terminate, and thus computing the strongest possible commutativity condition for a given pair of processes p_1 and p_2 is undecidable. We compute a conservative approximation by applying a Model Checker to the harness given as Program 2.

Program 2. Harness for the analysis of race conditions for a given pair of processes p1 and p2. The pre-condition ϕ is true initially, and is then iteratively strengthened

---

```
     assume (φ);
 2   s0 := current_state;
     p1 (); p2 ();
 4   s1,2 := current_state;
     current_state := s0;
 6   p2 (); p1 ();
     s2,1 := current_state;
 8   assert (s1,2 ≠ s2,1);
```

The basic idea of the harness is to run $p_1(); p_2()$, and compare the result with the result of running $p_2(); p_1()$ on the same initial state. The harness operates as follows: Initially, ϕ is set to *true*. The assume statement in the first line restricts the search to states that satisfy ϕ. Then the values of the visible variables are stored in s_0, the pair of processes $p_1(); p_2()$ is run, and the state is stored in $s_{1,2}$. The state is restored to s_0, and $p_2(); p_1()$ is run. The state is stored in $s_{2,1}$.

SCOOT passes the harness to a Model Checker to check the reachability of the last line, which is modeled by means of an assertion. If the Model Checker returns a counterexample, we have a trace π with an initial state satisfying the initial condition ϕ, passing through both processes, and ending in a state that violates the assertion. The path therefore begins in a state in which the two processes are commutative. SCOOT then computes the weakest precondition of $s_{1,2} = s_{2,1}$ alongside that path. Let P_π denote this condition. The executions of $p_1(); p_2()$ and $p_2(); p_1()$ from a state s terminate and yield an equal state if s satisfies P_π. Consequently, P_π is an under-approximation of the commutativity condition for p_1 and p_2. At this point, SCOOT strengthens ϕ using $\neg P_\pi$, yielding ϕ'. This removes the trace π and any trace similar to π that goes through the same control locations. SCOOT iterates this process until the Model Checker stops reporting counterexamples. At this point, the predicate $P = \bigvee_\pi P_\pi$ represents the weakest condition such that the executions of $p_1(); p_2()$ and $p_2(); p_1()$ terminate and that p_1 and p_2 are commutative.

In practice, we observe that the number of facts that SCOOT tracks during the computation of the weakest precondition of $s_{1,2} = s_{2,1}$ may explode. Therefore, instead of comparing the entire state vectors $s_{1,2}$ and $s_{2,1}$, we restrict the comparison to the variables written by the processes. This set is determined by means of a standard data-flow analysis.

In the following, we elaborate on our integration of the strengthening loop into SatAbs, a Model Checker based on predicate abstraction. Note that our approach is independent of the particular Model Checking engine. The general idea can be extended in different directions. As an example, we can adapt the strengthening loop to operate on infinite traces using a Model Checker for liveness properties such as Terminator [27], or we can replace the Model Checker with a testing engine to discover terminating traces at the cost of code-coverage guarantees.

Strengthening Using Predicate Abstraction. *Predicate Abstraction* is a technique that abstracts a transition system by mapping sets of concrete states to a new, smaller abstract state space in a way that conserves the relevant behaviors of the system [14,15]. Each predicate in the abstract model is represented by a Boolean variable, while the original variables are removed. The abstract program is created using existential abstraction, which is a conservative abstraction for reachability properties. If the property holds on the abstract model, it also holds on the original program. In case a trace in the abstract model violates the property, the feasibility of the counterexample must be tested in the concrete model. If the counterexample can be simulated on the original program, it is reported to the user. The counterexample is called *spurious* if it does not correspond to a concrete trace. In that case, a refinement procedure adds new predicates in a way that removes the spurious trace. This is automated by *Counterexample Guided Abstraction Refinement* (CEGAR) [28] and promoted by the Model Checker SLAM [13]. Predicate abstraction has been applied to SpecC [29] and SystemC [30]. Figure 3 shows the integration of our technique into SatAbs. After strengthening, SatAbs retains the abstract model obtained during previous iterations.

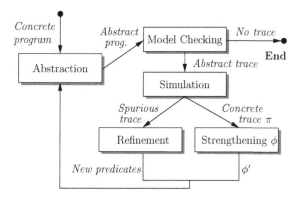

Fig. 3. Iterative computation of the process commutativity condition using predicate abstraction

4 Experimental Evaluation

In this section, we evaluate the benefits of integrating our partial-order reduction into a simulator that examines all schedules exhaustively using a backtracking search. The experiments that we present are difficult instances. Commutativity of processes depends on control flow and data, and the computation of the condition is susceptible to the state-space explosion problem. We obtained our results on a 3GHz Linux machine. We make the benchmarks and the tool available for experimentation by other researchers at *www.cprover.org/scoot/*.

4.1 The Running Example

We continue our running example (Program 1). Figure 4 depicts the number of explored transitions as a function of the number of simulation steps using persistent and sleep sets *(P+S)* and without partial-order reduction *(No-POR)*. We set *PMAX* to *10*. Our simulator performs a state-less search, that is, the simulator replays transitions to backtrack. Those transitions are counted only once. With this technique, the number of transitions explored during simulation grows quadratically with the number of steps, whereas without partial-order reduction, the curve grows exponentially. As mentioned before, a conventional dynamic analysis would always detect a read/write dependency between the two processes, forcing the simulator to explore all schedules.

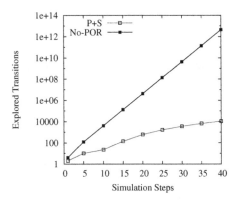

Fig. 4. Number of transitions explored at runtime as a function of the number of simulation steps

4.2 State Machines

We use two different benchmarks to evaluate the benefit of statically computed race conditions. The first benchmark (B1) consists of a synchronous model with three dependent processes. One process plays the role of a server waiting for requests, while the other two compete for access to the service. Program 3 contains the skeleton of the benchmark. When triggered, the clients and the server execute

Program 3. Skeleton of Benchmark B1

```
   bool locked; int op;
 2 void process_client() {
   if(!locked){ op=get_pid(); locked=true;}
 4 }
   void process_server(){
 6   switch(state) {
     ...
 8   case Idle: {switch(op) {...} break;}
     case End: {state = Idle; locked = false;}
10   }
   }
```

functions *process_client* and *process_server*, respectively. The clients communicate with the server via two shared variables *op* and *locked*. If *locked* is set, then the server is busy processing the request *op*. Otherwise, the clients compete for access to the service. The processes are sensitive to a clock. Figure 5 compares the number of explored transitions, and the total exploration time as a function of the number of simulation steps. We present results without partial-order reduction (*No-POR*) and using a combination of sleep sets and persistent sets (*P+S*). The exploration time is limited to thirty minutes (1800 seconds).

The results indicate that partial-order reduction using statically computed commutativity conditions is able to significantly reduce both the number of explored transitions and the exploration time by about two to three orders of magnitude. With partial-order reduction, the simulator can exhaustively cover all the relevant behaviors up to twelve simulation steps in less than thirty minutes, whereas the naive approach already times out after seven simulation steps.

Our second benchmark (B2) consists of two synchronous state machines communicating via shared variables. The model has three interdependent processes,

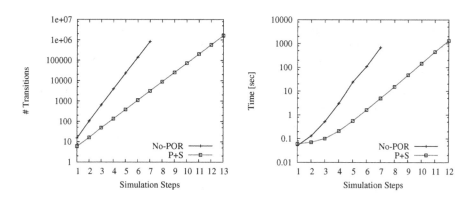

Fig. 5. Performance effect of static partial-order reduction on B1

Table 1. Time to compute the race conditions for each of the process-pairs using SATABS and CBMC. The timeout is set to ten minutes.

Benchmark	Pair	SATABS [s]	CBMC [s]
B1	0	< 1	< 1
B1	1	3	< 1
B1	2	3	< 1
B2	0	76	TO
B2	1	19	5
B2	2	19	2

which are sensitive to the clock. The state machines are implemented using case switches. On this benchmark, partial-order reduction reduces the simulation time and the number of explored transition by one order of one magnitude.

For each pair of processes, Table 1 shows the time required for the static analysis running SATABS and CBMC. The cost for B1 is negligible using both SATABS and CBMC. The results for B2 indicate that CBMC is faster than SATABS on the second and third pair of processes but times out on the first one, whereas SATABS provides a result within two minutes. Note that the computation of these conditions can be distributed onto multiple machines, as the computation for each pair of processes is independent. Furthermore, the precision of the analysis can be controlled by bounding the number of strengthening iterations, which yields a conservative approximation. Finally, as demonstrated by the experiments, the time required for a full exploration grows exponentially with the number of simulation steps, and therefore, the time spent statically for a precise analysis eventually pays off.

5   Conclusion

We presented SCOOT, a novel compiler for SystemC that integrates static analysis and formal verification techniques in order to improve simulation performance. We invoke a modified software Model Checker on each pair of dependent transitions in order to compute a sufficient condition for commutativity of the transitions. Our technique benefits from the fact that SystemC processes are not preempted, and thus, only few such pairs have to be checked. Note that the Model Checker is never applied to the entire model, but only to pairs of transitions – the static part of the analysis is therefore typically polynomial in the size and number of processes.

SCOOT uses the commutativity condition during simulation in order to eliminate unnecessary interleavings. Our analysis is fully automatic and requires no annotation of the source code by the user. Using Model Checking, our analysis is able to detect reduction opportunities that depend on subtle control-flow properties. The experimental results indicate that our formal race-analysis technique produces valuable information for pruning the state space at runtime.

References

1. Blanc, N., Kroening, D.: Race analysis for SystemC using model checking. In: Proceedings of ICCAD 2008, pp. 356–363. IEEE, Los Alamitos (2008)
2. Blanc, N., Kroening, D., Sharygina, N.: Scoot: A tool for the analysis of SystemC models. In: Ramakrishnan, C.R., Rehof, J. (eds.) TACAS 2008. LNCS, vol. 4963, pp. 467–470. Springer, Heidelberg (2008)
3. Clarke, E., Kroening, D., Sharygina, N., Yorav, K.: SATABS: SAT-based predicate abstraction for ANSI-C. In: Halbwachs, N., Zuck, L.D. (eds.) TACAS 2005. LNCS, vol. 3440, pp. 570–574. Springer, Heidelberg (2005)
4. Netzer, R.H.B., Miller, B.P.: What are race conditions? Some issues and formalizations. ACM Lett. Program. Lang. Syst. 1, 74–88 (1992)
5. Flanagan, C., Freund, S.N.: Type-based race detection for Java. In: Programming language design and implementation (PLDI), pp. 219–232. ACM, New York (2000)
6. Savage, S., Burrows, M., Nelson, G., Sobalvarro, P., Anderson, T.: Eraser: A dynamic data race detector for multithreaded programs. ACM Trans. Comput. Syst. 15, 391–411 (1997)
7. Engler, D., Ashcraft, K.: RacerX: Effective, static detection of race conditions and deadlocks. In: Operating systems principles (SOSP), pp. 237–252. ACM, New York (2003)
8. Naik, M., Aiken, A., Whaley, J.: Effective static race detection for Java. In: Programming language design and implementation (PLDI), pp. 308–319. ACM, New York (2006)
9. D'Silva, V., Kroening, D., Weissenbacher, G.: A survey of automated techniques for formal software verification. IEEE Transactions on Computer-Aided Design of Integrated Circuits and Systems (TCAD) 27, 1165–1178 (2008)
10. Vardi, M.Y.: Formal techniques for SystemC verification. In: Design Automation Conference (DAC), pp. 188–192. ACM, New York (2007)
11. Witkowski, T., Blanc, N., Kroening, D., Weissenbacher, G.: Model checking concurrent Linux device drivers. In: Automated software engineering (ASE), pp. 501–504. ACM, New York (2007)
12. Qadeer, S., Wu, D.: KISS: keep it simple and sequential. SIGPLAN Not. 39, 14–24 (2004)
13. Ball, T., Rajamani, S.K.: The SLAM project: debugging system software via static analysis. In: POPL 2002: Proceedings of the 29th ACM SIGPLAN-SIGACT symposium on Principles of programming languages, pp. 1–3. ACM, New York (2002)
14. Graf, S., Saïdi, H.: Construction of abstract state graphs with PVS. In: Grumberg, O. (ed.) CAV 1997. LNCS, vol. 1254, pp. 72–83. Springer, Heidelberg (1997)
15. Ball, T., Rajamani, S.: Boolean programs: A model and process for software analysis. Technical Report MSR-TR-2000-14, Microsoft Research (2000)
16. Godefroid, P.: Software model checking: The VeriSoft approach. Form. Methods Syst. Des. 26, 77–101 (2005)
17. Sen, A., Ogale, V., Abadir, M.S.: Predictive runtime verification of multi-processor SoCs in SystemC. In: Design Automation Conference (DAC), pp. 948–953. ACM, New York (2008)
18. Flanagan, C., Godefroid, P.: Dynamic partial-order reduction for model checking software. In: Principles of programming languages (POPL), pp. 110–121. ACM, New York (2005)
19. Lamport, L.: Time, clocks, and the ordering of events in a distributed system. Commun. ACM 21, 558–565 (1978)

20. Helmstetter, C., Maraninchi, F., Maillet-Contoz, L., Moy, M.: Automatic generation of schedulings for improving the test coverage of systems-on-a-chip. In: Formal Methods in Computer Aided Design (FMCAD), pp. 171–178. IEEE Computer Society, Los Alamitos (2006)
21. Kundu, S., Ganai, M., Gupta, R.: Partial order reduction for scalable testing of SystemC TLM designs. In: Design Automation Conference (DAC), pp. 936–941. ACM, New York (2008)
22. Wang, C., Yang, Z., Kahlon, V., Gupta, A.: Peephole partial order reduction. In: Ramakrishnan, C.R., Rehof, J. (eds.) TACAS 2008. LNCS, vol. 4963, pp. 382–396. Springer, Heidelberg (2008)
23. Peled, D.: All from one, one for all: On model checking using representatives. In: Courcoubetis, C. (ed.) CAV 1993. LNCS, vol. 697, pp. 409–423. Springer, Heidelberg (1993)
24. Peled, D.: Combining partial order reductions with on-the-fly model-checking. In: Dill, D.L. (ed.) CAV 1994. LNCS, vol. 818, pp. 377–390. Springer, Heidelberg (1994)
25. Godefroid, P.: Partial-Order Methods for the Verification of Concurrent Systems. LNCS. Springer, Heidelberg (1996)
26. Blanc, N., Groce, A., Kroening, D.: Verifying C++ with STL containers via predicate abstraction. In: 22nd IEEE International Conference on Automated Software Engineering (ASE), pp. 521–524. IEEE, Los Alamitos (2007)
27. Cook, B., Podelski, A., Rybalchenko, A.: Terminator: Beyond safety. In: Ball, T., Jones, R.B. (eds.) CAV 2006. LNCS, vol. 4144, pp. 415–418. Springer, Heidelberg (2006)
28. Clarke, E.M., Grumberg, O., Jha, S., Lu, Y., Veith, H.: Counterexample-guided abstraction refinement. In: Emerson, E.A., Sistla, A.P. (eds.) CAV 2000. LNCS, vol. 1855, pp. 154–169. Springer, Heidelberg (2000)
29. Clarke, E., Jain, H., Kroening, D.: Verification of SpecC using predicate abstraction. Form. Methods Syst. Des. 30, 5–28 (2007)
30. Kroening, D., Sharygina, N.: Formal verification of SystemC by automatic hardware/software partitioning. In: Formal Methods and Models for Co-Design (MEMOCODE), pp. 101–110. IEEE Computer Society, Los Alamitos (2005)

Partial Behaviour Modelling: Foundations for Incremental and Iterative Model-Based Software Engineering

Sebastian Uchitel[1,2]

[1] Department of Computing, Imperial College London,
180 Queen's Gate, London, SW7 2RH, UK
[2] Department of Computer Science, FCEN, Universidad de Buenos Aires,
Intendente Güiraldes 2160, C1428EGA, Argentina
`suchitel@dc.uba.ar, s.uchitel@doc.ic.ac.uk`

Abstract. Rigorous modelling of the intended behaviour of software in-
tensive systems has been shown to be successfull in uncovering requirements and design flaws. However, the impact that behaviour modelling
has had among practitioners is limited. The construction of behaviour
models remains a difficult and laborious task that requires significant
expertise. In addition, traditional approaches to behaviour models require complete descriptions of the system behaviour up to some level
of abstraction. This completeness assumption is limiting in the context
of software development process best practices which include iterative
development, adoption of use-case and scenario-based techniques and
viewpoint- or stakeholder-based analysis; practices which require modelling and analysis in the presence of partial information about system
behaviour. Our aim is to support the iterative and incremental construction of behaviour models by means of construction, composition and
analysis of partial, heterogeneous, yet formal, descriptions of behaviour.
In this talk we discuss how modal transitions systems can provide the
basis for such support and present some of the model synthesis and composition techniques we have developed.

1 Introduction

Software systems are amenable to analysis through the construction of behaviour
models. This corresponds to the traditional engineering approach to construction of complex systems. Models can be studied to increase confidence on the
adequacy of the product to be built. The advantage of using behaviour models
to describe systems is that they are cheaper to develop than the actual system.
Consequently, they can be analysed and mechanically checked for properties in
order to detect design errors early in the development process and allow cheaper
fixes.

Although behaviour modelling and analysis has been shown to be successful in
uncovering subtle requirements and design errors, adoption by practitioners has
been slow. Partly, this is due to the complexity of building behavioural models

M.V.M. Oliveira and J. Woodcock (Eds.): SBMF 2009, LNCS 5902, pp. 17–22, 2009.

in the first place – behaviour modelling remains a difficult, labour-intensive task that requires considerable expertise. To address this, a wide range of techniques for supporting automated and semi-automated synthesis of behaviour models have been investigated. In particular, synthesis from scenarios and use cases (e.g., [24,10,3,19]), has been studied extensively.

A current limitation of synthesis approaches is that the models being synthesized, e.g., labeled transition systems (LTSs) [14], are typically assumed to be complete descriptions of the system behaviour. That is, that they completely classify all behaviours with respect to some fixed alphabet as either behaviour that the system-to-be is required to exhibit or behaviour that the system-to-be is prohibited from exhibiting. The required behaviour is decribed by the transitions that appear in the behaviour model. The proscribed behaviour is defined as anything that is not described by the model's transitions. This completeness assumption that usually is attached to behaviour models is problematic if these models is to be built from a scenario based-specifications which is inherently partial as synthesis procedures are left to cope with completing the specification automatically, or the engineer is required to put in more information before any meaningful analysis can be performed. Utlimately, this completeness assumption is limiting in the context of software development process best practices which include iterative development, adoption of use- case and scenario-based techniques and viewpoint- or stakeholder-based analysis; practices which require modelling and analysis in the presence of partial information about system behaviour.

A workaround to the completeness assumption is to reinterpret the two sets of behaviours that a behaviour model describes. Rather than interpreting the behaviour that cannot be reproduced by the transitions of a model as proscribed behaviour, it can be interpreted as being "yet to be determined". This interpretation works for scenario-based specifications that have an existential semantics (e.g. MSCs [13]) as these specifications provide examples of what the system must do, but do not say anything about what it must not do. Consequently, a behaviour model synthesized from scenarios provides a *lower bound* from which to identify the behaviours that the system will provide but that have not been explicitly captured by the scenarios. As these new behaviours are identified, they are added to the scenario specification which is then used to synthesis a new behaviour model that includes these new behaviours. This elaboration process can be formalised at the behaviour level with some notion of refinements such as trace inclusion or *simulation* [20].

An alternative workaround is to consider the behaviour explicitly described by the transitions of a behaviour model as unclassified and to assume that the rest of the behaviour is known to be proscribed. This is the interpretation taken for senario-based specifications that have a universal semantics such as Constant LSCs [10]. In such approaches, as with approaches that do synthesis from declarative specifications such as goal models [19]. The specification prunes the acceptable space of behaviours as more universal properties are added to the specification. The fact that a behaviour satisfies a universal statement does not mean that the system is required to provide that trace; the trace could be violating another property, possibly one yet to be elicited. Consequently, a behaviour model synthesized from properties should characterize all possible behaviours that do not violate the properties. Such a model provides an *upper bound* on all the behaviours that the system will actually provide, once implemented. Validation of behaviour models synthesized from properties can prompt the elicitation of more properties, which in turn will further approximate from above the intended behaviour of the system to be. In other words, as new properties are elicited, the resulting synthesized model will be able to do *less* (notion that can be formally captured using a traditional notion of refinement such as simulation), describing behaviour that is closer to that of the system to be.

The problem is that if behaviour models are to be synthesised from rich scenario based languages that use combine existential and universal scenarios as first envisioned in [10], the target synthesis formalism cannot be in the form of traditional behaviour models such as LTS because these are not capable of capturing simultaneously both the upper and lower bounds [22] that universal and existential statements provide.

2   Partial Behaviour Models

Partial behaviour models, such as Modal Transition Systems (MTS) [17], disinguish between three kinds of behaviour, required, proscribed and unknown, and therefore can describe *both* an upper and a lower bound to the intended system behaviour, allowing both bounds to be refined simultaneously. For instance, MTS are equipped with two kinds of transitions *required* transitions and *possible* transitions. The former provide a lower bound to system behaviour, while the latter provide the lower bound to system behaviour.

The semantics of a partial behaviour model can be thought of as a set of traditional behaviour models. For instance, MTS semantics can be given in terms of sets of LTSs that provide all of the behaviour required by the MTS, do not provide any of the behaviour proscribed by the MTS, and make arbitrary decisions on the MTS's unknown behaviour. Intuitively, as more information becomes available, unknown or unclassified behaviour gets changed into either required or proscribed behaviour. The notion of refinement between MTSs capture this intuition formally and provides an elegant way of describing the process of behaviour model elaboration as one in which behaviour information is acquired and introduced into the behaviour model incrementally, gradually refining an MTS until it characterizes a single LTS.

The original notion of refinement was aimed at comparing MTS models with the same alphabet and no unobservable transitions and is referred to as strong refinement [17]. Although in [17] a notion of weak refinement that allows for unobservable actions was defined, this notion was then extended to account for models different alphabets [23]. More recently, an alternative, possibly more appropriate observational refinement, based on branching equivalence [25] has also been proposed [7].

A particularly useful notion in the context of software and requirements engineering is that of *merge*. Merging two consistent models is a process that should result in a minimal common refinement of both models where *consistency* is defined as the existence of one common refinement. Intuitively, merging builds a model that characterises the intersection of the LTS characterised by the models being merged. In other words, the merge characterises the LTSs that provide all the required behaviour of the MTS being merged, and that do not provide any of the proscribed behaviour of the MTS being merged.

MTS merging can be used as the conjunction of multiple partial operational descriptions. The original formulation of was done by Larsen in [16] where an incomplete merge algorithm was proposed for MTS under strong refinement, recently we have presented a correct and complete version [8]. The problem of merge under observational refinements is still open, a partial result can be found in [23] where incomplete algorithm for merging models with different alphabets under weak refinement is presented.

We have revisted the problem of behaviour model synthesis in the context of MTS. We have provided a generic extension of synthesis approaches that start from existential scenario-based specifications and build LTS models [22]. The extension, produces an MTS model instead of an LTS which captures appropriately the lower bound to intended system behaviour provided by such specifications. However, given that MTS are more expressive than LTS, we have explored opportunities for the defining novel synthesis approaches that start from more expressive scenarios notations. In particular, we have investigated triggered existential scenarios [21] which have been neglected in existing scenario description languages as it is impossible to adequately capture their semantics using traditional behaviour models.

3   Conclusions

In this talk we discuss Modal Transition Systems [17] and some of their theoretical foundations and semantics. We discuss how such models can support iterative and incremental behaviour modelling based on a notion of refinement that prunes the space of acceptable implementations of the system-to-be and based on model merging. We also discuss how merge and synthesis of Modal Transition Systems can aide in the analysis and elaboration of system behaviour from multiple, partial and heterogeneous descriptions of behaviour and demonstrate some of these ideas using the Modal Transition System Analyser, a tool that aims to support incremental elaboration of partial models [5] and that is available, open source, at `http://sourceforge.net/projects/mtsa/` . We finalise with a number of open problems and directions of future work.

Acknowledgments

Dario Fischbein, Nicolas D'Ippolito, German Sibay, Greg Brunet, Mathieu Sassoulas, Victor Braberman, and Marsha Chechik have all collaborated on parts of the work we present. The work we present has been funded in part by CONICET and grant ERC 204853/PBM.

References

1. Antonik, A., Huth, M., Larsen, K., Nyman, U., Wasowski, A.: EXPTIME-complete Decision Problems for Mixed and Modal Specifications. In: 15th International Workshop on Expressiveness in Concurrency (August 2008)
2. Antonik, A., Huth, M., Larsen, K.G., Nyman, U., Wasowski, A.: Complexity of decision problems for mixed and modal specifications. In: Amadio, R.M. (ed.) FOSSACS 2008. LNCS, vol. 4962, pp. 112–126. Springer, Heidelberg (2008)
3. Bontemps, Y., Heymans, P., Schobbens, P.-Y.: From live sequence charts to state machines and back: A guided tour. IEEE Transactions on Software Engineering 31(12), 999–1014 (2005)
4. Brunet, G., Chechik, M., Uchitel, S.: Properties of behavioural model merging. In: Misra, J., Nipkow, T., Sekerinski, E. (eds.) FM 2006. LNCS, vol. 4085, pp. 98–114. Springer, Heidelberg (2006)
5. D'Ippolito, N., Fischbein, D., Chechik, M., Uchitel, S.: Mtsa: The modal transition system analyser. In: 23rd IEEE/ACM International Conference on Automated Software Engineering (ASE 2008), L'Aquila, Italy, September 15-19, pp. 475–476. IEEE, Los Alamitos (2008), http://sourceforge.net/projects/mtsa/
6. Fantechi, A., Gnesi, S.: Formal modeling for product families engineering. In: Proceedings of Software Product Lines, 12th International Conference, SPLC 2008, Limerick, Ireland, September 8-12, pp. 193–202. IEEE Computer Society, Los Alamitos (2008)
7. Fischbein, D., Braberman, V., Uchitel, S.: A sound observational semantics for modal transition systems. In: Leucker, M., Morgan, C. (eds.) ICTAC 2009. LNCS, vol. 5684, pp. 215–230. Springer, Heidelberg (2009)
8. Fischbein, D., Uchitel, S.: On correct and complete strong merging of partial behaviour models. In: Harrold, M.J., Murphy, G.C. (eds.) Proceedings of the 16th ACM SIGSOFT International Symposium on Foundations of Software Engineering, Atlanta, Georgia, USA, November 9-14, pp. 297–307. ACM, New York (2008)
9. Fischbein, D., Uchitel, S., Braberman, V.A.: A foundation for behavioural conformance in software product line architectures. In: Hierons, R.M., Muccini, H. (eds.) ROSATEA, pp. 39–48. ACM, New York (2006)
10. Harel, D., Marelly, R.: Come, Let's Play: Scenario-Based Programming Using LSCs and the Play-Engine. Springer, Heidelberg (2003)
11. Huth, M.: Refinement is complete for implementations. Formal Aspects of Computing 17(2), 113–137 (2005)
12. Hüttel, H., Larsen, K.G.: The use of static constructs in a modal process logic. In: Meyer, A.R., Taitslin, M.A. (eds.) Logic at Botik 1989. LNCS, vol. 363, pp. 163–180. Springer, Heidelberg (1989)
13. ITU. Recommendation z.120: Message sequence charts. ITU (2000)
14. Keller, R.M.: Formal verification of parallel programs. Commun. ACM (1976)
15. Krka, I., Brun, Y., Edwards, G., Medvidovic, N.: Synthesizing partial component-level behavior models from system specifications. In: van Vliet, H., Issarny, V. (eds.) ESEC/SIGSOFT FSE, pp. 305–314. ACM, New York (2009)
16. Larsen, K.G., Steffen, B., Weise, C.: A constraint oriented proof methodology based on modal transition systems. In: Brinksma, E., Steffen, B., Cleaveland, W.R., Larsen, K.G., Margaria, T. (eds.) TACAS 1995. LNCS, vol. 1019. Springer, Heidelberg (1995)
17. Larsen, K.G., Thomsen, B.: A modal process logic. In: Proceedings, Third Annual Symposium on Logic in Computer Science, Edinburgh, Scotland, UK, July 5-8. IEEE Computer Society, Los Alamitos (1988)

18. Larsen, K.G., Xinxin, L.: Equation solving using modal transition systems. In: Proceedings, Fifth Annual IEEE Symposium on Logic in Computer Science, Philadelphia, Pennsylvania, USA, June 4-7, pp. 108–117. IEEE Computer Society, Los Alamitos (1990)

19. Letier, E., Kramer, J., Magee, J., Uchitel, S.: Deriving event-based transition systems from goal-oriented requirements models. Automated Software Engineering Journal 15(2), 175–206 (2008)

20. Milner, R.: Communication and Concurrency. Prentice-Hall, New York (1989)

21. Sibay, G., Uchitel, S., Braberman, V.A.: Existential live sequence charts revisited. In: Schäfer, W., Dwyer, M.B., Gruhn, V. (eds.) 30th International Conference on Software Engineering (ICSE 2008), Leipzig, Germany, May 10-18, pp. 41–50. ACM, New York (2008)

22. Uchitel, S., Brunet, G., Chechik, M.: Synthesis of partial behavior models from properties and scenarios. IEEE Transactions on Software Engineering 35(3), 384–406 (2009)

23. Uchitel, S., Chechik, M.: Merging partial behavioural models. In: Taylor, R.N., Dwyer, M.B. (eds.) Proceedings of the 12th ACM SIGSOFT International Symposium on Foundations of Software Engineering, Newport Beach, CA, USA, October 31 - November 6, pp. 43–52. ACM, New York (2004)

24. Uchitel, S., Kramer, J., Magee, J.: Incremental Elaboration of Scenario-Based Specifications and Behaviour Models using Implied Scenarios. ACM TOSEM 13(1) (2004)

25. van Gabbeek, R.J., Weijland, W.P.: Branching time and abstraction in bisimulation semantics. J. ACM 43(3), 555–600 (1996)

Satisfiability Modulo Theories: An Appetizer

Leonardo de Moura and Nikolaj Bjørner

Microsoft Research, One Microsoft Way, Redmond, WA 98074, USA
{leonardo,nbjorner}@microsoft.com

Abstract. Satisfiability Modulo Theories (SMT) is about checking the satisfiability of logical formulas over one or more theories. The problem draws on a combination of some of the most fundamental areas in computer science. It combines the problem of Boolean satisfiability with domains, such as, those studied in convex optimization and term-manipulating symbolic systems. It also draws on the most prolific problems in the past century of symbolic logic: the decision problem, completeness and incompleteness of logical theories, and finally complexity theory. The problem of modularly combining special purpose algorithms for each domain is as deep and intriguing as finding new algorithms that work particularly well in the context of a combination. SMT also enjoys a very useful role in software engineering. Modern software, hardware analysis and model-based tools are increasingly complex and multi-faceted software systems. However, at their core is invariably a component using symbolic logic for describing states and transformations between them. A well tuned SMT solver that takes into account the state-of-the-art breakthroughs usually scales orders of magnitude beyond custom ad-hoc solvers.

1 Introduction

Satisfiability is one of the most fundamental problems in theoretical computer science, namely the problem of determining whether a formula expressing a constraint has a solution. Constraint satisfaction problems arise in many diverse areas including software and hardware verification, type inference, extended static checking, test-case generation, scheduling, planning, graph problems, among others [1]. The most well-known constraint satisfaction problem is *propositional satisfiability* SAT, where the goal is to decide whether a formula over Boolean variables, formed using logical connectives, can be made true by choosing true/false values for its variables. Some problems require or are more naturally described in more expressive logics such as first-order logic. A first-order formula is formed using logical connectives, variables, quantifiers, function and predicate symbols. A solution, also known as a *model*, is an interpretation for the variable, function and predicate symbols that makes the formula true. Of particular recent interest is *satisfiability modulo theories* (SMT), where the interpretation of some symbols is constrained by a *background theory*. For example, the theory of *arithmetic* restricts the interpretation of symbols such as: $+$, $\leq$, 0, and 1.

M.V.M. Oliveira and J. Woodcock (Eds.): SBMF 2009, LNCS 5902, pp. 23–36, 2009.
© Springer-Verlag Berlin Heidelberg 2009

SMT draws on the most prolific problems in the past century of symbolic logic: the decision problem, completeness and incompleteness of logical theories, and finally complexity theory. The computational complexity of most SMT problems is very high. The problem of modularly *combining special purpose algorithms* for each domain is as deep and intriguing as finding new algorithms that work particularly well in the context of a combination. The theory of linear arithmetic, which is the basis of linear programming, is one prominent theory that is useful in many applications. Linear programming algorithms can be used to check satisfiability of conjunctions of linear arithmetic inequalities, but they do not directly apply for Boolean combinations. SMT solvers distinguish themselves by handling such combinations.

It is well-known that SAT is NP-complete and first-order logic is undecidable. Due to this high computational complexity, it is infeasible to build a procedure that can solve arbitrary SMT problems. Therefore, most procedures focus on the more realistic goal of efficiently solving problems that occur in practice. They rely on the assumption that, although potentially big, most formulas produced by verification and analysis tools are *shallow*. That is, only a small fraction of a formula is really critical for establishing satisfiability. The rest consists of irrelevant noise.

In recent years, there has been an enormous progress in the scale of problems that can be solved, thanks to innovations in core algorithms, data structures, heuristics, and paying attention to implementation details. Modern SAT procedures can check formulas with hundreds of thousands variables and millions of clauses. A similar progress has being observed for SMT procedures for the more commonly occurring theories. The annual competition for SAT and SMT procedures is a key ingredient in driving progress [2]. In this paper, we provide a brief overview of SMT and the main technical ideas.

1.1   An Example

We will introduce three theories used in SMT solvers using the following example:

$$b + 2 = c \land f(read(write(a, b, 3), c - 2)) \neq f(c - b + 1).$$

The formula uses the theory of arrays. It was introduced by McCarthy in [3] as part of forming a broader agenda for a calculus of computation. In the theory of arrays, there are two functions *read* and *write*. The term $read(a, i)$ produces the value of array a at index i, while the term $write(a, i, v)$ produces an array, which is equal to a except for possibly index i which maps to v. These properties can be summarized using the equations:

$$read(write(a, i, v), i) = v$$
$$read(write(a, i, v), j) = read(a, j) \text{ for } i \neq j.$$

They state that the result of reading $write(a, i, v)$ at index j is v for $i = j$. Reading the array at any other index produces the same value as $read(a, j)$. The formula also uses the function f, therefore for all t and s, if $t = s$, then $f(t) = f(s)$

(congruence rule). In other words, the only assumption about function f is that it always produce the same result when applied to the same arguments. The congruence rule implies that formulas remain equivalent when replacing equal terms. The example formula is unsatisfiable. That is, there is no assignment to the integers b and c and the array a such that the first equality $b + 2 = c$ holds and at the same time the second disequality also is satisfied. One way of establishing the unsatisfiability is by replacing c by $b + 2$ in the disequality, to obtain the equivalent

$$b + 2 = c \land f(read(write(a, b, 3), b + 2 - 2)) \neq f(b + 2 - b + 1),$$

which after reduction using facts about arithmetic becomes

$$b + 2 = c \land f(read(write(a, b, 3), b)) \neq f(3).$$

The theory of arrays implies that the nested array read/write functions reduce to 3 and the formula becomes:

$$b + 2 = c \land f(3) \neq f(3).$$

The congruence property of f entails that the disequality is false.

2   Preliminaries

A *propositional formula* φ can be a propositional variable p or a negation $\neg\varphi_0$, a conjunction $\varphi_0 \land \varphi_1$, a disjunction $\varphi_0 \lor \varphi_1$, an implication $\varphi_0 \Rightarrow \varphi_1$, or a bi-implication $\varphi_0 \Leftrightarrow \varphi_1$ of smaller formulas φ_0, φ_1. A *truth assignment* M for a formula φ maps the propositional variables in φ to $\{\mathsf{true}, \mathsf{false}\}$. We say a truth assignment M *satisfies* φ ($M \models \varphi$), if M makes φ evaluate to true under the usual truth table interpretation of the connectives. For instance, let φ be the formula $p \lor (\neg q \land r)$, then the truth assignment $M = \{p \mapsto \mathsf{false}, q \mapsto \mathsf{false}, r \mapsto \mathsf{true}\}$ satisfies φ. A formula φ is *satisfiable* if there is an M s.t. $M \models \varphi$, and φ is *valid* if for all M, $M \models \varphi$. We say φ_1 and φ_2 are *equisatisfiable* if φ_1 is satisfiable iff φ_2 is satisfiable. A literal is either a propositional variable p or its negation $\neg p$. A clause is a disjunction of literals $l_1 \lor \ldots \lor l_n$. A formula is in conjunctive normal form (CNF) if it is a conjunction of clauses $C_1 \land \ldots \land C_m$. We will write CNF formulas as set of clauses. Any propositional formula can be converted to CNF, in linear time, by introducing fresh variables for each compound subformula and adding suitable clauses. For example, let φ be the formula $\neg p \lor (q \land \neg r)$, in converting φ into CNF, we label $q \land \neg r$ as k_1 and encode $k_1 \Leftrightarrow (q \land \neg r)$ using the set of auxiliary clauses $\Delta_1 = \{\neg k_1 \lor q, \ \neg k_1 \lor \neg r, \ \neg q \lor r \lor k_1\}$, similarly, we label $\neg p \lor k_1$ as k_2 and encode $k_2 \Leftrightarrow (\neg p \lor k_1)$ using the clauses $\Delta_2 = \{p \lor k_2, \ \neg k_1 \lor k_2, \ \neg k_2 \lor \neg p \lor k_1\}$, hence, the formula φ is equisatisfiable to the set of clauses $\{k_2\} \cup \Delta_1 \cup \Delta_2$.

Many-sorted (first-order) logic is a commonly used formalism and framework for formulating SMT problems. A many-sorted *signature* is composed of a set of *sorts*, a set of *function symbols*, and a set of *predicate symbols*. Each function symbol f has associated with it an arity of the form $\sigma_1 \times \ldots \times \sigma_n \to \sigma$, where $\sigma_1, \ldots, \sigma_n, \sigma$ are sorts. If $n = 0$, we say f is a constant symbol. Similarly, each predicate symbol p has associated with it an arity of the form $\sigma_1 \times \ldots \times \sigma_n$. If $n = 0$, we say p is a propositional symbol. We assume a set of *variables* X, where each variable is associated with a sort. A *term* t with sort σ has the form x or $f(t_1, \ldots, t_n)$, where x is a variable with sort σ, and f is a function symbol with arity $\sigma_1 \times \ldots \times \sigma_n \to \sigma$, where for each $i \in \{1, \ldots, n\}$, t_i has sort σ_i. An *atom* is of the form $p(t_1, \ldots, t_n)$ where p is a predicate symbol with arity $\sigma_1 \times \ldots \times \sigma_n$, and for each $i \in \{1, \ldots, n\}$, t_i is a term with sort σ_i. A *formula* φ is an atom, or has the form $\neg\varphi_0$, $\varphi_0 \wedge \varphi_1$, $\varphi_0 \vee \varphi_1$, $\varphi_0 \Rightarrow \varphi_1$, $\varphi_0 \Leftrightarrow \varphi_1$, $(\forall x \colon \sigma. \varphi_0)$, or $(\exists x \colon \sigma. \varphi_0)$, where φ_0, φ_1 are smaller formulas. A *Σ-formula* φ is a formula where each symbol in φ is in Σ. We say a variable x is *free* in formula φ if it is not bound by any quantifier $\exists, \forall$. For example, x is free in $(\forall y \colon \sigma. p(x, y))$, but y is not. A *sentence* is a formula without free variables. We use $vars(\varphi)$ to denote the set of free variables in φ. A *quantifier-free formula* is a formula not containing $\exists$ or $\forall$.

A *structure* M for a signature Σ and variables X consists of non-empty domains $|M|_\sigma$ for each sort in Σ, for each $x \in X$ with sort σ, $M(x) \in |M|_\sigma$, for each function symbol f with arity $\sigma_1 \times \ldots \times \sigma_n \to \sigma$, $M(f)$ is a total map from $|M|_{\sigma_1} \times \ldots \times |M|_{\sigma_n}$ to $|M|_\sigma$, and for each predicate symbol p with arity $\sigma_1 \times \ldots \times \sigma_n$, $M(p)$ is a subset of $|M|_{\sigma_1} \times \ldots \times |M|_{\sigma_n}$. The interpretation of a term t is given by $M[\![x]\!] = M(x)$ and $M[\![f(t_1, \ldots, t_n)]\!] = M(f)(M[\![t_1]\!], \ldots, M[\![t_n]\!])$. We assume that, for each sort σ, the equality $=_\sigma$ is a *builtin* predicate symbol with arity $\sigma \times \sigma$ that does not occur in any signature and for every structure M, $M(=_\sigma)$ is the identity relation over $|M|_\sigma \times |M|_\sigma$. As a notational convention, we will always omit the subscript. We use $M\{x \mapsto \nu\}$ to denote a structure where the variable symbol x with sort σ is interpreted as ν, $\nu \in |M|_\sigma$, and all other variables, function and predicate symbols have the same interpretation as in M. Given a formula φ and a structure M, satisfaction $M \models \varphi$ is defined as:

$$
\begin{aligned}
M &\models p(t_1, \ldots, t_n) &&\Longleftrightarrow \langle M[\![t_1]\!], \ldots, M[\![t_n]\!]\rangle \in M(p) \\
M &\models \neg\varphi &&\Longleftrightarrow M \not\models \varphi \\
M &\models \varphi_0 \vee \varphi_1 &&\Longleftrightarrow M \models \varphi_0 \text{ or } M \models \varphi_1 \\
M &\models \varphi_0 \wedge \varphi_1 &&\Longleftrightarrow M \models \varphi_0 \text{ and } M \models \varphi_1 \\
M &\models (\exists x \colon \sigma. \varphi) &&\Longleftrightarrow M\{x \mapsto \nu\} \models \varphi \text{ for some } \nu \in |M|_\sigma \\
M &\models (\forall x \colon \sigma. \varphi) &&\Longleftrightarrow M\{x \mapsto \nu\} \models \varphi \text{ for all } \nu \in |M|_\sigma
\end{aligned}
$$

Note that an implication $\varphi_0 \Rightarrow \varphi_1$ is equivalent to $\neg\varphi_0 \vee \varphi_1$, and a bi-implication $\varphi_0 \Leftrightarrow \varphi_1$ is equivalent to $(\neg\varphi_0 \vee \varphi_1) \wedge (\varphi_0 \vee \neg\varphi_1)$. A formula φ is *satisfiable* if there is a structure M s.t. $M \models \varphi$, and is *valid* if for all structures M, $M \models \varphi$. A structure M satisfies a set of formulas S ($M \models S$) if $M \models \varphi$ for every $\varphi \in S$. A formula is in negation normal form (NNF) if the negation only occurs in literals of the form $\neg p(t_1, \ldots, t_n)$. A formula can be converted to NNF by using the equivalences such as: $\neg\neg\varphi \equiv \varphi$, $\neg(\varphi_0 \wedge \varphi_1) \equiv \neg\varphi_0 \vee \neg\varphi_1$, $\neg(\varphi_0 \vee \varphi_1) \equiv \neg\varphi_0 \wedge \neg\varphi_1$, $\neg(\exists x \colon \sigma. \varphi) \equiv (\forall x \colon \sigma. \neg\varphi)$, and $\neg(\forall x \colon \sigma. \varphi) \equiv (\exists x \colon \sigma. \neg\varphi)$. We use $t[s/x]$ to denote a term t' where the free variable x is replaced by the term s. *Skolemization* converts an NNF formula φ into an equisatisfiable formula φ' not containing $\exists$. It it is based on the observation that if φ is NNF, then any subformula $(\exists x \colon \sigma. \varphi_0)$ can be replaced by $\varphi_0[f(x_1, \ldots, x_n)/x]$, where $vars(\exists x \colon \sigma. \varphi_0) = \{x_1, \ldots, x_n\}$, and f is a new fresh function symbol. The resulting formula can then be converted in linear time into CNF using an approach similar to the one used for propositional formulas. The only difference is that if a subformula contains free variables in the context of universal quantifiers $\forall$, then the auxiliary clauses are universally quantified. For example, let φ be the formula $(\forall x \colon \sigma. (\forall y \colon \sigma. (q(y) \wedge p(y)) \vee \neg r(x, y)))$, the variable y is bound by an universal quantifier $\forall$, now suppose we want to label the subformula $q(y) \wedge p(y)$, then we create a new fresh predicate symbol s, and encode $\forall y \colon \sigma. s(y) \Leftrightarrow (q(y) \wedge p(y))$ using the auxiliary clauses $\{(\forall y \colon \sigma. \neg s(y) \vee q(y)), (\forall y \colon \sigma. \neg s(y) \vee p(y)), (\forall y \colon \sigma. s(y) \vee \neg q(y) \vee \neg p(y))\}$. In practice, solvers try to minimize the number of auxiliary clauses by using, when feasible, the distributivity rule: $\varphi_0 \vee (\varphi_1 \wedge \varphi_2) \equiv (\varphi_0 \vee \varphi_1) \wedge (\varphi_0 \vee \varphi_2)$. Note that, in the worst case, the repeatedly application of the distributivity rule may exponentially increase the size of the resulting formula. From now on, without loss of generality, we assume every formula that is being checked for satisfiability is in CNF. We also use $(\forall x_1 \colon \sigma_1, \ldots, x_n \colon \sigma_n. \varphi)$ to denote $(\forall x_1 \colon \sigma_1. \ldots (\forall x_n \colon \sigma_n. \varphi) \ldots)$, and $\forall^* \varphi$ to denote a formula with zero or more $\forall$.

3   Efficient Case-Analysis

Case-analysis is in the core of most automated deduction tools. Most SMT solvers rely on SAT procedures for performing case-analysis efficiently. In this section, we describe the basic techniques used in state-of-the-art SAT solvers. Later, we describe how SMT specific solvers are combined with SAT solvers.

Most successful SAT solvers are based on an approach called *systematic search*. The search space is a tree with each vertex representing a propositional variable and the out edges representing the two choices (i.e., true and false) for this variable. For a formula containing n variable, there are 2^n leaves in this tree. Each path from the root to a leaf corresponds to a truth assignment. Given a formula φ, a procedure, based on systematic search, searches the tree for a truth assignment M that satisfies φ. Most search based SAT solvers are based on the DPLL approach [4]. Given a CNF formula, the DPLL algorithm tries to build a satisfying truth assignment using three main operations: decide, propagate and backtrack. The operation decide heuristically chooses an unassigned propositional variable and assigns it to true or false. This operation is also called *branching* or *case-splitting*. The operation propagate deduces the consequences of a partial truth assignment using deduction rules. The most widely used deduction rule is the *unit-clause rule*, which states that if a clause has all but one literal assigned to false and the remaining literal l is unassigned, then the only way for this clause to evaluate to true is to assign l to true. Let C be the clause $p \vee \neg q \vee \neg r$, and M the partial truth assignment $\{p \mapsto \text{false}, r \mapsto \text{true}\}$, then the only way for C to evaluate to true is by assigning q to false. Given a partial truth assignment M and a clause C in the CNF formula φ such that all literals of C are assigned to false in M, then there is no way to extend M to a complete truth assignment M' that satisfies φ. We say this is a *conflict*, and C is a *conflicting clause*. A conflict indicates that some of the earlier decisions cannot lead to a truth assignment that satisfies φ, and the DPLL procedure must *backtrack* and try a different branch value. If a *conflict* is detected and there are no decisions to backtrack, then the formula φ is unsatisfiable. Many significant improvements of this basic procedure have been proposed over the years. The main improvements are: *lemma learning* [5], *non-chronological back-tracking* [5], efficient *indexing techniques* for applying the unit-clause rule [6], and *preprocessing* techniques.

4   What Is a Theory?

A theory is essentially a set of sentences. More formally, a Σ-theory is a collection of sentences over a signature Σ. Given a theory T, we say φ is *satisfiable modulo T* if $T \cup \{\varphi\}$ is satisfiable. We use $M \models_T \varphi$ to denote $M \models \{\varphi\} \cup T$. For example, let Σ be the signature containing the symbols 0, 1, $+$, $-$ and $<$, and $\mathbb{Z}$ be the structure that interprets these symbols in the usual way over the integers, then the theory of linear arithmetic is the set of first-order sentences that are true in $\mathbb{Z}$. Let Ω be a class of structures over a signature Σ, then we use $Th(\Omega)$ to denote the set of all sentences ϕ over Σ such that $M \models \phi$ for every M in Ω. In the literature, sometimes a theory T is defined as a class of structures, and φ is satisfiable modulo T if there is a structure M in T such that $M \models \varphi$. Note that these two definitions are not equivalent when checking the satisfiability of a formula φ over an expanded signature (see discussion at [7]).

We say the satisfiability problem for theory T is *decidable* if there is a procedure $\mathfrak{S}$ that checks whether any quantifier-free formula is satisfiable or not. In this case, we say $\mathfrak{S}$ is a *decision procedure* for T.

4.1   Theories

So which theories are integrated with SMT solves? The answer depends on the SMT solver, yet some theories have gained more attention than others. We summarize some of these here.

Linear Arithmetic. Linear arithmetic, also known as additive arithmetic, is the theory where the only arithmetical functions are $+$ and $-$. The functions may be applied to either numerical constants or variables. Multiplication of a numerical constant with a variable is also allowed, so $5 \cdot x$ is a legal term, and for arithmetic over the reals, $\frac{2}{3} \cdot x$ is allowed. The relations for equality and inequalities $(=, \leq, <)$ are used for forming atomic predicates. A conjunction of $=$ and $\leq$ atoms can be decided using a procedure based on the *dual* simplex algorithm [8]. A method for extending the procedure to strict inequalities is by working with non-standard reals that contain *infinitesimals*. This is achieved by adding a symbolic infinitesimal constant ϵ to strict inequalities to make them non-strict.

Difference arithmetic. is a fragment of linear arithmetic where predicates are restricted to be of the form $x - y \leq c$, for x, y variables and c a numeric constant. Conjunctions of difference arithmetic inequalities can be checked very efficiently for satisfiability by searching for negative cycles in weighted directed graphs. In the graph representation, each variable corresponds to a node, and an inequality of the form $x - y \leq c$ corresponds to an edge from y to x with weight c. Figure 1 shows a conjunction of difference inequalities and the corresponding graph, the negative cycle, with weight -1, is shown by dashed lines.

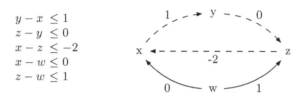

$$y - x \leq 1$$
$$z - y \leq 0$$
$$x - z \leq -2$$
$$x - w \leq 0$$
$$z - w \leq 1$$

Fig. 1. Difference inequalities example

Non-linear arithmetic. The theory of quantifier-free non-linear arithmetic over the reals is decidable. Tarski established a stronger result, that the full first-order theory of reals with addition and multiplication is decidable [9]. Modern methods for non-linear arithmetic over the reals use algorithms from computer algebra, such as computing a Gröbner basis from equalities [10]. The situation is completely different for integers. Hilbert's famous 10th problem was to develop an algorithm for solving non-linear equalities over the integers. Matiyasevich established that this problem was undecidable That is, there is no algorithm for solving such equalities. It is much worse with quantifiers, which is also known as Peano arithmetic: Gödel established there is not even a computable set of axioms for characterizing Peano arithmetic.

Free functions. The free theory over a signature Σ is the first-order theory with an empty set of sentences. The free theory was used in Section 1.1. It is also known as the theory of uninterpreted functions. Decision procedures for this theory are particularly important because the decision problem for many theories (e.g., arrays) can be reduced to this one. Given a conjunction of equalities between terms using free functions, a *congruence closure* can be used for representing the smallest set of implied equalities. This representation can be used to check if a mixture of equalities and disequalities are satisfiable. Simply check that the terms on both sides of each disequality are in different equivalence classes. Efficient algorithms for computing congruence closure has been the subject of long-running research [11]. In these algorithms, terms are represented as directed acyclic graphs (DAGS). Figure 2 shows the operation of a congruence closure algorithm in a small example.

Bit-vectors. The arithmetic of machines is not the same as arithmetic on mathematical integers. In machine arithmetic, integers fit in fixed size registers.

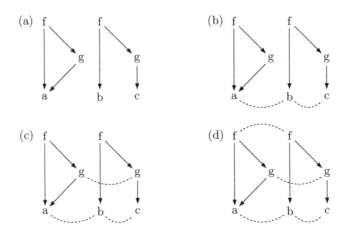

Fig. 2. Congruence closure example: $a = b$, $b = c$, $f(a, g(a)) \neq f(b, g(c))$. (a) A DAG for all terms in the example. (b) Equivalences $a = b$ and $b = c$ are shown by dashed lines. (c) Nodes $g(a)$ and $g(c)$ are congruent because $a = c$ is implied by first two equalities. (d) Nodes $f(a, g(a))$ and $f(b, g(c))$ are also congruent, hence the example is unsatisfiable because $f(a, g(a)) \neq f(b, g(c))$.

A more suitable domain for machine arithmetic is to represent every number as a fixed-size sequences of bits. On a 64 bit CPU, for instance, an integer is represented as a bit-vector with 64 bits. The theory of bit-vector arithmetic also allows mixing bit-wise operations. For example, when x is a 64-bit integer, then x is a power of two, if and only if $0 = ((x - 1)\&x)$. The theory of bit-vectors can be reduced to Boolean satisfiability by simply *blasting* bit-vector formulas to Boolean formulas. For example, assume x and y are bit-vectors of size 2, then the formula $x + y = 0$ can be blasted into:

$$(x_0 \text{ xor } y_0) \qquad\qquad \Leftrightarrow \text{ false}$$
$$(x_1 \text{ xor } y_1) \text{ xor } (x_0 \wedge y_0) \Leftrightarrow \text{ false}$$

where x_0, x_1, y_0, y_1 are propositions corresponding to the *bits* of x and y, xor is the exclusive-or operator, a xor b is defined as $a \Leftrightarrow \neg b$. In this example, we are essentially encoding a carry look-ahead adder as a Boolean formula. Current research into efficient decision procedures for bit-vectors seek taking advantage of methods for modular arithmetic, methods for lazy bit-blasting, and approximating long bit-vectors by short bit-vectors.

Arrays. We used the theory of (applicative) arrays in Section 1.1. The theory is useful for encoding state changes to programs with arrays. When a program updates an array a by setting the value of a field i to v it induces a state change. The side-effect can be encoded by referring to the updated array as $write(a, i, v)$. The problem of checking whether a quantifier-free formula is satisfiable modulo the theory of arrays is decidable, and it allows various extensions which have been pursued in recent literature [12,13].

Other theories. There are several other theories of interest and relevance in applications of SMT solvers. We cannot survey them all here, but mention a just few to give an idea of the scope. These include the theory of *pairs*, or more generally tuples, allows working with pairs and accessing components within pairs after they have been built. The basic theory of acyclic finite *lists* is tailored to the list data-structure found in functional programming languages. A theory of *strings* is closely related to the theory of lists. It is distinguished as *concatenation* is assumed as the basic way of building strings, as opposed to *consing* new elements to the front of a list. Concatenation is found in programs that manipulate strings. Of equal relevance for string-manipulating programs are operations for taking lengths of strings, indexing into strings, and checking membership in regular and context-free languages. Unfortunately not all combinations of these extensions remain decidable. The theory of acyclic finite *recursive data-types* generalizes both the theory of pairs and lists. It can be used for algebraic data-types, known from functional programming.

5   SAT + Theory Solvers

The previous section summarized an array of different theories, and described decision procedures for deciding the satisfiability of conjunction of literals modulo a given theory. From now on, we say these procedures are *theory solvers*. In practice, we are usually interested in deciding the satisfiability of arbitrary quantifier-free formulas. One simple idea is to integrate SAT techniques described in Section 3 with theory solvers [14,15,16,17].

First, we introduce an abstraction function α that maps a quantifier-free formula φ into a propositional formula $\alpha(\varphi)$ by replacing atoms in φ with (fresh) propositional variables. More formally, given a formula φ with atoms $A = \{a_1, \ldots, a_n\}$ and a set of propositional variables $P = \{p_1, \ldots, p_n\}$ not occurring in φ, the mapping α from formulas over A to propositional formulas over P is defined as the homomorphism induced by $\alpha(a_i) = p_i$. The inverse γ of such an abstraction mapping α simply replaces propositional variables p_i with their associated atom a_i. For instance, let φ be the formula $f(x) \not\simeq x \wedge f(f(x)) \simeq x$, $\alpha(f(x) \simeq x) = p_1$ and $\alpha(f(f(x)) \simeq x) = p_2$, then $\alpha(\varphi) = \neg p_1 \wedge p_2$. Moreover, the truth assignment M induces a set of literals

$$\gamma(M) = \{\gamma(p_i) \mid M(p_i) = \mathsf{true}\} \cup \{\neg\gamma(p_i) \mid M(p_i) = \mathsf{false}\}$$

Now, given a truth assignment $M = \{p_1 \mapsto \mathsf{false}, p_2 \mapsto \mathsf{true}\}$, $\gamma(M) = \{f(x) \not\simeq x, f(f(x)) \simeq x\}$.

Given an unsatisfiable set of literals S, we say a *justification* for S is any unsatisfiable subset J of S. Of course, any unsatisfiable set S is a justification for itself. We say a justification J is *non-redundant* if there is no strict subset J' of J that is also unsatisfiable.

The basic integration of a SAT solver with a theory solver is reported in Figure 3. The procedure SAT(φ) (satisfiability solver) returns a tuple $\langle r, M \rangle$ where r is *sat* if φ is satisfiable and *unsat* otherwise, and M is a truth assignment

SMT-Solver(φ)
    $\varphi' := \alpha(\varphi)$
    loop
        $\langle r, M \rangle := \text{SAT}(\varphi')$
        if $r = $ unsat then return unsat
        $\langle r, J \rangle := \text{T-Solver}(\gamma(M))$
        if $r = $ sat then return sat
        $C := \bigvee_{l \in J} \neg\alpha(l)$
        $\varphi' := \varphi' \wedge C$

Fig. 3. Basic SAT + Theory Solver integration

that satisfies φ if r is *sat*. The procedure T-Solver(S) (theory solver) returns a tuple $\langle r, J \rangle$ where r is *sat* if the set of literals S is satisfiable and *unsat* otherwise, and J is a justification for S if r is *unsat*. Note that $\bigvee_{l \in J} \neg\alpha(l)$ is a new clause not in φ', and we say it is a *theory lemma*.

The algorithm described in Figure 3 is also known as the *lazy offline* approach. There are many refinements for this basic algorithm. The basic idea is to have a tighter integration between the two procedures, where the T-solver is used to check partial truth assignments being explored by the SAT solver (*online integration*). In this refinement, additional performance gains can be obtained if the theory solver is incremental and backtrackable. Theory deduction rules can also be used to prune the search space being explored by the DPLL solver (*theory propagation*). More formally, let M be a partial truth assignment, and $\gamma(M)$ implies $\gamma(l_i)$, then l_i is assigned to true by theory propagation. Finally, it is desirable to have a theory solver that produces non-redundant justifications, because they may drastically reduce the search space. This observation follows from the fact that if $J \subset J'$, then the clause $\bigvee_{l \in J} \neg\alpha(l)$ is smaller than $\bigvee_{l \in J'} \neg\alpha(l)$, and consequently the number of truth assignments that satisfy the first clause is smaller than the second.

6   Combining Procedures

Section 4.1 summarized an array of different theories. Most of these theories are decidable and their decision procedures use specialized efficient algorithms. As the example in Section 1.1 illustrated, it does not always suffice to use one theory in isolation. A fundamental question arises: is the union of two solvable theories still solvable? If they are, how can procedures be combined? Can the glue for combining two procedures be defined without specific dependencies on the theories?

Given a Σ_1-theory T_1 and a Σ_2-theory T_2, we use $T_1 \oplus T_2$ to denote the $(\Sigma_1 \cup \Sigma_2)$-theory that is the union of the sentences of T_1 and T_2.

6.1   Strongly Disjoint Theories

We say Σ_1-theory T_1 and Σ_2-theory T_2 are *strongly disjoint* if Σ_1 and Σ_2 do not have sort symbols in common, and consequently no function and predicate symbols in common. For example, the theory of arithmetic and bit-vectors are strongly disjoint. Let $\mathfrak{S}_i$ be a decision procedure for theory T_i, then it is very easy to build a procedure $\mathfrak{S}$ for the $(\Sigma_1 \cup \Sigma_2)$-theory $T_1 \oplus T_2$. It is based on the simple observation that any set S of $\Sigma_1 \cup \Sigma_2$-literals is of the form $S_1 \cup S_2$ where S_i is a set of Σ_i-literals for $i = 1, 2$. Hence, S is satisfiable iff S_1 and S_2 are satisfiable.

6.2 Nelson-Oppen Combination

We say Σ_1-theory T_1 and Σ_2-theory T_2 are *disjoint* if Σ_1 and Σ_2 do not have function and predicate symbols in common. Note that Σ_1 and Σ_2 may have sort symbols in common. The Nelson-Oppen procedure [18] gives a method for combining decision procedures for disjoint theories T_1 and T_2 into one for $T_1 \oplus T_2$.

A theory T is *stably infinite* with respect to sort σ if for every formula φ satisfiable in T, there exists a structure M s.t. $M \models_T \varphi$ and $|M|_\sigma$ is infinite. We say a $(\Sigma_1 \cup \Sigma_2)$-formula φ is *pure* if every literal l in φ is a Σ_i-literal for $i = 1, 2$. Every quantifier-free $(\Sigma_1 \cup \Sigma_2)$-formula φ can be *purified* into a pure and equisatisfiable formula φ_p. The basic idea is to use the following satisfiability preserving transformation:

$$F[t] \rightsquigarrow F[u] \wedge u = t, \quad \text{where } u \text{ is a fresh variable.}$$

For example, let φ be the formula $f(x - 1) - 1 = x \wedge f(y) + 1 = y$, then after purification we obtain the equisatisfiable formula φ_p:

$$(u_2 - 1 = x \wedge u_3 + 1 = y \wedge u_1 = x - 1) \wedge (u_2 = f(u_1) \wedge u_3 = f(y))$$

A *partition* Π on a set of variables X is a disjoint collection of subsets $X_1, \ldots, X_n$ s.t. $(\bigcup_{i=1}^{n} X_i) = X$, and for all $x, y \in X_i$, x and y have the same sort. Given a partition Π, an *arrangement* A_Π is a union of the set of equalities $\{x \simeq y \mid$ for some i s.t. $x, y \in X_i\}$ and disequalities $\{x \not\simeq y \mid$ for some i, j s.t. $i \neq j, x \in X_i, y \in X_j\}$.

Given two disjoint theories T_1 and T_2 such that T_i is stably infinite with respect to each sort σ in Σ_1 and Σ_2, for $i = 1, 2$. The Nelson-Oppen combination theorem states that a pure formula $\varphi_1 \wedge \varphi_2$ is satisfiable in $T_1 \oplus T_2$ iff there exists an arrangement A_Π of the shared variables $X = vars(\varphi_1) \cap vars(\varphi_2)$ such that $\varphi_i \cup A_\Pi$ is satisfiable for $i = 1, 2$. The stable-infiniteness requirement in the Nelson-Oppen framework is used to bring the interpretation of the shared sorts to the same infinite cardinality.

A naïve implementation of the Nelson-Oppen combination method simply tries all possible arrangements. There are many refinements for this basic approach: the SAT solver is used to "guess" the arrangement (*delayed theory combination* [19]), candidate models (structures), produced by $\mathfrak{S}_i$, are used to "guess" the right arrangement (*model-based theory combination* [20]).

A theory T is *convex* iff for all finite sets S of literals and for all non-empty disjunctions $\bigvee_{i \in I} u_i \simeq v_i$ of variables, S implies $\bigvee_{i \in I} u_i \simeq v_i$ in T iff S implies $u_i \simeq v_i$ in T for some $i \in I$. Intuitively, a theory is convex if for every satisfiable set of literals there is a model where variables not implied to be equal have a distinct interpretation. The theory of linear rational arithmetic is convex, but the theory of linear integer arithmetic is not (e.g., if x, y and z are integers, then $\{x \simeq 0, y \simeq 1, 0 \leq z \leq 1\}$ implies $x \simeq z \vee y \simeq z$, but does not imply $x \simeq z$ or $y \simeq z$). For convex theories, instead of *guessing* a partition, one can *deduce* the equalities to be shared. The key idea is to propagate $x \simeq y$ to φ_2 whenever $T_1 \cup \varphi_1$ implies $x \simeq y$, and vice-versa. This process is repeated until no further equations can be propagated. Then, the individual procedures are used to decide whether φ_i is satisfiable. Sharing equalities in this case is sufficient, because $\mathfrak{S}_1$ can assume that in the structure M_2 produced by $\mathfrak{S}_2$ to satisfy φ_2, $M_2(x) \neq M_2(y)$ whenever $x \simeq y$ was not propagated and vice versa. So, for convex theories, there is an efficient way to construct a partition of the set of shared variables.

There are many extensions for the Nelson-Oppen combination method. For example, some of them are extensions for non-stably infinite theories [21,22] and for non-disjoint theories [23].

7   Meta-procedures

It is infeasible to implement a (semi-) decision procedure for every possible theory that may be useful in practice. Thus, some SMT solvers implement *meta-procedures* for classes of theories that can be described by a finite number of sentences. A *meta-procedure* $\mathfrak{S}$ is a (semi-) decision procedure for a class of theories Ω. Given a theory $T \in \Omega$ and a formula φ, $\mathfrak{S}$ can decide whether φ is satisfiable modulo T or not.

Instantiation Based Meta-procedures. The effectively propositional class, EPR, also known as the Bernays-Schönfinkel-Ramsey class of first-order formulas, comprises of formulas of the form $\forall^* \varphi$, where φ is a quantifier-free formula with predicate symbols and constant symbols, but without non-constant function symbols. The satisfiability problem for the EPR class can be reduced to Boolean satisfiability problem by instantiating the quantified formulas by all combinations of constants. Several useful theories, such as the theory of partial orders, are in the EPR class. The satisfiability problem for many other classes of formulas can be decided using instantiation methods [13,7,22].

Rewriting Based Meta-procedures. An *equational theory* is a theory containing only sentences of the form $\forall^* t = s$. Given a finite equational theory T, the Knuth-Bendix completion algorithm [24] is an algorithm for transforming the equations in T into a confluent term rewriting system. When the algorithm succeeds, it has effectively solved the satisfiability problem for T. Similarly, a *Superposition-Calculus* procedure [25] is a semi-decision procedure for the satisfiability problem for a finite set of many-sorted sentences. In many cases, superposition-calculus is a decision procedure [26].

8   Conclusion

In the last few years, satisfiability became the core engine underlying a wide range of powerful technologies. SMT is an active and exciting area of research with many practical applications [1]. We have presented some of the basic ideas, but a real implementation requires careful attention to a large number of details and heuristics that we have not covered. SAT and SMT solving technologies are already making a profound impact on a number of application areas. The theoretical challenges include better representations and algorithms, efficient methods for combining procedures, and various extensions to the basic search method.

References

1. Bjørner, N., de Moura, L.: Z3^{10}: Applications, Enablers, Challenges and Directions. In: CFV (2009)
2. Barrett, C., de Moura, L., Stump, A.: Design and Results of the 1st Satisfiability Modulo Theories Competition. JAR (2005)
3. McCarthy, J.: Towards a mathematical science of computation. In: IFIP Congress, pp. 21–28 (1962)
4. Davis, M., Logemann, G., Loveland, D.: A machine program for theorem proving. Communications of the ACM (1962)
5. Marques-Silva, J.P., Sakallah, K.A.: GRASP - A New Search Algorithm for Satisfiability. In: ICCAD (1996)
6. Moskewicz, M.W., Madigan, C.F., Zhao, Y., Zhang, L., Malik, S.: Chaff: Engineering an Efficient SAT Solver. In: DAC (2001)
7. Ge, Y., de Moura, L.: Complete instantiation for quantified SMT formulas. In: CAV (2009)
8. Dutertre, B., de Moura, L.: A Fast Linear-Arithmetic Solver for DPLL(T). In: Ball, T., Jones, R.B. (eds.) CAV 2006. LNCS, vol. 4144, pp. 81–94. Springer, Heidelberg (2006)
9. Tarski, A.: A decision method for elementary algebra and geometry. Technical report, 2nd edn. University of California Press, Berkeley (1951)
10. Buchberger, B.: Ein algorithmus zum auffinden der basiselemente des restklassenringes nach einem nulldimensionalen polynomideal. Technical report, Mathematical Institute, University of Innsbruck, Austria (1965)
11. Downey, P.J., Sethi, R., Tarjan, R.E.: Variations on the common subexpression problem. J. ACM 27, 758–771 (1980)
12. Stump, A., Barrett, C.W., Dill, D.L., Levitt, J.R.: A decision procedure for an extensional theory of arrays. In: LICS, pp. 29–37 (2001)
13. Bradley, A.R., Manna, Z., Sipma, H.B.: What's decidable about arrays? In: Emerson, E.A., Namjoshi, K.S. (eds.) VMCAI 2006. LNCS, vol. 3855, pp. 427–442. Springer, Heidelberg (2005)
14. de Moura, L., Rueß, H.: Lemmas on Demand for Satisfiability Solvers. In: SAT (2002)
15. Flanagan, C., Joshi, R., Ou, X., Saxe, J.B.: Theorem Proving Using Lazy Proof Explication. In: Hunt Jr., W.A., Somenzi, F. (eds.) CAV 2003. LNCS, vol. 2725, pp. 355–367. Springer, Heidelberg (2003)

16. Barrett, C., Dill, D., Stump, A.: Checking satisfiability of first-order formulas by incremental translation to SAT. In: Brinksma, E., Larsen, K.G. (eds.) CAV 2002. LNCS, vol. 2404, p. 236. Springer, Heidelberg (2002)

17. Nieuwenhuis, R., Oliveras, A., Tinelli, C.: Solving SAT and SAT Modulo Theories: From an abstract Davis–Putnam–Logemann–Loveland procedure to DPLL(T). J. ACM 53 (2006)

18. Nelson, G., Oppen, D.C.: Simplification by cooperating decision procedures. ACM Transactions on Programming Languages and Systems 1, 245–257 (1979)

19. Bruttomesso, R., Cimatti, A., Franzén, A., Griggio, A., Sebastiani, R.: Delayed Theory Combination vs. Nelson-Oppen for Satisfiability Modulo Theories: A Comparative Analysis. In: Hermann, M., Voronkov, A. (eds.) LPAR 2006. LNCS (LNAI), vol. 4246, pp. 527–541. Springer, Heidelberg (2006)

20. de Moura, L., Bjørner, N.: Model-based theory combination. In: Proc. 5th SMT Workshop, CAV 2007 (2007)

21. Jovanović, D., Barrett, C.: Polite Theories Revisited (to appear, 2009)

22. de Moura, L., Bjørner, N.: Generalized, Efficient Array Decision Procedures (to appear, 2009)

23. Tinelli, C., Ringeissen, C.: Unions of Non-Disjoint Theories and Combinations of Satisfiability Procedures. Theoretical Computer Science (2003)

24. Knuth, D.E., Bendix, P.B.: Simple word problems in universal algebras. Computational Problems in Abstract Algebra (1970)

25. de Moura, L., Bjørner, N.: Engineering DPLL(T) + saturation. In: Armando, A., Baumgartner, P., Dowek, G. (eds.) IJCAR 2008. LNCS (LNAI), vol. 5195, pp. 475–490. Springer, Heidelberg (2008)

26. Armando, A., Bonacina, M.P., Ranise, S., Schulz, S.: New results on rewrite-based satisfiability procedures. ACM TOCL 10, 129–179 (2009)

Interruption Testing of Reactive Systems

Wilkerson L. Andrade and Patrícia D.L. Machado

Federal University of Campina Grande (UFCG), Paraíba, Brazil
{wilker,patricia}@dsc.ufcg.edu.br

Abstract. Reactive systems may be composed of a number of concurrent processes and network distributed services, where interruptions in a flow of execution can occur at any time. These systems are very difficult to test. One of the reasons is that the possible number of combinations of allowed interruptions at different points of a flow of execution is huge. This makes exhaustive specification of each possibility infeasible. Without a specification, automated test case generation and selection is compromised. This work presents a strategy for testing interruptions in reactive systems that covers modelling (devoted to testing) of systems with interruptions, generation and selection of sound test cases. The strategy is supported by the LTS-BT tool. A case study is presented to illustrate its applicability in the mobile phone application domain.

1 Introduction

Reactive systems interact with their environment by accepting inputs and producing outputs. Apart from being inherently non-terminating, these systems are becoming more and more complex, for instance, by incorporating features such as interruptions that are caused by concurrent processes and network distributed services that demand instant execution in a given device. In this case, the process running in foreground is instantly suspended to release resources for the interrupting process. After the interruption, the interrupted process should resume from the point where it stopped. As an example, when a user is composing an e-mail by using a mobile phone device and an incoming call arrives in this device, the call feature interrupts the e-mail feature that must successfully resume later.

Considering that any interruption can occur at any point of a flow of execution, there are infinite possibilities of occurrences. This makes the exhaustive specification of each possibility infeasible and, consequently, automatic test case generation and selection is compromised. Effective testing requires a systematic investigation of all possibilities and, consequently, automation.

To provide an effective solution for interruption testing, it is crucial to define a model capable of representing such interruptions, and consequently, make the automatic test case generation process possible. In addition, the model has to be composable, allowing interruptions to be combined at different points of possibly different flows of execution. Moreover, due to the huge amount of possible test cases, selection strategies need to be applied to reduce the size of test suites.

M.V.M. Oliveira and J. Woodcock (Eds.): SBMF 2009, LNCS 5902, pp. 37–53, 2009.

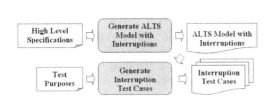
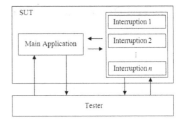

Fig. 1. Interruption Test Process   **Fig. 2.** Test Architecture

The particular problem of evaluating if a system implementation is in accordance with its specification by experimentation is referred to as conformance testing. Considerable progress has already been made in this area from both theoretical and practical point of view. The AGEDIS project [1] is an outstanding initiative. Nevertheless, to the best of our knowledge, approaches that handle applications with interruptions are practically nonexistent.

This paper presents a strategy for conformance testing of reactive systems with interruptions that covers modelling (devoted to testing), generation and selection of sound test cases. The model adopted is named Annotated Labelled Transition System (ALTS). This kind of Labelled Transition System (LTS) has special descriptions inserted into the model in order to make the test case generation process feasible. LTSs are good models for representing functional testing models because all information needed is the observable interactions between applications and environment and between applications. Also, they are the underlying formalism of most formal notations for reactive applications. The proposed model is implemented by the LTS-BT tool [2]. A case study illustrates the benefits of the strategy when compared to manual selection.

The remainder of this paper is structured as follows. Section 2 presents the general test process considered. Section 3 presents the ALTS behavioural model structure used to model interruptions. The interruption test case generation algorithm and a selection strategy based on test purposes are introduced in Section 4. In Section 5, some properties of the interruption test cases generated by LTS-BT are discussed. A case study is presented in Section 6. Finally, Section 7 presents related work and Section 8 concluding remarks.

2 Context

In general, the test process in the context of this work starts with the specification of the System Under Test (SUT) and interruptions. Given the high level specifications, an ALTS model is automatically generated. Finally, the ALTS model is combined with test purposes for interruption test case generation. The interruption test process uses test purposes in order to test at specific points of interest. A general view of this test process is presented in Figure 1.

The interruption test process considers the test architecture presented in Figure 2. In this test architecture, two elements are important: the SUT and

Main Flow

Description: The message is removed
From Step: START
To Step: END

Step Id	User Action	System State	System Response
1M	Go to "Message Center"		All folders are displayed
2M	Go to "Inbox"		All inbox messages are displayed
3M	Scroll to a message		Message is highlighted
4M	Select "Remove" option	Message is not blocked	"Message removed" is displayed

Alternative Flow

Description: The message is not removed because it is blocked
From Step: 3M
To Step: END

Step Id	User Action	System State	System Response
1A	Select "Remove" option	Message is blocked	"Blocked messages cannot be removed" dialog is displayed
2A	Confirm dialog		Message content is displayed

Fig. 3. *Remove Message* Specification

the tester. The SUT is composed by the main application and the interruptions allowed during the test process. The environment is assumed to be fully controllable by the tester, thus, during the test execution the tester has total control of the interruptions, deciding when they start and finish.

The SUT is specified as use cases using a controlled natural language [3]. An example of a use case of a mobile phone application is shown in Figure 3. This represents the behaviour of removing a message from inbox. A use case must have a main flow and can have some alternative flows. The flows are described through steps that include a user action and the respective system response. Besides the actor action and the system response, each step has a condition (System State) that determines if the system response will happen or not. If the condition is not satisfied, an alternative flow must be specified. As an example, the step "4M" of the main flow has one alternative flow (steps "1A" and "2A").

Considering the specification of interruptions, the adopted strategy is to specify an interruption in the same way and using the same use case template that is used to specify a simple behaviour of the SUT [4]. Once the interruption flow is specified, we assume that it can be executed at any time of another use case execution, i.e., between any step of another use case. With this, interruption behaviours are defined in a simple manner and all points where an interruption can occur do not need to be explicitly specified.

3   Interruption Model

This section presents the ALTS model structure capable of representing interruptions. Firstly, the semantics of an ALTS with interruptions is informally presented based on simple Input-Output Labelled Transition System (IOLTS)

Fig. 4. Simple IOLTS   **Fig. 5.** Modelling Interruptions Using IOLTS

models. Then the structure of the proposed model is defined and illustrated by an application in the mobile phone domain. Finally, conformance is discussed.

3.1 Representing Interruptions with IOLTS Models

Basically, LTS models are represented by graphs where nodes are possible system states and edges represent the action of moving between these states through occurrence of actions. Particularly, an IOLTS makes distinction between events of the system that are controllable by the environment (the inputs) and those that are only observable (the outputs). Internal actions can be represented too.

Figure 4 shows an example of an IOLTS. An input event is defined through the symbol "?" followed by the event name and an output event is defined through the symbol "!" followed by the event name.

It is possible to model interruptions using an IOLTS. For this, each possibility of interruption needs to have a specific set of states, implying that interruption flows must be duplicated. Figure 5 shows an example of how to model interruptions using IOLTS. Nodes from 0 to 4 are related to a behaviour that can be interrupted by another behaviour at nodes 1 and 3. Note that state 5 represents the possibility of interruption at node 1 and state 6 the possibility of interruption at node 3. Note that nodes 5 and 6 represent the same interruption behaviour.

The replication of the interruption model is due to the semantics of the behaviour. Suppose that only one state had been used to represent the interruption behaviour, then it would not be possible to associate a unique next state to the end of the interruption execution. After an interruption execution, the flow needs to continue from the same point where the interruption had started.

3.2 Annotated Labelled Transition Systems

ALTSs are capable of representing interruptions in a more compact way, following the same semantics presented in the previous section. This new kind of LTS follows the same classical LTS definition. The difference is that each label is associated with a description. This new description inserted into the model is called annotation. Before to define an ALTS we need to define a Generic Annotated Labelled Transition Systems (GALTS).

Definition 1 (GALTS). *A GALTS is a 5-tuple $\langle Q, A, L, q_0, T \rangle$, where:*

- *Q is a countable, non-empty set of locations;*
- *A is a countable, non-empty set of annotations;*
- *L is a countable, non-empty set of labels;*

- $q_0 \in Q$ *is an initial location;*
- T *is a set of transitions. Each transition consists of:*
  - *a location $q \in Q$, called the origin of the transition;*
  - *an annotation $a \in A$, called the annotation of the transition;*
  - *a label $l \in L$, called the label of the transition;*
  - *a location $q' \in Q$, called the destination of the transition.*

As said before, each label has an associated description (annotation). So in the GALTS definition (Definition 1) we have a set A that contains the possible descriptions of the labels. This set can be instantiated according to the information to be modelled or the context where the model will be used. In our case, we are interested in a model to support the test process, mainly a model capable of representing interruptions efficiently. Thus, we define a more specific GALTS where the set A of annotations has predefined elements.

Definition 2 (ALTS). *An ALTS is a 5-tuple $\langle Q, A, L, q_0, T \rangle$, where:*

- Q *is a countable, non-empty set of locations;*
- $A = \{steps, conditions, expectedResults, beginInterruption\_X, endInterruption\_X\}$ *is the set of annotations;*
- L *is a countable, non-empty set of labels;*
- $q_0 \in Q$ *is an initial location;*
- T *is a set of transitions. Each transition consists of:*
  - *a location $q \in Q$, called the origin of the transition;*
  - *an annotation $a \in A$, called the annotation of the transition;*
  - *a label $l \in L$, called the label of the transition;*
  - *a location $q' \in Q$, called the destination of the transition.*

These annotations were chosen with the following specific goals: (1) guide the test case generation process, by making the focus on particular interruptions easier; (2) make it possible for interruption models to be plugged and unplugged without interfering with the main model; (3) guide test case documentation; (4) make it possible for conditions to be associated with actions; (5) indicate points where interruptions can be reasonably observed externally.

The annotation *steps* is associated with a label $l \in L$ (we write $[steps]l$) to indicate that l is an input action. When a label $l \in L$ represents a condition associated with an input action, we use the annotation *conditions* and write $[conditions]l$. The expected results are indicated through *expectedResults* annotation ($[expectedResults]l$). The two other annotations are used to indicate the start and the end of an interruption and they are considered as special kinds of input actions and expected results, respectively. So the labels in L represent the observable actions or some condition associated to these actions.

Some more notations must be defined. Let $W = \langle Q, A, L, q_0, T \rangle$ be an ALTS. We write $q \xrightarrow{[a]l} q'$ for $(q, a, l, q') \in T$ and $q \xrightarrow{[a]l}$ for $\exists q' : q \xrightarrow{[a]l} q'$. An ALTS can be defined by its initial state, then we write $W \rightarrow$ for $q_0 \rightarrow$. Depending on the associated annotation, the labels can be classified as input actions, output actions, or conditions. Thus, let $L = L_I \cup L_O \cup L_C$, where L_I is the set of input actions, L_O is the set of output actions, and L_C is the set of conditions. Let $a_{(i)} \in A$ be some annotations, $\omega_{(i)} \in L$ be some labels, $\sigma \in ([A]L)^*$ a sequence of labels with their respective annotations, and q, $q' \in Q$ some states.

$\Omega(q) \triangleq \{a \in A, \omega \in L \mid q \xrightarrow{[a]\omega}\}$ is the set of firable locations in q. $Out(q) \triangleq \Omega(q) \cap [A \setminus \{steps, conditions, beginInterruption\_X\}]L_O$ is the set of firable outputs in q. The definition of $Out(q)$ can be extended for sets of states: for $P \subseteq Q$ we have $Out(P) \triangleq \{Out(q) \mid q \in P\}$. Denote $q \xrightarrow{[a_1]\omega_1...[a_n]\omega_n} q' \triangleq \exists [a_0]\omega_0, ..., [a_n]\omega_n : q = q_0 \xrightarrow{[a_1]\omega_1} q_1 \xrightarrow{[a_2]\omega_2} \cdots \xrightarrow{[a_n]\omega_n} q_n = q'$. The set q *after* $\sigma \triangleq \{q' \in Q \mid q \xrightarrow{\sigma} q'\}$ is the set of locations reachable from q, and P *after* $\sigma \triangleq \bigcup_{q \in P} q$ *after* σ is the set of locations reachable from the set P. $Traces(q) \triangleq \{\sigma \in ([A]L)^* \mid q \xrightarrow{\sigma}\}$ describes the set of labels with their respective annotations reachable from q. Considering the sequences of labels and annotations reachable from the initial location of an ALTS W, we define $Traces(W) \triangleq Traces(q_0)$.

Considering our running example presented in Section 2, Figure 6 presents an ALTS model that represents the behaviour of removing a message from inbox (locations from 0 to 13). This application is specified by the use case shown in Figure 3. This same model also represents the occurrence of interruptions (locations from 14 to 17). The incoming alert interruption specifies the arrival of a new kind of text messages where the text appears to the user inside a dialog box.

As we can see, in Figure 6, the interruption model is connected to the feature that can be interrupted (the main flow) using two new annotations: *beginInterrruption_X* and *endInterrruption_X*, where X is a counter. These annotations are used to memorise where the main flow has been interrupted. They are needed to represent the behaviour where the main flow continues its execution from the same point where it had been interrupted. For instance, if an interruption begins with the *beginInterruption_0* annotation it must finish with *endInterruption_0*.

One of the main advantages of using the Annotated LTS is that we can add the same interruption behaviour to many different points only manipulating the two new annotations (*beginInterrruption_X* and *endInterrruption_X*). Thus, we can represent interruptions in a more compact way than standard LTS, while preserving the same efficiency and precision in test generation.

Considering the time as being continuous, an interruption can occur at infinite points during the system execution. But considering the tester's point of view, each possibility of interruption can only be observed after each system response. This happens due to the fact that it is impractical to reproduce a scenario where an interruption occurs between an input action and the system response, mainly when tests are manually executed. It is important to remark that this is a limitation of the test process in general and not of the proposal presented in this paper. Thus, the intention is to represent only interruptions that occur immediately after the system responses. In this case, Figure 6 represents all possibilities of interruption from tester's point of view.

Note that, as we are considering an LTS model for testing, only functionalities to be tested are specified. Thus, we have a partial behavioural model. From

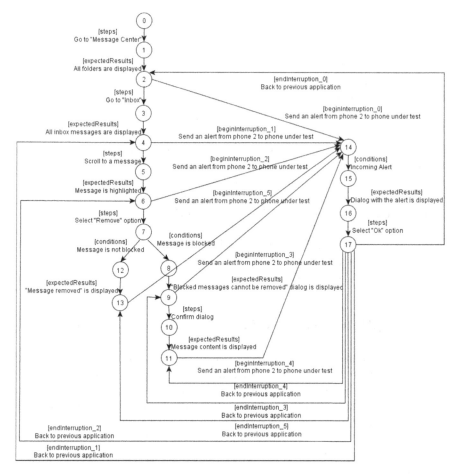

Fig. 6. *Remove Message* behaviour with Interruptions

tester's point of view, only the specified behaviour is observed, and with this, all other behaviours are not observed during the test, including other possible interruptions. We are assuming that the test execution environment is controlled by the tester, that is, one interruption only occurs when the tester wants.

In practice, this interruption model should not be written by hand because it is tiresome and not cost-effective. They must be generated directly from abstract specifications. The ALTS model presented in this section is automatically generated from those use case templates described in Section 2 by the LTS-BT tool [2]. This tool will be described in more details in the next section.

3.3   Testing Conformance

We are considering a testing theory that is based on the notions of *specification*, *implementation*, and a *conformance relation* between them [5]. The specification of a reactive system with interruption can be any notation with that semantics discussed in Subsection 3.1. But this work only considers use case templates or an ALTS that respects the constraints on labels use defined in Subsection 3.2. The implementation can be any computer system that can be interrupted at any time and can be modelled as an input-output labelled transition system [5] (Subsection 3.1). Moreover, we assume all interruptions to be controllable and implementations to be input-enabled, i.e., $\forall q \in Q, a \in A \setminus \{conditions, expectedResults, endInterruption\_X\}, \forall w \in L_I, q \overset{[a]w}{\rightarrow}$. The latter assumption is an usual limitation of testing techniques [5,6].

The conformance relation considered is the **ioco** relation defined by Tretmans in [5]. Informally, an implementation conforms to a specification for **ioco** if for all traces of the specification, the set of output actions of the implementation is contained in the set of output actions of the specification. This implementation relation is similar to the one considered by the TGV tool [6].

Definition 3 (ioco Conformance Relation). *Let the specification S be an ALTS and SUT be an input-enabled IOLTS:* SUT **ioco** $S \overset{\Delta}{=} \forall \sigma \in$ Traces(S), $Out(SUT$ after $\sigma) \subseteq Out(S$ after $\sigma)$.

4   Interruption Test Case Generation and Selection

This section presents the results related to the automation of the test process described in Section 2. Firstly, the algorithm developed to generate interruption test cases from ALTS is presented. Nevertheless, the algorithms used to translate use case templates to ALTS are not presented due to space restrictions. Finally, an interruption test case selection strategy based on test purposes is presented.

Intuitively, a test case (Definition 4) is a path from the root location to any leaf location. A test case can be obtained from ALTS model, using the Depth-First Search (DFS) method, by traversing the ALTS starting from the initial location. As a general coverage criterion, all transitions need to be covered, i.e., all transitions are visited at least once. In Figure 7, the algorithm to generate test cases is shown. As this algorithm is based on DFS method, its running time using the asymptotic notation is $O(|Q| + |T|)$, where $|Q|$ is the number of locations and $|T|$ is the number of transitions of the ALTS model.

Definition 4 (Test Case). *A test case is an ALTS TC* $= \langle Q^{TC}, A^{TC}, L^{TC}, q_0^{TC}, T^{TC} \rangle$. *The set of annotations is the same of the specification* $(A^{TC} = A^S)$ *and the set of labels is* $L^{TC} = L_I^{TC} \cup L_O^{TC} \cup L_C^{TC}$, *where* $L_I^{TC} \subseteq L_O^{SUT}$ *(outputs of the SUT are the inputs of the TC),* $L_O^{TC} \subseteq L_I^{SUT}$ *(TC emits only inputs allowed by the SUT), and* $L_C^{TC} \subseteq L_C^S$ *(the conditions are the same specified by the specification).*

The algorithm requires three parameters: *loc*, a location of the model, indicating the current one during execution; *path*, a set of transitions from the model, indicating the path visited during the processing; and *intCode*, the interruption code, indicates that a given interruption is being processed.

```
1   Decompose(Location loc, Path path, Integer intCode) {
2       if (loc.isLeaf() OR (loc.isRoot() AND path <> Ø)) {
3           // End of a path
4           recordTestCase(path);
5           return;
6       }
7       for each descendent in loc.getAdjacencies() {
8           edge := getEdgeBetween(loc, descendent)
9           if (edge.isBeginInterruption()) {
10              intCode := edge.getIntCode();
11          }
12          if ((edge.getIntCode() = -1 AND edge ∉ path) OR
                  (intCode >= 0 AND edge.getIntCode() = intCode)) {
13              path.add(edge);
14              if (edge.isEndInterruption()) {
15                  intCode := -1;
16              }
17              Decompose(descendent, path, intCode);
18          } else if (edge.getIntCode() = intCode) {
19              recordTestCase(path);
20          }
21      }
22      return;
23  }
```

Fig. 7. Test Case Generation Algorithm

The extraction is started from the root (the initial location of the ALTS model), verifying if the current location indicates the end of a path in the model, indicating that the test case has been extracted. In this case, it needs to be recorded. If the current location does not indicate the end of a path, then each of its descendants is visited through the depth-first search strategy.

To visit each of its descendants, the edge between the current location and its descendant is analysed. The search proceeds only if (Figure 7, Line 12): (i) the edge does not belong to the current analysed path, i.e., the edge has already been "visited" (note that when the algorithm is processing the main application, the value of $intCode$ is -1); or (ii) if it is an edge from an interruption behaviour (an edge with the $endInterruption\_X$ label). This precaution is necessary because after the interruption, the extraction process in the ALTS comes back to previous location (the last location of the main application before the interruption), therefore being possible to pass through the same interruption, in different parts of the model, and constraining that would cause inconsistency.

Due to these conditions, two scenarios are encountered: (1) Conditions (i) and (ii) are not satisfied: The search stops, recording the entire path as a test case avoiding loops in the main application and finishing an interruption with the correct $endInterruption\_X$ transition. In this case, the recursion step of the algorithm returns to the next branch that needs to be analysed, continuing the algorithm; (2) Condition (i) or (ii) is satisfied: The edge between the location and its descendent is added to the test case and the algorithm continues until it finds the end of the path, which happens when either a leaf in the graph or an edge going back to the root of the model are found.

These constraints over the extraction, when using the depth-first search approach, are required to avoid a burst of paths during the test case extraction caused by the loops in the ALTS model. This may reduce the number of extracted test cases, but without those constraints, the number of paths extracted becomes unfeasible, while most of them may be obtained by combining the extracted test cases. Also, practice has shown that these excluded paths generally add redundancy to the test suite, that is, they do not add test cases that would lead to uncover escaped faults.

An exhaustive interruption test case generation is impractical due to the huge amount of generated test cases. Particularly, in mobile phone applications context, the majority of test cases are manually executed. In this scenario, test case selection strategies are badly needed. The strategy used to reduce the test suite is a test case selection based on purposes. This strategy focuses on a coverage selection criterion, the test purpose, in order to test a particular system functionality. The defined test purpose is used to filter out the model, that is, it is used to remove all paths that do not lead to the desired behaviour to be tested. After that, the generation algorithm is executed, for then, generate the test cases.

Test purposes can be defined using a simple notation, where they are defined through transition sequences. In these sequences, an "*" (asterisk) indicates that, at this point, any transition can occur. A test purpose always finishes with a transition that has an *Accept* label (indicating that all test cases need to be in conformance with the purpose) or a *Refuse* label (otherwise).

Definition 5 (Test Purpose). *A test purpose is a deterministic LTS $TP = (Q^{TP}, L^{TP}, q_0^{TP}, T^{TP})$, equipped with the special labels Accept, Refuse, and "*", and with the same alphabet of the specification, i.e., $L^{TP} = L^S$. Q^{TP} is a countable, non-empty set of states, $q_0^{TP} \in Q^{TP}$ is the initial state, and T^{TP} is the transition relation.*

Some hints of how to define test purposes can be given as follows: (1) choose the behaviour to be observed in the implementation and identify its description in the specification; (2) if the behaviour to be observed is the first behaviour of the specification, then the test purpose should start with the description of this behaviour. Otherwise, add an asterisk followed by the description of the behaviour to be observed. This indicates that any behaviour can occur before the observation of the desired behaviour; (3) if there is more behaviours to be observed in the same test purpose, go back to the first step; (4) if the last behaviour description added to the test purpose is the last behaviour of the specification, then go to the next step. Otherwise, an asterisk should be added to the test purpose. This indicates that any other behaviour can occur after the desired behaviour; (5) the last step is to add an *Accept* or a *Reject* label to the test purpose. As mentioned before, the *Accept* label is used to indicate that all generated test cases must be in conformance with the test purpose. The *Reject* label is used otherwise.

As an example of a test purpose, we will use that ALTS model from Figure 6 (only locations from 0 to 13) in order to define a test purpose for a scenario where a message is not removed because it is blocked. For this scenario, the

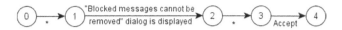

Fig. 8. LTS Model of a Test Purpose

following purpose could be defined: "*;'Blocked messages cannot be removed' dialog is displayed;*;Accept". The LTS model that represents this test purpose is showed in Figure 8.

It is very simple to define test purposes where an interruption can occur. Given that the behaviour to be interrupted has been chosen, the name of the interruption must appear immediately after the description of this behaviour in the test purpose. The ALTS model with interruptions from Figure 6 will be used to demonstrate how to define test purposes to check specific interruptions. A test purpose will be defined to test the scenario where an alert appears when the user is accessing the inbox folder. This scenario can be specified through the following test purpose: "*;All inbox messages are displayed;Incoming Alert;*;Accept".

Considering the defined test purpose, the model from Figure 6 is filtered out to meet it. So, the following edges are removed: *beginInterruption_0, endInterruption_0, beginInterruption_2, endInterruption_2, beginInterruption_3, endInterruption_3, beginInterruption_4, endInterruption_4, beginInterruption_5,* and *endInterruption_5*. The last step is to execute the test case generation algorithm.

All algorithms are implemented in the LTS-BT tool [2]. In order to make the test execution activity easier, considering that this activity is manual, the tool generates test cases in an alternative representation instead of ALTS. Each selected test case is transformed in matrices, where each condition is considered as an initial condition to execute the test case.

Figures 9 and 10 present the generated interruption test cases for the example above (the scenario where an alert appears when the user is accessing the inbox folder). Note that, in both generated test cases, the interruption occurs when the user is viewing the inbox folder, as it was specified by the test purpose. Moreover, all scenarios of the main feature are covered. In the test case of Figure 9, an interruption occurs in the scenario where the message is removed, whereas, in the test case of Figure 10, an interruption occurs in the scenario where the message is not removed because it is blocked.

Notably LTS-BT allows for a systematic and less error-prone coverage of all possible interruptions automatically, since the tester do not need to specify all possible points where an interruption can occur – this is assumed by the tool. Moreover, LTS-BT makes it easier to focus on particular points to be interrupted and interruptions. These LTS-BT characteristics allow the tester to obtain test cases in a faster and reliable way. Note that in the current version of LTS-BT, test cases are selected as paths in the ALTS model. Therefore, even though the model is capable of representing non-determinism, the tool suits only deterministic applications. This is currently being addressed.

Initial Condition	Message is not blocked

Steps	Expected Results
Go to "Message Center"	All folders are displayed
Go to "Inbox"	All inbox messages are displayed
Send an alert from phone 2 to phone under test	Dialog with the alert is displayed
Select "Ok" option	Back to previous application
Scroll to a message	Message is highlighted
Select "Remove" option	"Message removed" is displayed

Fig. 9. Test Case 01

Initial Condition	Message is blocked

Steps	Expected Results
Go to "Message Center"	All folders are displayed
Go to "Inbox"	All inbox messages are displayed
Send an alert from phone 2 to phone under test	Dialog with the alert is displayed
Select "Ok" option	Back to previous application
Scroll to a message	Message is highlighted
Select "Remove" option	"Blocked messages cannot be removed" dialog is displayed
Confirm dialog	Message content is displayed

Fig. 10. Test Case 02

5   Properties of the Interruption Test Cases

This section comments on properties of the interruption test cases generated by the generation algorithm presented in Section 4. Considering the execution of a test case against a SUT, three kinds of verdicts can be obtained indicating that the SUT should be approved or not: if the SUT emits the specified outputs for each input emitted by the test case, the verdict is *Pass*; if at least one of the outputs of the SUT is not specified by the specification, the verdict is *Fail*; and the *Inconclusive* verdict is emitted when the SUT conforms with the specification but the behaviour described by the test purpose is not exhibited by the SUT.

It is very important to formalize the execution of the test cases in order to establish some properties as soundness and exhaustiveness, where the conformance relation is linked to verdicts obtained during the test execution [6]. Interruptions are clearly asynchronous events, but as we are considering a test architecture where the environment is fully controllable by the tester, all interruptions can be analysed as synchronous events. Thus, test cases interact with the SUT through a synchronous communication, where the execution of a test case against a SUT is modelled by a parallel composition with synchronisation on common actions. Basically, the parallel composition is defined by the following rule: $P \parallel Q = \frac{p \xrightarrow{a}_P p', \ q \xrightarrow{a}_Q q'}{(p,q) \xrightarrow{a}_{P \parallel Q} (p',q')}$.

Considering the defined model of test case execution, $TC \parallel SUT$ will only finish when one of the following scenarios is reached: (1) if, at any moment, any unspecified output is emitted by the SUT, the execution is stopped and the resulting verdict is *Fail*; (2) if the SUT, at any moment, blocks or spends a lot of time to emit an output the resulting verdict is *Inconclusive* (a timer must be used in this case); (3) if the outputs of the SUT are specified by the specification but the behaviour specified by a test purpose is not exhibited the resulting verdict is *Inconclusive*; and (4) if all steps of the test case is executed and all expected results are observed, then the resulting verdict is *Pass*. Given the possible situations with their respective verdicts, the rejection of a SUT by a test case is defined as follows.

Definition 6 (may reject). *TC may reject SUT $\overset{\Delta}{=} \exists \sigma \in Traces(TC \parallel SUT)$, verdict$(\sigma)$ = Fail, where verdict(σ) = Fail $\overset{\Delta}{=} TC$ after $\sigma \not\subseteq Q^S$.*

The conformance relation of a SUT with respect to a specification is decided based on the verdicts obtained with the execution of the generated test cases. So, the next definition formally relates the previously defined conformance relation (Definition 3) to the verdicts of these executions.

Definition 7 (Soundness and Exhaustiveness). *A test case TC is said to be sound for S and **ioco** if $\forall SUT$, SUT **ioco** S $\Rightarrow \neg(TC$ may reject SUT) and it is said to be exhaustive for S and **ioco** if $\forall SUT$, $\neg(SUT$ **ioco** S) $\Rightarrow TC$ may reject SUT. Finally, a test suite is said to be complete if it consists of both sound and exhaustive test cases.*

Informally, a test suite is said to be sound if all correct implementations, and possibly some incorrect implementations, pass in the test (a sound test suite never rejects a correct implementation). On the other hand, a test suite is said to be exhaustive if all non-conforming implementations, and possibly some correct implementations, will not pass in the test. A test suite that can distinguish between all conforming and non-conforming implementations is called complete.

   A complete test suite is a very strong requirement for practical testing. Then, weaker requirements are accepted. In practice, sound test suites are more commonly accepted, since rejection of conforming implementations, by exhaustive test suites, may lead to unnecessary debugging. In this context, the test cases generated by LTS-BT have some properties stated by the following theorem:

Theorem 1. *For every specification S, all test suites generated by LTS-BT are sound. Moreover, the test suites can be considered as being exhaustive when they are associated with test purposes.*

The proofs of the Theorem 1 are not detailed here but the main ideas are discussed. For soundness, we need to prove that if a test case TC may reject a SUT (implementing the specification S), then ¬(SUT **ioco** S). In this case, we only need to prove that a *Fail* verdict of a test case only occur if the SUT emits an unspecified output. This was already discussed in this section and the unique case where a *Fail* verdict is obtained during a test case execution is exactly when the SUT emits un unspecified output. For exhaustiveness, we need to prove that for every non-conforming SUT there is a test purpose TP and a way of generating a test case TC from S and TP, such that TC may reject SUT. Given that ¬(SUT **ioco** S), then there is a trace σ of S such that an output of SUT after σ is not allowed by S. So, the trace σ can be used to define a TP, after that, this test purpose can be used to generate TCs where the SUT may be rejected.

6   Case Study

The objective of this section is to present a case study performed in order to evaluate a practical application of the proposed approach. As previously said, a scenario where interruptions are allowed may have infinite test cases. Thus, in practice, only a subset of interruption test cases are manually generated and executed. Considering this context, the main goal is to compare the manual process of test case generation with the automatic process implemented by LTS-BT [2]. In practice, this kind of testing is often conducted by manual processes of selection guided by expertise. Also, there are not related proposals of more systematic strategies that could make a good basis for comparison. As the amount of test cases is large, some test case selection strategy is needed. Particularly, in this case study, the strategy used to select the test suite was based on test purposes defined in order to cover a fault model defined based on real defects found in the past. The focus is on interruption testing, generation of test suites for manual execution, and the main metrics observed were the time wasted during the test case generation and selection and the coverage of the fault model.

This case study was performed using some reactive applications of the mobile phone domain. The feature chosen to be interrupted is the Aircraft Mode feature, it provides the functionality of allowing the user to turn off the radio frequency transceiver and still be able to use the applications of the phone. This feature allows the user to use applications of the phone while flying in an aircraft, but without receiving calls, messages, and so on. The other features of the case study (Incoming Call, Incoming Message, and Alarm Clock) are responsible for causing interruptions. It is important to remark that these four features represent 10 use cases and, considering the relationship between all them, the amount of interruption test cases is more than forty million tests.

The case study was conducted by three testers. Considering the knowledge of them, they had good test skills and none of them knew the features under test before the case study execution. They performed the case study based on the specification of the features according to that notation presented in Section 2 and a fault model defined based on common problems related to feature interruptions and real defects related to the features under test. The following topics describe the fault model: (1) after an interruption, the interrupted application does not maintain data entered by the user; (2) after an interruption, the interrupted application does not continue its execution of the same point where it was interrupted; (3) possible conflicts related to the use of shared resources (screen, network, and so on); (4) problems related to interruptions immediately before enabling the aircraft mode; (5) problems related to interruptions immediately after disabling aircraft mode; (6) problems related to interruptions when the aircraft mode is enabled. By measuring coverage of an instance of this specification with actual faults (instead of coverage of the specification), where one kind of fault may correspond to more than one actual fault, it is possible to analyse which approach can be more effective to systematically investigate the implementation by generating a more complete test suite.

All testers had the same preparation time (Table 1). Tester 1 generated the test suite through automatic process using LTS-BT [2], and Tester 2 and Tester 3 generated the tests through manual process. According to the results, from Table 1, Tester 1 generated the largest test suite (line "Number of TCs", where

Table 1. Metrics

Metrics	Tester 1	Tester 2	Tester 3
Preparation time	2 h	2 h	2 h
Number of TCs	115	15	12
Generation time	80 min	165 min	150 min
Productivity	86,5 TCs/h	5,4 TCs/h	4,8 TCs/h
Fault model coverage	57,14%	28,57%	28,57%
Number of valid TCs	115 (100%)	11 (73,33%)	8 (66,66%)
Number of ineffective TCs	23 (20%)	13 (86,66%)	7 (58,33%)
Most common TC size	5	6 and 8	8

TCs means Test Cases). Furthermore, Tester 1 generated the tests in less time (line "Generation time") implying in more productivity. The productivity was calculated observing the number of test cases generated per hour.

Considering the fault model coverage (Table 1, line "Fault model coverage"), Tester 1 reached the best coverage. However, as the process is guided by test purposes defined by the tester, the quality of the test cases depends on the tester's experience. On the other hand, test cases generated through manual process are error-prone. The line "Number of valid TCs" of Table 1 shows the number of test cases generated with errors, that is, test cases impossible to run, mainly because they miss information. Moreover, manually generated test suites tend to not take all scenarios of an interruption into account. This does not occur in the automatic process because when the tester decides, for example, to check the incoming call interruption at some point of the feature under test, the developed algorithms consider all scenarios of the interruption, for example, when the call is accepted and when it is rejected by the user.

Considering the number of test cases that actually do not find defects (line "Number of ineffective TCs"), Tester 1 reached the best results. The last line of Table 1 gives information about the most common size (w.r.t number of steps) of generated test cases. This is explained by the fact that test cases were generated based on a structured document that may induce the same general kind of test cases to be defined. In practice, manual testing is not usually based on structured documents and then test cases tend to be as simple as possible. However, not using the same input document would put a thread to validity of the results.

According to this preliminary investigation, it is possible to conclude that the proposed strategy contributes to better productivity and fault coverage, depending on the tester's experience. Moreover, some problems of the manual process such as erroneous test cases generation is solved by the automatic process since all generated tests are sound (Section 5).

7   Related Work

Lorentsen et al. [7] propose a way of identifying categories of interactions and create behavioural models that capture those interactions, where interruptions are a type of interaction. They use Colored Petri Nets to manually model the interactions and a model checker for interactive graphical simulation. As disadvantages, the process is manual and the work is not devoted to testing.

Another interesting work is that belonging to Jard and Jéron [6], where the TGV tool is presented. TGV receives a specification and a test purpose as input and produces abstract test cases as output. The TGV input format for both specification and test purpose is IOLTS (already defined in Subsection 3.1). As we saw in Subsection 3.1, it is possible to represent interruptions through IOLTS models. So the TGV tool can be used to generate interruption test cases, but an interruption behaviour needs to be replicated if it can occur at more than one place. Moreover, it is not possible to represent conditions associated to actions and due to the fact that the same interruption behaviour is replicated in the IOLTS model, the test purpose must specify the point where we want to verify the interruption and all other points where the interruption cannot occur. Thus, given that the tester needs to manipulate LTS models in the definition of the TGV test purposes, this notation is not useful in practice.

One possible solution is to consider the tools set proposed by the AGEDIS project that can generate test cases from high level models (e.g. UML diagrams) [1], where TGV is internally used to generate test cases. However, the tools set does not support interruption specifications directly as well as the newest version of UML (UML 2.0) with is greatly improved diagrams. In this case, the difficulties on interruption modelling and test purposes definition remain.

Finally, the process algebra CSP (Communicating Sequential Processes) was designed for describing systems of interacting components [8]. CSP has a specific operator for describing interruptions but its semantics is very different from our proposal. This operator specifies that when a process P_1 is interrupted by another process P_2, the process P_1 is discarded and P_2 begins its execution. In our context, the process P_1 executes again after the execution of P_2. Jovanovic et al. [9] have proposed an extension of CSP to represent this kind of behaviour but there is not any tool supporting their proposal. Figueiredo et al. [4] presents a behavioural model that represents interruptions in CSP without using the interruption operator, but the model is more suitable for representing the semantics of interruption behaviour (such as the ones that can be modelled by ALTS).

8   Concluding Remarks

This work proposes a strategy of interruption testing that is based on a model capable of representing interruptions for reactive systems. The model makes it possible for interruptions to be combined at different points of possibly different flows of execution. This model is supported by LTS-BT along with a test case generation algorithm and a test purpose selection technique. Test selection is crucial for interruption testing since the number of possible test cases is enormous. Also, in practice, not all possible points of interruption are fault-prone.

The current version of LTS-BT is restricted to deterministic systems. This may seem unrealistic. However, particularly, if embedded systems such as mobile phone applications are considered, the tool can be largely applied. For these systems, applications are often deterministic ones that run on single-processor, single and restricted screen, and so on. But have complex patterns of interruptions which clearly justify the need for modelling and systematic test selection. Furthermore, ALTS models are capable of representing non-determinism and the algorithms can be clearly extended to support non-deterministic systems since the semantics of ALTS and IOLTS are very similar.

As further work, this model is going to be extended to consider multiple processes and cascade interruptions in order to widen its applicability. Moreover, it is going to be extended to include timing requirements for extending its application to real-time systems. LTS-BT is going to be extended to support non-deterministic systems. The tool is also going to be extensively applied to case studies, particularly in the mobile phone applications domain. This is also going to be integrated with test code generation tools.

References

1. Hartman, A., Nagin, K.: The agedis tools for model based testing. SIGSOFT Softw. Eng. Notes 29(4), 129–132 (2004)
2. Cartaxo, E.G., Andrade, W.L., Neto, F.G.O., Machado, P.D.L.: LTSBT: A tool to generate and select functional test cases for embedded systems. In: SAC 2008: Proceedings of the 2008 ACM symposium on Applied computing, vol. 2, pp. 1540–1544. ACM Press, New York (2008)
3. Cabral, G., Sampaio, A.: Formal specification generation from requirement documents. In: Brazilian Symp. on Formal Methods (SBMF), Natal, pp. 217–232 (2006)
4. de Figueiredo, A.L.L., Andrade, W.L., Machado, P.D.L.: Generating interaction test cases for mobile phone systems from use case specifications. SIGSOFT Softw. Eng. Notes 31(6), 1–10 (2006); Proceedings of the AMOST 2006
5. Tretmans, J.: Test generation with inputs, outputs, and quiescence. In: Margaria, T., Steffen, B. (eds.) TACAS 1996. LNCS, vol. 1055, pp. 127–146. Springer, Heidelberg (1996)
6. Jard, C., Jéron, T.: TGV: theory, principles and algorithms: A tool for the automatic synthesis of conformance test cases for non-deterministic reactive systems. Int. J. Softw. Tools Technol. Transf. 7(4), 297–315 (2005)
7. Lorentsen, L., Tuovinen, A.P., Xu, J.: Modelling feature interactions in mobile phones. In: Feature Interaction in Composed Systems (ECOOP 2001), Budapest, Hungary, pp. 7–13 (2001)
8. Schneider, S.: Concurrent and Real-Time Systems: The CSP Approach. John Wiley & Sons, Inc., New York (2000)
9. Jovanovic, D.S., Orlic, B., Broenink, J.F.: On issues of constructing an exception handling mechanism for csp-based process-oriented concurrent software. In: Proc. of Comm. Process Architectures CPA 2005, Eindhoven, pp. 18–21. IOS Press, Amsterdam (2005)

Test Case Generation of Embedded Real-Time Systems with Interruptions for FreeRTOS*

Wilkerson L. Andrade, Patrícia D.L. Machado, Everton L.G. Alves, and Diego R. Almeida

Federal University of Campina Grande (UFCG), Brazil
{wilker,patricia,everton,diegor}@dsc.ufcg.edu.br

Abstract. This paper discusses issues raised in the construction of test models and automatic generation of test cases for embedded real-time systems with interruptions that can run on the FreeRTOS operating system. The focus is on the use of symbolic transition systems (STSs) as the formalism from which test cases are generated by using the STG tool. The solution presented considers a test case execution model for real-time systems with interruptions that can be based on the integrated use of FreeRTOS components. A case study is presented to illustrate all steps from the construction of the test model to test case generation.

1 Introduction

The correct functioning of real-time systems depends on the results produced by the system and the time at which they are produced [1]. These systems are also reactive systems that can receive both periodic and aperiodic stimuli. Moreover, these systems are usually organised as a set of concurrent processes, where interruption mechanisms are defined to handle aperiodic stimuli. Therefore, testing of these systems inherits all challenges presented by testing concurrent and reactive systems by additionally bring in issues on timing and interruption.

Real-time systems often run on a special kind of operating system called Real-Time Operating System (RTOS) that provides facilities to the programmer such as process execution predictability, data structures and mechanisms for inter-process communication, including interruption handling primitives. The focus of this work is on functional testing of real-time systems with interruptions that run on FreeRTOS [2] – a mini-kernel that can be used to develop real-time systems for embedded devices [2]. Embedded systems are usually critical systems with real-time requirements and interruptions. Therefore, dependability is a key issue that demands rigorous application of V&V activities and also relies on dependability of FreeRTOS. From a testing perspective, FreeRTOS requires at least two kinds of testing: 1) unit level, where components are tested in isolation; 2) integration level, where components work together to provide support for a system application. In both cases, a formal specification of the intended

---

* Supported by MCT/CNPq/CT-INFO 07/2007 - PD&I-TI - Process 550946/2007-1.

M.V.M. Oliveira and J. Woodcock (Eds.): SBMF 2009, LNCS 5902, pp. 54–69, 2009.

behaviour is needed to improve quality and confidence on testing results. As general strategies for event handling at application level, for instance interruption handling, must be implemented by the system developer based on the functionalities provided, integration testing of these functionalities can only be performed upon the existence of applications. In other words, application level integration testing of FreeRTOS can only be performed in the scope of applications that are developed on it: execution scenarios of the application are used to identify what needs to be tested (among a number of possible combinations) and how to test.

The main goal of this work is to propose a test case generation strategy for real-time systems with interruptions that are designed to run on FreeRTOS. As a result, the aim is to contribute to the definition of a strategy and an infrastructure that can support integration testing of the FreeRTOS components used. For this, a case study – an alarm system – will be considered so that issues on modelling, test case generation and execution can be investigated. The main challenges to be faced are: 1) to define an appropriate test model formalism supported by a well-founded theory that is capable of representing these systems and 2) to identify and design FreeRTOS infrastructure for running test cases for these systems. Solutions to both challenges must be encompassed by test case generation procedures to make test cases valid and executable. Although much progress has already been made in the theory and practice of testing real-time systems [3,4], these challenges still have open problems. For instance, interruptions and real-time requirements are not usually supported by the same formalism.

In this work, Symbolic Transition Systems (STSs) are considered as the formalism from which test cases are generated. The aim is to handle both timing and symbolic data manipulation that is not addressed by current timed automata-based approaches (avoiding the need for state space enumeration). Also, a solid theory along with tool support has already been developed for STSs and there is a growing interest to extend transition systems to handle real-time issues [5,6]. Transition systems have also been defined as the underlying semantics of many abstract formalisms and therefore they can be widely applied. In this paper, an extension of the model defined by Jéron et al. [7,8,9,10] that handles time requirements and interruptions is proposed. For the sake of abstraction, the specification of real-time systems starts with the construction of UML 2 [11] models that are translated into corresponding STSs models. To check whether behaviour is preserved, both UML and STS models are inspected. Test cases are generated by using the STG tool [8] based on test purposes that are defined according to testing goals.

This paper is structured as follows. Section 2 introduces FreeRTOS. Section 3 presents a test execution model that can be implemented in FreeRTOS. Section 4 presents a strategy to model interruptions and introduces an extension of STSs to handle time requirements. Section 5 presents transformation rules from UML 2 diagrams to STSs. Section 6 presents a case study and Section 7 presents concluding remarks and pointers to further work. We assume the reader to be familiar with basic concepts on UML 2 [11] diagrams and STSs [7].

2   FreeRTOS

FreeRTOS [2] is a portable, open source, mini real-time kernel that can be used to develop commercial applications for small embedded systems. It was developed with the goal to be small, simple and easy to use. By now, 17 official versions for different architectures are available and the code is predominantly written in C.

In a conventional operating system, each task is an executable program under control of the operating system that can only execute one task at a time. However, the rapid exchange between tasks can make it appear as a concurrent execution of them. In a real-time operating system, the principles are the same, but the goals are different since they are designed to respond to events with time requirements. The main difference is the scheduling policy. The policy of a conventional operating system is to provide a fair proportion of time for each task, whereas FreeRTOS uses a priority policy to ensure time requirements.

FreeRTOS has three scheduling modes: preemptive (a task can be interrupted at any time by the scheduler), cooperative (a task can block and enable the scheduler for context switching) and hybrid (preemptive and cooperative). It supports both tasks and co-routines and provides execution trace. In addition, it provides queues, semaphores and mutexes as mechanisms for communication and synchronisation between tasks, or between tasks and interruptions.

Considering the context of real-time systems, events can be classified into synchronous and asynchronous events. The former are those that occur at predictable points in the flow of control and are represented by conditional branches, invocation of procedures or methods, occurrence of internal trap interruptions (in the case of exception handling), etc. The latter occur at unpredictable points in the flow of control. An important characteristic of the asynchronous events is that they are usually caused by external sources, for instance, an alarm system of a building has sensors to detect intruders and once a movement is detected, the sensors interrupt the main application of the alarm system. In this scenario, the main application of the alarm system cannot predict when an event will occur because it is caused by external sources.

Real-time systems have to take actions in time to respond to events in order to guarantee time requirements. FreeRTOS does not impose any event processing strategy at the application level, but it provides features that allow simple implementation of an interruption scheme [12]. For example, a binary semaphore can be used to unblock a main task each time an interruption occurs. This strategy allows the interruption scheme to be implemented through a synchronised task named Interruption Service Routine (ISR). When an interruption occurs, ISR executes and uses a semaphore to unblock the task responsible for handling the interruption – the Handler task. Once unblocked and as the Handler task has the highest priority, it starts to execute immediately, leaving the interrupted task in the ready state. Finally, the Handler task blocks to wait for the next interruption, allowing a lower priority task to run again.

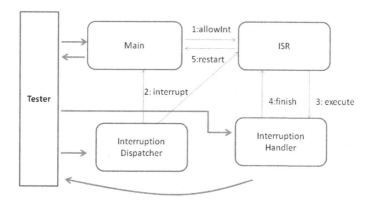

Fig. 1. A test execution model for FreeRTOS

3 Test Execution Model for FreeRTOS

The test execution model under FreeRTOS considered in this work is presented in Figure 1. This model is adapted from the one presented by Figueiredo *et al.* [13] for interruption handling at application level in mobile phone systems. The model is composed of modules responsible for interruption management, handling, the main application and testing monitoring and execution. `Interruption Handler` is a task responsible for treating a given interruption. `Interruption Dispatcher` is a task or external entity responsible for generating interruptions. `ISR` is a task responsible for delegating the interruption handling to the responsible task.

`Interruption Dispatcher` communicates with the `ISR` through two signals: *interrupt* and *noInterruption*. The *interrupt* signal indicates that an interruption has occurred in the system, for instance, an incoming message or incoming call. And with the *noInterruption* signal follows the information that no interruption has occurred. Communication with `ISR` is performed through four signals: *allowInterruption, interrupt, restart*, and *finish*. *allowInterruption* is used by the tasks to inform the `ISR` that interruptions are allowed. *interrupt* is used by `ISR` to inform the tasks that an interruption has occurred. *restart* is used by `ISR` to inform the task that it can continue its execution. Finally, *finish* is used by the tasks that handle interruptions to inform `ISR` that such handling has finished.

The arrows in Figure 1 are exemplifying the scenario where an interruption occurs. At some execution point, `Main` sends an *allowInterruption* signal to `ISR` informing that in that point interruptions are allowed (1); at this moment, `Interruption Dispatcher` can send a *noInterruption* signal informing that no interruption has occurred, or an *interrupt* signal (2), making `ISR` transfer the execution to `Interruption Handler` (3) that is responsible for the interruption handling. When it finishes the handling, a *finish* signal is sent to `ISR` (4) that sends a *restart* signal to `Main` (5), so it can continue its execution from the point where it stopped.

`Tester` is a task responsible for conducting and monitoring a given test execution, by providing input stimuli and observing output behaviours. It is assumed that it has total control of `Interruption Dispatcher`, deciding when and what interruptions may occur. Mechanisms for interprocess communication can be used for communications between `Tester` and `Main`, `Interruption Dispatcher` and `Interruption Handler` in order to control and observe behaviour produced by them.

In summary, when constructing systems with interruptions for FreeRTOS to be tested under this model, it is necessary to develop `ISR`, `Interruption Dispatcher` and one `Interruption Handler` for each interruption or group of interruptions to be handled. For test case generation, it is also necessary to model detailed behaviour that includes interaction between them and the system tasks as illustrated in Section 6. The `Tester` module is developed by the testing team according to the test cases defined.

It is possible to reuse parts of these modules for different systems, but this is out of the scope of this paper. As general guidelines, a binary semaphore can be used to unblock `Interruption Handler` each time the corresponding interruption occurs. When either this task is started or when it finishes to handle an interruption, it gets blocked on this semaphore. Moreover, it is crucial that this task priority is set as high as it is necessary to ensure it always preempts other tasks.

4   STSs with Interruptions and Time

This section presents the strategy used to model interruptions through STSs proposed by Andrade and Machado [14] and an extension capable of representing time requirements that is introduced here. In graphical representations of STSs, input actions are followed by the "?" symbol and output actions by the "!" symbol.

Figure 2 presents a symbolic model that represents the behaviour of an alarm system that monitors a room for detecting invasion by checking on occurrences of movement and door disclosure. This is represented by locations from 1 to 12. The monitoring process can be interrupted by a power failure handling process that will start a backup power supply (locations 13 to 21). The interruption is only allowed before and after checking the sensors (locations 3 and 11). Note that the interruption handling model is connected to the main process that can be interrupted (the main flow) using a special action named *Interrupt* carrying a parameter (*intCode*) that identifies the place where the interruption is allowed. Then, the value of the parameter *intCode* is saved in the variable *choice*. Each point where an interruption is allowed has a different integer value associated with it (see locations 3 and 11). Another important information is in the last action of the interruption: there is a guard used to guarantee that the main flow continues its execution from the same point where it had been interrupted. For instance, if an interruption begins with the parameter *intCode* equals to 1, then it must finish performing the action that has the following guard: *choice = 1*.

From the testers point of view, only interruptions that are interesting to test at specific points are added to this model. Also, the idea is that this model is

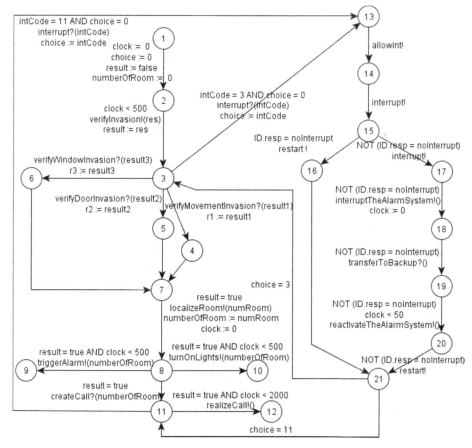

Fig. 2. STS model of an alarm system

automatically generated from a high level notation such as the one introduced by Figueiredo *et al.* [13]. Moreover, as only a few combinations will actually be tested, threats to scalability are so not considerable. For the sake of simplicity, nested interruptions are not allowed in this model. Nevertheless, this is not a severe constraint to its application since, in practice, usually only one interruption is tested at a time due to the complexity of the test execution itself and also to make it easier for faults to be pinpointed (the more complex a test is, the more error-prone and complex to analyse it is, particularly for concurrent systems).

Some hints of how to link a model with an interruption are: 1) identify the point where the interruption may occur; 2) link this point to the interruption behaviour using a transition labelled as follows: the guard is *intCode = X and choice = 0*, where X uniquely identifies this point of interruption; the action is *Interrupt?(intCode)*; the assignment is *choice := intCode*; 3) connect the last action of the interruption behaviour to the same point where the interruption started using a transition labelled with the guard *choice = X*, where X is the same value that uniquely identifies this point of interruption.

The test case generation strategy where only one interruption is allowed for each test case is reached because of the second part of the guard (*choice* = *0*) associated with the *Interrupt* actions. When an interruption is allowed, the value of the variable *choice* is changed to any value different from zero, then all other interruptions are automatically discarded during the test case generation.

Definition 1 presents an extension of STSs that considers time requirements.

Definition 1 (TIOSTS). *Formally, a Timed Input-Output Symbolic Transition Systems (TIOSTS) is a tuple* $\langle V, P, \Theta, L, l^0, \Sigma, C, \mathcal{T} \rangle$*, where:*

- *V is a countable set of typed variables;*
- *P is a countable set of parameters. For $x \in V \cup P$, type(x) is the type of x;*
- *Θ is the initial condition, a predicate with variables in $V \cup P$;*
- *L is a countable, non-empty set of locations;*
- *$l^0 \in L$ is the initial location;*
- *$\Sigma = \Sigma^? \cup \Sigma^! \cup \Sigma^\tau$ is a countable, non-empty alphabet, where $\Sigma^?$ is a countable set of input actions, $\Sigma^!$ is a countable set of output actions, and Σ^τ is a countable set of internal actions. Each action $a \in \Sigma$ has a signature sig(a) = $\langle t_1, ..., t_n \rangle$, that is a tuple of distinct parameters. The signature of internal actions is the empty tuple;*
- *C is a countable set of clocks;*
- *$\mathcal{T}$ is a countable set of transitions. Each one is a tuple $\langle l, a, G, A, d, l' \rangle$, where:*
  - *$l \in L$ is the origin location of the transition,*
  - *$a \in \Sigma$ is the action of the transition,*
  - *$G = \Xi \wedge \Psi$ is the guard of the transition, where Ξ is a predicate with variables in $V \cup P \cup sig(a)$ and Ψ is a clock constraint over C. Ψ is defined as a conjunction of constraints of the form $\alpha\#c$, where $\alpha \in C$, c is an integer constant and $\# \in \{<, \leq, =, \geq, >\}$,*
  - *$A = K \cup \Phi$ is the assignments of the transition. For each variable $x \in V$ there is exactly one assignment in K, of the form $x := K^x$, where K^x is an expression on $V \cup P \cup sig(a)$. $\Phi \subseteq C$ is a set of clocks to set to zero,*
  - *$d \in \{lazy, delayable, eager\}$ is the deadline of the transition,*
  - *$l' \in L$ is the destination location of the transition.*

The main idea is to introduce a new kind of variable for managing time. Figure 3 represents a scenario with a timing requirement: if a movement is detected, the lights must be switched on within 1 time unit. In Figure 3, note that, according to Definition 1, *clock* $\in C$.

Note that this is not intended to be a final solution to modelling time in STSs, but it will be enough for the purposes of this study, by assuming that the algorithms will handle the differences between regular and time variables.

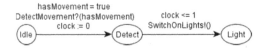

Fig. 3. TIOSTS Example

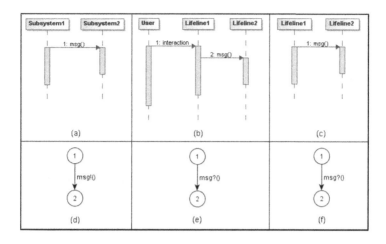

Fig. 4. Mapping messages

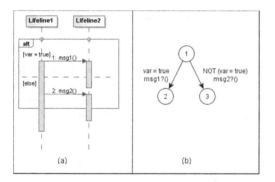

Fig. 5. Mapping ALT fragment

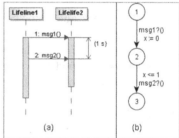

Fig. 6. Mapping time requirements

5   From UML 2 to STSs

This section briefly presents a few rules that can be used to transform UML models of real-time systems into STSs. The following UML diagrams can be used for modelling real-time systems: 1) Component diagram, used to specify interaction between subsystems; 2) State machine diagram, used to show which objects and/or components are susceptible to be interrupted; and 3) Sequence diagram, used to express the behaviour of the system including time requirements and structures like loops and conditional commands.

Mapping messages. There are three kinds of messages in sequence diagrams: 1) a message between subsystems: when a message is between two lifelines and these represent subsystems (this can be detected in the component diagram), a transition is created, where this one will have an output action labelled with the same name as the original operation from the message (Figure 4a and

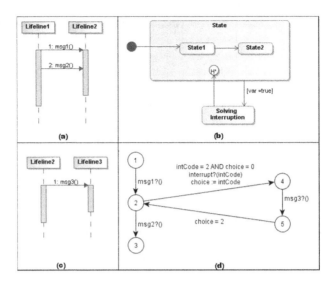

Fig. 7. Examples of mapping interruptions

Figure 4d); 2) a message from the user/environment to system: this one does not have mapping, but the following message will be mapped to a transition with an input action (Figure 4b and Figure 4e); and 3) a regular message: a regular message will be mapped to a transition with an action labelled with the same name as the original operation from the message (Figure 4c and Figure 4f).

Mapping ALT fragment. This allows the specification of alternate behaviours if a condition on the main flow cannot be satisfied. The flow is split into two paths. All the transitions of the first flow will have the guard from the first line. The second flow will have the negation of the same guard (Figure 5).

Mapping time requirements. On the transition that refers to the message of the initial time requirement, set the clock variable to zero. On the transition that refers to the message of the end time requirement, add a guard that verifies if the time constraint is satisfied (Figure 6).

Mapping interruptions. Interruptions can be modelled by: 1) sequence diagram modelling the regular behaviour of the system (Figure 7a); 2) state machines for each involved object (Figure 7b); and 3) sequence diagram that model the behaviour of the interruption (Figure 7c). Mapping can be made as follows. For each mapped message, if the state machine of the target object has a pseudo state history (Figure 7b), a transition T_1 is added to the current location L, having the interruption model as target. Next, a new transition T_2, from the end of the interruption model with target in L, is added too. T_1 will have three features: 1) a guard that verifies if no interruption occurred before; 2) a special action named *Interrupt* carrying a parameter ($intCode$) that identifies the place where the interruption is allowed; and 3) an assignment where a variable

V will receive a label from the location L. T_2 will have a guard that verifies if V corresponds to the label of L (Figure 7d).

6   Case Study

This section presents a case study using a practical example adapted from [1] of an application that can be implemented on FreeRTOS following the execution model presented in Section 3. The chosen example is a burglar alarm system, a real-time monitoring system. The objective of the system is to monitor sensors to detect the presence of intruders in a building. This system uses different kinds of sensors including movement detectors in individual rooms, window sensors, which detect the breaking of a window and door sensors, which detect the opening of doors. There are 50 window sensors, 30 door sensors, and 200 movement detectors. When a sensor indicates the presence of an intruder, the system automatically calls the police and, with a voice synthesiser, reports the position of the alarm. In addition, the system switches on lights around the area with active sensors and switches on an audible alarm. The system is normally powered by the central power supply system, but it is equipped with a battery backup. The loss of power is detected by a circuit monitor that monitors the main tension. The system switches automatically to backup power when a voltage drop is detected.

Firstly, an UML model of the system is constructed based on the generic model presented in Section 3. Some of the diagrams produced are presented in the sequel, focusing on interruption behaviour. Figure 8 shows structurally which components are part of the system and defines where communications, between those components, occur. The *Building Monitor* (**Main** in the generic model) and *Sensor Manager* components are responsible for implementing the regular system behaviour. The *Circuit Monitor Handler* component is responsible for the interruption behaviour (**Interruption Handler**). As in the generic model, the *Interruption Dispatcher* component is responsible for deciding if an interruption can occur and *ISR* is the component responsible for delegating the interruption handling to the responsible tasks. Figure 9 describes the regular alarm system behaviour evidencing how the interaction between its elements occurs.

Figure 10 and Figure 11 shows how the loss of power interruption behaviour is modelled. The first one shows how the interaction between the components responsible for treating the interruption occurs, following the guidelines presented in Section 3. If no interruption has been raised, then *Building Monitor* proceeds its execution. Otherwise, *Interruption Dispatcher* raises an interruption and control is transferred to *Circuit Monitor Handler*. Among the state machines relative to the system objects, Figure 11 shows the possibility of occurring an interruption during *Building Monitor* execution. When an interruption occurs, the *noPower* internal variable will be set to *true* and the behaviour of the **Running Backup** state will be executed. The pseudo state History (H*) guarantees that, after the interruption treatment, the system execution goes back to the most recent active configuration of the **Running** composite state that directly contains this pseudo state (the state configuration that was active when the **Running** composite state was interrupted).

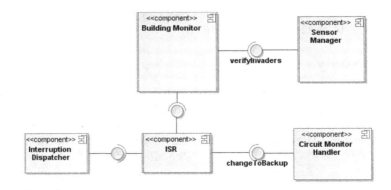

Fig. 8. Components diagram of the Alarm System

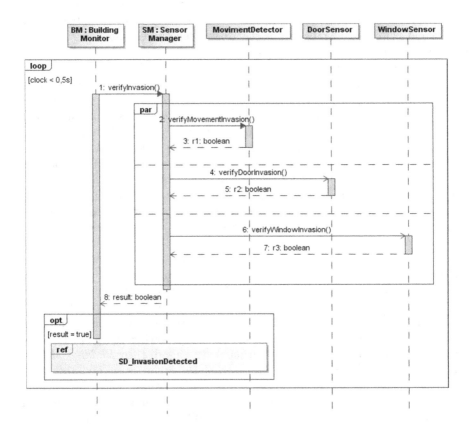

Fig. 9. Regular behaviour of the Alarm System

After validating these diagrams, the next step is to produce an STS model for test case generation. This is accomplished by applying mapping rules (Section 5) to the UML diagrams. As a result, the STS model represented in Figure 2 is

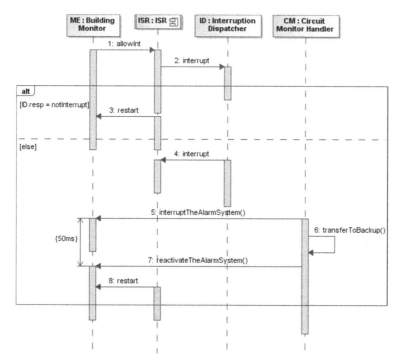

Fig. 10. Loss of power interruption behaviour

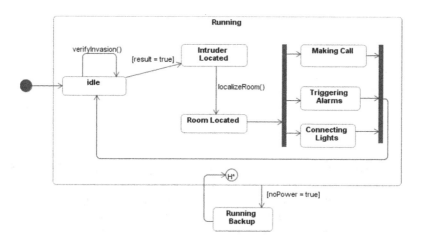

Fig. 11. State machine from Building Monitor component

obtained. This model also includes the intruder detection behaviour (its sequence diagram is omitted by the lack of space). This model was inspected to validate the intended behaviour and therefore to guarantee the validity of the test cases to be generated with respect to the system requirements.

Fig. 12. Test Purpose

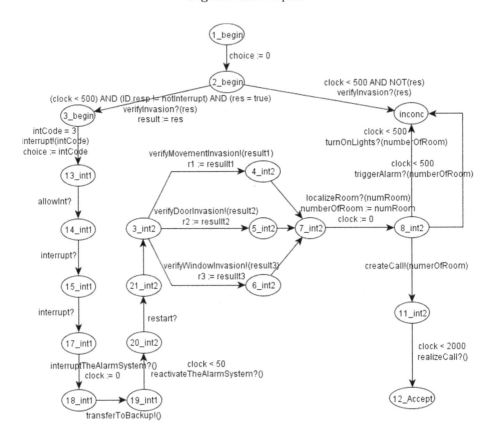

Fig. 13. Test Case

Having the STS model, the next step is test case generation. For this, the STG tool [8] was used. This tool is able to generate test cases from the STS model and a test purpose defined by the tester. For the sake of space, only a test case will be shown in the sequel. This is obtained by using the test purpose presented in Figure 12. As a result, the test case presented in Figure 13 is produced. Note that inputs and outputs are reversed in the test case when compared to the source model. The reason is that an input action in the STS model under test is actually an output that should be provided by **Tester** when executing the test case, whereas output actions of the STS are inputs to be observed by **Tester**.

As test purpose (Figure 12), it was chosen a situation that reflects an interesting scenario in the context of reactive systems with interruption testing. The situation forces an interruption, the loss of power, followed by the detection of an intruder. That is an interesting situation to test, because it makes the major locations and transitions of the model to be visited and it tests how the interruption treatment occurs.

The test case generated covers the occurrence of an interruption while verification of intruders' invasion is executed (verified by the building sensors). This interruption has as behaviour the following activities: 1) stopping the alarms system; 2) switching automatically the power to backup battery; and 3) reactivating the alarm system.

More specifically, the test case describes the following behaviour: at the beginning, from location 1_begin to 2_begin, the *choice* variable is initialised. From location 2_begin there are two possible paths (Tester can observe two possible behaviours). The first one has a guard with three conditions, this transition can only be covered if all the guard is true, that is: 1) the time is less than 500ms (*clock* < 500), 2) an interruption has occurred (*ID.resp* != *notInterrupt*), and 3) an invasion has been detected (*res* = *true*). To perform the entire test case, it is required that Tester forces that all conditions are true. Otherwise, if an invasion has not been detected, the test case verdict will be set to inconclusive. With the guard being true, then the *verifyInvasion* input action will be executed, and its parameter is stored in the *result* variable.

After the guard is satisfied, the value of the *res* variable is *true*, indicating that an intruder was located. Next, on the transition starting from location 3_begin, there is the *IntCode* = 3 guard that forces the system execution to go through the transition which induce to the interruption treatment. In other words, Tester has to force the occurrence of the loss of power interruption to test this behaviour. This can also be understood by the executed commands in sequence: *interrupt*, used to force the interruption; and the attribution of *intCode* to the *choice* variable, that will allow the execution flow returns to the exact point it was before the interruption be launched.

The next three transitions are responsible for the exchange of communication signals between the components that treat the interruption execution: *Building Monitor*, *ISR* and *Interruption Dispatcher* (Figure 10). In location 17_int1, Tester expects that the interruption behaviour is executed. This is represented by the following events: *interruptTheAlarmSystem*, *transferToBackup* and *reactivateTheAlarmSystem*. In 17_int1-18_int1 and 19_int1-20_int2, the clock is initialised and a time requirement is verified through a guard, respectively.

As soon as interruption treatment finishes, the *restart* signal should be emitted between *ISR* and *Building Monitor* components, allowing the return of the execution flow to the configuration before the interruption. From 3_int2, three actions are expected to verify the sensors (*verifyMovementeInvasion*, *verifyDoorInvasion* and *verifyWindowInvasion*) and their respective results will be assigned to the internal variables (*r1*, *r2* and *r3*). Then, in which room the intruder is at the moment should be located (action *localizeRoom*), the phone call is created (*createCall*) and then it should be executed (*realizeCall*), according to the time requirements. If this sequence of steps is completely done, the test case has as verdict the Accept value (location `"12_Accept"`).

This test case provides an interesting integration testing scenario that will exercise cooperation between the main modules of the system, including the ones deployed for providing FreeRTOS infrastructure. In practice, this scenario can be executed in full or in parts, depending on the integration strategy chosen (incremental or big-bang). Even though this case study addresses application level behaviour only, the same modelling and test case generation technique can be applied to model each of the components as a system in order to test lower level integration of FreeRTOS components. Finally, the case study illustrates the kind of interactions and behaviour that it is expected from an implementation of `Tester`: this should be provided in a way that do not interfere with behaviour of the application so that deadlines can be accurately checked.

7   Concluding Remarks

This work is part of a research cooperation between Brazilian Institutions (UFPE, UFCG, UFRN) aimed at the challenge of constructing high quality real-time embedded systems by combining formal methods and testing techniques. This is also part of a research cooperation with the VerTeCs team through the lNRIA's "Associate Team" programme - Project TReaTiES. Regarding testing, the goal of these cooperations is to investigate techniques for test case generation and selection for real-time embedded systems based on a well-founded testing theory and also by taking into account issues raised at test case execution in a real RTOS. In this sense, FreeRTOS was chosen as a platform for investigation and validation of the solutions provided. This paper presents work in progress in this direction by focusing on test case generation from an extension of STSs. Application modelling is based on a strategy of interruptions handling that can be implemented in FreeRTOS. This is illustrated by a case study.

Since reliability of the testing techniques and infrastructure to be provided is dependent on reliability of FreeRTOS itself, success of this work depends on initiatives that are being pursued in the same cooperation for modelling and verification of FreeRTOS functionalities, for instance, by using the B method [15]. As further work, the aim is to use the B specification to provide information on testing verdicts extracted from invariants, pre and post conditions. Also, a strategy of interruption management in the FreeRTOS is under implementation. This will provide a complete test execution environment. Moreover, mapping rules from UML to STS models are still only informally defined, demanding inspection for validity. Investigation on formal transformations and mapping from other formalisms will be conducted. Finally, empirical studies are planned.

References

1. Sommerville, I.: Software Engineering, 8th edn. International Computer Science Series. Addison-Wesley, Boston (2006)
2. The FreeRTOS.org Project: FreeRTOS, http://www.freertos.org/

3. Li, S., Wang, J., Dong, W., Qi, Z.C.: Property-oriented testing of real-time systems. In: APSEC 2004: Proceedings of the 11th Asia-Pacific Software Engineering Conference, Washington, DC, USA, pp. 358–365. IEEE Computer Society, Los Alamitos (2004)
4. Krichen, M.: Model-Based Testing for Real-Time Systems. PhD thesis, Universit Joseph Fourier (December 2007)
5. Krichen, M., Tripakis, S.: Black-box conformance testing for real-time systems. In: Graf, S., Mounier, L. (eds.) SPIN 2004. LNCS, vol. 2989, pp. 109–126. Springer, Heidelberg (2004)
6. Hessel, A., Larsen, K.G., Mikucionis, M., Nielsen, B., Pettersson, P., Skou, A.: Testing real-time systems using UPPAAL. In: Hierons, R.M., Bowen, J.P., Harman, M. (eds.) FORTEST. LNCS, vol. 4949, pp. 77–117. Springer, Heidelberg (2008)
7. Rusu, V., du Bousquet, L., Jéron, T.: An approach to symbolic test generation. In: Grieskamp, W., Santen, T., Stoddart, B. (eds.) IFM 2000. LNCS, vol. 1945, pp. 338–357. Springer, Heidelberg (2000)
8. Clarke, D., Jéron, T., Rusu, V., Zinovieva, E.: STG: A symbolic test generation tool. In: Katoen, J.-P., Stevens, P. (eds.) TACAS 2002. LNCS, vol. 2280, p. 470. Springer, Heidelberg (2002)
9. Jeannet, B., Jéron, T., Rusu, V., Zinovieva, E.: Symbolic test selection based on approximate analysis. In: Halbwachs, N., Zuck, L.D. (eds.) TACAS 2005. LNCS, vol. 3440, pp. 349–364. Springer, Heidelberg (2005)
10. Jéron, T., Marchand, H., Rusu, V.: Symbolic determinisation of extended automata. In: Proceedings of the 4th IFIP Int. Conference on Theoretical Computer Science. IFIP book series, vol. 209, pp. 197–212. Springer, Heidelberg (2006)
11. Object Management Group: UML superstructure, v2.1.1. Technical Report formal/07-02-05, OMG (2007),
    http://www.omg.org/cgi-bin/doc?formal/07-02-05
12. Barry, R.: Using the FreeRTOS Real Time Kernel: A practical Guide. FreeRTOS.org (2009)
13. de Figueiredo, A.L.L., Andrade, W.L., Machado, P.D.L.: Generating interaction test cases for mobile phone systems from use case specifications. SIGSOFT Softw. Eng. Notes 31(6), 1–10 (2006); Proceedings of the AMOST 2006
14. Andrade, W.L., Machado, P.D.L.: Modeling and testing interruptions in reactive systems using symbolic models. In: SAST 2008: Proceedings of the 2nd Brazilian Workshop on Systematic and Automated Software Testing, Porto Alegre, RS, Brazil, pp. 34–43. Brazilian Computer Society (2008)
15. Déharbe, D., Galvao, S., Moreira, A.M.: Report on an ongoing formal development of a real-time operating system with the B method. In: Oliveira, M.V.M., Woodcock, J. (eds.) SBMF 2009. LNCS, vol. 5902, pp. 54–69. Springer, Heidelberg (2009)

Concurrent Models of Flash Memory Device Behaviour[*]

Andrew Butterfield and Art Ó Catháin

School of Computer Science & Statistics
Trinity College Dublin
Rep. of Ireland
Andrew.Butterfield@cs.tcd.ie

Abstract. We present a CSP model of the internal behaviour of Flash Memory, based on its specification by the Open Nand-Flash Interface (ONFi) consortium. This contributes directly to the low-level modelling of the data-storage technology that is the target of the POSIX filestore mini-challenge. The key objective was to ensure that the internal behaviour was well-specified, and that it was consistent with the specification of the external interface of such devices. The FDR toolkit was used to perform the revelent refinement/model-checking. In addition to uncovering errors and possible sources of misinterpretation in the ONFi standard, this work also describes a methodology for model data-entry based on a "state-chart" dialect of XML (SCXML) using XSLT to translate into CSP, and HTML, to support validation.

1 Introduction

The "Grand Challenge in Computing" [Hoa03] on Verified Software [Woo06, HLMS07], has a stream focussing on mission-critical filestores, as required, for example, in space-probe missions [JH05]. Of particular interest are filestores based on the relatively recent NAND Flash Memory technology, now very popular in portable datastorage devices such as MP3 players and datakeys.

This paper follows on from initial formal models of NAND Flash Memory, reported in [BW07, BFW09] based on the specification published by the "Open NAND Flash Interface (ONFi)" consortium [H+06]. That work looked at a formal model of flash memory in terms of its internal data storage architecture, and the top-level operations that manipulate that storage.

Here we report work on modelling and analysing the finite-state machines in [H+06] that describe the internal behaviour of flash devices. The modelling was done using machine-readable CSP (CSP_M) [Ros97] and the FDR2 tool [For05] for the analysis, and was reported in detail in an M.Sc dissertation [Cat08]. The emphasis of our flash memory modelling to date has been to focus on the flash memory chips themselves, both their external interfaces as well as their internal behaviour and to interrelate the two. Whilst of interest to the ONFi

---

[*] Work reported in this paper was partially supported by Science Foundation Ireland.

M.V.M. Oliveira and J. Woodcock (Eds.): SBMF 2009, LNCS 5902, pp. 70–83, 2009.
© Springer-Verlag Berlin Heidelberg 2009

consortium, this work has a relevance to the broader community as using an ONFi device is not simply a matter or sequencing top-level atomic operations — in fact few of the operations are atomic, and most are designed to be interleaved, to exploit internal concurrency in the devices to improve performance. Indeed, depending on the hardware configuration, key operations like reading and writing may require interleaving with status checking operations in order to function at all.

In the next section (§2) we describe the relevant aspects of ONFi flash devices, and look at related work (§3). We then proceed to present the development of the CSP model (§4) the analyses performed with it (§5), and conclude (§6).

2   Background

There are two types of Flash Memory: (i) NOR flash, which can be programmed (written) at byte level, but suits random access; and (ii) NAND flash with higher speed and density, but where programming must be done at the page level, making it a sequential access device. The ONFi standard, and this paper, is solely concerned with NAND flash.

A flash memory device is best viewed as a hierarchy of nested arrays of bytes[1], plus additional state and storage facilities at various levels. At the bottom we have *pages*, arrays of bytes, which comprise the basic unit for both writing (programming) and reading (operations *PageProgram* and *Read*). The next level up is the *block*, an array of pages, that is the smallest level at which erasure (operation *BlockErase*) can take place. Blocks are aggregated together under the control of a *logical unit (LUN)*, which is the smallest entity capable of independent (concurrent) execution. A LUN also has one or more local registers the same size as a page (*page-registers*), used as temporary storage when transferring data to/from block pages, and a *status register* recording key information about ongoing operations, or those just completed. The status register has 8 bits, of which only bit 6 (a.k.a "SR[6]"), is of interest, used to indicate the ready/busy status of a LUN. LUNs are collected together into *targets*, which have their own means of communication off-chip. A physical flash memory chip (or *device*) may have several targets, depending on the number of available I/O pins. The work reported in this paper focusses on the target level and below, with a particular emphasis on the interactions between LUNs and their containing target.

2.1   Host-Target Communication

Following the ONFi standard [H+06], we use the term *host* to refer to any entity interacting with a flash memory device. Most communication between a host and target is mediated through a single bi-directional byte-wide I/O port, so the hardware interface is essentially serial. Conceptually, four types of transfer take place across this port:

---

[1] Some Flash devices are organised on "word" (16-bit) lines, but we ignore this detail in this paper.

Command Write (CW). A single byte denoting a command is sent by the host to the target.

Address Write (AW). A byte denoting part of an address is sent to the target.

Data Write (DW). A data-byte is sent to the target.

Data Read (DR). A data-byte is received from the target.

Additional single-bit control pins determine which of the above transfer types are taking place at any given moment. Executing a typical operation involves a series of transfers of the four types listed above, typically with some waiting inbetween. For example, a *Read* operation involves the following (typical) initial series of transfers:

$$CW(readOpcode); \ AW(addr_4); \ \ldots; \ AW(addr_0); \ CW(confirm)$$

The host has then to wait whilst the addressed data is pulled from the relevant page into the selected LUN's page-register. One way is to poll the target periodically, asking if the LUN is ready, using the *ReadStatus* operation:

$$CW(readStatus); \ DR(status)$$

Once the status indicates "ready", the data is drawn out, one byte at a time, until the number n of bytes specified in the read operation has been read.

$$DR(byte_0); \ DR(byte_1); \ \ldots; \ DR(byte_n)$$

The ready/busy part of the status can also be read by hardware directly through an output pin, so we distinguish between the "hardware" and "software" approaches to getting status information. The *WriteProtect* operation is also implemented by a single input pin, rather than via a transfer sequence.

2.2 Flash Translation Layers

The hardware/software subsystem that sits on top of unreliable serial-access flash memory and provides the abstraction of reliable parallel-addressable memory is called the *flash translation layer* (FTL). Most of the extant formal modelling of flash memory filesystems (see §3) assumes the existence of (at least) the hardware parts of the FTL. This paper is concerned with what happens *beneath* the FTL, and so we do not consider it further.

2.3 Flash Memory Operations

The ONFi standard defines a collection of operations that are to be supported by flash devices. Some of the operations are mandatory and must be provided in any ONFi-compliant implementation. The operations, *Read, PageProgram, BlockErase* and *ReadStatus*, have already been introduced. The other operations include: *Change ... Column* operations that support access to part of a page; *Reset* to allow software to reset a device,; *WriteProtect* to direct LUNs to be locked/unlocked against changes; and *ReadID* and *ReadParameterPage* that return data specific to a device such as manufacturer's name, and sizing information.

Other optional operations are also specified, typically providing enhanced performance-improving features that exploit the parallelism provided by the LUNs.

2.4   The ONFi State Machines

The internal behaviour of ONFi devices is described by two finite-state machines (FSMs) [H+06, §7], one describing the behaviour of a target, the other capturing the actions of a LUN. The target state machine is defined with the aid of seven state variables, and has a total of 77 state entries. The LUN state machines uses eight state-variables and 62 states. An example state entry, for the target state **T_RPP_ReadParams** (for the *ReadParameterPage* operation) is shown in Fig.1. We shall use this as a running example to describe our approach. The box at on the top-right describes the events that occur on entry to the state. The three rows below describe the subsequent conditional behaviour in this state. The left of each row describes a input event or condition whilst the right indicates the resulting state transition, with the conditions being evaluated in the order in which they appear.

T_RPP_ReadParams	The target performs the following actions:		
	1. Request LUN tLunSelected clear SR[6] to zero.		
	2. R/B# is cleared to zero.		
	3. Request LUN tLunSelected make parameter page data available in page register.		
	4. tReturnState set to T_RPP_ReadParams.		
	1. Read of page complete	→	T_RPP_Complete
	2. Command cycle 70h (Read Status) received	→	T_RS_Execute
	3. Read request received and tbStatusOut set to TRUE	→	T_Idle_Rd_Status

Fig. 1. ONFi Target State example [H+06]

3   Related Work

Formal model-checking techniques have been applied to the verification of the Samsung OneNAND flash device driver [KCKK08], with particular emphasis on a multi-sector read operation implemented within the FTL. This proved too complex for "conventional testing methods"[2] to the extent that even when tests failed, they were not adequate to pinpoint the cause of the error. The model-checkers explored were NuSMV, Spin and CBMC. The best tool was reported as CBMC[CKL04], a SAT-solver based model-checker, that works directly with C source code. It was able to uncover a number of previously unknown bugs in critical sub-systems of their FTL.

---

[2] Their words.

A fully automatic analysis, using Alloy, of a flash filesystem is described in [KJ08]. This was built on top of a simple flash model (at roughly the same level of abstraction as [BW07]). and implements wear-leveling and block mapping, so covering the "soft" parts of the FTL. Similar work, but very much a tools-integration approach to modelling (VDM/HOL/Alloy), is reported in [FSO08]. The key issue here is matching specific tools to specific verification tasks, and the need to translate between tool notations, in order to have a complete formal verification lifecycle. VDM is used as the main modelling tool, with Alloy and HOL called upon to verify proof obligations that arise.

At the other end of the scale, there is ongoing work on the modelling of the filesytem from the POSIX level down. This ranges from explorations of modelling the tree structures characteristic of filesystems (e.g. acyclic graphs), in Event-B using the Rodin platform [DBA08], to comprehensive machine verification of the POSIX Z model [FWF09] and part of the IBM CICS system [FWZ09]. Finally, we note recent work looking at computational models of flash memory devices with performance issues in mind [ABJ+09], of possible interest to the formal verification community as they suggest the kinds of optimisations to be considered during the later stages in the refinement to code.

In terms of automated translations from some notation into CSP, we note the Casper tool developed by Gavin Lowe [Low98], designed for cryptographical protocols — however this used a tailored notation not suitable for our purposes.

4   The CSP Model

The main objective of this work was to formalise the Target/LUN FSM descriptions in machine-readable CSP and then use this as a basis for checking their correctness using the FDR2 refinement checker [For05]. CSP was chosen because of its familiarity, and the availability of the FDR2 model checker, and because the basic mechanisms of CSP appeared to be a good match for the FSM model in the ONFi document.

The main criteria for correctness was that the behaviours possible for the interconnected FSMs was consistent with the behaviour patterns for the operations mandated by that same standard.

The state machine notation of the ONFi specification allows for a relatively direct conversion into CSP: there is a one-to-one mapping between ONFi states and CSP processes. The ONFi FSMs interact by passing messages and waiting to respond to same, dependent on both the named-state they are in and conditions over other state-variables. The conceptual match between this and CSP processes is very close, as examples later will show. The separation of target from LUNs also echoes the parallel composition features of CSP. Multiple LUN processes can be interleaved: required to synchronize on events with the target, but not with each other. The target-LUN communication events (*TLEvts*) are then hidden and this is put in parallel with a *HOST* process that models the behaviour of the environment that communicates with the flash device. In CSP notation this is written (for a single target and two LUNs) as:

$$SYSTEM \cong HOST \parallel ((\ TARGET \parallel (\ LUN(0) \ ||| \ LUN(1))) \setminus TLEvts)$$

Modelling the communication between host and target was straightforward as this is well documented as the external interface of ONFi devices, and had already been modelled in Z at an abstract level[BW07, BFW09]. In CSP_M we used events with names of the form ht_XXXX to model these communications, which basically consisted of the byte-level transfers of commands, addresses, data and the single-bit signals (e.g. write-protect input, ready/busy output).

Details of the target-LUN communication (CSP_M events of form tl_XXXX) were much more sketchy, precisely because these are viewed as implementation details to be resolved appropriately by individual device manufacturers. For example, during a *PageProgram* operation, the specification goes into some detail during the input of address bytes from the host to the target. For the transfer of the same address from the target to the appropriate LUN, it simply states "Target issues the [page] Program with associated row address to the LUN" [H+06, p84]. It is assumed that the target can transfer the address in one go, rather than serially, byte-by-byte.

Certain abstractions and simplifications had to be made so that the FDR2 model-checker could perform analysis without running out of memory. So, as just seen above, most data and address items were modelled as single bits, while the command datatype was restricted to the set of known command types, rather than being a full byte. An exception is the *column address* (address of byte within page), which was modelled as two bits to support the *ChangeXXXXColumn* operations.

The 7 state variables of the target FSM had also to be abstracted, and augmented with implicit state data, such as the state of the write protect pin, and the data and address information temporarily in transit, as well as a counter for the number of address chunks expected. This resulted in the addition of a further 12 state components. A similar exercise in augmenting the state had to be done for the LUN FSM as well, to a lesser degree (8 ONFi variables were augmented by a further 3).

4.1   CSP Data-Entry: A Challenge

Generating the CSP models for *TARGET* and *LUN* was a considerable challenge, best illustrated by considering the CSP encoding in Fig.2 of the state shown previously in Fig.1, where we explicitly list the 19 variables needed. A typical state transition is triggered by a condition on a small subset of those state-variables, and itself usually only modifies a few of them. Clearly the tasks of both entering the data for, and checking the correct encoding of, each of the state-tables, was a daunting and highly error-prone task.

An additional complication arose from the fact that textual ordering is used to determine which state transitions occur if more than one is possible. So given an ONFi table of the form on the left, we had to generate CSP_M in the form on the right:

c1 and e1 $\to$ S1	c1	& e1 -> S1
c2 and e2 $\to$ S2	(not c1) and c2	& e2 -> S2
c3 and e3 $\to$ S3	(not c1 and not c2) and c3 & e3 -> S3	

```
T_RPP_READPARAMS(tbStatusOut,tbChgCol,tCopyback,tLunSelected,tLastCmd,tReturnState,
    tbStatus78hReq,cmd,isReadyBusy,isWriteProtected,dataBit,addrReceived,lun0ready,
    lun1ready,intCounter,addr3Block,addr2Page,addr1ColH,addr0ColL) =
       tl.tLunSelected!targRequest -> tl_setSR6.tLunSelected!false ->
    tl.tLunSelected!targRequest -> tl.tLunSelected!retrieveParameters ->
              (tl.tLunSelected.readPageComplete -> T_RPP_COMPLETE(tbStatusOut,
                  tbChgCol,tCopyback,tLunSelected,tLastCmd,T_RPP_ReadParams,
                  tbStatus78hReq,cmd,false,isWriteProtected,dataBit,addrReceived,
                  lun0ready,lun1ready,intCounter,addr3Block,addr2Page,addr1ColH,
                  addr0ColL)
                  []
              ht_ioCmd.cmd70h -> T_RS_EXECUTE(tbStatusOut,tbChgCol,tCopyback,
                  tLunSelected,tLastCmd,T_RPP_ReadParams,tbStatus78hReq,cmd,false,
                  isWriteProtected,dataBit,addrReceived,lun0ready,lun1ready,
                  intCounter,addr3Block,addr2Page,addr1ColH,addr0ColL)
                  []
              (tbStatusOut==true)
                 & (ht_read -> T_IDLE_RD_STATUS(tbStatusOut,tbChgCol,tCopyback,
                  tLunSelected,tLastCmd,T_RPP_ReadParams,tbStatus78hReq,cmd,false,
                  isWriteProtected,dataBit,addrReceived,lun0ready,lun1ready,
                  intCounter,addr3Block,addr2Page,addr1ColH,addr0ColL)))
```

Fig. 2. CSP encoding

After some initial experimentation with small handcrafted examples, it became very clear that some form of automation was going to be needed if the CSP encoding was going to be completed in a timely fashion. The solution adopted was to use State Chart XML (SCXML), a "state-chart" dialect of XML [BAA+09] for initial data entry. This was chosen because SCXML provided a textual way to describe states, state-variables, and variable updates at a level very close to that used in the ONFi descriptions. Given an SCXML encoding, this could then be translated into the machine-readable form of CSP using XSL Transformations (XSLT) [W3C99]. The ready availability of parsers and tools to manipulate XML made this an easier prospect than trying to develop our own data-entry language with tool support.

The SCXML code to describe the T_RPP_ReadParam state is shown in Fig.3. The key feature to note is that the data-entry requirements are limited to the information that appears explicitly in the ONFi behaviour tables.

```
<state id=T_RPP_ReadParams>
    <onentry>
        <event name=tl.tLunSelected.setSR6!0"/>
        <assign location=readyBusy expr=0"/>
        <event name="tl.tLunSelected!retrieveParameters"/>
        <assign location="tReturnState" expr="T_RPP_ReadParams"/>
    </onentry>
    <transition event=tl.readPageComplete target=T_RPP_Complete/>
    <transition event=ht_Iocmd.cmd70h target=T_RS_Execute/>
    <transition cond=tbStatusOut == true
                event=ht_read target=T_Idle_Rd_Status/>
```

Fig. 3. SCXML encoding

One caveat has to be mentioned: the SCXML we used can be processed by the standard XSLT translation tools, but is not itself correct SCXML. We are using the `<event name="..."`> construct, but our 'names' are in fact portions of CSP_M event syntax. However, as we are simply using SCXML for data-entry to build a CSP model, the fact that we cannot use SCXML tools for analysis is not a concern.

Validating the data entry is important, and is facilitated by the fact that these same SCXML sources can also be used to generate HTML that renders in a style very close to that used by ONFi (Fig.4) — this greatly facilitates the checking and proof-reading of the entered data. The difference in the number of state-entry events (6 rather than 4) is that single events in the ONFi document are sometimes split into several at the SCXML/CSP level.

T_RPP_ReadParams	1. Event: tl.tLunSelected!targRequest 2. Event: tl_setSR6.tLunSelected!false 3. isReadyBusy set to false 4. Event: tl.tLunSelected!targRequest 5. Event: tl.tLunSelected!retrieveParameters 6. tReturnState set to T_RPP_ReadParams		
1. tl.tLunSelected readPageComplete		->	T_RPP_Complete
2. ht_ioCmd.cmd70h		->	T_RS_Execute
3. ht_read (if tbStatusOut==true)		->	T_Idle_Rd_Status

Fig. 4. HTML rendering

5   Model Analysis

The model analysis fell conceptually into two phases: the first focussed on debugging and validating the model, to ensure that it captured the intent of the ONFi specification. The second phase was using the model to analyse the consistency of the entire ONFi document.

5.1   Validating the Model

To model the behaviour of a flash device fully, several processes were necessary in addition to HOST, TARGET, and LUN. These processes were simpler than those derived directly from the ONFi state machine, and so were written in CSP directly rather than via SCXML. The need for these emerged as the model was being built and animated, using the CSP_M ProBE tool.

The first difficulty arose in trying to model the propagation of status information from the LUNs, via the target, to the host. In the ONFi document these are handled within the FSM framework, as events between the LUNs and target. A particular problem arose in relation to bit 6 of this register ("SR[6]"), used to record the "Ready/Busy" status of the system (Ready=1,Busy=0). The SR[6] values of the LUNs are propagated by the target to the host via a single bit pin called "R/B#". The ONFi document states (p19) that

" R/B# shall reflect the logical AND of the SR[6] (Status Register bit
6) values for all LUNs on the corresponding target. "

In effect the propagation of SR[6] from LUNs to target occurs asynchronously,
and concurrently with any other FSM behaviour — trying to model this behaviour exactly as described in the ONFi FSM descriptions led to a deadlocking
model. Attempting to augment the target model to sample the SR[6] events more
often did not resolve the deadlock in all cases, and so in order to get a deadlock-
free model that captured the behaviour intended by ONFi, we had to model the
SR[6] and R/B# bit communication using a separate process *READYBUSY*.
This allowed the asynchronous updating of SR[6] and hence R/B# to be decou-
pled from the target FSM, and made available directly to the host.

However, there were still circumstances that required the target itself to be
aware of changes in any SR[6] values, particularly where interleaved operations
were concerned. These situations essentially arose when the target was itself in
an idle state, so both the target and *READBUSY* processes had to be augmented
to communicate with each other at such times. The final architecure of the CSP
model now consisted of the main processes and linkages shown in Fig. 5.

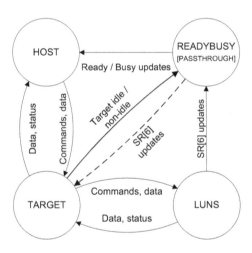

Fig. 5. Final CSP Process Structure

Whilst the bulk of the behaviour of the combined FSMs was deterministic,
there was one area of unpredictability that we modelled with non-deterministic
choice. This was related to the fact that the time it took for certain operations
(*Read,PageProgram*) to complete was variable, depending on how much data
was being processed. We used a process called *LUN_INNARDS* to model this,
using a counter to record the amount of remaining work, and non-deterministic
choice to decide on how much work (always non-zero) was done in one "step".
The effect of this was ensure that a bounded number of status reads would return
busy, before finally switching to ready.

5.2   Verifying the FSMs

The combination of Target and LUNs was not deadlock-free: they model passive hardware that is meant to be driven by an active host, and so if left to run freely together they quickly enter inconsistent states. So, our analysis had to consist of an appropriately chosen collection of hosts. We came up with two types of analysis: those where the host followed the device usage protocols described in the ONFi standard, which we expected to be deadlock- and livelock-free, and those where we deliberately modelled incorrect host behaviour, hoping to see deadlocks. Deadlock freedom ensured that the protocols were correct, in so far that both the target and LUN FSMs could follow through the required sequence of events. For deadlock checking we had to ensure that host itself did not terminate, so a typical test host was something that repeatedly performed arbitrary commands. Livelock freedom was checked in the case were all but target-host events were hidden, so ensuring that the host would never run the risk of having to wait forever for the target to complete some operation.

We used two host models — on assuming the hardware approach to status checking, the other that it would be done in software (i.e. explicit *ReadStatus* operations). Either type of host was implemented as an infinite loop that made a non-deterministic choice of an operation to execute on each iteration. The host would then be placed in parallel with a target and two LUNs.

```
TARGET_TWOLUNS = TARGET [| tl_events |] (LUN(lun0) ||| LUN(lun1))
HOST_SW_TARGET_TWOLUNS
          = INITIAL_HS_POWERON [| ht_sw_events |] TARGET_TWOLUNS
```

A key issue that arose early on was that some of the models were too large to even compile in FDR ("failed to compile ISM"), let alone model-check. These were the models that covered all the behaviour in the ONFi FSMs, including that for both the mandatory and optional operations. One of the FDR compression techniques, "diamond", was used, as was increasing the stack size (Unix command `ulimit -s 262144`), but in order to get results, the SCXML and XSLT sources were configured in such a way that a subset of the models containing only the states and transitions for the mandatory operators could be automatically generated — it was these `-mandatory` CSP_M files that were used for automated analysis. The one exception to this was that we included the non-mandatory operation *ReadStatusEnhanced*, as this was required in order to test the concurrent operation of two LUNs.

When checking `HOST_SW_TARGET_TWOLUNS` for deadlock freedom FDR2 reported 4490300 transitions during compilation, that it refined 32,338 states with 78469 transitions, and took 17mins to run on a dual 1.28Ghz UltraSPARC-IIIi processor with 4Gb RAM, and 20G swap disk.

For example, a test of the Read operation was set up as follows. We took the `HOST_SW_TARGET_TWOLUNS` process, hid all events except the host-target read-related commands and data transfers, and treated this as a specification.

```
READ_SPEC = HOST_SW_TARGET_TWOLUNS
              \ diff(Events,
                  union({ht_ioCmd.cmds
                        | cmds <-{cmd30h,cmd00h,cmd70h,cmdFFh}}
                      ,{|ht_ioDataOut|}))
```

We then defined a process that performed an expected sequences of host target protocol events for a *Read* (preceded by a *POWERON* behaviour, as it is present in the specification model),

```
POWERON
 = ht_ioCmd.cmdFFh -> ht_ioCmd.cmd70h -> ht_ioDataOut.true -> SKIP
READ_IMPL
 = POWERON;
   ht_ioCmd.cmd00h -> ht_ioCmd.cmd30h
   -> ht_ioCmd.cmd70h -> ht_ioDataOut.false -- status busy, so wait
   -> ht_ioCmd.cmd70h -> ht_ioDataOut.true -- read ready, so read
   -> ht_ioCmd.cmd00h -> ht_ioDataOut.false
   -> ht_ioCmd.cmd70h -> ht_ioDataOut.true -> STOP
```

We then used FDR to check for trace-refinement.

```
assert READ_SPEC [T= READ_IMPL
```

This check took 47mins on the dual 1.2GHz 4Gb 20Gb swap Sparc machine already mentioned.

We also tested for illegal usage of the device, looking at erroneous actions like the following: *BlockErase* followed by *ReadStatusEnhanced*; *Read* completed without *ReadStatus* (in software model); and Multiple *Read*s completed followed by busy indicator. Most of these came from gleaning the ONFi document for statements regarding required patterns of behaviour.

5.3 Anomalies Uncovered

We have already alluded to the difficulties in how the SR[6] and R/B# pin behaviour, asynchronous in nature, was described in the FSM format, and how we had to model it as a separate process — this was not an error in the ONFi document, but is rather a clarification of what correct behaviour was meant.

Several deadlocks were found the in *ReadParameterPage* operation, one ironically caused by the target requesting a status update just as a LUN decided, unsolicited, to provide such an update. In effect the ONFi standard talks about explicit status update messages when in fact this all occurs asynchronously via bit SR[6]. It was possible to fix this, by adding extra target-LUN synchronisation events (tl_sync), but this was now no longer consistent with the implicit requirement that a host can perform a Read Status at any time to determine the device's readiness.

Another deadlock resulted from the user of the tReturnState state variable to allow some states to 'return' to a saved 'calling state'. Essentially on return to the saved state, its entry events and state changes get re-executed, involving setup communication with the LUNs, which in certain cases were not expecting it, as they had already been setup.

A number of deadlocks were also found in the interaction between the *Reset* and *ReadStatus* operations.

All of the above were reported back to the ONFi consortium, some of which have lead to an ONFi Technical Errata notice being issued (Errata Id 008). It is worth pointing out that all the deadlock issues we have discovered are connected to the *ReadStatus* operation in some way, and seem to be consequences of trying to mix the asynchronous reporting of status with the synchronised behaviour of the FSMs.

6   Conclusions and Future Work

It is safe to say that to verify a specification as complex as ONFis by hand would have been impossible. Here the one-to-one correspondence between CSP processes and state machine states allowed for a fairly direct conversion, avoiding the need to abstract away too much detail.

Unfortunately the full ONFi model proved too much for the FDR2 model-checker, which failed to compile. The deadlocks described above were discovered in the mandatory-only model. With this limited model we found that the ONFi specification was basically sound, once we had resolved the synchronous/asynchronous mismatch in the description of status reporting. Feedback to ONFi has resulted in corrections to the published specification, now at version 2.1.

Using XSLT to convert the intermediate XML to CSP undoubtedly saved time and allowed a more thorough model to be developed. The conversion is not totally automatic, requiring manual intervention for the following: specification, in CSP, of channels, datatypes and sets to differentiate mandatory from optional commands; minor supplementary CSP processes (*LUN_INNARDS*, *READYBUSY*); parallel composition of host / target / LUN state machines; and specification of deadlock/livelock checks. The above totalled 583 lines of CSP, whereas the XSLT translations of the full target and LUN models resulted in a total of 1348 lines of CSP. These numbers belie the fact that the generated CSP is far more complex and inscrutable than the hand-generated material.

6.1   Future Work

The full model, including optional commands, remains to be verified. To succeed, some creativity will be required, since the CSP model (as it currently stands) runs into the resource limits of the FDR2 model-checker. One possible approach will be to use FDR Explorer [FW09] to assist us.

ONFi have since released version 2.0 and 2.1 of the specification. The state machine has not changed significantly, so it should be modelled in the same framework without much difficulty, which would also bring in changes due to any relevant errata.

At the time of writing, work is underway to take the SCXML sources and translate them to *Circus*[OCW06], to allow them to be analysed against the top-level Z models we already have. We also propose to use the same sources with new translations to do some comparative work by re-targeting at tools used with other formalisms. Finally, we intend to use an implementation of the "hard" FTL components as a case-study for a ongoing work on hardware compilation.

Acknowledgments

We'd like to thank Amber Huffman of Intel and Michael Abraham of Micron for their assistance and feedback regarding the ONFi standard, and Micheal Goldsmith of Formal Methods (Europe) Ltd., for his assistance with FDR2.

Sources of the material mentioned in this paper can be downloaded from `https://www.cs.tcd.ie/Andrew.Butterfield/Research/FlashMemory/`.

References

[ABJ$^+$09]   Ajwani, D., Beckmann, A., Jacob, R., Meyer, U., Moruz, G.: On computational models for flash memory devices. In: Vahrenhold, J. (ed.) SEA 2009. LNCS, vol. 5526, pp. 16–27. Springer, Heidelberg (2009)

[BAA$^+$09]   Barnett, J., Akolkar, R., Auburn, R.J., Bodell, M., Burnett, D.C., Carter, J., McGlashan, S., Lager, T.: State chart XML (SCXML): State machine notation for control abstraction. In: World Wide Web Consortium, Working Draft WD-scxml-20090507 (May 2009)

[BFW09]   Butterfield, A., Freitas, L., Woodcock, J.: Mechanising a formal model of flash memory. Science of Computer Programming 74(4), 219–237 (2009), Special Issue on the Grand Challenge

[BW07]   Butterfield, A., Woodcock, J.: Formalising flash memory: First steps. In: ICECCS, pp. 251–260. IEEE Computer Society, Los Alamitos (2007)

[Cat08]   Catháin, A.Ó.: Modelling flash memory device behaviour using CSP. Taught M.Sc dissertation, School of Computer Science and Statistics, Trinity College Dublin (2008), Also published as techreport TCD-CS-2008-47

[CKL04]   Clarke, E.M., Kroening, D., Lerda, F.: A tool for checking ANSI-C programs. In: Jensen, K., Podelski, A. (eds.) TACAS 2004. LNCS, vol. 2988, pp. 168–176. Springer, Heidelberg (2004)

[DBA08]   Damchoom, K., Butler, M., Abrial, J.-R.: Modelling and proof of a tree-structured file system. In: Liu, S., Maibaum, T., Araki, K. (eds.) ICFEM 2008. LNCS, vol. 5256, pp. 25–44. Springer, Heidelberg (2008)

[For05]   Formal Systems (Europe) Ltd. Failures-Divergence Refinement, FDR2 User Manual, 6th edn. (June 2005)

[FSO08]   Ferreira, M.A., Silva, S.S., Oliveira, J.N.: Verifying intel ash file system core specification. In: Larsen, P.G., Fitzgerald, J.S., Sahara, S. (eds.) Modelling and Analysis in VDM: Proceedings of the Fourth VDM/Overture Workshop, pp. 54–71. School of Computing Science, Newcastle University (2008), Technical Report CS-TR-1099

[FW09]   Freitas, L., Woodcock, J.: FDR explorer. Formal Asp. Comput. 21(1-2), 133–154 (2009)

[FWF09]   Freitas, L., Woodcock, J., Fu, Z.: POSIX file store in Z/eves: An experiment
           in the verified software repository. Sci. Comput. Program 74(4), 238–257
           (2009)
[FWZ09]   Freitas, L., Woodcock, J., Zhang, Y.: Verifying the CICS file control API
           with Z/eves: An experiment in the verified software repository. Sci. Com-
           put. Program 74(4), 197–218 (2009)
[H+06]   Hynix Semiconductor. Open NAND Flash Interface Specification. Techni-
           cal Report Revision 1.0, ONFI (December 28, 2006), http://www.onfi.org
[HLMS07]   Hoare, T., Leavens, G.T., Misra, J., Shankar, N.: The verified software
           initiative: A manifesto (2007),
           http://qpq.csl.sri.com/vsr/manifesto.pdf
[Hoa03]   Hoare, T.: The verifying compiler: A grand challenge for computing re-
           search. Journal of the ACM 50(1), 63–69 (2003)
[JH05]   Joshi, R., Holzmann, G.J.: A mini challenge: Build a verifiable file system.
           In: Proc. Verified Software: Theories, Tools, Experiments (VSTTE), Zürich
           (2005)
[KCKK08]   Kim, M., Choi, Y., Kim, Y., Kim, H.: Pre-testing flash device driver
           through model checking techniques. In: ICST, pp. 475–484. IEEE Com-
           puter Society, Los Alamitos (2008)
[KJ08]   Kang, E., Jackson, D.: Formal modeling and analysis of a flash filesystem
           in alloy. In: Börger, E., Butler, M., Bowen, J.P., Boca, P. (eds.) ABZ 2008.
           LNCS, vol. 5238, pp. 294–308. Springer, Heidelberg (2008)
[Low98]   Lowe, G.: Casper: A compiler for the analysis of security protocols. Journal
           of Computer Security 6(1-2), 53–84 (1998)
[OCW06]   Oliveira, M., Cavalcanti, A., Woodcock, J.: A denotational semantics for
           circus. In: REFINE 2006. ENTCS, pp. 1–16 (2006)
[Ros97]   Roscoe, A.W.: The Theory and Practise of Concurrency. Prentice-Hall
           (Pearson) (1997) (revised to 2000 and lightly revised to, 2005)
[W3C99]   W3C. XSL Transformations, XSLT (1999), http://www.w3.org/TR/xslt
[Woo06]   Woodcock, J.: First steps in the verified software grand challenge. IEEE
           Computer 39(10), 57–64 (2006)

Corecursive Algebras:
A Study of General Structured Corecursion

Venanzio Capretta[1], Tarmo Uustalu[2], and Varmo Vene[3]

[1] School of Computer Science, University of Nottingham, United Kingdom
[2] Institute of Cybernetics at Tallinn University of Technology, Estonia
[3] Department of Computer Science, University of Tartu, Estonia

Abstract. Motivated by issues in designing practical total functional programming languages, we are interested in structured recursive equations that uniquely describe a function not because of the properties of the coalgebra marshalling the recursive call arguments but thanks to the algebra assembling their results. Dualizing the known notions of recursive and wellfounded coalgebras, we call an algebra of a functor corecursive, if from any coalgebra of the same functor there is a unique map to this algebra, and antifounded, if it admits a bisimilarity principle. Differently from recursiveness and wellfoundedness, which are equivalent conditions under mild assumptions, corecursiveness and antifoundedness turn out to be generally inequivalent.

1   Introduction

In languages of total functional programming [17], such as Cockett's Charity [5] and type-theoretic proof assistants and dependently typed languages, unrestricted general recursion is unavailable. Instead, these languages support structured recursion and corecursion schemes for defining functions with inductive domains resp. coinductive codomains. For inductive types such schemes include iteration, primitive recursion and recursion on structurally smaller arguments ("guarded-by-destructors" recursion). Programming with coinductive types can dually be supported, e.g., by "guarded-by-constructors" corecursion [6,10].

Characteristically, schemes like this define a function as the unique solution of a recursive equation where the right-hand side marshals the arguments of recursive calls, makes the recursive calls and assembles their results. Operational intuition tells us that structured recursion defines a function uniquely as the argument is gradually consumed and structured corecursion because the result is gradually produced. More generally, instead of structurally smaller recursive call arguments one can allow arguments smaller in the sense of some wellfounded relation (not necessarily on an inductive type). We may ask: Does the "productivity" aspect of structured corecursion admit a similar generalization? What are some principles for reasoning about functions defined in this way? In this article we address exactly these questions in an abstract categorical setting.

General structured recursion and induction have been analysed in terms of recursive and wellfounded coalgebras. A *recursive coalgebra* (RCA) is a coalgebra

M.V.M. Oliveira and J. Woodcock (Eds.): SBMF 2009, LNCS 5902, pp. 84–100, 2009.

of an endofunctor F with a unique coalgebra-to-algebra morphism to any F-algebra. In other words, it is a coalgebra that guarantees unique solvability of any structured recursive diagram involving it. This abstract version of the wellfounded recursion principle was introduced by Osius [13]. It was also of interest to Eppendahl [9], and we have previously studied constructions to obtain recursive coalgebras from other coalgebras already known to be recursive, with the help of distributive laws of functors over comonads [4].

Taylor introduced the notion of *wellfounded coalgebra* (WFCA), an abstract version of the wellfounded induction principle, and proved that, under mild assumptions, it is equivalent to RCA [14,15],[16, Ch. 6]. Defined in terms of Jacobs's next-time operator [11], a wellfounded coalgebra is a coalgebra such that any subset of its carrier containing its next-time subset is isomorphic to the carrier, so that the carrier is the least fixed-point of the next-time operator. As this least fixed-point is given by those elements of the carrier whose recursive calls tree is wellfounded, the principle really states that all of the carrier is included in the "wellfounded core" (cf. Bove-Capretta's method [2] in type theory: a general-recursive definition is made acceptable by casting it as a definition by structured recursion on the inductively defined wellfounded core and proving that the whole domain is in the wellfounded core). A closely related condition has the coalgebra carrier reconstructed by iterating the next-time operator on the empty set.

Adámek et al. [1] provided additional characterizations for the important case when the functor has an initial algebra. Backhouse and Doornbos [8] studied wellfoundedness in a relational setting.

We look at the dual notions with the aim to achieve a comparable analysis of structured corecursion and coinduction. It is only to be expected that several differences arise from the fact that Set-like categories are not self-dual. More surprisingly, however, they turn out to be quite deep. The dual of RCA is the notion of *corecursive algebra* (CRA): we call an algebra corecursive if there is a unique map to it from any coalgebra. Here the first discrepancy arises: while it is well-known that initial algebras support primitive recursion and, more generally, a recursive coalgebra is parametrically recursive ([16, Ch. 6]), the dual statement is not true: corecursiveness with the option of an escape (complete iterativity in the sense of Milius [12]) is a strictly stronger condition than plain corecursiveness.

The dual of WFCA is the notion of *antifounded algebra* (AFA)[1]. The dual of the next-time operator maps a quotient of the carrier of an algebra to the quotient identifying the results of applying the algebra structure to elements that were identified in the original quotient. AFA is a categorical formulation of the principle of bisimilarity: if a quotient is finer than its next-time quotient, then it must be isomorphic to the algebra carrier. Here also the equivalence with CRA is not satisfied: both implications fail for rather simple algebras in Set.

Finally, we call an algebra *focusing* (FA), if the algebra carrier can be reconstructed by iterating the dual next-time operator. In the coalgebra case, one

---

[1] Our choice of the name was motivated by the relation to the set-theoretic antifoundation axioms.

starts with the empty set and constructs a chain of ever larger subsets of the carrier. Now, we start with the singleton set, which is the quotient of the carrier by the total relation, and construct an inverse chain of ever finer quotients. Intuitively, each iteration of the dual next-time operator refines the quotient. And while a solution of a recursive diagram in the recursive case is obtained by extending the approximations to larger subsets of the intended domain, now it is obtained by sharpening the approximations to range over finer quotients of the intended codomain. FA happens to be the strongest of the conditions, implying both AFA and CRA. The inverse implications turn out to be false.

The article is organized around these three notions, treated in Sections 2, 3 and 4, respectively, before we arrive at our conclusions in Section 5. Throughout the article we are interested in conditions on an algebra (A, α) of an endofunctor F on a category $\mathcal{C}$. We assume that $\mathcal{C}$ has pushouts along epis and that F preserves epis.[2] Our prime examples are $\mathcal{C}$ being Set and F a polynomial functor.

2   Corecursive Algebras

Our central object of study in this article is the notion of corecursive algebra, the dual of Osius's concept recursive coalgebra [13].

Definition 1. *An algebra (A, α) of an endofunctor F on a category $\mathcal{C}$ is called corecursive (CRA) if for every coalgebra (C, γ) there exists a unique coalgebra-to-algebra map, i.e., a map $f : C \to A$ making the following diagram commute:*

$$
\begin{array}{ccc}
C & \xrightarrow{\ \gamma\ } & FC \\
{\scriptstyle f}\downarrow & & \downarrow{\scriptstyle Ff} \\
A & \xleftarrow{\ \alpha\ } & FA.
\end{array}
$$

We write separately CRA-existence and CRA-uniqueness for the statements that the diagram has at least and at most one solution, respectively.

An algebra is corecursive if every structured recursive diagram (= coalgebra-to-algebra map diagram) based on it defines a function (in the sense of turning out to be a definite description). The inverse of the final F-coalgebra, whenever it exists, is trivially a corecursive F-algebra (in fact the initial corecursive F-algebra). However, there are numerous examples of corecursive algebras that arise in different ways.

Example 1. We illustrate the definition with a corecursive algebra in Set, for the functor $FX = E \times X \times X$, where E is some fixed set. The carrier is the set of streams over E, $A = \mathsf{Str}(E)$. The algebra structure α is defined as follows:

$$\alpha : E \times \mathsf{Str}(E) \times \mathsf{Str}(E) \to \mathsf{Str}(E) \qquad \mathsf{merge} : \mathsf{Str}(E) \times \mathsf{Str}(E) \to \mathsf{Str}(E)$$
$$\alpha(e, s_1, s_2) = e : \mathsf{merge}(s_1, s_2) \qquad \mathsf{merge}(e : s_1, s_2) = e : \mathsf{merge}(s_2, s_1).$$

---

[2] In the recursive case it makes sense to additionally require that F preserves pullbacks along monos. This assumption holds for typical functors of interest. In the presence of a subobject classifier in $\mathcal{C}$, it guarantees that recursiveness of a coalgebra implies wellfoundedness. The dual assumption, that F preserves pushouts along epis, is not as helpful. Moreover, it is too strong: it is false, e.g., for $FX = X \times X$. We drop it.

It is easy to see that this algebra is corecursive, although it is not the inverse of the final F-coalgebra, which is the set of non-wellfounded binary trees with nodes labelled by elements of E.

A simple example of recursive definition that could be justified by the corecursiveness of (A, α) is the following. Let $E = 2^*$ (lists of bits, i.e., binary words). We define a F-coalgebra $(C, \gamma : C \to 2^* \times C \times C)$ by $C = 2^*$ and $\gamma(l) = (l, 0l, 1l)$. We can now be certain that there is exactly one function $f : 2^* \to \mathsf{Str}(2^*)$ such that $f = \alpha \circ Ff \circ \gamma$. This function sends a binary word to the lexicographical enumeration of the binary words which have this given one as a prefix. In particular, the stream $f(\varepsilon)$ is the lexicographical enumeration of all binary words.

Example 2. We also obtain a corecursive algebra by endowing $A = \mathsf{Str}(E)$ with the following algebra structure of the functor $FX = E \times X$ (note that this is different from the inverse of the final F-coalgebra structure also carried by A):

$$\alpha : E \times \mathsf{Str}(E) \to \mathsf{Str}(E) \qquad \mathsf{double} : \mathsf{Str}(E) \to \mathsf{Str}(E)$$
$$\alpha(e, s) = e : \mathsf{double}(s) \qquad \mathsf{double}(e : s) = e : e : \mathsf{double}(s).$$

The next notion is an important variation.

Definition 2. *An algebra (A, α) is called* parametrically corecursive *(pCRA) if for every object C and map $\gamma : C \to FC + A$ (that is, coalgebra of $F(-) + A$), there exists a unique map $f : C \to A$ making the following diagram commute:*

$$
\begin{array}{ccc}
C & \xrightarrow{\;\;\gamma\;\;} & FC + A \\
{\scriptstyle f}\big\downarrow & & \big\downarrow{\scriptstyle Ff + \mathrm{id}_A} \\
A & \xleftarrow[{[\alpha, \mathrm{id}_A]}]{} & FA + A.
\end{array}
$$

This notion is known under the name of *completely iterative algebra* [12].[3] While this term is well-established and we do not wish to question its appropriateness in any way, we use a different term here, locally, for better fit with the topic of this article (the adjective "parametrically" remains idiosyncratic however).

To be parametrically corecursive, an algebra must define a function also from diagrams where, for some arguments, the value of the function is given by an "escape". The inverse of the final coalgebra always has this property [18]. Examples 1, 2 also satisfy pCRA. We leave the verification to the reader.

Proposition 1. *pCRA $\Rightarrow$ CRA : A parametrically corecursive coalgebra is corecursive.*

Proof. Given a coalgebra (C, γ), the unique solution of the pCRA diagram for the map $(C, C \xrightarrow{\gamma} FC \xrightarrow{\mathsf{inl}} FC + A)$ is trivially also the unique solution of the CRA diagram for (C, γ). □

---

[3] In this terminology inspired by iterative theories, the word "iterative" refers to iteration in the sense of tail-recursion. "Completely iterative" means that a unique solution exists for every coalgebra while "iterative" refers to the existence of such solutions only for finitary coalgebras, i.e., coalgebras with finitary carriers.

The following counterexamples show that the converse is not true (differently from the dual situation of recursive and parametrically recursive coalgebras). We exhibit an algebra that is corecursive but not parametrically corecursive.

Example 3. In the category Set, we use the functor $FX = X \times X$. An interesting observation is that any corecursive algebra (A, α) for this F must have exactly one fixed point, that is, one element a such that $\alpha(a, a) = a$. We take the following algebra structure on the three-element set $A = 3 = \{0, 1, 2\}$:

$$\alpha : 3 \times 3 \to 3$$
$$\alpha(1, 2) = 2$$
$$\alpha(n, m) = 0 \quad \text{otherwise.}$$

Proposition 2. *CRA $\not\Rightarrow$ pCRA-uniqueness: Example 3 is corecursive, but does not satisfy the uniqueness property for parametrically corecursive algebras.*

Proof. Example 3 satisfies CRA. Let (C, γ) be a coalgebra. We prove that the only possible solution f of the CRA diagram is the constant 0. In fact, for $c \in C$, it cannot be $f(c) = 1$, because 1 is not in the range of α. On the other hand, if $f(c) = 2$, then we must have $f(c) = \alpha((f \times f)(\gamma(c)))$. Let us call c_0 and c_1 the two components of $\gamma(c)$: $\gamma(c) = (c_0, c_1)$. Then we have $f(c) = \alpha(f(c_0), f(c_1))$. For $f(c)$ to be equal to 2, it is necessary that $f(c_0) = 1$ and $f(c_1) = 2$. But we already determined that $f(c_0) = 1$ is impossible. In conclusion, there is a unique solution: $f(c) = 0$ for every $c \in C$.

Example 3 does not satisfy pCRA-uniqueness. The pCRA diagram for $C = \mathbb{B}$ and $\gamma : \mathbb{B} \to \mathbb{B} \times \mathbb{B} + 3$ defined by $\gamma(\text{true}) = \text{inr}(1), \gamma(\text{false}) = \text{inl}(\text{true}, \text{false})$, has two distinct solutions:

$$
\begin{array}{ccc}
\mathbb{B} & \xrightarrow{\gamma} & \mathbb{B} \times \mathbb{B} + 3 \\
{\scriptstyle f_0}\downarrow\downarrow{\scriptstyle f_1} & {\scriptstyle f_0 \times f_0 + \text{id}}\downarrow\downarrow{\scriptstyle f_1 \times f_1 + \text{id}} & \\
3 & \xleftarrow{[\alpha, \text{id}]} & 3 \times 3 + 3
\end{array}
\qquad
\begin{array}{ll}
f_0(\text{true}) = 1 & f_1(\text{true}) = 1 \\
f_0(\text{false}) = 0 & f_1(\text{false}) = 2.
\end{array}
$$

(Note that Example 3 satisfies pCRA-existence: to construct a solution, put it equal to 0 on all argument values on which it is not recursively forced.) $\square$

Example 4. Consider the following algebra (A, α) for the functor $FX = X \times X$ in Set: We take A to be $\mathbb{N}$ and define the algebra structure by

$$\alpha : \mathbb{N} \times \mathbb{N} \to \mathbb{N}$$
$$\alpha(1, m) = m + 2$$
$$\alpha(n, m) = 0 \quad \text{if } n \neq 1.$$

Proposition 3. *CRA $\not\Rightarrow$ pCRA-existence: Example 4 is corecursive, but does not satisfy the existence property for parametrically corecursive algebras.*

Proof. Example 4 satisfies CRA, essentially by the same argument as for Example 3: the unique solution is forced to be the constant 0.

Example 4 does not satisfy pCRA-existence. Take $C = \mathbb{B}$ and define $\gamma : \mathbb{B} \to \mathbb{B} \times \mathbb{B} + \mathbb{N}$ by $\gamma(\text{true}) = \text{inr}(1)$ and $\gamma(\text{false}) = \text{inl}(\text{true}, \text{false})$. For this case, there is no solution to the pCRA diagram. Indeed, a solution should surely satisfy $f(\text{true}) = 1$. Therefore we should also have $f(\text{false}) = \alpha(f(\text{true}), f(\text{false})) = \alpha(1, f(\text{false})) = f(\text{false}) + 2$, which is clearly impossible.

(Note that Example 4 satisfies pCRA-uniqueness: the value of a solution $f(c)$ can be undetermined only if $\gamma(c) = \text{inl}(c_1, c_2)$ with $f(c_1) = 1$ and $f(c_2)$ undetermined in turn. But this cannot go on forever because it would give an unbounded value.) □

3   Antifounded Algebras

Now we turn to the dual of Taylor's wellfounded coalgebras. We state the definition with the help of the dual of the next-time operator of Jacobs [11]. Remember that we assume that the category C has pushouts along epis and that F preserves epis.

Definition 3. *Given an algebra* (A, α). *Let* $(Q, q : A \twoheadrightarrow Q)$ *be a quotient of* A *(i.e., an epi with A as the domain[4]). We define a new quotient* $(\text{nt}_A(Q), \text{nt}_A(q) : A \twoheadrightarrow \text{nt}_A(Q))$ *(the* next-time *quotient) by the following pushout diagram:*

$$
\begin{array}{ccc}
A & \xleftarrow{\ \ \alpha\ \ } & FA \\
{\scriptstyle \text{nt}_A(q)}\downarrow & & \downarrow{\scriptstyle Fq} \\
\text{nt}_A(Q) & \xleftarrow{\ \ \alpha[q]\ \ } & FQ
\end{array}
$$

Note that $\text{nt}_A(q)$ is guaranteed to be an epi, as a pushout along an epi.

Notice that we abuse notation (although in a fairly standard fashion): First, nt_A is really parameterized not by the object A, but the algebra (A, α). And further, nt_A operates on a quotient (Q, q) and returns another quotient given by the vertex and one of the side morphisms of the pushout. It is a convention of convenience to denote the vertex by $\text{nt}_A(Q)$ and the morphism by $\text{nt}_A(q)$.

In particular, in the category Set we can give an intuitive definition of nt_A in terms of quotients by equivalence relations. In Set, a quotient is, up to isomorphism, an epi $q : A \twoheadrightarrow A/\equiv$, where $\equiv$ is an equivalence relation on A, with $q(a) = [a]_\equiv$. Its next-time quotient can be represented similarly: $\text{nt}_A(A/\equiv) = A/\equiv'$, where $\equiv'$ is the reflexive-transitive closure of the relation

$$\{(\alpha(y_0), \alpha(y_1)) \mid y_0, y_1 \in FA, y_0\ (F\equiv)\ y_1\}.$$

Here $F\equiv$ is the lifting of $\equiv$ to FA: it identifies elements of FA that have the same *shape* and equivalent elements of A in corresponding *positions* (if $\equiv$ is given by a span $(R, r_0, r_1 : R \to A)$, $F\equiv$ is just (FR, Fr_0, Fr_1)).

The following definition is the dual of Taylor's definition of *wellfounded algebra* [14,15,16].

---

[4] We do not bother to identify equivalent epis, see below.

Definition 4. *An algebra (A, α) is called* antifounded *(AFA) if for every quotient $(Q, q : A \twoheadrightarrow Q)$, if $\mathsf{nt}_A(q)$ factors through q, then q is an isomorphism. In diagrams:*

$$
\begin{array}{c}
A \\
\mathsf{nt}_A(q) \swarrow \quad \searrow q \\
\mathsf{nt}_A(Q) \xleftarrow{\ u\ } Q
\end{array}
\quad \Rightarrow \quad
\begin{array}{c}
A \\
\downarrow q \\
Q
\end{array}
\quad \text{is an isomorphism.}
$$

Note that, if $\mathsf{nt}_A(q)$ factors, i.e., u exists, then it is necessarily unique, as q is an epi. Note also that q being an isomorphism means that id_A factorizes through q, i.e., that q is a split mono.

Example 1 is an antifounded algebra. Indeed, let $q : \mathsf{Str}(E) \twoheadrightarrow \mathsf{Str}(E)/\equiv$ be a quotient of $\mathsf{Str}(E)$ such that $\mathsf{nt}_A(q)$ factors through q. Let $\equiv'$ be the equivalence relation giving the next-time quotient, that is, $\mathsf{nt}_A(\mathsf{Str}(E)/\equiv) = \mathsf{Str}(E)/\equiv'$. It is the reflexive-transitive closure of the relation

$$
\{(e : \mathsf{merge}(s_{00}, s_{01}), e : \mathsf{merge}(s_{10}, s_{11}))
$$
$$
\mid e \in E, s_{00}, s_{01}, s_{10}, s_{11} \in \mathsf{Str}(E), s_{00} \equiv s_{10} \wedge s_{01} \equiv s_{11}\}
$$

This relation is already reflexive and transitive, so the closure is in fact unnecessary. The hypothesis that $\mathsf{nt}_A(q)$ factors through q tells us that $\equiv$ is finer than $\equiv'$, that is, $\forall s_0, s_1 \in \mathsf{Str}(E). s_0 \equiv s_1 \Rightarrow s_0 \equiv' s_1$. We want to prove that $\equiv$ must be equality. In fact, suppose $s_0 \equiv s_1$, then also $s_0 \equiv' s_1$. This means that they must have the same head element e_0 and that their *unmerged* parts must be equivalent: if $s_{00}, s_{01}, s_{10}, s_{11}$ are such that $s_0 = e_0 : \mathsf{merge}(s_{00}, s_{01})$ and $s_1 = e_0 : \mathsf{merge}(s_{10}, s_{11})$, then it must be $s_{00} \equiv s_{10}$ and $s_{01} \equiv s_{11}$; repeating the argument for these two equivalences, we can deduce that s_0 and s_1 have the same second and third element, and so on. In conclusion, $s_0 = s_1$ as desired.

Example 2 can be seen to be an antifounded algebra by a similar argument. The next-time equivalence relation $\equiv'$ of an equivalence relation $\equiv$ on $\mathsf{Str}(E)$ is the reflexive closure of the transitive relation

$$
\{(e : \mathsf{double}(s_0), e : \mathsf{double}(s_1)) \mid e \in E, s_0, s_1 \in \mathsf{Str}(E), s_0 \equiv s_1\}.
$$

Theorem 1. *AFA $\Rightarrow$ pCRA-uniqueness: An antifounded algebra (A, α) satisfies the uniqueness part of the parametric corecursiveness condition.*

Proof. Assume that (A, α) satisfies AFA and let f_0 and f_1 be two solutions of the pCRA diagram for some $(C, \gamma : C \to FC + A)$. We must prove that $f_0 = f_1$.

Let $(Q, q : A \to Q)$ be the coequalizer of f_0 and f_1. As any coequalizer, it is epi. We apply the next-time operator to it. We prove that $\mathsf{nt}_A(q) \circ f_0 = \mathsf{nt}_A(q) \circ f_1$; the proof is summarized by this diagram:

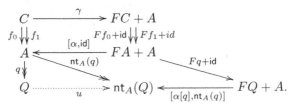

By the fact that f_0 and f_1 are solutions of the pCRA diagram, the top rectangle commutes for both of them. By definition of the nt_A operator, the lower-right parallelogram commutes. Therefore, we have that $\mathsf{nt}_A(q) \circ f_0 = [\alpha[q] \circ F(q \circ f_0), \mathsf{nt}_A(q)] \circ \gamma$ and $\mathsf{nt}_A(q) \circ f_1 = [\alpha[q] \circ F(q \circ f_1), \mathsf{nt}_A(q)] \circ \gamma$. But $q \circ f_0 = q \circ f_1$, because q is the coequalizer of f_0 and f_1, so the right-hand sides of the two previous equalities are the same. We conclude that $\mathsf{nt}_A(q) \circ f_0 = \mathsf{nt}_A(q) \circ f_1$.

Now, using once more that q is the coequalizer of f_0, f_1, there must exist a unique map $u : Q \to \mathsf{nt}_A(Q)$ such that $u \circ q = \mathsf{nt}_A(q)$. By AFA, this implies that q is an isomorphism. As $q \circ f_0 = q \circ f_1$, it follows that $f_0 = f_1$. $\qquad\square$

However, AFA does not imply CRA-existence (and therefore, does not imply pCRA-existence), as attested by the following counterexample.

Example 5. In Set, we use the identity functor $FX = X$ and the successor algebra on natural numbers: $A = \mathbb{N}$ and $\alpha : \mathbb{N} \to \mathbb{N}$ is defined by $\alpha(n) = n + 1$.

Proposition 4. *AFA $\nRightarrow$ CRA-existence: Example 5 satisfies AFA but not CRA-existence.*

Proof. Example 5 satisfies AFA. Let $q : A \to A/\equiv$ be a quotient of A such that $\mathsf{nt}_A(q)$ factorizes through q. Note that the definition of $\equiv'$ (the next-time equivalence relation of $\equiv$) is particularly simple, just the reflexive closure of

$$\{(m_0 + 1, m_1 + 1) \mid m_0, m_1 \in \mathbb{N}, m_0 \equiv m_1\}.$$

So two distinct numbers are equivalent according to $\equiv'$ if and only if they are the successors of elements that are equal according to $\equiv$. There is no need of a transitive closure in this case, since the relation is already transitive. By assumption $\equiv$ is finer than $\equiv'$, that is $\forall m_1, m_2 \in \mathbb{N}. m_0 \equiv m_1 \Rightarrow m_0 \equiv' m_1$. We want to prove that $\equiv$ is equality. We prove, by induction on m, that $[m]_\equiv = \{m\}$, that is, every equivalence class is a singleton:

- For $m = 0$ the statement is trivial: $0 \equiv m'$ implies, by hypothesis, that $0 \equiv' m'$, but since 0 is not a successor, this can happen only by reflexivity, that is, if $m' = 0$;
- Assume that $[m]_\equiv = \{m\}$ by induction hypothesis; we must prove that $[m + 1]_\equiv = \{m + 1\}$; if $m + 1 \equiv m'$, then $m + 1 \equiv' m'$, which can happen only if either $m + 1 = m'$ or m' is a successor and $m \equiv m' - 1$; by induction hypothesis, this implies that $m' - 1 = m$, so $m' = m + 1$.

Example 5 does not satisfy CRA-existence. Indeed, if we take the trivial coalgebra $(1 = \{0\}, \mathsf{id} : 1 \to 1)$, we see that a solution of the CRA diagram would require $f(0) = f(0) + 1$, which is impossible. $\qquad\square$

The vice versa also does not hold: CRA does not imply AFA, as evidenced by the following counterexample.

Example 6. We use the functor $FX = 2^* \times X$ in Set, where 2^* is the set of lists of bits (binary words). We construct an F-algebra on the carrier $A =$

$\mathsf{Str}(2^*)/\simeq$, where $\simeq$ is the equivalence relation defined below. We are particularly interested in streams of a special kind: those made of *incremental* components that stabilize after at most one step. Formally, if $l \in 2^*$ and $i, j \in 2$, we define $(l)^{ij} = (li, lij, lijj, lijjj, \ldots)$, that is,

$$(l)^{0\bar{0}} = (l0, l00, l000, l0000, l00000, \ldots) \quad (l)^{0\bar{1}} = (l0, l01, l011, l0111, l01111, \ldots)$$
$$(l)^{1\bar{0}} = (l1, l10, l100, l1000, l10000, \ldots) \quad (l)^{1\bar{1}} = (l1, l11, l111, l1111, l11111, \ldots).$$

The relation $\simeq$ is the least congruence such that $(l)^{0\bar{1}} \simeq (l)^{1\bar{0}}$ for every l. This means that two streams that begin in the same way but then stabilize in one of the two forms above will be equal: $(l_0, \ldots, l_{k-1}) + (l)^{0\bar{1}} \simeq (l_0, \ldots, l_{k-1}) + (l)^{1\bar{0}}$. In other words, the equivalence classes of $\simeq$ are $\{(l_0, \ldots, l_{k-1}) + (l)^{0\bar{1}}, (l_0, \ldots, l_{k-1}) + (l)^{1\bar{0}}\}$ for elements in one of those two forms, and singletons for elements not in those forms. Notice that we do not equate elements of the forms $(l)^{0\bar{0}}$ and $(l)^{1\bar{1}}$. For simplicity, we will write elements of A just as sequences, in place of equivalence classes. So if $s \in \mathsf{Str}(2^*)$, we will use s also to indicate $[s]_{\simeq}$. We leave it to the reader to check that all our definitions are invariant with respect to $\simeq$. We now define an algebra structure α on this carrier by:

$$\alpha : 2^* \times (\mathsf{Str}(2^*)/\simeq) \to \mathsf{Str}(2^*)/\simeq$$
$$\alpha(l, s) = l : s.$$

Proposition 5. *pCRA $\not\Rightarrow$ AFA: Example 6 satisfies pCRA but not AFA.*

Proof. First we prove that Example 6 satisfies pCRA. Given some $(C, \gamma : C \to 2^* \times C + A)$, we want to prove that there is a unique solution to the pCRA diagram. Given any element $c : C$, we have two possibilities: $\gamma c = \mathsf{inr}\, s$, in which case it must necessarily be $f c = s$; or $\gamma c = \mathsf{inl}\langle l_0, c_1 \rangle$, in which case it must be $f c = l_0 : (f c_1)$. In this second case, we iterate γ again on c_1. The kth component of $f c$ is decided after at most k such steps, therefore the result is uniquely determined by commutativity of the diagram.

Now we prove that Example 6 does not satisfy AFA. With this goal we define an equivalence relation $\equiv$ on $A = \mathsf{Str}(2^*)/\simeq$ such that $\mathsf{nt}_A(A/\equiv)$ factorizes through $A/\equiv$ but $\equiv$ is strictly coarser than $\simeq$. The relation $\equiv$ is the reflexive closure of the following: $\forall l \in 2^*, i_0, i_1, j_0, j_1 \in 2. (l)^{i_0 \bar{j_0}} \equiv (l)^{i_1 \bar{j_1}}$. In other words, $\equiv$ identifies all elements in the form $(l)^{ij}$ that have the same base sequence l. Contrary to the case of $\simeq$, we do not extend $\equiv$ to a congruence: $l_0 + (l_1)^{0\bar{0}} \not\equiv l_0 + (l_1)^{1\bar{1}}$, but still $l_0 + (l_1)^{0\bar{1}} \equiv l_0 + (l_1)^{1\bar{0}}$, because these elements are equivalent according to $\simeq$ and $\equiv$ is coarser. So if s_0 is not in the form $(l)^{ij}$, then $s_0 \equiv s_1$ is true only if $s_0 \simeq s_1$. This equivalence relation is strictly coarser than $\simeq$, since $(l)^{0\bar{0}} \equiv (l)^{1\bar{1}}$ but $(l)^{0\bar{0}} \not\simeq (l)^{1\bar{1}}$.

Let $\equiv'$ be the next-time equivalence relation of $\equiv$, i.e., such that $\mathsf{nt}_A(A/\equiv) = A/\equiv'$. Concretely, $\equiv'$ is the (already reflexive and transitive) relation

$$\{(l : s_0, l : s_1) \mid l \in 2^*, s_0, s_1 \in A, s_0 \equiv s_1\}.$$

We prove that $\equiv$ is finer than $\equiv'$, i.e., if $s_0 \equiv s_1$, then $s_0 \equiv' s_1$. There are two cases.

If s_0 or s_1 is not in the form $(l)^{i\bar{j}}$, then its equivalence class is a singleton by definition, so the other element must be equal to it and the conclusion follows by reflexivity.

If both s_0 and s_1 are in the form $(l)^{i\bar{j}}$, then their base element must be the same l, by definition of $\equiv$. There are four cases for each of the two elements, according to what their i and j parameters are. By considerations of symmetry and reflexivity, we can reduce the cases to just two:

- $s_0 = (l)^{0\bar{0}}$ and $s_1 = (l)^{0\bar{1}}$: We can write the two elements alternatively as $s_0 = l0 : (l0)^{0\bar{0}}$ and $s_1 = l0 : (l0)^{1\bar{1}}$; since $(l0)^{0\bar{0}} \equiv (l0)^{1\bar{1}}$, we conclude that $s_0 \equiv' s_1$;
- $s_0 = (l)^{0\bar{0}}$ and $s_1 = (l)^{1\bar{1}}$: By the previous case and its dual we have $s_0 \equiv'$ $(l)^{0\bar{1}}$ and $s_1 \equiv' (l)^{1\bar{0}}$; but $(l)^{0\bar{1}} \simeq (l)^{1\bar{0}}$ so $s_0 \equiv' s_1$ by transitivity.   □

We now turn to a higher-level view of antifounded algebras. This is in terms of the classical fixed point theory for preorders and monotone endofunctions.

For a (locally small) category $\mathcal{C}$ and an object A, we define the category of quotients of A, called $\mathbf{Quo}(A)$ as follows:

- an object is an epimorphism $(Q, q : A \twoheadrightarrow Q)$,
- a map between (Q, q), (Q', q') is a map $u : Q \rightarrow Q'$ such that $u \circ q = q'$.

Clearly there can be at most one map between any two objects, so this category is a preordered set. (In the standard definition of the category, equivalent epis are identified, so it becomes a poset. We have chosen to be content with a preorder; the cost is that universal properties define objects up to isomorphism.) We tend to write $Q \leq Q'$ instead of $u : (Q, q) \rightarrow (Q', q')$, leaving q, q' and the unique u implicit.

Clearly, $\mathbf{Quo}(A)$ has (A, id_A) as the initial and $(1, !_A)$ as the final object.

Now, nt_A sends objects of $\mathbf{Quo}(A)$ to objects of $\mathbf{Quo}(A)$. It turns out that it can be extended to act also on maps. For a map $u : (Q, q) \rightarrow (Q', q')$, we define $\mathrm{nt}_A(u) : (\mathrm{nt}_A(Q), \mathrm{nt}_A(q)) \rightarrow (\mathrm{nt}_A(Q'), \mathrm{nt}_A(q'))$ as the unique map from a pushout, as shown in the following diagram:

$$
\begin{array}{ccc}
A & \xleftarrow{\ \alpha\ } & FA \\
\downarrow{\scriptstyle \mathrm{nt}_A(q)} & & \downarrow{\scriptstyle Fq} \\
\mathrm{nt}_A(Q) & \xleftarrow{\ \alpha[q]\ } & FQ \\
\vdots\,{\scriptstyle \mathrm{nt}_A(u)} & & \downarrow{\scriptstyle Fu} \\
\mathrm{nt}_A(Q') & \xleftarrow{\ \alpha[q']\ } & FQ'
\end{array}
$$

Given that $\mathbf{Quo}(A)$ is a preorder, this makes nt_A trivially a functor (preservation of the identities and composition is trivial). In preorder-theoretic terms, we say that nt_A is a monotone function.

We can notice that (A, id_A) is trivially a fixed point of nt_A. Since it is the least element of $\mathbf{Quo}(A)$, it is the least fixed point.

The condition of (A, α) being antifounded literally says that, for any Q, $Q \leq \mathrm{nt}_A(Q)$ implies $Q \leq A$, i.e., that A is an upper bound on the post-fixed points of nt_A. Taking into account that A, by being the least element, is also trivially a post-fixed point, this amounts to A being the greatest post-fixed point. Fixed point theory (or, if you wish, Lambek's lemma) tells us that the greatest post-fixed point is also the greatest fixed point.

So, in fact, (A, α) being antifounded means that (A, id_A) is a unique fixed point of nt_A. (Recall that this is up to isomorphism.)

4   Focusing Algebras

Our third and last notion of focused algebra, introduced below in Def. 6, is the condition that an algebra is recoverable by iterating its next-time operator, starting with the final quotient.

At transfinite iterations, given by limits in $\mathcal{C}$ (so that we can prove Theorem 3), we are not guaranteed to still obtain a quotient. In Prop. 7 we will prove that, for Example 5, the iteration at stage ω is not a quotient anymore. However, to apply fixed point theory to $\mathbf{Quo}(A)$ in Lemma 6, we need to work with limits in $\mathbf{Quo}(A)$. Below, talking about the iteration at a limit ordinal, we require that it is a quotient (assuming that so are also all preceding stages), or else we take it to be undefined. Clearly, this is not a beautiful definition. We regard it as one possible way to partially reconcile the discrepancy between corecursiveness and antifoundedness that we have already witnessed.

Definition 5. *Given an algebra (A, α), for any ordinal λ we partially define (A_λ, a_λ) (the λ-th iteration of nt_A on the final object $(1, !_A)$ of $\mathbf{Quo}(A)$) and maps $p_\lambda : A_{\lambda+1} \to A_\lambda$, $p_{\lambda,\kappa} : A_\lambda \to A_\kappa$ (for λ a limit ordinal and $\kappa < \lambda$) in $\mathcal{C}$ by simultaneous recursion by*

$$
\begin{array}{lll}
A_0 = 1 & A_{\lambda+1} = \mathsf{nt}_A(A_\lambda) & A_\lambda = \lim_{\kappa<\lambda} A_\kappa \\
a_0 = !_A & a_{\lambda+1} = \mathsf{nt}_A(a_\lambda) & a_\lambda = \langle a_\kappa \rangle_{\kappa<\lambda} \\
p_0 = !_{A_1} & p_{\lambda+1} = \mathsf{nt}_A(p_\lambda) & p_\lambda = \langle p_\kappa \circ \mathsf{nt}_A(p_{\lambda,\kappa}) \rangle_{\kappa<\lambda} \\
& & p_{\lambda,\kappa} = \pi_{\lambda,\kappa} \quad if\ \kappa < \lambda
\end{array}
$$

where the third column applies if λ is a limit ordinal, the limit $\lim_{\kappa<\lambda} A_\kappa$ exists and the mediating map $\langle a_\kappa \rangle_{\kappa<\lambda}$ is epi; otherwise A_λ, a_λ, p_λ, and $p_{\lambda,\kappa}$ are left undefined.

Diagrammatically,

The limit in the limit ordinal case is of the following diagram in $\mathcal{C}$:

$$(A_\kappa, p_\kappa, p_{\kappa,\iota}\ (\kappa\ \text{lim. ord.}, \iota < \kappa))_{\kappa<\lambda}.$$

Lemma 1. *The above definition is well-formed: for any λ,*

1. *a_λ is an epi (so, for any λ, nt_A is applicable to (A_λ, a_λ), ensuring $(A_{\lambda+1}, a_{\lambda+1})$ is defined),*
2. *$p_\lambda \circ a_{\lambda+1} = a_\lambda$ and $p_{\lambda,\kappa} \circ a_\lambda = a_\kappa$ (if λ is a limit ordinal, $\kappa < \lambda$) (so, for any λ, $(A, (a_\kappa)_{\kappa<\lambda})$ in the definition of a_λ for λ a limit ordinal form a cone, ensuring a_λ is defined)*

Diagrammatically,

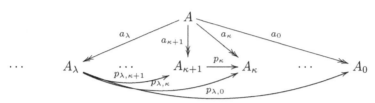

Proof. Both parts are proved by induction on λ.

(1) $a_0 =\, !_A$ is an epi. For the successor case, $a_{\lambda+1} = \mathsf{nt}_A(a_\lambda)$ is an epi, since nt_A takes quotients of A to quotients of A. Finally, for λ a limit ordinal, we have agreed to define a_λ as $\langle a_\kappa \rangle_{\kappa<\lambda}$ only if this mediating map is epi, leaving it undefined otherwise.

(2) It is trivial that $p_0 \circ a_1 =\, !_{A_1} \circ a_1 =\, !_A = a_0$.

For the successor case, $p_{\lambda+1} \circ a_{\lambda+2} = \mathsf{nt}_A(p_\lambda) \circ \mathsf{nt}_A(a_{\lambda+1}) = \mathsf{nt}_A(a_\lambda) = a_{\lambda+1}$ holds by the induction hypothesis $p_\lambda \circ a_{\lambda+1} = a_\lambda$, implying $\mathsf{nt}_A(p_\lambda) \circ \mathsf{nt}_A(a_{\lambda+1}) = \mathsf{nt}_A(a_\lambda)$ by the definition of the functorial extension of nt_A.

For λ a limit ordinal, $p_\lambda \circ a_{\lambda+1} = \langle p_\kappa \mathsf{nt}_A(p_{\lambda,\kappa}) \rangle_{\kappa<\lambda} \mathsf{nt}_A(a_\lambda) = \langle p_\kappa \mathsf{nt}_A(p_{\lambda,\kappa}) \circ \mathsf{nt}_A(a_\kappa) \rangle_{\kappa<\lambda} = \langle p_\kappa \circ \mathsf{nt}_A(a_\kappa) \rangle_{\kappa<\lambda} = \langle p_\kappa \circ a_{\kappa+1} \rangle_{\kappa<\lambda} = \langle a_\kappa \rangle_{\kappa<\lambda} = a_\lambda$, from the induction hypotheses $p_{\lambda,\kappa} \circ a_\lambda = a_\kappa$, implying $\mathsf{nt}_A(p_{\lambda,\kappa}) \circ \mathsf{nt}_A(a_\lambda) = \mathsf{nt}_A(a_\kappa)$ by the definition of the functorial extension of nt_A, and from the induction hypotheses $p_\kappa \circ a_{\kappa+1} = a_\kappa$.

For λ a limit ordinal and $\kappa < \lambda$, $p_{\lambda,\kappa} \circ a_\lambda = \pi_{\lambda,\kappa} \circ \langle a_\kappa \rangle_{\kappa<\lambda} = a_\kappa$.   □

It is very important to remember that we only accept $\lim_{\kappa<\lambda} A_\kappa$ (which is a limit in $\mathcal{C}$) as A_λ for λ a limit ordinal, if it is a quotient of A (otherwise we take A_λ to be undefined). This is by no means guaranteed. As the next proposition shows, this implies that A_λ is also a limit in $\mathbf{Quo}(A)$, but the vice versa need not be true. The carrier of a limit in $\mathbf{Quo}(A)$ is not necessarily a limit in $\mathcal{C}$, as evidenced by our analysis of Example 5 below.

Proposition 6. *If A_λ is defined for a limit ordinal (meaning that $(A_\lambda, (p_{\lambda,\kappa})_{\kappa<\lambda})$ is a limiting cone in $\mathcal{C}$ and $a_\lambda = \langle a_\kappa \rangle_{\kappa<\lambda}$ is epi), then $((A_\lambda, a_\lambda), (p_{\lambda,\kappa})_{\kappa<\lambda})$ is a limiting cone in $\mathbf{Quo}(A)$.*

Proof. To see that

$$((A_\kappa, a_\kappa), p_\kappa, p_{\kappa,\iota} \ (\kappa \text{ lim. ord.}, \iota < \kappa))_{\kappa<\lambda}$$

is a diagram in $\mathbf{Quo}(A)$ we need that $p_\kappa \circ a_{\kappa+1} = a_\iota$ and $p_{\kappa,\iota} \circ a_\kappa = a_\iota$ (κ a limit ordinal, $\iota < \kappa$) for $\kappa < \lambda$. To see that $((A_\lambda, a_\lambda), (p_{\lambda,\kappa})_{\kappa<\lambda})$ is a cone we also need $p_{\lambda,\kappa} \circ a_\lambda = a_\kappa$. But we have proved these equalities already.

To see that $((A_\lambda, a_\lambda), (p_{\lambda,\kappa})_{\kappa<\lambda})$ is a limiting cone, we observe that the sole map to it from a cone $((Q, q), (f_{\lambda,\kappa})_{\kappa<\lambda})$ in $\mathbf{Quo}(A)$ is given by the unique map from $(Q, (f_{\lambda,\kappa})_{\kappa<\lambda})$ to $(A_\lambda, (p_{\lambda,\kappa})_{\kappa<\lambda})$ in $\mathcal{C}$.   □

Given that $\mathbf{Quo}(A)$ is a preorder, we have learned that $(A_\kappa)_{\kappa<\lambda}$ is an inverse chain (if all A_κ are defined) and the limit is the infimum.

Lemma 2. *If A_λ is defined and $A_\lambda \leq A_{\lambda+1}$, then A_λ is the greatest fixed point of nt_A.*

Proof. This is standard fixed point theory for preorders. A_λ is a post-fixed point of nt_A, as $A_\lambda \leq A_{\lambda+1} = \mathrm{nt}_A(A_\lambda)$. And by induction one checks that $Q \leq A_\kappa$ holds for any post-fixed point Q of nt_A and any κ: $Q \leq 1 = A_0$ is trivial; $Q \leq \mathrm{nt}_A(Q) \leq \mathrm{nt}_A(A_\kappa) = A_{\kappa+1}$ follows from the induction hypothesis $Q \leq A_\kappa$, as nt_A is monotone; and, finally, $Q \leq \inf_{\iota<\kappa} A_\iota$ is immediate from the induction hypotheses $Q \leq A_\iota$ ($\iota < \kappa$).   □

Definition 6. *(A, α) is λ-focusing (λ-FA) if A_λ is defined and $A_\lambda \cong A$.*

We show that Example 1 is ω-focusing. In fact we claim that, in this case, $A_i = \mathsf{Str}(E)/\equiv_i$, where $\equiv_i$ is the equivalence relation defined by $s_0 \equiv_i s_1$ if the first $2^i - 1$ elements of s_0 and s_1 are the same. The claim is clearly true for $i = 0$, because $\equiv_0$ is the total relation. Assume, as an induction hypothesis, that $A_i = \mathsf{Str}(E)/\equiv_i$. Then $A_{i+1} = \mathrm{nt}_A(\mathsf{Str}(E)/\equiv_i) = \mathsf{Str}(E)/\equiv_{i+1}$. Now $s_0 \equiv_{i+1} s_1$ holds if $s_0 = e_0 : \mathsf{merge}(s_{00}, s_{01})$ and $s_1 = e_0 : \mathsf{merge}(s_{10}, s_{11})$ with $s_{00} \equiv_i s_{10}$ and $s_{01} \equiv_i s_{11}$. By the induction hypothesis, this means that the first $2^i - 1$ elements of s_{00} and s_{10} are the same and the first $2^i - 1$ elements of s_{01} and s_{11} are also the same. In conclusion, the first $1 + (2^i - 1) + (2^i - 1) = 2^{i+1} - 1$ elements of s_0 and s_1 are the same, that is $s_0 \equiv_{i+1} s_1$, as claimed.

We have proved that A_i is isomorphic to the set E^{2^i-1} of vectors of length $2^i - 1$, with p_i the projection giving the first $2^i - 1$ elements of a vector of length $2^{i+1} - 1$. Standard reasoning shows that $\lim_{i<\omega} A_i$ is $\mathsf{Str}(E)$.

Example 2 is also ω-focusing, but the equivalence relations $\equiv_i$ are different. For $s_0 \equiv_i s_1$ to hold, if $s_0 \neq s_1$, it is not enough that they share the first $2^i - 1$ elements, say $e_0, \ldots, e_{2^i-2}$. It must moreover be the case that $e_1 = e_2$, $e_3 = e_4 = e_5 = e_6$, $\ldots$, $e_{2^{i-1}-1} = \ldots = e_{2^i-2}$ and the remainders of s_0 and s_1 must both be in the image of double^i, i.e., consist of groups of 2^i equal elements.

There are examples of λ-focusing algebras that do not converge at the first limit ordinal ω but at later stages. Here is an example that converges at 2ω.

Example 7. Let us use the functor $FX = X + \mathbb{N} \times X$ in Set. We define an F-algebra with carrier $A = 2\omega + 1 = \{0, 1, \ldots, \omega, \omega + 1, \omega + 2, \ldots, 2\omega\}$:

$$\alpha : (2\omega + 1) + \mathbb{N} \times (2\omega + 1) \to 2\omega + 1$$
$$\alpha(\mathsf{inl}(x)) \quad = x + 1$$
$$\alpha(\mathsf{inr}(n, x)) = \min(\omega + x - n, 2\omega).$$

Theorem 2. *λ-FA $\Rightarrow$ AFA: If an algebra (A, α) is λ-focusing, it is antifounded.*

Proof. Assume that (A, α) is λ-focusing, i.e., that A_λ is defined and $A_\lambda \cong A$. Then $A_\lambda \cong A \leq A_{\lambda+1}$ trivially, as A is the least element in the preorder $\mathbf{Quo}(A)$. It follows by the previous lemma that A_λ, which is isomorphic to A, is the greatest fixed point of nt_A, i.e., that (A, α) is antifounded. $\qquad\square$

The converse does not hold: Some antifounded algebras are not focusing.

Proposition 7. *AFA $\nRightarrow \exists\lambda. \lambda$-FA: Ex. 5 satisfies AFA but not λ-FA for any λ.*

Proof. We already proved in Proposition 4 that Example 5 satisfies AFA. Now we prove that it is not focusing at any ordinal. In fact, we have the following sequence of iterations of nt_A:

$$A_0 = \{\bot\}, \quad A_1 = \{0, \bot\}, \quad A_2 = \{0, 1, \bot\}, \quad \ldots,$$
$$A_i = \{0, \ldots, i-1, \bot\}, \quad \ldots, \quad \lim_{i<\omega} A_i = \mathbb{N} \cup \{\bot\}.$$

At the limit, the element $\bot$ is not an equivalence class of natural numbers anymore and the limit $\lim_{i<\omega} A_i$ is not a quotient of $A = \mathbb{N}$. So, in this case, the limit exists in Set, but is not a limit in the quotient category $\mathbf{Quo}(A)$. The reason that this happens is that, the limit in Set of an inverse chain of quotients given by equivalence relations is not necessarily the quotient given by the intersection of these equivalence relations. $\qquad\square$

Notice that $(A_i)_{i<\omega}$ has the limit $\mathbb{N}$ in $\mathbf{Quo}(A)$. So we have to be mindful of the subtle distinction: λ-FA states that the limit exists in $\mathcal{C}$ and happens to be a quotient; this is a strictly stronger requirement than the condition that the limit exists in $\mathbf{Quo}(A)$.

Theorem 3. *λ-FA $\Rightarrow$ pCRA: If an algebra (A, α) is λ-focusing, it is parametrically recursive.*

The proof uses the inverse chain $(A_\kappa)_{\kappa<\lambda+1}$ as the sequence of codomains for *fuzzy* approximations of the solution. The fact that $A = A_\lambda$ is the inverse limit establishes that a (sharp) function is achieved. This is analogous to the dual situation where a (total) solution arises from a sequence of *partial* approximations defined on a chain of subsets of the given domain to which the chain is required to have as the direct limit.

Proof. Assume that (A, α) is λ-focusing, i.e., that A_λ is defined and $A_\lambda = A_{\lambda+1} = A$ (we ignore that in general we have isomorphisms, not equalities).

Given $(C, \gamma : C \to FC + A)$, we define, for any κ, a map $f_\kappa : C \to A_\kappa$ by

$$f_0 = !_C$$
$$f_{\kappa+1} = [\alpha[a_\kappa] \circ Ff_\kappa, a_{\kappa+1}] \circ \gamma$$
$$f_\kappa = \langle f_\iota \rangle_{\iota<\kappa} \qquad \text{if } \kappa \text{ is a lim. ord.}$$

Diagrammatically,

Simultaneously, we show that $p_\kappa \circ f_{\kappa+1} = f_\kappa$ and $p_{\kappa,\iota} \circ f_\kappa = f_\iota$.

The base case $p_0 \circ f_1 = {!}_{A_1} \circ f_1 = {!}_C = f_0$ holds trivially.

For the successor case, we conclude $p_{\kappa+1} \circ f_{\kappa+2} = \mathsf{nt}_A(p_\kappa) \circ [\alpha[a_{\kappa+1}] \circ F f_{\kappa+1},$ $]a_{\kappa+2}] \circ \gamma = [\mathsf{nt}_A(p_\kappa) \circ \alpha[a_{\kappa+1}] \circ F f_{\kappa+1}, \mathsf{nt}_A(p_\kappa) \circ \mathsf{nt}_A(a_{\kappa+1})] \circ \gamma = [\alpha[a_\kappa] \circ F(p_\kappa \circ f_{\kappa+1}), \mathsf{nt}_A(a_\kappa)] \circ \gamma = [\alpha[a_\kappa] \circ F f_\kappa, a_{\kappa+1}] \circ \gamma = f_{\kappa+1}$ from the induction hypothesis $p_\kappa \circ f_{\kappa+1} = f_\kappa$, using the fact $p_\kappa \circ a_{\kappa+1} = a_\kappa$, which implies $\mathsf{nt}_A(p_\kappa) \circ \alpha[a_{\kappa+1}] = \alpha[a_\kappa] \circ F p_\kappa$ and $\mathsf{nt}_A(p_\kappa) \circ \mathsf{nt}_A(a_{\kappa+1}) = \mathsf{nt}_A(a_\kappa)$ by the definition of the functorial extension of nt_A.

For κ a limit ordinal, $p_\kappa \circ f_{\kappa+1} = \langle p_\iota \circ \mathsf{nt}_A(p_{\kappa,\iota}) \rangle_{\iota < \kappa} \circ [\alpha[a_\kappa] \circ F f_\kappa, a_{\kappa+1}] \circ \gamma = \langle p_\iota \circ \mathsf{nt}_A(p_{\kappa,\iota}) \circ [\alpha[a_\kappa] \circ F f_\kappa, a_{\kappa+1}] \circ \gamma \rangle_{\iota < \kappa} = \langle p_\iota \circ [\mathsf{nt}_A(p_{\kappa,\iota}) \circ \alpha[a_\kappa] \circ F f_\kappa, \mathsf{nt}_A(p_{\kappa,\iota}) \circ \mathsf{nt}_A(a_\kappa)] \circ \gamma \rangle_{\iota < \kappa} = \langle p_\iota \circ [\alpha[a_\iota] \circ F(p_{\kappa,\iota} \circ f_\iota), \mathsf{nt}_A(a_\iota)] \circ \gamma \rangle_{\iota < \kappa} = \langle p_\iota \circ [\alpha[a_\iota] \circ F f_\iota, a_{\iota+1}] \circ \gamma \rangle_{\iota < \kappa} = \langle p_\iota \circ f_{\iota+1} \rangle_{\iota < \kappa} = \langle f_\iota \rangle_{\iota < \kappa} = f_\kappa$ follows from the induction hypotheses $p_{\kappa,\iota} \circ f_\kappa = f_\iota$ and $p_\iota \circ f_{\iota+1} = f_\iota$, using the facts $p_{\kappa,\iota} \circ a_\kappa = a_\iota$, which imply $\mathsf{nt}_A(p_{\kappa,\iota}) \circ \alpha[a_\kappa] = \alpha[a_\iota] \circ F p_{\kappa,\iota}$ and $\mathsf{nt}_A(p_{\kappa,\iota}) \circ \mathsf{nt}_A(a_\kappa) = \mathsf{nt}_A(a_\iota)$ by the definition of the functorial extension of nt_A.

For κ a limit ordinal and $\iota < \kappa$, it is straightforward that $p_{\kappa,\iota} \circ f_\kappa = \pi_{\kappa,\iota} \circ \langle f_\iota \rangle_{\iota < \kappa} = f_\iota$.

Given that $A_\lambda = A_{\lambda+1} = A$, which implies that $p_\lambda = \mathsf{id}_A$, $a_{\lambda+1} = \mathsf{id}_A$, $\alpha[a_\lambda] = \alpha$, it is immediate that f_λ is a solution (in f) of the equation

$$
\begin{array}{ccc}
C & \xrightarrow{\quad \gamma \quad} & FC + A \\
{\scriptstyle f}\big\downarrow & & \big\downarrow{\scriptstyle Ff + \mathsf{id}_A} \\
A & \xleftarrow[{[\alpha, \mathsf{id}_A]}]{} & FA + A
\end{array}
$$

Indeed, $f_\lambda = p_\lambda \circ f_{\lambda+1} = f_{\lambda+1} = [\alpha[a_\lambda] \circ F f_\lambda, a_{\lambda+1}] \circ \gamma = [\alpha \circ F f_\lambda, \mathsf{id}_A] \circ \gamma$.

To show that it is the only solution, i.e., that, for any other solution f, we have $f = f_\lambda$, we show that $a_\kappa \circ f = f_\kappa$. We do this by induction.

The base case $a_0 \circ f = {!}_A \circ f = {!}_C = f_0$ holds trivially.

We also have $a_{\kappa+1} \circ f = \mathsf{nt}_A(a_\kappa) \circ f = \mathsf{nt}_A(a_\kappa) \circ [\alpha \circ F f, \mathsf{id}_A] \circ \gamma = [\mathsf{nt}_A(a_\kappa) \circ \alpha \circ F f, \mathsf{nt}_A(a_\kappa)] \circ \gamma = [\alpha[a_\kappa] \circ F(a_\kappa \circ f), \mathsf{nt}_A(a_\kappa)] \circ \gamma = [\alpha[a_\kappa] \circ F f_\kappa, a_{\kappa+1}] \circ \gamma = f_{\kappa+1}$, from the induction hypothesis $a_\kappa \circ f = f_\kappa$, using that f is a solution.

For κ a limit ordinal, we get $a_\kappa \circ f = \langle a_\iota \rangle_{\iota < \kappa} \circ f = \langle a_\iota \circ f \rangle_{\iota < \kappa} = \langle f_\iota \rangle_{\iota < \kappa} = f_\kappa$ from the induction hypotheses $a_\iota \circ f = f_\iota$ (for $\iota < \kappa$).

From this basis, the desired result $f = f_\lambda$ is already immediate: as $a_\lambda = \mathsf{id}_A$, it is trivial that $f = a_\lambda \circ f = f_\lambda$. $\qquad\square$

Finally, notice that since pCRA does not imply AFA, it cannot imply λ-FA. Example 6 shows this: We proved that it satisfies pCRA but not AFA, hence it cannot satisfy λ-FA either.

5   Conclusion

We have looked at some notions of support for general structured corecursion/coinduction. They are all properties on an algebra (A, α) of a fixed functor

F. The conditions CRA/pCRA state that we can uniquely solve all structured recursive diagrams based on (A, α). The condition AFA asserts that the principle of bisimilarity holds for the carrier A: Every equivalence on A that is finer than its own structural refinement must be equality. Finally, λ-FA says that we can reconstruct A by iterating structural refinement.

The relations between the four conditions CRA, pCRA, AFA, and λ-FA are summarized by the following diagram. The solid lines indicate implications, the dotted lines indicate non-implications.

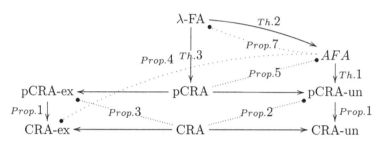

We conclude from this study that general structured corecursion/coinduction is more subtle and, at the same time, also more revealing than general structured recursion/induction from which we drew inspiration. In particular, we have seen that, for Set-like categories, straightforward dualization of the different equivalent conditions of recursion/induction leads to inequivalent conditions of corecursion/coinduction. This could be an indication that some of the conditions are not really the right ones: perhaps they work for recursion/induction in Set incidentally, but for smooth generalization to other categories and dualization one should proceed from different conditions. While we believe firmly that recursiveness [corecursiveness] are natural conditions, it may turn out that some yet unconsidered versions of wellfoundedness [antifoundedness] are more robustly equivalent to recursiveness [corecursiveness] than the versions we have considered here.

To achieve progress we must fully understand each of the conditions we have considered and the role that the different viable assumptions play for the implications and non-implications between them. We can then seek variants that are more in line with our intuitive grasp. We expect that this enquiry will produce new and exciting results.

We would like to be able to tell a type-theoretic version of the story, i.e., to develop a dual Bove-Capretta method (allowing a general corecursive definition to be justified by a productivity proof). For this, we must overcome the discrepancies already commented, but likewise it is important that all our constructions can be made constructively (computationally) meaningful.

We would also very much like to relate our work to approaches to recursion/corecursion based on Banach's fixed point theorem [7,3].

Acknowledgements. We thank Thierry Coquand and Peter Dybjer for comments and questions and likewise the referees. T. Uustalu and V. Vene were supported by the Estonian Science Foundation under grants No. 6940 and 6713. The research visits between the authors were financed by the EU FP6 IST coordination action TYPES and the Estonian Tiger University Plus programme. The latter programme also financed Varmo Vene's attendance of SBMF 2009.

References

1. Adámek, J., Lücke, D., Milius, S.: Recursive coalgebras for finitary functors. Theor. Inform. and Appl. 41(4), 447–462 (2007)
2. Bove, A., Capretta, V.: Modelling general recursion in type theory. Math. Struct. in Comput. Sci. 14(4), 671–708 (2005)
3. Buchholz, W.: A term calculus for (co-)recursive definitions on streamlike data structures. Ann. of Pure and Appl. Logic 136(1–2), 75–90 (2005)
4. Capretta, V., Uustalu, T., Vene, V.: Recursive coalgebras from comonads. Inform. and Comput. 204(4), 437–468 (2006)
5. Cockett, R., Fukushima, T.: About Charity. Yellow series report 92/480/18, Dept. of Comput. Sci., Univ. of Calgary (1992)
6. Coquand, T.: Infinite objects in type theory. In: Barendregt, H., Nipkow, T. (eds.) TYPES 1993. LNCS, vol. 806, pp. 62–78. Springer, Heidelberg (1994)
7. Di Gianantonio, P., Miculan, M.: A unifying approach to recursive and co-recursive definitions. In: Geuvers, H., Wiedijk, F. (eds.) TYPES 2002. LNCS, vol. 2646, pp. 148–161. Springer, Heidelberg (2003)
8. Doornbos, H., Backhouse, R.: Reductivity. Sci. of Comput. Program 26(1-3), 217–236 (1996)
9. Eppendahl, A.: Coalgebra-to-algebra morphisms. Electron. Notes in Theor. Comput. Sci. 29, 8 (1999)
10. Giménez, E.: Codifying guarded definitions with recursion schemes. In: Smith, J., Dybjer, P., Nordström, B. (eds.) TYPES 1994. LNCS, vol. 996, pp. 39–59. Springer, Heidelberg (1995)
11. Jacobs, B.: The temporal logic of coalgebras via Galois algebras. Math. Struct. in Comput. Sci. 12(6), 875–903 (2002)
12. Milius, S.: Completely iterative algebras and completely iterative monads. Inform. and Comput. 196(1), 1–41 (2005)
13. Osius, G.: Categorical set theory: a characterization of the category of sets. J. of Pure and Appl. Algebra 4, 79–119 (1974)
14. Taylor, P.: Intuitionistic sets and ordinals. J. of Symb. Logic 61(3), 705–744 (1996)
15. Taylor, P.: Towards a unified treatment of induction, I: The general recursion theorem. Unpublished draft 35 pp (1996); // A short version (1996) of 5 pp was distributed at Gödel 1996 Brno (August 1996), http://www.monad.me.uk/ordinals/
16. Taylor, P.: Practical foundations of mathematics. Cambridge Studies in Advanced Mathematics, vol. 59, xi+572. Cambridge Univ. Press, Cambridge (1999)
17. Turner, D.A.: Total functional programming. J. of Univ. Comput. Sci. 10(7), 751–768 (2004)
18. Uustalu, T., Vene, V.: Primitive (co)recursion and course-of-value (co)iteration, categorically. Informatica 10(1), 5–26 (1999)

Formalizing FreeRTOS: First Steps

David Déharbe, Stephenson Galvão, and Anamaria Martins Moreira

Departamento de Informática e Matemática Aplicada
Universidade Federal do Rio Grande do Norte
Natal, RN, Brazil

Abstract. This paper presents the current state of the formal development of FreeRTOS, a real-time operating system. The goal of this effort is to address a scientific challenge and is realized within the scope of the Grand Challenge on Verified Software. The development is realized with the B method. A model of the main functionalities of the FreeRTOS is now available and can be a starting point to establish an agreed formal specification of FreeRTOS that can be used by the research community.

1 Introduction

Computer Science is a fairly young discipline, but has a dramatic impact on our society and lifestyle. The pervasive nature of computing has given rise to a very large number of sub-areas and has fragmented the efforts of the research community. It seems now a good time for the community to pause and reflect to define scientific challenges that provide the opportunity for these different sub-areas to share and combine knowledge, efforts and results to achieve ground-breaking results that attend to existing needs of our societies.

One such initiative has been undertaken by the Brazilian Computer Society [1] and has identified five grand challenges. One such challenge is concerned with the *technological development of quality: dependable, scalable and ubiquitous systems*. Formal methods have shown to be a successful approach to build dependable systems. They are currently employed in applications requiring a high level of safety and integrity.

The work presented in this paper represents a small step in the direction of this challenge, but it more specifically addresses another one: the *International Grand Challenge on Verified Software* [2]. One of the activities associated to this challenge consists in setting up case studies of increasing complexity to measure and compare existing approaches to build verified software, to identify their weaknesses and how they can be improved. It is in that context that real-time operating system FreeRTOS has been proposed as a case study [3].

FreeRTOS is mainly written in C, with some parts in assembly language. It is available as a library of types and functions to build real-time, multi-tasking, embedded software. FreeRTOS is an interesting case study for many reasons. First, it has a large community of users and its verification would have a strong impact. Second, although FreeRTOS has a relatively large number of functions, its source code has medium size. Third, it is easily available, as it is open source

M.V.M. Oliveira and J. Woodcock (Eds.): SBMF 2009, LNCS 5902, pp. 101–117, 2009.

and it is well documented. Finally, and most importantly, modeling and verifying the kernel of an operating system is scientifically challenging [4]: for instance, the code includes many complex pointer-based operations.

The verification of a software aims at showing that it is free from errors (or to find some errors). In the context of this paper, we are interested in design errors, resulting in a discrepancy between the system behavior and its requirements. In the case of FreeRTOS, the requirements are distributed throughout the documentation, are expressed in natural language and are therefore not adequate as a source for a formal verification effort. The first step towards verifying FreeR-TOS is thus to build a functional specification of its intended behavior. The goal of this paper is to present the current state of the model of FreeRTOS, which covers a significant, and essential, subset of the available functionalities. This model is available for researchers interested in contributing to the challenge of the verification of FreeRTOS.

Several formalisms are candidates to specify the functional requirements of *software*. In this work, we have chosen the B method [5,6]: it provides not only a notation, but also a framework for the verification of a specification and its refinement towards an implementation. It is similar to other well-known formal specification notations, such as VDM [7] and Z [8]. One important criterion to choose the B method is that it has a solid tool support for all the development stages.

Overview of the paper. Sections 2 and 3 lay the ground for this paper by presenting respectively the main features of FreeRTOS and the B method. Section 4 then enumerates and describes the functionalities of FreeRTOS that have been selected for modeling. The resulting functional specification is presented in Section 5. Section 6 draws conclusions and presents future work.

2   FreeRTOS

FreeRTOS is a simple, easy-to-use real-time operating system. Its source code is written in C and assembly. It is open source and has little more than 2,200 lines of code. FreeRTOS has been officially ported to most architectures for embedded systems, such as 8051, PIC, ARM and Zilog's Z80.

One key assumption of FreeRTOS is that the target system has a single processing unit. FreeRTOS provides the following services: task management, inter-task communication and synchronization, memory management, real-time events, and control of input and output devices. These services are provided as a library of types and functions that needs to be linked to the compiled code of the application being developed. Typically, this code is divided in two parts: the first one contains the code of the tasks that are going to be executed during the operation of the system, while the second contains the code responsible for the system initialization; namely, registering the tasks and starting the scheduler. Consequently, the run of an application built with FreeRTOS starts with a boot phase, to set up the different tasks and communication channels, followed by an application execution phase, starting when the scheduler is activated: from that moment on, tasks are scheduled and executed.

2.1   Task Management

Tasks form the basic computation unit in multi-tasking applications. A task has a *state*, that may be one of running, ready, suspended and blocked, a *priority*, an integer value ranging from zero up to a maximum value defined at compile time, and the *execution context* storing the call stack and the register values when the task is not executing.

Task scheduling is based on priorities. The scheduler always chooses one task with the highest priority among those ready tasks. A direct consequence of that policy is that the priority of the running task is always greater than or equal to that of all ready tasks.

Scheduling also equally shares the processing time between tasks with the same priority. Thus, if there are two or more tasks having the highest priority among the ready tasks, they shall equally share the processing time.

Finally, FreeRTOS automatically creates a system task, called the *idle task*, that has the lowest possible priority. This task guarantees that the processor is always executing some task and also executes some administration duties of the operating system, such as memory management.

2.2   Communication and Synchronization

FreeRTOS provides message-passing communication facilities. Tasks may post messages to queues and read messages from queues. Queues have a fixed, limited capacity, defined when the task is created. Message-passing is blocking: whenever a task wants to read from an empty queue or to write to a full queue, it is blocked. There are however facilities to associate delays to queue access, or to make non-blocking accesses.

FreeRTOS also provides semaphores as a task synchronization primitive. Semaphores are actually implemented as queues with capacity one, with the convention that the semaphore is taken when the queue is empty and it is free when the queue is full. FreeRTOS also provides counting semaphores, to control the access to a resource by a maximum number of tasks. To avoid the priority inversion problem, FreeRTOS also provides mutexes with priority inheritance.

3   The B Method

The B method is a model-driven design methodology to build software components reliably, in the sense that the programs produced are guaranteed to implement the corresponding functional specification. The B method consists in the following steps: first, a functional specification of the requirements, or part thereof, is developed. In B, this initial specification is called a *machine*. This initial specification is then subject to different kinds of analysis, including type checking and theorem proving, to establish that it is implementable and that all executions are safe, in the sense that they may not reach an invalid state.

Once the specification has been built, it is used as the starting point of a series of refinements, each *refinement* resulting in an artifact providing a new model of the system. In B, refinements are usually constructed by the modeler, although automatic refinement support is now also possible [9]. Each such refinement may capture new functional requirements or introduce a more concrete description of the system, by introducing an algorithmic development or an implementable data representation. The former is called an *horizontal* refinement and the latter a *vertical* refinement [10]. Eventually, a sequence of horizontal and then vertical refinements shall lead to a fully algorithmic artifact, called an *implementation* in the B method. Such modules may then be translated to source code for programs in imperative languages such as C, Ada or Java.

The theoretical underpinnings of the B method are first-order logic, integer arithmetic, set theory, substitution calculus, and refinement theory. The different modules are written in a language called *abstract machine notation* (or AMN). An AMN module is divided into sections, each section being responsible for defining an aspect of the specification, e.g. parameters, basic types, constant values, state variables, initial states and transitions.

As an illustration, Figure 1 contains a module, called *Kernel*, specifying a system which allows to include new tasks up to a maximum number of ten. The **MACHINE** section identifies the nature (a functional specification) and the name of the module. The section **SETS** introduces a new type of entities, namely *TASK*. At this level, no further detail is provided on how this entity is going to be implemented. The **VARIABLES** section enumerates the name of the different state variables. Here, the state is composed of a single variable, named *tasks*. The **INVARIANT** section defines the possible values of the state variables: it defines their types and other restrictions that shall reflect the functional requirements of the system. Next, the **INITIALISATION** section provides a definition of the set of possible initial states of the system. Last is the **OPERATIONS** section, which is where the different types of events that the system may execute and the corresponding state transitions are defined. The example has a single operation that takes a task as parameter and adds it to *tasks*. In B, operations may have parameters (passed by value), results, and may change the value of the state variables. Operations are defined in a language called the *generalized substitution language*. The constructs of this language are syntactically similar to that of imperative programming languages, and semantically, they are predicate transformers.

In the B method, a machine must be verified to satisfy the correctness criteria stating that it is implementable, that all the states that are reachable are valid

MACHINE	**INVARIANT**	$task\_add(task) =$
Kernel	$tasks \in \mathbb{P}(TASK) \wedge$	**PRE**
SETS	$\mathbf{card}(tasks) \leq 10$	$task \in TASK \wedge task \notin tasks \wedge$
TASK	**INITIALISATION**	$\mathbf{card}(tasks) < 10$
VARIABLES	$tasks := \emptyset$	**THEN**
tasks	**OPERATIONS**	$tasks := tasks \cup \{task\}$
		END

Fig. 1. Functional specification of a simple task management system

states (i.e. they satisfy the condition expressed in the invariant clause), and that all expressions appearing in the specification are well-defined. This verification consists in checking proof obligations that are automatically generated from the text of the machine. The proof obligations are formulas of first-order logic and the user is responsible for proving that they are valid.

Consider the example of Figure 1. To guarantee that the machine is implementable, one needs to prove the satisfiability of the different constraints of the model. In the case of this example, one needs to show the validity of the existential quantification of the invariant:

$$\exists tasks \bullet tasks \in \mathbb{P}(TASK) \wedge \mathbf{card}(tasks) \leq 10.$$

To guarantee the correctness criterion stating that all reachable states are valid, one must check that each operation preserves the invariant: if the operation is applied to a state satisfying the invariant, and if the pre-condition of the operation is satisfied, then the resulting state must also be valid. The following formula, generated automatically by the proof obligation generator, states this property:

$$tasks \in \mathbb{P}(TASK) \wedge \mathbf{card}(tasks) \leq 10 \quad \wedge$$
$$task \in TASK \wedge task \in tasks \wedge \mathbf{card}(task) < 10 \Rightarrow$$
$$(tasks \cup \{task\}) \in \mathbb{P}(TASK) \wedge \mathbf{card}(tasks \cup \{task\}) \leq 10.$$

Finally, it is necessary to show that all the expressions occurring in the specification are well-defined. In the case of the example, one must show that *tasks* is a finite set in every context where the expression $\mathbf{card}(tasks)$ is evaluated.

The proof of these verification conditions is performed either by automatic theorem provers, or manually, by issuing commands to an interactive theorem prover. Typically, the automatic theorem prover manages to discharge a significant part of the verification conditions. The remaining conditions are either valid and the user must be able to build a proof of their validity, or are not valid. In the former case, it might happen that the user cannot build the proof, as the prover is inherently incomplete; he has then the choice of including additional rules or to check the condition manually and take responsibility for the verdict. In the latter case, the specification has some error and must be corrected or the formula cannot be proved. In the case of an erroneous specification, the information provided by the interactive theorem prover is often helpful to locate the error. Eventually, the user shall reach a point where all verification conditions have been proved and the refinement process may be initiated.

Note that the functional model may also be used to derive manually an implementation in a programming language. Moreover the functional specification may also be used as a reference to generate tests [11] of the implementation.

An example of refinement is presented in Figure 2. The state variable *tasks* is no longer a set of tasks but a sequence of tasks. Sequences are pre-defined in AMN and the operators **ran** and $\rightarrow$ return respectively the contents of the sequence (as a set) and addition of an element to the end of the sequence. The B method also defines a set of verification conditions which, when proved, guarantee that the refinement is correct with respect to the initial specification.

REFINEMENT INVARIANT	OPERATIONS
$Kernel\_r$	$tasks\_r \in \mathbf{seq}(TASK) \wedge$ $task\_add(task) =$
REFINES	$\mathbf{ran}(tasks\_r) = tasks$ **BEGIN**
$Kernel$	**INITIALISATION** $\quad tasks\_r := task \rightarrow tasks\_r$
VARIABLES	$tasks\_r := []$ **END**
$tasks\_r$	

Fig. 2. Refinement of the machine $Kernel$ (Figure 1)

4 Overview of the Modeling

Modeling a complex system with the B method may be facilitated by taking into account the following remarks:

1. Parts of the functional requirements may be abstracted in the initial speci-fication. Such requirements may be introduced later, by means of horizontal refinements, or by extending the specification. In order to adopt this ap-proach, one must first plan a sequence of incremental modeling steps, each introducing additional entities and functionalities of FreeRTOS. Such steps are described in Section 4.3.
2. When requirements do not present interdependency, they may specified in different modules. These modules will then be combined using the compo-sition mechanism of the B method (e.g inclusion, vision, etc.) The modular structure of the model is presented in Section 5.

In system development projects, (formal) specifications are usually performed in the initial stages. In the experience reported in this paper, the system already exists, its functionalities have been identified and implemented. The presented model is the result of the analysis of the documentation of the system as well as of the source code of its implementation.

Based on an informal analysis of FreeRTOS documentation and source code, we planned an incremental construction of the model. Such increments are pre-sented in section 4.3.

The main classes of entities provided by FreeRTOS are tasks, message queues, co-routines, semaphores and mutexes, and each such class has an associated set of functions. However in the case of FreeRTOS, semaphores are nothing more than specialized message queues. Therefore, to build a first functional model of FreeRTOS, two basic kinds of entities were initially chosen for formalization: tasks and message queues, which form the basic mechanism for task communi-cation and synchronization.

4.1 Tasks

Functions manipulating tasks can be divided into the functions that manage the tasks themselves and those that control the scheduler.

The task management functions that we have modeled are task creation (xTaskCreate), task destruction (xTaskDelete), an accessor to get the priority of a task (uxTaskPriorityGet), task suspension (vTaskSuspend), resumption of a suspended task, taking it to a **ready** state (vTaskResume), changing the priority of a task (vTaskPrioritySet), interruption of a task for a given time period, starting from the moment the function was called (vTaskDelay), or from the moment the task was resumed (vTaskDelayUntil).

With respect to the scheduling aspects, we have modeled functions to: access the currently executing task (xTaskGetCurrentTaskHandle), access to the state of the schedule, which may be **executing, suspended** or **uninitialized** (xTaskGetSchedulerState), get the number of existing tasks (uxTaskGetNumberOfTasks), get the time elapsed since the scheduler was initialized (xTaskGetTickCount), initiate the scheduler and start the so-called *idle* task (vTaskStartScheduler), finalize the activities of the scheduler and put it back in the uninitialized state, deleting all the entities created (vTaskEndScheduler), suspend the scheduler (vTaskSuspendAll), and resume the scheduler (xTaskResumeAll).

4.2   Message Queues

We have modeled the following functions related to message queues: construction of a new, empty, queue (xQueueCreate), sending a message to a queue (xQueueSend), sending a message to the back of a queue (xQueueSendToBack) or to the front of a queue (xQueueSendToFront), to retrieve a message from the front of a queue (xQueueReceive), to read a message from the front of a queue, without removing it (xQueuePeek), and to delete a message queue. The presented model does not take into account the (fixed) capacity of the queues, resulting in non-deterministic models of these functions.

4.3   Increments in the Model

Once the basic funcionalities of the system have been identified (namely, tasks and message queues), we identified modeling steps such that they could be defined in an incremental fashion:

1. **Basic model:** In this first step, we considered mainly the behavior of the functions related to the state of the tasks and the transitions between such states. The notion of priority was, at this level, left abstract. Also, the state of the scheduler was defined as well as the concept of elementary timing events called *ticks* in FreeRTOS. Message queues were also modeled, and their size was left abstract. In order to be able to abstract notions such as queue size and message priority, operations depending on these were defined non-deterministically.
2. **Priority:** In this second step, task priority was effectively taken into account in the model. The main consequence is that functions resulting in the scheduling of a new task were refined into more deterministic versions.
3. **Mutexes:** The third stage will consist in specifying this mechanism, that allows synchronizing tasks without provoking priority inversions.

4. **Queue size:** The fourth step shall consist in removing non-determinism related to queue sizes and actually specify the behavior related to the requirements with respect to full or empty queues.

5. **Addition of non-elementary entities:** We have already mentioned that a semaphore can be viewed as a message queue. Modeling semaphores and the related requirements will be performed last, by using the definitions already available for message queues.

5   The Functional Model

This section presents the first two steps to build the model of FreeRTOS as described in Section 4. The resulting model thus includes tasks, message queues, scheduling, and priorities. All the models presented in this section have been developed and verified using Atelier B 4.0 [12].

Even though only parts of the requirements are considered, the estimated size of the resulting model seemed large enough to consider a modular structure of the specification. The components of this structure are:

- The *Config* machine contains auxiliary definitions of constants that need to be be instantiated when building an application on top of FreeRTOS; for instance, the number of priority levels is configurable. Our model simply defines the domain of these constants.
- The *Types* machine declares the types of the different entities of the model of the system such as tasks, queues, messages, return codes.
- The *Task* machine defines the state variables modeling the tasks in the system, as well as the corresponding elementary functions.
- The *Queue* machine has a role similar to the *Task* machine, but related to message queues.
- The *Scheduler* machine is a very simple machine that justs maintains the current state of the scheduler.
- The machine *FreeRTOSBasic* includes an instance of the three machines *Task*, *Queue* and *Scheduler* and defines models of elementary message passing functions.
- Finally, the machine *FreeRTOS* includes an instance of *FreeRTOSBasic* and defines models of high-level message-passing functions. The intermediate machine *FreeRTOSBasic* is necessary as B does not allow operations in a machine to refer to operations in the same machine.

5.1   Tasks

The machine *Task* defines the entities and operations related to tasks (see excerpts in Figure 1). Several modeling approaches are possible: using disjoint sets, or using a state function mapping tasks to an enumerated set. We chose the former, as it allows expressing the invariant using simple sets and is thus easier to analyze using one of the available theorem provers.

The state variable *active* indicates whether the operating system is active or not (i.e. it is in the initialization phase of an instance of the system). Variable *tasks* represents all the created tasks. In addition, *running*, *ready*, *blocked* and *suspended* represent respectively the currently scheduled task, the set of tasks ready to be scheduled, the set of blocked tasks and the set of suspended tasks. Finally, variable *idle* represents the idle system task.

VARIABLES
    active, tasks, blocked, running, ready, suspended, idle
INVARIANT
    $active \in BOOL \wedge tasks \in \mathbb{F}(TASK) \wedge running \in TASK \wedge idle \in TASK$
    $\wedge\ blocked \in \mathbb{F}(TASK) \wedge ready \in \mathbb{F}(TASK) \wedge suspended \in \mathbb{F}(TASK)$

The invariant includes also constraints to model several requirements: (1) a task may be in a single state at any time; (2) while the scheduler has not been activated, tasks are ready to execute; when the scheduler has been activated, (3) the idle task is always either ready to execute or executing, and (4) there is always a running task.

$$blocked \subseteq tasks \wedge ready \subseteq tasks \wedge suspended \subseteq tasks \wedge$$
$$ready \cap blocked = \emptyset \wedge blocked \cap suspended = \emptyset \wedge suspended \cap ready = \emptyset \wedge$$
$$(active = FALSE \Rightarrow tasks = ready) \wedge$$
$$(active = TRUE \Rightarrow (idle = running \vee idle \in ready) \wedge$$
$$running \notin (blocked \cup ready \cup suspended) \wedge$$
$$tasks = \{running\} \cup suspended \cup blocked \cup ready)$$

In addition, the *Task* machine contains basic operations that model the elementary changes to the system state with respect to tasks and the scheduler. Such operations are used to specify the functions of FreeRTOS related to tasks. There is a total of twelve such elementary functions, from which two will be presented here[1].

The creation of a new task is specified by the operation *t_create*. This operation can only be applied when the scheduler has not been initialized. It takes as parameter the priority of the task, which will be taken into account in a refinement, and creates and returns a new task entity which is initially ready to execute:

$result \longleftarrow t\_create(priority) =$ **THEN**
PRE $tasks := \{task\} \cup tasks\ \|$
    $priority \in PRIORITY \wedge$ $ready := \{task\} \cup ready\ \|$
    $active = FALSE$ $result := task$
THEN   **END**
    ANY *task*   **WHERE**   **END**;
      $task \in TASK \wedge task \notin tasks$

---

[1] The full models and the corresponding interactive proofs are freely available at http://code.google.com/p/freertosb/source/browse

The second operation shown here is $t\_startScheduler$ that specifies the state transition when the scheduler is activated. This corresponds to the change from the initialisation phase to the execution phase of a FreeRTOS application. In that phase, the system task $idle$ is created and the scheduler chooses a task for execution. Again, recall that the priority has not been taken into account at this level of abstraction and is the subject of a further refinement. It is here left non-deterministic:

$t\_startScheduler =$
PRE
   $active = FALSE$
THEN
   $active := TRUE \parallel$
   $blocked, suspended := \emptyset, \emptyset \parallel$
   ANY $idle\_task$ **WHERE**
     $idle\_task \in TASK \wedge$
     $idle\_task \notin tasks$
   THEN

     $tasks := \{idle\_task\} \cup tasks \parallel$
     $idle := idle\_task \parallel$
     ANY $task$ **WHERE**
       $task \in ready \cup \{idle\_task\}$
     THEN
       $running := task \parallel$
       $ready := (ready \cup \{idle\_task\}) - \{task\}$
     END
   END
END;

The behavior of the task-related functions of FreeRTOS has then been modeled using these elementary operations. Here, we only show the function specification of the function $xTaskCreate$, that provides the task creation functionality in FreeRTOS. This specification uses the previously presented operation t_create. The $return$ value of the function $xTaskCreate$ indicates if the operation succeeded or failed (for instance due to a lack of available memory) and a handler to the new task is asssigned to to parameter $handler$, passed by reference.

$result, handle \longleftarrow$
   $xTaskCreate(\ code, name,$
        $stackSize, params,$
        $priority) =$
PRE
   $code \in TASK\_CODE \wedge$
   $name \in NAME \wedge$
   $stackSize \in NATURAL \wedge$
   $params \subset PARAMETER \wedge$
   $priority \in PRIORITY \wedge$
   $scheduler = NOT\_STARTED \wedge$
THEN

CHOICE
   $handle \longleftarrow$
     $\mathbf{t\_create}(priority) \parallel$
   $result := pdPASS$
OR
   $result := errMEMORY \parallel$
   $handle :\in TASK$
END
END

Note that in the notation of the B method, parameters are always passed by value, and operations may return multiple values. In the C implementation of FreeRTOS, operations such as xTaskCreate return more than one value and use pointer typed parameters to store these additional results. Wherever this is the case, the functional model includes an additional return parameter.

5.2   Message Queues

The machine *Queue* defines the basic functionality to handle message queues. There are two types of entities: *QUEUE*, the queues, *ITEM*, the messages. Its state is formed by a variable *queues* representing queues, and the variables *items*, *sending* and *receiving* associating each queue with its contents, the tasks waiting to write in the queue, and the tasks waiting to read from the queue, respectively.

VARIABLES   INVARIANT

queues,	$queues \in \mathbb{P}(QUEUE) \wedge$
items,	$items \in QUEUE \nrightarrow \mathbb{P}(ITEM) \wedge \mathbf{dom}(items) = queues \wedge$
receiving,	$receiving \in QUEUE \nrightarrow \mathbb{P}(TASK) \wedge \mathbf{dom}(receiving) = queues \wedge$
sending	$sending \in QUEUE \nrightarrow \mathbb{P}(TASK) \wedge \mathbf{dom}(sending) = queues$

The *Queue* machine also contains operations that define the basic functionality to manipulate the message queues. There is a total of six such operations. For instance, the operation *sendItem* defines the inclusion of a new message *item* at position *pos* of *queue*, and destination *task*:

$sendItem(queue, item, task, pos) =$ **THEN**
PRE $items(queue) :=$
    $queue \in queues \wedge$ $items(queue) \cup \{item\}$ ‖
    $item \in ITEM \wedge$ $receiving(queue) :=$
    $task \in TASK \wedge$ $receiving(queue) - \{task\}$
    $pos \in COPY\_POSITION \wedge$ **END**
    $task \in receiving(queue)$

Such low-level operations are used to specify the behavior of section of the FreeRTOS API dealing with communication. There are basically two classes of functions: one for read access, and one for write access. They can all be specified by means of two basic operations: *xQueueGenericSend* and *xQueueGenericReceive*, which, in our model, are defined in the machine *FreeRTOSBasic*. For instance, the operation *xQueueGenericSend* specifies a generic write access of a message *i* in a queue *q*. This operation is also parameterized by the access position *pos* and the maximum number of ticks *wait* that the sending task may be blocked waiting for the queue. The sending task is always the running task. Three different behaviors are possible. First, if the queue is already full, then the running task is inserted in the set of tasks waiting to write on the queue, and a deadline is associated to this task with operation *t_delayTask*. In this scenario, the result is the constant *pdTRUE*. Second, if the queue is full, but the task is not willing to wait, the operation returns the constant *errQUEUE_FULL*. Finally, in case the destination task is already blocked waiting to read from this queue, then this task is unblocked, and the operation returns *pdPASS*. Note that the capacity of the queues is not part of the abstract model, which is why the specification of this function is non-deterministic. This aspect will be included in the specification through a refinement.

$res \leftarrow xQueueGenericSend(q, i, wait, pos) =$
PRE
  $q \in queues \wedge i \in ITEM \wedge wait \in TICK \wedge$
  $pos \in COPY\_POSITION \wedge$
  $active = TRUE \wedge running \neq idle$
THEN
  CHOICE
    IF $wait > 0$ **THEN**
      $q\_insertTaskWaitingToSend(q, running) \parallel$
      $t\_delayTask(wait) \parallel$
      $res := pdTRUE$
    ELSE
      $res := errQUEUE\_FULL$
    END

OR
  ANY t **WHERE**
    $t \in TASK \wedge$
    $t \in blocked \wedge$
    $t \in receiving(q)$
  THEN
    $q\_sendItem(q, i, t, pos) \parallel$
    $t\_unblock(t) \parallel$
    $res := pdPASS$
  END
END
END

Finally, the machine *FreeRTOS* instantiates these generic operations to specify the behavior of FreeRTOS' functions providing task communication facilities. For instance, the operation *xQueueSend* specifies the behavior of the homonym FreeRTOS function, one of the three message sending variants in the API:

$res \longleftarrow xQueueSend(q, i, w) =$
PRE
  $q \in queues \wedge i \in ITEM \wedge w \in TICK \wedge$
  $active = TRUE \wedge running \neq idle$
THEN
  $res \leftarrow xQueueGenericSend(q, i, w, queueSEND\_TO\_BACK)$
END
END

5.3 Taking Priorities into Account

The functional requirements state that the running task should have a priority greater or equal than all the ready tasks. In order to take into account such requirement, the invariant needs to be strengthened to define task priorities and to specify the desired property. From the methodological viewpoint, starting from the first version of the *Task* machine (described in Section 5.1), we can either define a new version, or create a refinement. We chose the latter solution and we describe it now.

We defined a refinement module called *Task_r*. In it, we defined a type *PRIORITY* that represents tasks priorities. The state variable *prio* maps each task to its priority and the invariant states that when the scheduler has been initialised, no ready task has a priority greater than the running task. We also include restrictions on the priority of the idle task, which is the lowest possible priority.

CONSTANTS
  $MAX\_P, IDLE\_P$
PROPERTIES
  $PRIORITY = 0..(MAX\_P - 1)\wedge$
  $MAX\_P > 0 \wedge IDLE\_P = 0$
VARIABLES
  $prio$

INVARIANT
  $prio \in TASK \nrightarrow PRIORITY \wedge$
  $\mathbf{dom}(prio) = tasks \wedge$
  $(active = TRUE \Rightarrow$
    $prio(idle) = IDLE\_P\wedge$
    $\forall t.(t \in ready \Rightarrow prio(t) \leq prio(running))\wedge$
    $\forall t.(t \in ready \Rightarrow IDLE\_P \leq prio(t)))$

Most of the operations of the *Task* machine involve defining a new running task, and these operations need to be refined to maintain the new invariant. In order to simplify the definition of these refined operations, a scheduling function was introduced. It takes as input a set of tasks and a function mapping tasks to their priorities, and it returns those given tasks that have the highest priority:

CONSTANTS
  $schedule\_p$
PROPERTIES
  $schedule\_p : (\mathbb{F}(TASK) \times (TASK \nrightarrow PRIORITY)) \nrightarrow \mathbb{F}(TASK)\wedge$
  $schedule\_p = \lambda(tasks, prio)\bullet$
    $(tasks : \mathbb{F}(TASK) \wedge prio : TASK \nrightarrow PRIORITY \wedge tasks \neq \emptyset \wedge tasks \subseteq \mathbf{dom}(prio)$
    $\mid tasks \cap prio^{-1}(\max(prio[tasks]))))$

To illustrate the refinement of the operations, we present the case of the operations *t_create* and *t_startScheduler*:

$result \longleftarrow t\_create(priority) =$
PRE
  $priority \in PRIORITY\wedge$
  $active = FALSE$
THEN
  ANY $task$ **WHERE**
    $task \in TASK \wedge task \notin tasks$
THEN
  $tasks := tasks \cup \{task\} \parallel$
  $prio := prio \cup \{task \mapsto priority\} \parallel$
  $ready := ready \cup \{task\} \parallel$
  $result := task$
END
END

$t\_startScheduler =$
  BEGIN
    $active := TRUE \parallel$
    $blocked, suspended := \emptyset, \emptyset \parallel$
    ANY i **WHERE**
      $i \in TASK \wedge$
      $i \notin tasks$
    THEN
    $tasks := tasks \cup \{i\} \parallel$
    $prio := prio \cup \{i \mapsto IDLE\_P\} \parallel$
    $idle := i \parallel$
    ANY t **WHERE**
      $t \in TASK \wedge$
      $(ready = \emptyset \Rightarrow t = i)\wedge$
      $(ready \neq \emptyset \Rightarrow t \in ready \wedge$
      $t \in schedule\_p(ready, prio)$
    THEN
      $running := t \parallel$
      $ready := (ready \cup \{i\}) - \{t\}$
    END
    END
  END

In *t_create*, a substitution was added to update the information on the new task priority, and in *t_startScheduler*, *idle* is registered to have priority 0 and the new running task is selected among those ready tasks with highest priority (or *idle*, in case there are no ready tasks waiting to be executed).

5.4   Comments on the Verification of the Models

One of the main features of the B method is the tool support for project management, syntactic verification, and semantic analysis of the produced artifacts. In particular, the semantic analysis produces proof obligations the verification of which guarantees: (1) all expressions appearing in the text of the different artifacts are well-defined, (2) the logic consistency of the specification and its refinements. The development environment thus includes support for the construction of the proofs, by providing a number of theorem provers. However, due to the incomplete nature of the specification logic, as well as the computational complexity of finding proofs, human intervention is needed to establish part of the proofs. This is a time-consuming activity that pays off in two ways. First, when confronted with a proof obligation that is not valid, the developer has access to the context where such proof obligation was generated and has clues as where the artifact needs to be corrected. Second, when all proof obligations have been successfully validated, then the user has a very strong confidence in its models.

To give an idea of the effort needed to establish the correctness of the development, Table 1 provides the number of proof obligations generated for each artifact[2]. This table does not include however the effort needed to reach consistent models, as several iterations were needed to produce a correct definition of the invariant and of the operations.

6   Conclusion and Future Work

This paper presented the first steps of a formal modeling, using the B method, of a significant part of the real-time operating system FreeRTOS. This model provides a functional specification of the operations related to task management and message queues. This effort was initiated in response to the challenge set by Jim Woodcock to the Brazilian community on Formal Methods [3] to contribute with this case study to the *Verified Software Repository* [13], as part of the *International Grand Challenge on Verified Software*. Thus, a first contribution of this work is the execution of a case study for the development of a verified model of a moderately complex software library. We have already extended the presented model to specify semaphores and related functions; next, we will include the definition of functional specifications for mutexes and refine the scheduling policy to take into account fairness requirements.

---

[2] Professionals using the B method estimate that a seasoned practitioner averages sixteen interactive proofs per day.

Table 1. The table presents, for each module, the number of operations defined in the module, the total number of lines (including comments), the number of proof obligations (well-definedness lemas, correctness theorems, and total), and the number of interactive proofs required to establish the correctness theorems. Most of our interactive proofs have fewer than 10 steps. In the one case (lowering the priority of the running task below that of at least one ready task), we needed more than a hundred steps. We do not claim that we were able to find the shortest proofs.

Module	Size		Proof obligations			Interactive
	Operations	Lines	W.D.	Corr.	Total	proofs
Config	0	89	0	0	0	0
Types	0	103	1	1	2	1
Scheduler	5	90	0	0	0	0
Task	12	467	1	219	220	28
Queue	7	231	12	33	45	0
FreeRTOSBasic	19	562	37	46	83	2
FreeRTOS	19	562	43	3	49	0
Task_r	12	432	42	100	142	18
Total	55	1974	136	402	538	49

A relevant question in our context is the cost-effectiveness of the approach we have taken. For circumstantial reasons, this is a difficult question to answer. Indeed, the model was mainly developed by a student with little previous experience with formal methods, and even less with guiding an interactive prover. In retrospect, assuming that the development would be carried out by a professional with proficiency with the B method and its tool support (including the interactive prover), we estimate that the model could have been developed in a few weeks time. Also we are not sure that the modular approach we have taken is indeed the most suitable, compared to introduce system features such as queues incrementally, through horizontal refinements. It would certainly be useful for formal methods practicioners to have a published body of architectural patterns for large specifications.

Also, we feel that there is some space for improvement in the tool support. In the case of interactive proofs, hypothesis selection is often required, however the selection interface is a bit clumsy. Proof management is rudimentary and still has bugs: at times proofs are lost, at times the prover gets into an infinite loop and the whole interface needs to be restarted. Also the development environment was not designed for multi-user efforts and we have not found a satisfactory way to integrate Atelier B with a version control system. Since the graphical interface of Atelier B has recently gone open source, we hope that such improvements will soon be implemented by the community.

A second important question is: what is this model worth for? Several possible applications could be foreseen. The first would be to use it to verify existing implementations of FreeRTOS[3], or to derive formally a new implementation of

---

[3] It is important to have in mind that part of the implementation is written in assembly, thus needing to be rewritten and re-verified for each target platform.

FreeRTOS. To verify an existing application, we could proceed either by reviewing code, taking as a reference the functional specification and try to manually find errors in the source code, or by deriving tests from the specification, using techniques such as [11]. Another approach to verification would be to use the B specification to instrument the source code of FreeRTOS with assertions, using a formalism such as ACSL [14], and formally prove that they are satisfied using low-level code verifiers such as VCC [15] or Frama-C [16]. A third possibility would be to use the model of FreeRTOS in formal development of real-time applications based on this system. It remains to be seen if this is possible to do this strictly within the scope of the B method, or if it would be necessary to couple it with other formalisms to handle e.g. concurrency and real-time properties.

The B method could also be applied to build an implementation of FreeRTOS from the model. However the B method currently has some restrictions that would make this task more difficult than a straightforward application of existing techniques. Indeed, the B method is targeted to safety-critical applications where dynamic memory allocation is prohibited. So current C code generators do not have support for pointers. However, such functionality is required in the case of FreeRTOS. It would be necessary to develop solutions to represent and manage memory representation in B.

Finally, since FreeRTOS is a library to build real-time embedded applications, the functional model presented in this paper could be used, in combination with a model checker for B such as ProB [17], as as an oracle when testing real-time applications based on FreeRTOS as proposed in [18].

Acknowledgements. We thank the anonymous reviewers for many insightful and challenging comments.

References

1. SBC: Grandes Desafios da Pesquisa em Computação no Brasil: 2006–2016 (2006), http://www.sbc.org.br
2. Jones, C., O'Hearn, P., Woodcock, J.: Verified software: a grand challenge. Computer 39(4), 93–95 (2006)
3. Woodcock, J.: Grand challenge in software verification. In: Brazilian Symposium on Formal Methods, SBMF 2008 (2008)
4. Craig, I.D.: Formal Models of Operating System Kernels. Springer, Heidelberg (2007)
5. Abrial, J.R.: The B-Book: Assigning Programs to Meanings. Cambridge University Press, Cambridge (1996)
6. Schneider, S.: The B-Method: An Introduction. Palgrave, Oxford (2001)
7. Jones, C.B.: Systematic Software Development Using VDM. Prentice-Hall, Englewood Cliffs (1990)
8. Spivey, J.: The Z Notation: a Reference Manual, 2nd edn. Prentice-Hall International Series in Computer Science. Prentice Hall, Englewood Cliffs (1992)
9. Requet, A.: Bart: A tool for automatic refinement. In: Börger, E., Butler, M., Bowen, J.P., Boca, P. (eds.) ABZ 2008. LNCS, vol. 5238, pp. 345–345. Springer, Heidelberg (2008)

10. Abrial, J.R.: Faultless system: Yes we can! Technical Report 629, Department of Computer Science, ETH Zurich (2009)
11. Jaffuel, E., Legeard, B.: LEIRIOS test generator: Automated test generation from B models. In: The 7th International B Conference, pp. 277–280 (2007)
12. Clearsy: Atelier B 4.0 (2009), http://www.atelierb.eu
13. Bicarregui, J., Hoare, C., Woodcock, J.: The verified software repository: a step towards the verifying compiler. Formal Aspects of Computing 18(2), 143–151 (2006)
14. Baudin, P., Filliâtre, J.C., Marché, C., Monate, B., Moy, Y., Prevosto, V.: ACSL: ANSI/ISO C Specification Language (2008)
15. Dahlweid, M., Moskal, M., Santen, T., Tobies, S., Schulte, W.: Vcc: Contract-based modular verification of concurrent c. In: ICSE Companion, pp. 429–430. IEEE, Los Alamitos (2009)
16. CEA: Frama-c: Software analyzers (2009), http://frama-c.cea.fr
17. Leuschel, M., Butler, M.: ProB: A model checker for B. In: Araki, K., Gnesi, S., Mandrioli, D. (eds.) FME 2003. LNCS, vol. 2805, pp. 855–874. Springer, Heidelberg (2003)
18. Andrade, W.L., Alves, E.L.G., Almeida, D.R., Machado, P.D.L.: Test case generation of embedded real-time systems with interruptions for FreeRTOS. In: Brazilian Symposium on Formal Methods, SBMF 2009 (2009)

A Mechanized Strategy for Safe Abstraction of CSP Specifications

Adriana Damasceno, Adalberto Farias, and Alexandre Mota

Center for Informatics, UFPE, P.O. Box 7851, CEP 50740540, Recife-PE, Brazil
{acd,acf,acm}@cin.ufpe.br

Abstract. Infinite models cannot be directly analyzed by model checking. An alternative for achieving that is using data abstraction to derive a simpler (abstract) but finite model so that the properties can be verified using the abstract model instead. This work proposes a strategy and an algorithm for generating abstractions of systems modeled in the process algebra CSP. These abstractions are safe in the sense that they preserve trace-based refinements. We show the application of our strategy to an example.

1 Introduction

Model checking is an automatic technique used to check whether a given model satisfies a temporal formula [16]. For CSP [12] (Sect. 2.1), the subject language of this work, we have a variant known as refinement checking. In refinement checking, two models are compared in terms of a number of CSP semantic models (traces, failures, and failures-divergences).

Despite having most of its process automatic, model checking is applicable to systems that have a finite state space representation. Hence, several models cannot be analyzed by model checking directly because they are based on infinite domains (integers, for example). This is one of the causes of the problem known as the state explosion problem. The works reported in [4][11] present a number of techniques to tackle this problem: Symbolic algorithms, counterexample-guided abstraction, data abstraction and data independence.

Among these techniques, we consider two of them in this work that are orthogonal and complementary to each other; they can be used in a compositional way. CSP data independence was initially proposed in [11]. It consists in syntactically determining the degree (threshold) of polymorphism of a CSP process with respect to one of its types. The minimum threshold means the maximum degree of polymorphism, that is, any concrete type can assume the place of the independent type without modifying the process behavior. In such cases, a type can be instantiated by {0} to apply model checking.

Complementarily to data independence, the basic idea of data abstraction [17] is to use mappings of elements from a concrete domain (real domain of a system) to elements of an abstract domain. Such a mapping can be said safe when it preserves trace-based refinements and optimal when it preserves failures-divergences refinements. The relevance of safe abstractions in relation to optimal

M.V.M. Oliveira and J. Woodcock (Eds.): SBMF 2009, LNCS 5902, pp. 118–133, 2009.
© Springer-Verlag Berlin Heidelberg 2009

is that the safe ones is a weaker model, and it is enough to preserve the properties we want. Hence, safe abstraction can be found in an easier way than optimal ones.

Therefore, the main contributions of this paper are:

- **Extension of the formal definition of an abstraction:** We extend the safe abstraction definition given by [17] (Sect. 2.2).
- **An abstraction strategy that preserves trace-based properties:** We present a strategy for calculating a safe abstraction based on predicate satisfaction (Sect. 3.1).
- **An algorithmic implementation for deriving abstractions:** We propose an algorithm that implements the proposed strategy in Sect. 3.2. We present the algorithm in functional language and apply it to a simple example.

We assume basic knowledge of CSP and Z [18] in this paper. we use CSP to specify systems, while Z is used in the algorithmic description.

2   Background

We present Communicating Sequential Processes notation and data abstraction to show our strategy to mechanically generate safe abstractions.

2.1   Communicating Sequential Processes

The notation CSP is used to describe concurrent systems whose components interact with each other through communications [12]. The verification of properties of CSP specifications is achieved by using the model checker FDR [15], which accepts CSP_M — the machine-readable dialect of CSP. In this work we assume familiarity with CSP_M as well.

To exemplify this language and our abstraction strategy, we use the following simple but curious example. It defines the process Main with parameter x.

```
Main (x) = x ≤ 5 & a!x → Main(x + 1)
        [ ] x ≥ 5 & b!x → Main(x - 3)
        [ ] (x < 4 or x ≥ 6) & c!x → Main(2 * x)
```

Process Main uses the prefixed process x ≤ 5 & a!x → Main(x + 1) that is able to perform a!x and behaves as Main(x + 1) (a recursive call to Main with a different parameter). Note that there are values that enable more than one path (choices that determine processes behaviors) at the same time and all of then are integers. For example, when x = 5, the conditions x ≤ 5 and x ≥ 5 are both satisfied.

We can study this and other system behaviors through LTS (Labeled Transition Systems). For CSP, it is a tuple $S = (Q, A, T, q_0)$, where Q is a set of finite states, A is a set of finite labels, T is a transition relation $(Q \times A \times Q)$, and q_0 is the initial state $(q_0 \in Q)$. Figure 1 shows the LTS of our example. We can see that state 5 allows two paths to follow.

An LTS can be finite or infinite. A process is said to have finite states if we can represent it by a finite LTS. Figure 1 shows two LTS, an infinite (a) and another finite (b). Both LTSs have the same behavior. Our algorithm will generate a process that represents the finite LTS (Fig. 1 (b)) while simulating traces of the infinite one (Fig. 1 (a)).

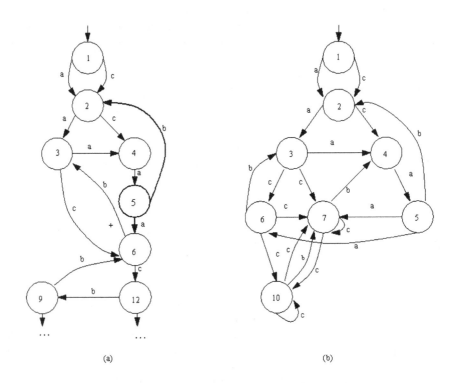

(a)   (b)

Fig. 1. LTS for concrete (a) and abstract (b) system

Furthermore, the LTSs in Fig. 1 can be seen as equivalent if we can abstract the specific integer being communicated by equivalent classes of integers. And obviously, by dealing with classes of integers we can obtain a finite representation for the LTS (a).

2.2   Data Abstraction

Data abstraction is an abstraction technique which is based on mapping a concrete domain into an abstract one [5]. Its idea is to interpret a program in an abstract domain, using abstract operations. The main gain is that the concrete program does not need to be completely executed, although it is possible to obtain information about its real execution. For example, if one wants to know the signal resulting from the expression 5 * -3, one can observe the number 5 simply as a positive number **pos**, -3 as a negative number **neg** and $\tilde{*}$ the new version of multiplication operator where only signs are observed, such that pos $\tilde{*}$ neg = neg. Hence, it is not necessary to evaluate the original expression to know its resulting signal.

The basic principle of formal verification is to inform if a property is valid in a given model. Thus, the state explosion problem can be overcame through the use of a less precise model, but being relevant for properties we want to prove.

In this way, the abstract system presents the same behavior of the concrete system. This correspondence is formalized by defining abstract interpretations for all operations, as well as mapping data from a concrete domain to the abstract one. In the context of this work, we consider abstractions that preserve the traces model (briefly explained at Sect. 2.1). In these abstractions, each concrete and infinite domain is partitioned in such a way that each infinite component of the partition is represented by a single element. This establishes equivalence classes of values that are mapped to a representant that preserve the execution of the same traces performed by the concrete system [17] .

This abstraction was originally developed for CSP-OZ [8], an integration of CSP and Object-Z [14]. In this way, CSP is responsible for dynamic aspects of the system, while Object-Z is used to describe the static ones. We assume that data domain to be abstracted are associated to state variables: $D_1, ..., D_n$ for variables $v_1, ..., v_n$ and domains associated to channels: $M_1, ..., M_k$ for channels $ch_1, ..., ch_k$ (messages). This is also adopted by the work reported in [17]. However, the work has some restrictions: for instance, it is completely dependent of user expertise along the abstraction process and a data in the concrete domain that corresponds to more than one element in the abstract domain cannot be expressed with that formalism.

Our work deal with [17] by using relations instead of functions. Systems that have states in the concrete domain with more than one corresponding in the abstract one cannot use functions, but relations. Hence, abstract data domains D_i^A and M_i^A, and relations α_{in} and α_{out}, which represent abstract relations for input and output channels from the concrete to the abstract domain, are used with the abstract relation α_S for a data (state) variable, as follows:

$$\alpha_s : (D_1 \times ... \times D_n) \leftrightarrow (D_1^A \times ... \times D_n^A)$$
$$\alpha_{in} : (M_1^{in} \times ... \times M_k^{in}) \leftrightarrow (M_1^{in,A} \times ... \times M_k^{in,A})$$
$$\alpha_{out} : (M_1^{out} \times ... \times M_j^{out}) \leftrightarrow (M_1^{out,A} \times ... \times M_j^{out,A})$$

The definition of safe abstraction uses functions and abstraction operations, each one defined by enable (pre condition) and effect (post condition) functions:

$$[\![enable_{op}]\!] : (D_1 \times ... \times D_n) \times (M_1^{in} \times ... \times M_k^{in}) \rightarrow \mathbb{B}$$

$$[\![effect_{op}]\!] : (D_1 \times ... \times D_n) \times (M_1^{in} \times ... \times M_k^{in}) \rightarrow$$
$$(D_1 \times ... \times D_n) \leftrightarrow (M_1^{out} \times ... \times M_j^{out})$$

Definition 1 formally shows safe abstraction.

Definition 1 (Safe Abstraction). *An abstract interpretation* $[\![op]\!]^S$ *of enable and effect predicates of an operation is safe with respect to* α_S, α_{in} *and* α_{out} *relations if and only if*

$\forall \, d \, \in D, \, in \in M^{in} \bullet \exists \, d^A \in D^A, in^A \in M^{in,A} \mid (d, d^A) \in \alpha_s \wedge (in, in^A) \in$
$\quad \alpha_{in} \bullet [\![enable_{op}]\!]^S (d^A, in^A) \Leftrightarrow [\![enable_{op}]\!](d, in)$

and

$\forall \, d \in D, in \in M^{in} \bullet \exists \, d^A \in D^A, in^A \in M^{in,A} \mid (d, d^A) \in \alpha_s \wedge (in, in^A) \in$
$\quad \alpha_{in} \bullet [\![effect_{op}]\!]^S (d^A, in^A) =$
$\quad \{(d'_A, out^A) \mid (d', out) \in [\![effect_{op}]\!](d, in) \wedge (d', d'_A) \in \alpha_s \wedge (out, out^A) \in \alpha_{out}\}$

So, for all concrete states d there exists a corresponding abstract state d^A that are α related such that their preconditions are equivalent. A safe abstraction interpretation assures that in a state of the abstract system, a communication over a channel is possible when there is a corresponding concrete one in which this communication is allowed. A particularity of a safe abstraction is that the generated abstract system P^S maintains the same traces as those of the corresponding concrete system P modulo a renaming function G. Therefore, $P^S \sqsubseteq_T P[\![G]\!]$ (P $[\![G]\!]$ is a refinement of P^S). This renaming function G is used to map infinite communications into finite ones (values from communications are abstracted). A safe abstraction allows more traces than its equivalent concrete system. In the concrete system, some movement cannot be allowed, but it happens in its corresponding abstract one. Theorem 1 [17] formally establishes this property.

Theorem 1 (Traces Refinement). *Let P be a CSP process, P^S an safe abstract interpretation and $\Sigma \rightarrow \Sigma$ the renaming function G in a way that $G(ch \, . \, x_{in} \, . \, x_{out}) = ch \, . \, g_{in}(x_{in}) \, . \, g_{out}(x_{out})$. Then,*

$$P^S \sqsubseteq_T P[\![G]\!]$$

3   Mechanized Generation of Safe Abstraction

Section 3.1 informally presents how our strategy works using the same example previously shown in Sect. 2.1. Hence, Sect. 3.2 shows the formal specification of our algorithm.

3.1   General Idea

Our strategy inputs the concrete system and requires user intervention to build the LTS, which is used to retain information necessary to our algorithm process the concrete system. In the sequence, this last outputs an abstraction relation for all the variables, and the user is required to manually build the abstracted system. Figure 2 shows this acquisition strategy.

The algorithm is based on finding subsets in the concrete domain that correspond to single elements in the abstract one. This is achieved by combining the guards of the original process, in a way that all the possible paths (a sequence of labels which are connected by transitions) of the system can be analyzed with respect to before and after state changes.

To keep the values of variables along a given path, we use the type *SBinding*, which establishes a mapping between variables and expressions. *SBinding*

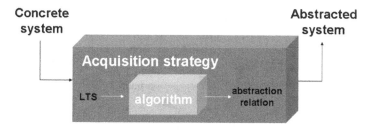

Fig. 2. Acquisition of the abstracted system

is defined as a partial function (available at Z language) from a set of *Variable* (system variables) to a set of *Expression* (mathematical expressions).

SBinding == *Variable* ↦ *Expression*

In the sequence, the type *SState* identifies the state of the system (a set of variables or one of the identifiers SKIP or STOP). We represent paths that finish with SKIP (a successful termination) or STOP (termination with deadlock) processes by the triple (*Predicate, Channel,* {}), as those processes do not change state variables. There is no difference between them because we want to study the behavior of variable values at system traces. Figure 3 shows the SLTS for our example.

SLabel == *Predicate* × ℙ *Channel* × *SBinding*
SState ::= var ⟨⟨*Variable*⟩⟩ | SKIP | STOP

Additionally, we define a symbolic LTS that we use in our strategy and algorithm. Definition 2 specifies this element using the abstract types *SState* and *SLabel*.

Definition 2 (Symbolic Labeled Transition System). *A Symbolic Labeled Transition System (SLTS) is a tuple* S = (Q, A, T, q_0) *where* Q *is a finite set of states of SState type,* A *is a finite set of labels of type SLabel,* T *is a transition relation* (Q × A × Q) *and* q_0 *is the initial state, where* (q_0 ∈ Q).

We point out that our current algorithm can only be applied to a CSP process that satisfies the normal form of Definition 3. It establishes a class of processes defined by a recursion in which its body is an (external or internal) choice regarding to operations in *Ops*. If a guard $enable_i(state)$ is true, the event op_i is given to the system and process $P(effect_i(state))$ is performed. Although our normal form can be rather restrictive, we can reduce any CSP process to this normal form by applying the CSP algebraic laws [12].

Definition 3 (Normal Form). *Let P(state) be a CSP process with a state, a set of events Ops and the indexed operator* ∇ ∈ {[], |∼|}. *The process P(state) is in our proposed normal form whether it can be written as*

$P(state) = ∇\ op_i{:}Ops@enable_i(state)\ \&\ op_i → P(effect_i(state))$

where none variable names can be repeated.   ◇

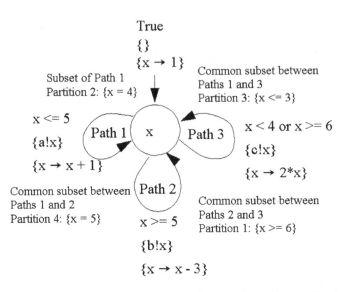

Fig. 3. SLTS of a process where there are three paths with non-disjoint sets

Our abstraction strategy consists of two main steps: (1) Determine which guard (or combination of guards) can be satisfied by the current state of the system; (2) After the changes of variable paths, which guard (or combination of them) can be satisfied in this new state *SState* of the current path. As, in general, guards usually do not form a partition, we only determine the specific values for variables in the Step (2). Step (1) is performed to avoid trying to satisfy more complex (after state) non-satisfiable predicates. Thus, Table 1 shows three guards (columns) combined in rows (each row defines a partition and the satisfiable ones will be used to define other tables) forming the respective partitions. The column **Satisfiability** is used to show which combination is satisfiable (True) or not (False).

Table 1. Guard combinations to find out available partitions of the concrete domain

Path 1 ($x \le 5$)	**Path 2** ($x \ge 5$)	**Path 3** ($x < 4$ or $x \ge 6$)	**Satisfiability**
$\neg x \le 5$	$\neg x \ge 5$	$\neg(x < 4$ or $x \ge 6)$	False
$\neg x \le 5$	$\neg x \ge 5$	$x < 4$ or $x \ge 6$	False
$\neg x \le 5$	$x \ge 5$	$\neg(x < 4$ or $x \ge 6)$	False
$\neg x \le 5$	$x \ge 5$	$x < 4$ or $x \ge 6$	**True**
$x \le 5$	$\neg x \ge 5$	$\neg(x < 4$ or $x \ge 6)$	**True**
$x \le 5$	$\neg x \ge 5$	$x < 4$ or $x \ge 6$	**True**
$x \le 5$	$x \ge 5$	$\neg(x < 4$ or $x \ge 6)$	**True**
$x \le 5$	$x \ge 5$	$x < 4$ or $x \ge 6$	False

Based on the satisfiable partitions (rows) of Table 1, we build the similar Table 2 where the columns are now divided as: **Input** has the satisfiable combinations of Table 1 to **Path 1** (**Partitions 2**, **3** and **4**), **Output** has all the partitions of Table 1 but with its variables renamed by the corresponding recursive call. Finally, column **Result** shows a pair of sets where the first is a binding between variables and values, indicating a solution to the corresponding predicate, and the second is the simplified predicate representation of the conjunction between the predicates **Input** and **Output**. So, **Output** considers the truth branches of the satisfiable partitions with the recursive call (actual parameters) substituted appropriately.

Table 2. Predicate combinations for **Path 1** (**Partition 2**, **3** and **4**)

Input	Output	Result
$(x \leq 5) \wedge \neg (x{\geq}5) \wedge \neg (x < 4 \vee x \geq 6)$	$\neg (x+1 \leq 5) \wedge (x+1 \geq 5) \wedge (x+1 < 4 \vee x+1 \geq 6)$	$\{\{\}, \{\text{False}\}\}$
$(x \leq 5) \wedge \neg (x \geq 5) \wedge \neg (x < 4 \vee x \geq 6)$	$(x+1 \leq 5) \wedge \neg (x+1 \geq 5) \wedge \neg (x+1 < 4 \vee x+1 \geq 6)$	$\{\{\}, \{\text{False}\}\}$
$(x \leq 5) \wedge \neg (x{\geq}5) \wedge \neg (x < 4 \vee x \geq 6)$	$(x+1 \leq 5) \wedge \neg (x+1 \geq 5) \wedge (x+1 < 4 \vee x+1 \geq 6)$	$\{\{\}, \{\text{False}\}\}$
$(x \leq 5) \wedge \neg (x \geq 5) \wedge \neg (x < 4 \vee x \geq 6)$	$(x+1 \leq 5) \wedge (x+1 \geq 5) \wedge \neg (x+1 < 4 \vee x+1 \geq 6)$	$\{\{x \rightarrow 4\}, \{x == 4\}\}$
$(x \leq 5) \wedge \neg (x \geq 5) \wedge (x < 4 \vee x \geq 6)$	$\neg (x+1 \leq 5) \wedge (x+1 \geq 5) \wedge (x+1 < 4 \vee x+1 \geq 6)$	$\{\{\}, \{\text{False}\}\}$
$(x \leq 5) \wedge \neg (x \geq 5) \wedge (x < 4 \vee x \geq 6)$	$(x+1 \leq 5) \wedge \neg (x+1 \geq 5) \wedge \neg (x+1 < 4 \vee x+1 \geq 6)$	$\{\{x \rightarrow 3\}, \{3 \leq x < 4\}\}$
$(x \leq 5) \wedge \neg (x \geq 5) \wedge (x < 4\vee x \geq 6)$	$(x+1 \leq 5) \wedge \neg (x+1 \geq 5) \wedge (x+1 < 4 \vee x+1 \geq 6)$	$\{\{x \rightarrow 1\}, \{x < 3\}\}$
$(x \leq 5) \wedge \neg (x \geq 5) \wedge (x < 4 \vee x \geq 6)$	$(x+1 \leq 5) \wedge (x+1 \geq 5) \wedge \neg (x+1 < 4 \vee x+1 \geq 6)$	$\{\{\}, \{\text{False}\}\}$
$(x \leq 5) \wedge (x \geq 5) \wedge \neg (x < 4 \vee x \geq 6)$	$\neg (x+1 \leq 5) \wedge (x+1 \geq 5) \wedge (x+1 < 4 \vee x+1 \geq 6)$	$\{\{x \rightarrow 5\}, \{x == 5\}\}$
$(x \leq 5) \wedge (x \geq 5) \wedge \neg (x < 4 \vee x \geq 6)$	$(x+1 \leq 5) \wedge \neg (x+1 \geq 5) \wedge \neg (x+1 < 4 \vee x+1 \geq 6)$	$\{\{\}, \{\text{False}\}\}$
$(x \leq 5) \wedge (x \geq 5) \wedge \neg (x < 4 \vee x \geq 6)$	$(x+1 \leq 5) \wedge \neg (x+1 \geq 5) \wedge (x+1 < 4 \vee x+1 \geq 6)$	$\{\{\}, \{\text{False}\}\}$
$(x \leq 5) \wedge (x \geq 5) \wedge \neg (x < 4 \vee x \geq 6)$	$(x+1 \leq 5) \wedge (x+1 \geq 5) \wedge \neg (x+1 < 4 \vee x+1 \geq 6)$	$\{\{\}, \{\text{False}\}\}$

Concerning to **Path 2**, only **Partitions 1** and **4** are solvable for it. So, we only consider the variable effect $x \mapsto x{-}3$ to generate predicates (See Fig. 3), in the same way as we made for **Path 1**. We show these results in Table 3.

Finally, **Path 3** is satisfiable to **Partitions 1** and **3**. So, we perform the combination between this partition with all the predicates from the truth table, as we show at Table 4. Although some intervals from column **Result** are rational, all the variable values are integers.

Table 3. Predicate combinations for **Path 2** (**Partition 1** and **4**)

Input	Output	Result
$\neg$ (x $\leq$ 5) $\wedge$ (x $\geq$ 5) $\wedge$ (x < 4 $\vee$ x $\geq$ 6)	$\neg$ (x-3 $\leq$ 5)$\wedge$ (x-3 $\geq$ 5) $\wedge$ (x-3 < 4 $\vee$ x-3 $\geq$ 6)	({x $\rightarrow$ 10}, {x $\geq$ 9})
$\neg$ (x $\leq$ 5) $\wedge$ (x $\geq$ 5) $\wedge$ (x < 4 $\vee$ x $\geq$ 6)	(x-3 $\leq$ 5) $\wedge$ $\neg$ (x-3 $\geq$ 5) $\wedge$ $\neg$ (x-3 < 4 $\vee$ x-3 $\geq$6)	({x $\rightarrow$ 7}, {7 $\leq$ x < 8})
$\neg$ (x $\leq$ 5) $\wedge$ (x $\geq$ 5) $\wedge$ (x < 4 $\vee$ x $\geq$ 6)	(x-3 $\leq$ 5) $\wedge$ $\neg$ (x-3 $\geq$ 5) $\wedge$ (x-3 < 4 $\vee$ x-3 $\geq$ 6)	({x $\rightarrow$ 6}, {6 $\leq$ x < 7})
$\neg$ (x $\leq$ 5) $\wedge$ (x $\geq$ 5) $\wedge$ (x < 4 $\vee$ x $\geq$ 6)	(x-3 $\leq$ 5) $\wedge$ (x-3 $\geq$ 5) $\wedge$ $\neg$ (x-3 < 4 $\vee$ x-3 $\geq$ 6)	({x $\rightarrow$ 8}, {x == 8})
(x $\leq$ 5) $\wedge$ (x$\geq$5) $\wedge$ $\neg$	$\neg$ (x-3 $\leq$ 5) $\wedge$ (x-3 $\geq$ 5) $\wedge$ (x-3 < 4 $\vee$ x-3 $\geq$ 6)	{{}, {False}}
(x $\leq$ 5) $\wedge$ (x $\geq$ 5) $\wedge$ $\neg$	(x-3 $\leq$ 5) $\wedge$ $\neg$ (x-3 $\geq$ 5) $\wedge$ $\neg$ (x-3 < 4 $\vee$ x-3 $\geq$ 6)	{{}, {False}}
(x $\leq$ 5) $\wedge$ (x $\geq$ 5) $\wedge$ $\neg$ (x < 4 $\vee$ x $\geq$ 6)	(x-3 $\leq$ 5)$\wedge\neg$(x-3 $\geq$ 5) $\wedge$ (x-3 < 4 $\vee$ x-3 $\geq$ 6)	{{x $\rightarrow$ 5}, {x == 5}}
(x $\leq$ 5) $\wedge$ (x $\geq$ 5) $\wedge$ $\neg$ (x < 4 $\vee$ x $\geq$ 6)	(x-3 $\leq$ 5) $\wedge$ (x-3 $\geq$ 5) $\wedge$ $\neg$ (x-3 < 4 $\vee$ x-3 $\geq$ 6)	{{}, {False}}

Table 4. Predicate combinations of **Path 3** (**Partitions 1** and **3**)

Input	Output	Result
$\neg$ (x $\leq$ 5) $\wedge$ (x $\geq$ 5) $\wedge$ (x < 4 $\vee$ x $\geq$ 6)	$\neg$ (2*x $\leq$ 5) $\wedge$ (2*x $\geq$ 5) $\wedge$ (2*x < 4 $\vee$ 2*x $\geq$ 6)	({x $\rightarrow$ 7}, {x $\geq$ 6})
$\neg$ (x $\leq$ 5) $\wedge$ (x $\geq$ 5) $\wedge$ (x < 4 $\vee$ x $\geq$ 6)	(2*x $\leq$ 5) $\wedge$ $\neg$ (2*x $\geq$ 5) $\wedge$ $\neg$ (2*x < 4 $\vee$ 2*x $\geq$ 6)	({}, {False})
$\neg$ (x $\leq$ 5) $\wedge$ (x $\geq$ 5) $\wedge$ (x < 4 $\vee$ x $\geq$ 6)	(2*x $\leq$ 5) $\wedge$ $\neg$ (2*x $\geq$ 5) $\wedge$ (2*x < 4 $\vee$ 2*x $\geq$ 6)	({}, {False})
$\neg$ (x$\leq$5) $\wedge$ (x $\geq$ 5) $\wedge$ (x < 4 $\vee$ x $\geq$ 6)	(2*x $\leq$ 5) $\wedge$ (2*x $\geq$ 5) $\wedge$ $\neg$ (2*x < 4 $\vee$ 2*x $\geq$ 6)	({}, {False})
(x $\leq$ 5) $\wedge$ $\neg$ (x $\geq$ 5) $\wedge$ (x < 4 $\vee$ x $\geq$ 6)	$\neg$ (2*x $\leq$ 5) $\wedge$ (2*x $\geq$ 5) $\wedge$ (2*x < 4 $\vee$ 2*x $\geq$ 6)	{{x $\rightarrow$ 3}, {3 $\leq$ x < 4}}
(x $\leq$ 5) $\wedge$ $\neg$ (x $\geq$ 5) $\wedge$ (x < 4 $\vee$ x $\geq$ 6)	(2*x $\leq$ 5) $\wedge$ $\neg$ (2*x $\geq$ 5) $\wedge$ $\neg$ (2*x < 4 $\vee$ 2*x $\geq$ 6)	{{x $\rightarrow$ 2},{2 $\leq$ x < $\frac{5}{2}$}}
(x $\leq$ 5) $\wedge$ $\neg$ (x $\geq$ 5) $\wedge$ (x < 4 $\vee$ x $\geq$ 6)	(2*x $\leq$ 5) $\wedge$ $\neg$ (2* $\geq$ 5) $\wedge$ (2*x < 4 $\vee$ 2*x $\geq$ 6)	{{ x $\rightarrow$ 1}, {x < 2}}
(x $\leq$ 5) $\wedge$ $\neg$ (x $\geq$ 5) $\wedge$ (x < 4 $\vee$ x $\geq$ 6)	(2*x $\leq$ 5) $\wedge$ (2*x $\geq$ 5) $\wedge$ $\neg$ (2*x < 4 $\vee$ 2*x $\geq$ 6)	{{}, {False}}

From the Tables 2, 3 and 4 we take (collect) the rows which are satisfiable to build the abstraction relation α_{Main}. We can conclude that all the concrete domain is related to abstract data through this relation.

$$\alpha_{Main} = \begin{array}{l} \{xV\colon \mathbb{Z} \,|xV < 3 \bullet (\text{`x'}, xV) \mapsto (\text{`x'}, 1)\} \cup \\ \{xV\colon \mathbb{Z} \,|2 \le xV < 5/2 \bullet (\text{`x'}, xV) \mapsto (\text{`x'}, 2)\} \cup \\ \{xV\colon \mathbb{Z} \,|3 \le xV < 4 \bullet (\text{`x'}, xV) \mapsto (\text{`x'}, 3)\} \cup \\ \{xV\colon \mathbb{Z} \,|xV == 4 \bullet (\text{`x'}, xV) \mapsto (\text{`x'}, 4)\} \cup \\ \{xV\colon \mathbb{Z} \,|xV == 5 \bullet,(\text{`x'}, xV) \mapsto (\text{`x'}, 5)\} \cup \\ \{xV\colon \mathbb{Z} \,|xV \ge 6 \bullet (\text{`x'}, xV) \mapsto (\text{`x'}, 7)\} \cup \\ \{xV\colon \mathbb{Z} \,|6 \le xV < 7 \bullet (\text{`x'}, xV) \mapsto (\text{`x'}, 6)\} \cup \\ \{xV\colon \mathbb{Z} \,|7 \le xV < 8 \bullet (\text{`x'}, xV) \mapsto (\text{`x'}, 7)\} \cup \\ \{xV\colon \mathbb{Z} \,|xV \ge 9 \bullet (\text{`x'}, xV) \mapsto (\text{`x'}, 10)\} \end{array}$$

Note that α_{Main} has bindings mapping into bindings, where the name of the variable is relevant; in this case, variable x. The first bindings contain concrete domain instances for x whereas the second bindings abstract domain instances. This example shows the construction of relations instead of functions (Definition 1). One element in the concrete domain leads to more than one element in the abstract one. For example, if x = 6 in the concrete domain, it can assume values 6 or 7 in its corresponding abstract one. Figure 4 shows the correspondence between the concrete and the abstract domain for process Main.

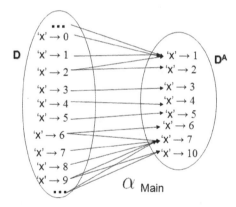

Fig. 4. Mapping between bindings for process Main

Finally, the safe abstract version of the original CSP specification is built based on the previous abstract relation α_{Main}. The enabling conditions did not need to be changed in the abstract process, because they were used to originate the abstract representers. However, the effects must be abstracted so that the resulting new state is always inside the abstract domain of the abstraction relation. To get the abstract result corresponding to evaluating the recursive call (effect) of the process, we first compute the relational image using the concrete binding (name of the variables with corresponding effects), and thus for each variable of the abstract binding we construct an indexed non-deterministic choice between these values (ran). This index (abstract variable) is finally used in the corresponding recursive call. The indexed non-determinism causes no problem for the kind of properties we can prove with the abstract version because the safe abstraction can only guarantee trace-based properties, which cannot distinguish between deterministic and non-deterministic processes. A library containing the implementation of these operators in CSP notation is available at [6].

```
Main(x) = x≤5 & a!x→ |~|xᵃ:ran(α_Main({('x',x+1)}))@Main(xᵃ)
        [ ] x≥5 & b!x→|~|xᵃ:ran(α_Main({('x',x-3)}))@Main(xᵃ)
        [ ](x< 4 or x≥6) & c!x→ |~|xᵃ:ran(α_Main({('x',2*x)}))
              @Main(xᵃ)
```

The abstraction relations for channels are not performed because they depend on the value of x, so they do not need to be abstracted. We show SLTS for the concrete system (a) and the abstract one (b) at Fig. 1. Note that all the LTS states of the abstracted system from Fig. 1 are represented at relation α_{Main}.

3.2   Algorithm

In Sect. 2.2, we showed that for each variable v_i with infinite type, there is an abstraction relation α_{v_i}. Then, these relations were grouped according to state variables ($\alpha_s \in (D \leftrightarrow D^A)$), data input ($\alpha_{in} \in (M^{in} \leftrightarrow M^{in,A})$) and output ($\alpha_{out} \in (M^{out} \leftrightarrow M^{out,A})$) in such a way that $\alpha_s = (\alpha_{v_1}, \alpha_{v_2}, \ldots, \alpha_{v_n})$, $\alpha_{in} = (\alpha_{v_1}^{in}, \alpha_{v_2}^{in}, \ldots, \alpha_{v_j}^{in})$ and $\alpha_{out} = (\alpha_{v_1}^{out}, \alpha_{v_2}^{out}, \ldots, \alpha_{v_k}^{out})$.

Therefore, this section presents the algorithm to map data from concrete to abstract domain. We assume there are two sets *Variable* and *Value*. From these sets we build the type *Binding* and define α_v as a relation between bindings. This type differ from *SBinding* because it represents concrete instances of expressions, that is, it does not allow expression usage, but concrete values.

Binding == *Variable* × *Value*
α_v == *Binding* ↔ *Binding*

So, the concrete domain D has *Bindings* $b = (b_1, b_2, \ldots, b_n)$ and the abstract domain D^A has *Bindings* $b^A = (b_1^A, b_2^A, \ldots, b_n^A)$, such that $b_i = (v_i \mapsto val_i)$ and $b_i^A = (v_i \mapsto val_i^A)$, where v_i is a variable and val_i and val_i^A are values, with each variable having a corresponding value. Furthermore, recall from Sect. 2.2 that the abstract relation α_v maps a set of values to variables from the concrete domain D to the abstract domain D^A.

As Definition 1 (safe abstraction) needs an abstract relation for each variable and we use all the variables *Variable* of a path in the relation, the abstraction relations for each variable can be calculated by:

$$(val, val^A) \in \alpha_v \Leftrightarrow val^A \in ran(\alpha_v(\{('v',val)\}))$$

The algorithm starts with the top level function findAbstraction, which accepts an SLTS as input and returns the relation of *Bindings* between concrete and abstract domains.

The labels representing *paths* of the system are found by the function build-Paths. The set of predicates obtained from paths is used by the function build-TruthTable to find the possible partitions from the guards.

The variable *predicates* has the set of tuples (*Predicate*, $\mathbb{P}$ *Variable*). It is built by a union between two sets. The first has the predicates obtained with paths finished by SKIP or STOP (they have an empty set of *Bindings* where $bin = 0$) and the second by the paths that finish with recursions ($bin \neq 0$). The set related to SKIP and STOP processes do not need combinations because they lead to terminal paths.

Finally, the function safeAbs is responsible for receiving the set of tuples and returning the relation between the concrete and abstract domains, that is, the safe abstraction.

---

findAbstraction :: $SLTS \rightarrow (D \leftrightarrow D^A)$
findAbstraction (Q, A, T, q_0) =
   let
        $paths$ = buildPaths T
        $partitions$ = buildTruhTable $\{(pred, ch, bin): paths \bullet pred\}$
        $predicates$ = $\{(pred, ch, bin): paths \mid bin = \{\} \bullet pred\} \cup$
   buildPredicates $\{g_{before}, g_{after}: partitions; (pred, ch, bin): paths \mid bin \neq \{\}$
   $\bullet (g_{before}, (pred, ch, bin), g_{after})\}$
        $\bullet$
        safeAbs *predicates*

The function buildPaths receives a set of labels from SLTS and returns all the labels, except the starting one. This happens as the determined values for each variable belongs to one of the resulting partitions in the abstraction and we cannot take them into account. As we use normal form, we assume there are recursions ($q_{in} == q_{out}$) or each path finishes with SKIP/STOP processes. The use of the operator minus for sets at the recursive call in the function happens because the pattern combination with the input set allows the possibility of the element be in the set given as parameter.

---

buildPaths :: $\mathbb{P}(SState \times SLabel \times SState) \rightarrow \mathbb{P}\ SLabel$
buildPaths $\{\}$ = $\{\}$
buildPaths $\{(q_{in}, r, q_{out})\} \cup s$ =
   if $q_{in} == q_{out} \vee q_{out} ==$ SKIP $\vee$ $q_{out} ==$ STOP then
      $\{r\} \cup$ buildPaths $s \setminus \{(q_{in}, r, q_{out})\}$
   else
      buildPaths $s \setminus \{(q_{in}, r, q_{out})\}$

The function buildTruthTable is responsible for combination guards from the paths to perform the truth table, returning a new set of predicates and it uses recursion. We need to make a call with the element $\{g_{cur}\}$ by himself because this function must return this element and its negation.

---

buildTruthTable :: $\mathbb{P}$ *Predicate* $\rightarrow$ $\mathbb{P}$ *Predicate*
buildTruthTable $\{\} = \{\}$
buildTruthTable $\{g_{cur}\} = \{g_{cur}, \neg g_{cur}\}$
buildTruthTable $\{g_{cur}\} \cup s =$
   combine $\{g_{cur}\}$ buildTruthTable $s \setminus \{g_{cur}\} \cup$ combine $\{\neg g_{cur}\}$
buildTruthTable $s \setminus \{g_{cur}\}$

The function buildTruthTable uses the function combine which is responsible for joining predicates in sets in such a way that the compatibility among elements of each line is maintained. The partial function denotes the relation when g_1 is the empty set and the contrary case.

---

combine :: $\mathbb{P}$ *Predicate* $\nrightarrow$ $\mathbb{P}$ *Predicate* $\rightarrow$ $\mathbb{P}$ *Predicate*
combine $\{g_1\} \{\} = \{\}$
combine $\{g_1\} \{g_2\} \cup s =$
   $\{g_1 \wedge g_2\} \cup$ combine g_1 $s \setminus \{g_2\}$

After renaming all paths and the truth table combination is generated, function buildPredicates receives the previous guard g_{before}, and verifies if it is satisfiable to the current path predicate through the function reduceGuard. If it is true, we perform this guard conjunction with the subsequent guard g_{after}, which is renamed by function renamePredicate using the corresponding set of bindings. Besides that, it returns the set of variables for the channels and bindings in an input tuple.

---

buildPredicates :: $\mathbb{P}(Predicate \times SLabel \times Predicate) \rightarrow \mathbb{P}$ *Predicate*
buildPredicates $\{\} = \{\}$
buildPredicates $\{g_{before}, (pred, ch, bind), g_{after}\} \cup s =$
   if reduceGuard($g_{before} \wedge pred$) $\neq$ False then
      $\{g_{before} \wedge$ renamePredicate($g_{after}, bind$)$\} \cup$
buildPredicates $s \setminus \{g_{before}, (pred, ch, bind), g_{after}\}$
   else
      buildPredicates $s \setminus \{g_{before}, (pred, ch, bind), g_{after}\}$

The function reduceGuard receives a predicate and returns its simplified version. For example, reduceGuard($x > 5 \wedge x > 7$) $= x > 7$ and reduceGuard($x < 5 \wedge x > 7$) $=$ False. In order to update variable values when a recursive call is performed, the function renamePredicate receives the predicate and a set of symbolic bindings, returning this predicate renamed by the set of elements.

---

renamePredicate :: *Predicate* $\rightarrow$ $\mathbb{P}$ *SBinding* $\rightarrow$ *Predicate*
renamePredicate $p \{\} =$ True
renamePredicate $p \{x \mapsto e\} \cup s =$
   renamePredicate $p[e/x]$ $s \setminus \{x \mapsto e\}$

In the sequence, function safeAbs simplifies the predicates (using reduceGuard again) and finds their corresponding values. In this step, we find mappings among elements of the abstract and concrete domains and the abstract relation for the system is returned. We only use reduceGuard to simplify predicates and guarantee a better visualization to the user.

We need to create bindings of variables and values in a domain (given by the function Type) in the abstract domain using the function findValues. This function receives a simplified predicate p through the usage of reduceGuard and it returns the set of bindings if p can be solved or it is the empty set, otherwise. We also use the domain restriction operator $\lhd$ [18] to set bindings from the abstract domain apart from other bindings that do not correspond to a certain element.

---

safeAbs $:: \mathbb{P} \, Predicate \rightarrow (D \leftrightarrow D^A)$
safeAbs $\{\} = \{\}$
safeAbs $\{p\} \cup s =$
    if reduceGuard $p \neq$ False then
        $\{dVar$: vars p; $dValue$: Type($dVar$); $dBind$: findValues $p \mid$ reduce-Guard $p \wedge dBind \in \{dVar\} \lhd$ findValues $p \bullet (dVar, dValue) \mapsto dBind\}$
    $\cup$ safeAbs $s \setminus \{p\}$
    else
        safeAbs $s \setminus \{p\}$

---

4   Related Work

As far as we know, there is no work which can automate the process of finding a safe abstraction from a CSP system. The use of automatic abstractions through predicate abstraction is reported in [10]. With predicate abstraction, concrete states of the system are mapped to abstract states according to the evaluation of a set of finite predicates.

The strategy presented in [1] shows the use of the tool $C2_{BP}$. It performs the abstraction of C programs through predicate abstraction, giving solutions to problems as procedure calls. However, there is no selection of data instances, as the abstraction replaces a predicate that represents a decision point in the program by true or false values. The automatic verification of concurrent C programs [19] from safe abstractions, considering many sequential C programs, is an evolution of [1].

The work [2] describes techniques for concrete and abstract interpretation of C/C++ programs represented in a language intermediary level called GIMPLE, which basically produces a control flow graph model for each C/C++ function or method. The results are implemented in a tool and they are currently applied for integrated module testing and static analysis of safety-critical embedded systems software in the railway and avionic domains.

Safe abstraction for CSP-OZ systems was initially proposed by [17] and it establishes general procedures for obtaining safe abstraction, using abstraction functions. In addition to this, it gives procedures for abstracting systems using parallelism and process composition. However, in spite of what is presented in our work, the choice about abstraction functions does not establishes procedures, so it is dependent on the user experience.

There is an strategy similar to ours that concentrates on finding optimal abstractions [6] for CSP-Z systems instead of safe ones, preserving failures-divergences model of a system. Nevertheless, it never terminates if a sequence of events repetition is not detected.

An evolution of [6] is shown in [7]. Using the data independence criteria, they apply an internal partitioning to the Z part of a CSP-Z specification. An algorithm to find a optimal abstraction is build, but channel variables are not treated if they are dependent of a certain type.

We propose to mechanize safe abstractions. Our work gives a more general theory where [17] can be inserted, but minimizes the class of systems to be treated by the usage of a normal form. Our strategy is able to deal with more general classes of systems than [7], while requiring less computational effort. Besides that, we can lead with channel and data variable abstractions in any kind of system which obey our normal form (Definition 2).

5   Conclusions and Future Work

In this paper we proposed a strategy and an algorithm to generate safe abstractions of CSP systems [12]. We used an example in Sect. 3.1 to introduce the proposed strategy and in Sect. 3.2 we presented the proposed algorithm based on a functional Z-based language.

We used data abstraction (Sect. 2.2) to abstract part of the CSP specification in such a way that this abstraction can always satisfy the abstraction for the data dependent part of the CSP specification. In particular, by assuming data independence [11], we can focus our attention completely on the data dependent part.

Our technique always gives an answer, as it deals with non-determinism and traces model when using non-parallel systems. Furthermore, we can define abstraction relations through a mechanized technique, independently from user expertise, but we left to the user the work of building our SLTS. Our technique cover systems which are in the normal form (Definition 3). We intend to use our strategy into Motorola [13] and Embraer [9] projects, research programs that are result of a partnership between CIn/UFPE and these companies, as their main focus is formal testing.

For future work, we have to prove that our algorithm always provides a safe abstraction from a CSP specification in the proposed normal form. After that, we plan to investigate the inclusion of parallelism in our strategy based on the compositional results reported in [17]. Another research interest includes reformulating our algorithm to consider OBDDs [3] instead of truth tables as the current version. And finally we intend to implement our algorithm in a program to make the usage of it easier.

Acknowledgements

The authors would like to thank the Brazilian Government for the financial support through one of its agencies, FACEPE/CAPES. We also thanks Augusto Sampaio and Marcio Cornelio for criticisms which helped us to improve our work.

References

1. Ball, T., Majumdar, R., Millstein, T., Rajamani, S.: Automatic predicate abstraction of C programs. ACM SIGPLAN Notices 36(5), 203–213 (2001)
2. Bourdoncle, F.: Abstract interpretation by dynamic partitioning. Journal of Functional Programming 2(04), 407–435 (2008)
3. Bryant, R.: Symbolic Boolean manipulation with ordered binary-decision diagrams. ACM Computing Surveys (CSUR) 24(3), 293–318 (1992)
4. Clarke, E., Grumberg, O., Jha, S., Lu, Y., Veith, H.: Progress on the state explosion problem in model checking. Informatics-10 Years Back 10, 176–194 (2001)
5. Cousot, P., Cousot, R.: Abstract Interpretation Frameworks. Journal of Logic and Computation 2(4), 511–547 (2004)
6. Farias, A., Mota, A., Sampaio, A.: Efficient CSP-Z Data Abstraction. In: Boiten, E.A., Derrick, J., Smith, G.P. (eds.) IFM 2004. LNCS, vol. 2999, pp. 108–127. Springer, Heidelberg (2004)
7. Farias, A., Mota, A., Sampaio, A.: Compositional abstraction of CSP-Z processes. Journal of the Brazilian Computer Society 14, 23–44 (2008)
8. Fischer, C.: CSP-OZ: A combination of Object-Z and CSP. In: Formal Methods for Open Object-Based Distributed Systems (FMOODS 1997), vol. 2, pp. 423–438 (1997)
9. Forjaz, M.: The origins of Embraer. Tempo Social 17, 281–298 (2005)
10. Graf, S., Saidi, H.: Construction of abstract state graphs with PVS. In: Grumberg, O. (ed.) CAV 1997. LNCS, vol. 1254, pp. 72–83. Springer, Heidelberg (1997)
11. Lazic, R., Roscoe, A.: A semantic study of data independence with applications to model checking. Bulletin-European Association For Theoretical Computer Science 71, 259–260 (2000)
12. Roscoe, A.: The Theory and Practice of Concurrency. Prentice Hall, Englewood Cliffs (1998)
13. Sampaio, A., Albuquerque, C., Vasconcelos, J., Cruz, L., Figueiredo, L., Cavalcante, S.: Software test program: a software residency experience. In: ICSE 2005: Proceedings of the 27th international conference on Software engineering, pp. 611–612. ACM Press, New York (2005)
14. Smith, G.: The Object-Z Specification Language. Springer, Heidelberg (2000)
15. Systems, F.: Failures-Divergence Refinement - FDR2 User Manual, June 2005. Formal Systems (Europe) Ltd. (June 2005)
16. Visser, W., Havelund, K., Brat, G., Park, S., Lerda, F.: Model Checking Programs. Automated Software Engineering 10(2), 203–232 (2003)
17. Wehrheim, H.: Data Abstraction Techniques in the Validation of CSP-OZ Specifications. Formal Aspects of Computing 12(3), 147–164 (2000)
18. Woodcock, J., Davies, J.: Using Z: specification, refinement, and proof. Prentice-Hall, Inc., Upper Saddle River (1996)
19. Yorav, S., Clarke, E.: Automated Compositional Abstraction Refinement for Concurrent C Programs: A Two-Level Approach. Electronic Notes in Theoretical Computer Science 89(3), 105–127 (2003)

Applying Event and Machine Decomposition to a Flash-Based Filestore in Event-B⋆

Kriangsak Damchoom and Michael Butler

University of Southampton
United Kingdom
{kd06r,mjb}@ecs.soton.ac.uk

Abstract. Event-B is a formal method used for specifying and reasoning about systems. Rodin is a toolset for developing system models in Event-B. Our experiment which is outlined in this paper is aimed at applying Event-B and Rodin to a flash-based filestore. Refinement is a useful mechanism that allows developers to sharpen models step by step. Two uses of refinement, feature augmentation and structural refinement, were employed in our development. Event decomposition and machine decomposition are structural refinement techniques on which we focus in this work. We present an outline of a verified refinement chain for the flash filestore. We also outline evidence of the applicability of the method and tool together with some guidelines.

Keywords: refinement, event decomposition, machine decomposition, file system, flash memory, proof, Event-B, Rodin.

1 Introduction

Hoare and Misra [14] outline the importance of undertaking experiments involving the application of theories and tools in order to push forward scientific progress in formal methods. Experiments help us to understand the strengths and weaknesses of theories and tools. A flash-based filestore has been selected as case study for our experiment. This case study was proposed as a challenging system by Joshi and Holzmann [19]. As stated in [19], the challenge is how to deal with accidental failures that may occur while performing operations on a flash memory. For example, how do we cope with power loss or sudden reboot? How do we manage the data consistency when flash instructions being performed fail? The flash architecture we chose is the ONFI (Open NAND Flash Interface) specification proposed in [16]. This specification is open and is commonly referenced by researchers who are working in this area.

A flash array has physical characteristics that constrain the way it is used. Taking account of physical characteristics and failure management is required.

⋆ This work was part of the EU research project ICT 214158 DEPLOY (Industrial deployment of system engineering methods providing high dependability and productivity) www.deploy-project.eu.

M.V.M. Oliveira and J. Woodcock (Eds.): SBMF 2009, LNCS 5902, pp. 134–152, 2009.
© Springer-Verlag Berlin Heidelberg 2009

Reading and writing of files to the flash array are expected to be consistent with an abstract model of a filesystem.

Our experiment presented in this paper is the development of a verified refinement chain for a flash-based filestore using Event-B and the Rodin platform. This experiment is an extension of the work we presented in [11] where we outlined a model of a tree-structured file system. The extension we address here consists of replacing the abstract file system by the flash specification and dealing with fault-tolerance. In Section 12 we discuss some related work on applying formal methods to the file store problem. A distinguishing feature of our treatment of the file store problem is the use of multiple levels of refinement to relate an abstract model, with large atomic reads and writes on abstract data structures, to a model with more complex concrete data structures and more fine-grained atomic steps. The use of multiple levels of refinement means that the abstraction gap is relatively small at each stage which means the gluing invariants required for refinement verification are relatively simple. Simpler gluing invariants are easier for modellers to formulate and lead to simpler proof obligations. We believe the relative ease of the proof effort, reported in Section 11, testifies to this. Another distinguishing feature of our development is the use of machine decomposition to partition the development after several refinement steps. The partitioning led to sub-models that were refined separately. While it is well-known that decomposition is critical for scaling of formal development, it is rare to find examples of its application in practice. Our file store development represents an exemplar of multi-level refinement and of machine decomposition that we believe others could learn from. This role as an exemplar is the main contribution of the paper.

Two uses of refinement were employed in our development: horizontal and vertical refinements (details are given in Section 3). The horizontal development was mainly presented in [11]. (In this paper, we focus on the vertical refinement.) We first used horizontal refinement in an incremental way to construct the file system model. The model started with an abstract tree structure. After that, new features were gradually added in each refinement step. We finally got five layers of specification describing an abstract file system.

Vertical refinement was later used to introduce more design details in order to map the abstract file system to the flash architecture. In the case of vertical refinement, while refining the file system down to the flash specification, the event-decomposition technique [6] was used to decompose events like *readfile* (read the whole content of the given file from the storage into the memory buffer) and *writefile* (write the whole content of the given file on the buffer to the storage) into three sub-events, *start, step* (read or write a page) and *end*.

We also applied the machine decomposition technique [6] to decompose the machine of the last refinement into two sub-machines representing the specification of the file system layer and the flash interface layer. The reason we do this is to explore further refinements of the flash model separately from the file system model.

The paper begins with an introduction to Event-B and Rodin in Section 2. The refinement and event-decomposition techniques used in our development are outlined in Section 3 and 4. An overview of an abstract file system is given in Section 5. Vertical refinement and event-decomposition used to link the file system to the flash specification are discussed in Section 6–8. Machine decomposition and further refinement focusing on the flash specification are outlined in Section 9 and 10. Proof statistics, related work and conclusion are discussed in Section 11, 12 and 13, respectively.

Note: An archive of our development in Rodin may be downloaded[1]. This can be imported by the Rodin tool release 0.9.2.1 or later[2].

2   Event-B and Rodin

Event-B [3] is an extension of the B-method [1] for specifying and reasoning about systems. An Event-B model is described in terms of contexts and machines. Contexts [4,5] contain the static parts of a model. Each context may consist of carrier sets and constants as well as axioms that are used to describe the properties of those sets and constants. Contexts may contain theorems which are required to follow from the preceding axioms and theorems. Machines [4,5] represent the dynamic part of an Event-B model consisting of variables and actions. A machine is made of a state, which is defined by means of variables, invariants, events and theorems. The theorems of a machine are required to follow from the context and the invariants of that machine. Variables are typed as mathematical objects such as sets, relations, numbers, etc. Variables are constrained by invariants. Invariants are expected to be preserved whenever variable values change. This must be proved through the discharge of proof obligations [4].

A machine contains a number of atomic events which model the way that a system may evolve. In general, an event is composed of four elements: name, parameter, guard and action. The guard is the necessary condition for the event. The action determines the way in which the state variables are going to evolve when performing the event [4]. An event is guarded and atomic and may be performed only when its guard holds. When the guards of several events hold at the same time, then only one event may be performed at that time. The event to be performed is non-deterministically chosen.

Refinement is the main development method supported by Event-B. In Event-B, an event of an abstract machine may be refined by several corresponding events in a refined machine. A refined machine may also have additional events that are refinements of *skip* rather than being refinements of abstract events. Note this is more flexible than the usual approach in, for example, Z, VDM or "classical" B, where there is a strong one-to-one correspondence between abstract and concrete events.

Rodin [4] is an open and extensible toolset for specifying and verifying system models in Event-B. It contains a database of modelling elements used for constructing system models such as variables, invariants, events, etc. The Rodin toolset is accompanied by various useful plug-ins such as a proof-obligation generator, provers, model-checkers, UML transformers, etc [9].

---

[1] http://deploy-eprints.ecs.soton.ac.uk/125/
[2] www.event-b.org

3   Refinement Strategy

Incremental refinement has been used as our strategy to develop a model of a flash-based file system. Two uses of refinement were employed in our development: *feature augmentation* (or horizontal refinement) and *structural refinement* (or vertical refinement) [8]. Feature augmentation is aimed at introducing new requirements or properties which are not addressed in the initial model or may be postponed to other levels. Thus, in each refinement step, additional state variables and related events might be added to incorporate those features which are introduced. The system models will be enlarged gradually when new properties are introduced. The purpose of structural refinement, on the other hand, is to replace an abstract structure with more design details in each refinement step down to an implementation. This kind of refinement may involve data refinement, event decomposition and machine decomposition.

In the development presented in [11], feature augmentation was used in an incremental way to develop a model of a flash-based file system. That is, we began with a small set of features and then enlarged the model by introducing new features in each refinement step. We finally got five levels of a specification describing an abstract file system. That is, the specification is the abstract model plus a series of feature augmentations. As stated in [11], we regard the full chain of augmentation (horizontal) refinements as constituting *the specification*, not just the most abstract level.

Structural refinement, which is the focus of this paper, was used to relate the abstract file system with the specification of the flash interface layer. This kind of refinement was used to decompose the events *readfile* and *writefile* into sub-events in order to map them with *page-read* and *page-program* interfaces provided by the flash interface layer. Details will be given in Section 6 and 7.

4   Event Decomposition in Event-B

While refining a model we may find that some (atomic) events can be split into sub-events. We can decompose this kind of event through a refinement step. Among those sub-events which are split, at least one event refines the abstract event, while other sub-events refine *skip*. In our case, for example, instead of writing the whole content in one step, the abstract file write can be partitioned into sub-events: (i) start write (set an initial state and buffers), (ii) write a single page (occurs once for each page of a file) and (iii) end write (reset the state and buffers of the given file). Note that we achieve this form of event decomposition using the standard refinement rules of Event-B which allows for the introduction of events that refine *skip* in a refinement [3].

To understand more about event decomposition, event refinement diagrams proposed in [6] will be used to explain how an atomic event can be decomposed into sub-events. Fig. 1 shows an example of such a diagram. In the figure, the root represents an abstract event which is partitioned into events *start*, *step*, and *end* in a refinement. A solid line indicates that the *end* event refines the *abs_evt* event. That means the *end* event will be proved to refine the abstraction. The dashed lines state that both *start* and *step* refine *skip*. The oval represents a quantifier that specifies multiple interleaved instances of an event (i will range over some set). Order, from left to right, constrains the order in which events have performed. A *step(i)* event can be performed only when the *start* event is completed, and *end* can be performed only when all *step(i)* events have been occurred. The order amongst the *step(i)* events is nondeterministic. In Event-B, there are no explicit sequencing operations. Events are non-deterministically performed when their guards hold. Thus, in order to control the order of event execution, each event must be guarded by using additional states or flag variables. For example, in order to start writing a single page, the given file must be in the writing state. Thus, a *writing* state should be introduced and used to construct guards of events that we want to control.

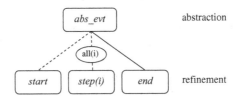

Fig. 1. An example of event refinement diagram

The event refinement diagrams are used as an aid to constructing and understanding the formal models rather than being formal objects themselves. As outlined in [6] , the diagrams were inspired by Jackson Structured Design (JSD) diagrams [18]. In the future, we plan to investigate a more formal incorporation of event refinement diagrams into the refinement proof obligations.

5   Outline of Abstract File System

In the development presented in [11], feature augmentation was used in an incremental way to develop the model of an abstract file system. That is, we began with a small set of features and then augmented the model by adding new features in refinement steps. Additional state variables and events which are related to the new features were introduced in each step. The event-extension feature[3] provided by the tool was mainly used to develop this refinement chain. In each refinement step, when new features were introduced the related events were extended by adding more details or constraints corresponding to those features. The event extension may involve adding new parameters, guards and actions.

The layered specification of the abstract file system is briefly described as follows.

---

[3] Event extension is a new feature of Rodin.

Abstraction. Tree properties and basic operations affecting the tree structure (*create*, *delete*, *move* and *copy*) were firstly specified in this level. No-loop and reachability (all objects in a tree are reachable from the *root*) are two main properties which were the focus of verification effort.

First refinement. Files and directories were introduced. In the abstraction, files and directories are treated in the same way as *objects* which are nodes of the tree structure. In this level, *objects* was replaced by *files* and *directories*. That means an object can be either a file or a directory. The abstract event *create* was refined into *crtfile* (create a file) and *mkdir* (make a directory).

Second refinement. File content was introduced in this level. Additional constraints and events related to file content are also addressed. For example, each file has a content, an existing file must be opened before reading or writing.

Third refinement. Access permissions and related constraints were introduced. For instance, each object has an owner, a group-owner and a list of permissions. The user who issues read- or write-request must have the right to read or write on the given file.

Fourth refinement. Additional properties which were not addressed in [11] – such as objects' name, creation date and last modification date – were introduced here.

Fig. 2 shows the definitions of three variables of the abstract specification along with an abstract file write event, named *writefile*, of the abstract file system. The *writefile* event writes the whole content of the given file f from the write buffer (*wbuffer*) into the storage in one step. Here *fcontent* represents the content of each file on the storage, *w_opened* is a set of files which are opened for writing, and *CONTENT* is defined as a sequence of *DATA* in a context seen by this abstract machine.

$$\ldots$$
$$fcontent \in files \rightarrow CONTENT$$
$$w\_opened \subseteq files$$
$$wbuffer \in w\_opened \rightarrow CONTENT$$
$$\ldots$$

Event *writefile* $\widehat{=}$
  Any f Where
    grd1 : $f \in w\_opened$
  Then
    act1 : $fcontent(f) := wbuffer(f)$
  End

Fig. 2. Event *writefile* of the abstract file system

6   Vertical Refinement

The purpose of this section is to outline the decomposition of the abstract events *readfile* and *writefile*. The decomposition is based on the assumption that the content of the file is read from or written to the storage one page at a time. As shown in Fig. 3 (b), for example, instead of writing the buffer content into the storage in one step, we introduced an intermediate variable named *fcont_tmp*. This variable behaves like a shadow disk used for accumulating the content of the pages as they are written one at a time. This shadow becomes the actual content of that file only when all pages have been written to the shadow. The use of this shadow allows us to deal with faults that may occur during writing a file – if a fault occurs, we discard the shadow and keep the original. The use of the shadow is an abstraction of the fact that when writing a file at the implementation level we use fresh pages on the flash array rather over-writing the pages used for the previous version of the file. Additional details are explained in Section 7.

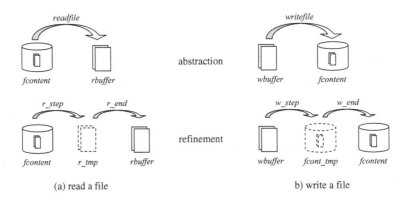

Fig. 3. A diagram of refining events *readfile* and *writefile*

Note: Because of space constraints, instead of detailing the decomposition of both file read and file write which are similar, we will present only file write which is more interesting. Full details of the specification can be found in the archive mentioned in Section 1.

7   Decomposing Event *writefile*

Fig. 4 (a) shows an event refinement diagram for the *writefile* event which is decomposed into three sub-events: *w_start* (start write), *w_step* (write one page at a time) and *w_end* (end write, when all pages are written completely). Event *w_end* refines *writefile* of the abstraction while *w_start* and *w_step* refine *skip*. This diagram states that *w_start* must be performed before *w_step*. Event *w_step* will be repeated until all pages are written or programmed into the flash device.

In case of failures (see Fig. 4 (b)), in the abstraction, the *writefileFail* event does nothing (i.e. *skip*). The content of file on the storage is not changed and all memory buffers are released.

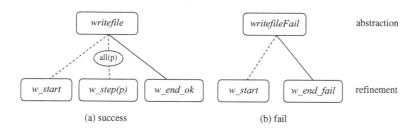

Fig. 4. Refinement diagram of event *writefile*

Fig. 5 shows machine invariants in this refinement step. Variable *fcont_tmp* represents temporary content of the file while it is in the writing state. This variable behaves like a shadow content of the file being written, as already discussed. This shadow content becomes an actual content (*fcontent*) when all pages have been written to the shadow. No change is made to *fcontent* if writing a file fails at any point from the start to the end of writing a file. That means the content of that file will be same as the previous state. We specified *writing* as a set of opened files which are in the writing state. Variable *wbuffer* represents a write-buffer of each writing file. Invariant *inv6.3* states that for any file f which is in the writing state, the temporary contents of f will be a subset or equal to the content on its writing buffer.

$inv6.1 : writing \subseteq w\_opened$
$inv6.2 : fcont\_tmp \in writing \rightarrow CONTENT$
$inv6.3 : \forall f \cdot f \in writing \Rightarrow fcont\_tmp(f) \subseteq wbuffer(f)$

Fig. 5. Machine invariants of the refinement

Fig. 6 shows the refinement of event *writefile* when it is split into *w_start*, *w_step* and *w_end* (in cases of *success* and *fail*). Consider the *w_start* event. In order to start writing a file, the given file must be opened for writing and not already in the writing state (see *grd1* and *grd2* of event *w_start*). Event *w_step* writes the contents of page i from the write buffer (*wbuffer*) into *fcont_tmp*. In order to do this the given file must be in the writing state (see *grd1*). The page being written must be a page in the write buffer that has not already been written to the storage (see guards *grd4* and *grd5* of event *w_step*). Event *w_end_ok* is enabled when all pages have been written (*grd2*) and the file is in the writing

Event $w\_start \mathrel{\widehat{=}}$
  Any f Where
    $grd1 : f \in w\_opened$
    $grd2 : f \notin writing$
  Then
    $act1 : writing := writing \cup \{f\}$
    $act2 : fcont\_tmp(f) := \varnothing$
  End

Event $w\_step \mathrel{\widehat{=}}$
  Any f, i, cnt Where
    $grd1 : f \in writing$
    $grd2 : i \in \mathbb{N}$
    $grd3 : cnt \in DATA$
    $grd4 : i \mapsto cnt \in wbuffer(f)$
    $grd5 : i \notin dom(fcont\_tmp(f))$
  Then
    $act1 : fcont\_tmp(f) := fcont\_tmp(f) \cup \{i \mapsto cnt\}$
  End

Event w_end_ok refines $writefile \mathrel{\widehat{=}}$
  Any f Where
    $grd1 : f \in writing$
    $grd2 : dom(wbuffer(f)) = dom(fcont\_tmp(f))$
  Then
    $act1 : fcontent(f) := fcont\_tmp(f)$
    $act2 : writing := writing \setminus \{f\}$
    $act3 : fcont\_tmp := \{f\} \lhd fcont\_tmp$
  End

Event $w\_end\_fail \mathrel{\widehat{=}}$
  Any f Where
    $grd1 : f \in writing$
  Then
    $act1 : writing := writing \setminus \{f\}$
    $act2 : fcont\_tmp := \{f\} \lhd fcont\_tmp$
  End

Fig. 6. Decomposition of the *writefile* event

state. The effect of *w_end_ok* is to overwrite the existing file content with the shadow content.

Guard *grd2* of the *w_end_ok* event and Invariant *inv6.3* play an important role in proving that the *w_end_ok* event is a correct refinement of the *writefile* event (given in Fig 2). Namely, the gluing invariant, *inv6.3*, is used to show that *fcont_tmp(f)* is equal to *wbuffer(f)* when the guards of the *w_end_ok* event holds.

8   Linking the Abstract File System to the Flash Interface Layer

This section outlines our model of the flash specification, which is based on the ONFI specification given in [16], and shows how it is related to the abstract file system via data refinement. We first describe an abstract specification of the flash in Section 8.1 and then show the refinement of the file system layer when the flash specification is included.

8.1   Abstract Flash Interfaces Layer

An ONFI-based flash device is a collection of LUNs (Logical Units). Each LUN is composed of a number of blocks. Each block has a number of pages. Each page is a sequence of data items.

Flash pages are accessed via row addresses consisting of a LUN, a block number within a LUN and a page number within a block. A flash device can be specified as an array of pages which are identified by row addresses:

$$flash \in RowAddr \rightarrow PDATA$$

where *RowAddr* is a set of possible row addresses. *PDATA* represents a page data within each page. To realise the file system layer, we assume that each *PDATA* is composed of file data, the object identity to which the data belongs, the logical page-id (or page index in the view of file system) and a version number. Fig. 7 represents the structure of *PDATA*. We model each component of *PDATA* by a projection function. For example, the file data stored in a *PDATA* is modelled by *dataOfpage* (*axm1*). The other projections represent file object, page index and version number. A set of version numbers (*VERNUM*) is used to record the version of data which is programmed in each page.

The flash interface layer provides two main interfaces to the file system layer. The first is *page_read*, read a page of data from a given row address, and the second is *page_program* (or *page_write*), write a page of data into the flash device at a given row address. These two interfaces will become part of the events *r_step* and *w_step* of the file system layer.

$$
\begin{aligned}
&axm1 : dataOfpage \in PDATA \rightarrow DATA \\
&axm2 : objOfpage \in PDATA \rightarrow OBJECT \\
&axm3 : pidxOfpage \in PDATA \rightarrow \mathbb{N} \\
&axm4 : verOfpage \in PDATA \rightarrow VERNUM
\end{aligned}
$$

Fig. 7. A structure of PDATA

8.2   Relating the File System Layer with the Flash Interface Layer

In this refinement step, flash properties are introduced together with variables used to relate those two layers. Variables *fcontent* and *fcont_tmp* of the file system layer are replaced by *fat* and *fat_tmp* respectively. The variable *fat* represents the table of contents of each file. This table is a mapping of each file to a table that maps each logical page-id of the file to its corresponding row address in the flash. The corresponding row address represents the location (in the flash) in which the content of that page is stored.

The properties mentioned above are described by the invariants given in Fig. 8. Invariants *inv7.3* and *inv7.4* are gluing invariants introduced to relate the abstract variables *fcontent* and *fcont_tmp* with the concrete variables *fat* and *fat_tmp* respectively. They play an important role in proving the correctness of this refinement. Variable *programmed_pages* represents the row addresses of pages that have already been programmed or written, while *obsolete_pages* is a set of programmed pages that are invalid to be used. Invariants *inv7.8* and *inv7.9* were introduced to relate the content of file with the actual content on the flash device. For instance, *inv7.8* says that for any page whose version equals to the current version of the file to which the page belongs, the data of that page will be the data of the given page-id of that file.

Fig. 9 illustrates how the file write of the abstract file system is replaced by the flash specification. The top diagram represents the abstract file write which is composed of three sub-events: *w_start*, *w_step* and *w_end*. The bottom diagram represents the refinement where *w_step* is refined by event *pagewrite*.

$inv7.1 : fat \in files \rightarrow (\mathbb{N} \nrightarrow RowAddr)$

$inv7.2 : fat\_tmp \in writing \rightarrow (\mathbb{N} \nrightarrow RowAddr)$

$inv7.3 : \forall f \cdot f \in files \Rightarrow dom(fat(f)) = dom(fcontent(f))$

$inv7.4 : \forall f \cdot f \in files \wedge f \in writing \Rightarrow dom(fat\_tmp(f)) = dom(fcont\_tmp(f))$

$inv7.5 : flash \in RowAddr \rightarrow PDATA$

$inv7.6 : programmed\_pages \subseteq RowAddr$

$inv7.7 : obsolete\_pages \subseteq programmed\_pages$

$inv7.8 : \forall p \cdot p \in PDATA \wedge objOfpage(p) \in files$
$\quad \wedge verOfpage(p) = curr\_version(objOfpage(p)) \wedge pidxOfpage(p) \neq 0$
$\quad \Rightarrow pidxOfpage(p) \mapsto dataOfpage(p) \in fcontent(objOfpage(p))$

$inv7.9 : \forall p \cdot p \in PDATA \wedge objOfpage(p) \in writing$
$\quad \wedge verOfpage(p) = writing\_version(objOfpage(p)) \wedge pidxOfpage(p) \neq 0$
$\quad \Rightarrow pidxOfpage(p) \mapsto dataOfpage(p) \in fcont\_tmp(objOfpage(p))$

...

Fig. 8. Machine invariants of replacing the file system by the flash specification

In this event, *page_program* will be called in order to write the content of each page into the flash device. When each page has been programmed successfully, the *fat_tmp* will be updated. Finally, the *fat_tmp* will be copied to *fat* when all pages have been completely programmed into the flash device.

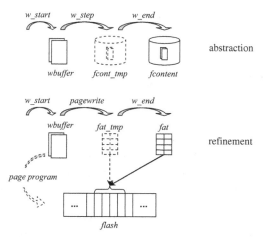

Fig. 9. A diagram of mapping *writefile* to the flash specification

---

Event *pagewrite* refines *w_step* $\widehat{=}$
    Any $f, i, cnt, r, pdata$ Where
        $grd1 : f \in writing$
        $grd2 : i \in \mathbb{N}$
        $grd3 : cnt \in DATA$
        $grd4 : i \mapsto cnt \in wbuffer(f)$
        $grd5 : i \notin dom(fat\_tmp(f))$
        $grd6 : r \in RowAddr$
        $grd7 : r \notin programmed\_pages$
        $grd8 : pdata \in PDATA$
        $grd9 : verOfpage(pdata) = writing\_version(f)$
        $grd10 : objOfpage(pdata) = f$
        $grd11 : lpidOfpage(pdata) = i$
        $grd12 : dataOfpage(pdata) = cnt$
    Then
        $act1 : fat\_tmp(f) := fat\_tmp(f) \cup \{i \mapsto r\}$
        $act2 : flash(r) := pdata$
        $act3 : programmed\_pages := programmed\_pages \cup \{r\}$
    End

Fig. 10. The refinement of the *w_step* event

Fig. 10 shows the *pagewrite* event which is a refinement of the *w_step* event. The *pagewrite* event will look for an available page on the flash (*grd6-grd7*) in order to write the content of page number i on the *wbuffer*. Parameter r represents a row address within the flash. Guards *grd9-grd12* describe the contents of *pdata* to be written to the flash. Action *act1* updates the temporary *fat* table of the file f. Action *act2* sets the content of the flash at row number r equal to *pdata*. The row address identifying that page will be set as a programmed page by *act3*.

9   Machine Decomposition

The aim of this section is to decompose the machine into a file system machine, modelling the file system layer, and a flash machine, modelling the flash interface layer. As a result, further refinements of the flash interface layer can be explored separately. The machine decomposition we apply here follows the style described in [6]. Namely, machine variables and events are partitioned into sub-machines. Sub-machines interact with each other via synchronisation over shared parameterised events.

Fig. 11 shows a diagram of machine decomposition illustrating the decomposition of the events *pagewrite* and *pageread*. The top layer represents the file system sub-machine consisting of machine variables *fat*, *fat_tmp*, *wbuffer*, and so on. The lower layer represents the flash interface sub-machine which contains machine variables named *flash*, *programmed_pages* and *obsolete_pages*. The ovals represent synchronisation over shared parameterised events between the sub-machines. In this case, both sub-machines interact by synchronising over the *page_write* and the *page_read* events.

At this point, for example, we partitioned the *pagewrite* event given in Fig. 10 following the approach of [6] and got a specification of the *page_program* event of the flash interface layer which is shown in Fig. 12. We also got a specification of the *pagewrite* event of the file system layer given in Fig 13. Parameters r and

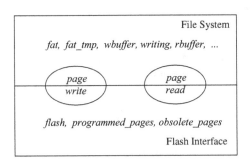

Fig. 11. A machine-decomposition diagram focusing on events *page_read* and *page_write*

Event $page\_program \mathrel{\widehat{=}}$
   Any $r, pdata$ Where
      $grd6 : r \in RowAddr$
      $grd7 : r \notin programmed\_pages$
      $grd8 : pdata \in PDATA$
   Then
      $act2 : flash(r) := pdata$
      $act3 : programmed\_pages := programmed\_pages \cup \{r\}$
   End

Fig. 12. An abstract *page_program* of the flash interface layer

Event $pagewrite \mathrel{\widehat{=}}$
   Any $f, i, cnt, r, pdata$ Where
      $grd1 : f \in writing$
      $grd2 : i \in \mathbb{N}$
      $grd3 : cnt \in DATA$
      $grd4 : i \mapsto cnt \in wbuffer(f)$
      $grd5 : i \notin dom(fat\_tmp(f))$
      $grd6 : r \in RowAddr$
      $grd8 : pdata \in PDATA$
      $grd9 : verOfpage(pdata) = writing\_version(f)$
      $grd10 : objOfpage(pdata) = f$
      $grd11 : lpidOfpage(pdata) = i$
      $grd12 : dataOfpage(pdata) = cnt$
   Then
      $act1 : fat\_tmp(f) := fat\_tmp(f) \cup \{i \mapsto r\}$
   End

Fig. 13. Event *pagewrite* of the file system layer

pdata represent shared parameters which are used for an interaction between these two events.

After decomposition we finally got a machine specifying the flash interface layer which consists of events *page_program* and *page_read* that can later be refined separately from the specification of the file system. We also got a machine specifying the file system with *pagewrite* and *pageread* plus the other events from earlier refinement such as *w_start* and *w_end*.

10   Further Refinements

Further refinements are focused on the flash interface layer. After decomposition, the flash model is refined separately by adding more details of the flash specification. For example, each LUN has at least one page register used for buffering data. Writing a page is done in two phases. The first is writing the given data into a page register within the selected LUN and the second is programming the data on the page register into the flash array at the given row address. Similarly for reading page data, the data will be first transferred to the page register before it is read off chip into the memory buffer.

An additional event that we specify is *block-erase*. This event has the effect of erasing a given block in order to be reused for writing. The number of erasures per block is limited (the number is dependent on its manufacturing). The block which fails to erase will become a bad block which is no longer to be used. In order to reclaim a dirty block, the block should contain obsolete data and may have one or more pages whose data is still valid. All valid pages within the block being reclaimed must be relocated (moved to another fresh block). After all valid pages have been relocated, the given block becomes obsolete and ready to be erased. That means only obsolete blocks are allowed to be erased.

These further refinements mentioned are the refinements of the flash interface layer which are refined separately from the model of the file system layer.

Note that the *wear-levelling* process[4] is an important feature that has not been covered in our development yet. It is in our on-going work.

11   Proofs

The proof statistics, given in Table 1[5], show that 540 proof obligations (POs) were generated by the Rodin tool. 501 POs (or 93%) were proved automatically while others were discharged by interactive proof. In the case of interactive proofs, almost 80% of proof steps involved instantiation of universal quantifiers while the rest involved adding hypotheses, case distinctions, etc. In this table, MCH0 represents an abstract model; MCH1 up to MCH4 represent the first up to the fourth horizontal refinements, MCH5 – MCH7 represent the vertical refinements. MCH_FL0 up to MCH_FL3 represent an abstract model (MCH_FL0) of the flash interface layer and its refinements.

In each step of iteration of modelling, modification and proof, POs generated by the tool were used as guidelines for modelling and reasoning about the model. For example, they were used to determine which gluing invariant should be added to the machine (e.g. *inv*6.3 given in Fig. 5), which guard should be added to the event in order to strengthen the model, as well as which form of expressions should be specified to make prove easier. For instance, specifying an expression

---

[4] A technique used for prolonging the life time of flash memory covering reclaiming and erasing blocks within a flash chip.

[5] These proof statistics are slightly different from the table given in [11] because we have introduced events for deleting a file and removing an empty directory in MCH1.

Table 1. Proof statistics

Machines	Total POs	Automatic	Interactive
MCH0	35	22	13
MCH1	57	49	8
MCH2	33	32	1
MCH3	37	34	3
MCH4	26	26	0
MCH5	27	26	1
MCH6	31	30	1
MCH7	109	97	12
MCH_FL0	8	8	0
MCH_FL1	110	110	0
MCH_FL2	57	57	0
MCH_FL3	9	9	0
Overall	540	501 (93%)	39 (7%)

like $pg \mapsto obj \in objOfpage$ is easier to discharge than $objOfpage(pg) = obj$. As a result, this technique means we get a higher degree of automatic proof.

Results for automatic proof are good, but there is room for improvement. In principle, when any change is made, Rodin has the ability to avoid re-running proofs that are still valid. However, in some cases, some (unnecessary) proofs need to be re-run when some changes are made. As a result, if there is a large number of POs to be reproved and it can take a lot of time to re-run unnecessary proofs whenever the model changes.

12   Related Work

A number of formalisations of a file system have been developed by other researchers. For example, a specification of a visual file system in Z by Hughes [15] is focussed on tree properties and basic file operations affecting the tree structure, but file content and a manipulation of file content were not specified. The commonly referenced model developed by Morgan and Sufrin presented in [21] is a specification of a Unix file system in Z. In this specification, instead of using a tree structure, the location of each object is formulated as a sequence of directory names, which is the path of each object. This work is focused on file contents and naming operations used for manipulating these rather than structure manipulation operations such as directory copy and move. Based on the specification of Morgan and Sufrin, Freitas, Woodcock and Fu [13] have developed a verified model of the POSIX filestore accompanied with a representation and proof using the Z/Eves proof system. Since the filestore challenge was proposed by Joshi and Holzmann [19] in 2005, other researchers have addressed this challenge. For example, Butterfield, Freitas and Woodcock [10] have developed an abstract specification in Z of the ONFI specification [16]. In addition, Ferreira et al. [12] have developed and verified a specification of the Intel Flash File

System Core [17] in VDM. HOL and Alloy were used as a theorem prover and model checker, respectively. Other work developed by Kung and Jackson [20] is a formal specification and analysis of a flash-based filestore in Alloy. [20] focusses on basic operations of a file system, such as *read* and *write*, and addresses fault tolerance and *wear-levelling* process.

The approach of refining *skip* events to achieve decomposition of the atomicity of events was used by Woodcock and Davies [22] to refine a file write operation with the Z notation. Like us, they use a shadow disk in the refinement. They show how the decomposition of the file write can be cast as either a forwards simulation or a backwards simulation. In our case, we work only with forward simulation as Rodin only supports forward simulation. We have not found this restriction in Rodin to cause any difficulties.

Other researchers mentioned above also report statistics from mechanical proof efforts. However, we found it difficult to perform a like-for-like comparison of our results with others. Any comparison would depend heavily on the nature of the proof obligations and on the proof support provided in the language. For example, in Rodin, refined events may contain 'witness' clauses that are used to instantiate existential proof obligations. Without this, we would have a lot more interactive proofs whose only interactive step would be the provision of witnesses for existential quantifiers. By providing the witnesses directly in the model, we achieve a higher degree of automatic proof and the proofs are more robust against model changes. In the future it would be useful for researchers in this area to attempt to develop a common framework for comparing proof effort.

13   Conclusion and Discussion

We have presented a model of a flash-based filestore which was developed by using Event-B and Rodin. In this development, we have outlined the use of refinement for two different purposes. First refinement was used in feature augmentation (or horizontal refinement) and second for structural refinement (or vertical refinement).

Feature augmentation is a mechanism used for constructing a model of an abstract file system which was presented in [11]. Instead of specifying everything in one level that may give rise of proof difficulty, we decided to split the whole system features into sub-features. These sub-features were chosen to be introduced in refinement steps. We have found that this approach makes the model easier to construct and prove. In addition, we have found that the event-extension feature provided by the Rodin tool (release 0.9.x) makes models easier to refine. Namely, some changes can be made to the abstract levels individually and are propagated down automatically. This is in contrast to when we were developing the model of [11] using the Rodin tool release 0.8.2 that has no support for event-extension.

Structural refinement was used to relate the abstract file system with the flash specification. Event-decomposition is a structural refinement on which we focused in this paper. We have shown how the decomposition technique can be applied to our case study. This technique was used to partition atomic events *readfile* and *writefile* into a number of sub-events as explained in Section 7.

We have found that the event-decomposition technique is very effective for breaking an atomic event. It can be applied to other work whose events may require to be decomposed in order to cope with fault-tolerance or concurrency. An atomic event can be partitioned into sub-events that can be performed in an interleaved fashion. In addition, as can be seen in Section 7, we could deal with file write that may fail at any point between the start and the end of writing a file.

Additionally, in Section 9, the machine decomposition was employed to separate part of the flash interface layer from the file system layer. The purpose is to deal with further refinements of the flash interface layer separately. Those two layers interact with each other via the shared parameterised events. Based on this evidence, we believe that machine decomposition is useful for other developments whose specification involves a number of sub-systems that can be partitioned and refined separately. Rodin does not provide any tool to decompose machines directly, we still need to decompose machines manually using the editor of the Rodin tool. Thus, in the future, it would be useful if a machine-decomposition tool could be developed.

Although the proof statistics show a high degree of automatic proof, some improvements are still required. As explained in Section 11, in some cases, proofs are required to be re-run every time the model changes although they have already been proved. This is because Rodin currently uses a mixture of new and legacy provers and, while the new provers maintain sufficient information about used hypotheses to be able to avoid re-running proofs, the legacy provers do not. This is an engineering issue that is being addressed in Rodin.

As mentioned in the introduction, our file store development represents an exemplar of multi-level refinement and of machine decomposition that we believe others could learn from.

References

1. Abrial, J.-R.: The B Book. Cambridge University Press, Cambridge (1996)
2. Abrial, J.-R.: A system development process with Event-B and the Rodin platform. In: Butler, M., Hinchey, M.G., Larrondo-Petrie, M.M. (eds.) ICFEM 2007. LNCS, vol. 4789, pp. 1–3. Springer, Heidelberg (2007)
3. Abrial, J.-R.: Modelling in Event-B: System and Software Engineering. Cambridge University Press, Cambridge (2009) (to be published)
4. Abrial, J.-R., Butler, M., Hallerstede, S., Voisin, L.: An open extensible tool environment for Event-B. In: Liu, Z., He, J. (eds.) ICFEM 2006. LNCS, vol. 4260, pp. 588–605. Springer, Heidelberg (2006)
5. Abrial, J.-R., Hallerstede, S.: Refinement, decomposition and instantiation of discrete models: Application to Event-B. Fundamentae Infomatica, 1001–1026 (2006)
6. Butler, M.: Decomposition structures for Event-B. In: Leuschel, M., Wehrheim, H. (eds.) IFM 2009. LNCS, vol. 5423, pp. 20–38. Springer, Heidelberg (2009)
7. Butler, M., Yadav, D.: An Incremental development of the Mondex system in Event-B. Formal Aspects of Computing 20(1), 61–77 (2008)
8. Butler, M., Abrial, J.-R., Damchoom, K., Edmunds, A.: Applying Event-B and Rodin to the filestore. VSRNet, ABZ 2008 (2008)

9. Butler, M.: Rodin deliverable D31: Public versions of plug-in tools. Technical report, University of Southampton, UK (2007)
10. Butterfield, A., Freitas, L., Woodcock, J.: Mechanising a formal model of flash memory. Science of Computer Programming 74(4), 219–237 (2009)
11. Damchoom, K., Butler, M., Abrial, J.-R.: Modelling and proof of a tree-structured file system in Event-B and Rodin. In: Liu, S., Maibaum, T., Araki, K. (eds.) ICFEM 2008. LNCS, vol. 5256, pp. 25–44. Springer, Heidelberg (2008)
12. Ferreira, M.A., Silva, S.S., Oliveira, J.N.: Verifying Intel Flash File System Core Specification. Technical report, University of Minho (2008)
13. Freitas, L., Woodcock, J., Fu, Z.: POSIX file store in Z/Eves: An experiment in the verified software repository. Science of Computer Programming 74(4), 238–257 (2009)
14. Hoare, T., Misra, J.: Verified software: theories, tools, experiments; Vision of a Grand Challenge project (2005)
15. Hughes, J.: Specifying a visual file system in Z. Technical report, Department of Computing Science, University of Glasgow (1989)
16. Cemicondutor, H., et al.: Open NAND Flash Interface Specification, Revision 2.0. Technical report, ONFI (February 2008), http://www.onfi.org
17. Intel Flash File System Core Reference Guide, version 1. Technical report 304436001, Intel Coorporation (October 2004)
18. Jackson, M.A.: System Development. Prentice Hall, Englewood Cliffs (1983)
19. Joshi, R., Holzmann, G.J.: A mini challenge: Build a verifiable filesystem. In: Verified Software: Theories, Tools, Experiments (2005)
20. Kang, E., Jackson, D.: Formal modeling and analysis of a flash filesystem in Alloy. In: Börger, E., Butler, M., Bowen, J.P., Boca, P. (eds.) ABZ 2008. LNCS, vol. 5238, pp. 294–308. Springer, Heidelberg (2008)
21. Morgan, C., Sufrin, B.: Specification of the Unix filing system. IEEE Transaction on Software Engineering 10, 128–142 (1984)
22. Woodcock, J., Davies, J.: Using Z: Specification, Refinement, and Proof. Prentice Hall, Englewood Cliffs (1996)

An Integrated Formal Methods Tool-Chain and Its Application to Verifying a File System Model

Miguel Alexandre Ferreira[1] and José Nuno Oliveira[2]

[1] Software Improvement Group, The Netherlands
m.ferreira@sig.nl
[2] Universidade do Minho, Portugal
jno@di.uminho.pt

Abstract. Tool interoperability as a mean to achieve integration is among the main goals of the international Grand Challenge initiative. In the context of the Verifiable file system mini-challenge put forward by Rajeev Joshi and Gerard Holzmann, this paper focuses on the integration of different formal methods and tools in modelling and verifying an abstract file system inspired by the Intel® Flash File System Core. We combine high-level manual specification and proofs with current state of the art mechanical verification tools into a tool-chain which involves Alloy, VDM++ and HOL. The use of (pointfree) relation modelling provides the glue which binds these tools together.

1 Introduction

There is a healthy trend in formal methods for computer science driven by the idea of a *Grand Challenge* (GC). Hoare [21] revisited an old challenge in computer science: a verifying compiler, capable of performing extended static analysis of the programs it compiles. Hoare's paper defines a set of criteria for an international effort to drive research in computer science forward towards automatic software verification. Hoare *et al* [22] proposed that the conditions set in [21] were met, and that the time to start such a long term international research project had arrived.

The GC project is expected to *"deliver a comprehensive and unified theory of programming"*, *"prototype for a comprehensive and integrated suite of programming tools"*, and *"deliver a repository of verified software"*. [22, Section 2]

The current paper is focused on the integration of both programming and logical tools [22, Section 2.2] that aid in the verification of formally specified operations. We propose to combine different formal specification languages, and make their tool sets interoperate, to form a tool-chain supporting a development and verification life cycle process that yields checked specifications. We assume our target audience to be already using formal specification and verification techniques, thus benefiting from a structured approach to break down software complexity through design, backed up by automated verification tools. The tool-chain should fulfil the following requirements:

M.V.M. Oliveira and J. Woodcock (Eds.): SBMF 2009, LNCS 5902, pp. 153–169, 2009.
© Springer-Verlag Berlin Heidelberg 2009

- promote incremental development and verification of specifications;
- be agile enough to encourage users to verify even the smallest unit of their specifications;
- be capable of producing immediate feedback to unveil problems;
- be capable of performing fully automated consistency proofs;
- be amenable to automatic code generation.

As a case study for checking the proposed tool-chain life cycle, a formal model of an abstract file system was developed [8,9], inspired by the "mini-challenge" proposed in [26]. Although not yet covering the robustness or hardware requirements of [26], the model built in [8,9] is realistic while following the API of the File System Layer of the architecture for flash file systems designed by Intel Corporation [6, Section 4.14]. Such a model is given in the current paper stripped of its many details so as to convey the basic idea and method rather than not so relevant technicalities.

Paper structure. Sections 2 and 3 address the integration of languages and tools in an agile tool-chain. Section 4 presents the basics of our abstract modelling strategy, based on diagrams expressing model constraints. In Section 5 the abstract (pointfree) model of Section 4 is converted to Alloy, where it is model checked for the correctness of the operations. Section 6 describes the refinements to which the Alloy model is subject to so as to render it as a VDM++ executable specification. Section 7 introduces a proof system for VDM++ that uses the HOL theorem prover to discharge proof obligations. Section 8 addresses limitations of the tool-chain and a possible implementation. Finally, some concluding remarks are given in Section 10.

It is assumed that the reader has basic knowledge of the Alloy and VDM++ languages, model checking and theorem proving.

2   Tool-Chain

The main motivation for the proposed tool-chain is to combine formal method tools for model checking, theorem proving, model animation, etc, in a way such that each tool is placed in the "right" step of the given life-cycle. The version of the tool-chain which has been the subject of our experimentation involves the following languages and tools.

Relational PF-notation. Following Tarski's *formalization of set theory without variables* [37], relation algebra has emerged as a language for expressing and reasoning about logical formulae in a very concise, pointfree (PF) way. References [32,33] show how to reason about data models using PF-notation, in a typed way supported by categorial diagrams. This paper exploits the same approach by regarding PF-notation and diagrams as the starting point of the proposed verification life-cycle.

Alloy. This is a lightweight modelling language for software design developed by the Software Design Group at MIT [24]. Its foundations are first order logic and relational calculus. Alloy's lemma "everything is a relation" makes the language very simple, highly declarative, and well integrated with the relational PF-notation, as will be explained later. Alloy's tool support is provided by the Alloy Analyzer that supports both development and verification of models.

VDM. The Vienna Development Method [4] is a mature formal method whose origins go back to the IBM Vienna Laboratory in the 1970s. The use of VDM associated languages to specify and guide the development of software has been widely described in the literature [12,13]. VDM++ [29] is a widespread VDM dialect which, compared to ISO standard VDM-SL [34], introduces object oriented and concurrency features in the language. Tool support is one of the key strengths of VDM in general. From the wide variety of tools available we single out the Overture [28] Automatic Proof System (APS) [38] and the VDMTools [14] for type checking, interpretation and code generation.

HOL. This theorem prover [18,36] (a descendant of the LCF theorem prover) was developed with hardware verification in mind. It is an interactive proof assistant designed for higher order logic, with a vast set of ready to use theories and proof tactics. Its function definition mechanism provides termination proofs for recursive functions for free.

3   "All-in-One" Strategy

To effectively build a tool-chain it is necessary to have a strategy for each component as well as for the overall set of tools. The main goal of the strategy is to provide better verification techniques for formal development of software.

Better development means that the first steps in specifying a given problem should be taken at the most abstract level possible, capturing all the key aspects of the artifact under specification. This should be followed by incremental refinement of the specification in order to obtain an executable version, that can be used to validate functional requirements with stakeholders. Once verified, the executable specification is translated to source code in some mainstream programming language. The leap from abstract specification to executable specification must allow for early detection of failing functional requirements.

Better verification means that before tackling full-fledged proofs, confidence in the specification should be gained. In this way, one avoids attempting proofs that could be demonstrated impossible by counterexamples, or that add no value to the development since they fail the user requirements.

The kind of proof which is illustrated in the remainder of this paper is known as *satisfiability* [25]: for every operation Op whose input is of type A and whose output is of type B, proof obligation (PO)

$$\forall\, a \,\cdot\, a \in A \wedge \text{pre-}Op\, a \Rightarrow \exists\, b \,\cdot\, b \in B \wedge \text{post-}Op(b,a) \tag{1}$$

should be discharged. Because $a \in A$ and $b \in B$ check for the data type invariants associated to A and B, respectively, this PO is also referred to as *invariant preservation* [25]. Since in our case all our operations are total and deterministic, the POs we have in hands are actually simpler:

$$\forall a \cdot a \in A \wedge \text{pre-}Op\ a \Rightarrow Op(a) \in B \ . \tag{2}$$

The following situations can take place:

1. While specifying the overall architecture of a system, several interests are at stake. Often these interests are contradictory. A well founded notation which is paradigm-, platform- and technology-independent is welcome to enable reasoning about the high level design.
2. During the design phase, several experiments are performed to assess different design options for Op. A *model checker* able to automatically generate counterexamples to (2) and thus suggest how to improve Op is welcome.
3. Op satisfies (2) but is semantically wrong, for it ends up not behaving according to the requirements. To prevent this situation, running the model as a prototype in an interpreter is welcome.
4. Both the model checker and the test suite above do not find any flaws. In this case, a theorem prover is welcome to mechanically check (2).
5. PO (2) is too complex for the theorem prover. In this situation, the ultimate hope is a pen-and-paper manual proof, or some kind of exercise able to decompose the too complex PO into smaller sub-proofs.

This 5-step design scenario calls for a PO discharge strategy based on, respectively:

1. A highly abstract mathematical notation, providing for agile algebraic manipulation and diagrammatic representation of data models — we have chosen the PF-transform [33] and associated calculus of binary relations.
2. A model checker for timely generation of uninterpreted, unexpected counterexamples — we have chosen Alloy for this purpose.
3. An interpreter enabling one to carry out semantically meaningful animation and testing — for this purpose we have chosen the VDMTools.
4. A theorem prover — HOL in our case, thanks to the Overture proof system.
5. A pen-and-paper proof strategy regarding POs as "mathematical objects" which can be calculated upon. For this stage we have been using the PO calculus described in [33], where POs are represented by arrows which can be put together or decomposed into simpler ones.

This "all-in-one" strategy is depicted in Figure 1. The process starts from a highly abstract model of the architectural design of the target system, either in relational pointfree notation or directly in Alloy. Note the dashed line of the topmost box in Figure 1 (PF-notation), meaning that it is an optional stage. Although Alloy is not able to prove properties, it is very useful in finding counterexamples spotting where and why these properties fail.

After validating the design in Alloy, the model is translated to VDM++, where more detail is introduced. (Due to Alloy's notational compactness, the equivalent VDM++ specification becomes more verbose.) In the VDM++ stage it is already possible to validate all functional requirements, since the specification becomes executable. Validation can be carried out through unit tests [13, Section 9.5], combinatorial tests [30], or by interpreting (animating) the specification. Should dynamic analysis performed at VDM++ level detect any design flaw, the process goes back to the Alloy stage to suppress defective behaviour. Once the specification looks *adequate* and captures all functional requirements, the Overture APS is used to generate all the POs arising from the VDM++ model and attempt to mechanical discharge them in HOL.

The last stage (pen-and-paper proof) caters for POs which HOL could not prove and Alloy could not refute: the worst scenario. The idea is to use PF-calculation at this stage, aiming at simplifying POs or dividing them into smaller goals, which are fed back to HOL.

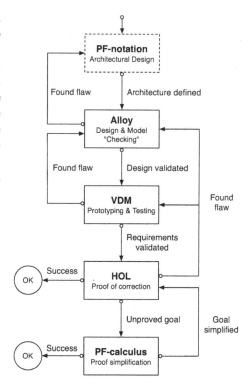

Fig. 1. Tool-chain operation

4   Relational Model of a (Simplified) File System

At the highest level of abstraction, a file system model should only capture the top level relationships among its main components. Capturing the properties which constrain the system's overall state is an essential part of This exercise. The challenge is doing so in a way which helps in reasoning about operations over such constrained state. At this level, the less detail the better, as long as no key aspect is overlooked.

A very abstract relational model of a file system is presented using PF-notation. Relational point-free models are built by depicting binary relations as arrows between data types in diagrams. The

$$Path \xleftarrow{\;dirName\;} Path$$

diagrams have a strong formal semantics, based on category/allegory theory [16], thus ensuring the move from diagrams to symbols, back and forth. At such an abstract level, a file system *stores* files in a way such that their data becomes *accessible* through paths. Paths play the double role of *identifying* files and revealing the *hierarchy* under which they are stored. Following POSIX terminology, we define the relation *dirName* that for a given path yields its parent path. This relation establishes the hierarchy of files within a file system: a file a is said to be the parent of a file b if, in the hierarchy, b lies exactly underneath a, that is, $(path\ a)dirName(path\ b)$ holds.

Just by thinking of paths one pictures a file system as an hierarchic structure, in fact a tree like structure, provided some properties of *dirName* hold. This does not necessarily mean that a file store must be a tree structure. As long as it is possible to navigate throughout it, any structure can implement a file store. Given a file system s, its file store component *fileStore s* is abstractly specified as a partial function.

$$Path \xleftarrow{\;(fileStore\ s)\;} File$$

Partial functions are often termed *simple* relations [3], and we shall use this terminology too.

$$FileHandle \xleftarrow{\;(table\ s)\;} FileDescriptor$$

Simple relations are so important in our data models (as elsewhere) that we use special harpoon looking arrows to depict them in diagrams, as above. Files can be handled by applications through the file system API, provided that all applications relying on files can reach them, and the files they are using do not get moved or removed. Applications do not handle files directly, instead they do it through file handlers. It is the file system's task to manage the relation between file handlers and the corresponding file descriptors. These descriptors keep relevant run-time information about files that are open, and in use by applications.

This leads us to a file system model with two sub-components: a file store, and an open-file table. The file system requires from the file store the ability to find a file given its path,

$$FileDescriptor \xleftarrow{\;table\ s\;} FileHandle$$
$$\downarrow{path}$$
$$Path \xrightarrow{\quad\quad\quad} File$$
$$\uparrow{dirName}\quad fileStore\ s$$
$$Path$$

and that the open-file table keeps track of the files requested by applications.

Files are the basic unit of a file system, and POSIX [23, Section 3.163] defines several types of files: regular file, directory, character special file, block special file, fifo special file, symbolic link and socket. Only regular files and directories are of interest at this topmost level of abstraction, and to distinguish these two types of file we introduce the *fileType* relationship, cf.:

$$FileDescriptor \xleftarrow{\;table\ s\;} FileHandle$$
$$\downarrow{path}$$
$$Path \xrightarrow{\quad\quad\quad} File \xrightarrow{\;fileType\;} FileType$$
$$\uparrow{dirName}\quad fileStore\ s$$
$$Path$$

The next step in the modelling consists of "gluing" the data structures in the diagram with constraints spelling out their static semantics (data type invariants, in the VDM terminology). The following pair of constraints is easily extracted from [6]:

- **Referential integrity:** non existing files cannot be handled by applications.
- **Paths closure:** parent directories always exist and are indeed directories.

In diagrams, constraints take the shape of rectangles, each labelled by the appropriate relational inclusion symbol[1]:

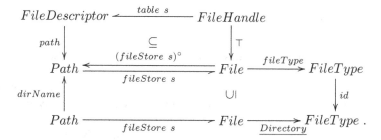

The diagram above depicts the two constraints that were identified: *referential integrity* (*ri*) is the top rectangle, *paths closure* (*pc*) is the bottom rectangle. Let us explain the meaning of these diagrams. A rectangle as displayed aside depicts PF-formula $R \cdot S \subseteq U \cdot V$. Once the meaning of relational composition is spelt out, this PF-formula becomes predicate

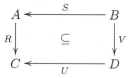

$$\forall\, c \in C, b \in B\ \cdot (\exists\, a \in A\ \cdot cRa \wedge aSb) \implies (\exists\, d \in D\ \cdot cUd \wedge dVb)\ .$$

Should any of R, S, U, V be the top relation $\top$, the corresponding conjunct is deleted from the formula above because $y \top x$ always holds, for any choice of x and y. Should it be a converse relation, say R°, then the variables of the corresponding conjunct are swapped, because $yR^\circ x$ means the same as xRy. Finally, should it be a function f, then $y\, f\, x$ means the same as $y = f\, x$, thus cancelling quantification over y. In the particular case of f being the everywhere-k constant function $\underline{k}$, $y\, f\, x$ shrinks to $y = k$.

In this way, the rectangle picturing referential integrity — which in symbols is $path \cdot (table\ s) \subseteq (fileStore\ s)^\circ \cdot \top$ — unfolds (for all $b \in FileHandle$) into predicate:

$$(\exists\, a \in FileDescriptor\ \cdot a(table\ s)b) \implies (\exists\, d \in File\ \cdot d(FileStore\ s)(path\ a))\ .$$

Drawing constraints in this fashion, as rectangles in diagrams, allows for great notation economy while providing for the visualization of the design in a "UML-like" style. The interested reader will want to do the exercise of spelling out the predicate which is pictured by the other rectangle in the diagram.

---

[1] In category/allegory terminology, these rectangles are referred to as "commutative squares".

Regarding the file system API, we specify operations as arrows again. Aside we con-

$$System \times Path \xrightarrow{\ open\ } System \times FileHandle$$

$$System \times Path \times FileType \xrightarrow{\ create\ } System$$

sider the two operations *open* and *create*, which open a given (regular) file and create a new (regular or directory) file, respectively. Opening files results in a new state with a new entry in the open-file table and a file handle referring to it. Creating a file only modifies the file store, by adding the new file.

In the next section the relational pointfree diagrammatic specification is translated to Alloy in an almost effortless exercise.

5   From PF Diagrams to Alloy

Transposing the above relational specification to Alloy is almost direct, since Alloy relations are first class citizens. Still, more detail is required in the Alloy specification to more accurately specify the file system state and operations. Once the specification is transliterated to Alloy, and the Alloy Analyzer is asked to instantiate it, it will display instances where: *(a)* there are cycles in paths; *(b)* there are directories being referenced in the open-file table. Both these situations should be avoided either because they are erroneous states of the file system *(a)* or because they display undesired behaviour *(b)*. To overcome this situation, more constraints must be added to the specification, and to a certain extent more detail has to be introduced in signatures (Alloy data types). Considering the file store only an additional constraint should be enforced:

Paths structure: the *dirName* relation should be such that: (a) the root directory is its own parent; (b) it is acyclic for all paths other than the root directory (thus no links are allowed in the file system).

Regarding the open-file table, one more constraint should be enforced:

Files table: only regular files can be opened, ie. no entry in the open-file table should refer to a directory.

The two simple relations of the diagrams lead to the Alloy top-level signature aside. In the system definition, the harpoon arrow of the relational

```
sig System {
    fileStore: Path -> lone File ,
    table: FileHandle -> lone FileDescriptor
}
```

diagram becomes the *lone* (one or less) multiplicity factor. Hence simplicity is ensured.

We specify *dirName* as a simple and total relation on paths, thus a function from *Path* to *Path*. Both simplicity and totality of the relation are specified with the *one* multiplicity factor in the range of the relation. This means that no path has more than one parent path and that, at the same time, every path (in the relation) has a parent path.

Note the use of the *abstract* keyword in declaring the

```
abstract sig Path {dirName: one Path}
```

Path signature, meaning that there can be no instances of *Path*. Using this keyword only makes sense if one extends the signature later on. In Alloy, the extension mechanism is similar to OO-extension in the sense of inheriting the structure and properties of the extended entity. Furthermore, by extending an abstract signature one creates a partition of that signature.

The root path is different from any other path, and this reflects the hierarchy of a file system, where the root is the topmost element. To differentiate the root from the other paths, we introduce it as an extension to *Path*. Fur-

```
one sig Root extends Path
```

```
sig FileNames extends Path {}
```

thermore, the root path is declared to be unique, through signature multiplicity factor *one*. The remaining paths are instances of the *FileNames* signature. Upon root path differentiation, separate properties can be specified for each type of path present in the *dirName* relation, namely:

```
pred ps[] {
  Reflexive[id[Root].dirName,Root]
  Acyclic[id[FileNames].dirName,FileNames]
} .
```

The *path structure* (*ps*) predicate enforces the paths structure constraint, by declaring that: *(a)* *dirName* is reflexive on the root path, ie. root is parent of itself; *(b)* *dirName* is acyclic for all other paths.

To specify the remaining constraint (*files table*) it is necessary to differentiate files by their type. Although we have already intro-

```
sig File {fileType : one FileType}
```

duced file types in the relational specification, we left room for choice on this matter.

```
abstract sig FileType{}
```

```
one sig RegularFile, Directory extends FileType {}
```

One way to make such differentiation explicit is to partition files, as done before concerning paths. However, in this case, it is not necessary to define separate relational properties for each type of file, and therefore, it suffices to use a flag as differentiation mechanism. File types are

```
pred ft[s: System] {
  (s.table).path.(s.fileStore).fileType
    in (FileHandle -> RegularFile)
}
```

```
pred inv_System[s: System] {
  ri[s] and pc[s] and ft[s] and ps[]
}
```

defined as a partition composed of regular files and directories.

The *files table* (*ft*) constraint predicate (above) enforces that only (regular) files can be requested by applications to read and write. (Without prejudice of directories being browsable.) The overall invariant for the system is then defined as a conjunction of the two constrains *referential integrity* (*ri*) and *paths closure* (*pc*) defined in the relational specification, and the above described constraints *files table* (*ft*) and *path structure* (*ps*).

Once the state of the system is defined we proceed to the specification of the operations. Each operation is specified as *n*-ary relation *Op* between an initial system *s* and a final state *s'*, for instance:

```
pred openFile[fh': FileHandle, s',s: System, p: Path] {
  s'.fileStore = s.fileStore
  fh' !in s.table.dom
  (one fd: OpenFileInfo {
      fd !in s.table.ran and fd.path = p
      s'.table = s.table + (fh' -> fd)
  })
} .
```

The operation *openFile* does not affect the file store and produces a new entry in the open-file table. It is guarded by a precondition made of two conjuncts. The first is meant to preserve referential integrity, and the second to preserve the open-file table invariant.

```
pred pre_openFile[s: System, p: Path] {
  p in s.fileStore.dom
  p.(s.fileStore).fileType = RegularFile
}
```

With the Alloy Analyzer it is possible to start verifying this operation straight away, and we do so by first simulating and afterwards verifying. Either because the scope is too narrow, or because a predicate is a contradiction, verifying assertions will always succeed if there is no possible instantiation. To detect these situations, we make sure that the predicate can be instantiated by simulating it. Simulation with Alloy Analyzer can easily reveal problems as the instances of the model are depicted in simple (but expressive) diagrams. We have checked the *openFile* operations for satisfiability, with a scope of 10 elements[2], and found no counterexamples.

The *create* operation creates a new file, of a given type, in the file store.

```
pred create[s',s: System, p: Path, ft: FileType] {
  s'.table = s.table
  one f: File {
    f.fileType = ft
    s'.fileStore = s.fileStore + (p -> f)
  }
}
```

---

[2] In Alloy the state space is limited by the scope. The scope defines how many elements will be used for each top level signature. Top level signatures are those which do not extend other signatures.

The operation is guarded by a precondition again made of two conjuncts. The first prevents from creating files that already exist in the file store. The second is composed of a disjunction of two other sub-clauses. The first of these allows one to create the root directory (note that this is only possible if the file store is empty due to the first clause). The second preserves the paths closure invariant, in case a path other than the root is passed as argument.

```
pred pre_create [s: System , p: Path , ft: FileType] {
  p !in s.fileStore.dom
  ((p = Root and ft = Directory )
   or
   (p.dirName in s.fileStore.dom and
    p.dirName.(s.fileStore).fileType = Directory ))
}
```

After simulation and verification, no counterexamples where found for the *create* operation, also for a scope of 10 elements.

6   From Alloy to VDM++

Model translation to VDM++ involves additional effort and increases the steepness of the learning curve. However, it helps in further refining the specification, while giving access to a comprehensive set of tools.

VDM++ translation is guided by the rules described in [9,8]. The outcome is a sizeable VDM++ model of which we only address an example of where the abstraction level is lowered, in order for the specification to become executable.

The refinement that has greater impact in the model relates to paths. Paths in the Alloy model are so abstract that it suffices to differentiate the root and declare a relation (*dirName*) recording the path-hierarchy. There are two obvious models for paths in VDM++: either as a linear recursive data type, or as a sequence of file names.

The first option would clash with the mapping we chose to use for the file store, because it would introduce inductive reasoning (which we decided to avoid). The second option, which was chosen, allows us to avoid inductive reasoning, but introduces some more constraints. The resulting VDM++ data type that specifies paths is defined as a co-product of root and remaining paths, as in Alloy. The difference resides in the specification of the remaining paths, now sequences of tokens.

```
Path = <Root > | seq1 of token ;

dirName : Path -> Path
dirName (p) ==
  cases p:
    <Root > -> <Root >,
    [-]     -> <Root >,
    others  -> allButLast (p)
  end ;
```

The refinement of paths introduces a new constraint preventing paths, which are sequences, from being empty. The relation that navigates through paths (above) must also be refined according to the changes in the data type, where the alternative pattern [−] matches any singleton sequence.

Recall, from the specification of *openFile*, that the entry to be created in the open-file table should consist of a new file handle and a new file descriptor. In Alloy it was possible to declare that the file handle should not belong to the original table; in VDM++ it is necessary to operationalize this behaviour.

```
open: System * Path -> System * FileHandle
open(s,p) ==
  let newFh  = newFileHandle(dom s.table),
      entry  = { newFh |-> mk_OpenFileInfo(p) },
      table' = s.table munion entry in
  mk_(mu(s, table |-> table'),newFh)
pre p in set dom s.fileStore and
    s.fileStore(p).fileType = <RegularFile>;
```

In the above definition a new file handle is mapped to a new open-file element using the binary operator |->. The initial state is mutated using the *mu* operator, whereby the original *table* field is replaced by the newly created *table'*.

7   From VDM++ to HOL

For each PO arising from the specification, the Overture proof system can yield three different results:

1. the PO evaluates to *true* (discharged) — no inconsistency found;
2. the PO evaluates to *false* — a design inconsistency exists;
3. the PO evaluates to an unproven goal — no conclusion from proof.

In the case of a discharged PO (Item 1) the life cycle is over for this particular PO. If, on the contrary, the PO evaluates to false (Item 2) then it is clear that a flaw exists in the specification and some action must be taken to correct it. At this stage the adequate corrective action depends on the kind of flaw detected. It might be the case that the proof failed because of some error introduced in one of the previous stages, Alloy or VDM++. So the process should go back to the appropriate stage to correct the specification. The last possible outcome (Item 3) might result from a proof that stopped before reaching any of the Boolean values, or from a proof that times out.

Through the Overture proof system the specification was analysed to generate the two satisfiability proof obligations for the specified operations [8]. A HOL theory was automatically translated from the VDM++ specification, and a proof script produced. (Neither the theory nor the proof script are described in this paper, due to space constraints — see [8] for details.) It followed that the proof system was able to mechanically discharge the satisfiability proof for

$$inv \xleftarrow{\quad open \quad} inv \ , \tag{3}$$

but not for

$$inv \xleftarrow{\quad create \quad} inv \ . \tag{4}$$

(We adopt the arrow notation of [33] for satisfiability proof obligations.)

Recall that *inv* is a conjunction of four predicates: *referential integrity, paths closure, files table* and *path structure*. The last is no longer necessary because it is ensured by the *dirName* function once refined to the VDM level. Following the *splitting by conjunction* rule of the PO-calculus of [33, Section 15], (4) splits into:

$$ ri \xleftarrow{\quad create \quad} inv \ , \tag{5} $$

$$ pc \xleftarrow{\quad create \quad} inv \ , \tag{6} $$

$$ ft \xleftarrow{\quad create \quad} inv \ . \tag{7} $$

Sub-goals (5) and (7) were mechanically discharged by the proof system, whereas (6) produced an intermediate goal. Further decomposition applied to (6) branches the proof into: *(a)* the case where the argument path is the root directory; *(b)* the remainder cases. By manipulating the theorems made available to the prover for term rewriting, the two branches of (6) where interactively discharged in HOL.

The success of the proof was due to initially limiting the theorems used by the re-writing procedures. The first attempt to discharge this proof used all available theorems from the specification theory to re-write and simplify the goal. However, this approach lead to an intermediate goal whose semantics could only be perceived by inspecting every proof step to identify all relevant decisions that took place.

By not allowing the prover to use the theorems for *dirName* and *pc* (paths closure invariant), and re-invoking the same proof tactic we obtained branches *(a)* and *(b)*. In this way, goal (6) was split in two sub-goals (one per branch), the theorems for *dirName* and *pc* were made available for the re-writing tactics, and the remaining proof was carried out automatically by the APS.

8   Discussion

This paper presents a formal methods tool-chain that promotes tool interoperability while transforming abstract models through an iterative process of development. The tool-chain disciplines the use of different tools and techniques ranging from simulation, model checking, testing, interpretation and code generation, to mathematical proof of correctness.

For the tool-chain to be applicable in the verification of large and complex models some issues have to be addressed. First of all, not every step in the tool-chain is automated. Although the Overture APS automates the connection between VDM++ and HOL, the one between Alloy and VDM++ is still manual. First steps towards this automation have been taken in [9,8] by defining a set of rules to translate VDM++ data types into Alloy signatures. In the current paper similar rules are applied, however from Alloy to VDM++. We agree that the agility of the tool-chain is compromised until all steps are fully automated. Although code generation was not addressed in the paper, the tool-chain "borrows" this capability from the VDMTools.

Of the tool-chain requirements set up in Section 1, only fully automated proofs are still far from being a reality. These should eventually include those of the refinements implicit in translating from one notation (eg. Alloy) to another (VDM++). It is our intention to experiment with the presented tool-chain to verify the different refinements it promotes. Extending the verification capabilities of the tool-chain to support refinement proofs would indeed increase its usefulness and soundness. Surely, there is much work to be carried out in this respect.

With the file system case study we show how a small model can be fully verified in a multi-stage process. Stage after stage (Figure 1), more confidence is gained on the consistency of the model. Throughout this case study care was taken to independently check small units of models, by constructing the model piece by piece on a tight loop of development and verification. However, when verifying models whose development is out of the verifier control, *slicing* tools [39] are of great value, since they can isolate the smallest sub-model that accommodates some target property, operation or data type. This is another aspect which calls for automation: operation-wise manual slicing carried throughout the project [9,8] proved to be very time-consuming.

Both the languages and principles adopted in devising the tool-chain are generically applicable to software development and verification. We therefore envisage its integration in the Overture platform in the near future. Overture includes a framework for generation of abstract syntax trees (ASTs) for languages modelled in VDM++. This framework is supported by the AST generator (AstGen) tool, which (for example) was used to generate the Overture Modelling Language (OML) AST from a VDM specification. OML AST is the pillar that supports all other Overture tools that manipulate VDM dialects. Both OML AST and surrounding tools can be automatically implemented in Java (or C++) [19]. The Overture proof system stands as an example of such automated implementation. Adding to these features, efforts are currently under way to integrate the complete Overture tool set in the Eclipse platform, where Alloy is already integrated [31]. All these conditions together with the fact that the VDM++ connection to HOL is a component of the Overture tool set, make this the most interesting option to foster the tool-chain put forward in this paper.

9   Related and Future Work

Verifiable file system. Since the VFS mini-challenge was put forward, contributions have been made at different levels, either focusing on verification or refinement [27,15,7]. Reference [27] already contemplates NAND flash memory peculiarities, such as wear levelling, erase unit reclamation, and tolerance to power loss. More recently, new papers [35,20] on file system formalization have become available. Theorem proving is used in [20], which follows a top down approach in formalizing a hierarchical file system. [35] reports on the bottom up verification of the UBIFS implementation for Linux.

Other file system implementations have also been mechanically verified by model checking [17,40]. [40] found several errors in widely used file system implementations that were reported back to the respective developers. [17] analysed a concurrent model of the Linux Virtual File System, which bridges between the Linux kernel and the miscellaneous file system implementations that it supports.

Integration of formal tools. There has been a proliferation of independent languages and tools that support formal specification and verification. However, it is already possible to see the results of the effort made towards integrating these tools in development environments that are more agile and sophisticated. Good examples of such integration are Alloy4Eclipse [31], the Rodin [5] tool for Event-B and the Overture tools for VDM.

Part of the tool-chain presented in the current paper is already implemented in the Overture project, thanks to our work on the APS workflow [10]. Current efforts go into improving interoperability among Overture internal components, the VDMTools and HOL. This will hopefully produce a cross platform proof system, capable of mechanically discharging all VDM-standard POs.

On flash-level refinement. As for current work on the VFS project itself, our implementation (refinement) strategy is based on the following design principle: whatever abstract model one writes for file systems, it can be refined into diagrams of "atomic" (1NF) simple relations using *data transformation by calculation* [32]. Inspired by [35], one just has to consider a further, generic refinement step in moving towards the flash level: that of implementing every simple relation by a 4-tuple made of the relation itself, the corresponding RAM and flash indices and the *journal*. We are currently busy in proving the correctness of this refinement strategy [11].

10   Summary

The research described in this paper is intended to contribute to the GC trend while focusing on tool interoperability as a means to obtain an integrated verification tool-chain taking advantage of the capabilities of each tool in the chain. Furthermore the approach is tool independent, and other tools like SPIN [2] or Perfect Developer [1] could also be integrated.

The integration of formal language tool sets in modern development environments such as Eclipse is today a reality. We propose that communities take an extra step towards interoperability. This can be done through translators based on public ASTs, that can be distributed to developers of other communities as open source code, or binary libraries. However, the soundness of such integration still needs to be demonstrated through refinement proofs.

This paper shows how the principles of abstraction, iterative development and proof decomposition help in overcoming the difficulties implicit in verifying complex operations on states subject to elaborate invariants. Operation can be broken down in sub-operations that are independently verified. Invariants can be factored into sub-invariants. In the case study reported in this paper [8,9], decomposition helped in identifying properties and sub-operations that were preventing the proof system from automatically discharging the proof.

In retrospect, the improvements in verification obtained following our "single-PO, multiple-proof-technology" approach need to be balanced against the fact that the learning curve becomes steeper and steeper as new technologies are added to the system. This can only be avoided via automation and transparent integration.

References

1. Escher Technologies - Products, `http://www.eschertech.com/products`
2. Spin - Formal Verification, `http://spinroot.com`
3. Bird, R., de Moor, O.: Algebra of Programming. Series in Computer Science. Prentice-Hall International, Englewood Cliffs (1997), C.A.R. Hoare, series editor
4. Bjørner, D., Jones, C.B.: The Vienna Development Method: The Meta-Language. LNCS, vol. 61. Springer, Heidelberg (1978)
5. Coleman, J., Jones, C., Oliver, I., Romanovsky, A., Troubitsyna, E.: RODIN (Rigorous open Development Environment for Complex Systems). In: WORDS, pp. 23–26. IEEE Computer Society, Los Alamitos (2005)
6. Intel Corporation. Intel® Flash File System Core Reference Guide. Technical report 304436-001, Intel Corporation (2004)
7. Damchoom, K., Butler, M., Abrial, J.: Modelling and Proof of a Tree-Structured File System in Event-B and Rodin. In: Liu, S., Maibaum, T., Araki, K. (eds.) ICFEM 2008. LNCS, vol. 5256, pp. 25–44. Springer, Heidelberg (2008)
8. Ferreira, M.: Verifying Intel® Flash File System Core. Master's thesis, Minho University (January 2009)
9. Ferreira, M., Silva, S., Oliveira, J.N.: Verifying Intel Flash File System Core Specification. In: Fourth VDM/Overture Workshop (CS-TR-1099) (May 2008)
10. Ferreira, M.A.: Implementing the Overture Automatic Proof System (submitted for publication, 2009)
11. Ferreira, M.A., Oliveira, J.N.: Verifying the (generic) flash memory implementation of abstract mappings (in preparation, 2009)
12. Fitzgerald, J., Larsen, P.G.: Modelling Systems: Practical Tools and Techniques in Software Development. Cambridge University Press, Cambridge (1998)
13. Fitzgerald, J., Larsen, P.G., Mukherjee, P., Plat, N., Verhoef, M.: Validated Designs for Object-oriented Systems. Springer, New York (2005)
14. Fitzgerald, J., Larsen, P.G., Sahara, S.: VDMTools: advances in support for formal modeling in VDM. SIGPLAN Notices 43(2), 3–11 (2008)
15. Freitas, L., Fu, Z., Woodcock, J.: POSIX file store in Z/Eves: an experiment in the verified software repository. In: ICECCS 2007, Washington, DC, USA, pp. 3–14. IEEE Computer Society, Los Alamitos (2007)
16. Freyd, P.J., Ščedrov, A.: Categories, Allegories. Math. Lib., vol. 39. North-Holland, Amsterdam (1990)
17. Galloway, A., Lüttgen, G., Mühlberg, J.T., Siminiceanu, R.: Model-checking the linux virtual file system. In: Jones, N.D., Müller-Olm, M. (eds.) VMCAI 2009. LNCS, vol. 5403, pp. 74–88. Springer, Heidelberg (2009)
18. Gordon, M.: From LCF to HOL: a short history, pp. 169–185. MIT Press, Cambridge (2000)

19. The VDM Tool Group. The VDM++ to Java Code Generator. Technical report, CSK Systems (January 2008)
20. Hesselink, W.H., Lali, M.I.: Formalizing an Hierarchical File System. Submitted to FM 2009 (2009)
21. Hoare, C.A.R.: The verifying compiler: A grand challenge for computing research. J. ACM 50(1), 63–69 (2003)
22. Hoare, T., Misra, J.: Verified Software: Theories, Tools, Experiments Vision of a Grand Challenge Project. In: Meyer, B., Woodcock, J. (eds.) VSTTE 2005. LNCS, vol. 4171, pp. 1–18. Springer, Heidelberg (2008)
23. IEEE and The Open Group. Standard for information technology - POSIX®. Base Definitions, Issue 6. IEEE Std 1003.1-2001. The Open Group Tech. Std. (2004)
24. Jackson, D.: Software Abstractions: Logic, Language, and Analysis. MIT Press, Cambridge (2006)
25. Jones, C.B.: Systematic Software Development Using VDM, 2nd edn. Prentice-Hall International, Englewood Cliffs (1990)
26. Joshi, R., Holzmann, G.J.: A Mini Challenge: Build a Verifiable File system. In: Meyer, B., Woodcock, J. (eds.) VSTTE 2005. LNCS, vol. 4171, pp. 49–56. Springer, Heidelberg (2008)
27. Kang, E., Jackson, D.: Formal Modeling and Analysis of a Flash Filesystem in Alloy. In: Börger, E., Butler, M., Bowen, J.P., Boca, P. (eds.) ABZ 2008. LNCS, vol. 5238, pp. 294–308. Springer, Heidelberg (2008)
28. Larsen, P.G., Batle, N., Fitzgerald, J., Lausdahl, K., Ferreira, M., Verhoef, M.: The Overture Initiative Integrating all VDM tools (in preparation, 2009)
29. Larsen, P.G., Fitzgerald, J.S., Riddle, S.: Practice-oriented courses in formal methods using VDM++. Formal Asp. Comput. 21(3), 245–257 (2009)
30. Larsen, P.G., Lausdahl, K., Batle, N.: Combinatorial Testing for VDM++. Submitted for publication (2009)
31. Leberre, D., Delorme, F.: An eclipse plugin for the alloy4 tool, http://code.google.com/p/alloy4eclipse/
32. Oliveira, J.N.: Transforming Data by Calculation. In: Lämmel, R., Visser, J., Saraiva, J. (eds.) GTTSE 2007. LNCS, vol. 5235, pp. 134–195. Springer, Heidelberg (2008)
33. Oliveira, J.N.: Extended Static Checking by Calculation using the Pointfree Transform. In: Bove, A., et al. (eds.) LerNet ALFA Summer School 2008. LNCS, vol. 5520, pp. 195–251. Springer, Heidelberg (2009)
34. Plat, N., Larsen, P.G.: An overview of the ISO/VDM-SL standard. SIGPLAN Notices 27(8), 76–82 (1992)
35. Schierl, A., Schellhorn, G., Haneberg, D., Reif, W.: Abstract Specification of the UBIFS File System for Flash Memory. Submitted to FM 2009 (2009)
36. Slind, K., Norrish, M.: A Brief Overview of HOL4. In: Mohamed, O.A., Muñoz, C., Tahar, S. (eds.) TPHOLs 2008. LNCS, vol. 5170, pp. 28–32. Springer, Heidelberg (2008)
37. Tarski, A., Givant, S.: A Formalization of Set Theory without Variables. American Math. Soc., vol. 41. AMS Colloq. Pub., Providence (1987)
38. Vermolen, S.: Automatically Discharging VDM Proof Obligations using HOL. Master's thesis, Radboud University, Computer Science Department (2007)
39. Weiser, M.: Program slicing. In: 5th Int. Conf. on Software Eng., San Diego, California (March 1981)
40. Yang, J., Twohey, P., Engler, D.R., Musuvathi, M.: Using model checking to find serious file system errors. ACM Trans. Comput. Syst. 24(4), 393–423 (2006)

Towards Safe Design of Synchronous Bus Protocols in Event-B

Ricardo Bedin França[1], Leandro Buss Becker[1], Jean-Paul Bodeveix[2],
Jean-Marie Farines[1], and Mamoun Filali[2]

[1] Universidade Federal de Santa Catarina
Campus Universitário – Departamento de Automação e Sistemas
88040-970 Florianópolis
[2] Université de Toulouse – IRIT CNRS
118 Route de Narbonne
F-31062 Toulouse – France

Abstract. In this paper[1], we address the problem of developing synchronous bus protocols with Event-B. The interest of using Event-B lies in its parameterized nature, as well as its refinement-based modeling methodology and its formal verification semantics. A synchronous, generic model was created to serve as a basis for synchronous bus protocols with a centralized arbiter. Bus protocols and their properties can then be specified as refinements of the generic model: properties are specified and verified with the Event-B proof semantics, their preservation being enforced in the construction of correct refinements. We use the AMBA bus protocol as an application example of our synchronous model, with emphasis in its arbitration phase and the mutual exclusion property.

Keywords: Event-B, bus protocols, parameterized systems, synchronous systems.

1 Introduction

The increasingly complex modern embedded systems demand powerful design techniques in order to avoid prohibitive costs in the development and maintenance of such systems. In this context, formal methods are being widely employed in the specification and verification of embedded systems: formal specifications enforce early design decisions and may be used in high-level property verification.

A communication bus can be seen as the backbone of an embedded system: the overall communication speed depends on its hardware aspects, such as bandwidth capacity, and also on the communication protocol that describes how it is accessed and shared by its connected devices. Since it affects the system performance in a direct manner, it is important to specify and verify its behavior with sound methods that are able to cope with the parameterized nature of bus specifications.

---

[1] This work was partially funded by CAPES (Coordenação de Aperfeiçoamento de Pessoal de Nível Superior) and TOPCASED (http://www.topcased.org).

In this paper, we use the Event-B method to design synchronous bus protocols, with emphasis in an incremental modeling and a formal, parameterized verification based on theorem proving. The Event-B refinement-based approach is used to devise a generic model for synchronous bus protocols with a centralized arbiter; the protocols are then specified as refinements of this generic model.

The paper is structured as follows: Section 2 depicts the most important aspects of bus protocols in the scope of this paper, Section 3 presents the B and Event-B methods, Section 4 presents our generic synchronous bus model and how it is used to specify and verify an actual protocol and Section 5 discusses the results of our work and similar ones. The final remarks of this paper are presented in Section 6.

2   Basic Bus Concepts

A bus is, basically, a transmission medium that connects the devices which share it. This connection is made by a certain number of 'lines' that may transmit data, control, or both, and are accessible by all the connected devices. Since the bus is, by definition, a shared resource, there must be an access control in order to avoid data overwriting or inconsistencies; usually, one of the devices – a bus arbiter – manages the use of the bus by the other devices, which shall be referred in this paper as the bus controllers.

Stallings [17] classifies buses according to their type (dedicated or multiplexed lines), method of arbitration (a centralized or distributed arbitration) and timing (synchronous or asynchronous), as well as the quantity of available lines and data transfer types.

The behavior of a bus is defined by the control flow among it, its arbiter and the controllers. Among the main control lines seen in common buses, there are those who deal with bus access requests, I/O and interruption commands, and transfer acknowledgments. The data transmissions across the bus are achieved by two stages: firstly there is an arbitration period, where the bus controller shall decide what component will be able to use the bus and thus become a transfer 'master', and a transfer period, where the master sends or receives data from a slave.

In this work, we shall deal with synchronous bus protocols with only one device (the arbiter) being responsible for the arbitration process. In a synchronous protocol, the bus lines are read every clock cycle, before any line is updated by a controller or the arbiter. The bus controllers and the arbiter send data and control through the communication lines in any order – all devices update their outputs before the next clock cycle. Hence, the synchronous data read ensures a synchronous protocol even if the whole protocol behavior is not completely deterministic.

2.1   The AMBA Protocol

The *Advanced Microcontroller Bus Architecture* (AMBA [2]) protocol was developed in 1995 by ARM[2]. Initially used in the ARM processors, it has been

---

[2] http ://www.arm.com/

widely employed in systems-on-a-chip (SoCs). The AMBA specifications presented in this work are based in the version 2 of this protocol. According to the classification seen in [17], this protocol has synchronous timing, centralized arbitration, dedicated lines, 32-bit data bus width and several transfer types. The AMBA may be implemented as a standard system bus (ASB), high-performance system bus (AHB, used in this work) or peripheral communication bus (APB). The most important bus lines in the scope of this work are:

HBUSREQ. Control lines that are used to send access requests from the controllers to the arbiter. The bus has one *HBUSREQ* line for each controller – we assume that all controllers are able to become masters.

HGRANT. Control lines used by the arbiter to grant bus access to a controller. There is one *HGRANT* line for each controller.

HMASTER. Control line used by the arbiter to display the current bus master.

HTRANS. Two control lines used by the master to specify the current transfer type.

HADDR. 32 address lines used by the master to specify the slave address.

HWDATA. 32 data lines used in write operations.

HRDATA. 32 data lines used in read operations.

HREADY. Control line set by the slave when it is ready to write or read data.

CLK. The system clock line.

The arbitration in the AMBA protocol is "hidden", therefore, no clock cycles are wasted in a master change: in a single cycle the *HGRANT* line of the current master is reset and the *HGRANT* line of another one is set. While some transfer types have a fixed length in clock cycles, others can last until the *HBUSREQ* signal of the master reset. In the end of a transfer, the arbiter passes bus control to a controller which has set its *HBUSREQ* line in order to require bus access. If there is no controller waiting to carry out a transfer, control is given to a "default master". In such cases, the default master sets the *HTRANS* lines with a special value to show that no transfer is taking place.

One period after setting a *HGRANT* line, the arbiter puts the master address in *HMASTER* line and the master puts the slave address in the HADDR line. In the following clock cycles, the master puts data in the *HWDATA* lines and the slave puts data in the *HRDATA* ones. Since the arbiter changes masters in the last clock cycle of a transfer in order not to waste cycles, the current master must reset its *HBUSREQ* line in the next-to-last cycle if the transfer has no fixed length. Figure 1 shows the behavior of the *HBUSREQ* and *HGRANT* lines in a typical arbitration timeline.

2.2   Issues with Synchronous Bus Protocols

In order to have proper synchronous specifications and meaningful results with formal verification, their synchronous, parameterized nature must be taken into account. The design approaches that use model checking to verify system specifications are not the most suitable for our objectives: the general case of parameterized temporal verification was proven undecidable in [3], because of the

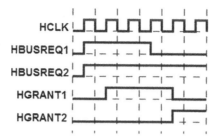

Fig. 1. Simplified arbitration in the AMBA protocol

infinite state space generated by a parameterization. In some cases, such as ring topologies, the problem of parameterized verification can be solved with the use of model checking, as shown by Emerson and Namjoshi [9]: They proved that a parameterized verification in a ring may be obtained by a normal model-checking on a small instance of the parameterized ring. However, such proofs are not trivial and non-ring topologies would require other proofs.

One alternative to the verification with model checking is the theorem proving approach. Its main drawback is the user interaction that is often required to finish the proofs, but the set representation of data structures can be seen as a natural system parametrization. As parameterized verification is a main issue of this work, this approach is the one used in our work. The bus protocols are specified and verified with Event-B, a refinement-oriented method that uses invariant and theorem proving to validate its specifications.

3 The B Method

The B Method is a formal, refinement-based, method for designing discrete systems. It "essentially deals with the central aspects of the software life cycle, namely: the design by successive refinement steps, the layered architecture, and the executable code generation" [1].

This method uses set theory as its notation, thus variables are either sets or elements of a set. This notation enables the design of parameterized systems, since the sets do not need to be enumerated to be used.

The basis of a B specification is the *machine*. A machine specification describes a system module with its static and dynamic characteristics. The static part is given mainly by variables, which denote the system state, and invariants - first-order logic predicates that describe constraints over the state. The dynamic part of a machine is given by its operations: variable substitutions guarded by pre-conditions.

The specification is then validated by means of proof obligations: assuming that all invariants hold before an operation, they must be proven to hold after the operation, too. B Method tools usually include automatic theorem provers to help in this validation.

A most useful feature in the B Method is the notion of refinement. When a machine is refined, its proven invariants are kept in its lower-level specifications, thus ensuring the validity of high-level properties. In the new machine, new events can be created and the old ones can be refined. New variables can also be created and abstract variables can be replaced by concrete ones, their mapping being described with a *gluing invariant*. Besides the gluing invariant, the mapping of variables relies on *witness* declared inside events: a witness maps an abstract variable to a concrete one in an event refinement. A witness must respect the gluing invariant, correct witnesses underline the mapping between abstract and concrete guards and actions.

3.1   Event-B

Event-B [13] is a variation of the B Method, that focuses less in low-level aspects such as software behavior and code generation. In Event-B, operations are replaced by events (which are simpler and represent reactive behaviors very well) and sets, constants and axioms are declared inside *contexts*. Each machine can "see" one or more contexts. Figure 2 shows a typical context declaration.

Events have a "any...where...then" basic form, with instantiated variables in the *any* clause, the guard predicates in the *where* clause and the actions (substitutions) in the *then* part. Figure 4 shows events where the *any* or both *any* and *where* clauses are not used.

In this work, the Event-B specifications were verified with the Rodin[3] tool. The proof obligations can be satisfied either with the available automatic provers or interactively, with direct interference from the user.

4   Synchronous Bus Protocols in Event-B

4.1   The Synchronization Model

As the Event-B method has the notion of refinement, it is clear that the bus protocols should be designed in several steps, instead of specifying them monolithically. Thus, each refinement may represent a different abstraction layer of a protocol, making the specifications easier to understand.

Modeling a synchronous bus protocol in Event-B is not completely straightforward: the controller and arbiter actions are specified with events, but such events are not simultaneous, while the controller actions in actual buses are seen as simultaneous. Since all synchronous protocols must have this modeling problem solved, it is useful to have a generic, synchronous model that can be used as a basis for synchronous protocols. Each protocol may then be specified as a refinement of this basis, using events to describe its actions, and avoiding any problems related to the synchronization of actions. Such a model has much in common with the emerging concept of patterns in Event-B [4,12,7], in the sense that Event-B variables and events are reused in several specifications, but our model is refined in protocol specifications, while patterns are usually seen as snippets of code embedded in a B specification.

---

[3] http://www.event-b.org/platform.html

CONTEXT synchronous_c
SETS   *CONTROLLERS*
  CTR_STATES
END

Fig. 2. The basic context

VARIABLES
  finishedArb
  globalstateCtr
  preglobalstateCtr
  busbusy
  prebusbusy
INVARIANTS
  typinv_fa : *finishedArb* ∈ *BOOL*
  typinv_gstate : *globalstateCtr* ∈ *CONTROLLERS* ↠ *CTR_STATES*
  typinv_pgstate : *preglobalstateCtr* ∈ *CONTROLLERS* → *C̄TR_STATES*
  typinv_busbusy : *busbusy* ∈ *BOOL*
  typinv_prebusbusy : *prebusbusy* ∈ *BOOL*

Fig. 3. Abstract specification variables and type invariants

The model comprises a context (*synchronous_c*) and two machines (*synchronous* and *ctr_async*). We decided to use two machines for methodological reasons: *synchronous* depicts the system in a fully synchronous view, while *ctr_async* "desynchronizes" the controllers.

The context *synchronous_c* contains two nonempty[4] sets, shown in Figure 2 – the carrier set *CONTROLLERS* for the controllers and the enumerated set *CTR_STATES* for the controller abstract states. This structure could be modified in order not to have abstract state variables, however, in the Event-B refinement-based approach, it makes sense to start modeling a protocol with high-level state machines before specifying the concrete variables: abstract variables are often useful to prove high-level properties and such properties are preserved in the concrete variables by means of correct gluing invariants. As different protocols might have different states, the basic model does not define the elements of the *CTR_STATES* set.

In the machine *synchronous*, we have a fully synchronous view of the system. The most abstract variables of the synchronization model are seen in Figure 3. We need two flags to show that every controller has acted in the period (we assume that controllers do act every clock cycle) and the arbiter has also taken a decision; these flags are the *globalstateCtr* and *finishedArb* variables. Also, the *globalstateCtr* variable stores the state of each controller, and *busbusy* shows the bus internal state. We also create "pre" variables to store past values of the state variables. Only type invariants are shown here, as system properties shall be given within actual protocol descriptions.

The desired behavior of the controllers and the arbiter, as well as the clock mechanism, is represented by the four events of Figure 4: one mandatory initialization event, one for the synchronous system clock, one that triggers an arbiter

---

[4] In B, abstract sets are considered as finite and nonempty.

action in a given period, and another that comprises the actions of all controllers in a period.

The bus state variable *busbusy* and its "pre" counterpart, as well as *preglobalstateCtr*, are initialized nondeterministically, since at this level the controller state set is abstract and the arbiter state is not important. The initialization of *globalstateCtr* with the empty set means that the controller states for the current period are not yet defined – as it will be shown, this enables the controller actions event and disables the clock event.

The *next_step* event represents a clock step, saving the current state variable values in their "pre" variables and resetting other variables. It may be triggered only if the arbiter and the controllers have taken their actions in the current period: this guard represents the assumption that every controller manages to operate its bus lines before the end of the current period. As it updates all the state variables simultaneously, it is the key to the system synchronization.

A generic arbiter action is given by the *generic_arbiter_action* event, it states that if the arbiter did not act in the current cycle, it may take an action, seen in the *action_taken* clause. This action must be refined lately, as it is nondeterministic in order to keep the model as generic as possible. The *controllers_sync* event depicts a simultaneous action by all the controllers – in the highest abstraction level, one should have a synchronous view of the controllers.

The machine *ctr_async* refines the machine *synchronous* and goes further in representing the controller actions. It uses the same context as *synchronous*, and adds a new variable and a new event to underline the real, independent way each controller or group of controllers act. The declarations added in this

EVENTS
INITIALISATION BEGIN
  $ini\_pbusbusy : prebusbusy :\in BOOL$
  $ini\_busbusy : busbusy :\in BOOL$
  $ini\_pgstate : preglobalstateCtr :\in CONTROLLERS \rightarrow CTR\_STATES$
  $ini\_gstate : globalstateCtr := \varnothing$ /∗ the set of pairs defining the partial function is empty ∗/
  $ini\_fa : finishedArb := FALSE$
  END
EVENT next_step   WHEN
  $arb\_done : finishedArb = TRUE$
  $ctr\_sync : globalstateCtr \in CONTROLLERS \rightarrow CTR\_STATES$
  THEN
  $update\_states : preglobalstateCtr := globalstateCtr$
  $update\_arb : prebusbusy := busbusy$
  $reset\_gstate : globalstateCtr := \varnothing$
  $reset\_fa : finishedArb := FALSE$
  END
EVENT generic_arbiter_action   WHEN
  $arb\_rdy : finishedArb = FALSE$
  THEN
  $arb\_done : finishedArb := TRUE$
  $action\_taken : busbusy :\in BOOL$
  END
EVENT controllers_sync   WHEN
  $not\_sync : globalstateCtr = \varnothing$
  THEN
  $ctr\_sync : globalstateCtr :\in CONTROLLERS \rightarrow CTR\_STATES$
  END

Fig. 4. Basic events of the machine *synchronous*

VARIABLES
  $stateCtr$
INVARIANTS
  $typinv\_stateCtr : stateCtr \in CONTROLLERS \nrightarrow CTR\_STATES$

EVENTS
INITIALISATION BEGIN
  $ini\_state : stateCtr := \varnothing$
  END
EVENT generic_controller_action
  ANY
  C, ns
  WHERE
  $some\_ctrls : C \in \mathbb{P}(CONTROLLERS)$
  $didnt\_act : C \cap dom(stateCtr) = \varnothing$
  $new\_states : ns \in C \rightarrow CTR\_STATES$
  THEN
  $statechange : stateCtr := stateCtr \cup ns$
  END
EVENT next_step   REFINES next_step
  THEN
  $reset\_state : stateCtr := \varnothing$
  END
EVENT controllers_sync   REFINES controllers_sync
  WHEN
  $not\_sync : globalstateCtr = \varnothing$
  $ctr\_done : stateCtr \in CONTROLLERS \rightarrow CTR\_STATES$
  THEN
  $ctr\_sync : globalstateCtr := stateCtr$
  END

Fig. 5. Added features in the machine ctr_async

machine are depicted in Figure 5 – the clauses of Figures 3 and 4 are preserved but they were omitted due to space restrictions. The new variable $stateCtr$ has the same type of $globalstateCtr$ and is also initialized with the empty set, but it can be modified in several steps, instead of a single step like in the global variable.

The $generic\_controller\_action$ event describes generic actions taken by a group of controllers that have not yet taken an action in the current period. The $next\_step$ event has an extra action to reset the new variable, and the $controllers\_sync$ event has an extra guard to ensure that the synchronization happens only after the actions of all controllers.

This model can be used regardless of the system topology, assuming that all the values can be read and written in time. If the generic controller and arbiter events are correctly refined, each controller will trigger one of the refined events in any order, the arbiter will also trigger one event, and the synchronizing events ($controllers\_sync$ and $next\_step$) will ensure that the same values are read by all the controllers and the arbiter. As this behavior is expected in synchronous protocols, the model can be used to specify any synchronous protocol with a centralized arbiter.

4.2   Applying the Synchronization Model: The AMBA Protocol

In order to show how our model can be used in an actual protocol specification, we specified a simplified version of the AMBA protocol as a refinement of the synchronization model. We use three levels of abstraction: level 0 models the protocol states and its desired protocol property (mutual exclusion), level 1 gives an abstract view of the protocol (with its abstract transitions) and level 2 refines the arbitration phase in order to represent the concrete bus arbitration variables. We keep the transfer phase at an abstract level, since an actual AMBA transfer is very detailed and we did not intend to verify any properties at a concrete level.

All Event-B components of this AMBA specification have the *amba_* prefix, followed by a letter (*c* for a context, *m* for a machine) and a number to indicate its level.

Level 0 - A High-Level Invariant. The most abstract machine in the Event-B specification contains only the necessary elements to state the basic property we wanted to verify at this level – the bus data lines being used by at most one controller. Taking into account only the arbitration phase, we have three states: *idle*, *request* and *master* – at this level, we do not need to model slave controllers. These states are represented in the automaton of Figure 6.

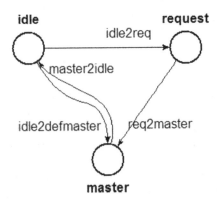

Fig. 6. Abstract controller behavior for the AMBA protocol

We make use once again of the refinements to model the abstract states at level 0. As the transitions are not essential to create the invariant that will state the mutual exclusion property, they will be specified in the next level. The context *amba_c0*, created to specify the controller states, is seen in Figure 7.

In order to express the property, new variables had to be created in the specification presented in the previous section. The variable *owner* contains the controller which has the permission to use the bus data lines. As other state variables, it also has a "pre" counterpart to store its past value.

The basic invariant to express the mutual exclusion property is seen with the new variables in Figure 8: The set of controllers which are in the *master* state must be included in the singleton *preowner*. It must be noted that the "pre" value is used because it represents the value seen in the clock cycle – in the actual protocol, the arbiter and controllers have access only to past values

CONTEXT amba_c0 **REFINES** synchronous_c
CONSTANTS $idle, request, master$
AXIOMS $axm1 : CTR\_STATES = \{idle, request, master\}$
  $axm2 : idle \neq request$
  $axm3 : idle \neq master$
  $axm5 : request \neq master$

END

Fig. 7. The $amba\_c0$ context

VARIABLES
  $owner, preowner$
INVARIANTS
  $typinv\_owner : owner \in CONTROLLERS$
  $typinv\_preowner : preowner \in CONTROLLERS$
  $singlemaster : stateCtr^{-1}[\{master\}] \subseteq \{preowner\}$

Fig. 8. Variables and invariants to express the level 0 basic property

EVENT generic_controller_action **REFINES** generic_controller_action   **ANY**
  C, ns
  WHERE
  $some\_ctrls : C \in \mathbb{P}(CONTROLLERS)$
  $didnt\_act : C \cap dom(stateCtr) = \varnothing$
  $new\_states : ns \in C \rightarrow CTR\_STATES$
  $correct\_master : ns^{-1}[\{master\}] \subseteq \{preowner\}$
  THEN
  $statechange : stateCtr := stateCtr \cup ns$
  END

Fig. 9. The controller event with a guard to ensure the invariant

of other components. The "pre" values shall be used in property verification whenever the properties are synchronous – we say a property is synchronous if it must be checked over the synchronized variable values.

As the invariant *singlemaster* must be respected, one must specify events carefully. Since the event *generic_controller_action* changes the values of the variable *stateCtr*, it must be proved that it will never assign the "master" value to a controller that is not the bus owner of the last period. A new guard (*correct_master*) was created in the generic controller event, as Figure 9 shows. This guard ensures that if a subset of controllers will go to the "master" state, this subset shall be a subset of *{preowner}*, as required by the invariant. Thus, every correct refinement of this generic event will have to refine this generic guard and the property will be preserved at more concrete levels.

Level 1 - An Abstract Event-B View of the AMBA Protocol. Together with the synchronization model, level 0 presented the synchronization process of the bus controllers, as well as the mutual exclusion invariant. At level 2, it was intended to present the most elementary interactions of the protocol. These interactions model the arbitration phase of the protocol, when the controllers try to receive bus access. This level was specified with an Event-B machine (*amba_m1*) which refines the abstract synchronous model. No new invariants were created, as there are no new variables and the invariant was already created and proven in Level 0.

The generic controller event is now decomposed into four new events which specify the state changes seen in Figure 6: idle to request, request to master, idle to master (in the case of a default master) and master to idle. Figure 10 shows the event *req2master*, which changes the state of a controller from "request" to "master": at levels 1 and 2, a controller event changes the state of only one controller. The *witness* shows the relations between the abstract set C and the refined variable c, as well as the set of new states to the state of the single controller which is involved in the refined event. The guard *is_req* ensures that this state transition will happen only with a controller that was waiting for bus control, as the event *req2master* is a transition from the "request" to the "master" state. The guard *is_owner* refines the guard *correct_master* seen in level 0: the event can be triggered only for a controller which was the bus owner in the last period.

EVENT req2master **REFINES** generic_controller_action
  ANY c
  WHERE
    $a\_ctrl : c \in CONTROLLERS$
    $didnt\_act : c \notin dom(stateCtr)$
    $is\_req : preglobalstateCtr(c) = request$
    $is\_owner : prebusbusy = TRUE \land preowner = c$
  WITNESSES $C = \{c\} \land ns = \{c \mapsto master\}$
  THEN
    $going\_master : stateCtr := stateCtr \lhd \{c \mapsto master\}$
  END

Fig. 10. A controller event from level 1

The arbiter generic event is refined into three main events: one that represents an idle bus granting access to a controller, another for owner changes, and another one for the busy to idle transition. These events show the concept of "hidden arbitration" seen in AMBA, since no clock cycles are wasted due to arbitration. As the arbitration specification is still abstract, the "master" controller has its access removed nondeterministically.

In addition to these events, there are two "default" events, one for the arbiter and one for the controllers, which are triggered in situations where their states shall not be changed. The clock cycle event is refined in order to update the variables created in this level.

At this level, the default master will be chosen randomly. In case of an idle bus, the default master will have the same "master" state as a normal master, however, the *busbusy* variable will store the false value to state that no transfer is taking place.

Level 2 - Introducing AMBA Arbitration Lines. The Level 2 specification presents the arbitration phase in a more concrete way, using the *HMASTER*, *HBUSREQ* and *HGRANT* lines (as well as their *pre* values) which are seen in the AMBA buses. The presence of these lines permits a further refinement of the arbitration events which change the bus owner – now the bus access can be removed when the current master turns off its *HBUSREQ* line. This level contains a context (*amba_c2*) and a machine (*amba_m2*). The context contains only the declaration of a default master: a constant called *DefCtr* which is one of the controllers. The machine *amba_m2* contains the new variables and the necessary mapping between them and their abstract counterparts, as well as invariant and event refinements.

As we shall deal with actual AMBA arbitration lines, the abstract arbitration variables *owner* and *preowner* are no longer necessary. Hence, these two variables are excluded from the *amba_m2* machine, but a gluing invariant is necessary to specify how the mapping between abstract and concrete variables works.

MACHINE amba_m2 **REFINES** amba_m1 **SEES** amba_c1
VARIABLES

...
HGRANT
preHGRANT
prepreHGRANT
preprebusbusy
HMASTER
preHMASTER
INVARIANTS

...
$inv1 : HGRANT \in CONTROLLERS \rightarrow BOOL$
$inv2 : HGRANT = (CONTROLLERS \times \{FALSE\}) \Leftleftarrows \{owner \mapsto TRUE\}$
$inv3 : preHGRANT \in CONTROLLERS \rightarrow BOOL$
$inv4 : preHGRANT = (CONTROLLERS \times \{FALSE\}) \Leftleftarrows \{preowner \mapsto TRUE\}$

Fig. 11. Gluing invariants in the AMBA arbitration refinement

Since the AMBA protocol always has a master, the value of the *owner* abstract variable will always be the same as the controller which has the true value in the concrete *HGRANT* variable. Therefore, there is a gluing invariant that links the concrete variable to its abstract counterpart. The conjunction of invariants *inv2* and *inv4* of Figure 11 are the gluing invariant: the *HGRANT* variable maps all controllers to the false value, except for the owner. A similar correspondence is made to the *preHGRANT* variable. Among the new variables of this level, there are two with the *prepre* prefix. These variables are inspired by synchronous languages, where the memory used to store past values of a given variable depends on the quantity of nested *pre* operators. In our case, the *HMASTER* variable calculates its value in period n with values from the period (n-2), thus we need "pre" and "prepre".

The initialization event must have *witnesses* which state the mapping between abstract and concrete variable initializations, when the abstract variables have a non-deterministic initialization and the concrete ones are initialized with concrete values. As it can be seen in Figure 12, the initialization specification starts with mappings for the *owner'* and *preowner'* variables. The *DefCtr* value is now assigned to the *HMASTER* variable and its *HGRANT* line is initialized as true, placing the default master as the bus owner in its initialization.

EVENTS

INITIALISATION

WITNESSES
$owner' : owner' = DefCtr$
$preowner' : preowner' = DefCtr$
$ini\_fa : finishedArb := FALSE$
BEGIN
$ini\_state : stateCtr := \varnothing$
$ini\_busbusy : busbusy := FALSE$
$ini\_HGRANT : HGRANT := (CONTROLLERS \times \{FALSE\}) \Leftarrow \{DefCtr \mapsto TRUE\}$
$act2 : globalstateCtr := \varnothing$
$act4 : HMASTER := DefCtr$
...
END

Fig. 12. Initialization in the AMBA arbitration refinement

The other events of *amba_m2* are refined by means of the inclusion of concrete variables where abstract variables were used, validating these changes with the verification of the gluing invariant. Also, a new event is created to specify the behavior of the *HMASTER* variable.

5   Discussion and Related Work

5.1   Synchronous Protocol Modeling in Event-B

The specification of a synchronous bus protocol in an asynchronous environment such as the one seen in Event-B is not a trivial task, however, the synchronous structure presented here makes it possible to reason about synchronous invariants (such as the mutual exclusion property, which involves the whole set of controllers) without changing the controllers individual reasoning – events that modify one controller at a time. The same generic model was used to specify the PCI Protocol, its specifications and the complete code of the AMBA specification presented here are available in [11].

It is important to note that this generic model can be used outside our intended domain with minor changes: it can be used in synchronous bus protocols with distributed arbitration if the arbiter variables and its event are removed. Also, the *next_step* event can be used as a pattern in synchronous specifications, storing past system states and resetting system flags and the current state.

Synchronous languages may be seen as natural tools for designing synchronous bus protocols. Indeed, the Esterel language was used by Berry *et al* [5] in the modeling and verification of a system which uses the CoreConnect bus. However, system modeling with such languages does not solve the parameterization issues described in section 2.

The Event-B method was already used in previous works with bus protocols. Cansell *et al* [6] used Event-B to prove the consumer-producer property in the PCI protocol. In their work, the protocol synchronization issues were not dealt with: their main concern were the complex proof obligations that could arise, thus an incremental modeling was important to reduce the proving efforts during the verification phase. Zimmermann [18] used a bus protocol as a case study to illustrate his circuit development methodology, which involves formal modeling and verification with Event-B and generation of VHDL code. As neither of these works was concerned with synchronous bus protocols, our synchronization model for bus protocols is the main contribution of our work.

5.2 Protocol Verification Issues

The use of Event-B ensured a parameterized verification of our specifications, fulfilling a main concern of this paper. As the necessary proof obligations of these specifications are fairly simple, the Rodin automatic theorem prover was able to cope with most proofs. As it can be seen in table 1, there are indeed some manual proof obligations, but in such cases it was sufficient to change the automatic theorem prover inside Rodin.

Table 1. Proof obligations of all machines

Specification	Automatic POs	Manual POs
synchronous	8	0
ctr_async	4	0
amba_m0	5	1
amba_m1	14	13
amba_m2	37	23
Sum	68	37

In such cases where there are not too many complex proofs, and if parameterization is more prioritary than automation, it is interesting to use the B and Event-B methods instead of approaches that use model checking. On the other hand, if the maximum number of controllers connected in a bus is known beforehand (e.g. if one wants to design a bus protocol for a bounded number of controllers), the user's interactions seen in Event-B may be a major disadvantage, while model checking works well in finite-state systems (with a reasonable size).

There is a number of bus-related works that use model checking for system validation. Clarke et al [8] use the PCI protocol as an example for their modeling methodology that employs Abstract Binary Decision Diagrams to create efficient system specifications for model checking. Their technique enables state space reduction, but does not cope with the infinite state space generated by parameterized systems. The PCI protocol is also used by Shimizu et al [16] in a monitor-based specification for model checking. The use of monitors is aimed to ease system modeling, but once again the parameterized verification problem is not dealt with. Oumalou et al [14] also use the PCI protocol in a design strategy that involves UML in a high-level modeling, Abstract State Machines for verification with model-checking, and a SystemC-based implementation. This methodology helps in the formal verification of SystemC implementations but once again the protocol is not verified in a parameterized fashion. A bus-specific language was created by Pal *et al* [15] for modeling and verification with model checking. It has features that enable hierarchical and parameterized modeling, however, the property verification with model checking requires concrete system instances. In [10], TLA+ was used for PCI bus modeling purposes, however, at that time TLA+ did not offer a proof manager to assist system verification.

6   Conclusion

In this paper, we have presented an approach for modeling and verification of synchronous bus protocols. As refinement-based modeling and parameterized verification were our top priorities, the Event-B method was chosen to carry out both modeling and verification.

The main contribution of this work is a reusable, generic synchronous structure created to specify synchronous bus protocols. This structure eases the abstract specification of protocols with events that describe independently the behavior of controllers and the bus arbiter. The necessary verifications in our example (the AMBA protocol) were carried out by means of refinement and invariant verification. In spite of the interactive nature of this verification, no considerable user interference was necessary. With the use of our synchronous Event-B model, it is possible to put together synchronization (even if the environment is asynchronous), parameterization and incremental design.

Possible future works include the application of our structure in the development of protocols to an implementation level, as well as further investigation about other bus-related properties and their representation in Event-B.

References

1. Abrial, J.-R.: The B Book: Assigning Programs to Meanings. Cambridge University Press, Cambridge (1996)
2. AMBA Specification (Rev. 2). ARM Limited (1999)
3. Apt, K., Kozen, D.: Limits for automatic verification of finite-state concurrent systems. Inf. Process. Lett. 22(6), 307–309 (1986)
4. Ball, E., Butler, M.: Event-B patterns for specifying fault-tolerance in multi-agent interaction. In: Workshop on Methods, Models and Tools for Fault Tolerance, Oxford, pp. 4–13 (2007)
5. Berry, G., Kishinevsky, M., Singh, S.: System Level Design and Verification Using a Synchronous Language. In: ICCAD 2003: Proceedings of the 2003 IEEE/ACM international conference on Computer-aided design, San Jose, p. 433 (2003)
6. Cansell, D., Gopalakrishnan, G., Jones, M., Méry, D., Weinzoepflen, A.: Incremental proof of the producer/consumer property for the PCI Protocol. In: Bert, D., P. Bowen, J., C. Henson, M., Robinson, K. (eds.) B 2002 and ZB 2002. LNCS, vol. 2272, pp. 22–41. Springer, Heidelberg (2002)
7. Cansell, D., Méry, D., Rehm, J.: Time constraint patterns for event B development. In: Julliand, J., Kouchnarenko, O. (eds.) B 2007. LNCS, vol. 4355, pp. 140–154. Springer, Heidelberg (2006)

8. Clarke, E., Jha, S., Lu, Y., Wang, D.: Abstract BDDs: A technique for using abstraction in model checking. In: Pierre, L., Kropf, T. (eds.) CHARME 1999. LNCS, vol. 1703, pp. 172–187. Springer, Heidelberg (1999)
9. Emerson, E., Namjoshi, K.: Reasoning about rings. In: POPL 1995: Proceedings of the 22nd ACM SIGPLAN-SIGACT, pp. 85–94. ACM, New York (1995)
10. França, R.B., Farines, J.-M., Bodeveix, J.-P., Becker, L.B., Filali, M.: Modeling a Bus Protocol: an Incremental Approach. In: 9th WTR. Belém (2007)
11. França, R.B.: An Approach for Modeling and Verification of Synchronous Bus Protocols (Uma Abordagem para Modelagem e Verificação de Protocolos Síncronos de Barramentos de Comunicação). Master's dissertation, SAID/Université de Toulouse (2008), UFSC, Florianópolis (2009),
www.tede.ufsc.br/teses/PEAS0008-D.pdf
12. Lliasov, A.: Refinement patterns for rapid development of dependable systems. In: Workshop on Engineering Fault Tolerant Systems, article no. 10. ACM, Dubrovnik (2007)
13. Metayer, C., Abrial, J.-R., Voisin, L.: Rodin Deliverable D7: Event B language. Project IST-511599, School of Computing Science, University of Newcastle (2005)
14. Oumalou, K., Habibi, A., Tahar, S.: Design for Verification of a PCI Bus in System C. In: Proceedings of the 2004 International Symposium on System-on-Chip (SOC 2004), pp. 201–204. IEEE, Tampere (2004)
15. Pal, B., Banerjee, A., Dasgupta, P., Chakrabarti, P.: The BUSpec Platform for Automated Generation of Verification Aids for Standard Bus Protocols. In: MEM-OCODE 2004, San Diego, pp. 119–128 (2004)
16. Shimizu, K., Dill, D., Hu, A.: Monitor-based formal specification of PCI. In: Johnson, S.D., Hunt Jr., W.A. (eds.) FMCAD 2000. LNCS, vol. 1954, pp. 335–353. Springer, Heidelberg (2000)
17. Stallings, W.: Computer Organization and Architecture - Designing for Performance. Prentice Hall, Englewood Cliffs (1994)
18. Zimmermann, Y.: Développement formel de circuits électroniques par la méthode B. In: Approches Formelles dans l'Assistance au Développement de Logiciels, pp. 181–198. ACM, Namur (2007)

Mechanising Data-Types for Kernel Design in Z

Leo Freitas

Department of Computer Science
University of York, UK
leo@cs.york.ac.uk

Abstract. We present results from the mechanisation of a priority queue and its operations. Our interest comes from its use in the specification and refinement of a scheduler for OS kernels for embedded real-time devices. It is part of a pilot project within the international Grand Challenge in Verified Software. Our work uncovers important hidden and missing properties, and their relation to kernel design.

1   Introduction

Formal methods for software development allow the construction of an accurate characterisation of a problem domain that is firmly based on mathematics; by applying standard mathematical analyses, these methods can be used to prove the correctness of systems. The survey presented in [25] describes over 60 industrial projects, and discusses the effect formal methods have on time, cost, and quality. It shows that with tools backed by mature theory, formal methods are becoming cost effective, and their use is easier to justify, not as an academic or legal requirement, but as part of a business case. These recent advances in theory and tool support have inspired industrial and academic researchers to join up in an international Grand Challenge (GC) in Verified Software [12,23]. Work has started with the creation of a Verified Software Repository (VSR) with two principal aims: (i) the construction of verified software components; and (ii) industrial-scale verification experiments to drive future research in the development of theory and tool support [2].

This paper is an experiment undertaken as part of a pilot project on verifying operating system (OS) kernels within the GC. It explores the mechanisation of proofs of correctness of the formal specification and design of several operating systems kernels for real-time embedded systems constructed by Craig [5]. In particular, we focus in this paper on the underlying basic data structures used by the various kernel components [10]. This is not to be confused with another pilot project: the mechanisation of FreeRTOS [6], the real-time operating system. One key difference in Craig's kernel is the use of refinement from an abstract specification down to code. We have already mechanised the abstract parts of the scheduler, which is being prepared for publication [26]. Our contribution in this paper is in the mechanisation of a priority queue data type used to used to account for the known kernel's processes, and their scheduling policy.

M.V.M. Oliveira and J. Woodcock (Eds.): SBMF 2009, LNCS 5902, pp. 186–203, 2009.

Since these models are all in the Z notation [20], it naturally follows that we use a Z tool, and for us that is the Z/Eves theorem prover (v. 2.4) [19,18]. The choice is based on its ease of use, long previous experience and, most importantly for involving students, its gentle learning curve. We had many successful cases with MSc. students. The next section briefly set the scene, and Sections 3 and 4 present the mechanised abstract data types used in the kernel scheduler design, together with a collection of interesting properties. After that, in Section 5, we discuss some of the most important lessons learned through this experiment. Finally, in Section 6 we present some conclusions.

Related work. In 2006, the first VSR pilot project was undertaken on the verification of the Mondex smart card [21] to ITSEC Level 6 (Common Criteria Level 7) [14]. The work is reported in [16], where a summary of Mondex and its original development and certification are described [16, p.5–19]. The experiment mechanised the original manual proofs in Alloy [16, p.21–39], ASM [16, p.41–59], Event-B [16, p.61–77], OCL [16, p.79–100], π-calculus [15], Raise [16, p.101–116], and Z [16, p.117–139]. A second pilot project on POSIX compliant flash file stores followed [11]. A domain model with widely used terminology and well-understood requirements is needed, and we have based our mechanised domain model based on the formal refinement of OS kernel designs [5].

There are two other related GC pilot projects: FreeRTOS [6] and the Microsoft Hypervisor [4]. FreeRTOS is an open-source real-time embedded operating system written in pointer-rich C, and it does not have a specification, making it an attractive topic for research in formal analysis and top-down development. The extensive use of pointers offers two complementary challenges: (i) the annotation of the code with suitable assertions and the verification of the code against these assertions; and (ii) the top-down development of the code, starting from a suitable specification of its abstract behaviour. The goal of the Microsoft Hypervisor Verification Project is to develop an industrially viable verification methodology for low-level code, and to use this methodology to verify the functional correctness of the Microsoft Hypervisor [17]. The hypervisor is a 60kLoC C and assembler program that turns a multi-processor (MP) x64 machine into a number of virtual MP x64 machines.

2   Verified OS Kernels Pilot Project

An OS kernel is a central component of most operating systems, providing an interface to the management of hardware and software resources, including memory, processors, and I/O devices. It offers this interface to application processes through inter-process communication mechanisms and system calls. Among its features, the most important are: low-level scheduling of processes; inter-process communication; process synchronisation; context switching; manipulation of process control blocks; hardware interrupt handling; process creation and destruction; *etc.*. Kernel development has a reputation for being a very difficult and complex programming task for two prime reasons. First, every computing system requires the OS kernel to provide correct functionality and good performance. Second, because the kernel cannot make (direct) use of the abstractions it provides (*e.g.,* processes, semaphores, *etc.*), which would make higher-level programming of embedded and real-time systems easier.

Our pilot project is inspired by Iain Craig's book on the formal refinement of OS kernels [5]. The objectives are to demonstrate feasibility of top-down OS kernel development using formal specification and verification, with refinement down to a C implementation. Craig uses the Z notation [20,24,13] for specification and refinement, and recording correctness arguments in hand-written proofs. Our pilot project investigates the tractability of mechanising all the models in each kernel development, including formalising all proofs. A key principle is to retain these models as far as possible, making changes only for correctness, not for easing the task of mechanisation.

Part of this investigation involves constructing prototype tool chains for the development process from specification through design and down to code. For the specification and verification we use Z theorem provers like Z/Eves [19]. Data refinement [24] links the abstract specification to a concrete design that is closer to code, and we use a Z theorem prover. After that, we use the Z refinement calculus (ZRC) [3] to go down to the guarded command language. The invariants and pre- and postconditions for each programming statement are then converted to a formal annotation language for C, such as Spec# [1]. Finally, tools like Boogie/PL and the Microsoft Verified C Compiler can be used to perform static and partial correctness analysis. All results, including models, mechanisation lemmas, papers, tools, *etc.* are being curated in the VSR.

The pilot project is currently in an exploratory phase, having mechanised the whole of the simple kernel [26]. We have found some interesting issues, including missing and hidden invariants. Although Craig's models have great insight from an OS engineer in necessary underlying data types, a series of mistakes are introduced, both clerical and more substantial design decisions. On the other hand, despite these errors, the work is carried out using the refinement calculus [3] and goes down to a real ANSI-C implementation running on embedded processors, like the Intel IA32 architecture. With this work, our attempt is to straight up all that effort more rigorously, hence laying out a solid foundation for the development of formally verified kernels.

This paper is dedicated to our more intimate understanding of the invariants for the kernel's basic data structures that are relevant to scheduler design. We take a step back from OS kernel design and verify its basic data structures to see which invariants are fundamental, and which can be relaxed and proved as properties instead. We have reports (summarised in this paper) with all definitions and proofs that can be found in [7,8,9].

3   Process Table

In Craig's kernel [5, Ch. 3], processes are represented uniformly (*i.e.,* they all have the same kind of information). A process table is used to represent a finite list of unique process identifiers, together with the relevant information the kernel keeps for each of them, such as scheduling priority, execution state and stack pointer, sleeping timeout, interprocess message exchanges, and so on. It represents a simple storage for used and free process identifiers.

In this section we present an improved version, where mistakes have been corrected, and a less verbose modelling approach was adopted. Wherever differences emerged due to style, rather than mistakes, equivalence theorems have been proved to show that we are indeed talking about the same mathematical artefacts. We follow the style of using Z advocated by Woodcock & Davies [24] separates two concerns in the specification of data types: the successful behaviour of each operation is first specified; once this is complete, each operation's precondition is analysed and appropriate error handling is added. Other specification patterns for Z exist [22], and a few patterns overlap. The ones used in this work came directly from previous experience, and our own catalogue (to appear), which is tailored for proof in Z/Eves. We are also undertaking an interesting experiment in proving this model together with our catalogue in a different theorem prover for Z. That should give us some parameter on whether the catalogue is tool-oriented or general enough for the VSR. Details on proof strategies within Z/Eves are beyond the scope of this paper, yet are available in the MSc course material at York.

We first define a set of valid process identifiers (PID) as a strictly positive range over some bounded maximum ($maxpid \in \mathbb{N}_1$), where the invalid identifier ($null$) is outside this range. This is an axiomatic definition: it introduces global constants for the specification, where $maxpid$ constrains process identifier values to be strictly positive, and $min/maxprio$ will be used to define a non-empty process priority range.

$$
\begin{array}{|l}
maxpid : \mathbb{N}_1; \ minprio, maxprio : \mathbb{Z} \\
\hline
\langle\!\langle\, \text{rule RangePPRIO} \,\rangle\!\rangle \ \ maxprio \leq minprio
\end{array}
$$

These global constants are said to be loosely specified, since although it has a single value, we do not say precisely which one it is. The label "rule RangePPRIO" gives a name to the fact that the range of priorities has at least one element, and that the lowest value represents the highest priority. The **rule** mark identifies it as a kind of rewrite rule that needs to be explicitly invoked. Next, the actual ranges for process identifiers (PID) and their priorities ($PPRIO$) are declared as an abbreviation for the set of integers bound by these constants. We also add an abbreviation to represent time (as positive milliseconds) in process waking delays. The $null$ PID is an invalid number outside PID.

$$
\begin{array}{ll}
PID \ == \ 1 \,.. \, maxpid & PPRIO \ == \ maxprio \,.. \, minprio \\
null \ == \ 0 \qquad GPID \ == \ PID \cup \{null\} & TIME \ == \mathbb{N}
\end{array}
$$

We introduce $GPID$ as including the set PID and the $null$ PID. Next, we add an non-interpreted type to represent memory addresses and messages to be exchanged between processes. These abstractly specify a set of values as a specific type. Finally, the different states a process can have is defined.

$$[MSG, ADDR] \qquad PSTATE ::= psterm \mid psrunning \mid psready \mid \ldots$$

It is given as a Z free-type that characterises in this case an enumeration of (unique) possible states a process may be in. The process table itself has seven variables: the finite sets ($\mathbb{F}$) of *used* and *free* PIDs; and partial functions ($\nrightarrow$) mapping for each used PID, process specific information. The state of the data type is specified using one of the most characteristics elements of Z: the schema. PTAB is a named mathematical structure describing an arbitrary instance of the process table with an invariant constraining the relationship between the variables. The invariants on *free* and *used* identifiers are disjoints and partitions the whole of PIDs, and we only store process information for identifiers being used. In other words, the process information mappings are total with respect to PIDs in use. A PID is in use when it is known within the kernel: its corresponding process state might then be either running, sleeping, ready, and so on.

PTAB

$used, free : \mathbb{F} \; PID; \; prio : PID \nrightarrow PPRIO; \; state : PID \nrightarrow PSTATE$
$stacktop : PID \nrightarrow ADDR; \; smsg : PID \nrightarrow MSG; \; waking : PID \nrightarrow TIME$

$free = (PID \setminus used) \land used = \mathrm{dom} \; prio$
$\mathrm{dom} \; prio = \mathrm{dom} \; state = \mathrm{dom} \; smsg = \mathrm{dom} \; waking = \mathrm{dom} \; stacktop$

Process information is used by the scheduler whilst performing context switches. Process priority (*prio*) is used to sort the scheduler's ready queue. Process state (*state*) documents what actions can be taken by the scheduler. The stack (*stacktop*) pointers to the top of the process' stack. As processes can communicate using synchronous message passing, *smsg* stores the latest message sent to each process. Finally, some system calls may put the process to wait for a specific amount of sleeping time (*waking*). Once "awake", a process is returned to the scheduler's ready queue for subsequent execution. The refinement to code use a linked list of (pointers to) process identifiers, a data structure modelled and mechanised elsewhere [10].

Craig models error cases with separate schemas for the error reports from the actual error conditions. First, we define some error cases as a free-type. The complete list is rather long, and we mention only those used here. We also only add one example schema to save space. It contains an output variable *serr!* with the corresponding error case.

$$SYSERR \quad ::= \quad sysok \mid pdinuse \mid unusedpd \mid ptabfull \mid pqfull \mid pqempty \mid \ldots$$
$$ErrSysOk \quad \hat{=} \quad [\, serr! : SYSERR \mid serr! = sysok \,]$$

The conditions for each error case is given in the PTAB operations defined next. Schema ErrSysOk reports the successful cases.

3.1   *PTAB* **Operations**

Schema *PTInit* establish the initial state as an empty set *PID*s. As it represents the domain of all functions, they are also empty, where *free* is the whole *PID*. Next, two query operations are defined. *UsedPID* determines for a input *p?* whether it is being used, whereas *PIDSFree* enquires whether there are any free *PID*s left, which is the case if *used* is a proper subset of *PID*.

$$PTInit \;\widehat{=}\; [\,PTAB' \mid used' = \emptyset\,] \quad PIDSFree \;\widehat{=}\; [\,\Xi PTAB \mid used \subset PID\,]$$
$$UsedPID \;\widehat{=}\; [\,\Xi PTAB;\; p? : PID \mid p? \in used\,]$$

In Z, *PTAB'* represents the *PTAB* schema, where all variables names have been dashed; they represent the after state for *PTAB*. Similarly, the *ΞPTAB* schema represents the inclusion of *PTAB* and *PTAB'*, where all variables remain unchanged (*i.e., used' = used, prio' = prio*, etc.). For instance, because the *PTAB* functions are partial within *used*, whenever function application over an input *p?* occurs in a *PTAB* operation, a proof obligation that *p?* belongs to the domain of the function needs to be discharged (*e.g., p?* ∈ dom *smsg*). As these proof obligations will appear quite often, to discharge those easily enough and without the need to expand definitions, we add a few lemmas like ∀ *UsedPID* • *p?* ∈ dom *prio*. We define two operations that allocate and free *PID*s, respectively. *AllocPID* has an output *p!* that is not being used, and then updates *used* to know about its nondeterministically chosen value. If *p?* ∉ *used*, this operation does not affect the state. In the Z schema calculus *ΔPTAB* represents the inclusion of *PTAB* and *PTAB'*, where all variable values are left unconstrained.

$$AllocPID \;\widehat{=}\; [\,\Delta PTAB;\; p! : PID \mid p! \notin used \wedge used' = used \cup \{p!\}\,]$$

The *FreePID* schema removes a given *p?* ∈ *PID* from *used*, as well as from each function. Note the invariant about keeping the remainder of the *PID* information constant was missing from the original model.

```
┌─ FreePID ──────────────────────────────────────────────
│ ΔPTAB;  p? : PID
├────────────────────────────────────────────────────────
│ used' = used \ {p?}
│ prio' = {p?} ⩤ prio
│ state' = {p?} ⩤ state
│ smsg' = {p?} ⩤ smsg
│ wakingtime' = {p?} ⩤ wakingtime
│ stacktop' = {p?} ⩤ stacktop
└────────────────────────────────────────────────────────
```

An update operation is then defined for each one of the *PTAB* functions. We collapse them all in one schema (*AddPDESC*) below for simplicity. It updates each corresponding function with a given *PID* to its corresponding information. For priorities, that is an input *pr?* ∈ *PPRIO*; for the current process state, a

$st? \in PSTATE$ is used; and for the process waiting time, a $t? \in TIME$ to sleep after a system call is given. Finally, the complete process descriptor without pending message to exchange is shown below.

```
┌─ AddPDESC ─────────────────────────────────────────────
│ ΔPTAB; p? : PID; pr? : PPRIO; st? : PSTATE; t? : TIME
├────────────────────────────────────────────────────────
│ prio' = prio ⊕ { (p? ↦ pr?) } ∧ state' = state ⊕ {(p? ↦ st?)}
│ waking' = waking ⊕ { (p? ↦ t?) } ∧ smsg' = smsg ⊕ { (p? ↦ nullmsg) }
│ {p?} ◁ stacktop' = {p?} ◁ stacktop
└────────────────────────────────────────────────────────
```

The relational override ($\_ \oplus \_$) operator updates each function with the new mapping between input $p?$ and its corresponding values. That is, if $p?$ already belongs to the function, then its value is updated; otherwise, a new mapping is added. This ensures the after state with information about $p?$ remains functional. For $stacktop'$, the effect of the operation is to nondeterministically choose it, as this is what the model intended. Nevertheless, the original model does not even mention $stacktop'$, meaning that previous mappings would have been lost, and we fix that by saying that everywhere else but on $p?$, the mappings remain constant. The mapping for $p?$ in $stacktop'$ is what remains nondeterministically chosen. Finally, the complete successful operation, which involves allocating a PID and updating the corresponding functions accordingly, is defined next.

$$AddPDOk \;\hat{=}\; (PIDSFree \;\fatsemi\; AllocPID) \wedge AddPDESC[p!/p?] \wedge ErrSysOk$$

This definition suggests a very operational approach to the specification: first you check whether there are any free PIDs, then you try allocating one together with the corresponding updates over each function holding information over PIDs. In Z, schema composition ($S \;\fatsemi\; T$) makes the after state of S the before state of T, which is kept hidden via existential quantification; the overall before state is that of S, whereas the overall after state is that of T. Although this is not wrong, we find it unnecessarily long winded. Instead, we use a simpler, expanded and simplified version of the above definition, When conjoining schemas, all common variable names must be type-compatible and no repetition is involved. This gives the whole schema signature. The invariants are combined according to the underlying logical operator: Z schemas can be both expressions or predicates, depending on the context. In order to ensure we are dealing with the same modelling artefact, we prove a theorem that both definitions are equivalent (*e.g.*, $AddPDOK \Leftrightarrow AddPDOkSimp$). This is important to keep modifications sound.

A PID that is already in use cannot be reused, and the appropriate error message is reported in the original. Nevertheless, the condition for such situation is encompassed by the precondition of $AddPDOk$, hence we removed this operation here. That means, such an error case is actually just a check of a condition that would enable successful adding. When $used$ reaches PID, $AddPDTabFull$ reports that the process table is full. Finally, following Woodcock & Davies' style of modelling [24], the complete operation $AddPD$ is the disjunction between successful and error cases accordingly.

$$AddPDPTABFull \; \widehat{=} \; [\, \Xi PTAB; \; ErrPTABFull \mid \neg \, used \subset PID \,]$$
$$AddPD \qquad\qquad \widehat{=} \; AddPDOk \vee AddPDPTABFull$$

A few query operation over a known (*i.e.*, $p? \in used$) *PID* are added to extract information as outputs for each relevant function in the process table.

$$ProcPrio \qquad \widehat{=} \; [\, UsedPID; \; pr! : PPRIO \mid pr! = prio \, p? \,]$$
$$WaitingTime \; \widehat{=} \; [\, UsedPID; \; t! : TIME \mid t! = waking \, p? \,]$$

At last, we define the complete operation that corresponds to deleting a *PID* and all its information from the *PTAB*. There are two cases: either the input $p?$ is being used, in which case it is freed and success is reported by *DelPDOk*; or else the *PID* is unknown, in which case it does not make sense to free it and an error is reported by *DelUnusedPID*. The complete case is the disjunction of possibilities, as in *DelPD*.

$$DelPDOk \qquad\quad \widehat{=} \; (UsedPID \,\fatsemi\, FreePID) \wedge ErrSysOk$$
$$DelUnusedPID \; \widehat{=} \; [\, \Xi PTAB; \; p? : PID; \; ErrUnusedPID \mid p? \notin used \,]$$
$$DelPD \qquad\qquad \widehat{=} \; DelPDOk \vee DelUnusedPID$$

A final comment is that although Craig's operational approach to modelling is not wrong, it can sometimes add a unnecessary burden of proof due to its verboseness. For these reasons, we will refactor his original specification in the more complex data structures that follow. As we mentioned before, whenever such changes take place, an equivalence theorem is added to ensure the correctness of the model. On the other hand, errors of design and indeed modelling do occur later on. In such cases where an equivalence theorem is not feasible, a thorough explanation or a weaker (refinement) claim is proved (*i.e.*, Corrected $\Rightarrow$ Original). Thus, the corrected specification is at least as good as the original, even if changed for the sake of easing the proofs.

3.2   *PTAB* Operations Preconditions

A precondition proof is required for each operation, where one can assume inputs $(p?)$ and the before state $(PTAB)$. These preconditions are summarised in Table 1. We also prove that the *PTAB* can be initialised: $(\exists \, PTAB' \bullet PTInit)$, hence we can establish the state invariant assumed in the precondition proofs.

Table 1. *PTAB* operations preconditions

PIDSFree, AllocPID, AddPDOk	$used \subset PID$
AddPDPTABFull	$\neg \, used \subset PID$
UsedPID, AddPDESC, ProcPrio, DelPDOk, DelUnusedPID	$p? \in used$
FreePID, AddPD, DelPD	**true**

Although these precondition proofs were rather trivial, they exposed a few automation lemmas needed for the mechanisation (more details in [9]). The precondition for the other *ProcXXX* query operations are the same as *ProcPrio*. The important aspect to notice is that the top-level operations (marked in bold) have a robust interface: all execution cases are accounted for.

4   Priority Queue

The priority queue is used in the kernel's scheduler. When a process is added to this queue, its priority is used to determine where it should be inserted. Its underlying implementation uses linked lists of processes identifiers with an extended version of a *Chain* data type [10].

Capturing the properties of mid-point insertions within ordered lists can be more complex than one might expect and has certainly be the most difficult to mechanise. We avoided the operational style in favour of a more straightforward model. It extends *PTAB* with a queue variable *pq* bound by a maximum *maxs*, and within the allocated processes identifiers. Although *maxs* bounds *pq*, *maxs* is itself also (implicitly) bound by $\# used$ because of the $\subseteq$ for *pq* with respect to *used*. The queue is ordered so that the highest priority (*e.g.,* lowest *PPRIO* value) corresponds to the sequence's lowest index.

$$
\begin{array}{|l}
\hline
\_PRIOQ \underline{\hspace{4cm}} \\
PTAB;\ pq : \text{seq } PID;\ maxs : \mathbb{N}_1 \\
\hline
\# pq \leq maxs \wedge \text{ran } pq \subseteq used \\
\forall i : \text{dom } pq \mid i < \# pq \bullet prio\,(pq\ i) \leq prio\,(pq\,(i+1)) \\
\hline
\end{array}
$$

We relaxed the restriction over the sequence elements being strictly within ($\subset$) *used*. It adds unnecessary burden of proof too early. For instance, to keep the data structure general — the scheduler may add the restriction if needed. Of course, that invariant is accounted for at the scheduler, when it makes use the priority queue. As one would expect, these modifications are carried along during the refinement chain towards code. Here it seems sensible for the scheduler in order to avoid kernel starvation. This modification is a refinement of the original, with improved modelling decisions presented next. We modified the original universal quantifier to the (proved) equivalent one presented here. Instead of using ($i \in 1 .. \#pq - 1$) as in the original, we prefer dom *pq* with the added side condition that *i* must not be the last one (*i.e.,* $i < \# pq$). This small change is crucial because since *pq* is a partial function over sequence indexes, when *i* varies over $1 .. \#pq-1$, we end up with proof obligations about *i* belonging to the domain of *pq*, which is obvious, as dom $pq = 1 .. \# pq$. For a similar reason, we add a rewriting rule to say that, providing some *PID* is within the queue range, it is an allocated one in *PTAB*'s *used PIDs* That is, many *PRIOQ* operations mention $prio\,(pq\ n)$, where both *n* and $pq\,(n)$ must be within the domain of *pq* and *prio*, respectively. The goal is easily proved since ran $pq \subseteq used$ from *PRIOQ*, and $used = $ dom $prio$ from *PTAB*. The point it is that the concept that one should shape ones model for the tool at hand is paramount. Error reporting schemas are just as before for $PTAB$ and are omitted here. The conditions for each error case are given next.

4.1 $PRIOQ$ Operations

For the operations, we strengthen the original invariants to say that $PTAB$ within the $PRIOQ$ cannot be modified. The priority queue is initialised by $PQInit$, which makes pq empty, and binds its maximum to an input on $mps?$. In the original specification, the underlying $PTAB$ initialisation is left unconstrained, and we initialise it here accordingly.

$$PQInit \;\widehat{=}\; [\, PRIOQ'; \; mps? : \mathbb{N}_1 \mid PTInit \wedge maxs' = mps? \wedge pq' = \langle\rangle \,]$$

The priority queue specify two top-level operations: enqueue, and dequeue, each of which is split in several possible cases. First, we define a few reusable operation signatures; this application of the schema calculus is useful to increase the specification's modularity while keeping it small and simple, if compared to the rather lengthy equivalent in the original model [5, Sect.3.5].

$$
\begin{aligned}
PQOp \qquad\qquad &\widehat{=}\; [\, \Delta PRIOQ; \; \Xi PTAB \mid maxs' = maxs \,] \\
KnownPIDPQ \qquad &\widehat{=}\; [\, PQOp; \; p? : PID \mid p? \in used \,] \\
KnownPIDNEmptyPQ \;&\widehat{=}\; [\, KnownPIDPQ \mid pq \neq \langle\rangle \,] \\
CanEnqPQ \qquad\quad &\widehat{=}\; [\, KnownPIDNEmptyPQ \mid \# pq < maxs \,]
\end{aligned}
$$

Schema $PRIOOp$ provides the general signature that keeps $PTAB$ and $maxs'$ constant, since $PRIOQ$ should not change $PTAB$, and after initialisation the upper bound cannot change. Schema $KnownPIDPQ$ extends $PRIOOp$ to mention an allocated PID input. Similarly, schema $KnownPIDNEmptyPQ$ extends $KnownPIDPQ$ for the non-empty priority queue. Finally, schema $CanEnqPQ$ encompass the whole set of conditions necessary for enqueuing over non-empty priority queues: (i) $PTAB$ and $maxs$ are constant; (ii) a PID input to be enqueued is allocated; (iii) the queue is not empty; and (iv) there is room for enqueuing, as the size of pq has not reached the maximum bound yet.

Prioritised Enqueue. The complete enqueue operation in the original specification is given as

$$
\begin{aligned}
PRIOQEnqueue \;\widehat{=}\; &ErrFullPQ \vee (CanEnqPQ \wedge ErrSysOk \\
&((IsEmptyPQ \wedge PRIOQAddSingleton) \vee \\
&(ShouldAddPRIOQHd \wedge PRIOQEnqueueHd) \vee \\
&(ShouldAddPRIOQLast \wedge PRIOQEnqueueLast) \vee PRIOQInsert))
\end{aligned}
$$

Either one can enqueue with success or fail because the queue is full. If enqueue is possible, then either: it is empty and a singleton can be added; or, we can add to either the head or tail; otherwise, mid-point insertion takes place. Although this may sound intuitive enough, even a cleric error like the missing conditions for the full queue error report ($ErrFullPQ$) can be disastrous. When $CanEnqPQ$ is not the case, the other disjunct does not contain something like the negation of $CanEnqPQ$'s invariants, and simply leave the state unconstraint. So, a report that the "scheduler is full" could non-deterministically happen inside the kernel! More serious design errors appeared when investigating mid-point insertion, a rather complex operation due to the priority ordering of the queue. We start our refactoring by modelling enqueue over an empty queue. We need an allocated PID, as defined by the schema $EnqEmptyPQ$.

$$EnqEmptyPQ \ \widehat{=} \ [\, KnownPIDPQ \mid pq = \langle\rangle \wedge pq' = \langle p?\rangle \,]$$

We enqueue at the front, in which case priority order must be observed: the element $p?$ concatenated at the front of pq must have a priority strictly higher than the head of the queue, which has the highest-priority queued PID. This strict ordering at the front is important to avoid starving the scheduler, say through a denial-of-service attack, in which a process with priority at least as high as the currently running process is to be scheduled. This could still happen with mid-point priorities mentioned later, yet is avoided by preserving the FIFO-ordering of elements with same priority. Although in usual embedded devices architectures are closed, the data structure may be used in a more general setting.

$$EnqHeadPQ \ \widehat{=} \ [\, CanEnqPQ \mid prio\ p? < prio\ (head\ pq) \wedge pq' = \langle p?\rangle \frown pq\,]$$
$$EnqLastPQ \ \widehat{=} \ [\, CanEnqPQ \mid prio\ (last\ pq) < prio\ p? \wedge pq' = pq \frown \langle p?\rangle\,]$$

Conversely, we can also add to the end of the queue if the priorities of the input $p?$ is strictly higher than the priority at the end of the queue. The original design allows $prio\ p?$ to be within the queue. We insist that the known input $p?$ is outside the priority queue. Although in itself the original design does not have a problem here, it creates a more complex proof obligation for the robustness of the complete enqueue operation, since negating the two original preconditions from the book for head / last enqueue would give

$$= \neg\ (prio\ p? < prio\ (head\ pq) \vee prio\ (last\ pq) \le prio\ p?)$$
$$= prio\ (head\ pq) \le prio\ p? < prio\ (last\ pq) \qquad \text{[original cond. negated]}$$

It characterises the case when one could enqueue anywhere before the last element, including the head of the queue itself. In this negated case, the original model is allowing unwanted scenarios. For instance, suppose we have pq and the queue of corresponding priorities with the sequence mapping / composition $(prio \circ pq)$ as

$$pq0 \ = \ \langle pd_1, pd_2, pd_3, pd_4, pd_5\rangle \qquad (prio \circ pq0) \ = \ \langle pr_0, pr_1, pr_2, pr_3\rangle$$

for some identifier $pd_n \in PID$ and corresponding priority $pr_n \in PPRIO$. Now, if we enqueue some $p?$ with $prio\ p? = pr_2$ to pq, the model allows $p?$ to be enqueued anywhere before/after/between pd_3 and pd_4. Thus, process $p?$ might "jump the queue" in the case where its priority $prio\ p?$ is known within pq.

Therefore, although queue priority ordering is preserved, actual first-in-first-out (FIFO) ordering within elements with equal priority is not. With our small modification on priority strictness near the queue edges, the same negation of our preconditions (see Table 2) would lead to

$$= \neg\, (prio\ p? < prio\ (head\ pq) \lor prio\ (last\ pq) < prio\ p?)$$
$$= prio\ (head\ pq) \leq prio\ p? \leq prio\ (last\ pq) \qquad \text{[refactored cond. neg.]}$$

So, the priority of the input $p?$ is within some known priority in the queue. Although this does not solve the FIFO ordering problem, it does keep it outside the cases for empty, head, or last enqueuing. That means such "fall-back" case needs to be addressed by queue mid-point insertion.

With some expansion, the original mid-point operation in the next schema states that, given enqueuing is possible, we can find two non-empty sequences l and r that split pq, such that the priority of the element being inserted $prio\ p?$ is within the priorities of the last element on l and first element on r.

$PRIOQInsert$ _____
$CanEnqPQ$

$\exists\, l, r : \text{seq}_1\ PID \mid pq = l \frown r \land$
$\qquad prio\ (last\ l) \leq prio\ p? < prio\ (head\ r) \bullet pq' = l \frown \langle p? \rangle \frown r$

It repeats the idea for head/last inclusion, yet with respect to a mid-point between sequences *left* and *right* splitting pq. If we negate and simplify the original operations preconditions we would have

$$= \neg\, (prio\ p? < prio\ (head\ pq) \lor prio\ (last\ pq) \leq prio\ p? \lor$$
$$(\exists\, l, r : \text{seq}_1\ PIDpq = l \frown r \land prio\ (last\ l) \leq prio\ p? < prio\ (head\ r)))$$
$$= prio\ (head\ pq) \leq prio\ p? < prio\ (last\ pq) \land (\forall\, l, r : \text{seq}_1\ PID \bullet$$
$$pq = l \frown r \land prio\ (last\ l) \leq prio\ p? \Rightarrow prio\ (head\ r) \leq prio\ p?)$$

It says $p?$'s priority is within pq before the last, and for all possible mid-points available for pq such that the priority of $p?$ is at least within the end of the left side, then it should be within the right side. The trouble is that we need to prove this for all possible mid-point cases, which also includes overlapping cases where $prio\ p?$ could be on either side. This leads to a lengthy induction proof on the sizes of l and r with respect to the corresponding length of pq! We propose a different model for mid-points that provides both simpler proof and deals with the mistake of loosing FIFO ordering for elements with the same priority as those previously enqueued. The next auxiliary schema *PQMidPoint* arranges the queue's indexes in three finite sets: *left*, *mid*, and *right*, which contains indexes with priorities strictly *higher*, *eq*, or *lower* than the priority of the $p?$ being inserted, respectively.

---PQMidPoint---
| $PRIOQ$; $p?$: PID; $left, mid, right$: $\mathbb{F}\ \mathbb{N}$; $higher, eq, lower$: $\mathbb{P}\ PPRIO$
|_____
| $p? \in used \land eq = \{prio\ p?\} \land higher = \{ ph : PPRIO \mid ph < prio\ p? \}$
| $lower = \{pl : PPRIO \mid priop? < pl\} \land left = (prio \circ pq)^{\sim}(\!\lvert\ higher\ \rvert\!)$
| $right = (prio \circ pq)^{\sim}(\!\lvert\ lower\ \rvert\!) \land mid = (prio \circ pq)^{\sim}(\!\lvert\ eq\ \rvert\!)$
|_____

Sets $higher$, mid, and $lower$ gather the disjoint set of priorities. By composing priorities with the queue ($prio \circ pq$), we go from the queue's domain ($\mathbb{N}$) of indexes to $prio$'s range ($PPRIO$) of priorities via the mid-points (PID) of process identifiers. We then take the relational image ($R(\!\lvert\ S\ \rvert\!)$) of the composed function inverted ($prio \circ pq)^{\sim}$ with respect to each set of priorities. The inverted function returns a relation between priorities and indexes; it is not a function since various indexes might have the same priority. Relational image over a set returns all the pairs in the range of R that have been filtered by the set S (*i.e.*, $R(\!\lvert\ S\ \rvert\!) =$ ran $(S \lhd R)$). It is a general case of (function) application for relations: if R is function and S is a singleton set within the domain of R, then the result set is a singleton that is equivalent to applying the element of S to R. For instance, since $p? \in$ dom $prio$, $prio (\!\lvert\ \{ p? \}\ \rvert\!) = \{ prio\ p? \}$. Thus, taking the relational image of $(prio \circ pq)^{\sim}$ with respect to each disjoint set of priorities gives their disjoint queue indexes. For instance, for our example queue above where $prio\ p? = pr_2$, we would have the follow scenario

$$
\begin{array}{llll}
pq0 & = \langle pd_1, pd_2, pd_3, pd_4, pd_5 \rangle & & [\text{queued } PIDs] \\
prio \circ pq0 & = \langle pr_0, pr_1, pr_2, pr_2, pr_3 \rangle & & [\text{prio per } PID] \\
(prio \circ pq0)^{\sim} & = \{ (pr_0, 1), (pr_1, 2), (pr_2, 3), (pr_2, 4), (pr_3, 5) \} & & [\text{prio idx}] \\
left & = \{ 1, 2 \} & \text{where, } higher = \{ pr_0, pr_1 \} & [\text{idx for } pr_0, pr_1]
\end{array}
$$

With these sets partitioning the queue's indexes by the input's priority ($prio\ p?$), we ensure that both priority and FIFO-orderings are maintained. Mid-point insertion is defined next. Providing that there is room for enqueuing, and that we can find a mid-point partition for pq with respect to the input's $p?$ priority, the operation updates the queue (pq') by concatenating its elements appropriately. Strictly higher priorities than $prio\ p?$ go first on the left. Then, the equal priorities are concatenated in the middle. Only after that $p?$ is enqueued, hence FIFO-ordering is preserved. Lastly, strictly lower priorities than $prio\ p?$ go at the right, hence priority ordering is also preserved. Finally, the mid-point enqueue hides the auxiliary partitioning sets as they are not part of the queue's state.

$$
\begin{array}{ll}
EnqMidPQ0 & \hat{=}\ [\ CanEnqPQ;\ PQMidPoint\ \mid \\
& \qquad pq' = left \upharpoonright pq \frown mid \upharpoonright pq \frown \langle p? \rangle \frown right \upharpoonright pq\ ] \\
EnqMidPQ & \hat{=}\ EnqMidPQ0 \setminus (higher, eq, lower, left, mid, right) \\
EnqueuePQ0 & \hat{=}\ (EnqEmptyPQ \lor EnqHeadPQ \lor \\
& \qquad EnqLastPQ \ \lor EnqMidPQ) \land ErrSysOk
\end{array}
$$

Schema hiding in Z existentially quantify the list of variables on the right from the schema on the left. The successful cases is combined as usual in schema

*EnqueuePQ*0. For the error cases, when one can no longer enqueue elements, it is because *pq* has reached its maximum size as in schema *EnqFullPQ*, in which case the report is returned. The other case is when the identifier is not yet allocated as in schema *EnqUnkwnPQ*.

$$
\begin{aligned}
EnqFullPQ &\;\widehat{=}\; [\,\Xi\,PRIOQ \mid \#pq = maxs\,] \\
EnqUnkwnPQ &\;\widehat{=}\; [\,\Xi\,PRIOQ;\; p? : PID \mid p? \notin used\,] \\
EnqueuePQ &\;\widehat{=}\; (EnqFullPQ \wedge ErrFullPQ)\; \vee \\
&\qquad (EnqUnkwnPQ \wedge ErrUnusedPID) \vee EnqueuePQ0
\end{aligned}
$$

The complete specification for enqueuing combines the successful and error cases with their corresponding error reports as usual. The mechanisation of dequeuing is also interesting and similar to enqueue. We leave it out due to space limitations.

4.2 *PRIOQ* Operations Preconditions

As before, to prove preconditions (see Table 2), we can assume the before state *PRIOQ* and an input *p?*. We also prove that the *PRIOQ* can be initialised: $(\exists\, PRIOQ' \bullet PQInit)$, hence we can establish state invariant. These

Table 2. *PRIOQ* operations preconditions

EnqEmptyPQ	$p? \in used \wedge pq \neq \langle\rangle$
CanEnqPQ	$p? \in used \wedge pq \neq \langle\rangle \wedge \# pq < maxs$
EnqHeadPQ	pre *CanEnqPQ* $\wedge$ *prio p?* $<$ *prio (head pq)*
EnqLastPQ	pre *CanEnqPQ* $\wedge$ *prio (last pq)* $<$ *prio p?*
EnqMidPQ	pre *CanEnqPQ* $\wedge$ *prio (head pq)* $\leq$ *prio p?* $\leq$ *prio (last pq)*
EnqueuePQ0	$p? \in used \wedge \# pq < maxs$
EnqFullPQ	$\# pq = maxs$
EnqUnkwnPQ	$p? \notin used$
EnqueuePQ	*true*

precondition proofs are rather complex, mainly due to the nature of FIFO-ordering on mid-point insertion, and the state invariant on priority ordering. Many general properties were found as a result of these proofs.

4.3 Priority Queue Properties

We summarise the proved lemmas on key properties about the priority queue in Table 3. Lemma L1 is a more general result about priority ordering: it is useful when proving ordering among elements that are not close to each other, as the *PRIOQ* invariant requires (*e.g.,* $prio\,(pq\,i) \leq prio\,(pq\,(i+1))$). It is proved by induction on the length of *pq*. Next, lemma L2 establishes that new valid identifiers *p?* within the queue ($p? \in ran\,pq$) must be at least within the queue's highest priority ($prio\,(head\,pq)$). Obviously, this side condition implies that the

Table 3. Properties about priority queues

L1	$\vdash \forall\, PRIOQ \bullet \forall\, i,j : \mathrm{dom}\ pq \mid i < j \bullet prio(pq\ i) \le prio\,(pq\ j)$
L2	$\vdash \forall\, PRIOQ \mid p? \in \mathrm{ran}\ pq \bullet prio\,(head\ pq) \le prio\ p?$
L3	$\vdash \forall\, PQMidPoint \bullet \{left, mid, right\} \subseteq \mathbb{P}\,(\mathrm{dom}\ pq)$
L4	$\vdash \forall\, PQMidPoint \bullet \langle left, mid, right\rangle\ \mathsf{partition}\ (\mathrm{dom}\ pq)$

queue is not empty and that $p? \in used$, since ran $pq \subseteq used$ from $PRIOQ$, and $used = \mathrm{dom}\ prio$ from $PTAB$. Finally, lemmas L3 and L4 ensure that all the queue's indexes are split in three disjoint sets (*i.e.,* sets without common elements), and that they partition dom pq (*i.e.,* their union equals to dom pq). This ensures both priority ordering at the strictly different priority cases, as well as FIFO-ordering at the middle case where elements have the same priority.

5   Interesting Lessons

Mechanising the verification of these data types has led to a deeper understanding of the kernel's components. We attempted simplifications by weakening some of the invariants that could have been derived as properties, in order to make our proofs simpler, but without compromising the specification. The lack of mechanisation in [5] led to missing invariants and other errors at the most crucial data structure in the kernel scheduler: the priority queue. This exercise shows the importance of tools in formal modelling in general, and theorem proving in particular, when one wants to provide greater levels of assurance. In practice, kernels use a matrix of priorities per sequences of identifiers, hence many problems of having a flat sequence might be simplified. This could be a good candidate for data refinement of the priority queue.

In fairness to Craig's original model, despite the mistakes mentioned, the sheer effort undertaken was considerable and worthwhile. His expertise in operating systems implementation is clear through the book. Luckily, many of the mistakes were consistent and easy to spot, which makes correcting them a simple task. And that is despite its serious consequences at times, like loosing scheduled processes FIFO ordering when priorities are the same. Overall, the whole exercise has proved worthwhile in establishing a solid foundation upon which one can build the top-level kernel components. Work in this front, as well as in the modelling of a Separation Kernel are under way.

Overall, we tried to strike a balance between reusing good parts of the models and remodelling from scratch based on the intended goals to capture the underlying requirements. The motivation for doing that is to save important invariants already discovered and modelled by a domain expert.

5.1   Going Back to the Scheduler Design

These data types presented are the core data structures within the kernel. Craig starts by designing a simple kernel, which later develops into a Separation Kernel. In the latter, all user process address spaces are disjoint, and all process execution times are disjoint. We model the list table of process identifiers and their corresponding information, as well as a queue for the kernel's semaphore, and priority queue for the kernel's scheduler. Other familiar OS components are also modelled, such as a global semaphore table, a synchronous message passing system, a process sleeping mechanism, and so on. The model is for an embedded/real-time system application, where unique *PID*s are sequentially allocated for every process, where an idle process is allocated first, and an initial (system) process is allocated second.

The process table is used to represent both these two initial processes, and the user processes in a uniform manner. It is implemented as an array-based structure similar to Linux, with the following structure: a stack pointer is used for context switching; priority is used for sorting the scheduler's ready queue; a state variable records whether the process is running, waiting, has terminated, and so on; an incoming message queue records all pending messages; and a waking time variable records how long should a process sleep until it becomes ready for scheduling again. The scheduler itself is a simple priority ready queue, which is refined to a chain of process identifiers with functional mapping encoded in the process table. Rescheduling occurs when a non-empty ready queue is present, where the current process's priority is lower than ready queue head, or the current process is neither ready nor running.

Other services like semaphores, message passing, and system calls are also available. Processes can synchronise using counting semaphores, FIFO queues, and so on. They are defined as separate mathematical data type, later refined to a chain of process identifiers [10]. Message passing enable processes to exchange messages, where the discipline that *receivers wait* and *senders retry* is observed. System calls can be used to: create or terminate processes; retrieve process identifiers; send or receive synchronous messages; allocate and release semaphores; put processes to wait or to sleep, as well as signal them; *etc.*.

6   Conclusions

The Grand Challenge's pilot projects help us to learn the best ways to model various application domains and how to verify those models. The intention is to make it easier for the next team who want to work in the application domain. In that direction, a series of data types and useful lemmas are needed if one is to make progress in tackling the central problems with OS kernel scheduling.

The experiments that started with mechanising the refinement of simple OS kernel schedulers led to the mechanisation of a set of abstract data types useful for this kind of modelling in general. This in itself instigated thinking about general properties for injective functions, transitive closure, sequences, and started few reports [7,8,9] that are good candidates to become part of the VSR as reusable mathematical data types. In more detail: we already have most (95%) of [5, Ch. 3], which is discussed in [26,10] and in here. Our model contains a series of declarations from Craig's book, and mechanically verified theorems. The general theories contain well over 120 theorems about various mathematical data types [7]. As a result of this work, our library of general theorems grew by 20 theorems; for the declared types, we needed 34 automation lemmas. The three components have a total of 145 schemas, type, and axiomatic declarations, with 44 precondition proofs, and 16 lemmas about the data type's properties. In total, these proofs were discharged with around 1540 proof commands, of which more than 2/3 were trivial, whereas the reminder 1/3 was divided in either creative steps involving quantifier's witnesses, or knowledge on how the tool works.

We improved the specification of most data structures used in the simple kernel and in the Separation Kernel described in [5]. The work incurred mostly in identifying useful properties about these data types and their use, as well as calculating the preconditions for each operation, and later proving data refinement about them. This mechanisation enabled both a better understanding of the various data structures, and a clearer definition of the Separation Kernel's scheduler specification use of it. As its use in [5] had modelling errors on data types, as well as the missing error cases uncovered here, we believe this to be an important contribution in building theories for formal modelling of OS kernels.

Future work. We are currently writing up reports about the various parts of the simple kernel, and how they are woven together. We have one MSc student working on the modelling of the Separation Kernel, as well as the refinement of the core data structures presented here. Colleagues from another research group in Brazil are working on combining all the kernel's components into a single top-level user-interface. With that in place, we will start to apply the refinement calculus to derive the kernel's code. Another approach is to go bottom-up from the already available C-code up towards the refined specifications.

Acknowledgements. We are grateful to QinetiQ Malvern for its long term support for our research. We are thankful to Juan Perna and Osmar Santos for fruitful discussions about properties of various parts of the kernel. We are also grateful to Iain Craig for producing an useful account of the formal specification and refinement of OS kernels.

References

1. Barnett, M., Leino, K.R.M., Schulte, W.: The Spec# programming system: An overview. In: Barthe, G., Burdy, L., Huisman, M., Lanet, J.-L., Muntean, T. (eds.) CASSIS 2004. LNCS, vol. 3362, pp. 49–69. Springer, Heidelberg (2005)
2. Bicarregui, J., Hoare, T., Woodcock, J.: The verified software repository: a step towards the verifying compiler. FACJ 18(2), 143–151 (2006)
3. Cavalcanti, A.: A Refinement Calculus for Z. PhD thesis, Oxford (1997)
4. Cohen, E.: Validating the Microsoft Hypervisor. In: Misra, J., Nipkow, T., Sekerinski, E. (eds.) FM 2006. LNCS, vol. 4085, p. 81. Springer, Heidelberg (2006)
5. Craig, I.: Formal Refinement of OS Kernels, 1st edn. Springer, Heidelberg (2007)
6. FreeRTOS, `http://www.freertos.org`
7. Freitas, L.: Extended Z mathematical toolkit. Technical Report CRG13, University of York (April 2008)

8. Freitas, L.: Formal model of a reusable Chain data type. Technical Report CRG14, University of York (April 2008)
9. Freitas, L.: Mechanising data-types for Kernel design in Z. Technical Report CRG15, University of York (March 2009)
10. Freitas, L., Woodcock, J.: A Chain Datatype in Z. International Journal of Software Informatics (2009) (in press)
11. Freitas, L., Woodcock, J., Buterfield, A.: POSIX and the Verification Grand Challenge: a Roadmap. In: IEEE Proceedings of 13th ICECCS, Belfast, pp. 153–162. IEEE, Los Alamitos (2008)
12. Hoare, T.: The verifying compiler: A grand challenge for computing research. Journal of the ACM 50(1), 63–69 (2003)
13. ISO/IEC 13568. Information Technology—Z Formal Specification Notation—Syntax, Type System and Semantics. ISO/IEC, 1st edn. (2002)
14. ITSEC. Information technology security evaluation criteria: primary harmonised criteria. Technical Report COM(90) 314, Commission of the European Communities, version 1.2 (June 1991)
15. Jones, C., Pierce, K.: What can the π-calculus tell us about the mondex purse system. In: 12th International Conference on Engineering of Complex Computer Systems (ICECCS), pp. 300–306. IEEE, New Zealand (2007)
16. Jones, C., Woodcock, J.: Formal Aspects of Computing — special issue on Mondex, vol. 20(1). Springer, Heidelberg (2008)
17. Neil, M., et al.: Hypervisor Top Level Functional Specification v0.83. Technical report, Microsoft Coorporation (December 2007)
18. Saaltink, M.: Z/Eves 2.0 Math. Toolkit. ORA, TR-99-5493-05b (October 1999)
19. Saaltink, M.: Z/Eves 2.0 User's Guide. ORA Canada, TR-99-5493-06a (1999)
20. Spivey, J.M.: The Z Notation: A Reference Manual. Prentice Hall, Englewood Cliffs (1998)
21. Stepney, S., et al.: An Electronic Purse: Specification, Refinement, and Proof. PRG 126, Oxford University (July 2000)
22. Stepney, S., et al.: A z patterns catalogue vol 1. Technical Report YCS-349, University of York (2003)
23. Woodcock, J.: First steps in the verified software grand challenge. IEEE Computer 39(10), 57–64 (2006)
24. Woodcock, J., Davies, J.: Using Z: Specification, Refinement, and Proof. Prentice Hall, Englewood Cliffs (1996)
25. Woodcock, J., et al.: Formal methods: practice and experience. ACM Computing Surveys (in press, 2009)
26. Woodcock, J., Freitas, L., Craig, I.: A Verified Simple Operating System Kernel. In: Workshop on the Verified Software Repository as part of FM Symposium, Turku, Finland (2008), Formal Methods Europe

A Complete Set of Object Modeling Laws for Alloy

Rohit Gheyi, Tiago Massoni, Paulo Borba, and Augusto Sampaio

Department of Computing Systems – Federal University of Campina Grande
Informatics Center – Federal University of Pernambuco
{rohit,massoni}@dsc.ufcg.edu.br, {phmb,acas}@cin.ufpe.br

Abstract. Applying transformations to object-oriented systems usually affects source code and its associated models, involving complex maintenance efforts to keep those artifacts up to date. Most projects abandon design information in the form of models early in the life cycle, as their maintenance becomes extremely expensive. In this paper, we propose a complete catalog of object model laws (bidirectional semantics-preserving transformations) for Alloy, a formal object-oriented modeling language. We address relative completeness through a reduction process that transforms an arbitrary Alloy model into an equivalent model in a core language (normal form). We evaluate our completeness result using two distinct normal forms.

1 Introduction

An *object model refactoring*, which is a structural model transformation that improves design structure while preserving semantics, may be useful, for instance, to maintain the consistency when refactoring programs that are conforming to the model invariants. It can be derived from more primitive semantics-preserving transformations usually referred to as *algebraic laws*. Our earlier work [1] shows an example of how an object modeling law can be synchronized with a sequence of equivalent program refactorings, ensuring semantic preservation. In this approach, some program refactorings may have more powerful automation considering model invariants. In this kind of work, it is important to have a comprehensive set of laws in order to derive more synchronizations.

In current practice, most object model refactorings rely on informal argumentation. It is difficult to prove that they are sound with respect to a formal semantics since each transformation may have an impact on a number of well-formedness rules and on different parts of the semantics. So, defining all enabling conditions required for a transformation to preserve semantics is not an easy task. Even a number of object model transformations proposed in the literature may lead to models with type errors or subtle semantic changes in some situations [2]. To our knowledge, there is no comprehensive set of object model refactorings to help designers to improve their models.

In this paper, we propose a complete catalog of transformation laws (Section 4) for Alloy [3], which is a formal object-oriented modeling language (Section 2).

M.V.M. Oliveira and J. Woodcock (Eds.): SBMF 2009, LNCS 5902, pp. 204–219, 2009.

Two new laws (splitting a relation and introducing a scalar relation), which were not published before, are presented. We prove that this catalog is *relatively complete* (Section 5), in the sense that it is sufficient to reduce an arbitrary Alloy model to an equivalent one expressed in a restricted subset of the language. We evaluate the completeness result using two different reduction strategies. Both reductions use all laws, except for one reduction that does not use the introducing a subsignature law. This result is important in order to show that our set of laws is representative enough to derive a large number of refactorings.

Our previous work [4] shows how some of our laws can be used to formally introduce Alloy design patterns (idioms). By using our catalog, we can derive a refactoring that allows us to formally switch between idioms. The Alloy laws are proven sound in the Prototype Verification System (PVS) [5], which encompasses a formal modeling language and a theorem prover. Our earlier work [6] proposes a formal semantics for Alloy in PVS and shows in detail how we proved one law in PVS. Another work [7] proposes a refinement notion, which is used in our laws, for Alloy encoded in PVS. All details about this formalization and proofs can be found elsewhere [2]. In this present paper, we focus on proving *completeness* for our catalog of Alloy laws. This is the main difference of this work and the related work (Section 6). So, the contributions of this paper are the following:

- propose two new laws (Section 4);
- show that our catalog is relatively complete (Section 5).

2   Alloy

An Alloy model or specification is an sequence of *paragraphs* of two kinds: signatures that are used for defining new types, and constraint paragraphs, such as facts, used to record constraints. Each signature comprises a set of objects, which associate with other objects by relations declared in the signatures. A signature paragraph introduces a type and a collection of relations, called fields, along with their types and other constraints on their included values.

Next, we model part of the banking system in Alloy, on which each bank is related to sets of accounts. The following fragment declares some signatures and relations. In Bank's declaration, the **set** qualifier specifies that accs associates each element in **Bank** to a set of elements in **Account**. All *top level signatures*, such as **Account** and **Bank**, are implicitly disjoint. Moreover, accounts may be checking or savings. In Alloy, one signature can extend another, establishing that the extended signature (subsignature) is a subset of the parent signature. Signature extension introduces a subtype. Alloy supports single inheritance. The extensions of a signature are mutually disjoint.

```
sig Bank {
  accs: set Account,
  custs: set Customer
}
```

```
sig Customer {}
sig Account { owner: set Customer }
sig ChAcc, SavAcc extends Account {}
fact BankInvs { all acc:Account | one acc.owner }
```

A fact packages formulae that always hold, such as invariants about the elements. The previous example introduces a fact named BankInvs, establishing general properties about the previously introduced signatures. It contains one formula stating that each account is owned by exactly one customer. The all keyword represents the universal quantifier. The one keyword, when applied to an expression, denotes that the expression has exactly one element. In Alloy, the fact formulae are implicitly conjoined.

3 Equivalence Notion

Before presenting object modeling laws for Alloy, we first define an equivalence notion (bidirectional refinement), which states when two object models are equivalent. Figure 1 describes two object models of a banking system. Figure 1(a) shows a model stating that each bank is related directly to a set of accounts, whereas the model in Figure 1(b) establishes that each bank is related to a collection, which is directly related to a set of accounts.

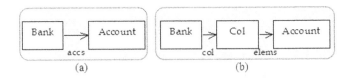

Fig. 1. Part of Two Models of a Banking System

The *usual notion* of equivalence states that object models are equivalent if they have *exactly* the same semantics. The models in Figure 1 are intuitively equivalent, but they are not equivalent using this notion since they have different elements. This notion is useful, but it is not flexible enough to compare equivalent models with auxiliary elements such as Col, or with different forms for representing the same concept, such as accs in Figure 1(a).

In order to compare models in such a scenario, we propose a more flexible notion. Our approach compares the semantics of two object models only for a number of relevant model elements, abstracting away the values assigned to the others. The set of relevant elements names is called *alphabet* (Σ). The names that are not in the alphabet are auxiliary, or not relevant for the comparison. For instance, suppose that Σ contains only the Bank and Account names in Figure 1. If both models have the same instances for those names, they are considered to be equivalent under this equivalence notion. Other names, such as elems, are regarded as auxiliary.

Sometimes we might have model elements that, although relevant, cannot be compared, since they are not part of both models. For instance, suppose that we include accs to Σ. In this case, we cannot compare the models in Figure 1, since accs is not part of the model in Figure 1(b). However, it can actually be expressed as the composition of col and elems. In those cases, our notion has a *view* (*v*), establishing how an element of one model can be interpreted using elements of another model. Views consist of a set of items such as $n{\rightarrow}exp$, where n is an element's name and exp is an expression. In Figure 1, we may choose a view containing the following item: $accs{\rightarrow}col.elems$. Now we can infer that both models are equivalent under this notion.

4   Modeling Laws

In this section, we propose a set of primitive laws for Alloy. They are summarized in Table 1. Each law has the form of an equation and defines two fine-grained semantics-preserving model transformations, with two templates of models (on the left and on the right-hand sides of the equations). They are primitive in the sense that they cannot be derived from other transformations. We have proposed laws for signatures, relations and formulae.

Table 1. Summary of Semantics-Preserving Transformations

Law	Name	Law	Name
1	Introduce signature	10	Remove Relation's Expression
2	Introduce generalization	11	Introduce Formula
3	Introduce subsignature	12	Introduce Empty Fact
4	Replace Abstract Qualifier	13	Remove Attached Empty Fact
5	Replace Signature Qualifier	14	Remove Form. from Attached Fact
6	Separate Signature Declaration	15	Split Relation
7	Introduce Relation	16	Introduce One Relation
8	Remove Relation Qualifier	17	Introduce Predicate
9	Separate Relation Declaration	18	Replace Predicate

Each law consists of two templates (patterns) of equivalent Alloy models, on the left-hand (LHS) and right-hand (RHS) sides. A law is applicable wherever one of the templates matches a given Alloy model. A matching is an assignment of all variables occurring in LHS/RHS models to concrete values. Each law may declare some meta-variables. We use *ps* to denote a set of signatures and facts, and *forms* to denote a set of formulae. Moreover, *rs* denotes a set of relations. The *exp* variable denotes an expression. A variable remains constant if it appears on both models. We write ($\rightarrow$), before a condition, to indicate that the condition is required when applying the law from left to right. Similarly, we use ($\leftarrow$) to indicate what is required when applying the law in the opposite direction, and we use ($\leftrightarrow$) to indicate that a condition is necessary in both directions.

The first law establishes that we can always introduce an empty signature declared with a fresh name. It also indicates that we can remove an empty signature that is not being used. Since a module cannot have two paragraphs with the same name, we have a condition stating that the new signature name does not appear in ps.

Law 1 ⟨introduce signature⟩

$$
\boxed{ps} \quad =_{\Sigma,v} \quad \boxed{\begin{array}{l} ps \\ \textbf{sig } S \; \{\} \end{array}}
$$

($\leftrightarrow$) (1) S is not in Σ; (2) for all names in Σ that are not in the resulting model, v must have exactly one valid item for it;
($\rightarrow$) ps does not declare any paragraph named S;
($\leftarrow$) S does not appear in ps.

It must be stressed that we can only introduce and remove signatures whose names do not belong to Σ. For instance, suppose that S belongs to Σ and the $S{\rightarrow}U$ item belongs to v, where U is declared in ps with the **one** cardinality qualifier. So, S is mapped to exactly one element on the left side of the law. However, after applying the law, any number of elements can be assigned to S, hence not preserving semantics. We would need to add the $S = U$ formula on the RHS of the law in order for S to have the same values in both models. Since S and U have different types, the formula is only valid when they are empty. However, if U is not empty, the $S = U$ formula introduces an inconsistency in the model. So, in case a signature name belongs to Σ, Law 2 must be used since it introduces a parent signature along with a formula.

The next law allows us to introduce a generalization into a model (applying from left to right); similarly it can also be used to remove a generalization from a model (applying from right to left). This law establishes that we can always introduce a generalization declared with a new name. Since in Alloy a module cannot have two paragraphs with the same name, we have a condition stating that the new parent signature name does not appear in the module. It also indicates that we can remove a parent signature that is not being used.

We can propose a similar law for introducing a generalization between any number of signatures. Besides conditions for ensuring that the well-formedness rules are preserved, this law presents other constraints for semantics preservation. For instance, if U belongs to Σ then v must have the $U{\rightarrow}S + T$ item in order for the left side model to have the same semantics of the right side model. The $+$ operator denotes the set union operator. There is another condition applied to all names in the alphabet that are not in the resulting model, ensuring that v represents them unambiguously. Adding a new name may turn an unused item in v to be valid. Similarly, removing a name may turn a valid item in v to be invalid. So, all laws that add or remove names have this condition. Notice that all conditions in all laws are syntactic. So, it is straightforward to implement tool support to verify those automatically. Observe that the new parent signature is

Law 2 ⟨introduce generalization⟩

$$
\begin{array}{|l|}
\hline
ps \\
\textbf{sig } S \text{ \{} \\
\quad rs \\
\text{\}} \\
\textbf{sig } T \text{ \{} \\
\quad rs' \\
\text{\}} \\
\textbf{fact } F \text{ \{} \\
\quad forms \\
\text{\}} \\
\hline
\end{array}
\quad =_{\Sigma,v} \quad
\begin{array}{|l|}
\hline
ps \\
\textbf{sig } U \text{ \{\}} \\
\textbf{sig } S \textbf{ extends } U \text{ \{} \\
\quad rs \\
\text{\}} \\
\textbf{sig } T \textbf{ extends } U \text{ \{} \\
\quad rs' \\
\text{\}} \\
\textbf{fact } F \text{ \{} \\
\quad forms \\
\quad U = S + T \\
\text{\}} \\
\hline
\end{array}
$$

($\leftrightarrow$) (1) if U belongs to Σ, v contains the $U \rightarrow S + T$ item; (2) for all names in Σ that are not in the resulting model, v must have exactly one valid item for it;
($\rightarrow$) ps does not declare any paragraph named U;
($\leftarrow$) U does not appear in ps, rs, rs' or $forms$.

always abstract. If S and T do not partition U, then we first introduce an empty signature applying Law 1 before applying Law 2. This new empty signature will contain all elements that belong to U but do not belong to S or T.

Law 3 allows us to introduce and remove a subsignature. We can introduce an empty subsignature declared with a new name along with its definition. Notice that this definition makes U an abstract signature, indicating that all its elements

Law 3 ⟨introduce subsignature⟩

$$
\begin{array}{|l|}
\hline
ps \\
\textbf{sig } U \text{ \{} \\
\quad rsU \\
\text{\}} \\
\textbf{sig } S \textbf{ extends } U \text{ \{} \\
\quad rsS \\
\text{\}} \\
\textbf{fact } F \text{ \{} \\
\quad forms \\
\text{\}} \\
\hline
\end{array}
\quad =_{\Sigma,v} \quad
\begin{array}{|l|}
\hline
ps \\
\textbf{sig } U \text{ \{} \\
\quad rsU \\
\text{\}} \\
\textbf{sig } S \textbf{ extends } U \text{ \{} \\
\quad rsS \\
\text{\}} \\
\textbf{sig } X \textbf{ extends } U \text{ \{\}} \\
\textbf{fact } F \text{ \{} \\
\quad forms \\
\quad X = U - S \\
\text{\}} \\
\hline
\end{array}
$$

($\leftrightarrow$) (1) if X belongs to Σ, v contains the $X \rightarrow (U - S)$ item; (2) for all names in Σ that are not in the resulting model, v must have exactly one valid item for it;
($\rightarrow$) (1) ps does not declare any paragraph named X; (2) there is no signature in ps that extends U;
($\leftarrow$) (1) X does not appear in ps, rsU, rsS and $forms$; (2) there does not exist an expression exp, such that $exp \leq U$ and $exp \not\leq S$, in ps or v.

belong to exactly one of its subsignatures. Similarly, the subsignature can be removed if not used elsewhere, and there is no expression in the model with its type, in order to avoid type errors.

The $\leq$ operator denotes the subtype relationship. For instance, if X is direct or indirect subsignature of Y then X is a subtype of Y ($X{\leq}Y$). Similarly, if a signature is not a subtype of another, we use the $\not\leq$ operator. We can propose a similar law when there are any number of subsignatures extending U. Notice that in order to preserve semantics, there is a condition when X belongs to Σ. In this case, v must have the item $X{\rightarrow}(U - S)$. The other conditions make sure that we preserve the well-formedness rules.

Besides laws for dealing with signatures, we also define laws for manipulating relations. Law 7 states that we can introduce a new relation along with its definition, which is a formula of the form $r = exp$, establishing a value for the relation. We can also remove a relation that is not being used.

Law 7 ⟨introduce relation⟩

($\leftrightarrow$) (1) if r belongs to Σ, r does not appear in exp and v contains the $r{\rightarrow}exp$ item; (2) for all names in Σ that are not in the resulting model, v must have exactly one valid item for it;
($\rightarrow$) (1) S's family in ps does not declare any relation named r; (2) T is a signature name declared in ps or is S; (3) r does not appear in exp, or exp is r; (4) $exp{\leq}r$ in the resulting model;
($\leftarrow$) r does not appear in ps or $forms$.

Law 7 can also be applied to S when it extends a signature. The family of a signature is the set of all signatures that extend or are extended by it direct or indirectly. Alloy does not allow two relations with the same name in the same family. Moreover, exp's type must be a subtype of r on the right side model in order to avoid inconsistencies, since r cannot be related to a value that does not belong to its type. Law 7 can also be applied for multirelations. The only difference is that we should not use the **set** relation qualifier. As explained before, omitting a relation qualifier denotes the unconstrained qualifier different from a binary relation, in which it represents a total function.

Besides proposing some laws for signatures and relations, Law 11 establishes that we can add or remove a formula from a fact, as long as it can be deduced

Law 15 ⟨split relation⟩

$$
\begin{array}{|l|}
\hline
ps \\
\textbf{sig } S \ \{ \\
\quad rs, \\
\quad r : \ \textbf{set } T \\
\} \\
\textbf{fact } F \ \{ \\
\quad forms \\
\} \\
\\
\hline
\end{array}
\quad =_{\Sigma,v} \quad
\begin{array}{|l|}
\hline
ps \\
\textbf{sig } S \ \{ \\
\quad rs, \\
\quad r : \ \textbf{set } T \\
\} \\
\textbf{sig } Col \ \{ \\
\quad x : \ \textbf{set } S, \\
\quad y : \ \textbf{set } T \\
\} \\
\textbf{fact } F \ \{ \\
\quad forms \\
\quad r = \ \tilde{}x.y \\
\} \\
\hline
\end{array}
$$

(↔) (1) Col, x and y do not belong to Σ; (2) for all names in Σ that are not in the resulting model, v must have exactly one valid item for it;
(→) ps does not declare any paragraph named Col;
(←) Col, x and y do not appear in ps, rs or $forms$.

from other formulae in the specification. Since f is derived from other formulae, we guarantee that both specifications have the same meaning. Notice that we assume that f must be well-typed. The constraints imposed by this formula are already imposed by the others.

Finally, we propose two new (previously unpublished) laws for relations. For instance, Law 15 introduces a relation. However, the definition of the new relation is different from Law 7. By using Law 15, we can split the relation r between two signatures into x and y. We can also remove the relation x, if it is not being used elsewhere.

Law 16 ⟨introduce one relation⟩

$$
\begin{array}{|l|}
\hline
ps \\
\textbf{sig } S \ \{ \\
\quad rs \\
\} \\
\textbf{fact } F \ \{ \\
\quad forms \\
\quad \# \ T \ != 0 \\
\} \\
\\
\hline
\end{array}
\quad =_{\Sigma,v} \quad
\begin{array}{|l|}
\hline
ps \\
\textbf{sig } S \ \{ \\
\quad rs, \\
\quad r : \ \textbf{one } T \\
\} \\
\textbf{fact } F \ \{ \\
\quad forms \\
\quad \# \ T \ != 0 \\
\} \\
\hline
\end{array}
$$

(↔) (1) r does not belong to Σ; (2) for all names in Σ that are not in the resulting model, v must have exactly one valid item for it;
(→) S's family in ps does not declare any relation named r;
(←) r does not appear in ps or $forms$.

After Law 15 from left to right, notice that the r relation can be removed from the model by applying Law 7 from right to left and Law 11 from left to right and vice-versa, since its definition is present. Moreover, this law can also be applied to S when it extends a signature. If one desires to move a relation from rs to the T signature, x and y must be bijective. Law 16 allows us to introduce a relation that is a function. This law is similar to Law 7. However, the new relation should not belong to the alphabet. Furthermore, the image of the new relation must be non-empty.

Although each law defines two semantics-preserving transformations, in fact, we have more than 36 primitive transformations. Some other laws can be similarly proposed for more than two signatures, such as Laws 2, 3 and 4. Other laws can be used with a signature extending another, such as Laws 4 and 7. We prefer to focus on laws for Alloy's main constructs: signatures, relations and formulae.

5   The Completeness Result

In this kind of work, it is important to show that our catalog is relatively complete, in order to establish that some clearly defined subset of all truths can be deduced directly from our laws.

In order to do that, we define a *reduction strategy* (based on primitive laws) showing how to transform any Alloy model into an equivalent one expressed in the Alloy normal form (*core language*). The Alloy core language is defined by Jackson [3]. It may declare unconstrained signatures without subtyping, and unconstrained relations. Moreover it includes subset (in), equality, negation, conjunction and universal quantification formulae. The other kinds of formulae, such as existential quantification and disjunction, can be derived from those. It includes binary (union (+), intersection (&), join (.) and product (->)) and unary (transpose (~) and transitive closure (^)) expressions. So, in this reduction strategy, we remove the signature hierarchy. In Section 5.6, in order to evaluate our result, we apply our laws to a different reduction strategy that preserves the signature hierarchy and pulls up all relations to the parent signature.

If two models have the same resulting model after applying the reduction strategy, they are equivalent. By defining a reduction strategy, the relative completeness result implies that our catalog can derive a comprehensive set of object model refactorings. We follow the same approach adopted by Tony Hoare for imperative languages [8]. Next we show an example, in which we apply the reduction strategy, in which Σ must contain all names in the initial model, in Sections 5.2-5.4. In Section 5.5, we generalize the reduction strategy (removing signature hierarchy).

5.1   Example

As an example, we show how our laws can be used to apply the reduction strategy to an Alloy model of a banking system presented in Figure 2 to an equivalent one in the core language. Account is an abstract signature, which is represented

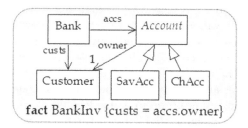

Fig. 2. Initial Model of a Banking System

by a box with an italic name. We focus on Alloy's main constructs and do not show other syntactic sugar constructs, such as functions and predicates.

Since we will remove all signatures that have subtypes (such as `Account`), the view v contains only mappings for them and all relations that refer to it, such as `owner` and `accs`. For instance, the item $Account \rightarrow ChAcc + SavAcc$ belongs to v since `Account` has subtypes. The other items are very similar to this one, relating a signature or relation name to the union of other names.

5.2   Removing Syntactic Sugar Constructs

In our reduction strategy, firstly we replace all syntactic sugar constructs by explicit formulae. We apply Laws 4 and 8 from left to right in order to replace the `Account` abstract signature qualifier and the one relation qualifier (`owner`) and express them by formulae in the `BankInv` fact, as declared next.

```
fact BankInv {
   custs = accs.owner
   Account = SavAcc + ChAcc
   all a:Account | one a.owner
}
```

Removing most of syntactic sugar laws do not have enabling conditions, except for Laws 4 and 10. However, Law 4 can also be applied to more than two subsignatures. So, its condition is always satisfied. Therefore, the syntactic sugar laws can always be applied. Moreover, all syntactic sugar laws do not introduce another syntactic sugar construct. Therefore, removing syntactic sugar constructs always *terminates* and *converges* to a model that does not have them. We can apply these laws in any order that the result is always the same.

5.3   Removing Top-Level Signatures

The core language does not have subtyping. Now we are aiming at removing all *top-level signatures*, which are signatures that have subtypes and do not extend another signature. First we must convert them to abstract in order to remove it later on. In the Figure 2 model, the only parent signature is abstract (`Account`), hence we do not need to apply Law 3 to introduce a subsignature (from left to right). Avoiding name conflicts, we can always apply Law 3 from left to right. So, any top-level signature can always be converted to abstract.

As mentioned before, Σ contains all elements in the original model. So, in this reduction, since the new elements introduced do not belong to Σ, the laws' conditions related to Σ are always valid. The conditions related to v can always be satisfied by choosing an appropriate name in order to preserve its validity.

Now that the top-level signature is abstract, our aim is to remove any reference to each parent signature in order to remove it later on. It can be referred by relations and formulae. For each relation whose type refers to `Account`, we have to introduce a corresponding relation for each subsignature of `Account` by applying Law 7 from left to right. In our example, `accs` and `owner` refer to `Account`. So, we introduce four new relations (`ownerCh`, `ownerSav`, `accCh` and `accSav`). `BankInv` contains their definitions.

```
fact BankInv {
   custs = accs.owner
   Account = SavAcc+ChAcc
   all a:Account | one a.owner
   ownerCh = owner&(ChAcc->Customer)
   ownerSav = owner&(SavAcc->Customer)
   accCh = accs&(Bank->ChAcc)
   accSav = accs&(Bank->SavAcc)
}
```

Notice that each introduced relation is similarly defined, which satisfies the conditions (the relation does not appear in its definition and the expression has the same type of the relation) required by applying Law 7 from left to right. All introduced relations must be equivalent to the intersection of the original relation with its new type, which is equivalent to the old type but it refers to a subsignature instead of the parent signature. This law can always be applied avoiding name conflicts. The same approach should be done for relations with arity greater than two.

We introduce new relations in order to eventually remove all relations that refer to a top-level parent signature. For example, using Law 11, we can deduce that `owner = ownerCh+ownerSav` from the definitions of the new relations and because the top-level signature is abstract. By replacing `owner` by its definition using Law 11, we can remove every occurrence of it in the model, except for its declaration and definition. Then, we can remove `owner` by applying Law 7 from right to left since it does not appear in the model. Since the relation name belongs to Σ, v must have an item for it $(owner \rightarrow ownerCh + ownerSav)$. As mentioned before, all items in v relate a name to a union of other names. In order to remove `accs`, we follow a similar approach.

Now our aim is to remove all references of the top-level signatures from formulae. Firstly we replace every occurrence of `Account` by its definition `SavAcc+ChAcc` in every formula using Law 11. Remember that we always deal with abstract parent signatures; hence they have a definition. Now `Account` only appears in its declaration, definition and in each subsignature extension. So, we

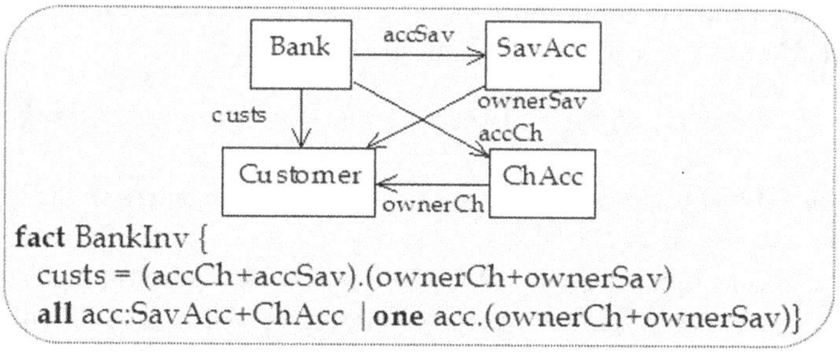
Bank
accSav
SavAcc
custs
ownerSav
accCh
Customer
ChAcc
ownerCh
fact BankInv {
custs = (accCh+accSav).(ownerCh+ownerSav)
all acc:SavAcc+ChAcc | one acc.(ownerCh+ownerSav)}

Fig. 3. Final Model of a Banking System

can always apply Law 2 from right to left in order to remove it from the model. Notice that `Account` encompasses a valid item for it in v. The resulting model is depicted in Figure 3.

We have to follow the same approach in order to remove all top-level signatures. This step of the reduction always terminates and converges because the number of top-level signatures always decreases. We only add a signature when the top-level signature is not abstract. However, this signature is not top-level since it does not have subtypes. Additionally, the number of relations introduced is finite since the number of subsignatures of the top-level signature is finite. Moreover, notice that we justify why we can always apply a law in each step. The only required condition is that the introduction of new names does not cause name conflicts.

5.4 Replacing Formulae

Finally, we apply Law 11 to every formula in order to transform it into an equivalent one in the core language. Applying Law 14, we can always remove all signature's attached formulae. When facts are empty, we can always use Laws 12 and 13 from right to left in order to remove them. Moreover we can move all formulae to one fact by applying Law 11. In Alloy, a formula can be declared in any fact.

5.5 Generalization

Applying a similar approach used in the previous example, we can always transform any Alloy model into an equivalent one in the core language, as stated by the following theorem.

Theorem 1. *Any Alloy model can always be reduced to Alloy's core language by applying Laws 1-14.*

The proof of the previous theorem is similar to the details given in the previous example. We use the same strategy in terms of the applicability of the laws discussed in each individual step in the example. The reduction strategy for an Alloy model M involves the following major steps:

1. remove all syntactic sugar constructs by applying Laws 4-6 and 8-10 from left to right;
2. apply the following steps to all top-level parent signatures S until there are no subsignatures in M:
   (a) make S an abstract signature by applying Law 3 from left to right;
   (b) push down every relation, whose type refers to S, for each subsignature of S by applying Laws 7 and 11;
   (c) replace every occurrence of S in all formulae by its definition using Law 11;
   (d) remove S by applying Law 2 from right to left;
3. replace all formulae by an equivalent one in Alloy's core language by applying Law 11, and move all formulae to one fact by using Laws 11-14.

In some situations, the resulting model can also be reduced into an equivalent one containing less signatures and relations. By applying Laws 1 and 15 from right to left, we can remove all auxiliary signatures and merge relations.

5.6   A Different Reduction Strategy

Our approach uses a normal form, in which there is no signature hierarchy, for Alloy proposed by Jackson [3]. In order to give more evidence of the previous result, next we present a reduction strategy for a different normal form, which is similar to the one proposed for ROOL [9] (a Java-like language). In ROOL's reduction, all attributes and methods are pulled up to the super class Object. In this normal form, the signature hierarchy is preserved in contrast to Jackson's one.

Next we present a reduction strategy for a normal form similar to ROOL. Any Alloy model is reduced to another one expressed, in which all relations are declared in the parent signature $Object$. In this new reduction strategy, we have to apply the same first (removing syntactic sugar constructs) and last step (replacing formulae) of the previous strategy. The only difference is in the second step. First, we have to apply Law 2 from left to right in order to introduce the $Object$ signature. This signature must be the parent signature of all top-level signatures. We can always apply Law 2 from left to right avoiding naming conflicts. Then, we pull up all relations from the subsignatures to $Object$. In order to do that, we apply Laws 7 and 11. By composing those laws, we can derive the Pull Up Relation refactoring. We can always apply this refactoring from left to right avoiding naming conflicts. In this reduction, we use the same laws of the previous strategy except for Law 3, which is not used in this reduction.

We summarize the new reduction strategy next:

1. remove all syntactic sugar constructs by applying Laws 4-6 and 8-10 from left to right;

2. introduce *Object* by applying Law 2 from left to right. All top-level signatures must have *Object* as a parent signature;
3. for each relation that is not declared in *Object*:
   (a) apply the Pull Up Relation refactoring from left to right;
4. replace all formulae by an equivalent one in Alloy's core language by applying Law 11, and move all formulae to one fact by using Laws 11-14.

So, the normal form proposed by Jackson [3] is better than the previous one because it allowed us to propose Law 3. In this kind of approach for proving the relatively completeness result, a normal formal is better than another if it allows us to propose more laws.

6   Related Work

Banerjee et al. [10] propose a set of primitive transformations for object-oriented database schemas. These schemas can be represented by a subset of UML class diagrams. They propose well-formedness rules for schemas and argue that their transformations preserve well-formedness. They have transformations for adding and removing signatures, relations, inheritance and methods. We proposed similar transformations, but we also focus on semantics preservation. Actually some of their transformations do not preserve semantics. Moreover, our language considers formulae differently from their work.

Bergstein [11] proposed five primitive *object-preserving* class transformations. Four of his transformations are very similar to our transformations defined by Law 2 and Pull Up Refactoring. The other transformation deals with multiple inheritance, which is not supported by signature extension in Alloy 4. The conditions for each transformation are not precisely defined as presented in our work. The set of transformations was shown to be complete under his language, which did not have multiplicities and constraints, and equivalence notion. He presented a full completeness result by showing that any two models that are equivalent under his notion can be related using his primitive transformations. So, if two models m and m' are equivalent, he showed that is always possible to rewrite them m=m1=m2=...=m' by applying his transformations. He has a stronger completeness result than our work. In his approach, he did not consider a normal formal different from our work. Since he did not consider formulae, it is much easier to remove a relation and a signature. The modeling language and transformations considered in our work are more complex then his. In our case, before removing any name, we have to deduce from the model's constraints a definition for it, which is not always possible, and replace it in every constraint.

Sunyé et al. [12] present a set of class diagram refactorings for adding, removing and moving features. Enabling conditions are informally presented, but some of them are not feasible in practice to be implemented in a tool. Gogolla and Richters [13] show some transformations for class diagrams and OCL constraints. Both approaches fail to propose a formal semantics for class diagrams and an equivalence notion. None of them guarantee the type system preservation differently from our work. So, OCL constraints can become ill-typed by applying some transformations. In some situations, some of the transformations proposed do not preserve semantics [2].

Lano and Bicarregui [14] present semantics for some class diagrams, and a set of transformations for structural and behavioral diagrams. They propose some structural refactorings, such as the *Extract Interface* refactoring. Nevertheless, they do not precisely state the enabling conditions. Some class diagram transformations consider OCL constraints. Evans [15] proposes deductive transformations for a subset of UML class diagrams. A formal semantics is proposed for a subset of UML class diagrams. He proposes five transformations, such as the *Pull Up Attribute*. These transformations can introduce type errors when considering OCL constraints. None of the previous approaches except for Bergstein's work attempts to propose a relatively complete set of transformations. McComb [16] investigated refactorings for Object-Z models. He proposed three refactoring rules and showed that they were complete in the sense that any Object-Z specification that does not have unbounded recursive constructs, any design may be derived, which represents a refinement of the original specification.

Frias et al. [17] specified a formal semantics for Alloy 2 (we focus on Alloy 4), in which there is no notion of subtyping. They consider signatures as syntactic sugar, different from our work. So, we can propose some interesting transformations changing the signature hierarchy.

7   Conclusions

We propose a comprehensive catalog of object modeling laws for Alloy. They are a powerful tool for reasoning about object model transformations. We prove that this set of transformations is relatively complete, through two reduction strategies (transforming any Alloy model to another one in the core language): destroying signature hierarchy, and preserving hierarchy and pulling up all relations. One of the strategies allowed us to discover Law 3. By composing these transformations, we can derive a representative set of model transformations. In our earlier work [4], we derived refactorings that allow us to change between Alloy idioms and, more generally, reason about models. In addition, the laws from this work help formalizing model-driven program refactoring, based on model invariants, as described before [1].

Suppose that two models are equivalent with respect to an alphabet and a view. The *full completeness* result states that we can always relate both models by applying our laws. Our catalog does not have the full completeness property due to our approach of proposing laws with syntactic conditions. Introducing formulae may introduce inconsistencies in a model. So, our laws are very conservative in the sense that some of them, such as Law 7, only introduce equality formulae. We assure that introducing equalities do not introduce inconsistencies and preserve semantics based on syntactic conditions. We do not have a law for introducing relations with any kind of formula because we do not want to leave to the user the burden of checking whether the new formulae preserve semantics since it is not a trivial task.

Acknowledgments

We thank the anonymous referees for useful suggestions. This work was partially supported by the National Institute of Science and Technology for Software Engineering, funded by CNPq and FACEPE, grants 573964/2008-4 and APQ-1037-1.03/08.

References

1. Massoni, T., Gheyi, R., Borba, P.: Formal model-driven program refactoring. In: Fiadeiro, J.L., Inverardi, P. (eds.) FASE 2008. LNCS, vol. 4961, pp. 362–376. Springer, Heidelberg (2008)
2. Gheyi, R.: A Refinement Theory for Alloy. PhD thesis, UFPE (2007)
3. Jackson, D.: Software Abstractions: Logic, Language and Analysis. MIT Press, Cambridge (2006)
4. Gheyi, R., Massoni, T., Borba, P.: Formally introducing alloy idioms. In: Brazilian Symposium on Formal Methods, Brazil, pp. 22–37 (2007)
5. Owre, S., et al.: PVS language reference (2007), http://pvs.csl.sri.com
6. Gheyi, R., Massoni, T., Borba, P.: A rigorous approach for proving model refactorings. In: 20th Automated Software Engineering Conference, pp. 372–375 (2005)
7. Gheyi, R., Massoni, T., Borba, P.: An abstract equivalence notion for object models. Electronic Notes in Theoretical Computer Science 130, 3–21 (2005)
8. Hoare, C., et al.: Laws of programming. CACM 30(8), 672–686 (1987)
9. Borba, P., et al.: Algebraic Reasoning for Object-Oriented Programming. Science of Computer Programming 52, 53–100 (2004)
10. Banerjee, J., et al.: Semantics and implementation of schema evolution in object-oriented databases. In: Int. Conf. on Management of Data, pp. 311–322 (1987)
11. Bergstein, P.: Object-preserving class transformations. In: OOPSLA, pp. 299–313 (1991)
12. Sunyé, G., et al.: Refactoring UML models. In: UML, pp. 134–148 (2001)
13. Gogolla, M., Richters, M.: Equivalence rules for UML class diagrams. In: UML, pp. 87–96 (1998)
14. Lano, K., Bicarregui, J.: Semantics and transformations for UML models. In: UML, pp. 97–106 (1998)
15. Evans, A.: Reasoning with UML class diagrams. In: 2nd IEEE Workshop on Industrial Strength Formal Specification Techniques, pp. 102–113 (1998)
16. McComb, T.: Refactoring Object-Z specifications. In: Wermelinger, M., Margaria-Steffen, T. (eds.) FASE 2004. LNCS, vol. 2984, pp. 69–83. Springer, Heidelberg (2004)
17. Frias, M., Pombo, C., Baum, G., Aguirre, N., Maibaum, T.: Reasoning about static and dynamic properties in alloy: A purely relational approach. ACM Transactions on Software Engineering Methodology 14(4), 478–526 (2005)

Undecidability Results for Distributed Probabilistic Systems*

Sergio Giro

FaMAF, Universidad Nacional de Córdoba - CONICET
Ciudad Universitaria - 5000 Córdoba - Argentina
sgiro@famaf.unc.edu.ar

Abstract. In the verification of concurrent systems involving probabilities, the aim is to find out the maximum/minimum probability that a given event occurs (examples of such events being "the system reaches a failure state","a message is delivered"). Such extremal probabilities are obtained by quantifying over all the possible ways in which the processes may be interleaved. Interleaving choices are considered a particular case of *nondeterministic* behaviour. Such behaviour is dealt with by considering *schedulers* that resolve the nondeterministic choices. Each scheduler determines a Markov chain for which actual probabilities can be calculated. In the recent literature on distributed systems, particular attention has been paid to the fact that, in order to obtain accurate results, the analysis must rely on partial information schedulers, instead of full-history dependent schedulers used in the setting of Markov decision processes. In this paper, we present undecidability results for *distributed schedulers*. These schedulers were devised in previous works, and aim to capture the fact that each process has partial information about the actual state of the system. Some of the undecidability results we present are particularly impressive: in the setting of total information the same problems are inexpensive and, indeed, they are used as preprocessing steps in more general model checking algorithms.

1 Introduction

Markov decision processes (MDPs) are widely used in diverse fields ranging from ecology to computer science. They are useful to model and analyse systems in which both probabilistic and nondeterministic choices interact. Particularly, composition oriented versions of MDPs like probabilistic I/O automata [6,23], or probabilistic modules [8] are aimed to model concurrent and distributed systems.

Model checking is a push-button technique to check properties about the behaviour of probabilistic systems. Given a property and a model of the system, model checking algorithms are able to determine whether the formula holds in the model or not. *Probabilistic* model checking can be applied to MDPs [22,2]. Moreover, probabilistic model checkers have been developed, notably PRISM [17] and LiQuor [7].

---

* Supported by ANPCyT project PICT 26135 and CONICET project PIP 6391.

M.V.M. Oliveira and J. Woodcock (Eds.): SBMF 2009, LNCS 5902, pp. 220–235, 2009.

The set of execution paths that are relevant to the property being checked is defined using temporal logic formulae. Such formula rely on the usual modal operators *finally* (written F or ◇) and *globally* (written G or □). As concrete example, we may consider the paths in which "globally, the system is not in a critical state" or "finally, the system reaches a stable state". Given that MDPs involve nondeterminism, the probability that a given formula holds depends on how nondeterminism is resolved (in the concrete case of concurrent systems, it depends on the order in which the components execute). Verification techniques are concerned with properties that are required to hold in all possible resolutions, and so the goal of probabilistic model checking is to find out the maximum (or minimum) probability value of a formula. Such extrema are safe bounds on the actual probability that the property holds, and so they can be used to state that "the probability of reaching a failure state is less than 0.05, no matter the order in which components execute". To obtain such extrema, the technique requires to universally quantify on all possible resolutions of the nondeterminism inherent to the MDP. The resolution of nondeterminism is carried out by the so-called *schedulers* (called also adversaries or policies, see e.g. [22,2,20]). Schedulers transform MDPs into Markov chains (MC) by selecting one of the enabled transitions at every step in the execution of the system. In case we are analysing a concurrent system, the next component to perform a transition in the MC is determined by the scheduler's choice. Therefore, the goal of probabilistic model checking is to find out the maximum (or minimum) probability value of a temporal formula over all possible schedulers.

Existing model checking techniques consider the *full-history dependent* schedulers used traditionally in the MDP setting. Such schedulers are functions mapping execution paths (representing the history of the system) to enabled transitions. In this way, the scheduler can choose a different enabled transition in each path. In the case of concurrent systems, a compound model is obtained by interleaving the models corresponding to the components, thus considering all the full-history dependent schedulers in the compound model.

There is a research trend focusing on the fact that, in case not all information is available to all components, some full-history dependent schedulers represent unrealistic resolutions of nondeterminism (see [1,3,4,6,8], just to name a few). Another consequence of full-history dependent schedulers is that properties cannot be proven in a compositional fashion: already in seminal works [20], this impossibility has been revealed as a rough edge in the theory.

The fictitious availability of information results in fictitious behaviours in which the system does not necessarily complies with its specification. The following examples show fictitious resolutions of nondeterminism and their impact on the maximum probability that certain states are reached.

In these examples, we see the execution of the system as a game, and the failure states we want to avoid as states in which one of the players has lost the game. The automata in Fig. 1a represent a game in which player T plays against the team comprising players G_H and G_T. In such a game, T tosses a coin and the team G_H, G_T has to guess. Since we have not introduced the

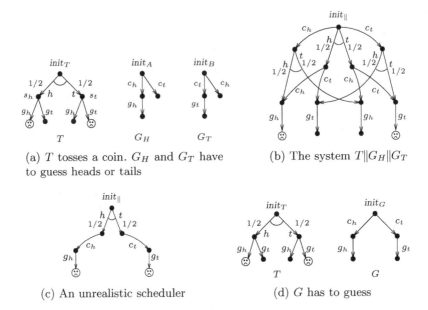

(a) T tosses a coin. G_H and G_T have to guess heads or tails

(b) The system $T\|G_H\|G_T$

(c) An unrealistic scheduler

(d) G has to guess

Fig. 1. Full-history dependent schedulers are unrealistic

formalism we use, we describe the problem informally. Players G_H and G_T take the guess in the following fashion: in case G_H believes that the coin landed heads, it executes c_h and then g_h. Conversely, in case G_T believes that the coin landed tails, it executes c_t and then g_t. The components synchronize in a CSP fashion. In particular, the transition labelled with c_h must be executed in both G_T and G_H during the same transition step. So, as soon as one of the players chooses an option, the other one accepts it and stays quiet. Player T loses if it receives a g_h and the coin has landed heads (the intended meaning being that G_H and G_T have correctly guessed heads), and similarly for g_t and tails[1]. Intuitively, since neither G_H not G_T have any information about the outcome of the coin, they cannot arrange in such a way that T loses all the time. However, in the compound system $T \parallel G_H \parallel G_T$ (shown in Fig. 1b) there is a full-history dependent scheduler in which T loses with probability 1. Such scheduler chooses T in the first place. Then it chooses G_H, in case the coin lands heads; and G_T, in case it lands tails (this scheduler is depicted in Fig. 1c). However, in the real system, the time that G_H and G_H spend in their initial states (and, consequently, the order in which they execute their transitions) cannot depend on information that is not available to them. Hence, full-history dependent schedulers are not a convenient way to model nondeterminism. The same observation applies to *internal* nondeterministic choices (which are used to model failures or user inputs). Figure 1d depicts players T and G, and the intended meaning is that T loses in case G guesses the outcome of the coin. Again, the compound system is that of Fig. 1b, and the scheduler in Fig. 1c

---

[1] Note that T gets very sad in case he loses.

unrealistically assumes that G can change its choice according to the outcome of the coin (note that G is the parallel composition $G_H \parallel G_T$) and so the probability that T loses is 1. This is the probability that we obtain using the algorithms behind existing model checkers such as PRISM [17] or LiQuor [7]. In both examples we would like the maximum probability of reaching ☺ to be $1/2$ since, if we repeat the game several times, the player G (or the team comprising G_H and G_T) will guess correctly half of the times in the long run.

In general, it may be the case that a program is deemed incorrect by an algorithm, while all the behaviours that violate the specification according to the algorithm (that is, the counterexamples) are fictitious. The bottom line is that some correct systems may be deemed incorrect by existing algorithms. In this sense, we can say that such algorithms are "sound" (that is, no incorrect systems are deemed correct) but not "complete" (some correct systems are deemed incorrect).

In order to limit the variety of behaviours introduced by full-history dependent schedulers, classes of schedulers that only consider partial information were proposed in the literature. In particular, we are interested in the class of so-called *distributed schedulers*. Such schedulers were studied in [8] in a synchronous setting and in [5,13] in an asynchronous setting. A distributed scheduler is constructed from *local* schedulers, which are schedulers for single components of the system defined in the usual way, and a mechanism to combine such schedulers. Such mechanism could be related to a projection function [8], a passing token [6,5], execution rates of the components [14], or schedulers that define the way in which components interleave [13]. These approaches result in different types of distributed schedulers. We remark that the scheduler of Fig. 1c would not be a valid scheduler for $T \parallel G$ in this new setting, since the choice for G depends only on information which is external to (and not observed by) G. In fact, a local scheduler for G yielding such a behaviour would not be definable, since the local scheduler depends only on the local history of G, which is certainly the same as long as G does not execute any transition.

In conclusion, we would like to calculate the extremal probabilities *under distributed schedulers*.

In this paper, we present several undecidability results concerning distributed schedulers. First, the maximum probability that a state is reached under distributed schedulers cannot be approximated, even in systems that do not exhibit internal nondeterminism. This result is of a *quantitative* nature, in the sense that the problem concerns the calculation of a probability value. Still more interesting are the results concerning *qualitative* properties: namely, there is no algorithm to decide whether there exists a scheduler reaching a set of states with probability one (nor whether the supremum quantifying over all schedulers is 1). In particular, it cannot be calculated whether there is a distributed strategy in which the system stabilizes with probability 1 (let alone calculating such an strategy).

These results are original contributions, and we complete the picture by recalling a theorem in [12]. In Sec. 4, we compare the results in this paper against existing undecidability results for partial information schedulers.

2   Interleaved Probabilistic I/O Automata

Our results are presented in the framework of Interleaved Probabilistic I/O Automata (IPIOA) [13]. This framework is based on the Switched PIOA introduced by Cheung et al. [6] It uses reactive and generative structures (see [16]). For a finite set S, we denote by $DiscDist(S)$ the set of all discrete probability distributions over the set S. Given a set ActLab of action labels and a set S of states, the set of generative transitions T_G on $(\mathsf{S}, \mathsf{ActLab})$ is $DiscDist(\mathsf{S} \times \mathsf{ActLab})$, and the set T_R of reactive transitions is $DiscDist(\mathsf{S})$. A generative structure on $(\mathsf{S}, \mathsf{ActLab})$ is a function $G : \mathsf{S} \to \mathcal{P}(T_G)$ and a reactive structure on $(\mathsf{S}, \mathsf{ActLab})$ is a function $R : \mathsf{S} \times \mathsf{ActLab} \to \mathcal{P}(T_R)$. Figure 2 depicts an example of these structures. Generative transitions model both communication and state change.

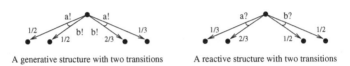

A generative structure with two transitions   A reactive structure with two transitions

Fig. 2. Reactive and generative structures

The component executing a generative transition chooses both a label a to output (the ! in the figure represents output) and a new state s according to a given distribution. Reactive transitions specify how a component reacts to a given input (the ? in the figure represents input). Since the input is not chosen, reactive transitions are simply distributions on states. A generative transition such that $g(a_1, s_1) = p_1$ and $g(a_2, s_2) = p_2$ is denoted by $p_1 \xrightarrow{a_1!} s_1 + p_2 \xrightarrow{a_2!} s_2$ and similarly for reactive transitions.

In our framework, a system is obtained by composing several *probabilistic I/O atoms*. Each atom is a probabilistic automata having reactive and generative transitions.

Definition 1. *A probabilistic I/O atom is a 5-tuple* $(\mathsf{S}, \mathsf{ActLab}, G, R, \mathsf{init})$, *where* S *is a finite set of states,* ActLab *is a finite set of actions labels, and* G *(R, resp.) is a generative (reactive, resp.) structure in* $(\mathsf{S}, \mathsf{ActLab})$. $\mathsf{init} \in \mathsf{S}$ *is the initial state. We require the atoms to be input-enabled[2], so* $R(s, a) \neq \emptyset$ *for every* $s \in \mathsf{S}$, $a \in \mathsf{ActLab}$. *We often write* S_i *to denote the set of states of an atom* A_i *and similarly for the other elements of the 5-tuple. In addition, we write* T_{G_i} *(T_{R_i}, resp.) for the set of generative (reactive, resp.) transitions on* $(\mathsf{S}_i, \mathsf{ActLab}_i)$.

An interleaved probabilistic I/O system P is a set $Atoms(P)$ of probabilistic I/O atoms $A_1, \cdots, A_N$. The set of states of the system is $\prod_i \mathsf{S}_i$, and the initial state of the system is $\mathsf{init} = (\mathsf{init}_1, \cdots, \mathsf{init}_N)$. The *parallel composition* of two systems P, Q (denoted by $P \parallel Q$) is the system having $Atoms(P \parallel Q) = Atoms(P) \cup Atoms(Q)$. Given two atoms A and B, we denote by $A \parallel B$

---

[2] This requirement is already present in seminal works introducing I/O automata [18].

the parallel composition of the systems P with $Atoms(P) = \{A\}$ and Q with $Atoms(Q) = \{B\}$.

In order to define how the system evolves, we define *compound transitions*, which are the transitions performed by the system as a whole. In such compound transitions, all the atoms having the same action label in their alphabet must synchronize and *exactly one* of them must participate with an output (generative) transition (thus modelling multicasting). Formally, a compound transition is a tuple $c = (g_i, a, r_{j_1}, \cdots, r_{j_m})$ (we require $i \neq j_k$ and $j_k \neq j_{k'}$ for all $k \neq k'$) where g_i is a generative transition in the atom A_i (the *active* atom, denoted by $\mathsf{active}(c)$), $a \in \mathsf{ActLab}_i$ is an action label, the r_{j_k} are reactive transitions in the atoms A_{j_k} (the *reactive* atoms) and $\{A_i, A_{j_1}, \cdots, A_{j_m}\}$ is the set of all the atoms such that $a \in \mathsf{ActLab}_j$. We say that $A_i, A_{j_1}, \ldots, A_{j_m}$ are the atoms *involved* in the compound transition. A compound transition $(g_i, a, r_{j_1}, \cdots, r_{j_m})$ is enabled in a given state $(s_1, \cdots, s_N)$ if $g_i \in G_i(s_i)$ and $r_{j_k} \in R_{j_k}(s_{j_k}, a)$. The action label a of a compound transition c is indicated by $label(c)$. The (sub)probability $c(s, s')$ of reaching a state $s' = (s'_1, \cdots, s'_N)$ from a state $s = (s_1, \cdots, s_N)$ using a compound transition $c = (g_i, a, r_{j_1}, \cdots, r_{j_m})$ is $g_i(s'_i, a) \cdot \prod_{k=1}^{m} r_{j_k}(s'_{j_k})$ if $s_t = s'_t$ for every atom not involved in the transition. Otherwise, $c(s, s') = 0$. So, for all A we have $\sum_{\{c | \mathsf{active}(c) = A\}} \sum_s c(s, s') = 1$.

In order to ease some definitions, we introduce a fictitious "stutter" compound transition ς. Intuitively, this transition is executed iff the system has reached a state in which no atom is able to generate a transition. The probability $\varsigma(s, s')$ of reaching s' from s using ς is 1, if $s = s'$, or 0, otherwise.

A path σ of P is a sequence of the form $s_1.c_1.s_2.c_2 \cdots c_{n-1}.s_n$ where each s_i is a (compound) state such that $c(s_{i-1}, s_i) > 0$ and each c_i is a compound transition enabled in s_{i-1}. A path can be finite or infinite. We denote the set of finite paths by $Paths(P)$. For a path σ as before, we define $\sigma(i) = s_i$. For all finite σ, we define $last(\sigma) = s_n$ and $len(\sigma) = n$. The set $\sigma^\uparrow$ contains all the infinite paths starting with σ. Given a set of states U, the set of infinite paths $\{\rho \mid \exists i \bullet \rho(i) \in U\}$ is denoted by $reach(U)$.

In the following, we suppose that input-enabled atoms $A_1, \ldots, A_N$ are given, and we are considering the system P comprising all the atoms A_i. We call this system "the compound system". The states (paths, resp.) of the compound system are called global states (global paths, resp.) and the states (paths, resp.) of each atom are called local states (local paths, resp.).

The probability of a set of executions depends on how the nondeterminism is resolved. A scheduler resolves a nondeterministic choice by selecting one of the available transitions. Given a system and a scheduler, the probability of a set of executions is completely determined.

Usually, schedulers assign probabilities to the available transitions taking into account the complete history of the system. So, *arbitrary* schedulers are defined as functions mapping paths to transitions. As we have seen, it may be unrealistic to assume that the schedulers are able to see the full history of all the components in the system. In the following, we define restricted classes of schedulers in order to avoid considering unrealistic behaviours.

For simplicity, in this paper we restrict to non-randomized schedulers. Proofs of the results we present under randomized schedulers can be found in [15].

2.1   Distributed Schedulers

In a distributed setting as the one we are introducing, different kinds of nondeterministic choices need to be resolved. An atom needs a corresponding *output* scheduler to choose the next generative transition. In addition, it may be the case that many reactive transitions are enabled for a single label in the same atom. So, for each atom we need an *input* scheduler in order to choose a reactive transition for each previous history and for each label. Output and input schedulers are able to make their decisions based only on the local history of the atom. So, we need the notion of *projection*.

Given a path σ, the projection $[\sigma]_i$ of the path σ over an atom A_i is defined inductively as follows: **(1)** $[(\text{init}_1, \cdots, \text{init}_N)]_i = \text{init}_i$, **(2)** $[\sigma.c.s]_i = [\sigma]_i$ if $label(c) \notin \mathsf{ActLab}_i$ and **(3)** $[\sigma.c.s]_i = [\sigma]_i.label(c).\pi_i(s)$ (where π_i is the usual projection on tuples), otherwise. The set of all the projections of paths over an atom A_i is denoted by $\mathsf{Proj}_i(P)$.

An output scheduler for the atom A_i is a function $\Theta_i : \mathsf{Proj}_i(P) \to T_{G_i}$ such that, if $G_i(last(\sigma)) \neq \emptyset$ then $\Theta_i([\sigma]_i) = g \implies g \in G_i(last([\sigma]_i))$. An input scheduler for an atom A_i is a function $\Upsilon_i : \mathsf{Proj}_i(P) \times \mathsf{ActLab}_i \to T_{R_i}$ such that $\Upsilon_i([\sigma]_i, a) = r \implies r \in R_i(last([\sigma]_i), a)$. Note that, if the output scheduler Θ_i fixes a generative transition for a given local path $[\sigma]_i$, then the actions in the generative transition can be executed in every global path σ' such that $[\sigma']_i = [\sigma]_i$, since we require the atoms to be input-enabled.

An important difference with respect to the original framework introduced by Cheung et al. [5] is the addition of an *interleaving scheduler* that chooses the next component to perform an output. (For a detailed comparison of previous approaches to interleaving, see Sec. 4.)

We start by considering arbitrary interleaving schedulers that are able to see the complete history of the whole system. We restrict interleaving schedulers in the next subsection.

An interleaving scheduler is a map that, for a given (global) history, chooses an active atom that will be the next to execute an output transition (according to its output scheduler). Formally, an *interleaving scheduler* is a function $\mathcal{I} : Paths(P) \to \{A_1, \cdots, A_N\}$ such that, if there exists i such that $G_i(last([\sigma]_i)) > 0$ (that is, if there is some atom being able to generate a transition) then $\mathcal{I}(\sigma) = A_i \implies G_i(last([\sigma]_i)) \neq \emptyset$. Note that, even if interleaving schedulers are unrestricted, compound schedulers for the compound system are still restricted, since the local schedulers can only see the portion of the history corresponding to the component.

A scheduler for the compound system results from the appropriate composition of the interleaving scheduler and the output and input schedulers of each atom.

Definition 2. *Given an interleaving scheduler $\mathcal{I}$, input schedulers Υ_i and output schedulers Θ_i for each atom i, the* distributed scheduler η *obtained by* *composing* $\mathcal{I}$, Θ_i *and* Υ_i *is defined as* $\eta(\sigma)(g_i, a, r_{j_1}, \cdots, r_{j_m}) = 1$ *iff* $A_i = \mathcal{I}(\sigma)$, $\Theta_i([\sigma]_i) = g_i$ *and* $\Upsilon_{j_k}(\sigma, a) = r_{j_k}$ *for all* $j = 1, \cdots, m$. *In case there is no generative transition enabled, we require* $\eta(\sigma)(c) = 1$ *iff* $c = \varsigma$. *The set of distributed schedulers of* P *is denoted by* $Dist(P)$.

Since each generative transitions may output several different labels, the global scheduler η does not choose a single transition. The reader familiar with randomized schedulers may notice that $\sum_c \eta(\sigma)(c) > 1$ whenever the generative transition in c outputs more than one label. (This is in contrast with randomized schedulers, which choose probability distributions on transitions.) However, for every label a, we have $\sum_{\{c|label(c)=a\}} \eta(\sigma)(c) = 1$.

The probability of the extension sets $\sigma^\uparrow$ is inductively defined as follows: the probability $\Pr^\eta(\text{init}^\uparrow)$ of the extensions of the initial state is 1. The probability of $\Pr^\eta(\sigma.c.s^\uparrow)$ is $\Pr^\eta(\sigma) \cdot \eta(\sigma)(c) \cdot c(last(\sigma), s)$.

Simple arithmetic can be used to show that $\sum_{c,s'} \eta(\sigma)(c) \cdot c(last(\sigma), s') = 1$, and so, as usual (namely, by resorting to the Carathéodory extension theorem), this probability can be extended to the least σ-field containing all the extension sets.

2.2   Strongly Distributed Schedulers

Strongly distributed schedulers were introduced in [13] as a smaller but yet meaningful class of distributed schedulers.

Distributed schedulers as in Def. 2 provide an accurate model in case the interleaving scheduler has access to all information. As an example, suppose that the atoms represent processes running on the same computer, and the interleaving scheduler plays the role of the operating system scheduler. In case such an scheduler assigns priorities to the processes by gathering information from all processes states, a total information interleaving scheduler is a natural model.

On the contrary side, if we are analysing an agreement protocol and each atom models an independent node in a network, then the order in which two nodes execute cannot change according to information that is not available to them. We recall the example in the introduction to show how the worst-case probability is affected by the information available to the interleaving scheduler.

Figure 3, depicts the example in Fig. 1a in terms of our formalism. Given the input-enabledness requirement, we add an input transition in the initial state of T, thus modelling that the game ends in case G_H and G_T take their guess before the coin has been tossed.

In case we consider the system $T \parallel G_H \parallel G_T$, the unrealistic scheduler in Fig. 1c is distributed according to Def. 2, since distributed schedulers restrict the resolution of internal nondeterministic choices, and these atoms have no such choices (note that there

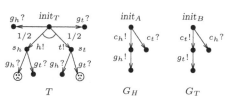

Fig. 3. Motivating strongly distributed schedulers

is at most one output transition in each state, and at most one input transition for each pair state/label). In particular, the interleaving scheduler can arrange the execution of G_H and G_T according to the hidden information in T.

Next, we present a condition on the interleaving scheduler. This restriction prevents the use of external information to change the order in which two components execute. The information available to atoms A and B can be defined as $[\sigma]_{A,B} = ([\sigma]_A, [\sigma]_B)$. Note that $[\sigma_{heads}]_{G_H,G_T} = [\sigma_{tails}]_{G_H,G_T} = (\text{init}_{G_H}, \text{init}_{G_T})$. In addition, in the unrealistic scheduler $\mathcal{I}(\sigma) = G_H$ and $\mathcal{I}(\sigma') = G_T$. Intuitively, for all atoms A, B there cannot be two paths σ, σ' such that: **(1)** $[\sigma]_{A,B} = [\sigma']_{A,B}$ and **(2)** atom A is scheduled in σ and **(3)** atom B is scheduled in σ'. Formally:

$$\forall A, B \in Atoms(P) \bullet \forall \sigma \bullet \nexists \sigma' \bullet [\sigma]_{AB} = [\sigma']_{AB} \wedge \mathcal{I}(\sigma) = A \wedge \mathcal{I}(\sigma) = B . \quad (1)$$

Definition 3. *A scheduler η is* strongly distributed *iff η is distributed and (1) holds on the interleaving scheduler $\mathcal{I}$ that defines η. The set of strongly distributed schedulers of P is denoted by $SDist(P)$.*

In [13] (where strongly distributed schedulers are introduced for the first time) we prove some properties to further support the fact that (1) is a natural restriction whenever the interleaving nondeterminism is resolved a distributed fashion. In particular, we prove that (1) implies a more general condition in which A and B are replaced with two disjoint sets of atoms $\mathcal{A}$ and $\mathcal{B}$. Strongly distributed schedulers also generalize the *rate schedulers* of [14], in the sense that the set of rate schedulers is included in the set of strongly distributed schedulers.

3   Undecidability

We start with a quantitative problem for strongly distributed schedulers, namely, to calculate the supremum probability that a state in a given set U is reached. Then, we consider the qualitative problem of deciding whether there exists a scheduler reaching some state in U with probability 1, and the problem of deciding whether the supremum probability quantifying over all schedulers is 1. These latter problems are not trivially equivalent. In [13] we show that, in some cases, the supremum probability is 1 and, although there are schedulers reaching U with probabilities arbitrarily close to 1, there is no scheduler yielding exactly such probability.

3.1   Quantitative Results

The following theorem is stated in its more "particular" form (that is, restricting the IPIOA to have no internal nondeterminism), since the stronger undecidability results are those concerning smaller input sets. Of course, the problem is also undecidable if we consider unrestricted IPIOA. The fact that the result holds for systems without internal nondeterminism shows that the condition we impose to strongly distributed schedulers introduce undecidability on its own, independently of the restrictions imposed by the mechanism of input/output schedulers.

Theorem 1. *There is no algorithm such that, for all IPIOA P having no internal nondeterministic choices, for all sets U, and for all $\epsilon > 0$, the algorithm computes r such that*

$$\left| \sup_{\eta \in SDist(P)} \Pr^{\eta}(\text{reach}(U)) - r \right| \leq \epsilon .$$

Proof. In order to prove Theorem 1, we reduce the supremum acceptance problem for probabilistic finite-state automata (PFA) to the supremum reachability problem for PIOA with unspecified rates. The supremum acceptance problem for PFA was proven undecidable in [19].

A PFA is a quintuple (Q, Σ, l, q_i, q_f) where Q is a finite set of *states* with $q_i, q_f \in Q$ being the *initial* and *accepting state* respectively, Σ is the *input alphabet*, and $l : \Sigma \times Q \rightarrow (Q \rightarrow [0, 1])$ is the *transition function* such that $l(\alpha, q)$ is a distribution for all $\alpha \in \Sigma$ and $q \in Q$. A word w is an infinite sequence of symbols from Σ. The probability $\Pr(\text{accept}(w))$ of accepting a word w is the probability of all paths ρ starting from q_i and reaching q_f according to $l(w_k, s_{k+1})$, where w_k is the k-th symbol in w and s_{k+1} is the $k + 1$-th state in ρ (the first state in ρ is q_i.

We recall Corollary 3.4 in [19]:

For any fixed $0 < \epsilon < 1$, the following problem is undecidable: Given a PFA F_A such that either

1. F_A accepts some word with probability greater than $1 - \epsilon$, or
2. F_A accepts no word with probability greater then ϵ;

decide whether case 1 holds.

Given a PFA F_A, we can construct an atom A_F having only reactive transitions. Such atom A_F is defined as follows: $S_F = Q$, $\text{ActLab}_F = \Sigma$, $G_F(s) = \emptyset$ for all s, $R_F(s, \alpha) = \{l(\alpha, s)\}$ and $\text{init}_F = q_i$.

In addition to A_F, we construct atoms A_α. For each $\alpha \in \Sigma$, the atom A_α is defined as follows: $S_{A_\alpha} = \{\text{init}_\alpha\}$, $\text{ActLab}_F = \{\alpha\}$, $G_F(\text{init}_\alpha) = \{g_\alpha\}$ where $g_\alpha(\alpha, \text{init}_\alpha) = 1$ and $R_\alpha(\text{init}_\alpha, \alpha) = \{r_\alpha\}$ where $r_\alpha(\text{init}_\alpha) = 1$ (although r_α is not used, it is required by the input-enabledness condition).

We consider the system $P = A_F \|_{\alpha \in \Sigma} A_\alpha$. In this system, every $\eta \in SDist(P)$ defines a word w for F. In fact, if $\mathcal{I}$ (i.e., the interleaving that defines η) chooses A_{α_1} in the initial state, then the first symbol of the word is α_1. After executing $l(\alpha, s)$, atom A_F can be in several states, but the choice of $\mathcal{I}$ must be the same in all of them, since

$$[s. (\, g_{\alpha_1}, \alpha_1, l(\alpha_1, s)\,). \, s']_{A_\alpha} = [s. (\, g_{\alpha_1}, \alpha_1, l(\alpha_1, s)\,). \, s'']_{A_\alpha} = \text{init}_\alpha . \alpha_1 . \text{init}_\alpha$$

for all α. So, if $\mathcal{I}(s.(g_{\alpha_1}, l(\alpha_1, s)).s') = \alpha_2$ for all s', then α_2 is the second symbol in the word, and so on.

Similarly, every word defines a strongly distributed scheduler. Then, we have

$$\sup_{w} \Pr(\text{accept}(w)) = \sup_{\eta \in SDist(P)} \Pr^{\eta}(\text{reach}(\{q_f\})) .$$

And so the result follows from Corollary 3.4 in [19].

By checking the definitions of A_α and A_F, we can see that the constructed system P has no internal nondeterminism.

In order to complete the picture, we state a theorem by Giro and D'Argenio in [12]. This theorem concerns the undecidability introduced by the fact that output schedulers can only look at the local history. In fact, the formalism used to prove the results in [12] is the one of synchronous probabilistic modules introduced by de Alfaro et al. in [8], and so there are no interleaving issues.

We say that a system has no interleaving nondeterminism if, for all states s, there is at most one atom A_i in which there are generative transitions enabled in s (that is, $G_i(\pi_i(s)) \neq \emptyset$ and for all $i' \neq i$ we have $G_{i'}(\pi_{i'}(s)) = \emptyset$).

Theorem 2. *There is no algorithm such that, for all IPIOA P without interleaving nondeterminism, for all sets U, and for all $\epsilon > 0$, the algorithm computes r such that*

$$\left| \sup_{\eta \in Dist(P)} \Pr^\eta(\text{reach}(U)) - r \right| \leq \epsilon .$$

In [12] this result is proven using the formalism in [8] and there it is explained how the proof can be adapted to a PIOA setting as the one in this paper.

3.2   Qualitative Undecidability

In the following proofs, we use reductions of the Post correspondence problem (PCP), which is a well-known undecidable problem [21].

The PCP problem can be stated as follows: given *finite* words $u_1, \ldots, u_n$ and $v_1, \ldots, v_n$ over an alphabet S. Is there a finite non-empty sequence of indices $k = k_1 \cdots k_m$ such that $u_{k_1} \cdots u_{k_m} = v_{k_1} \cdots v_{k_m}$? We remark that (in contrast to the PFA acceptance problem explained before) the PCP problem only concerns finite words.

Intuitively, we can think that we are given n blocks with two words, as shown in the following example:

aba	c
a	bacab
1	2

These blocks depict the instance $u_1 = $ aba, $u_2 = $ c, $v_1 = $ a and $v_2 = $ bacab. The sequence of indices $1, 2, 1$ is a solution, since $u_1 \cdot u_2 \cdot u_1 = $ abacaba $= v_1 \cdot v_2 \cdot v_1$.

We say that (w, k) is an upper pair iff $k = k_1 \cdots k_n$ and $w = u_{k_1} \cdots u_{k_n}$. We say that (w, k) is a lower pair iff $w = v_{k_1} \cdots v_{k_n}$. Note that a word w can appear in an upper pair (in this case, we say that the word is an *upper word*) iff w is in the regular language $(u_1 + \ldots + u_n)^*$ (which we call the *upper language*), and similarly for the words that can appear in a lower pair. Then, an instance of the PCP problem has a solution iff there exists an upper pair (w, k) such that (w, k) is also a lower pair. We denote by $\text{len}(w)$ the length of a word w.

Next, we prove the qualitative undecidability result for distributed schedulers.

Theorem 3. *There is no algorithm that, for all IPIOA P without interleaving nondeterminism, for all sets U, the algorithm decides whether or not*

$$\sup_{\eta \in Dist(P)} \Pr^{\eta}(\mathrm{reach}(U)) = 1 .$$

There is no algorithm that, for the same input as above, decides whether or not there exists $\eta \in Dist(P)$ such that $\Pr^{\eta}(\mathrm{reach}(U)) = 1$.

Proof. Given a PCP instance $u_1, \ldots, u_n, v_1, \ldots, v_n$, we construct three atoms W, S, I and consider the system $P = W \parallel S \parallel I$. Roughly speaking, W chooses either "upper" or "lower". If W chooses "upper", then W probabilistically chooses an upper word w , communicating the symbols in w to S and the indices k_i to I (and similarly if W chooses "lower"). Once w ends (the end of w is also decided probabilistically), then W outputs *stop*. After *stop*, I is able to output any sequence of indices to S (some of the behaviours we will be interested in are the behaviours in which I communicates the indices it has received from W). Then, S has to guess whether W has chosen either "upper" or "lower". The set of states U is the set in which S has guessed correctly.

The set ActLab_W is $\mathcal{S} \cup \{1, \cdots, n\} \cup \{stop, \tau_W\}$. The behaviour of W is as follows: W has no nondeterministic choices. In the initial state there is a probabilistic transition $(\frac{1}{2} \xrightarrow{\tau_W!} initUp + \frac{1}{2} \xrightarrow{\tau_W!} initLo)$. The states $initUp$ and $initLo$ represent the fact that W has chosen "upper" or "lower" respectively. In $initUp$ there is a probabilistic transition $(\frac{1}{n} \xrightarrow{1!} startU_1 + \cdots + \frac{1}{n} \xrightarrow{n!} startU_n)$. The states $startU_i$ represent the fact that the word w will start with u_i. Similarly, the states $startL_i$ represent the fact that word w will start with v_i. In each state $startU_i$ there is a transition $(1 \xrightarrow{u_{i_1}!} U_{i_1})$, where u_{i_1} is the first symbol in u_i[3] and U_{i_1} represents the fact that the first symbol in U_i has been output. From each state U_{i_j} with $j < \mathrm{len}(u_i) - 1$ there is a transition $(1 \xrightarrow{u_{i_{j+1}}!} U_{i_{j+1}})$. In the state $U_{i_{\mathrm{len}(u_i)-1}}$, there is a transition $(\frac{1}{2} \xrightarrow{u_{i_{\mathrm{len}(w)}}!} initUp + \frac{1}{2} \xrightarrow{stop!} endWU)$. The state $endWU$ indicates that the upper word has ended (similar definitions must be done in case W chooses "lower", where we have the state $endWL$). Since W must be input-enabled, each state has input transitions for each $l \in \mathsf{ActLab}_W$. However, because of the definition of the atoms, the paths in which the labels are output by other atoms have probability 0 for all schedulers, and so the definitions of the input transitions are irrelevant.

The set ActLab_I is $\mathcal{S} \cup \{1, \cdots, n\} \cup \{1', \cdots, n'\} \cup \{stop, stop'\}$. The labels $\{1', \cdots n'\}$ are indices to be communicated to S. However, such labels must be different from the labels $\{1, \cdots, n\}$ output by W, since S is not allowed to see such labels. The label $stop'$ simplifies the construction for similar reasons. In the initial state $init_I$ there are input transitions $(1 \xrightarrow{i?} init_I)$ for each $1 \leq i \leq n$ and also an input transition $(1 \xrightarrow{stop?} outputI)$. Other input transitions are irrelevant.

---

[3] For simplicity, we omitted the case in which some of the words u_k (v_k, resp.) are empty. In this case, when the index k is output in the state $initUp$, W returns to $initUp$ instead of moving to $startU_k$.

In the state *outputI* there are transitions $(1 \xrightarrow{i'!} outputI)$ for each $1 \le i \le n$, and also a transition $(1 \xrightarrow{stop'!} endI)$.

The set ActLab_S is $\mathcal{S} \cup \{1', \cdots, n'\} \cup \{stop', \tau_S\}$. In the initial state there are input transitions $(1 \xrightarrow{a?} init_S)$ for every $l \in \mathcal{S} \cup \{1', \cdots, n'\}$ and transition $(1 \xrightarrow{stop'?} guessS)$. In *guessS* there are two transitions: $(1 \xrightarrow{\tau_S!} tryUp)$ and $(1 \xrightarrow{\tau_S!} tryLo)$.

So, the set U to be reached is $\{(endWU, endI, tryUp), (endWL, endI, tryLo)\}$. We prove the following statement: there exists a distributed scheduler such that $\Pr^{\eta}(reach(U)) = 1$ iff the PCP problem has no solution. In addition, $\sup_{\eta \in Dist(P)} \Pr^{\eta}(reach(U)) = 1$ iff the PCP problem has not a solution.

Suppose that the problem has no solution. Then every pair (w, k) can be an upper or a lower pair, but it cannot be both. So, there exists a function $\mathcal{F}$ such that $\mathcal{F}(w, k) = Up$ ($\mathcal{F}(w, k) = Lo$, resp.) iff (w, k) is an upper pair (a lower pair, resp.). We can construct the following distributed scheduler for P: input and output schedulers for W are uniquely defined (there are no nondeterministic choices). The output scheduler for I chooses the transitions that output the indices in order as they were output by W. The output scheduler for S has to decide only between going to *tryUp* or going to *tryLo*. The only paths with probability greater than 0 in which this choice is performed have a sequence of action labels of the form $a_1 \cdots a_q k_1 \cdots k_r stop'$. If $\mathcal{F}(a_1 \cdots a_q, k_1 \cdots k_r) = Up$, then the output scheduler chooses *tryUp*, otherwise it chooses *tryLo*. If the path has positive probability, and $a_1 \cdots a_r k_1 \cdots k_q$ is an upper pair, then (by construction of W) we know that W is in state *endWU*. Conversely, if $a_1 \cdots a_r k_1 \cdots k_q$ is a lower pair, then W is in state *endWL*, and so the scheduler we constructed reaches U with probability 1.

Now assume that the PCP problem has a solution. Then, let $(w, k = k_1 \cdots k_r)$ be an upper pair that is also a lower pair. Let ϵ be $\frac{1}{2}(\frac{1}{n}\frac{1}{2})^r$. We prove that $\Pr^{\eta}(reach(U)) \le 1 - \epsilon$ for all $\eta \in Dist(P)$. Given the existence of $(w, k = k_1 \cdots k_r)$, there exist two paths σ, σ' whose projection on I is of the form $k_1 \cdots k_r stop$ and, in σ, W has chosen "upper" while in σ' it has chosen "lower". Let η^q be any scheduler in $Dist(P)$. For both σ and σ', the output scheduler Θ_I^q starts to choose transitions in such a way that a certain sequence $l_1 \cdots l_{r'} stop'$ is output (if $stop'$ is never output, then a state in U cannot be reached and so η^q yields a probability less than or equal than $1 - \epsilon$). Then, in both σ, σ' the projection to S is $wl_1 \cdots l_{r'} stop'$. So, if the scheduler for S chooses "upper" in σ, then it also chooses "upper" in σ'. Since σ' has probability ϵ and U cannot be reached after "upper" has been chosen in σ', we have $\Pr^{\eta^q}(reach(U)) \le 1 - \epsilon$. The same happens in case the scheduler for S chooses "lower".

Therefore, every $\eta^q \in Dist(P)$ reaches U with probability less than or equal to $1 - \epsilon$, and hence the supremum is less than or equal to $1 - \epsilon$, and there is no scheduler reaching U with probability 1.

The constructed system P has no interleaving nondeterminism, since first W selects a word, then I outputs the indices and finally S decides.

Note that the theorem above is the qualitative analogous of Theorem 2 (concerning distributed schedulers). Now, we consider the qualitative analogous of Theorem 1.

Theorem 4. *There is no algorithm that, for all IPIOA P without internal nondeterminism, for all sets U, the algorithm decides whether or not*

$$\sup_{\eta \in SDist(P)} \mathrm{Pr}^{\eta}(reach(U)) = 1 .$$

There is no algorithm that, for the same input as above, decides whether or not there exists $\eta \in SDist(P)$ such that $\mathrm{Pr}^{\eta}(reach(U)) = 1$.

Proof. We use the same idea as in the case of distributed schedulers. When proving such result, we defined three atoms W, S and I. Here, we reuse the atom W, excepting for a little modification explained later. The atom S is replaced by two atoms S_{Up} and S_{Lo}. Atom I is replaced by a set of atoms $\{I_i\}_{i=1}^n \cup \{I_{stop}\}$. The intended meaning is that S_{Up} and S_{Lo} are a team that must guess whether the word is an upper or a lower one, according to the same information that S receives in the other reduction (namely, the sequence of symbols output by W and the sequence of indices output by I, such sequence being now output by the team comprising atoms $\{I_i\}_{i=1}^n$). Atoms S_{Up} and S_{Lo} take the guess in the following fashion: if S_{Up} believes that it is an upper word, then it outputs u. Conversely, if S_{Lo} believes that it is a lower word, then it outputs l. So, both S_{Up} and S_{Lo} behave as S, until the point in which S decides, i.e. at the state $guessS$. In this state, S_{Up} has enabled the transition $(1 \xrightarrow{u!} tryUp)$, and S_{Lo} has enabled the transition $(1 \xrightarrow{l!} tryLo)$. In W, the state $endWU$ has the following input transitions: $(1 \xrightarrow{u?} good)$ and $(1 \xrightarrow{l?} bad)$. The state $endWL$ has the following transitions $(1 \xrightarrow{u?} bad)$ and $(1 \xrightarrow{l?} good)$. Then, the state $good$ is reached in the cases in which the team $\{S_{Up}, S_{Lo}\}$ guesses correctly "upper" or "lower".

Each atom I_i has all the input transitions in I. In addition, in the initial state there is an input transition $(1 \xrightarrow{stop'?} endI_i)$. The atom I_{stop} has all the input transitions in I, and only one output transition $(1 \xrightarrow{stop'!} endI_{stop})$. So, once I_{stop} decides to stop, all the I_i reach the state $endI_i$. Each atom I_i has enabled the output transition $(1 \xrightarrow{i'!} init_I)$.

Since we deal with strongly distributed schedulers, in case the indices output by W coincide in two given paths, the sequence of indices output by the atoms I_i also coincides, regardless of the symbols output by W. The argument thus follows as in the case of distributed schedulers (Theorem 3): given two paths σ, σ', such that σ (σ', resp.) represents an upper word (lower word, resp.) followed by the same sequence of indices, if the upper word in σ and lower word in σ' coincide, then the indices output by the atoms A_i also do. So, the projections to S_{Lo} and S_{Up} are the same in both σ and σ'. Hence, if "upper" is chosen in σ, so it is in σ', and the team comprising S_{Lo} and S_{Up} chooses incorrectly in at least one of these paths.

Therefore, the same argument as in the proof for distributed schedulers applies, thus proving that the supremum probability of reaching *good* is 1 (there exists a scheduler reaching *good* with probability 1, resp.) iff the PCP problem has no solution.

4   Impact and Related Work

An important aspect of Theorems 1 and 4 (concerning strongly distributed schedulers) is that they are valid for systems with no internal nondeterminism. A quick look to the case studies in [10] reveals that several protocols (and models in general) do not involve such nondeterminism. However, the interleaving nondeterminism is present in all concurrent systems. Therefore, these theorems have a wider impact than the theorem in [12], which says nothing about systems without internal nondeterminism.

Since the notion of strongly distributed schedulers was introduced by Giro and D'Argenio very recently[4] in [13], it is quite unlikely that results similar to Theorems 1 and 4 exist. It is worth mentioning that [14] presents a quantitative undecidability result for a mechanism to resolve interleaving nondeterminism using rates, in a fashion similar to the probabilistic I/O automata in [23].

Theorems 3 and 4 (concerning a qualitative problem) are really negative, since in a total information setting the problem can be solved using simple graph calculations (see [9, Algorithm 3.2, p. 56]). In fact, in [9] this calculation is presented as a fast preprocessing step to alleviate the computation of maximal reachability probabilities.

A concrete problem affected by Theorems 3 and 4 is that of *stabilization* [11]. If we take U to be the set of *correct* states, then these theorems imply that it cannot be told whether there is a distributed strategy that leads the system to a correct state with probability 1 (i.e. a strategy in which the system complies with the so-called *convergence* property).

The problem concerning the infimum probability is not symmetrical with respect to the supremum, and no clue about its decidability was given in related previous papers such as [12] or [19]. Completing the picture in this sense will then require an additional effort.

References

1. Aumann, Y.: Efficient asynchronous consensus with the weak adversary scheduler. In: PODC, pp. 209–218 (1997)
2. Bianco, A., de Alfaro, L.: Model checking of probabalistic and nondeterministic systems. In: FSTTCS, pp. 499–513 (1995)
3. Canetti, R., Cheung, L., Kirli Kaynar, D., Lynch, N.A., Pereira, O.: Compositional security for Task-PIOAs. In: CSF, pp. 125–139. IEEE CS, Los Alamitos (2007)
4. Chatzikokolakis, K., Norman, G., Parker, D.: Bisimulation for demonic schedulers. In: FOSSACS, pp. 318–332 (2009)

---

[4] As explained in [13], the previous approaches involved mechanisms other than schedulers such as token passing, equivalence classes, arbiters, rates, etc.

5. Cheung, L.: Reconciling Nondeterministic and Probabilistic Choices. PhD thesis, Radboud Universiteit Nijmegen (2006)
6. Cheung, L., Lynch, N., Segala, R., Vaandrager, F.: Switched Probabilistic PIOA: Parallel composition via distributed scheduling. Theor. Comput. Sci. 365(1-2), 83–108 (2006)
7. Ciesinski, F., Baier, C.: LiQuor: A tool for qualitative and quantitative linear time analysis of reactive systems. In: QEST 2006, pp. 131–132. IEEE CS, Los Alamitos (2006)
8. de Alfaro, L., Henzinger, T.A., Jhala, R.: Compositional methods for probabilistic systems. In: Larsen, K.G., Nielsen, M. (eds.) CONCUR 2001. LNCS, vol. 2154, pp. 351–365. Springer, Heidelberg (2001)
9. de Alfaro, L.: Formal Verification of Probabilistic Systems. PhD thesis, Stanford University (1997), Technical report STAN-CS-TR-98-1601
10. PRISM development team. Prism case studies, http://www.prismmodelchecker.org/casestudies/index.php
11. Dijkstra, E.W.: Self-stabilizing systems in spite of distributed control. Commun. ACM 17(11), 643–644 (1974)
12. Giro, S., D'Argenio, P.R.: Quantitative model checking revisited: neither decidable nor approximable. In: Raskin, J.-F., Thiagarajan, P.S. (eds.) FORMATS 2007. LNCS, vol. 4763, pp. 179–194. Springer, Heidelberg (2007)
13. Giro, S., D'Argenio, P.R.: On the expressive power of schedulers in distributed probabilistic systems. In: Proc. of QAPL 2009 (2009). Extended version to appear in ENTCS, cs.famaf.unc.edu.ar/~sgiro/QAPL09-ext.pdf
14. Giro, S., D'Argenio, P.R.: On the verification of probabilistic i/o automata with unspecified rates. In: SAC 2009: Proceedings of the 2009 ACM symposium on Applied Computing, pp. 582–586. ACM, New York (2009)
15. Giro, S.: On the automatic verification of Distributed Probabilistic Automata with Partial Information. PhD thesis, Universidad Nacional de Córdoba (to appear)
16. van Glabbeek, R.J., Smolka, S.A., Steffen, B.: Reactive, generative, and stratified models of probabilistic processes. Information and Computation 121, 59–80 (1995)
17. Hinton, A., Kwiatkowska, M., Norman, G., Parker, D.: PRISM: A tool for automatic verification of probabilistic systems. In: Hermanns, H., Palsberg, J. (eds.) TACAS 2006. LNCS, vol. 3920, pp. 441–444. Springer, Heidelberg (2006)
18. Lynch, N.A., Tuttle, M.R.: An introduction to input/output automata. CWI Quarterly 2(3), 219–246 (1989)
19. Madani, O., Hanks, S., Condon, A.: On the undecidability of probabilistic planning and related stochastic optimization problems. Artif. Intell. 147(1-2), 5–34 (2003)
20. Segala, R.: Modeling and Verification of Randomized Distributed Real-Time Systems. PhD thesis, Laboratory for Computer Science, MIT (1995)
21. Sipser, M.: Introduction to the Theory of Computation, 2nd edn., pp. 199–205. Thomson Course Technology (2005)
22. Vardi, M.Y.: Automatic verification of probabilistic concurrent finite state programs. In: Procs. of 26th FOCS, pp. 327–338. IEEE Press, Los Alamitos (1985)
23. Wu, S.-H., Smolka, S.A., Stark, E.W.: Composition and behaviors of probabilistic I/O automata. Theor. Comput. Sci. 176(1-2), 1–38 (1997)

Formalisation and Analysis of Objects as CSP Processes

Renata Kaufman, Augusto Sampaio, and Alexandre Mota

Centro de Informática, Universidade Federal de Pernambuco, P.O. Box 7451, Brazil

Abstract. CSP-OZ is a formal specification language. It is a formal combination of the process algebra CSP and Object-Z, an object-oriented version of the model-based Z language. CSP-OZ lacks tool support, having only a type checker and a model-checking strategy. Unfortunately, the model-checking strategy for CSP-OZ does not deal with the object-oriented features of this language. In this work, we propose design patterns for CSP to capture such features and for CSP-OZ. Our approach complements the original model-checking strategy by also considering object-oriented characteristics.

Keywords: CSP, Object-Z, Object-Oriented Specification, Design Pattern.

1 Introduction

In the formal methods area there has been a lot of interest in the integration of formalisms in such a way that several facets (data, control, time, mobility, probability) can be coherently combined in software development. Several efforts have been dedicated to combine process algebras and model-based specification languages [1,2,3]. CSP-OZ [1] is a combination of the process algebra CSP [4] and Object-Z [5], an object-oriented extension of the model-based formalism Z [6].

There are several complex issues to be considered in the integration of languages: syntax, semantics, proof theory, development methods, analysis techniques, reuse and so on. This paper contributes to the model-checking strategy for CSP-OZ. The existing model-checking strategy for CSP-OZ [7] is based on the translation of a CSP-OZ specification into CSP and then on the use of FDR [8] to carry out the analysis. Unfortunately, this strategy does not deal with object-oriented features, such as clientship, polymorphism and inheritance. To extend the existing approach to consider object-oriented constructs, we define a set of patterns in terms of CSP_M [9] (the machine-readable version of CSP supported by the model checker FDR) that mimic object-oriented features, such as classes, subclasses, creation and dynamic removal of objects.

Our approach to capture object-oriented features purely in terms of CSP can be used both as a target for translations from combined formalisms like CSP-OZ and Circus [2], but also as a more structured style of writing and analysing process algebra specifications.

M.V.M. Oliveira and J. Woodcock (Eds.): SBMF 2009, LNCS 5902, pp. 236–250, 2009.

The work was motivated by the need to formalize specifications of an EHRS (Electronic Health Record System). Other works on formal methods to health applications have been published. Dallien et all. [10] safety check workflows of healthcare systems to avoid problems on patient care. Closer to our work, Baksi [11] uses π-calculus to ensure that service provided by diverse healthcare entities will interact correctly.

This paper is organised as follows. Section 2 introduces CSP-OZ through an example. It assumes some basic knowledge of both CSP and Object-Z. Section 3 presents the proposed patterns to capture object-oriented features in CSP. Section 4 shows the application of the patterns to a Bank System case study, including both the specification and analysis of the system. In the final section, we summarize our results and discuss related and future work.

2   CSP-OZ through an Example

A CSP-OZ specification describes a system as a collection of interacting objects, each one with its own structure and behaviour. Communication takes place via channels as in CSP. In general, a CSP-OZ specification consists of several paragraphs, introducing classes, global variables, functions and types. A CSP-OZ class has an interface (channels), a control behaviour (expressed in CSP), a state, and operations over this state (described in Z).

We introduce CSP-OZ through an example of a hypothetical Bank System. It consists basically of three entities: an *Account*, a *SavingsAccount* and the *Bank* itself.

The Bank System specification has the given set *Password*, which represents the user passwords; the *Value* and *Number* abbreviations, which represent banking operation values and account numbers, respectively as naturals; and the free-type *Message* whose values are the system messages.

> [*Password*]
> *Value* $==$ $\mathbb{N}$
> *Number* $==$ $\mathbb{N}$
> *Message* ::= *AccountDoesNotExist* | *InsufficientBalance*

As presented in Figure 1, an *Account* is modelled as a CSP-OZ class that is declared using the Z language style, together with the parameters to initialize the state of the class instance. The first elements of a class are public/private channel or method declarations. In the case of the *Account* class, we use method declarations (keyword *method*) because this class provides services to other classes. If we used public channel (keyword *channel*) declarations this class should be requiring services from other classes. Finally, we could also use private channel declarations (keyword *local_channel*) in which case the class will resolve its behaviour internally.

Following the interface elements of a class, we have its behaviour. It is given in terms of CSP, where the process *main* captures the initial behaviour of the class.

___ $Account(n : Number;\ v : Value;\ p : Password)$ _____

$\quad$ $method\ \ deposit : [v? : Value]$

$\quad$ $method\ \ withdraw : [v? : Value]$

$\quad$ $method\ \ getBalance : [v! : Value]$

$\quad$ $method\ \ withdrawOk, withdrawNotOk : [v : Value]$

$\quad$ $main = (deposit?v \rightarrow main\ \square\ getBalance!v \rightarrow main\ \square\ WD)$

$\quad$ $WD = withdraw?v \rightarrow (withdrawOk.v \rightarrow main\ \square\ withdrawNotOk.v \rightarrow main)$

$\quad$ _____

$\quad$ $num : Number;\ bal : Value;\ passw : Password$

$\quad$ _____

$\quad$ $bal \geq 0$

$\quad$ _____

$\quad$ $INIT \triangleq [num = n \wedge bal = v \wedge passw = p]$

$\quad$ _ $effect\_deposit$ _____ $\quad$ _ $effect\_getBalance$ _____

$\quad$ $\Delta(bal);\ v? : Value$ $\qquad\qquad\qquad$ $\Delta();\ v! : Value$

$\quad$ _____ $\qquad\qquad\qquad$ _____

$\quad$ $bal' = bal + v?$ $\qquad\qquad\qquad\quad$ $v! = bal$

$\quad$ _ $enable\_withdrawOk$ _____ $\quad$ _ $effect\_withdrawOk$ _____

$\quad$ $v : Value$ $\qquad\qquad\qquad\qquad\qquad$ $\Delta(bal);\ v : Value$

$\quad$ _____ $\qquad\qquad\qquad$ _____

$\quad$ $bal \geq v$ $\qquad\qquad\qquad\qquad\qquad$ $bal' = bal - v$

$\quad$ ___ $enable\_withdrawNotOk$ _____

$\quad$ $v : Value$

$\quad$ _____

$\quad$ $bal < v$

Fig. 1. Class Account

It always offers *deposit* and *getBalance* events to the environment or behaves like the auxiliary process WD, which offers *withdraw* and then *withdrawOk* or *withdrawNotOk*. After any choice, it behaves like *main* again.

After describing the behavioural part, we need to characterize the class structural part as well. The state space of *Account* has three elements: the account number, its balance and its password. And the state invariant is $bal \geq 0$.

We are ready to add the operation that initializes the state of the system.

For each channel c, declared in the interface, there must be an *effect_c* schema and an *enable_c* schema. When the schema is omitted, it means that the predicate is true. For example, we omitted schemas for *effect_withdrawNotOk* and *enable_deposit* as can be seen in the schemas of the *Account* class.

According to the semantics of CSP-OZ, the behaviour of a class is the parallel composition of the Z part (interpreted as a CSP process) with the CSP part, synchronizing on all elements of the class's interface after the initialization takes place. Thus, for instance, in the *Account* class, when the event, say *withdrawOk*, can be engaged the corresponding Z operation (*effect_withdrawOk*) is executed, as long as its enabling condition (*enable_withdrawOk*) is satisfied.

We now introduce *SavingsAccount* (Figure 2), which illustrates the inheritance aspect of CSP-OZ. The syntax of this class is similar to the previous one, except for the *inherit* keyword. This class inherits the interface, behaviour and Z schemas (operations) from the *Account* class. Apart from the events inherited, a new event (*interest*) is introduced, as well as the attribute *ratio* to record the interest rate.

Semantically, inheritance is interpreted as the conjunction of the Z part and the parallel composition of the CSP part of a CSP-OZ specification.

The third class is *Bank* (Figure 3), which models our hypothetical bank. This class is responsible for creating and recovering accounts and savings account, and for delegating some services to them as, for example, deposit, withdraw, balance and interest (this last one only from *SavingsAccount*). The state of the *Bank* class has the declaration *accounts:* $\mathbb{P} \downarrow Account$, which means that the set *accounts* may contain *SavingsAccount* and *Account* objects. A polymorphic declaration is made with the symbol $\downarrow$.

As we said previously, channel types can assume three possibilities: *method*, *chan* and *local_chan*. The first one indicates that the corresponding Z operation, for example *enterAcc*, is implemented in the class itself. The second one means that the operation, like *deposit*, is implemented by another class (*Account*). And the third one is used when the operation, for example *found*, cannot be observed from the environment; it is only accessible by the class itself.

$\underline{\quad SavingsAccount(n : Number; \; v : Value; \; p : Password) \underline{\qquad\qquad\qquad}}$
$method \; interest : [t? : Ratio]$
$inherit \; Account$
$main = interest?t \rightarrow getBalance?s \rightarrow deposit!(t * s) \rightarrow main$

$\quad ratio : Ratio$

$INIT \mathrel{\hat{=}} [ratio = 0]$

$\underline{\quad effect\_interest \underline{\qquad\qquad\qquad\qquad\qquad}}$
$\Delta(ratio); \; t? : Ratio$

$\quad ratio' = t?$

Fig. 2. Class SavingsAccount

We observe that operations on *SavingsAccount* are the same as those for *Account* (polymorphism), except for *interest*, which is exclusive for *SavingsAccount* objects. Furthermore, objects are created using the keyword *New* followed by the class's name and the real parameters as usual in object-oriented systems; for instance, the *New c : Account(r, 0, p)* in the Bank class.

Bank(*sqId* : seq *Number*)

---

method *createAccount* : [*p*? : *Password*]

local_chan *getIndObj* : [*ind* : *Number*]

method *enterAcc*, *enterSav* : [*n*? : *Number*]

method *depositB* : [*v*? : *Value*]

method *exit*, *getBalanceB* : []

method *interestB* : [*r*? : *Ratio*]

chan *getBalance* : [*b*? : *Value*]

chan *deposit* : [*v*! : *Value*]

chan *message* : [*m*? : *Message*]

chan *interest* : [*r*! : *Ratio*]

local_chan *notFound* : [*n* : *Number*]

local_chan *add*, *update* : [*cp* : ↓ *Account*]

local_chan *found* : [*n* : *Number*; *cp*? : ↓ *Account*] . . .

main = *createAccount*?*p* → (*getIndObj*?*r* → *New c* : *Account*(*r*, 0, *p*) •

$$\qquad\qquad\qquad\qquad add.c \to main \;\square\; \ldots)$$

□ *enterAcc*?*n* → (*found*.*n*?*ac* → *MovAcc*(*ac*)

$$\qquad\qquad\qquad \square\; notFound.n \to message?m \to main)$$

□ *enterSav*?*n* → (*found*.*n*?*s* → *MovSav*(*s*)

$$\qquad\qquad\qquad \square\; notFound.n \to message?m \to main)$$

MovAcc(*ac*) = *depositB*?*v* → (*ac* [| *deposit* |] (*deposit*!*v* → *SKIP*));

$$\qquad\qquad\qquad MovAcc(ac) \ldots$$

□ *getBalanceB* → (*ac* [| *getBalance* |] (*getBalance*?*b* → *SKIP*)); *MovAcc*(*ac*)

□ *exit* → *update*.*ac* → *main*

MovSav(*s*) = *depositB*?*v* → (*s* [| *deposit* |] (*deposit*!*v* → *SKIP*)); *MovSav*(*s*) . . .

□ *getBalanceB* → (*s* [| *getBalance* |] (*getBalance*?*b* → *SKIP*)); *MovSav*(*s*)

□ *interestB*?*t* → (*s* [| *deposit* |] (*deposit*!*t* → *SKIP*)); *MovSav*(*s*) □ . . .

---

accounts : ℙ ↓ *Account*; *msg* : *Message*

∀ *a*, *b* : *Account* | *a*, *b* ∈ *accounts* ∧ *a*.*num* = *b*.*num* • *a* = *b*

INIT ≙ [*accounts* = ∅]   *enable_getIndObj* ≙ [*seqIds* ≠ ⟨⟩]

effect_getIndObj ≙ [Δ(*seqIds*); *ind*? : *Number* | *ind*? = head *seqIds* ∧

$$\qquad\qquad\qquad seqIds' = tail\; seqIds]$$

effect_add ≙ [Δ(*accounts*); *cp* :↓ *Account* | *accounts*′ = *accounts* ∪ {*cp*}]

enable_found ≙ [*n* : *Number* | ∃ *c* : *Accounts* | *c*.*num* = *n*]

effect_found ≙ [Δ(); *n* : *Number*; *cp*? :↓ *Account* | ∃ *c* : *Accounts* |

$$\qquad\qquad\qquad c.num = n \bullet cp? = c]$$

enable_notFound ≙ [*n* : *Number* | ∄ *c* : *Accounts* | *c*.*num* = *n*]

effect_notFound ≙ [Δ(*msg*); *n* : *Number* | *msg*′ = *AccountDoesNotExist*]

---

effect_update

Δ(*accounts*); *c* :↓ *Account*

∃ *as* : *accounts* | *as*.*num* = *c*.*num* • *accounts*′ = (*accounts* \ {*as*}) ∪ {*c*}

. . .

Fig. 3. Class Bank

3   CSP Patterns for Object-Orientation

Concerning tool support, CSP-OZ has only a type-checker [12] and a model-checking strategy [7], which transforms a CSP-OZ specification into a CSP_M one. Unfortunately, the proposed model-checking strategy for CSP-OZ does not deal with its object-oriented aspects. In [1,13], inheritance, for example, is not dealt appropriately. Implicitly, it is assumed that the inheritance hierarchy is flattened, according to the semantics. This means the conjunction of the Z part of the superclass with the Z part of the subclass, and the parallel composition of the CSP parts of both classes synchronizing on all events of their interfaces. The process equations of the superclass are inherited by the subclass.

3.1   Polymorphism

A CSP-OZ polymorphic variable is declared by using the polymorphic declaration symbol ↓ followed by the type of the superclass. Recall from Section 2 that the *Bank* class has the attribute *accounts:↓Account*. This declaration allows the variable *accounts* to reference *Account* and *SavingsAccount* objects.

To obtain such a polymorphic feature in CSP_M, we need to explicitly state the possible varieties using a union type. Thus, to allow *Account* and *SavingsAccount* objects to be referenced we need to create a new type (`ObjectContext`), which is the union of `AccCtxt.AccountContext` and `SavCtxt.SavingsAccountContext`.

```
datatype ObjectContext = AccCtxt.AccountContext |
                         SavCtxt.SavingsAccountContext
```

The constructors `AccCtxt` and `SavCtxt` represent Account and SavingsAccount, respectively. The `AccountContext` set has account state tuples and the `Savings-AccountContext` set savings account state tuples.

3.2   Dynamic Object Creation

Dynamic object creation is obtained by a function whose input parameters are the type of a process and its state initialisation:

```
procName = proc(objectType,objectState)
```

The call `proc(objectType,objectState)` is a kind of constructor which returns an object (process) of the class `ObjectType`, initialised with `objectState`.

We use the creation of an object (process) `Account` to illustrate a CSP specification of the pattern. The part of the code presented in Figure 4 belongs to the flow of the process `Bank`. The process `main` receives the account identifier (`?an`) by the `enterAcc` event. If the account is found (`found`) then a process `Account` is created using the `proc` function, with parameters `TACCOUNT` (the type of the object) and `e` (the state of the process). The state `e` is recovered by a call to the function `recoverTuple(obj)`. This function receives one entity of type Account (`AccCtxt.(ind,b,p,v)`) and yields the tuple (`ind,b,p,v`) that represents its state. If the account does not exist (`notFound`), the `Bank` notifies the environment and

```
main =
        . . .
        enterAcc?an -> (found?obj:ObjectAcc ->
                       (let
                          e = recoverTuple(obj)
                          procAcc = proc(TACCOUNT,e)
                          Flow = ...
                          within (procAcc[|{|...|}|] Flow);
                          main)
                       []
                       notFound -> message?m -> main)
        . . .
```

Fig. 4. Creation of processes without inheritance

offers its initial events again. The process `Flow` will be detailed later. As the channel `found` is polymorphic (see Section 3.1), we had to constrain its values to the set `ObjectAcc`, which only has objects of type Account.

3.3 Object Values

An interesting feature of CSP-OZ is that processes are also communicating values [1]. This means that we can declare a channel whose type is a process.

However, as CSP does not support such a feature directly [14,8], a possible solution is to communicate the state of the process as a tuple, using the process name as a constructor type.

To illustrate how this simple pattern is specified in CSP, we present part of the process `Bank` that creates an entity of type `Account` (Figure 5). The environment demands that the process `Bank` creates an account (`createAccount`). After performing the `createAccount` event, the process `Bank` searches for the next available index (`getObjInd`) and then creates a new account (`AccCtxt.(ind,0,p,0)`). The elements of the tuple (`ind,0,p,0`) stand for account number, balance, password and amount respectively. After that, it adds this account to the set of accounts (`add`), and offers its initial events again. Otherwise (`NotGetObjInd`), the environment is notified with an error message (`message`) and offers its initial events again. The channel `add` is polymorphic because it can receive entities of `Account` or `SavingsAccount` types as parameters.

3.4 Pattern for the Object Lifecycle

The pattern we propose here assumes the general form presented in Figure 6. In this template, `procName` captures the behaviour of an object, which is the result of the function `proc(objectType,objectState)`[1]. This process represents an object (in the original CSP-OZ specification) of class `ObjectType`. `ObjectState` is a tuple

---

[1] CSP_M includes a functional language which can yield processes as results.

```
main = createAccount?p ->
        (getObjInd?ind -> add.(AccCtxt.(ind,0,p,0)) -> main
        []
        NotGetObjInd -> message?m -> main)
    []
    ...
```

Fig. 5. Creation of entities of type Account

```
let
    procName = proc(objectType, objectState)
    Flow = PEvents
        []
        exit -> getStateName.y -> [action] -> terminate -> SKIP
within (procName[|{|...|}|] Flow)
```

Fig. 6. Pattern for the object lifecycle

that holds the current values to initialize the state of the process. `Flow` is the client process (for example, a collection) that has the control flow to be performed by the reference process `procName`. It also has other events that synchronize with the environment. It is formed of two processes. The first process, `PEvents`, contains the events for the execution flow itself. The second process, `exit -> getStateName?y -> [action] -> terminate -> SKIP`, has the events needed for synchronizing with the process `procName` until termination. In which case the state of the object `procName` is obtained or passed through channel `getStateName`; some actions (optional) can be performed; Z part finalizes(`terminate`); and CSP part ends(`SKIP`). The last sentence `within (procName[|{|...|}|] Flow)` stands for the parallel composition between `procName` and `Flow`. The events in which they synchronize are listed in the set `{|...|}`.

This pattern works in the following way: `procName` is a passive object (process) that offers its events to the active process `Flow`. Process `Flow` then selects the events to be realized by `procName`. An operation is performed when both (`procName` and `Flow`) synchronize in the event corresponding to that operation.

Representing object-oriented features as CSP processes involves several patterns. In the following sections we present each identified pattern illustrating its use in our case study.

3.5 Delegation

Once we have shown how objects are created, in this section we discuss how such objects are used by a client. For the sake of conciseness, we omit the generic pattern, which is presented in [15].

The patterns are illustrated using the examples presented in Figures 7 and 8 which show the description of the processes `Bank` and `Account` in CSP_M. To ease

```
main = ...
 enterAcc?an ->
 (found?obj:ObjectContextAcc ->
    (let
       e = recoverTuple(obj)
       procAcc = proc(TACCOUNT,e)
       Flow = depositB?v -> deposit.v -> Flow
             []withdrawB?v -> withdraw.v ->
                                (withdrawOk -> getMoney -> Flow
                                 []
                                 withdrawNotOk -> message?m -> Flow)
             []getBalanceB -> getBalance?b -> Flow
             []exit -> getStateAcc?st2 -> update.(AccCtxt.st2) ->
                terminate -> SKIP
          within (procAcc [|{|deposit,withdraw,withdrawOk,
             withdrawNotOk,getBalance,getStateAcc,exit|}|] Flow);
             main)
 []notFound -> message?m -> main)
 ...
```

Fig. 7. Behaviour of the Bank in relation to interaction with Account

reading our specifications, we use the name of the related process (or part of it) to build the name of our events. For instance, the event getStateAcc belongs to the process Account due to the suffix Acc. Bank can receive requests from a user. For example: depositB, withdrawB, getBalanceB and exit. After that, Bank delegates to the process Account the responsibility to execute the relevant operation (as in a standard object oriented modelling). Termination is captured by the event exit, which allows Bank to obtain the state of Account (getStateAcc), updates its account collection and finalizes. The Account finalizes after sending its state.

We observe in Figure 7 that the process Flow synchronizes with the process Account in the events deposit, withdraw, withdrawOk, withdrawNotOk, getBalance, getStateAcc and exit. The other events of the Flow allow it to synchronize with the environment. After Account and Flow terminate together, the process Bank offers its initial events again. The events getBalanceDup and depositDup (Figure 8) are discussed in the next section.

3.6   Delegation with Inheritance

In our proposal, inheritance is captured using parallelism. That is, if a class C inherits from a class A then our process representation of C, say P_C, must create an instance of A, say process P_A, and behave synchronously with it. This composition handles the following situations:

- An event specific to process P_C: only process P_C handles it.
- An event of process P_C inherited from process P_A, but not redefined in process P_C: P_A handles it.

```
main = deposit?v -> main
       [] withdraw?v ->
          (withdrawOk -> main
           []
           withdrawNotOk -> main)
       [] getBalance?v -> main
       [] getBalanceDup?v -> main
       [] depositDup?b -> main
       [] exit -> getStateAcc?st -> terminate -> SKIP
```

Fig. 8. Behavioural part of the process Account

- An event of process P_C inherited from process P_A and redefined: P_A and P_C synchronize and each one is responsible for a part of the task. P_A carries out its original responsibility concerning this event, and P_C performs the complement related to the redefinition.

It is worth observing that our specification assumes that, regarding redefinition, the original behaviour of the process is preserved by behavioural subclassing [16].

We observe in Figure 9 that the creation of the process SavingsAccount generates a process of type Account with the values of the variables (inherited) from SavingsAccount. The operator "\" (*hiding*), that appears in the innermost within, is used to hide the events that should not synchronize with the environment (Bank). The function Semantics translates the Z part into a process and puts this process in parallel with the CSP part. See [17] for further details on this function.

To illustrate our model of inheritance in further details, we use the processes Bank (Figure 11), SavingsAccount (Figure 10) and Account (Figure 8). We can observe that Bank receives the same requests of the Account and SavingsAccount, in addition to interestB, which is responsible to pay interest. When the requests are the same as those of Account, they are delegated to the process Account, as

```
SavingsAccount(nu,bl,ps,va,rt) =
           let
           ...
             main =
             let
                  e = (nu,bl,ps,va)
                  procAcc = proc(TACCOUNT,e)
                  Flow = ...
             within (procAcc [|{|...|}|] Flow)\ {|...|}
           within Semantics(...)
```

Fig. 9. Creation of the process SavingsAccount

```
...
main =
let
  e = (nu,bl,ps,va)
  procAcc = proc(TACCOUNT,e)
  Flow = interest?t -> getBalanceDup?b -> depositDup.(b*t) -> Flow
         []
         exit -> getStateAcc?st1 -> recoverState?st ->
         getStateSav!makeContext(st1,st) -> terminate -> SKIP
within (procAcc
        [|{|getStateAcc,getBalanceDup,depositDup, terminate,exit|}|]
        Flow)\ {|getBalanceDup,depositDup|}
```

Fig. 10. Behavioural part of the process SavingsAccount

already explained: SavingsAccount behaves as Account in relation to the events
that were inherited from Account.

Regarding the event interestB, the process Bank receives it and thus delegates it to the process SavingsAccount, which invokes the event interest. Then
SavingsAccount requests from Account the balance and the deposit of the interest, through the respective getBalanceDup and depositDup events. These events
are called duplicates (Dup) because they do exactly the same as deposit and
getBalance events from Account. The duplication is used to allow the synchronization between Account and SavingsAccount, without Bank interference. We
must distinguish local from global synchronization. Furthermore, these duplicated events are not problematic because we hide them at the top level of the
process.

```
...
main = ...
  enterSav?sn ->
  (found?obj:ObjectContextSav ->
   (let
      e = recoverTuple(obj)
      procSav = proc(TSAVING,e)
      Flow = depositB?v -> deposit.v -> Flow
             ...
             [] interestB?r -> interest.r -> Flow
             [] exit -> getStateSav?st1 -> update.(SavCtxt.st1) ->
                terminate -> SKIP
    within (procSav [|{|deposit,...,interest,getStateSav,exit|}|] Flow);
           main)
  [] notFound -> message?m -> main)
...
```

Fig. 11. Behaviour of the Bank in relation to interaction with SavingsAccount

Finally, the event `exit` makes `Bank` to request the state of `SavingsAccount` (`getStateSav`), which asks for the state of `Account` (`getStateAcc`). `Account`, after providing its state, finalizes Z and CSP parts. `SavingsAccount`, after receiving part of the state that is in `Account`, recovers its own state (`recoverState`), returns the complete state to `Bank` (`getStateSav`), finalizes Z and CSP parts. And `Bank`, after receiving the state of `SavingsAccount`, updates its account collection (`update`), finalizes Z and CSP parts and then offers its initial events again.

4   Applying the Patterns

In this section we further consider the bank account example, and illustrate how the approach proposed in [7] (to translate CSP-OZ specifications to CSP_M) together with our translation patterns can be used to translate and analyse CSP specifications preserving the object-oriented structure.

The `ObjType` set has the constants `TACCOUNT`, `TBANK` and `TSAVING`, that represent the types of the objects. These constants can be passed as parameters to the function `proc`, which is responsible for the creation of the corresponding process.

```
datatype ObjType = TACCOUNT | TBANK | TSAVING
```

The function `proc` creates the processes dynamically. Its input parameters are the type of the process and the initial values of the state variables. These parameters determine the active process.

```
proc(TBANK,(cc,sa)) = Bank(cc,sa)
proc(TACCOUNT,(n,b,p,v)) = Account(n,b,p,v)
proc(TSAVING,(n,b,p,v,r)) = SavingsAccount(n,b,p,v,r)
```

The specification uses several channel types. Among them we have `Number`, `ObjectContext` and `Value`. From the channel types, we can present the declaration of the channels.

```
channel enterSav:Number
channel update,add,found:ObjectContext
channel depositB,depositDup,getBalanceDup:Value
...
```

The process `Bank` is defined as follows. The identifier `Ops` keeps the names of the channels used by the process concerning the Z part and `LocOps` the names of the local channels.

```
Bank(cts,sqId) =
let
 Ops = {enterSav,found,notFound,...,update}
 LocOps = {update,found,...}
 main = ...
  enterSav?sn ->(found?obj:ObjectContextSav ->
  (let
```

```
e = recoverTuple(obj)
procSav = proc(TSAVING,e)
Flow = depositB?v -> deposit.v -> Flow
            ...
         [] interestB?r -> interest.r -> Flow
         [] exit -> getStateSav?st1 ->update.(SavCtxt.st1) ->
             terminate -> SKIP
      within (procSav[|{|deposit,...,interest,getStateSav,exit|}|]
             Flow); main)
         ...
within Semantics(Ops,LocOps,in,out,enable,effect,init,...,main,
                 event)
```

The process `Account` is partially defined as (see Figure 8 for its complete definition):

```
Account(nu,bl,ps,va) =
 let ...
   main = deposit?v -> main
           ...
         [] getBalanceDup?v -> main
         []depositDup?b -> main
         []exit -> getStateAcc?st -> terminate -> SKIP
           ...
within Semantics(Ops,LocOps,in,out,enable,effect,init,...,main,
                 event)
```

and the process `SavingsAccount` as (see Figure 7):

```
SavingsAccount(nu,bl,ps,va,rt) =
let ...
  main =
   let e = (nu,bl,ps,va)
      procAcc = proc(TACCOUNT,e)
      Flow = interest?t -> getBalanceDup?b -> depositDup!(b*t)->
             Flow
                []
             exit -> getStateAcc?st1 -> recoverState?st ->
                 getStateSav!makeContext(st1,st) -> terminate ->
                 SKIP
      within (procAcc [|{|getStateAcc,getBalanceDup,depositDup,
            terminate,exit|}|] Flow)\{|getBalanceDup,depositDup|}
        ...
within Semantics(Ops,LocOps,in,out,enable,effect,init,...,main,
                 event)
```

The process `main` includes the creation of the process `Account` that performs the inherited events of the class `Account` . The process `Flow` has specific `SavingsAccount` events only. The inherited events are not in `Flow` because its process `Account` realize those events.

The Bank system specification in this section shows that the application of the design patterns together with the extended model-checking strategy [7] allows to create CSP_M specifications using object-oriented concepts. This specification was analysed using the FDR tool, considering classical properties like deadlock freedom; clearly, other domain specific properties can be analysed in a similar way.

5   Conclusions

This paper has presented a way to deal with object-oriented concepts in the CSP process algebra concerning both specification and analysis (model-checking). In particular, we have shown that inheritance, dynamic binding, creation and dynamic removal of objects and polymorphic structures, can all be elegantly modelled in CSP_M. The proposed patterns have been applied to a Bank system specification, where the use of all proposed patterns has been illustrated.

The formalisation of a more realistic and extensive case study can be found in [15], where the patterns are used to formalise and analyse a healthcare record protocol.

We conclude that there is a systematic way to apply the FDR tool to object-oriented concurrent systems to perform property analysis, in particular, the deadlock freedom analysis.

As far as we are concerned, the contribution of this work is original in the sense of capturing object-oriented aspects in a process algebra aiming at model checking. We could not find any work in the literature which shows how object-oriented concepts can be captured by a process algebra. Nevertheless, in the field of formal semantics of object-oriented languages, there are works [18,19] that use process algebras to define the semantics of the language.

For future research, we intend to formalize and to develop a conversion tool that converts CSP-OZ specifications into CSP_M notation using patterns.

Acknowledgments

We deeply thank Ana Lucia Caneca Cavalcanti for her cosupervision in the Masters thesis that originated this paper. We would also like to thank Adalberto Farias, Rafael Duarte and Leonardo Lucena for their comments on early drafts of this paper.

References

1. Fischer, C.: Combination and Implementation of Processes and Data From CSP-OZ to Java. PhD thesis, Oldenburg University (2000)
2. Sampaio, A., Woodcock, J., Cavalcanti, A.: Refinement in Circus. In: Eriksson, L.-H., Lindsay, P.A. (eds.) FME 2002. LNCS, vol. 2391, pp. 451–470. Springer, Heidelberg (2002)

3. Galloway, A.J., Stoddart, W.: An operational semantics for ZCCS. In: Hinchey, M., Liu, S. (eds.) International Conference of Formal Engineering Methods (ICFEM), pp. 272–282. IEEE Computer Press, Los Alamitos (1997)
4. Hoare, C.: Communicating Sequential Processes. Prentice-Hall International, Englewood Cliffs (1985)
5. Smith, G.: A semantic integration of Object-Z and CSP for the specification of concurrent systems. In: Fitzgerald, J.S., Jones, C.B., Lucas, P. (eds.) FME 1997. LNCS, vol. 1313, pp. 62–81. Springer, Heidelberg (1997)
6. Spivey, J.M.: Z notation (1998), http://spivey.oriel.ox.ac.uk/mike/zrm/zrm.pdf
7. Fischer, C., Wehrheim, H.: Model-checking CSP-OZ specifications with FDR. In: Proceedings of the 1st International Conference on Integrated Formal Methods (IFM), pp. 315–334 (1999)
8. Formal Systems(Europe) Ltd.: Failures–Divergence Refinement, Revision 2.0 (1997)
9. Scattergood, B.: The Semantics and Implementation of Machine–Readable CSP. PhD thesis, Programming Research Group, Oxford University (1998)
10. Dallien, J., MacCaull, W., Tien, A.: Initial work in the design and development of verifiable workflow management systems and some applications to health care. In: 5th International Workshop on Model-based Methodologies for Pervasive and Embedded Software, 2008. MOMPES 2008, Budapest, Hungary, pp. 78–91. IEEE, Los Alamitos (2008)
11. Baksi, D.: Formal interaction specification in public health surveillance systems using π-calculus. Computer Methods and Programs in Biomedicine 92(1), 115–120 (2008)
12. Garrel, J.V.: Parsing, Typechecking und Transformation von CSP-OZ nach jass. Master's thesis, University of Oldenburg (1999)
13. Olderog, E.R., Wehrheim, H.: Specification and (Property) inheritance in CSP-OZ. Science of Computer Programming 55, 227–257 (2004)
14. Roscoe, A.W.: The Theory and Practice of Concurrency. Prentice-Hall, Englewood Cliffs (1997)
15. Kaufman, R.E.M.: Modelling and Analysis of Objects as CSP Processes: Design Pattern and Case Study. Master's thesis, Federal University of Pernambuco (2003)
16. Liskov, B.H., Wing, J.M.: A behavioral notion of subtyping. ACM Transactions on Programming Languages and Systems 16, 1811–1841 (1994)
17. Mota, A., Sampaio, A.: Model-checking CSP-Z: strategy, tool support and industrial application. Sci. Comput. Program. 40(1), 59–96 (2001)
18. Jones, C.B.: Process-algebraic foundations for an object-based design notation. Technical report, University of Manchester, Technical Report, UMCS-93-10-1 (1993)
19. Walker, D.: π-calculus semantics of object-oriented programming languages. Technical report, Computer Science Department, Edinburgh University, Technical Report, ECS-LFCS-90-122 (1990)

Concolic Testing of the Multi-sector Read Operation for Flash Memory File System*

Moonzoo Kim and Yunho Kim

CS Dept. KAIST
Daejeon, South Korea
moonzoo@cs.kaist.ac.kr,
kimyunho@kaist.ac.kr

Abstract. In today's information society, flash memory has become a virtually indispensable component, particularly for mobile devices. In order for mobile devices to operate successfully, it is essential that flash memory be controlled correctly through file system software. However, as is typical for embedded software, conventional testing methods often fail to detect hidden flaws in the software due to the difficulty of creating effective test cases. As a different approach, model checking techniques guarantee a complete analysis, but only on a limited scale.

In this paper, we describe an empirical study wherein a *concolic testing* method is applied to the multi-sector read operation for a flash memory. This method combines a symbolic static analysis and a concrete dynamic analysis to automatically generate test cases and perform exhaustive path testing accordingly. In addition, we analyze the advantages and weaknesses of the concolic testing approach on the domain of the flash file system compared to model checking techniques.

1   Introduction

Due to attractive characteristics such as low power consumption and strong resistance to physical shock, flash memory has become a crucial component for mobile devices. Accordingly, in order for mobile devices to operate successfully, it is essential that the file system software of the flash memory operates correctly. However, conventional testing methods often fail to detect hidden bugs in the file system software for flash memory, since it is very difficult to create effective test cases that provide a check of all possible execution scenarios generated from the complex file system software. Thus, the current industrial practice of manual testing does not achieve high coverage or provide cost-effective testing. In another testing approach, randomized testing can save human effort for test case generation, but does not achieve high coverage, because random input data does not necessarily guarantee high coverage of a target program.

---

* This work was supported by the Engineering Research Center of Excellence Program of Korea Ministry of Education, Science and Technology(MEST)/Korea Science and Engineering Foundation(KOSEF) (grant number R11-2008-007-03002-0) and the MKE(Ministry of Knowledge Economy), Korea, under the ITRC(Information Technology Research Center) support program supervised by NIPA(National IT Industry Promotion Agency) (NIPA-2009-(C1090-0902-0032)).

These deficiencies of conventional testing incur significant overhead to manufacturers. In particular, ensuring reliability and performance are the two most time-consuming tasks to produce high quality embedded software. For example, a multi-sector read (MSR) function was added to the flash software to improve the reading speed of a Samsung flash memory product [2]. However, this function caused numerous errors in spite of extensive testing and debugging efforts, to the extent that the developers seriously considered removing the feature. Considering that MSR is a core logic used for most flash software with variations, and that improvement of the reading speed through MSR can provide important competitive power to flash memory products, research on the effective analysis of MSR is desirable and practically rewarding.

In spite of the importance of flash memory, however, little research work has been conducted to formally analyze flash file systems. In addition, most of such work [8,10,4] focuses on the specification of file system design, not real implementation. In this paper, we describe experiments we carried out to analyze the MSR code of the Samsung flash file system using CREST [12], an open source *concolic testing* [22,20,5] tool for C programs. With a given compilable target C code, a concolic (CONCrete + symbOLIC) testing combines both a concrete dynamic analysis and a symbolic static analysis [13,23] to *automatically* generate test cases that achieve high coverage. However, it is necessary to check the effectiveness of concolic testing on a flash file system through empirical studies, since the success of this testing approach depends on the characteristics of the target program under test. MSR has complex environmental constraints between sector allocation maps and physical units for correct operation (see Section 2.2) and these constraints may cause insufficient coverage and/or high runtime cost for the analysis when concolic testing is applied.

Furthermore, we compare the empirical results obtained from analyzing MSR through concolic testing with those yielded by model checking [9]. As an alternative solution to achieve high reliability, model checking guarantees complete analysis results; the authors reported on the effectiveness of model checking for the verification of MSR in [15]. However, model checking has a limitation with respect to scalability, and thus the analysis results can be applied on a small scale only. Thus, comparison of these two different techniques to analyze MSR can clearly show their relative strengths and weaknesses and will serve as a basis for developing an advanced analysis technique suitable for flash file systems.

The organization of this paper is as follows. Section 2 overviews the file system for the flash memory and describes multi-sector operation in detail. Section 3 briefly explains the concolic testing algorithm. Section 4 describes the experimental results obtained by applying concolic testing to MSR. Section 5 discusses observations from the experiments. Section 6 concludes the paper with directions for future work.

2   Overview of Multi-sector Read Operation

Unified storage platform (USP) is a software solution to operate a Samsung flash memory device [2]. USP allows applications to store and retrieve data on flash memory through a file system. USP contains a flash translation layer (FTL) through which data and programs in the flash memory device are accessed. The FTL consists of three layers - a sector translation layer (STL), a block management layer (BML), and a low-level device driver layer (LLD). Generic I/O requests from applications are fulfilled through the file system, STL, BML, and LLD, in order. MSR resides in STL.[1]

2.1 Overview of Sector Translation Layer (STL)

A NAND flash device consists of a set of *pages*, which are grouped into *blocks*. A *unit* can be equal to a block or multiple blocks. Each page contains a set of *sectors*.

When new data is written to flash memory, rather than overwriting old data directly, the data is written on empty physical sectors and the physical sectors that contain the old data are marked as invalid. Since the empty physical sectors may reside in separate physical units, one logical unit (LU) containing data is mapped to a linked list of physical units (PU). STL manages this mapping from logical sectors (LS) to physical sectors (PS). This mapping information is stored in a sector allocation map (SAM), which returns the corresponding PS offset from a given LS offset. Each PU has its own SAM.

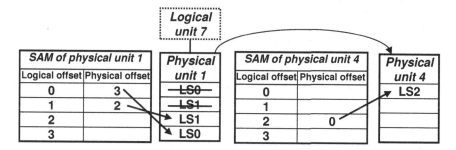

Fig. 1. Mapping from logical sectors to physical sectors

Figure 1 illustrates a mapping from logical sectors to physical sectors where 1 unit consists of 1 block and 1 block contains 4 pages, each of which consists of 1 sector. Suppose that a user writes LS0 of LU7. An empty physical unit PU1 is then assigned to LU7, and LS0 is written into PS0 of PU1 (SAM1[0]=0). The user continues to write LS1 of LU7, and LS1 is subsequently stored into PS1 of PU1 (SAM1[1]=1). The user then updates LS1 and LS0 in order, which results in SAM1[1]=2 and SAM1[0]=3. Finally, the user adds LS2 of LU7, which adds a new physical unit PU4 to LU7 and yields SAM4[2]=0.

2.2 Multi-sector Read Operation

USP provides a mechanism to simultaneously read as many multiple sectors as possible in order to improve the reading speed. The core logic of this mechanism is implemented in a single function in STL. Due to the non-trivial traversal of data structures for logical-to-physical sector mapping (see Section 2.1), the function for MSR is 157 lines long and highly complex, having 4-level nested loops. Figure 2 describes simplified pseudo code

---

[1] This section is taken from [15].

of these 4-level nested loops. The outermost loop iterates over LUs of data (line 2-18) until the numScts amount of the logical sectors are read completely. The second outermost loop iterates until the LS's of the current LU are completely read (line 5-16). The third loop iterates over PUs mapped to the current LU (line 7-15). The innermost loop identifies consecutive PS's that contain consecutive LS's in the current PU (line 8-11). This loop calculates conScts and offset, which indicate the number of such consecutive PS's and the starting offset of these PS's, respectively. Once conScts and offset are obtained, BML_READ rapidly reads these consecutive PS's as a whole (line 12).

```
01:curLU = LU0;
02:while(numScts > 0) {
03:  readScts = # of sectors to read in the current LU
04:  numScts -= readScts;
05:  while(readScts > 0 ) {
06:    curPU = LU->firstPU;
07:    while(curPU != NULL ) {
08:      while(...) {
09:        conScts = # of consecutive PS's to read in curPU
10:        offset = the starting offset of these consecutive PS's
11:      }
12:      BML_READ(curPU, offset, conScts);
13:      readScts = readScts - conScts;
14:      curPU = curPU->next;
15:    }
16:  }
17:  curLU = curLU->next;
18:}
```

Fig. 2. Loop structures of MSR

For example, suppose that the data is "ABCDEF" and each unit consists of four sectors and PU0, PU1, and PU2 are mapped to LU0 ("ABCD") in order and PU3 and PU4 are mapped to LU1 ("EF") in order, as depicted in Figure 3(a). Initially, MSR accesses SAM0 to find which PS of PU0 contains LS0('A'). It then finds SAM0[0]=1 and reads PS1 of PU0. Since SAM0[1] is empty (i.e., PU0 does not have LS1('B')), MSR moves to the next PU, which is PU1. For PU1, MSR accesses SAM1 and finds that LS1('B') and LS2('C') are stored in PS1 and PS2 of PU1 consecutively. Thus, MSR reads PS1 and PS2 of PU1 altogether through BML_READ and continues its reading operation.

The requirement for MSR is that the content of the read buffer should be equal to the original data in the flash memory when MSR finishes reading, as given by assert($\forall i.LS[i]$==buf[i]) inserted at the end of MSR.

In these analysis tasks, we assume that each sector is 1 byte long and each unit has four sectors. Also, we assume that data is a fixed string of distinct characters (e.g., "ABCDE" if we assume that data is 5 sectors long, and "ABCDEF" if we assume that data is 6 sectors long). We apply this data abstraction, since the values of logical sectors

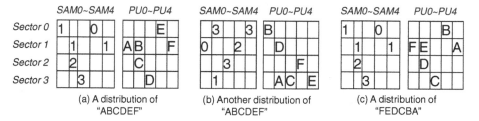

Fig. 3. Possible distributions of data "ABCDEF" and "FEDCBA" to physical sectors

should not affect the reading operations of MSR, but the distribution of logical sectors into physical sectors does. For example, for the same data "ABCDEF", the reading operations of MSR are different for Figure 3(a) and Figure 3(b), since they have different SAM configurations (i.e. different distributions of "ABCDEF"). However, for "FEDCBA" in Figure 3(c), which has the same SAM configuration as the data shown in Figure 3(a), MSR operates in exactly same manner as for Figure 3(a). Thus, if MSR reads "ABCDEF" in Figure 3(a) correctly, MSR reads "FEDCBA" in Figure 3(c) correctly too.

In addition, we assume that data occupies 2 logical units. The number of possible distribution cases for l LS's and n physical units, where $5 \leq l \leq 8$ and $n \geq 2$, increases exponentially in terms of both n and l, and can be obtained by

$$\sum_{i=1}^{n-1} \left({}_{(4 \times i)}C_4 \times 4! \right) \times \left({}_{(4 \times (n-i))}C_{(l-4)} \times (l-4)! \right)$$

For example, if a flash has 1000 physical units with data occupying 6 LS's, there exist a total of 3.9×10^{22} different distributions of the data. Table 1 shows the total number of possible cases for 5 to 8 logical sectors and various numbers of physical units, respectively, according to the above formula.

MSR has characteristics of a control-oriented program (4-level nested loops) and a data-oriented program (large data structure consisting of SAMs and PUs) at the same time, although the values of PS's are not explicitly manipulated. As seen from Figure 3, the execution paths of MSR depend on the values of SAMs and the order of PUs linked to LU. In other words, MSR operates deterministically, once the configuration of the SAMs and PUs is fixed.

Table 1. Total number of the distribution cases

PUs	4	5	6	7	8
$l = 5$	61248	290304	9.8×10^5	2.7×10^6	6.4×10^6
$l = 6$	239808	1416960	5.8×10^6	1.9×10^7	5.1×10^7
$l = 7$	8.8×10^5	7.3×10^6	3.9×10^7	1.5×10^8	5.0×10^8
$l = 8$	3.4×10^6	4.2×10^7	2.9×10^8	1.4×10^9	5.6×10^9

3 Overview of the Concolic Testing Approach

This section presents an overview of the concolic testing algorithm [22,20,5]. The concolic testing algorithm executes a target program both concretely and symbolically [13,23] at the same time. Note that the symbolic path is built following the path that the concrete execution takes. The concolic testing algorithm proceeds in the following five steps:

1. *Instrumentation*
   A target C program is statically instrumented with probes, which record symbolic path constraints from a concrete execution path when the target program is executed.
2. *Concrete execution*
   The instrumented C program is executed with given input values and the concrete execution part of the concolic execution constitutes the normal execution of the program. For the first execution of the target program, initial input values are assigned with random values. For the second execution and onward, input values are obtained from step 5.
3. *Symbolic execution*
   The symbolic execution part of the concolic execution collects symbolic constraints over the symbolic input values at each branch point encountered along the concrete execution path. Whenever each statement S_j of the original target program is executed, a corresponding probe P_j inserted at S_j updates the symbolic map of symbolic variables if S_j is an assignment statement, or collects a corresponding symbolic path constraint C_j if S_j is a branch statement. Thus, a complete symbolic path formula ϕ_i is built at the end of the ith execution by combining all path constraints C_j's.
4. *Deciding the next execution path*
   Given a symbolic path formula ϕ_i obtained in step 3, ϕ_{i+1} (the next execution path to test) is created by negating one path constraint C_j. For example, if depth first search (DFS) is used, ϕ_{i+1} is generated by negating the last symbolic path constraint of ϕ_i. If there is no further new paths to test, the algorithm terminates.
5. *Selecting the next input values*
   A constraint solver such as a Satisfiability Modulo Theory (SMT) solver [3] generates a model that satisfies ϕ_{i+1}. This model assigns concrete values to input values and the whole concolic testing procedure iterates from stage 2 again with these input values.

Note that the above algorithm does *not* raise any false alarms, since it executes a concrete path. However, there is a clear limitation in step 5. A constraint solver cannot solve complex path formulas to compute concrete values; most constraint solvers cannot handle statements containing arrays, pointers, and non-linear arithmetic. To address this difficulty, symbolic constraints are simplified by replacing some of the symbolic values with concrete values, which may result in incomplete coverage.

4 Empirical Study on Concolic Testing MSR

In this section, we describe two series of experiments for concolically testing MSR, both of which target the same MSR code, but with different environment models - a *constraint-based model* and an *explicit model*. Our hypotheses are as follows:

- H_1: Concolic testing is effective for analyzing the MSR code
- H_2: Concolic testing is more efficient than model checking for analyzing the MSR code

Regarding H_1, we expect that concolic testing can detect bugs effectively, since it tries to explore all feasible execution paths. For H_2, considering that model checking analyzes all possible value combinations of variables, concolic testing may analyze the MSR code faster (note that different value combinations of variables may execute a same path).

4.1 Testbed for the Experiments

All experiments were performed on 64 bit Fedora Linux 9 equipped with a 3 GHz Core2Duo processor and 16 gigabytes of memory. We used CREST [1] as a concolic testing tool for our experiments, since it is an open source tool and we could obtain more detailed experimental results by modifying the CREST source code for our purposes. However, since the CREST project is in its early stage, CREST has several limitations such as lack of support for dereferencing of pointers and array index variables in the symbolic analysis. Consequently, the target MSR code was modified to use an array representation of the SAMs and PUs. We used CREST 0.1.1 (with DFS search option), gcc 4.3.0, Yices 1.0.19 [6], which is a SMT solver used as an internal constraint solver by CREST for solving symbolic path formulas.

For model checking experiments, CBMC 2.6 [7] and MiniSAT 1.14 [18] were used. The target MSR codes used for concolic testing and model checking are identical, except nominal modification replacing the assumption statements in CBMC experiments with `if` statements to terminate testing if the assumptions are evaluated false (i.e. invalid test cases (see Section 4.2)). Model checking experiments were performed on the same testbed as that of concolic testing experiments.

To evaluate the effectiveness of concolic testing, we applied *mutation analysis* [14] by injecting the following three types of frequently occuring bugs (i.e. mutation operators), each of which has three instances:

1. *Off-by-1 bugs*

   - b_{11}: `while(numScts>0)` of the outermost loop (line 2 of Figure 2) to `while(numScts>1)`
   - b_{12}: `while(readScts>0)` of the second outermost loop (line 5 of Figure 2) to `while(readScts>1)`
   - b_{13}: `for(i=0;i<conScts; i++)` of `BML_READ()` (line 12 of Figure 2) to `for(i=0;i<conScts-1;i++)`

2. *Invalid condition bugs*

   - b_{21}: `if(SAM[i].offset[j]!=0xFF)` in the third outermost loop to `if(SAM[i].offset[j]==0xFF)`
   - b_{22}: `readScts=((4-j)>numScts)?numScts:4-j` in the innermost loop to `readScts=((4-j)<numScts)?numScts:4-j`
   - b_{23}: `if((firstOffset+nScts)==SAM[i].offset[j])` in the innermost loop to `if((firstOffset+nScts)!=SAM[i].offset[j])`

3. *Missing statement bugs*

   - b_{31}: missing `nScts=1` in the second outermost loop
   - b_{32}: missing `nReadScts--` in the second outermost loop
   - b_{33}: missing `nLun++` corresponding the line 17 of Figure 2

Furthermore, we injected an artificial corner case bug b_c by changing line 13 of Figure 2 as follows:

```
readScts = readScts - conScts -
              (PU[1].sect[3]=='A' && PU[0].sect[0]=='B' &&
              PU[2].sect[3]=='C' && PU[1].sect[1]=='D' &&
              PU[4].sect[3]=='E' && PU[3].sect[2]=='F')
```

Note that b_c causes an error only when the configuration of the PUs and SAMs satisfies the given condition illustrated in Figure 1.(b). b_c is very hard to detect, since the probability of detecting b_c through testing is extremely low (e.g. $7 \times 10^{-8} = 1/1416960$ when 6 logical sectors are distributed over 5 PUs (see Table 1)). Therefore, although b_c is not a realistic bug, the effectiveness of concolic testing can be shown more clearly by detecting b_c.

4.2   Experiments with a Constraint-Based Environment Model

Constraint-based Environment Model. As described in Section 2.2, a test case for MSR is a configuration of SAMs and PUs (see Figure 3). MSR assumes randomly written logical data on PUs and a corresponding SAM records the actual location of each LS. Unfortunately, however, the writing is *not* purely random, but is subject to several constraint rules; the following are some of the representative rules applied to the random writing. For example, the last two rules can be enforced by the constraints in Figure 4.

1. One PU is mapped to at most one LU.
2. If the i_{th} LS is written in the k_{th} sector of the j_{th} PU, then the $(i \bmod m)_{th}$ offset of the j_{th} SAM is valid and indicates the PS number k, where m is the number of sectors per unit (4 in our experiments).
3. The PS number of the i_{th} LS must be written in *only* one of the $(i \bmod m)_{th}$ offsets of the SAM tables for the PUs mapped to the $\lfloor \frac{i}{m} \rfloor_{th}$ LU.

$$\forall i, j, k \ (LS[i] = PU[j].sect[k] \rightarrow (SAM[j].valid[i \bmod m] = true$$
$$\& \ SAM[j].offset[i \bmod m] = k$$
$$\& \ \forall p.(SAM[p].valid[i \bmod m] = false)$$
$$\text{where } p \neq j \ \text{and } PU[p] \text{ is mapped to} \lfloor \frac{i}{m} \rfloor_{th} \ LU))$$

Fig. 4. Environment constraints for MSR

If a given configuration of SAMs and PUs satisfies the constraints, this configuration is *valid*; invalid, otherwise. It is important to check whether a given test case is valid or not, since an invalid test case may produce an incorrect testing result. Therefore, for accurate unit testing, it is essential to provide a precise environment model to feed valid test cases only.

To enforce the constraint-based environment model on the test cases, all elements of the SAM tables and PUs are declared to be analyzed symbolically through CREST_unsigned_char(PU[i].sect[j]) and CREST_unsigned_char(SAM[i].offset[j]) statements for all valid i and j. Then, a test driver/ environment model checks whether concrete values assigned by CREST to those variables satisfy the constraints in Figure 4. If not, the execution terminates immediately without testing MSR. Note that these constraints are encoded as if statements in nested loops handling universally quantified i, j, k, and p, which results in a complex environment model.

Experimental Results. Due to a time limitation, we could perform 4 experiments with 4 to 5 PUs with 5 to 6 LSes. The total numbers of test cases generated and the ratios of the valid test cases over the total test cases are depicted in Figure 5. For example, CREST generated a total of 5.6×10^5 test cases for 4 PUs with 5 LSes, and only 61248 test cases (around 11% of the total test cases) among them were valid. Note that the numbers of the valid test cases for these 4 experiments are equal to the numbers of all possible configurations of the SAMs and PUs (see Table 1). This means that the concolic testing covers all possible execution scenarios of MSR.[2] Consequently, all injected bugs b_{11} to b_{33} as well as b_c were detected; most of them were detected in a few seconds through the first few hundred test cases.

The performance of the concolic testing is shown in Figure 6. For example, CREST took 2594 seconds for the experiments with 4 PUs and 5 LSes. The amount of time to analyze MSR increases exponentially in terms of the number of PUs and LSes. Figure 6(a) shows that CREST is several hundred times slower than CBMC. Figure 6.(b) shows that symbolic execution, Yices, and system execution (e.g. launching a target program) take around 40%, 40%, and 20% of the total execution time. However, all experiments use around 10 megabytes of memory only, since the DFS search in CREST needs

---

[2] We tried to perform the same experiments with CUTE (32 bit binary) [22] but failed; CUTE crashed after consuming 4 gigabytes of memory at the constraint solving step at the third iteration. We could not continue the experiments with CUTE, since neither the source code nor user support was available.

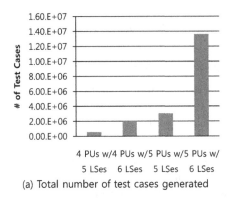 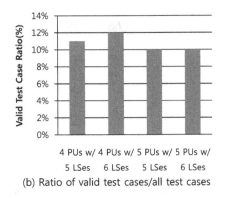

(a) Total number of test cases generated   (b) Ratio of valid test cases/all test cases

Fig. 5. Generated test cases with constraint-based environment model

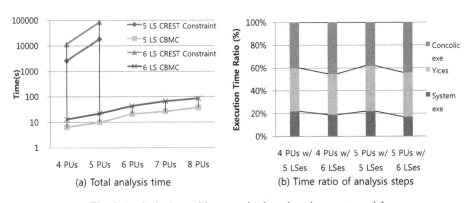

(a) Total analysis time   (b) Time ratio of analysis steps

Fig. 6. Analysis time with constraint-based environment model

only a small amount of information regarding the previous execution path, not the whole execution tree. In comparison, CBMC consumed 40 megabytes and 89 megabytes for 4 PUs with 5 LSes and 5 PUs with 6 LSes, respectively. Therefore, the memory bottleneck problem associated with model checking does not exist for concolic testing.

4.3 Experiments with an Explicit Environment Model

Explicit Environment Model. As we have seen from Figure 5(b), the constraint-based environment model generated too many invalid test cases. Thus, we decided to use an explicit environment model that generates test cases *explicitly* by selecting a PU and its sector to contain the l th logical sector (`PU[i].sect[j]=LS[l]`) and setting the corresponding SAM accordingly (`SAM[i].offset[l]=j`). Therefore, most of the generated test cases satisfy the constraints between SAMs and PUs.

However, since CREST cannot support accessing array elements through a symbolic array index variable, we have to modify assignments of SAMs and PUs in the environment model so that these assignments access array elements through constants, not index variables. This workaround solution is depicted in Figure 7. `idxPU` and `idxSect`,

```
01:for (i=0; i< NUM_LS; i++){
02: unsigned char idxPU, idxSect;
03: CREST_unsigned_char(idxPU);
04: CREST_unsigned_char(idxSect);
05: ...
06: //The switch statements encode the following two statements:
07: //   PU[idxPu].sect[idxSect]= LS[i];
08: //   SAM[idxPu].sect[i]= idxSect;
09: switch(idxPU){
10:    case 0: switch(idxSect) {
11:            case 0: PU[0].sect[0] = LS[i];
12:                    SAM[0].offset[i] = idxSect; break;
13:            case 1: PU[idxPU].sect[1] = LS[i];
14:                    SAM[0].offset[i] = idxSect; break;
15:            ... }
16:            break;
17:    case 1: switch(idxSect) {
18:            ...
```

Fig. 7. Explicit environment model for MSR

which indicate the physical location of the ith logical sector data (LS[i]), are declared to be handled symbolically (lines 3 and 4). In the explicit environment model, the switch statements starting at line 9 and line 10/17 respectively handle idxPU and idxSect case by case. Note that, although this explicit environment model does not generate many invalid test cases, it increases the total number of execution paths due to these additional switch statements.

Experimental Results. Due to a time limitation, we could perform only 4 experiments with 4 to 5 PUs with 5 to 6 LSes with the explicit environment model. The total numbers of test cases generated and the ratios of the valid test cases over the total test cases are depicted in Figure 8. For example, CREST generated a total of 10^5 test cases for 4 PUs with 5 LSes, 61248 test cases (around 60% of the total test cases) among them

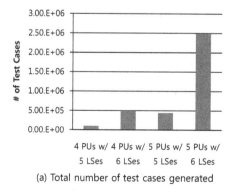

(a) Total number of test cases generated

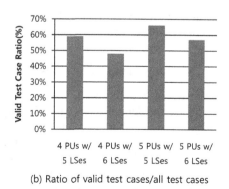

(b) Ratio of valid test cases/all test cases

Fig. 8. Statistics on the generated test cases with explicit environment model

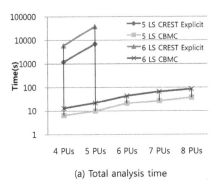
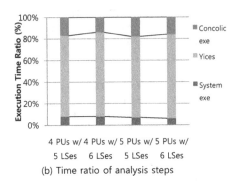

(a) Total analysis time   (b) Time ratio of analysis steps

Fig. 9. Analysis time with explicit environment model

being valid. Thus, the explicit environment model generates test cases more efficiently compared to the constraint-based model. Similar to the experiments with the constraint-based model, the numbers of valid test cases for these 4 set of experiments are equal to the numbers of all possible configurations of the SAMs and PUs (see Table 1). All injected bugs b_{11} to b_{33} and b_c were detected, but within fewer test cases; most of them were detected in 3 seconds through the first 50 test cases.

The performance of the concolic testing approach with the explicit environment model is depicted in Figure 9. For example, CREST took 1203 seconds for the experiments with 4 PUs and 5 LSes. Although the concolic testing with the explicit model is twofold faster than the testing with the constraint-based model, it is still a hundred times slower compared to CBMC (see Figure 6). Yices takes around 75% of the total execution time, since invalid test cases are significantly reduced, which thus decreases the portion of symbolic execution time and system execution time. Note that the symbolic execution path formulas for invalid test cases are very short and are solved quickly. Therefore, improvement of the SMT solver is an important issue with regard to the success of concolic testing.

5   Discussion

In this section, several issues are discussed on the basis of our experience of applying concolic testing to MSR.

5.1   Weaknesses of Concolic Testing

Although our hypothesis H_1 is accepted through the empirical study (i.e. the concolic testing method demonstrates capability of detecting bugs through high coverage), H_2 is rejected (i.e. its performance on MSR is worse than the performance of model checking MSR by CBMC (see Figure 6 and Figure 9)). This poor performance was caused by several steps of the concolic testing algorithm (see Section 3).

First, for a target program with a complex environmental model such as MSR, the concolic testing wastes a large amount of time to generate invalid test cases. In the experiments with the constraint-based environment model and the explicit environment model, around 90% and 45% of the total test cases generated were invalid respectively (see Figure 5 and Figure 8). Considering a unit under testing often has preconditions or constraints enforced by its interacting components, the concolic testing framework should provide an efficient way to control the generation of concrete input values so as to generate only valid test cases. Second, concolic execution (see steps 2 and 3 of the algorithm in Section 3) causes high overhead, since each original C statement is supplemented with a probe reflecting a concrete execution in a symbolic manner; around 40% and 15% of the total execution times were spent for the concolic executions with the constraint-based model and the explicit model, respectively (see Figure 6 and Figure 9). Note that the original MSR code takes less than 0.1% of the concolic execution time. Lastly, the performance of the constraint solver Yices was slow, although the path formulas of MSR are conjunctions of only linear arithmetic conditions and can be solved rapidly by many efficient algorithms [21]. Therefore, from our experiments, we can conclude that CREST needs to be improved for practical usage.

5.2 Importance of an Environment Model

Through the various experiments carried out to analyze MSR, including conventional testing [16], concolic testing, and model checking [15], we found that it is important to build an accurate and efficient environment model for the analysis of a flash file system. Also, it was found that different analysis techniques can commonly use the same environment model. For example, the constraint-based environmental model (see Section 4.2) was originally designed for model checking through CBMC and used as is with only nominal modification. Similarly, the explicit environmental model was originally designed for model checking through SPIN [11]. We used this environmental model for SPIN with slight modification due to the limitation of CREST (i.e., array index variables are not symbolically handled). Furthermore, the design of the environment model substantially affects the analysis performance (see Section 4.2 and Section 4.3).

Considering the importance of an environment model in unit testing, the claim of automated test case generation by concolic testing is only partially true, since an experienced user has to build an environment model.

5.3 Comparison with Model Checking

Concolic testing can be considered as a light-weight model checking method, since it generates all test cases corresponding to all possible execution paths. However, these two different analysis techniques have as many different characteristics as common characteristics. Table 2 compares these techniques briefly based on our experience, although this comparison result might not be applicable to other target programs.

In general, model checking provides better accuracy, since the coverage of concolic testing may not be complete if a target program contains complex statements that cannot be solved by a constraint solver (note that this was not the case for MSR). Also, constraint solvers used for concolic testing are not sufficiently advanced to manipulate symbolic execution path formulas efficiently. However, in terms of applicability, concolic testing has notable advantages, since it can analyze a target program with

Table 2. Comparison of concolic testing and model checking

	Accuracy	Analysis speed	Memory usage	User effort	Applicability
Concolic testing	High	Slower	Low	Middle	High
Model checking	Highest	Slow	High	High	Low

underlying binary libraries as it is, without manual abstraction, which is necessary for model checking.

5.4   Hard Characteristics of MSR for Concolic Testing

It was found that MSR is a hard instance for concolic testing. Concolic testing can efficiently analyze programs whose data domain can be significantly abstracted. For example, concolic testing can analyze binary search programs or sort programs quickly. The data domain of MSR (especially SAMs), however, cannot be abstracted, since every different value in every single element of SAMs leads to a unique execution path. Thus, as shown in Section 4.2 and Section 4.3, the total number of valid test cases generated is exactly the same as the number of all possible configurations of the PUs and SAMs (see Table 1). In other words, in the analysis of MSR, concolic testing is burdened by as much complexity as model checking. The same difficulty in analysis of MSR applies to model checking and a scalability issue remains.

6   Conclusion and Future Work

We reported our experience of applying a concolic testing method to analyze the MSR code, a complex unit of a flash file system, and analyzed the strengths and weaknesses of the approach empirically. Although several goals of the concolic testing method could be achieved through the experiments (e.g., automated test case generation, high coverage, and detection of bugs), CREST suffered from a few limitations including slow analysis speed and lack of support for array index variables. We expect that CREST will be able to overcome these limitations in the near future.

As future study, we plan to build a flash file system model that can be used by file-system-dependent applications in a concolic testing framework. One inspiring related work was carried out by Microsoft [17], where an intelligent mock object (an environment model in our terminology) for a file system was developed to test target applications in the PEX framework [19]. The mock file system automatically generates various possible test cases necessary to test applications, which can save significant effort to test file-system-dependent applications.

Acknowledgments

We would like to thank Hotae Kim at Samsung Electronics and Prof. Yunja Choi at Kyungpook National University for their valuable discussion on the environment models for flash file systems.

References

1. CREST - automatic test generation tool for C, http://code.google.com/p/crest/
2. Samsung OneNAND fusion memory,
   http://www.samsung.com/global/business/semiconductor/
   products/fusionmemory/Products_OneNAND.html
3. SMT-LIB: The satisfiability module theories library,
   http://combination.cs.uiowa.edu/smtlib/
4. Butterfield, A., Freitas, L., Woodcock, J.: Mechanising a formal model of flash memory. Science of Computer Programming 74(4) (February 2009)
5. Cadar, C., Dunbar, D., Engler, D.: KLEE: Unassisted and automatic generation of high-coverage tests for complex systems programs. In: Operating System Design and Implementation, OSDI (2008)
6. Dutertre, B., Moura, L.: A fast linear-arithmetic solver for DPLL(T). In: Ball, T., Jones, R.B. (eds.) CAV 2006. LNCS, vol. 4144, pp. 81–94. Springer, Heidelberg (2006)
7. Clarke, E., Kroening, D., Lerda, F.: A tool for checking ANSI-C programs. In: Jensen, K., Podelski, A. (eds.) TACAS 2004. LNCS, vol. 2988, pp. 168–176. Springer, Heidelberg (2004)
8. Kang, E., Jackson, D.: Formal modeling and analysis of a flash filesystem in Alloy. Abstract state machines, B and Z (2008)
9. Clarke, E.M., Grumberg, O., Peled, D.A.: Model Checking. MIT Press, Cambridge (2000)
10. Ferreira, M.A., Silva, S.S., Oliveira, J.N.: Verifying Intel flash file system core specification. In: 4th VDM-Overture Workshop (2008)
11. Holzmann, G.J.: The Spin Model Checker. Wiley, New York (2003)
12. Burnim, J., Sen, K.: Heuristics for scalable dynamic test generation. Technical Report UCB/EECS-2008-123, EECS Department, University of California, Berkeley (September 2008)
13. King, J.C.: Symbolic execution and program testing. Communications of the ACM 19(7) (1976)
14. Andrews, J.H., Briand, L.C., Labiche, Y.: Is mutation an appropriate tool for testing experiments? In: International Conference on Software Engineering (2005)
15. Kim, M., Choi, Y., Kim, Y., Kim, H.: Formal verification of a flash memory device driver - an experience report. In: Havelund, K., Majumdar, R., Palsberg, J. (eds.) SPIN 2008. LNCS, vol. 5156, pp. 144–159. Springer, Heidelberg (2008)
16. Kim, M., Kim, Y., Choi, Y., Kim, H.: Pre-testing flash device driver through model checking techniques. In: IEEE Int. Conf. on Software Testing, Verification and Validation (2008)
17. Marri, M., Xie, T., Tillmann, N., de Halleux, J., Schulte, W.: An empirical study of testing file-system-dependent software with mock objects. In: Automation of Software Test (2009)
18. Een, N., Sorensson, N.: An extensible sat-solver. In: Giunchiglia, E., Tacchella, A. (eds.) SAT 2003. LNCS, vol. 2919, pp. 502–518. Springer, Heidelberg (2004)
19. Tillmann, N., Schulte, W.: Parameterized unit tests. In: European Software Engineering Conference/Foundations of Software Engineering (2005)
20. Godefroid, P., Klarlund, N., Sen, K.: Dart: Directed automated random testing. In: Programming Language Design and Implementation, PLDI (2005)
21. Berezin, S., Ganesh, V., Dill, D.L.: An online proof-producing decision procedure for mixed integer linear arithmetic. In: Garavel, H., Hatcliff, J. (eds.) TACAS 2003. LNCS, vol. 2619, pp. 521–536. Springer, Heidelberg (2003)
22. Sen, K., Marinov, D., Agha, G.: CUTE: A concolic unit testing engine for C. In: European Software Engineering Conference/Foundations of Software Engineering (2005)
23. Visser, W., Pasareanu, C.S., Khurshid, S.: Test input generation with Java PathFinder. In: International Symposium on Software Testing and Analysis (2004)

Low-Level Code Verification Based on CSP Models

Moritz Kleine and Steffen Helke

Technical University of Berlin
Institute for Software Engineering and Theoretical Computer Science
Berlin, Germany
{mkleine,helke}@cs.tu-berlin.de

Abstract. This paper contributes to the broad field of software verification by proposing a methodology that uses CSP to verify implementations of real-life multithreaded applications. We therefore use CSP to formalize the compiler intermediate representation of a program. Our methodology divides the low-level representation into three parts: an application-specific part, describing the behavior of threads; a domain-specific part, which encapsulates low-level software concepts such as scheduling; and a platform-specific part, which is the hardware model. These three parts form a low-level CSP model that enables us to prove properties, e.g. the absence of race conditions in the model, by either model checking or theorem proving. The application-specific part is synthesized from the LLVM intermediate representation of a multithreaded program.

1   Introduction

In this paper, we address the problem of developing methods to increase confidence in safety-critical systems. To verify the C++ implementations of concurrent systems, we propose an approach that builds on the automated extraction of a CSP model of the Low Level Virtual Machine (LLVM) compiler intermediate representation (IR) of programs and the use of established CSP tools such as the refinement checker FDR2 [1] and the LTL model checker ProB [2] to analyze the generated model. Our methodology divides the low-level representation of a concurrent system into three parts: an application-specific one, which describes the behavior of threads; a domain-specific one, which encapsulates low-level software concepts such as scheduling; and a platform-specific one, which is the hardware model. The latter two are parameterized and highly reusable. The application-specific part as well as most of the parameters for the platform-specific and domain-specific parts are to be automatically generated from the LLVM IR of the program. Examples of such parameters are typing information for the channels and the set of thread identifiers.

We outline an algorithm that extracts the parameters for the domain-specific and platform-specific parts from the LLVM IR and gathers the information

M.V.M. Oliveira and J. Woodcock (Eds.): SBMF 2009, LNCS 5902, pp. 266–281, 2009.

needed for synthesizing the application-specific model of the program. Conformance of the implementation to its CSP-based specification is shown by proving that the generated model is a refinement of the system's specification. Unlike methods that require a formally proven refinement chain from the specification down to executable code, the approach presented in this paper retains the option of manually tweaking the performance of the final implementation without losing conformance of the implementation to its specification. As an example application of our method, we investigate a system of multiple threads accessing a shared counter variable to illustrate our verification methodology. To our knowledge, this is a new approach to relating CSP specifications and implementations.

1.1 Structure of the Paper

The following two subsections introduce the process calculus CSP and its machine-readable form CSP_M in Sect. 1.2, and the LLVM compiler infrastructure in Sect. 1.3. These form the basis of the framework presented in this paper. The paper begins by investigating the current role of CSP in software engineering in Sect. 2 and motivates the approach to developing a new CSP-based software engineering methodology. The example of a simple concurrent program is introduced which is used throughout the paper to illustrate our concepts. Our approach of verifying low-level code using CSP models is presented in Sect. 3. The three different parts of the resulting CSP_M model are introduced and we explain how they fit together. In Sect. 4 we present the application-specific part of the low-level model and show how it is obtained from the LLVM IR of a concurrent program. The paper closes with pointers to related work in Sect. 5, and conclusions and ideas for future work in Sect. 6.

1.2 Brief Introduction to CSP

Communicating Sequential Processes (CSP) is a process calculus developed in the early 1980s [5]. It is capable of specifying and verifying reactive and concurrent systems, where the modeling of communication plays a key role. CSP is equipped with a rich set of process operators for defining possibly infinite transition systems by, e.g., prefixing $(a \rightarrow P)$, sequential composition $(P_1; P_2)$, hiding $(P \backslash A)$ and parallel composition $(P_1 [\![A]\!] P_2)$. The semantics of CSP processes can be given in different ways. The most popular semantics are trace semantics, failure semantics and failure-divergence semantics [12]. In the trace semantics of CSP, a process is represented by the set of all its possible communication sequences. By contrast, the failure semantics additionally records the refusals of a process, i.e. the events a process can refuse after a particular communication sequence. Both these semantics are unable to recognize processes with infinite internal behavior. The failure-divergence semantics fills exactly this gap. All these semantics are supported by the automatic refinement checker FDR2 [1], which is one of the tools we use for verification purposes.

CSP_M[13] is a machine-readable version of CSP that has been developed as the input language for the FDR2 tool. CSP_M extends CSP by a small but powerful functional language, which offers constructs such as lambda and let expressions and supports advanced concepts like pattern matching and currying. The language provides a number of predefined data types, e.g. booleans, integers, sequences and sets, and also allows user-defined data types. The global event set is defined by the set of typed channel declarations of a CSP_M script.

CSP_M is now the de facto standard of machine-readable CSP. Besides FDR2, the model checker and animator ProB supports CSP_M, so CSP_M models can also be explored by animation and verified by LTL model checking.

1.3 Brief Introduction to LLVM

The LLVM compiler infrastructure provides a modular framework that can be easily extended by user-defined compilation passes. It also offers a diverse set of predefined analyses, i.e. points-to analysis by Steensgaard [16], and optimizations that can be used out of the box. This makes LLVM a great platform for the development of source code transformation and analysis tools. The heart of the compiler infrastructure project is its intermediate representation (IR). It is a typed assembler-like language [8], which is used internally as the basis for compiler optimizations. The LLVM framework provides gcc-based frontends for a variety of programming languages, including C++. The existence of the gcc-based front-end enables us to adapt our approach, which currently only supports C++, to a couple of other programming languages with little effort because it is source-language-independent and relies on the LLVM IR only.

2 Motivation: Relating CSP Models to Programs

In this section, we first present the example that is used throughout the paper to illustrate our verification methodology, and discuss how CSP is commonly used to model and analyze such systems. As a consequence of the discussion, we propose another way of using CSP for the verification of the example.

2.1 A Simple Concurrent Program

We consider a concurrent program composed of a finite number of threads that increase a shared counter. The most obvious unwanted phenomena are that the system deadlocks or that a race condition occurs. Access to shared resources may be controlled using a counting semaphore, which offers the two methods P and V that must enclose the critical region to protect it. The example application is implemented on a minimal C++ library operating system, BOSS [10], realizing preemptive multithreading. BOSS offers an abstract class *Thread* requiring that implementations override the *run* method. It also offers primitives that allow us to enable and disable preemption of threads. Its *InterruptLock* class disables interrupts within its constructor and enables interrupts within its destructor. Our example application is realized by two classes *Thread1* and *Semaphore*. The constructor of the *Semaphore* class takes the initial value of the semaphore's counter as argument. The method *Semaphore::P* blocks if the semaphore's counter is less than one. Otherwise, it decreases the counter and returns. This has to be done atomically. One way of realizing this atomicity is temporarily disabling preemption. The method *Semaphore::V* is used to release the shared resource. It increases the semaphore's counter and returns. The implementation of the class *Thread1* calls *Semaphore::P*, increases the shared counter, calls *Semaphore::V* and repeats this sequence in a loop as its *run* method. As the implementation of the semaphore is obviously crucial for the correct functioning of the program, the most important question that arises is, Does the implementation of the semaphore work as expected? This question is answered in the sequel.

2.2   Discussion: Modeling and Analyzing the Example with CSP

As stated above, a number of threads sharing a single resource must use some kind of synchronization mechanism to avoid interfering with each other when accessing the shared resource. A simple CSP model of such a system can be made up of a set of processes that run in parallel, synchronizing on events that model acquirement and release of a lock to protect the critical regions. The following process P models such a process:

$$P(id) = Q_0; \; claim?x \rightarrow (\text{if } x = id \text{ then } Q_1 \text{ else } SKIP \text{ fi}); \; release.x \rightarrow P(id)$$

Within this process the channels $claim, release : T$ communicate the thread identifiers from the set T. P is parameterized with a process identifier $id \in T$, which determines which process claims and releases the lock. The processes Q_0 and Q_1 define unprotected and protected regions of the processes, respectively. In our example, we define the set $N = \{0..3\}$ of valid values of the shared counter and the channels $read, write : N$. Then we let $Q_0 = SKIP$ and

$$Q_1 = read?y \rightarrow (\text{if } y < 3 \text{ then } write.(y + 1) \rightarrow SKIP \text{ else } STOP \text{ fi}).$$

This definition of Q_1 requires synchronization with another process E that stores the value of the shared counter and allows read and write access to it. A system P_{sys} of P processes that synchronize on the event set modeling the lock can now be composed and synchronized with the process E. The resulting processes are:

$$P_{sys} = \underset{\{|claim|\}}{\|} \; x : T \bullet P(x) \qquad E(v) = read.v \rightarrow E(v) \;\square\; write?x \rightarrow E(x)$$

$$S = P_{sys} \underset{\{|write,read|\}}{\|} E(0)$$

S can be encoded in CSP_M easily. With the help of a tool such as FDR2 or ProB, it can then be proved that S fulfills the requirement that the critical region may not be entered by two processes in parallel, which implies that no race condition on the shared counter can occur. The CSP_M encoding of S serves as specification for the implementation that is sketched in the previous section. To

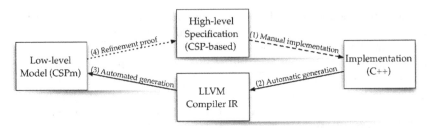

Fig. 1. Overview of the relations between high-level specification, source code, compiler IR and low-level CSP model in our verification methodology

prove the specification S race-condition-free, we used the LTL model checker ProB to verify the LTL formula:

$$G(([claim] \Rightarrow X[read]) \wedge ([read] \Rightarrow X(deadlock \vee [write])) \wedge ([write] \Rightarrow X[release]))$$

This formula can be informally rephrased as "it is always the case, that a claim is followed by a read, a read is followed by either a deadlock or a write and a write is followed by a release". Thus, racing cannot occur, because it is impossible that thread A reads the counter and before writing the increased counter, thread B reads it. Note that ProB supports keywords such as **deadlock** in LTL formulas. The brackets test if the enclosed channel name is enabled in a state. This formula checks for a deadlock state because the CSP_M encoding of S has a bounded counter variable. In the case that the counter variable reaches its maximum value, the variable can be read once more, then the process deadlocks. In the other case, the variable is increased and then written.

Nevertheless, this model does not in any way describe the lock itself. However, executable code of such a system must provide implementations of locks, so stepwise refinement is commonly used to push the specification as close to the implementation as possible.

It is clear that we cannot generate machine code for a single-processor system directly from an arbitrary CSP specification because parallelism and synchrony have to be resolved beforehand. Furthermore, any sensible specification of any system should abstract away technical details such as context switches. Since the strength of CSP lies in modeling concurrent systems, it is not advisable to limit oneself to using CSP in a way that avoids nondeterminism and parallelism in the first place. CSP is not a programming language, though programming languages inspired by CSP like OCCAM [3] do exist.

2.3   Overview: Analyzing the Implementation with CSP

Rather than exploring the classical approach of refining specifications down to executable code again, we propose that the software engineering process begin with the development of a high-level specification in some CSP-based formalism on the top level, as shown in Fig. 1. On the top level, either a CSP_M specification or a specification in an arbitrary CSP-based formalism for which a transformation into CSP_M exists, is required. For the reasons given in the last paragraph of Sect. 2.2, we cut the refinement chain at a level that still abstracts from implementation details, instead of automatically refining the specification down to executable code by CSP-based code generators. It is then the programmer's job to produce efficient and robust code – symbolized by arrow (1). Unlike code obtained using automatic code generators, our approach makes it more feasible to create high-performance code that meets the application's needs in terms of memory and power consumption.

This procedure induces a semantic gap between the high-level specification and the final implementation, which we bridge by generating another CSP model. This model is generated from the LLVM IR, which is automatically obtained during the compilation process with an LLVM-based compiler (arrow (2)). The generation process of the low-level model, which is described by arrow (3) in Fig. 1, is the subject of this paper.

The basic idea behind synthesizing a CSP_M model from a low-level representation of a program is that a CSP event is an arbitrary observation point inside a program. We would have to deal with the interpretation of events if we tried to automatically generate code from a given CSP model. This need is avoided by our approach, which extracts a detailed CSP model from the implementation of a concurrent program and includes data access, function calls and annotated observation points.

Fig. 1 also relates the generated CSP_M model to the high-level specification by arrow (4), which stands for a refinement proof. This is necessary to prove that the implementation meets its specification. Steps (3) and (4) can be used to investigate the implementation from different points of view. Especially if independent aspects have to be met by the implementation, they should be explored separately. This reduces the size of the low-level model, which is desirable for analysis by refinement and model checking.

As shown later on, to prove that the implementation for specification S is race-condition- and deadlock-free, the low-level CSP_M model is created with respect to any of the accesses to the shared counter and to the behavior of the semaphore.

3 Low-Level Verification with CSP

The generation of the low-level model relies on data dependence analyses and alias analyses such as the points-to analysis by Steensgaard[1], which computes the set of memory locations to which a variable can point. As will be explained in the sequel, the low-level CSP_M model abstracts from all function calls and data accesses that none of the data to be considered depends on. If, for example, concurrent accesses to a shared counter variable have to be proved race-condition-free, it is sufficient to build the model from the accesses to this shared counter and the locks protecting it.

---

[1] Even though data dependence analyses are not in general automatic, several analyses have been implemented in the LLVM framework. These analyses can be reused for the implementation of tools that work on the LLVM IR of programs, such as the LLVM IR to CSP_M transformation tool that we are currently implementing.

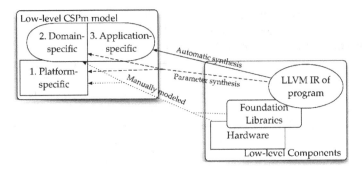

Fig. 2. Illustration of the relations between hardware and software of a multithreading system with the three components of our verification methodology

Fig. 2 refines and extends arrow (3) in Fig. 1. The low-level CSP_M model contains not only processes, types and channels that are generated from the LLVM IR of a program but also some predefined parts which require thorough explanation. The complete low-level model presented in this paper is an example of the overall methodology adopted to verify multithreaded applications running on a single-processor system because it describes the behavior of such a system in great detail.

First of all, the low-level model is divided into three distinct parts. The platform-specific part comprises the environment model and hardware details, while the domain-specific part encompasses aspects that are common to a domain of applications, e.g. system startup and scheduling, which are provided as foundation libraries that the program builds on. These two parts are mostly manually modeled but are parameterized so that they can be reused by all applications of the domain they have been designed for. The platform-specific and domain-specific parts together make up a model of interleaved concurrency that describes the behavior of a single-processor computing system and which is suitable for verifying multithreaded programs without considering the concrete concurrency implementation. The third part is the application-specific one, which describes the behavior of the threads of a multithreaded program with respect to a set of given variable names, function calls and annotations. Applications make up a single sequential process which is the interleaving of sequences belonging to one of the implemented threads. Threads are identified by a bijective mapping from the set `thread_ids` = {0 .. (number of threads −1)} to the thread instances. Data storage is modeled by zero-indexed lists. Per thread data is modeled by lists, which hold the data belonging to a thread at the index being the thread's identifier.

Any peculiarity that is introduced by a manual abstraction to keep the model a reasonable size for analysis with FDR2 or ProB is made explicit by a subprocess of the structure `error_code -> STOP` where `error_code` is a fresh event introduced to mark the violation of that very abstraction. This is necessary to maintain the soundness of our methodology. An example of such an abstraction

```
ENV = ENV1(global_vars_list)
ENV1(l) = env_read?t.i!elemAt(l, i) -> ENV1(l)
  [] env_write?t.i.e -> ENV1(insertAt(l, i, e))
  [] p_lock?t -> ENV2(l,t, 0) [] preempt -> ENV1(l)
ENV2(l, t, c) =  ...
  [] p_release.t -> (if (c == 0) then ENV1(l) else ENV2(l, t, c-1))
  [] p_lock.t -> (if c < max_lock_depth then
                  ENV2(l, t, c + 1) else e_terminate -> STOP)
```

Fig. 3. The ENV process models the global memory and preemption

is that (unsigned) integers are commonly reduced to a much smaller range (e.g. zero to three instead of zero to $2^{32} - 1$). If an integer increases beyond three in this example, the process would only offer the event that is the error code for this incident and then deadlock. Note that the shared counter variable of our program can safely be reduced to such a small range without loss of generality: the concrete values are irrelevant to race condition detection; all that matters is the order of read/write accesses to it.

The platform-specific and domain-specific parts used to verify the example presented in Sect. 2 are described in the sequel. Sect. 4 is devoted to the application-specific part.

3.1 The Platform-Specific Part

For the platform-specific part, we developed an environment model that describes the very basic behaviors of a computing system, such as read/write access to global data, enabling and disabling of preemption and triggering preemption itself. The environment is modeled as a recursive process ENV (Fig. 3) that carries a fixed-size list global_vars_list of the global variables along as it evolves. In our example, the list is <0, 1>. The first element is the initial value of the shared counter, the second element is the initial value of the semaphore's counter. The list is accessed whenever an event representing read or write access is consumed. Preemption, modeled by the preempt event, is enabled at any point in time, provided that preemption has not been locked. If it is locked, preemption is disabled until the preemption lock is released again. To facilitate verification of systems that allow nesting of preemption locks, our model also supports nesting of preemption locks[2]. Due to the restrictions of FDR2, the nesting depth is bounded by the predefined constant max_lock_depth, which must be adjusted to fit the application's needs. The error code for violating the predefined lock nesting depth is e_terminate. The list of global variables global_vars_list is

---

[2] Preemption is commonly implemented by a timer interrupt. Enabling and disabling of preemption thus can be understood as enabling and disabling of interrupts, respectively. The reason for explicitly modeling nesting of preemption locks is that it is often allowed by operating systems even though the outer-most lock is the one that affects the system's behavior.

```
channel intern_read_0, intern_write_0 : thread_ids . { 0 .. max_int}
channel intern_read_1, intern_write_1 : thread_ids . { 0 .. max_int}
ThreadState(l) = intern_read_0?t!elemAt(elemAt(l,t),0) -> ThreadState(l)
    [] intern_read_1?t!elemAt(elemAt(l,t),1) -> ThreadState(l)
    [] intern_write_0?t?val ->
        ThreadState(insertAt(l, t, insertAt(elemAt(l,t), 0, val)))
    [] intern_write_1?t?val -> ...
```

Fig. 4. The `ThreadState` process handles thread-internal data

a parameter of the platform-specific model. It can be derived from the typing information inherent to the LLVM IR of the program to be analyzed.

Data being read from or written to the main memory of the computing system is transferred to the near memory or first written to the near memory, which might be a register or a cache. This is done by the application-specific processes that are explained in the next section. The process modeling the near memory is called `ThreadState`. This process keeps track of the values to be transferred from or to the main memory. Its CSP_M encoding that suits the variables and typing of our example is shown in Fig. 4. Like the environment process, this process maintains the values in a fixed-size list that must match the memory-consumption needs of the applications. The typed channel definitions for the process are also parameters of the platform-specific model and have to be generated according to the typing information of the LLVM IR of the program under consideration. The channels `intern_read_0` and `intern_write_0` communicate the value of the semaphore's counter, while `intern_read_1` and `intern_write_1` communicate the value of the shared counter. Thus the types of the variables used by threads are represented by the typing of the channels used by the `ThreadState` process. Note that local variables and intermediate results of the methods (e.g. condition evaluations) are stored in the near memory as well. The `ThreadState` process runs in parallel to the application-specifc part and synchronizes with it on the `intern_read` and `intern_write` events as shown at the end of this section. Each communication carries the id of the owning thread, so the threads cannot interfere with each other when communicating with their local memories. In the shared counter example, the process `ThreadState` is initialized with the list `initialState = <<0,0>,<0,0>,<0,0>>`. This initialization means that the model supports up to three threads, each assuming the shared counter and the semaphore's counter to be zero.

3.2   The Domain-Specific Part

The domain-specific part models aspects such as scheduling and the entry to the application-specific processes. The entry to the application-specific processes is the initial choice of a thread to run, while scheduling happens after each of the atomic steps of a thread and is the act of deciding which thread to run next. Both aspects require the two lists `procDefs` and `threadStacks`. The former is an

```
procDefs = <Thread1_run, Semaphore_P, Semaphore_V>
threadStacks = <(<0>,<0>),(<0>,<0>),(<0>,<0>)>
AppSpecific = [] t: thread_ids @ CONTINUE(t, 0, threadStacks)
CONTINUE(t,pc,s) =
    let s' = setPC(t, s, pc) within (getProc(t, s)(t,pc,s) []
    (preempt -> []x : thread_ids@getProc(x, s')(x, getPC(x, s'), s')))
TS = {|intern_read_0, intern_write_0, intern_read_1,
intern_write_1|} TE = {|env_read,env_write, p_lock, p_release,
preempt|} Threads = ThreadState(initialState) [| TS |] AppSpecific
LowLevelModel = Threads [| TE |] ENV
```

Fig. 5. Important lists, processes and sets of the domain-specific part

unmodifiable list of the process definitions defined by the application-specific part. It is thus a mapping from integers to process definition names where each process definition represents one of the program's methods as explained in Sect. 4. The latter is a list of pairs in which each pair models the stack of a thread. The first component of any pair is a list recording the index of the process definition that describes the method a thread is currently executing. The second component is the program counter within the same method. A thread starting with process definition x of the procDefs list at program counter p has the stack (<x>,<p>). The entry to the application-specific part is the process called AppSpecific. Fig. 5 shows these two lists and the definition of AppSpecific as they occur in our example. The model of the system startup is a very simple one, which nondeterministically picks a thread identifier and allows it to start a program position 0 with the initial list of thread stacks. The definition of the CONTINUE process is far more interesting because it describes the advancement of the system. This process is a very abstract model of a scheduler: either the currently running thread continues at its current position or it is preempted. In the latter case, the state of the currently running thread is pushed onto the stack, then another thread is chosen, its state is popped from the stack and control is passed to this thread. Passing control to a thread is modeled by the process continuing with the process definition, id and program counter of the new thread. The function getProc returns the process definition (which itself is a function) for a given thread identifier according to its current stack state. It is important to notice, that any process obtained by getProc is an application-specific one, which finally evolves to the CONTINUE process. The CSP_M model of this process is also shown in Fig. 5. The set thread_ids is another parameter that has to be generated from the LLVM IR of the program. CALL and RETURN are two more important process definitions in the domain-specific part of the model. They model method calls and returns and use the threadStack list to record the positions of threads in the application-specific process definitions. Furthermore, the two processes have to deal with stack overflow and underflow. The error codes are channel e_call_stack_overflow : thread_ids and channel e_call_stack_underflow : thread_ids, respectively. Stack overflow is computed with respect to an unmodifiable predefined stack size, while stack underflow simply tests for emptiness of the stack. If none of the error cases occurs, both processes evolve to the CONTINUE process. The final system is represented by the process LowLevelModel, which is the parallel composition of the running threads with the environment over the following event set TE. The running threads are modeled by the process Threads, which is the parallel composition of the thread's state-holding process and the threads themselves, synchronized over the event set TS. The CSP_M encoding of these event sets and the processes Threads and LowLevelModel is also shown in Fig. 5. The process LowLevelModel is the one that, according to arrow (4) of Fig. 1, must be proved to be a refinement of the high-level specification.

4   Extracting a CSP Model from a Program

In this section we outline an algorithm for synthesizing the application-specific part of a program in LLVM IR. The synthesized CSP_M model is a set of functions that yield processes that match the control flow graph of the IR. To reduce the size of the resulting models, the synthesis procedure keeps track of the accesses to a predefined set of variables. For example, to prove that the implementation of the threads concurrently increasing a shared counter is race-condition-free, it is sufficient to track the accesses to this counter, to the counter of the semaphore as well as disabling and locking preemption. The set of variables to be tracked has to be extended with all variables that influence any of the variables under consideration. The extended set of variables is called D in the sequel. To compute D, we use the points-to analysis [16]. The mapping of function calls to be tracked is limited to functions that do not modify any variable that is a member of D. In addition to data access and function calls, arbitrary user-defined observation points can be included within the synthesized model. Such an observation point can be defined by using the ghost method *llvm2csp_annotate* within the program's source code[3].

Our *llvm2csp* algorithm is sketched in Fig. 6. It takes as input the LLVM IR of the implementation, a mapping M of function names to events and a list of data variables V. It outputs chunks of a CSP_M script that make up the application-specific part. It also creates the parameters for the platform- and domain-specific parts of the resulting CSP_M model, i.e. the data types and channel definitions, by exploiting the typing information that is present in the LLVM IR.

In Fig. 6, CSP_M code is typeset in typewriter font and LLVM-IR code in *cursive* typewriter font. The algorithm uses the following auxiliary variables: f records the name of the function currently being analyzed, c is a per method line counter and b is a flag indicating whether or not a sequential process has been opened but not yet been closed. Furthermore, we use the function $(\!|\ \_\ |\!)$ which translates the address of a variable into an integer being the index of that same variable in the global_vars_list that is passed to the ENV process (see Fig. 3).

---

[3] A ghost method is a method that modifies ghost variables only while a ghost variable is a variable that is used for verification purposes only.

Input: $L \mathrel{\widehat{=}}$ LLVM IR of program, $V \mathrel{\widehat{=}}$ List of variables to be tracked
$\qquad M \mathrel{\widehat{=}}$ Mapping from function names to events
Perform dependence analysis and compute the set D
Gather typing information, emit CSP_M data types and channel definitions
$f = nil, c = 0$ and $b = false$
for all lines $l \in L$ **do**
$\quad$ **if** l is inside a method definition **then**
$\qquad$ **if** $\neg b$ **then**
$\qquad\quad$ $b = true$ and emit process declaration, i.e. emit $f(\texttt{t}, c, \texttt{state})$ = ...
$\qquad$ **end if**
$\qquad$ **if** l loads $v \in D$ **then**
$\qquad\quad$ read $(\!| v |\!)$ from environment and write $[v]$ to state holder,
$\qquad\quad$ i.e. transform `%8 = load i32* %a`
$\qquad\quad$ into `env_read.t.(|%a|)?val -> intern_write.t.[ %8]!val -> ...`
$\qquad$ **else if** l is an event annotation **then**
$\qquad\quad$ emit event $A(l)$, i.e. transform
$\qquad\quad$ `call void (i8*, ...)* @_Z17llvm2csp_annotatePKvz(i8* %a1)`
$\qquad\quad$ into `a -> ...`
$\qquad$ **else if** l is a call to a method m that modifies any $v \in D$ **then**
$\qquad\quad$ emit `CALL(t,` m`, c, state)`
$\qquad$ **else if** l is a call to $m \in \text{dom}\, M$ **then**
$\qquad\quad$ emit event $M(l)$, i.e. transform
$\qquad\quad$ `call void @_ZN13InterruptLockD1Ev(%struct.InterruptLock* %1)`
$\qquad\quad$ into `p_lock.t -> ...`
$\qquad$ **else if** ... **then**
$\qquad\quad$ { descriptions of store, arithmetic, comparison, branch and return omitted}
$\qquad$ **else**
$\qquad\quad$ **continue**
$\qquad$ **end if**
$\qquad$ **if** l is neither a branch operation, nor function call nor return **then**
$\qquad\quad$ terminate the process by emitting `CONTINUE(t, c, state)`
$\qquad$ **end if**
$\qquad$ $b = false$ and increase c by one
$\quad$ **else if** l is a method declaration **then**
$\qquad$ record the method's name in f
$\quad$ **end if**
end for

Fig. 6. Sketch of the *llvm2csp* algorithm

Analogously, $[\_]$ is the function that gives the variable's index of the threads' variables in the `initialState` list (see Fig. 5). Method definitions are translated into CSP_M functions, which yield a sequential process that models the behavior of a thread executing that same function. The sketch of the algorithm demonstrates the intended use of the annotation ghost method *llvm2csp_annotate*. Whenever a call to such a method is encountered in the LLVM IR, the original name of the first variable passed to it is determined by the function A and translated into a single event. The mapping M makes it possible to match a function call in the IR with an arbitrary event. An example of this is the matching of the methods

```
Thread1_run(t, 0, state) = CALL(t, 1, 1, state)
Thread1_run(t, 1, state) = env_read.t.0?sharedVal ->
    intern_write_0.t!sharedVal -> CONTINUE(t,2, state)
Thread1_run(t, 2, state) = intern_read_0.t?sharedVal -> let
    nval = sharedVal+1 within write_int(t,0,nval,CONTINUE(t, 3, state))
Thread1_run(t, 3, state) = CALL(t, 2, 4, state)
Thread1_run(t, 4, state) = CONTINUE(t, 0, state)


Semaphore_P(t, 0, state) = p_lock.t -> CONTINUE(t, 1, state)
Semaphore_P(t, 1, state) =
    env_read.t.1?sem -> intern_write_1.t!sem -> CONTINUE(t, 2, state)
Semaphore_P(t, 2, state) = intern_read_1.t?sem ->
    if sem < 1 then CONTINUE(t,3, state) else CONTINUE(t, 4, state)
Semaphore_P(t, 3, state) = p_release.t -> CONTINUE(t, 0, state)
Semaphore_P(t, 4, state) = intern_read_1.t?sem ->
    let nsem = sem-1 within write_int(t,1,nsem,CONTINUE(t, 5, state))
Semaphore_P(t, 5, state) = p_release.t -> CONTINUE(t, 6, state)
Semaphore_P(t, 6, state) = claim.t -> CONTINUE(t, 7, state)
Semaphore_P(t, 7, state) = RETURN(t, state)
```

Fig. 7. Generated CSP code for a simple thread using a semaphore to protect access to a shared counter variable

that disable or enable preemption with the events p_lock.t and p_release.t, respectively. Calling the constructor of the *InterruptLock* class, which realizes locking of preemption, is translated into the event p_lock.t, for example.

Fig. 7 shows the generated model of the thread introduced in Sect. 2.1 that uses a semaphore to protect a global counter variable. The implementation of the semaphore is that the P method waits until the semaphore becomes greater than zero and then reduces the semaphore by one. The semaphore is incremented by one in the V method. The CSP_M model of the *Thread1::run* method consists of five sequential processes, modeling the calls to *Semaphore::P* and *Semaphore::V* at positions 0 and 3, the accesses to the shared counter at positions 1 and 2 and finally the jump back to the entry of the method at position 4. Thus, increasing and decreasing an integer is not modeled as an atomic operation, so race conditions can be detected in the case of bad locking. The Semaphore_P process is also of great interest. At position 0 the p_lock.t event is emitted, which models a method call that is mapped to an event by M as explained above. Conditional branching is used at position 2, while position 3 models unconditional branching.

Interestingly, there are no env_write events in Thread1_run and Semaphore_P. Instead, the function write_int is used. This function returns a process, that either emits the env_write event and then terminates successfully or deadlocks in the case of integer overflow. Fig. 7 also shows the use of annotations at position 6 of the process modeling *Semaphore::P*. Before the method returns, the claim.t event is emitted, which is introduced for verification purposes as explained later on. As explained in Sect. 3, the process Thread1_run is used by the domain-specific part of the model. The entry point to this process is the process CONTINUE which is first used by the model of the startup routine AppSpecific.

In Sect. 2.2, we have proved by LTL model checking that the specification is race-condition-free. As stated in [9], failures refinement of finitely-branching CSP processes preserves satisfaction of LTL formulas. Thus, to conclude that the implementation is race-condition-free, the low-level model must be a failures refinement of the specification. Before this can be checked with FDR2, some of the events of either of the two processes have to be renamed. Furthermore, we are not interested in the implementation of the semaphore anymore. It is sufficient to know that the methods *Semaphore::P* and *Semaphore::V* have been executed. This means that the events of these methods, apart from the annotated claim.t and release.t events, can be hidden. The events modeling read and write accesses to the shared counter are the ones of interest. They are therefore renamed so that they match those of the specification, resulting in the process LowLevelModel2. The final assertion that has been successfully checked with FDR2 is:

```
assert S [F= LowLevelModel2\diff(Events,{|read, write, claim, release|})
```

In addition to race conditions, we checked the low-level model for deadlock freedom in the failures-divergences semantics. FDR2 comes up with an error trace that ends with the t_terminate event. This is the error code for overflow of the shared counter variable. We therefore slightly modified the implementation so that the counter is increased modulo its maximum value and checked for deadlock freedom again. The modified system is deadlock-free, which means that the implementation is deadlock-free as well.

5   Related Work

Our approach is related to work that verifies source code using CSP models. The following tools use CSP as a basis to enable the detection of racing conflicts, deadlocks and livelocks. A CSP-based model for Java multithreading was presented by Welch and Martin in [18]. They used that model as the foundation of the JCSP library that offers CSP-like concurrency for Java programs. The model focuses on locks, offering no support for thread-internal data, global variables or a model of the underlying machine as our model does. In [15], an experimental tool called *Java2CSP* is presented. It translates concurrent Java programs into CSP processes to verify deadlock and livelock using the model checker FDR, but the work is poorly documented. An automatic generation of CSP specifications is presented in [14]. As in our work, the authors divide a CSP specification into two parts. One part is generated from a behavioral model and the other comes from the source code. In contrast to our work, the authors use state machines to describe the model part, and data variables are not supported.

Finally, there are a number of projects tackling software verification issues on the level of LLVM IR, e.g. the SAFECode project [7] and the Nasa MCP, a software model checker for LLVM IR [17]. The SAFECode project aims to provide memory safety guarantees to C/C++ programs. This is the project from which

LLVM stems. MCP is an explicit state model checker that operates on LLVM IR and has been successfully applied to verify C++ aerospace applications. In [19], the model checker SPIN is used to verify multithreaded C programs based on LLVM byte code. The authors apply a model-driven verification approach, by which a virtual machine executes LLVM bytecode during the verification process.

6   Conclusions and Future Work

In this paper, we presented a CSP-based methodology for verifying the implementations of concurrent systems. Verifying such a system requires both its abstract CSP-based specification and its C++ implementation. Our methodology determines how significant parts of a low-level model can be synthesized from the LLVM IR of the implementation and it requires that the low-level model be a refinement of the specification. The low-level model of the implementation is divided into application-, domain- and platform-specific parts. We illustrated our methodology by specifying and implementing a system composed of threads concurrently incrementing a shared counter. We proved the specification to be deadlock- and race-condition-free. For the domain- and platform-specific parts, we presented a low-level CSP model of a computing system implementing interleaved concurrency by employing a nondeterministic preemptive scheduler. Finally, we presented the application-specific part of the system and proved that it is a failures refinement of the specification. This proved that the implementation is indeed deadlock- and race-condition-free.

Our approach enables us to use state-of-the-art CSP tools such as FDR2 and ProB for the automated verification of concurrent programs written in a high-level programming language supported by the LLVM system. Furthermore, the presented model of concurrency is reusable for other applications developed for a great number of multithreading library implementations. It is well suited for verifying the absence of any unwanted phenomenon of concurrency thanks to its nondeterministic abstract scheduler.

Instead of outputting a CSP_M script for animation, model and refinement checking, we plan to output Isabelle/HOL code. Propitious target theories are those of the CSP Prover [6] and, in case we move from CSP to Timed CSP, the Isabelle/HOL formalization of Timed CSP [4] as well. Targeting an Isabelle/HOL theory would enable us to use a much more powerful type system than that of CSP_M. Additionally, it would eliminate the need to justify the abstractions introduced when reducing the ranges of the types so that model and refinement checking can be applied to the CSP_M model. Switching from CSP to Timed CSP is promising for the analysis of implementations of real-time systems. This can be supported by integrating tools for worst-case execution time analysis on LLVM IR, such as the one presented by Oechslein in [11].

Acknowledgements. We thank the anonymous referees for their helpful comments on preliminary versions of this paper. We also thank Björn Bartels and Thomas Göthel for fruitful discussions on this work. This work is funded by the German Research Foundation (DFG).

References

1. FDR2 User Manual (2005), http://www.fsel.com/documentation/fdr2/
2. ProB Manual (2005), http://www.stups.uni-duesseldorf.de/ProB/
3. Barrett, G.: occam 3 Reference Manual. Inmos Ltd. (1992)
4. Göthel, T., Glesner, S.: Machine Checkable Timed CSP. In: The First NASA Formal Methods Symposium (2009)
5. Hoare, C.A.R.: Communicating Sequential Processes. Prentice Hall Int., Englewood Cliffs (1985)
6. Isobe, Y., Roggenbach, M.: A generic theorem prover of CSP refinement. In: Halbwachs, N., Zuck, L.D. (eds.) TACAS 2005. LNCS, vol. 3440, pp. 108–123. Springer, Heidelberg (2005)
7. Lattner, C., Adve, V.: Automatic pool allocation for disjoint data structures. In: ACM SIGPLAN Workshop on Memory System Performance, Germany (2002)
8. LLVM Reference Manual (2008), http://llvm.org/docs/LangRef.html
9. Leuschel, M., Massart, T., Currie, A.: How to make FDR Spin: LTL model checking of CSP using refinement. In: Oliveira, J.N., Zave, P. (eds.) FME 2001. LNCS, vol. 2021, p. 99. Springer, Heidelberg (2001)
10. Montenegro, S., Briess, K., Kayal, H.: Dependable Software (BOSS) for the BEESAT pico satellite. In: DASIA 2006 - Data Systems In Aerospace, Germany (2006)
11. Oechslein, B.: Statische WCET Analyse von LLVM Bytecode. Master's thesis, Universität Erlangen (2008)
12. Roscoe, A.W.: The Theory and Practice of Concurrency. Prentice Hall PTR, Upper Saddle River (1997)
13. Scattergood, B.: The semantics and implementation of machine-readable CSP PhD thesis, University of Oxford (1998)
14. Scuglik, F., Sveda, M.: Automatically generated CSP specifications. Journal of Universal Computer Science 9(11), 1277–1295 (2003)
15. Shi, H.: Java2CSP: A system for verifying concurrent Java programs. In: Workshop on Tools for System Design and Verification (FM-TOOLS), Ulmer Informatik-Berichte (2000)
16. Steensgaard, B.: Points-to analysis in almost linear time. In: Int. Symposium on Principles of programming languages (POPL), pp. 32–41. ACM, New York (1996)
17. Thompson, S., Brat, G.: Verification of C++ Flight Software with the MCP Model Checker. In: Aerospace Conference, pp. 1–9. IEEE, Los Alamitos (2008)
18. Welch, P.H., Martin, J.M.R.: A CSP model for Java multithreading. In: Software Engineering for Parallel and Distributed Systems, pp. 114–122. IEEE, Los Alamitos (2000)
19. Zaks, A., Joshi, R.: Verifying multi-threaded C programs with Spin. In: Havelund, K., Majumdar, R., Palsberg, J. (eds.) SPIN 2008. LNCS, vol. 5156, pp. 325–342. Springer, Heidelberg (2008)

Formal Modelling of a Microcontroller Instruction Set in B

Valério Medeiros Jr. and David Déharbe

Federal University of Rio Grande do Norte, Natal RN 59078-970, Brazil

Abstract. This paper describes an approach to model the functional aspects of the instruction set of microcontroller platforms using the notation of the B method. The paper presents specifically the case of the Z80 platform. This work is a contribution towards the extension of the B method to handle developments up to assembly level code.

1   Introduction

The B method [1] supports the construction of safety systems models by verification of proofs that guarantees its correctness. So, an initial abstract model of the system requirements is defined and then it is refined until the implementation model. Development environments based on the B method also include source code generators for programming languages, but the result of this translation cannot be compared by formal means. The paper [4] presented recently an approach to extend the scope of the B method up to the assembly level language. One key component of this approach is to build, within the framework of the B method, formal models of the instruction set of such assembly languages.

This work gives an overview of the formal modelling of the instruction set of the Z80 microcontroller [6][1]. Using the responsibility division mechanism provided by B, auxiliary libraries of basic modules were developed as part of the construction of microcontroller model. Such library has many definitions about common concepts used in the microcontrollers; besides the Z80 model, it is used by two other microcontrollers models that are under way.

Other possible uses of a formal model of a microcontroller instruction set include documentation, the construction of simulators, and be possibly the starting point of a verification effort for the actual implementation of a Z80 design. Moreover the model of the instruction set could be instrumented with non-functional aspects, such as the number of cycles it takes to execute an instruction, to prove lower and upper bounds on the execution time of a routine. The goal of this project, though, is to provide a basis for the generation of software artifacts at the assembly level that are amenable to refinement verification within the B method.

This paper is focused on the presentation of the Z80 model, including elementary libraries to describe hardware aspects. The paper is structured as follows.

---

[1] The interested reader in more details is invited to visit our repository at: http://code.google.com/p/b2asm.

M.V.M. Oliveira and J. Woodcock (Eds.): SBMF 2009, LNCS 5902, pp. 282–289, 2009.
© Springer-Verlag Berlin Heidelberg 2009

Section 2 provides a short introduction to the B method. Section 3 presents the elementary libraries and the modelling of some elements common to microcontrollers. Section 4 presents the B model of the Z80 instruction set. Section 5 provides some information on the proof effort needed to analyze the presented models. Related work is discussed in Section 6. Finally, the last section is devoted to the conclusions.

2 Introduction to the B Method

The B method for software development [1] is based on the B Abstract Machine Notation (AMN) and the use of formally proved refinements up to a specification sufficiently concrete that programming code can be automatically generated from it. Its mathematical basis consists of first order logic, integer arithmetic and set theory, and its corresponding constructs are similar to those of the Z notation.

A B specification is structured in modules. A module defines a set of valid states, including a set of initial states, and operations that may provoke a transition between states. The design process starts with a module with a so-called functional model of the system under development. In this initial modelling stage, the B method requires that the user proves that, in a machine, all the its initial states are valid, and that operations do not define transitions from valid states to invalid states.

Essentially, a B module contains two main parts: a header and the available operations. Figure 1 has a very basic example. The clause *MACHINE* has the name of module. The next two clauses respectively reference external modules and create an instance of an external module. The *VARIABLES* clauses declares the name of the variables that compose the state of the machine. Next, the *INVARIANT* clause defines the type and other restrictions on the variables. The *INITIALIZATION* specifies the initial states. Finally, operations correspond to the transitions between states of the machine.

MACHINE   *micro*
SEES   *TYPES, ALU*
INCLUDES   *MEMORY*
VARIABLES   *pc*
INVARIANT   *pc* ∈ *INSTRUCTION*

INITIALISATION *pc* := 0
OPERATIONS
JMP(jump) =
   PRE *jump* ∈ *INSTRUCTION*
   THEN *pc* := *jump*
   END
END

Fig. 1. A very basic B machine

3 Model Structure and Basic Components

We have been developed a reusable set of basic definitions to model hardware concepts and data types concepts. These definitions are grouped into two separate development projects and are available as libraries. A third project is devoted to the higher-level aspects of the platform. Thus, the workspace is composed of: a hardware library, a types library and a project for the specific platform, in this case the Z80. The corresponding dependency diagram is depicted in Figure 2; information specific to each project is presented in the following.

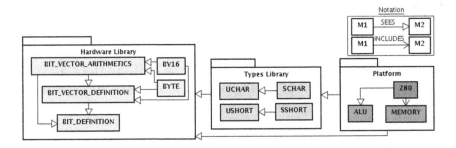

Fig. 2. Dependency diagram of the Z80 model

3.1   Bit Representation and Manipulation

The entities defined in the module $BIT\_DEFINITION$ are the type for bits, logical operations on bits (negation, conjunction, disjunction, exclusive disjunction), as well as a conversion function from booleans to bits.

First, bits are modelled as a set of integers: $BIT = 0..1$. The negation is an unary function on bits and it is defined as:

$$bit\_not \in BIT \rightarrow BIT \wedge \forall(bb).(bb \in BIT \Rightarrow bit\_not(bb) = 1 - bb)$$

The module also provides lemmas on negation that may be useful for the users of the library to develop proofs:

$$\forall(bb).(bb \in BIT \Rightarrow bit\_not(bit\_not(bb)) = bb)$$

Conjunction is an unary function on bits and it is defined as:

$$bit\_and \in BIT \times BIT \rightarrow BIT \wedge$$
$$\forall(b1, b2).(b1 \in BIT \wedge b2 \in BIT \Rightarrow$$
$$((bit\_and(b1, b2) = 1) \Leftrightarrow (b1 = 1) \wedge (b2 = 1)))$$

The module provides the following lemmas for conjunction, either:

$$\forall(b1, b2).(b1 \in BIT \wedge b2 \in BIT \Rightarrow$$
$$(bit\_and(b1, b2) = bit\_and(b2, b1))) \wedge$$
$$\forall(b1, b2, b3).(b1 \in BIT \wedge b2 \in BIT \wedge b3 \in BIT \Rightarrow$$
$$(bit\_and(b1, bit\_and(b2, b3)) = bit\_and(bit\_and(b1, b2), b3)))$$

The module provides definitions of bit_or (disjunction) and bit_xor (exclusive disjunction), as well as lemmas on those operators. These are standard and their expression in B is similar as for bit_and, they are thus omitted.

Finally, the conversion from booleans to bits is simply defined as:

$$bool\_to\_bit \in \mathbf{BOOL} \rightarrow BIT \wedge bool\_to\_bit = \{\mathbf{TRUE} \mapsto 1, \mathbf{FALSE} \mapsto 0\}$$

Observe that all the lemmas that are provided in this module have been mechanically proved by the theorem prover included with our B development environment. None of these proofs requires human insight.

3.2   Representation and Manipulation of Bit Vectors

Sequences are pre-defined in B, as functions whose the domain is an integer range with lower bound 1 (one). Indices in bit vectors usually range from 0 (zero) upwards and the model we propose obeys this convention by making an one-position shift where necessary. This shift is important to use the predefined functions of sequences. We thus define bit vectors as non-empty sequences of bits, and BIT_VECTOR is the set of all such sequences: $BIT\_VECTOR = \text{seq}(BIT)$.

The function bv_size returns the size of a given bit vector. It is basically a wrapper for the predefined function **size** that applies to sequences.

$$bv\_size \in BIT\_VECTOR \to \mathcal{N}_1 \wedge$$
$$bv\_size = \lambda\, bv.(bv \in BIT\_VECTOR \mid \textbf{size}(bv))$$

We also define two functions bv_set and bv_clear that, given a bit vector, and a position of the bit vector, return the bit vector resulting from setting the corresponding position to 0 or to 1, and a function bv_get that, given a bit vector, and a valid position, each one returns the value of the bit at that position. Only the first definition is shown here:

$$bv\_set \in BIT\_VECTOR \times \mathcal{N} \to BIT\_VECTOR \wedge bv\_set =$$
$$\lambda\, v, n.(v \in BIT\_VECTOR \wedge n \in \mathcal{N} \wedge n < bv\_size(v) \mid v \Leftplus\{n+1 \mapsto 1\})$$

Additionally, the module provides definitions for the classical logical combinations of bit vectors: bit_not, bit_and, bit_or and bit_xor. Only the first two are presented here. Observe that the domain of the binary operators is restricted to pairs of bit vectors of the same length:

$$bv\_not \in BIT\_VECTOR \to BIT\_VECTOR \wedge$$
$$bv\_not = \lambda\, v.(v \in BIT\_VECTOR \mid \quad \lambda\, i.(1..bv\_size(v)) \mid bit\_not(v(i))) \wedge$$
$$bv\_and \in BIT\_VECTOR \times BIT\_VECTOR \to BIT\_VECTOR \wedge$$
$$bv\_and = \lambda\, v_1, v_2.(v_1 \in BIT\_VECTOR \wedge v_2 \in BIT\_VECTOR \wedge$$
$$bv\_size(v_1) = bv\_size(v_2) \mid \lambda\, i.(1..bv\_size(v_1)) \mid bit\_and(v_1(i), v_2(i)))$$

We provide several lemmas on bit vector operations. These lemmas express properties on the size of the result of the operations as well as classical algebraic properties such as associativity and commutativity.

3.3   Modelling Bytes and Bit Vectors of Length 16

Bit vectors of length 8 are bytes. They form a common entity in hardware design. We provide the following definitions:

$$BYTE\_WIDTH = 8 \wedge BYTE\_INDEX = 1 .. BYTE\_WIDTH \wedge$$
$$PHYS\_BYTE\_INDEX = 0 .. (BYTE\_WIDTH\text{-}1) \quad \wedge$$
$$BYTE = \{\, bt \mid bt \in BIT\_VECTOR \wedge bv\_size(bt) = BYTE\_WIDTH\} \quad \wedge$$
$$BYTE\_ZERO \in BYTE \wedge BYTE\_ZERO = BYTE\_INDEX \times \{0\}$$

The *BYTE_INDEX* is the domain of the functions modelling bytes. It starts at 1 to obey a definition of sequences from B. However, it is common in hardware architectures to start indexing from zero. The definition *PHYS_BYTE_INDEX* is used to provide functionalities obeying this convention. The *BYTE* type is a specialized type from *BIT_VECTOR*, but it has a size limit. Other specific definitions are provided to facilitate further modelling: the type *BV16* is created for bit vector of length 16 in a similar way.

3.4   Bit Vector Arithmetics

Bit vectors are used to represent and combine numbers: integer ranges (signed or unsigned). Therefore, our library includes functions to manipulate such data, for example, the function *bv_to_nat* that maps bit vectors to natural numbers:

$bv\_to\_nat \in BIT\_VECTOR \rightarrow \mathcal{N} \land$
$bv\_to\_nat = \lambda v.(v \in BIT\_VECTOR \mid \sum i.(i \in \mathsf{dom}(v).v(i) \times 2^{i-1}))$
An associated lemma is: $\forall n.(n \in \mathcal{N}_1 \Rightarrow bv\_to\_nat(nat\_to\_bv(n)) = n)$

3.5   Basics Data Types

The instruction set of microcontrollers usually have common data types. These types are placed in the types library. Each type module has functions to manipulate and convert its data. There are six common basics data types represented by modules, see details in table 1.

Table 1. Descriptions of basic data types

Type Name	UCHAR	SCHAR	USHORTINT	SSHORTINT	BYTE	BV16
Range	0..255	-128..127	0..65.535	-32.768..32.767	–	–
Physical Size	1 byte	1 byte	2 bytes	2 bytes	1 bytes	2 bytes

Usually, each type module just needs to instantiate concepts that were already defined in the hardware modelling library. For example, the function *bv_to_nat* from bit vector arithmetics is specialized to *byte_uchar*. As the set *BYTE* is a subset of the *BIT_VECTOR*, this function can defined as follows:

$byte\_uchar \in BYTE \rightarrow \mathcal{N} \land$
$byte\_uchar = \lambda(v).(v \in BYTE \mid bv\_to\_nat(v))$

The definitions of the library types reuse the basic definitions from the hardware library. This provides greater confidence and facilitates the proof process, because the prover can reuse the previously defined lemma.

The inverse function *uchar_byte* is easily defined:

$uchar\_byte \in UCHAR \rightarrow BYTE \land$
$uchar\_byte = (byte\_uchar)^{-1}$

Similarly, several other functions and lemmas were created for all other data types.

4 Description of the Z80 B Model

The *Z80* is a CISC microcontroller developed by *Zilog* [6]. It supports 158 different instructions and all of them were specified. These instructions are classified into these categories: load and exchange; block transfer and search; arithmetic and logical; rotate and shift; bit manipulation; jump, call and return; input/output; and basic cpu control.

The main module includes an instance of the memory module and accesses the definitions from basic data types modules and the *ALU* module.

MACHINE
  Z80
INCLUDES
  MEMORY
SEES
  ALU, BIT_DEFINITION, BIT_VECTOR_DEFINITION,
  BYTE_DEFINITION, BV16_DEFINITION,
  UCHAR_DEFINITION, SCHAR_DEFINITION,
  SSHORT_DEFINITION ,USHORT_DEFINITION

Each instruction is represented by a B operation in the module Z80. By default, all parameters from operations are either predefined elements in the model or integers values in the decimal representation. The internal registers contain 208 bits of reading/writing memory. It includes two sets of six general purpose registers which may be used individually as 8-bits registers or as 16-bits register pairs. The working registers are represented by variable *rgs8*. The domain of *rgs8* (*id_regs8*) is a set formed by identifiers of registers of 8 bits. These registers can be accessed in pairs, forming 16-bits, resulting in another set of identifiers of 16-bits registers, named *id_reg16*. The main working register of Z80 is the accumulator (*rgs8(a0)*) used for arithmetic, logic, input/output and loading/storing operations.

4.1 Modelling Registers, Input and Output Ports and Instructions

The Z80 has different types of registers and instructions. The CPU contains general-purpose registers (*id_reg_8*), a stack pointer (*sp*), program counter (*pc*), two index registers (*ix* and *iy*), an interrupt register (*i_*), a refresh register (*r_*), two bits (*iff1*, *iff2*) used to control the interruptions, a pair of bits to define the interruption mode (*im*) and the input and output ports (*i_o_ports*). Below, part of the corresponding definitions are replicated from the **INVARIANT**:

$$rgs8 \in id\_reg\_8 \rightarrow BYTE \land pc \in INSTRUCTION \land$$
$$sp \in BV16 \land ix \in BV16 \land iy \in BV16 \land$$
$$i\_ \in BYTE \land r\_ \in BYTE \land iff1 \in BIT \land iff2 \in BIT \land$$
$$im \in (BIT \times BIT) \land i\_o\_ports \in BYTE \rightarrow BYTE$$

A simple example of instruction is a *LD_n_A*, as shown below. Many times, to model an instruction is necessary to use the predefined functions, these help the construction of model. This instruction use the *updateAddressMem* function from *Memory* module and it receives an address memory and its new memory value. Finally it increments the program counter (*pc*) and update the refresh register (r_-).

> **LD_n_A** (*nn*) =
>   **PRE** *nn* ∈ *USHORT*
>   **THEN**
>   **updateAddressMem** (*ushort_to_bv16* (*nn*) , *rgs8* (*a0*)) ||
>   *pc* := *instruction_next* (*pc*) || r_- := *update_refresh_reg*(r_-)
> **END**

The microcontroller model can specify security properties. For example, the last operation could have a restriction to write only in a defined region of memory.

5   Proofs

The proof obligations allow to verify the data types, important system properties and if the expressions are well-defined (WD)[2]. The properties provide additional guarantees, because they can set many safety rules. However, the model can be very difficult to prove.

Several iterations were needed to provide the good library definitions as well as to fine-tune the model of the microcontroller instructions by factoring common functionalities into auxiliary definitions.

However, few proof commands[3] need to be used to prove most proof obligations. As there are many similar assembly instructions, some human-directed proofs, when replayed, could discharge other proof obligations. A good example is a set of 17 proof commands that quickly aided the verification of 99% (2295) of WD proofs. We also set up a proving environment consisting of networked computers to take advantage of the distribution facilities now provided in the B development environment. Finally, all of the 2926 proof obligations were proved using the tool support of the development environment.

6   Related Works

There are in the literature of computer science some approaches [2,3] to model hardware and the virtual machines using the B method. Then, in both works the B method has been used successfully to model the operational semantic. However the cost of modelling was still expensive and this paper quoted some techniques to lower the cost of modelling.

---

[2] An expression is called "well-defined" (or unambiguous) if its definition assigns it a unique interpretation or value.

[3] The proof commands are steps that direct the prover to find the proof, and cannot introduce false hypothesis.

In general, the researchers employing the B method have focused on more abstract level of description of software. Considering low-level aspect, there has been previous work on modelling the Java Virtual Machine [3].

The main motivation of our research is the development of verified software up to the assembly level, which requires specifying the semantics of the underlying hardware. Thus, some aspects were not modelled in our work such as the execution time of the instructions. Also we did not consider the microarchitecture of the hardware as the scope of our work does not include hardware verification. However, there are many other specialized techniques to verify these questions.

7 Conclusions

This work has shown an approach to the formal modelling of the instruction set of microcontrollers using the B method. During the construction of this model, some ambiguities and errors were encountered in the official reference for Z80 microcontroller [6]. As the B notation has a syntax that is not too distant from that of imperative programming languages, such model could be used to improve the documentation used by assembler programmers. Besides, the formal notation used is analyzed by software that guarantees the correctness of typing, the well-definedness of expressions, in addition to safety properties of the microcontroller state.

Future works comprise the development of software with the B method from functional specification to assembly level, using the Z80 model presented in this paper. The mechanic compilation from B algorithmic constructs to assembly platform is also envisioned.

Acknowledgements. This work received support from ANP (*Agência Nacional do Petróleo, Gás Natural e Biocombustíveis*) and CNPq (*Conselho Nacional de Desenvolvimento Científico e Tecnológico*).

References

1. Abrial, J.R.: The B Book: Assigning Programs to Meanings, 1st edn. Cambridge University Press, USA (1996)
2. Aljer, P.D., Boulanger, S.T.J.-L., Bhdl, G.M.: Circuit Design in B. A. In: ACSD, Third International Conference on Application of Concurrency to System Design, pp. 241–242 (2003)
3. Casset, L., Lanet, J.L.: A Formal Specification of the Java Bytecode Semantics using the B method. Technical Report, Gemplus (1999)
4. Dantas, B., Déharbe, D., Galvão, S.L., Moreira, A.M., Medeiros Jr., V.G.: Applying the B Method to Take on the Grand Challenge of Verified Compilation. In: SBMF, Savaldor (2008), SBC
5. Hoare, C.A.R.: The verifying compiler, a grand challenge for computing research. In: Cousot, R. (ed.) VMCAI 2005. LNCS, vol. 3385, p. 78. Springer, Heidelberg (2005)
6. Zilog. Z80 Family CPU User Manual,
   http://www.zilog.com/docs/z80/um0080.pdf

Defining Behaviours by Quasi-finality

Elisabete Freire[1] and Luís Monteiro[2]

[1] CITI, Departamento de Matemática, Universidade dos Açores,
9501-801 Ponta Delgada, Portugal
`freire@notes.uac.pt`
[2] CITI, Departamento de Informática, Faculdade de Ciências e Tecnologia,
Universidade Nova de Lisboa, 2829-516 Caparica, Portugal
`lm@di.fct.unl.pt`

Abstract. This paper proposes a notion of quasi-final object for any concrete category, by relegating to the underlying category some of the requirements that final objects must satisfy in the main category. We present some very basic properties of quasi-final objects and show how known behaviours like traces and failures for transition systems, and behaviours extracted from the final sequence of an arbitrary endofunctor (here restricted to the first ω terms) can be described by quasi-final objects.

1 Introduction

For over a decade now the theory of coalgebras has been hailed as the appropriate mathematical framework for the study of state-based computational systems. This framework provided a uniform treatment of a great variety of types of systems and facilitated novel insights into the notions of behaviour, bisimilarity and coinductive definition and proof, among others. The basic constituents of a coalgebra are simple: a state space and a function that specifies the dynamics of the system in a stepwise fashion. By iterating the dynamics, we obtain the behaviours of the system. Often the set of these behaviours can itself be structured into a coalgebra and the assignment of a behaviour to each state is a morphism of coalgebras, and in fact the unique morphism from the given coalgebra to the coalgebra of behaviours. This coalgebra is then a final object in the category of coalgebras under consideration. This is the standard way to view behaviour in coalgebraic terms.

For many types of systems, however, notions of behaviour have been proposed that do not fit into this pattern. There may be at least two reasons for this. One is that we may be interested in notions of behaviour for a given class of systems that are different from the one offered by final coalgebras. The other is that the category of interest may not even have final coalgebras. For transition systems, for example, we find the two types of situations. On the one hand, if we consider general transition systems and not just say finitely-branching or image-finite ones, there is no final transition system. On the other hand, many non-equivalent notions of behaviour have been proposed for transition systems, which raises the question of describing them coalgebraically.

M.V.M. Oliveira and J. Woodcock (Eds.): SBMF 2009, LNCS 5902, pp. 290–305, 2009.
© Springer-Verlag Berlin Heidelberg 2009

This paper proposes a coalgebraic notion of behaviour that relaxes the requisite of finality and still retains some of its familiar properties, like the uniqueness of morphisms to final objects. Specifically, we propose the notion of quasi-final object for any concrete category, by relegating to the underlying category some of the requirements that final objects must satisfy in the main category. (In this paper we shall assume for simplicity that the underlying category is the category of sets and functions.) It turns out that morphisms (in the main category) preserve behaviours with respect to quasi-final objects, but there may be behaviour-preserving functions in the underlying category of sets that are not morphisms in the main category. By extending the main category with all behaviour-preserving functions, the quasi-final object becomes a final object. This way, quasi-final objects still satisfy a uniqueness property similar to that for final objects, that may prove useful for defining quasi-final semantics.

The structure of the paper is simple. After this section, there is a section introducing quasi-final objects and some basic properties. There follow two sections with examples: the first of the two presents traces and failures for transition systems as quasi-final objects, and the second one does the same for behaviours extracted from the final sequence (here restricted to the first ω terms) of an arbitrary endofunctor. The paper ends with some conclusions and future work.

The research reported in this paper started in [1], where a notion of "behaviour object" was introduced. The notion of quasi-final object is a simplification and a generalization of that notion. In [1] it was shown that some behaviours in van Glabbeek's spectrum [2], namely traces, ready-traces and failures can be described in coalgebraic terms using behaviour objects. In the present paper we have restricted ourselves to traces and failures for illustrative purposes, but several other notions could equally well have been considered. For the examples on the final sequence of a functor we rely on the work of Worrell in [3]. Some of the results we obtained appear also in the work of Kurz and Pattinson [4], but with a somewhat different presentation. The fact that there is a final $\mathcal{P}_{\text{fin}}(A \times -)$-coalgebra was proved by Barr [5], based on a quotient construction, which differs from our proof, which is based on a kind of coinductive argument. Other works on trying to capture in coalgebraic terms traces of systems that are not necessarily transition systems appear in [6, 7, 8]. As prerequisites we assume familiarity with the notions of trace and failure as can be found in [2]; these notions will be defined in the present paper but no motivation for them will be supplied. From category theory we only assume knowledge of the basic notions of category, functor, natural transformation and final object. From the theory of coalgebras we will only need the notions of coalgebra itself, morphism of coalgebras and bisimulation. All these notions will be recalled here; for further motivation and information see [9].

2   Quasi-final Coalgebras

A final object $\mathbb{Z}$ in a category $\mathbf{C}$ may be characterized by saying that there is a natural transformation $\beta : I \to \mathbb{Z}$ from the identity functor I to the constant functor $\mathbb{Z}$ such that $\beta_{\mathbb{Z}} : \mathbb{Z} \to \mathbb{Z}$ is the identity morphism. Indeed, if such a β exists and $f : \mathbb{S} \to \mathbb{Z}$ is a morphism, $\beta_{\mathbb{Z}} \circ f = \mathrm{id}_{\mathbb{Z}} \circ \beta_{\mathbb{S}} = \beta_{\mathbb{S}}$ by the naturality of β, so $f = \beta_{\mathbb{S}}$ because $\beta_{\mathbb{Z}} = \mathrm{id}_{\mathbb{Z}}$; thus, $\beta_{\mathbb{S}}$ is the only morphism from $\mathbb{S}$ to $\mathbb{Z}$; conversely, if $\mathbb{Z}$ is a final object, the unique morphism $\beta_{\mathbb{S}} : \mathbb{S} \to \mathbb{Z}$ is natural in $\mathbb{S}$ and $\beta_{\mathbb{Z}} = \mathrm{id}_{\mathbb{Z}}$.

Now suppose $\mathbf{C}$ is a concrete category over $\mathbf{Set}$, that is, there is a faithful forgetful functor $U : \mathbf{C} \to \mathbf{Set}$. As usual, we identify morphisms f in $\mathbf{C}$ with the functions Uf.

Definition 1. *An object $\mathbb{Z}$ in $\mathbf{C}$ is said to be* quasi-final *if there is a natural transformation $\beta : U \to U\mathbb{Z}$ from U to the constant functor $U\mathbb{Z}$ from $\mathbf{C}$ to $\mathbf{Set}$ such that $\beta_{\mathbb{Z}} : U\mathbb{Z} \to U\mathbb{Z}$ is the identity $\mathrm{id}_{U\mathbb{Z}}$. The behavioural equivalence $\overset{\mathbb{Z}}{=}_{\mathbb{S}}$ induced on $\mathbb{S}$ is the kernel of $\beta_{\mathbb{S}}$, $\mathrm{Ker}(\beta_{\mathbb{S}}) = \{(s,t) \in (U\mathbb{S})^2 : \beta_{\mathbb{S}}(s) = \beta_{\mathbb{S}}(t)\}$.*

An object $\mathbb{I}$ such that $U\mathbb{I}$ is a singleton is quasi-final, each $\beta_{\mathbb{S}}$ being the unique function from $U\mathbb{S}$ to $U\mathbb{I}$; in this case, $\overset{\mathbb{I}}{=}_{\mathbb{S}}$ is $(U\mathbb{S})^2$. For example, in a category of labelled transition systems with say transition preserving functions as morphisms, any transition system with a single state (and arbitrary transitions) is quasi-final. This already shows that there can be many non-isomorphic quasi-final objects, even on the same underlying set. More elaborate examples will be presented later.

Definition 2. *A function $f : U\mathbb{S}_1 \to U\mathbb{S}_2$ is a β-morphism from $\mathbb{S}_1$ to $\mathbb{S}_2$ if $\beta_{\mathbb{S}_2} \circ f = \beta_{\mathbb{S}_1}$. Let $\mathbf{C} \downarrow \beta$ be the category with the same objects as $\mathbf{C}$ and with β-morphisms as morphisms.*

Clearly, morphisms in $\mathbf{C}$ are β-morphisms. Since $\beta_{\mathbb{Z}} \circ \beta_{\mathbb{S}} = \beta_{\mathbb{S}}$, the $\beta_{\mathbb{S}}$ are β-morphisms; furthermore, $\beta_{\mathbb{S}}$ is the only β-morphism from $\mathbb{S}$ to $\mathbb{Z}$.

Proposition 1. *A quasi-final object $\mathbb{Z}$ in $\mathbf{C}$ with respect to β is final in $\mathbf{C} \downarrow \beta$.*

We have noticed that quasi-final objects need not be isomorphic, giving rise in general to different behavioural equivalences. The next result gives a sufficient condition for a behavioural equivalence to be a refinement of another one. This situation will be illustrated later with the equivalences induced by traces and failures.

Definition 3. *Suppose $\mathbb{Z}$ and $\mathbb{Z}'$ are quasi-final with respect to β and β', respectively. We say β' preserves β if $\beta'_{\mathbb{S}}$ is a β-morphism for every $\mathbb{S}$.*

Proposition 2. *Let $\mathbb{Z}$ and $\mathbb{Z}'$ be quasi-final with respect to β and β', respectively. If β' preserves β, then $\overset{\mathbb{Z}'}{=}_{\mathbb{S}} \subseteq \overset{\mathbb{Z}}{=}_{\mathbb{S}}$.*

Proof. We have $\beta_{\mathbb{Z}'} \circ \beta'_{\mathbb{S}} = \beta_{\mathbb{S}}$, since β' preserves β. In particular, $\mathrm{Ker}(\beta'_{\mathbb{S}}) \subseteq \mathrm{Ker}(\beta_{\mathbb{S}})$, that is, $\overset{\mathbb{Z}'}{=}_{\mathbb{S}} \subseteq \overset{\mathbb{Z}}{=}_{\mathbb{S}}$.

In the sequel we shall see examples of quasi-final objects in the category $\mathbf{C}$ of coalgebras over an endofunctor F on $\mathbf{Set}$. We recall here the main definitions; for more information see [9]. A *coalgebra* for F, or *F-coalgebra*, is a pair $\mathbb{S} = \langle S, \psi \rangle$ where S is a set and ψ is a function $\psi : S \to F(S)$, called the *dynamics* of the coalgebra. A morphism $f : \mathbb{S}_1 \to \mathbb{S}_2$ of F-coalgebras is a function $f : S_1 \to S_2$ such that the following diagram commutes:

$$
\begin{array}{ccc}
S_1 & \xrightarrow{\ f\ } & S_2 \\
{\scriptstyle \psi_1}\downarrow & & \downarrow{\scriptstyle \psi_2} \\
FS_1 & \xrightarrow[Ff]{} & FS_2 \ .
\end{array}
\tag{1}
$$

When the functor F is clear from the context, we just say coalgebra instead of F-coalgebra. The forgetful functor U applies any coalgebra $\mathbb{S} = \langle S, \psi \rangle$ to its underlying set S and any coalgebra morphism to itself as a function.

In the next section we consider quasi-final transition systems qua coalgebras based on traces and failures. Let $A \neq \emptyset$ be a set of *actions*. Recall that a (labelled) transition system with labels in A is a pair $\langle S, \to \rangle$, where S is a set of *states* and $\to$ is a ternary relation $\to\ \subseteq S \times A \times S$; as usual, we write $s \xrightarrow{a} t$ instead of $(s, a, t) \in\to$. There are several ways to view a transition system as a coalgebra $\mathbb{S} = \langle S, \psi \rangle$; in this paper we assume that ψ maps S to $\mathcal{P}(A \times S)$, where $\psi(s) = \{(a, t) : s \xrightarrow{a} t\}$ for all $s \in S$. Thus, transition systems are basically coalgebras for the functor $\mathcal{P}(A \times -)$; in the sequel we shall still often write $s \xrightarrow{a} t$ as an abbreviation of $(a, t) \in \psi(s)$, for clarity; sometimes we write $s \xrightarrow{a}$ to mean that $s \xrightarrow{a} t$ for some t. If $\mathbb{S}' = \langle S', \psi' \rangle$ is another transition system, a *morphism* $f : \mathbb{S} \to \mathbb{S}'$ is just a $\mathcal{P}(A \times -)$-coalgebra morphism, this is, a function $f : S \to S'$ such that $\psi' \circ f = \mathcal{P}(A \times f) \circ \psi$. It is easy to see that this notion is equivalent to the following two conditions taken together:

- whenever $s \xrightarrow{a} t$ in $\mathbb{S}$, then $f(s) \xrightarrow{a} f(t)$ in $\mathbb{S}'$;
- if $f(s) \xrightarrow{a} t'$ in $\mathbb{S}'$, there is $t \in S$ such that $s \xrightarrow{a} t$ in $\mathbb{S}$ and $f(t) = t'$.

For the rest of this section we fix a quasi-final coalgebra $\mathbb{Z} = \langle Z, \zeta \rangle$ with respect to a natural transformation $\beta : U \to U\mathbb{Z}$.

From a coalgebra $\mathbb{S} = \langle S, \psi \rangle$ we can build a new coalgebra $\langle FS, F\psi \rangle$, to be denoted $F\mathbb{S}$. Applying F to all objects and arrows in (1), we conclude that Ff is a morphism $F\mathbb{S}_1 \to F\mathbb{S}_2$; this shows F extends to an endofunctor on $\mathbf{C}$, also denoted F. Drawing the appropriate instance of (1), it is easy to conclude that ψ is a morphism from $\mathbb{S}$ to $F\mathbb{S}$. Thus, ψ is a β-morphism, so that $\beta_{F\mathbb{S}} \circ \psi = \beta_{\mathbb{S}}$. If we replace $\langle S, \psi \rangle$ with $\langle Z, \zeta \rangle$, we further conclude that $\beta_{F\mathbb{Z}} \circ \zeta = \beta_{\mathbb{Z}} = \mathrm{id}_Z$; thus, ζ is injective, hence is monic in $\mathbf{C}$ [9].

It is interesting to compare behaviour equivalences with bisimulations, a notion that can be defined as follows [9]. Given coalgebras $\mathbb{S}_1$ and $\mathbb{S}_2$, a relation $R \subseteq U\mathbb{S}_1 \times U\mathbb{S}_2$ is a *bisimulation* if there is a coalgebra $\mathbb{R}$ such that $R = U\mathbb{R}$ and the projections $p_1 : \mathbb{R} \to U\mathbb{S}_1$ and $p_2 : \mathbb{R} \to U\mathbb{S}_2$ are coalgebra morphisms.

When applied to transition systems, this definition coincides with the classical one [10]: for all $(s,t) \in R$, whenever $s \xrightarrow{a} s'$, there is t' such that $t \xrightarrow{a} t'$ and $(s',t') \in R$, and whenever $t \xrightarrow{a} t'$, there is s' such that $s \xrightarrow{a} s'$ and $(s',t') \in R$. In the sequel we only consider the case where $\mathbb{S}_1 = \mathbb{S}_2 = \mathbb{S}$. There is a largest bisimulation on any $\mathbb{S}$, called the *bisimilarity* relation and denoted $\sim_{\mathbb{S}}$, which is an equivalence relation. On final coalgebras, bisimilarity coincides with the identity relation, which constitutes the so-called coinduction proof principle. As we shall see shortly, the same principle holds for quasi-final coalgebras.

Proposition 3. *Suppose* $\mathbf{C}$ *has a quasi-final coalgebra* $\mathbb{Z}$ *with respect to* β*. The behavioural equivalence* $\overset{\mathbb{Z}}{=}_{\mathbb{S}} = \mathrm{Ker}(\beta_{\mathbb{S}})$ *is larger than any bisimulation in* $\mathbb{S}$*, that is, is larger than* $\sim_{\mathbb{S}}$*.*

Proof. Let $R \subseteq U\mathbb{S} \times U\mathbb{S}$ be a bisimulation in $\mathbb{S}$, that is, there is a coalgebra $\mathbb{R}$ such that $R = U\mathbb{R}$ and the projections $p_1 : \mathbb{R} \to U\mathbb{S}$ and $p_2 : \mathbb{R} \to U\mathbb{S}$ are coalgebra morphisms. As coalgebra morphisms are β-morphisms, $\beta_{\mathbb{S}} \circ p_1 = \beta_{\mathbb{R}} = \beta_{\mathbb{S}} \circ p_2$, hence, for all (s_1, s_2) in R, $\beta_{\mathbb{S}}(s_1) = \beta_{\mathbb{S}}(p_1(s_1,s_2)) = \beta_{\mathbb{S}}(p_2(s_1,s_2)) = \beta_{\mathbb{S}}(s_2)$. Thus, $s_1 \overset{\mathbb{Z}}{=}_{\mathbb{S}} s_2$, so $R \subseteq \overset{\mathbb{Z}}{=}_{\mathbb{S}}$.

Note that $\overset{\mathbb{Z}}{=}_{\mathbb{S}}$ may be much larger than $\sim_{\mathbb{S}}$. For example, if $U\mathbb{Z}$ is a singleton, then $\overset{\mathbb{Z}}{=}_{\mathbb{S}}$ is $(U\mathbb{S})^2$, but if $\mathbb{S}$ is e.g. a final coalgebra, $\sim_{\mathbb{S}}$ is $\Delta_{U\mathbb{S}}$ (the identity or diagonal relation on $U\mathbb{S}$). It can be shown that if the functor F preserves weak pullbacks, the relations $\overset{\mathbb{Z}}{=}_{\mathbb{S}}$ and $\sim_{\mathbb{S}}$ coincide whenever $\beta_{\mathbb{S}}$ is a coalgebra morphism. Here, as a corollary to the previous proposition, we just prove that any quasi-final coalgebra satisfies the coinduction proof principle.

Corollary 1. *Any quasi-final coalgebra* $\mathbb{Z}$ *satisfies the coinduction proof principle: for every bisimulation* R *on* $\mathbb{Z}$*,* $R \subseteq \Delta_{U\mathbb{Z}}$*.*

Proof. Since $\beta_{\mathbb{Z}}$ is the identity function on $U\mathbb{Z}$, $\overset{\mathbb{Z}}{=}_{\mathbb{Z}}$ is $\Delta_{U\mathbb{Z}}$. The conclusion follows from the previous proposition.

3   Quasi-final Transition Systems

Here we consider just traces and failures as examples of behaviours than can be viewed as quasi-final transition systems. In [1] these notions together with ready-traces have been shown to give rise to so-called "behaviour objects", which are essentially equivalent to quasi-final objects, and the presentation below can be seen as a simplification of the one in that paper. Note that the category of $\mathcal{P}(A \times -)$-coalgebras does not have final elements due to cardinality reasons [9].

3.1   Traces

Let $\mathbb{S} = \langle S, \psi \rangle$ be a transition system. A finite string $x = a_1 \cdots a_n \in A^*$ is a *trace* of $s \in S$ if $s \xrightarrow{a_1} \cdots \xrightarrow{a_n} t$, which we abbreviate to $s \xrightarrow{x} t$ (note that $s \xrightarrow{\varepsilon} s$

for all s, where ε is the null string). The set $Tr_{\mathbb{S}}(s) = \{x : \exists t, s \xrightarrow{x} t\}$ of traces from $s \in S$ is nonempty and prefix-closed, that is, $\varepsilon \in Tr_{\mathbb{S}}(s)$ and whenever $xy \in Tr_{\mathbb{S}}(s)$, then $x \in Tr_{\mathbb{S}}(s)$. Let $\mathcal{T}$ be the set of all nonempty and prefix-closed subsets of A^*, often called "trace languages"; we turn $\mathcal{T}$ into a transition system $\mathbb{T} = \langle \mathcal{T}, \zeta_{\mathbb{T}} \rangle$ by defining $\zeta_{\mathbb{T}} : \mathcal{T} \to \mathcal{P}(A \times \mathcal{T})$ by the transitions

$$L \xrightarrow{a} \{x : ax \in L\}$$

for $a \in L$ (to guarantee that $\{x : ax \in L\} \neq \emptyset$). Note that $Tr_{\mathbb{S}} : S \to \mathcal{T}$ is not in general a morphism from $\mathbb{S}$ to $\mathbb{T}$. We next show that $Tr : U \to U\mathbb{T}$ is a natural transformation and $Tr_{\mathbb{T}}$ is the identity, so that $\mathbb{T}$ is a quasi-final transition system. The next two lemmas are folklore; the proposition that follows is new in the present form though a different version appeared previously in [1].

Lemma 1. *If $f : \mathbb{S}_1 \to \mathbb{S}_2$ is a morphism of transition systems and s is a state of $\mathbb{S}_1$, then s and $f(s)$ have the same traces. Thus, $Tr_{\mathbb{S}_2} \circ f = Tr_{\mathbb{S}_1}$, so $Tr : U \to U\mathbb{T}$ is a natural transformation.*

Proof. More precisely, we show that if $s \xrightarrow{x} t$ in $\mathbb{S}_1$, then $f(s) \xrightarrow{x} f(t)$ in $\mathbb{S}_2$; and if $f(s) \xrightarrow{x} t'$ in $\mathbb{S}_2$, there is $t \in U\mathbb{S}_1$ such that $s \xrightarrow{x} t$ in $\mathbb{S}_1$ and $f(t) = t'$. For the first statement, it is immediate that $s \xrightarrow{a_1} s_1 \xrightarrow{a_2} \cdots \xrightarrow{a_n} s_n$ in $\mathbb{S}_1$ implies $f(s) \xrightarrow{a_1} f(s_1) \xrightarrow{a_2} \cdots \xrightarrow{a_n} f(s_n)$ in $\mathbb{S}_2$. Conversely, if $f(s) \xrightarrow{a_1} s_1' \xrightarrow{a_2} \cdots \xrightarrow{a_n} s_n'$ in $\mathbb{S}_2$, there is s_1 such that $s \xrightarrow{a_1} s_1$ and $f(s_1) = s_1'$; since $f(s_1) \xrightarrow{a_2} s_2'$, there is s_2 such that $s_1 \xrightarrow{a_2} s_2$ and $f(s_2) = s_2'$; continuing in this way, we conclude that $s \xrightarrow{a_1} s_1 \xrightarrow{a_2} \cdots \xrightarrow{a_n} s_n$ in $\mathbb{S}_1$ and $f(s_n) = s_n'$.

Lemma 2. *If L is in $\mathcal{T}$, then $Tr_{\mathbb{T}}(L) = L$. Thus, $Tr_{\mathbb{T}} = \mathrm{id}_{\mathcal{T}}$.*

Proof. Both $Tr_{\mathbb{T}}(L)$ and L contain the empty string ε; now consider a nonempty string $x = a_1 \cdots a_n$ ($n > 0$). If $x \in L$, then $a_1 \in L$ by prefix closure, so $L \xrightarrow{a_1} L_1$ with $L_1 = \{y : a_1 y \in L\}$. Since $a_2 \cdots a_n \in L_1$, we can repeat the reasoning $n - 1$ times to find a sequence of transitions $L \xrightarrow{a_1} L_1 \xrightarrow{a_2} \cdots \xrightarrow{a_n} L_n$ that show that $x \in Tr_{\mathbb{T}}(L)$. Conversely, from $L \xrightarrow{a_1} L_1 \xrightarrow{a_2} \cdots \xrightarrow{a_n} L_n$ we obtain successively $\varepsilon \in L_n, a_n \in L_{n-1}, a_{n-1} a_n \in L_{n-2}, \ldots, a_1 \cdots a_n \in L$.

Proposition 4. *$\mathbb{T}$ is quasi-final in $\mathbf{C}$.*

3.2   Failures

In this section a pair $(x, X) \in A^* \times \mathcal{P}(A)$ will be called a *failure*. Given a transition system $\mathbb{S} = \langle S, \psi \rangle$ and $s \in S$, $I(s) = \{a : \exists t, s \xrightarrow{a} t\}$ is the set of *initials* of s. We say $(x, X) \in A^* \times \mathcal{P}(A)$ is a *failure* of $s \in S$ if there exists t such that $s \xrightarrow{x} t$ and $I(t) \cap X = \emptyset$; thus, (x, X) states that s has trace x but may end in a state where no action in X is possible. The set of failures of s will be written $Fl_{\mathbb{S}}(s)$. What follows is a much reduced version of the treatment of failures in [1] with the purpose of deriving Proposition 9, which is new in the present form.

A *failure-set* over A is any set $F \subseteq A^* \times \mathcal{P}(A)$ such that the following conditions hold:

F1 $(\varepsilon, \emptyset) \in F$.
F2 $(\varepsilon, X) \in F \Rightarrow \forall a \in X, (a, \emptyset) \notin F$.
F3 $(xy, X) \in F \Rightarrow (x, \emptyset) \in F$.
F4 $(x, X) \in F \wedge Y \subseteq X \Rightarrow (x, Y) \in F$.
F5 $(x, X) \in F \wedge \forall a \in Y, (xa, \emptyset) \notin F \Rightarrow (x, X \cup Y) \in F$.

Let $\mathcal{F}$ be the set of all failure-sets. The following is easy to check.

Proposition 5. *For any state s of a transition system $\mathbb{S}$, $Fl_{\mathbb{S}}(s)$ is a failure-set. Thus, $Fl_{\mathbb{S}}$ is a function $Fl_{\mathbb{S}} : S \to \mathcal{F}$.*

Given $F \in \mathcal{F}$ and $x \in A^*$, let $C_F(x) = \{a \in A : (xa, \emptyset) \in F\}$ be the set of *continuations* of x in F. Using continuations, conditions **F2** and **F5** above can be rewritten as follows:

F2' $(\varepsilon, X) \in F \Rightarrow X \cap C_F(\varepsilon) = \emptyset$.
F5' $(x, X) \in F \wedge Y \cap C_F(x) = \emptyset \Rightarrow (x, X \cup Y) \in F$.

Given $F \in \mathcal{F}$, we call $(a, X) \in F$ a *primary failure* of F if $X \subseteq C_F(a)$. We then put

$$F \xrightarrow{a, X} F'$$

where

$$F' = \{(\varepsilon, Y) : Y \cap (C_F(a) - X) = \emptyset\}$$
$$\cup$$
$$\{(bx, Y) : (abx, Y) \in F, b \notin X\}.$$

Proposition 6. *F' in the previous definition is a failure-set.*

Proof. The conditions defining failure-set are easy to check, except **F2** and **F5**. For **F2**, or rather **F2'**, first note that $C_{F'}(\varepsilon) = \{b : (b, \emptyset) \in F'\} = \{b : (ab, \emptyset) \in F, b \notin X\} = C_F(a) - X$. Now if $(\varepsilon, Y) \in F'$, then $Y \cap C_{F'}(\varepsilon) = Y \cap (C_F(a) - X) = \emptyset$, by definition of F', so **F2'** holds. Next consider **F5'**. Assume $(y, Y) \in F'$ and $Z \cap C_{F'}(y) = \emptyset$; we must conclude that $(y, Y \cup Z) \in F'$. By definition of F', we must distinguish the cases where $y = \varepsilon$ and $y = bx$. In the first case, to conclude that $(\varepsilon, Y \cup Z) \in F'$ we must show that $(Y \cup Z) \cap (C_F(a) - X) = \emptyset$; this is certainly the case since $Y \cap (C_F(a) - X) = \emptyset$, by **F2'**, and $Z \cap (C_F(a) - X) = Z \cap C_{F'}(\varepsilon) = \emptyset$, by hypothesis. In the second case, by definition of F', $(abx, Y) \in F$ and $b \notin X$. But given that $b \notin X$, we have $C_{F'}(bx) = C_F(abx)$, since $b \notin X$ implies that $(bxc, \emptyset) \in F'$ iff $(abxc, \emptyset) \in F$ for every $c \in A$; thus, the hypothesis $Z \cap C_{F'}(bx) = \emptyset$ is equivalent to $Z \cap C_F(abx) = \emptyset$; this condition together with $(abx, Y) \in F$ allows to conclude that $(abx, Y \cup Z) \in F$, by **F5'** applied to F; by definition of F', $(bx, Y \cup Z) \in F'$.

The relations $\xrightarrow{a, X}$ turn $\mathcal{F}$ into a transition system with label set $A \times \mathcal{P}(A)$. To obtain a transition system with label set A put $F \xrightarrow{a} F'$ if $F \xrightarrow{a, X} F'$ for some X. This defines a transition system $\mathbb{F} = \langle \mathcal{F}, \varsigma_{\mathbb{F}} \rangle$.

Proposition 7. *If $f : \mathbb{S}_1 \to \mathbb{S}_2$ is a morphism of transition systems and s is a state of $\mathbb{S}_1$, then s and $f(s)$ have the same failures. Thus, $Fl_{\mathbb{S}_2} \circ f = Fl_{\mathbb{S}_1}$, so $Fl : U \to U\mathbb{F}$ is a natural transformation.*

Proof. Let (x, X) be a failure of s, so that there exists t such that $s \xrightarrow{x} t$ and $I(t) \cap X = \emptyset$. Since f is a morphism, $f(s) \xrightarrow{x} f(t)$ and $I(t) = I(f(t))$; it follows that (x, X) is a failure of $f(s)$. Conversely, if we start with a failure of $f(s)$, the proof that it is a failure of s is similar.

Lemma 3. *Let F be a failure-set.*

1. $I(F) = C_F(\varepsilon)$.
2. *If $F \xrightarrow{a,X} F'$, then $I(F') = C_F(a) - X$.*

Proof. For the first statement, it is easy to see that $F \xrightarrow{a}$ iff $(a, \emptyset) \in F$ for all $a \in A$, so $I(F) = \{a \in A : (a, \emptyset) \in F\} = C_F(\varepsilon)$. For the second statement, if $F \xrightarrow{a,X} F'$, then $I(F') = \{b \in A : (b, \emptyset) \in F'\} = \{b \in A : (ab, \emptyset) \in F, b \notin X\} = C_F(a) - X$.

Proposition 8. *For all $F \in \mathcal{F}$, $F = Fl_{\mathbb{F}}(F)$. Thus, $Fl_{\mathbb{F}} = \mathrm{id}_{\mathbb{F}}$.*

Proof. Let us show first that $F \subseteq Fl_{\mathbb{F}}(F)$. Given $(x, X) \in F$, we must find F' such that $F \xrightarrow{x} F'$ and $I(F') \cap X = \emptyset$. Note that $I(F) = C_F(\varepsilon)$, by Lemma 3. We treat separately the case where $x = \varepsilon$ and prove the remaining cases by induction on the length of x. When $x = \varepsilon$, from $(\varepsilon, X) \in F$ we deduce, by **F2'**, that $I(F) \cap X = C_F(\varepsilon) \cap X = \emptyset$, hence $(\varepsilon, X) \in Fl_{\mathbb{F}}(F)$. For $x = a$, let $Y = X \cap C_F(a)$ and $Z = X \cap (A - C_F(a))$; then (a, Y) is a primary failure and there is a transition $F \xrightarrow{a,Y} F'$. We have $I(F') = C_F(a) - Y$, by Lemma 3, so $I(F') \cap Y = \emptyset$ and $I(F') \cap Z = \emptyset$. Thus, $I(F') \cap X = \emptyset$, hence $(a, X) \in Fl_{\mathbb{F}}(F)$. Finally, suppose $x = aby$. Since $(a, \emptyset) \in F$, by **F3**, there is a transition $F \xrightarrow{a,\emptyset} F'$. By definition of the transition relation, $(by, X) \in F'$, so $(by, X) \in Fl_{\mathbb{F}}(F')$, by induction hypothesis. Thus, there exists F'' such that $F' \xrightarrow{by} F''$ and $I(F'') \cap X = \emptyset$. But then $F \xrightarrow{aby} F''$ and $I(F'') \cap X = \emptyset$, so $(aby, X) \in Fl_{\mathbb{F}}(F)$.

We next prove that $Fl_{\mathbb{F}}(F) \subseteq F$. Given $(x, X) \in Fl_{\mathbb{F}}(F)$, there is F' such that $F \xrightarrow{x} F'$ and $I(F') \cap X = \emptyset$. Like before, we proceed by induction on the length of x, the case $x = \varepsilon$ being treated separately. When $x = \varepsilon$, we have $F' = F$; since $I(F) = C_F(\varepsilon)$, by Lemma 3, it follows that $I(F') \cap X = \emptyset$ is equivalent to $C_F(\varepsilon) \cap X = \emptyset$; from $(\varepsilon, \emptyset) \in F$ and $X \cap C_F(\varepsilon) = \emptyset$, we conclude that $(\varepsilon, X) \in F$, by **F5'**. Next, assume $x = a$. Let $W \subseteq C_F(a)$ such that $F \xrightarrow{a,W} F'$. First note that $(a, W) \in F$, hence $(a, X \cap W) \in F$, by **F4**. Second, by Lemma 3, $I(F') = C_F(a) - W = (A - W) \cap C_F(a)$, so the condition $I(F') \cap X = \emptyset$ reads $(X - W) \cap C_F(a) = X \cap (A - W) \cap C_F(a) = \emptyset$. Thus, $(a, X \cap W) \in F$ and $(X - W) \cap C_F(a) = \emptyset$, so $(a, X) \in F$, by **F5'**. Finally, if $x = aby$, there is F'' such that $F \xrightarrow{a} F'' \xrightarrow{by} F'$. The condition $I(F') \cap X = \emptyset$ implies $(by, X) \in Fl_{\mathbb{F}}(F'')$, hence $(by, X) \in F''$, by induction hypothesis. By the definition of the transition relation, it follows immediately that $(aby, X) \in F$.

Proposition 9. $\mathbb{F}$ *is quasi-final in* **C**.

Proposition 10. *The relation of failure equivalence is finer than trace equivalence.*

Proof. Note that failures preserve traces and apply Proposition 2.

4   Quasi-final Coalgebras from the Final Sequence of a Functor

Here we investigate the existence of quasi-final coalgebras associated with the final sequence of a functor, restricted to the first ω terms. Only the results on quasi-finality are new. For the rest we rely heavily on [3] and in part on [4].

4.1   The Final Sequence of a Functor

Let $F : \mathbf{Set} \to \mathbf{Set}$ be a functor, where we assume that $FX \neq \emptyset$ if $X \neq \emptyset$. We shall also assume, without loss of generality, that the functor F preserves set inclusion and function restriction; this means that $FX \subseteq FY$ whenever $X \subseteq Y$ and if $g : V \to W$ is a restriction of $f : X \to Y$ with $V \subseteq X$ and $W \subseteq Y$, then $F(g)$ is a restriction of $F(f)$. The *final sequence* of F is a sequence of sets Z_n indexed by the ordinals n together with a family of functions $p_m^n : Z_n \to Z_m$ for all ordinals $m \leq n$ such that:

- $p_n^n = \mathrm{id}_{Z_n}$ and $p_k^n = p_k^m \circ p_m^n$ for $k \leq m \leq n$.
- If n is a limit ordinal, $(Z_n, p_m^n)_{m<n}$ is a limit; in particular, Z_0 is a singleton.
- $Z_{n+1} = FZ_n$, $p_{m+1}^{n+1} = Fp_m^n$ and p_k^{n+1} is the mediating function $Z_{n+1} \to Z_k$ for a limit ordinal k.

Here is a summary of this section. For every coalgebra $\mathbb{C} = \langle C, \gamma \rangle$, there is a standard way to define a function $\gamma_n : C \to Z_n$ for every ordinal n. Our main result is that if n is a limit ordinal, it is possible to find a subset Z of Z_n, containing the images $\gamma_n(C)$ for all $\langle C, \gamma \rangle$, on which can be defined an F-coalgebra which is quasi-final and has essentially the γ_n as behaviour functions. For reasons of space, we shall restrict ourselves here to the finite ordinals and ω, and prove the existence of a quasi-final F-coalgebra as a subset of Z_ω (the general case will be dealt with in a forthcoming paper). We then apply the results to general and to finitely-branching transition systems.

Let us recast the definition of the final sequence when it is restricted to the finite ordinals. By the first clause above, we only need to define the p_n^{n+1}, which we abbreviate to p_n. Let 1 be a singleton and denote by $!_X$ the unique function $X \to 1$ for any set X. For every $n \geq 0$, we have $Z_n = F^n 1$ and $p_n = F^n !_{F1}$. Thus, $p_0 = !_{F1} : F1 \to 1$ and in general $p_n : Z_{n+1} \to Z_n$. We also need Z_ω, which we shall write $\bar{Z}$ henceforth; in the same vein, the functions p_n^ω will be written π_n. By the second clause above, $\bar{Z}$, together with the π_n, is a limit of the Z_n, p_n for finite n. We may write $\bar{Z} = \{(z_n)_{n \geq 0} : \forall n \geq 0, z_n \in Z_n \text{ and } z_n = p_n(z_{n+1})\}$ and $\pi_n : \bar{Z} \to Z_n$ is given by $\pi_n(\bar{z}) = z_n$, where $n \geq 0$ and $\bar{z} = (z_n)_{n \geq 0}$.

We have $p_n \circ \pi_{n+1} = \pi_n$ for all n. If $p_n \circ f_{n+1} = f_n$ for all n, we denote by $\bar{f}$ the function determined by the f_n, that is, the unique function $X \to \bar{Z}$ such that $\pi_n \circ \bar{f} = f_n$ for all n. In particular, the functions π_n determine $\bar{\pi} = \mathrm{id}_{\bar{Z}}$. Other functions to $\bar{Z}$ are obtained by applying the next result.

Lemma 4. *Any function $\bar{f} : X \to \bar{Z}$ can be lifted to a function $\bar{f}^F : F(X) \to \bar{Z}$ with components $f_n^F = p_n \circ F(f_n)$ for all n:*

$$\begin{array}{ccc} X & & F(X) \\ {\scriptstyle f_n}\downarrow & {\scriptstyle f_n^F}\nearrow & \downarrow {\scriptstyle F(f_n)} \\ Z_n & \xleftarrow{\ p_n\ } & Z_{n+1}. \end{array} \qquad (2)$$

Furthermore, $f_{n+1}^F = F(f_n)$ for all n.

Proof. We calculate $p_n \circ f_{n+1}^F = p_n \circ p_{n+1} \circ F(f_{n+1}) = p_n \circ F(p_n \circ f_{n+1}) = p_n \circ F(f_n) = f_n^F$, so $\bar{f}^F$ is well-defined. Finally, $f_{n+1}^F = p_{n+1} \circ F(f_{n+1}) = F(p_n \circ f_{n+1}) = F(f_n)$.

4.2   Quasi-final Coalgebras Based on $\bar{Z}$

Let $\langle C, \gamma \rangle$ be an F-coalgebra. We define functions $\gamma_n : C \to Z_n$ by $\gamma_0 = !_C$ and $\gamma_{n+1} = F(\gamma_n) \circ \gamma$ as in the diagram:

$$\begin{array}{ccccc} & & C & \xrightarrow{\ \gamma\ } & FC \\ {\scriptstyle \gamma_0}\nearrow & {\scriptstyle \gamma_n}\downarrow & & {\scriptstyle \gamma_{n+1}}\searrow & \downarrow {\scriptstyle F(\gamma_n)} \\ Z_0 & \cdots & Z_n & \xleftarrow{\ p_n\ } & Z_{n+1} & \cdots \end{array} \qquad (3)$$

Lemma 5. *For all n, $p_n \circ \gamma_{n+1} = \gamma_n$.*

Proof. This is clear for $n = 0$ because both γ_0 and $p_0 \circ \gamma_1$ are $!_C$. Assuming the conclusion for n, we calculate: $p_{n+1} \circ \gamma_{n+2} = F(p_n) \circ F(\gamma_{n+1}) \circ \gamma = F(p_n \circ \gamma_{n+1}) \circ \gamma = F(\gamma_n) \circ \gamma = \gamma_{n+1}$.

This allows us to define $\bar{\gamma} : C \to \bar{Z}$ and $\bar{\gamma}^F : F(C) \to \bar{Z}$.

Lemma 6.   *If $f : \langle C, \gamma \rangle \to \langle D, \delta \rangle$ is a coalgebra morphism, then $\bar{\delta} \circ f = \bar{\gamma}$.*

Proof. Clearly, $\delta_0 \circ f = \gamma_0$. Assuming $\delta_n \circ f = \gamma_n$, we calculate $\delta_{n+1} \circ f = F(\delta_n) \circ \delta \circ f = F(\delta_n) \circ F(f) \circ \gamma = F(\delta_n \circ f) \circ \gamma = F(\gamma_n) \circ \gamma = \gamma_{n+1}$.

For our next result, recall that we are assuming that the functor F preserves set inclusion and function restriction. Also, for any function $f : A \to B$ and any $X \subseteq A$, we denote by $f[X] = \{f(x) : x \in X\}$ the image of X under f.

Theorem 1. *Let* $\langle Z, \zeta \rangle$ *be a coalgebra such that: (i)* $Z \subseteq \bar{Z}$ *and* $\bar{\zeta} : Z \to \bar{Z}$ *is the inclusion; (ii)* $\bar{\gamma}[C] \subseteq Z$ *for every coalgebra* $\langle C, \gamma \rangle$. *Then* $\langle Z, \zeta \rangle$ *is a quasi-final coalgebra whose behaviour function for any coalgebra* $\langle C, \gamma \rangle$ *is the restriction of* $\bar{\gamma}$ *to* $C \to Z$. *Furthermore, if every such restriction is a coalgebra morphism, then* $\langle Z, \zeta \rangle$ *is final.*

Proof. In view of condition (ii), every $\bar{\gamma}$ restricts to a function $C \to Z$. In general the restriction is also denoted by $\bar{\gamma}$, for simplicity, but in this proof it is convenient to keep things separate so we denote the restriction here by $\hat{\gamma}$. Now for the first statement, we prove that the family of the $\hat{\gamma}$ satisfies two properties: (1) if $f : \langle C, \gamma \rangle \to \langle D, \delta \rangle$ is a coalgebra morphism, then $\hat{\delta} \circ f = \hat{\gamma}$ as functions $C \to Z$; (2) $\hat{\zeta} = \mathrm{id}_Z$ as a function $Z \to Z$. The first property was proved in Lemma 6, and the second property is condition (i). For the second statement, we have a coalgebra morphism $\hat{\gamma} : C \to Z$ for every coalgebra $\langle C, \gamma \rangle$, by hypothesis, and uniqueness follows from the fact that $\langle Z, \zeta \rangle$ is quasi-final.

We next prove the existence of a coalgebra $\langle Z, \zeta \rangle$ in the conditions of the previous theorem. In the first version of this paper the proof employed a technique adapted from previous work on sets with families of equivalences [11]; this is no longer the case in the current version, which contains a rather simplified and more compact proof.

Theorem 2. *Let* $\langle Z, \zeta \rangle$ *be an F-coalgebra where:*

- $Z \subseteq \bar{Z}$ *is the greatest fixed point of the function* $X \mapsto \bar{\pi}^F[F(X)]$ *from* $\mathcal{P}(\bar{Z})$ *to itself.*
- $\zeta : Z \to F(Z)$ *is a right inverse of the restriction of* $\bar{\pi}^F$ *to* $F(Z) \to Z$.

Then $\langle Z, \zeta \rangle$ *is a quasi-final coalgebra whose behaviour function for any coalgebra* $\langle C, \gamma \rangle$ *is the restriction of* $\bar{\gamma}$ *to* $C \to Z$.

Proof. Let us denote the function $X \mapsto \bar{\pi}^F[F(X)]$ by $\bar{\pi}^F[F(-)]$. By our assumption on F, $\bar{\pi}^F[F(-)]$ is monotone, so has a gretest fixed point Z by Tarski's lemma. Since $\bar{\pi}^F[F(Z)] = Z$, the restriction of $\bar{\pi}^F$ to $F(Z)$ is surjective, so ζ is well defined. To establish the result we show that $\bar{\zeta} : Z \to \bar{Z}$ is the inclusion and $\bar{\gamma}[C] \subseteq Z$ for every coalgebra $\langle C, \gamma \rangle$, and apply Theorem 1. To show that $\bar{\zeta}$ is an inclusion, we show that $\zeta_n(\bar{z}) = z_n$ for all n. For $n = 0$ this immediate; for the inductive case we obtain a sequence of equalities, whose justification is given below:

$$
\begin{aligned}
\zeta_{n+1}(\bar{z}) &= F(\zeta_n)(\zeta(\bar{z})) && (i) \\
&= F(\pi_n)(\zeta(\bar{z})) && (ii) \\
&= \pi_{n+1}^F(\zeta(\bar{z})) && (iii) \\
&= p_{n+1}(\bar{\pi}^F((\zeta(\bar{z})))) && (iv) \\
&= p_{n+1}(\bar{z}) && (v) \\
&= z_{n+1}. && (vi)
\end{aligned}
$$

Justification: (i) By (3), instantiated to $\zeta : Z \to FZ$; (ii) by induction hypothesis, ζ_n is a restriction of π_n, so $F(\zeta_n)$ is a restriction of $F(\pi_n)$ by our assumption on F; (iii) by Lemma 4 with π_n in place of f_n; (iv) by definition of the mediating function $\bar{\pi}^F$; (v) by hypothesis, ζ is a right inverse of the restriction of $\bar{\pi}^F$; (vi) by definition of p_{n+1}. Next, to prove that $\bar{\gamma}[C] \subseteq Z$ for every coalgebra $\langle C, \gamma \rangle$ it is enough, by the proof of Tarski's lemma, to show that $\bar{\gamma}[C]$ is a post-fixed point of $\bar{\pi}^F[F(-)]$, that is, $\bar{\gamma}[C] \subseteq \bar{\pi}^F[F(\bar{\gamma}[C])]$; more precisely, given $c \in C$, we must find $u \in F(\bar{\gamma}[C])$ such that $\bar{\gamma}(c) = \bar{\pi}^F(u)$, that is, $\gamma_n(c) = \pi_n^F(u)$ for all n. We put $u = F(\bar{\gamma})(\gamma(c))$, which makes sense because $F(\bar{\gamma})$ applies $F(C)$ to $F(\bar{\gamma}[C])$ (F preserves restrictions) and $\gamma(c) \in F(C)$. We calculate (see justification below):

$$
\begin{aligned}
\pi_n^F(u) &= \pi_n^F(F(\bar{\gamma})(\gamma(c))) & (i)\\
&= (p_n \circ F(\pi_n))(F(\bar{\gamma})(\gamma(c))) & (ii)\\
&= p_n(F(\pi_n \circ \bar{\gamma})(\gamma(c))) & (iii)\\
&= p_n((F(\gamma_n) \circ \gamma)(c)) & (iv)\\
&= (p_n \circ \gamma_{n+1})(c) & (v)\\
&= \gamma_n(c). & (vi)
\end{aligned}
$$

Justification: (i) By definition of u; (ii) by definition of π_n^F; (iii) functors preserve composition; (iv) $\bar{\gamma}$ is a mediating function; (v) by (3); (vi) by Lemma 5. This ends the proof.

We now consider the two extreme cases in which $Z = \bar{Z}$ or $\langle Z, \zeta \rangle$ is a *final* coalgebra, and investigate conditions under which these cases hold. The results will be applied below to powerset functors and more specifically to transition systems. Recall that given a coalgebra $\langle C, \gamma \rangle$, the function $\bar{\gamma} : C \to \bar{Z}$ is defined by (3) and $\bar{\gamma}^F : F(C) \to \bar{Z}$ is defined by (2).

Lemma 7. *For any coalgebra $\langle C, \gamma \rangle$, the diagram*

$$
\begin{array}{ccc}
C & \xrightarrow{\;\bar{\gamma}\;} & \bar{Z} \\
\gamma \downarrow & & \uparrow \bar{\pi}^F \\
F(C) & \xrightarrow[\;F(\bar{\gamma})\;]{} & F(\bar{Z})
\end{array}
$$

commutes.

Proof. We have $\pi_n^F \circ F(\bar{\gamma}) \circ \gamma = p_n \circ F(\pi_n) \circ F(\bar{\gamma}) \circ \gamma = p_n \circ F(\pi_n \circ \bar{\gamma}) \circ \gamma = p_n \circ F(\gamma_n) \circ \gamma = p_n \circ \gamma_{n+1} = \gamma_n$ for all n, hence the conclusion.

Proposition 11. *Let $\langle Z, \zeta \rangle$ be the quasi-final coalgebra of Theorem 2. Consider the function $\bar{\pi}^F : F(\bar{Z}) \to \bar{Z}$.*

- *If $\bar{\pi}^F$ is surjective, then $Z = \bar{Z}$.*
- *If $\bar{\pi}^F$ is injective, then $\langle Z, \zeta \rangle$ is a final coalgebra.*

Proof. To say $\bar{\pi}^F$ is surjective is the same as saying that $\bar{Z} = \bar{\pi}^F[F(\bar{Z})]$. Thus, $\bar{Z}$ is the greatest fixed point of $\bar{\pi}^F[F(-)]$ and the first statement follows. Next assume $\bar{\pi}^F$ is injective. The proof of Theorem 2 shows that $\langle Z, \zeta \rangle$ satisfies the conditions of Theorem 1; by the last statement of that theorem and in the notation introduced in its proof, we only need to show that for any coalgebra $\langle C, \gamma \rangle$, the restriction $\hat{\gamma} : C \to Z$ of $\bar{\gamma}$ is a coalgebra mophism. Since F preserves inclusions and restrictions, $F(\hat{\gamma}) : F(C) \to F(Z)$ is the restriction of $F(\bar{\gamma})$. Denoting by $\hat{\pi}^F : F(Z) \to Z$ the restriction of $\bar{\pi}^F$, the diagram

$$
\begin{array}{ccc}
C & \xrightarrow{\hat{\gamma}} & \bar{Z} \\
{\scriptstyle\gamma}\downarrow & & \uparrow{\scriptstyle\hat{\pi}^F} \\
F(C) & \xrightarrow[F(\hat{\gamma})]{} & F(\bar{Z})
\end{array}
$$

commutes, by Lemma 7, that is, $\hat{\gamma} = \hat{\pi}^F \circ F(\hat{\gamma}) \circ \gamma$. Since $\bar{\pi}^F$ is injective, $\hat{\pi}^F$ is bijective, with inverse ζ. It follows that $\zeta \circ \hat{\gamma} = \zeta \circ \hat{\pi}^F \circ F(\hat{\gamma}) \circ \gamma = F(\hat{\gamma}) \circ \gamma$, thus showing that $\hat{\gamma}$ is a coalgebra morphism.

4.3 Examples from Transition Systems

We first consider $F = \mathcal{P}(A \times -)$ for a fixed nonempty set A. It is convenient in this case to put $1 = \{\emptyset\}$. We turn $\bar{Z}$ into a $\mathcal{P}(A \times -)$-coalgebra by defining $\zeta : \bar{Z} \to \mathcal{P}(A \times \bar{Z})$ by

$$\zeta(\bar{z}) = \{(a, \bar{u}) : \forall k, (a, u_k) \in z_{k+1}\}.$$

Note that this definition makes sense because $z_{k+1} \in Z_{k+1} = \mathcal{P}(A \times Z_k)$, that is, $z_{k+1} \subseteq A \times Z_k$, so indeed $u_k \in Z_k$.

Proposition 12. $\langle \bar{Z}, \zeta \rangle$ *is a quasi-final coalgebra.*

Proof. We show that ζ is a right inverse of $\bar{\pi}^F$ and the conclusion will follow from Theorem 2 and Proposition 11. Specifically, we show that $\pi_m^F(\zeta(\bar{z})) = z_m$ for every m. For $m = 0$ we have $\pi_0^F(\zeta(\bar{z})) = \emptyset = z_0$. For $m = n + 1$, first recall by Lemma 4 that $\pi_{n+1}^F = \mathcal{P}(A \times \pi_n)$, so that for $M \subseteq A \times \bar{Z}$ we have $\pi_{n+1}^F(M) = \{(a, z_n) : (a, \bar{z}) \in M\}$. Given this we calculate $\pi_{n+1}^F(\zeta(\bar{z})) = \{(a, u_n) : (a, \bar{u}) \in \zeta(\bar{z})\} = \{(a, u_n) : \bar{u} \in \bar{Z}, \forall k.(a, u_k) \in z_{k+1}\} = z_{n+1}$, where we still have to justify the last equality. The inclusion $\subseteq$ is immediate. For $\supseteq$ take $(a, u) \in z_{n+1}$; we must find $\bar{u} \in \bar{Z}$ with $(a, u_k) \in z_{k+1}$ for all k and $u_n = u$. The sequence of the z_k starts with the empty set $z_0 = \emptyset$ and for $k > 0$, since $z_k = p_k(z_{k+1}) = \mathcal{P}(A \times p_{k-1})(z_{k+1})$, the function $A \times p_{k-1}$ applies z_{k+1} surjectively onto z_k. So we obtain a sequence of pairs $(a, u_k) \in z_{k+1}$ for $k \geq 0$ as follows. We start at position n with $(a, u_n) = (a, u)$; for lower indices we put $(a, u_{n-1}) = (a, p_{n-1}(u_n))$ and so on; for upper indices, we let (a, u_{n+1}) be some element in z_{n+2} mapped to (a, u_n) by $A \times p_n$ and so on. The sequence of the u_k defines an element $\bar{u} \in \bar{Z}$ satisfying the required properties.

Proposition 13. *The behaviour equivalence generated by $\langle \bar{Z}, \zeta \rangle$ is finer than failure equivalence.*

Proof. This is another application of Proposition 2, since it is easy to see that for any transition system $\langle S, \psi \rangle$, the function $\bar{\psi} : S \to \bar{Z}$ preserves failures.

We end with a remark concerning finitely branching transition systems, that is, coalgebras for the functor $\mathcal{P}_{\text{fin}}(A \times -)$ where $\mathcal{P}_{\text{fin}}$ is the finite powerset. In this case $Z \neq \bar{Z}$, but $\bar{\pi}^{\mathcal{P}_{\text{fin}}(A \times -)} : \mathcal{P}_{\text{fin}}(A \times \bar{Z}) \to \bar{Z}$ is injective, so by Proposition 11 this gives another proof that there is a final $\mathcal{P}_{\text{fin}}(A \times -)$-coalgebra.

Lemma 8. *For $F = \mathcal{P}_{\text{fin}}(A \times -)$, $\bar{\pi}^F : F(\bar{Z}) \to \bar{Z}$ is injective.*

Proof. Suppose M, N are finite subsets of $A \times \bar{Z}$ and $\bar{\pi}^F(M) = \bar{\pi}^F(N)$, that is, $\pi_{n+1}^F(M) = \pi_{n+1}^F(N)$ for all n. Let $(a, \bar{u}) \in M$. Since $\pi_{n+1}^F(M) = F(\pi_n)(M) = \{(a, u_n) : (a, \bar{u}) \in M\}$, we have $(a, u_n) \in \pi_{n+1}^F(N)$. There is $\bar{v}^{(n)} \in \bar{Z}$ such that $(a, \bar{v}^{(n)}) \in N$ and $v_n^{(n)} = u_n$. Note that

$$v_k^{(n)} = p_k(\cdots p_{n-1}(v_n^{(n)}) \cdots) = p_k(\cdots p_{n-1}(u_n) \cdots) = u_k \quad (4)$$

for all $k < n$. Since N is finite, the $(a, \bar{v}^{(n)})$ can not be all distinct, so there is $(a, \bar{v}) \in N$ such that $\bar{v} = \bar{v}^{(n)}$ for infinitely many n. By (4), $v_k = u_k$ for all k, so $\bar{v} = \bar{u}$. Thus, $(a, \bar{u}) \in N$, hence $M \subseteq N$. By symmetry, $N \subseteq M$, therefore $M = N$.

Proposition 14 (Barr [5]). *There is a final $\mathcal{P}_{\text{fin}}(A \times -)$-coalgebra.*

Proof. By Lemma 8 and Proposition 11.

5   Concluding Remarks

This paper presents another attempt at capturing coalgebraically notions of behaviour that can not be described in terms of final coalgebras of the category under consideration. The examples considered so far seem to suggest that the notion of quasi-final object proposed here has the potential to be a useful tool for describing behaviours of systems and study their properties. But this is work still in progress, and much remains of course to be done. To begin with, since distinct quasi-final objects are not necessarily isomorphic, we need to understand better the structure of the "space" of quasi-final objects. This paper is a very first step in that direction. For example, given quasi-final objects $\mathbb{Z}, \beta$ and $\mathbb{Z}', \beta'$, the relation defined by $\mathbb{Z}, \beta \sqsubseteq \mathbb{Z}', \beta'$ if β' preserves β is a preorder, but what are its properties? It is easy to see that any coalgebra on a singleton (recall the remark after Definition 1) is a minimal element and a final object is the greatest element, but most properties remain to be studied. Also, it was shown that the ωth element of the final sequence of a non-trivial endofunctor contain a largest subset on which a quasi-final coalgebra can be defined. The same is true for the 0th element: just take any coalgebra on a singleton. Actually, this result can be extended to all ordinals (work in preparation). What role (if any) play these quasi-final objects in the space of all quasi-final objects? And in the characterization of final coalgebras, as in the work of Adámek [12] and Worrell [3]? Another line of work is to adapt the bialgebraic semantics of Turi and Plotkin [13], based on previous work by Rutten [14] and by Rutten and Turi [15]. We intend to define in those terms the semantics of CSP and compare it with other coalgebraic semantics of CSP like the one studied by Wolter [16]. It seems also that the bialgebraic setting with distributive functors may be the appropriate framework to compare the present approach based on quasi-finality with the work of Jacobs and his co-workers [7, 8]. As a general final remark, we note that any topic involving final objects may in principle lend itself to a study in terms of quasi-final objects.

Acknowledgements. We thank the anonymous referees for their comments, which have led to several improvements.

References

[1] Monteiro, L.: A coalgebraic characterization of behaviours in the linear time - branching time spectrum. In: Corradini, A., Montanari, U. (eds.) WADT 2008. LNCS. Springer, Heidelberg (2009)

[2] van Glabbeek, R.: The linear time–branching time spectrum I: the semantics of concrete, sequential processes. In: Bergstra, J., Ponse, A., Smolka, S. (eds.) Handbook of process algebra, pp. 3–99. Elsevier, Amsterdam (2001)

[3] Worrell, J.: On the final sequence of a finitary set functor. Theoretical Computer Science 338(1-3), 184–199 (2005)

[4] Kurz, A., Pattinson, D.: Coalgebraic modal logic of finite rank. Mathematical Structures in Computer Science 15(03), 453–473 (2005)

[5] Barr, M.: Terminal coalgebras in well-founded set theory. Theoretical Computer Science 114(2), 299–315 (1993)

[6] Power, J., Turi, D.: A coalgebraic foundation for linear time semantics. In: Hofmann, M., Rosolini, G., Pavlovic, D. (eds.) CTCS 1999, Conference on Category Theory and Computer Science. Electronic Notes in Theoretical Computer Science, vol. 29, pp. 259–274. Elsevier, Amsterdam (1999)

[7] Jacobs, B.: Trace semantics for coalgebras. In: Adamek, J., Milius, S. (eds.) Coalgebraic Methods in Computer Science. Electronic Notes in Theoretical Computer Science, vol. 106, pp. 167–184. Elsevier, Amsterdam (2004)

[8] Hasuo, I., Jacobs, B., Sokolova, A.: Generic trace semantics via coinduction. Logical Methods in Computer Science 3(4:11), 1–36 (2007)

[9] Rutten, J.: Universal coalgebra: a theory of systems. Theoretical Computer Science 249(1), 3–80 (2000)

[10] Milner, R.: Communication and Concurrency. International Series in Computing Science. Prentice Hall International, Englewood Cliffs (1989)

[11] Monteiro, L.: Semantic domains based on sets with families of equivalences. In: Jacobs, B., Moss, L., Reichel, H., Rutten, J. (eds.) Coalgebraic Methods in Computer Science (CMCS 1998). Electronic Notes in Theoretical Computer Science, vol. 11, pp. 73–106. Elsevier, Amsterdam (1998)

[12] Adámek, J.: On final coalgebras of continuous functors. Theoretical Computer Science 294, 3–29 (2003)

[13] Turi, D., Plotkin, G.: Towards a mathematical operational semantics. In: Proc. 12th LICS Conf., pp. 280–291. IEEE Computer Society Press, Los Alamitos (1997)

[14] Rutten, J.: Processes as terms: non-well-founded models for bisimulation. Mathematical Structures in Computer Science 15, 257–275 (1992)

[15] Rutten, J., Turi, D.: Initial algebra and final coalgebra semantics for concurrency. In: de Bakker, J.W., de Roever, W.-P., Rozenberg, G. (eds.) REX 1993. LNCS, vol. 803, pp. 530–582. Springer, Heidelberg (1994)

[16] Wolter, U.: CSP, partial automata, and coalgebras. Theoretical Computer Science 280, 3–34 (2002)

Verifying Compiled File System Code

Jan Tobias Mühlberg and Gerald Lüttgen

Software Engineering and Programming Languages Research Group,
University of Bamberg, 96052 Bamberg, Germany
{jan-tobias.muehlberg, gerald.luettgen}@swt-bamberg.de

Abstract. This paper presents a case study on retrospective verification of the Linux Virtual File System (VFS), which is aimed at checking for violations of API usage rules and memory properties. Since VFS maintains dynamic data structures and is written in a mixture of C and inlined assembly, modern software model checkers cannot be applied. Our case study centres around our novel verification tool, the SOCA Verifier, which symbolically executes and analyses compiled code. We describe how this verifier deals with complex program features such as memory access, pointer aliasing and computed jumps, while reducing manual modelling to the bare minimum. Our results show that the SOCA Verifier is capable of reliably analysing complex operating system components such as the Linux VFS, thereby going beyond traditional testing tools and into niches that current software model checkers do not reach.

1 Introduction

In the context of the grand challenge proposed to the program verification community by Hoare [16], a mini challenge of building a verifiable *file system* (FS) as a stepping stone was presented by Joshi and Holzmann [17]. As FSs are vital components of operating system kernels, bugs in their code can have disastrous consequences. Unhandled failure may render all application-level programs unsafe and gives way to serious security problems.

This paper applies an analytical approach to verifying an implementation of the *Virtual File System* (VFS) layer [5] within the Linux operating system kernel, using our novel, automated *Symbolic Object-Code Analysis* (SOCA) technique. As described in Sec. 2, the VFS layer is of particular interest since it provides support for implementing concrete FSs such as EXT3 and ReiserFS [5], and encapsulates the details on top of which C POSIX libraries are defined; such libraries in turn provide functions, e.g., *open* and *remove*, that facilitate file access. Our case study aims at checking for violations of API usage rules and memory properties within VFS, and equally at assessing the feasibility of our SOCA technique to reliably analysing intricate operating system components such as the Linux VFS implementation. We are particularly interested in finding out to what degree the *automatic* verification of complex properties

M.V.M. Oliveira and J. Woodcock (Eds.): SBMF 2009, LNCS 5902, pp. 306–320, 2009.

involving pointer safety and the correct usage of locking APIs within VFS is possible.[1]

Since the Linux VFS implementation consists of more than 65k lines of complex C code including inlined assembly and linked dynamic data structures, its verification is not supported by current software model checkers such as BLAST [15] and CBMC [8]. Thus, previous work by us focused on the question whether and how an appropriate model of the VFS can be reverse engineered from its implementation, and whether meaningful verification results can be obtained using model checking on the extracted model [13]. This proved to be a challenging task since automated techniques for extracting models from C source code do not deal with important aspects of operating system code, including macros, dynamic memory allocation, function pointers, architecture-specific and compiler-specific code and inlined assembly. Much time was spent in [13] on extracting a model by hand and validating this model via reviews and simulation runs, before it could be proved to respect data-integrity properties and to be deadlock-free using the SMART model checker [7]. Our SOCA technique addresses these shortcomings, providing automated verification support that does away with manual modelling and ad-hoc pointer analysis.

The contributions of this paper are threefold. In Sec. 3 we summarise our *SOCA technique* for automated analysis of compiled programs by means of bounded symbolic execution, using the SMT solver *Yices* [11] as execution and verification engine. Analysing the object code enables us to bypass limitations of software model checkers with respect to the accepted input language, so that analysing code sections written in inline assembly does not represent a barrier for us. Our technique is especially designed for programs employing complex heap-allocated data structures and provides full counterexample paths for each bug found. While generating counterexamples is often impossible for static analysis techniques due to precision loss in join and widening operations [14], traditional model checking requires the manual construction of models or the use of techniques such as predicate abstraction [3] which do not work well in the presence of heap-allocated data structures. Hence, symbolic execution is our method of choice over static analysis and model checking. Despite only employing path-sensitive and heap-aware slicing, the SOCA technique scales well for the Linux VFS. Moreover, manual modelling efforts are reduced to a bare minimum, namely to the abstract specification of a program's execution context that specifies input and initial heap content.

The paper's second contribution lies in demonstrating how verification properties can be expressed for symbolic object-code analysis, for which two different approaches are employed in Sec. 4. Firstly, properties may be presented to the SMT solver as assertions on the program's register contents at each execution point. Alternatively, the program may be instrumented during its symbolic execution, by adding test and branch instructions to its control flow graph.

---

[1] Doing so is in the remit of Joshi and Holzmann's mini challenge: "researchers could choose any of several existing open-source filesystems and attempt to verify them" [17].

Verifying a particular property then involves checking for the reachability of a specific code section. While the first approach allows us to express safety properties on pointers, we use the latter technique for checking preconditions of kernel API functions reflecting particular API usage rules.

Our last, but not least, contribution is the formal verification of a group of commonly used VFS functions, namely those for creating and removing files and directories, which we report in Sec. 5. By applying symbolic execution and leaving the parameters of these functions as unspecified as possible, our analysis covers low-probability scenarios. In particular, we look for program points where pointers holding invalid values may be de-referenced or where the violation of API usage rules may cause the VFS to deadlock. The experimental results show that the SOCA technique works well on the Linux VFS and that it produces a relatively low number of false-positive counterexamples while achieving high code coverage. Therefore, the absence of any flagged errors contributes to raising confidence in the correctness of the Linux VFS implementation.

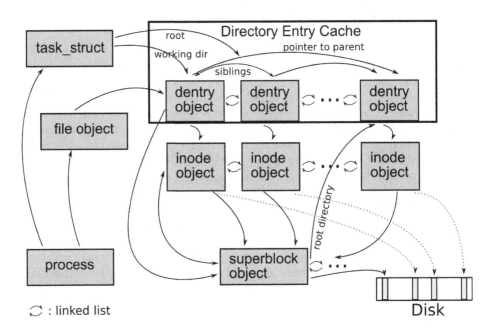

Fig. 1. VFS environment and data structures, where arrows denote pointers

2 The Linux Virtual File System

This section introduces the Linux FS architecture and, in particular, the *Virtual File System* layer; the reader is referred to [5] for a more detailed description. An overview of the VFS internals and data structures is presented in Fig. 1.

The Linux FS architecture consists of multiple layers. The most abstract is the *application* layer which refers to the user programs; this is shown as "process" in Fig. 1. Its functionality is constructed on top of the file access mechanisms offered by the *C POSIX library*, which provides functions facilitating file access as defined by the POSIX Standard, e.g., open file `open()`, delete file `remove()`, make directory `mkdir()` and remove directory `rmdir()`. The next lower layer is the *system call interface* which propagates requests for system resources from applications in user space to the kernel, e.g., to the VFS.

The *Virtual File System* layer is an indirection layer, providing the data structures and interfaces needed for system calls related to a standard Unix FS. It defines a common interface that allows many kinds of specific FSs to coexist, and enables the default processing needed to maintain the internal representation of a FS. The VFS runs in a highly concurrent environment as its interface functions may be invoked by multiple, concurrently executing application programs. Therefore, mechanisms implementing mutual exclusion are widely used to prevent inconsistencies in VFS data structures, such as atomic values, mutexes, reader-writer semaphores and spinlocks. In addition, several global locks are employed to protect the global lists of data structures while entries are appended or removed. To serve a single system call, typically multiple locks have to be obtained and released in the right order. Failing to do so could drive the VFS into a deadlock or an undefined state, effectively crashing the operating system.

Each *specific file system*, such as EXT3 and ReiserFS, then implements the processing supporting the FS and operates on the data structures of the VFS layer. Its purpose is to provide an interface between the internal view of the FS and physical media, by translating between the VFS data structures and their on-disk representations. Finally, the lowest layer contains *device drivers* which implement access control for physical media.

The most relevant data structures in the VFS are *superblocks*, *dentries* and *inodes*. As shown in Fig. 1, all of them are linked by various pointers inside the structures. In addition, the data structures consist of sets of function pointers that are used to transparently access functionality provided by the underlying FS implementation. The most frequently used data objects in the VFS are dentries. The *dentry* data structures collectively describe the structure of all currently mounted FSs. Each dentry contains a file's name, a link to the dentry's parent, the list of subdirectories and siblings, hard link information, mount information, a link to the relevant super block and locking structures. It also carries a reference to its corresponding inode and a reference count that reflects the number of processes currently using the dentry. Dentries are hashed to speed up access; the hashed dentries are referred to as the *Directory Entry Cache*, or *dcache*, which is frequently consulted when resolving path names.

In our initial verification attempt to the VFS [13], our work was focused on manually abstracting these data structures and their associated control flow, so as to obtain a sufficiently small model for automated verification via model checking. Hence, much effort was put into discovering relations between the different data structures employed by the VFS [13]. The focus of this paper differs in the sense that *no* models of data structures, memory layout or control flow are derived from the implementation. Instead, each path of the compiled program is translated automatically into a corresponding constraint system which is then analysed by an SMT solver, thus fully automating the verification process.

3   The SOCA Technique

One of the disadvantages of today's model checking tools results from their restriction to the analysis of source code. They usually ignore powerful programming constructs such as pointer arithmetic, pointer aliasing, function pointers and computed jumps. Furthermore they suffer from not being able to consider the effects of program components that are not available in the desired form of source code: functions linked in from libraries and the use of inlined assembly are common examples for this. In addition, many errors, especially in operating system components, arise because of platform-specific and compiler-specific details such as the byte-alignment in memory and registers, memory-layout, padding between structure fields and offsets [1]. Thus, software model checkers including BLAST [15] and SLAM/SDV [4] assume either that the program under consideration "does not have wild pointers" [2] or, as we show in [20], perform poorly when analysing such software.

Analysis outline. In this paper we employ a novel approach to verifying properties in software components based on *bounded path-sensitive symbolic execution of compiled and linked programs* as illustrated in Fig. 2. As shown in the illustration, we automatically translate a program given in its *object code* into an *intermediate representation* (IR), borrowed from the Valgrind binary instrumentation framework [21], by iteratively following each program path and resolving all target addresses of computed jumps and return statements. From the IR we generate systems of bit-vector constraints for each execution path, which reflect the path-relevant register and heap contents of the program under analysis. We then employ the *Yices* SMT solver [11] to check the satisfiability of the resulting constraint systems and thus the validity of the path. This approach also allows us to add in a range of pointer safety properties, e.g., whether a pointer points to an allocated address, as simple assertions over those constraint systems, while more complex properties such as preconditions for functions can be expressed by instrumenting the program. These instrumentations are also performed on the IR, and whence access to the source code is not required.

In contrast to other methods for software verification checking, our technique does not employ program abstraction but only *path-sensitive and heap-aware program slicing*, which means that our slices are not computed over the entire program but only over a particular path during execution. Furthermore, we do not consider the heap as one big data object but compute slices in respect of those heap locations that are data-flow dependents of a location in a program path for which a property is being checked. A safe over-approximation is used for computing these slices. In addition, our technique leaves most of the program's input (initially) unspecified in order to allow the SMT solver to search for subtle

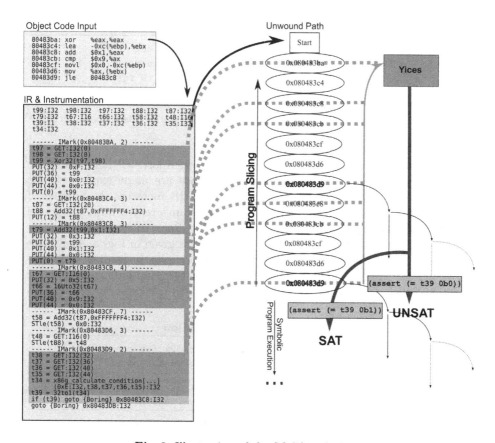

Fig. 2. Illustration of the SOCA technique

inputs that will drive the program into an error. Obviously, our analysis by symbolic execution cannot be complete: the search space has to be bounded since the total number of execution paths and the number of instructions per path in a program is potentially infinite. However, our experimental results on the Linux VFS reported in Sec. 5 will show that this boundedness is not a restriction in practice: many programs are relatively "shallow" and may still be analysed either exhaustively or up to an acceptable depth.

Valgrind's IR language. Valgrind's IR language is a typed assembly language in static-single-assignment form [9, 19] using *temporary registers* and some memory for storing the *guest state*, i.e., the registers available in the architecture for which the program under analysis is compiled. The language consists of a set of *basic blocks* containing a group of statements such that all transfers of control to the block are to the first statement in the group. Once the block has been entered, the statements in that block are executed sequentially.

In Valgrind's IR all arithmetic expressions including address arithmetic are decomposed into simple expressions with a fixed number of operands using

IA32 Assembly	IR Instructions
xor %eax,%eax	t9 = GET:I32(0) ;; t9 := eax
	t8 = GET:I32(0) ;; t8 := eax
	t7 = Xor32(t9,t8) ;; t7 := t9 xor t8
	PUT(0) = t7 ;; eax := t7

Fig. 3. Intel assembly instruction and its respective IR statements (types omitted)

temporary registers for intermediate results. Furthermore, all load and store operations to memory cells and to the guest state are made explicit. While normalising a program by transforming it into its IR increases the number of instructions, it reduces the complexity of the program's representation because IR instructions are relatively simple and side-effect free. An example for an assembly statement and its respective IR statements is given in Fig. 3. The figure shows how the xor statement is decomposed into explicitly loading (GET) the source register 0 into the temporary registers t8 and t9, and performing the xor operation followed by storing (PUT) the result back to the guest state.

IR Instruction	Constraint Representation
t9 = GET:I32(0)	(define t9::(bitvector 32) (bv-concat (bv-concat r3 r2) (bv-concat r1 r0))
t8 = GET:I32(0)	(define t8::(bitvector 32) (bv-concat (bv-concat r3 r2) (bv-concat r1 r0))
t7 = Xor32(t9,t8)	(define t7::(bitvector 32) (bv-xor t9 t8))
PUT(0) = t7	(define r0::(bitvector 8)(bv-extract 31 24 t7))
	(define r1::(bitvector 8)(bv-extract 23 16 t7))
	(define r2::(bitvector 8)(bv-extract 15 8 t7))
	(define r3::(bitvector 8)(bv-extract 7 0 t7))

Fig. 4. IR statements from Fig. 3 and their constraint representation in Yices

From IR to bit-vector constraints. Having a sequence of instructions decoded in the above way makes it relatively easy to generate a bit-vector constraint system for that sequence. An example with respect to the above IR instructions is given in Fig. 4, illustrating how the GET instruction can be implemented in Yices as the concatenation (bv-concat) of byte-aligned CPU registers (i.e., the parameter of the GET:I32 instruction, which is denoted as r0 to r3 in the constraint representation) from the guest state to word-aligned temporary registers. The PUT instruction is handled as bit-vector extraction (bv-extract <end> <start> <source>), respectively.

Note that CPU registers are assigned in "reverse byte order" to the temporary registers, i.e. with the least significant 8 bits in $r0$ and the most significant bits in $r3$. This is because the above constraints are generated from a binary compiled for Intel 32-bit CPUs (IA32), while arithmetic expressions in Yices are implemented for bit vectors that have the most significant bit at position 0. Since access operations to the guest state may be 8, 16, 32 or 64 bit aligned, we have to use two encodings here.

Furthermore, the IR is in static-single-assignment form only for the temporary registers within a single IR block. Hence, we have to be more precise when generating variable names for Yices: we simply append the instruction's location and the invocation number to each variable. Finally, since our analysis handles loops by unrolling them while exploring a path, a single instruction might appear multiple times in the path.

Heap-aware program slicing. Most difficulties in program analysis arise from the need to analyse accesses to a program's heap and stack. Valgrind's IR language provides two instructions, LD and ST, for loading and storing values from and to memory, respectively. While these instructions are in principle as easily mapped to constraints as the above GET and PUT instructions, handling them in the analysis phase requires care: including the entire 32-bit address space of a program into the constraint systems and performing access operation on pointer variables that hold potentially symbolic address values quickly becomes infeasible. Our approach tackles this problem by employing *heap-aware program slicing*: for each pointer used along a program's execution path we compute its potential target address range. When checking a property regarding some value obtained by de-referencing a particular pointer p, we only add those store instructions and their dependents to the constraint system that may have updated the value pointed to by p. The slicing mechanism used here is inspired by the interprocedural algorithm presented in [12]; our adaptation focuses on computing dynamic slices over a given program path.

4   VFS Execution Environment and Properties

This section discusses our model of the VFS execution environment and also presents the pointer safety properties and locking API usage rules relevant for the Linux VFS implementation.

Modelling the environment. One problem for program verification arises when program functions make use of an external data environment, i.e., de-reference pointers to data structures that are not created by the function under analysis. This is particularly common in case of the VFS as the majority of the VFS code operates on dentries that are assigned either when an FS is mounted or during previous path-lookup operations. The problem becomes particularly awkward since all these data structures are organised as linked lists which contain function pointers for accessing the specific file system underlying the VFS layer. This is because symbolic execution can easily cope with symbolic data objects of which only a pointer to the beginning of the structure is defined, while the remainder of the structure is left unspecified. However, in the case of linked data structures, some unspecified component of a given data object may be used as a pointer to another object. Treating the pointer symbolically will not only result in many false warnings since the pointer may literally point to any memory location, but may also dramatically increase the search space.

In our case study we "close" the VFS system to be analysed by defining a small number of dentries and associated data structures as static components of the kernel binary. As far as necessary, these data structures are directly defined in the VFS C source code by assigning a static `task_struct` (cf. `include/linux/sched.h` in the Linux source hierarchy) defining the logical context, including the working directory and a list of 15 dentries describing the FS's mount point and a simple directory hierarchy. The data objects are partially initialised by a handcrafted function that is used as a preamble in our analysis process. Note that the actual parameters to the VFS interface functions and the majority of data fields in the predefined data objects are still treated as symbolic values. Our modelling of the external environment is conducted by successively adding details to the initial memory state while carefully avoiding to be over-restrictive. We only intend to reduce the number of false warnings by eliminating impossible initial memory states to be considered in our analysis.

Pointer safety properties. We check three basic safety properties for every pointer that is de-referenced along an execution path:

1. The pointer does not hold value NULL.
2. The pointer only points to allocated data objects.
3. If the pointer is used as a jump target (call, return or computed jump), it may only point inside the `.text` section of the kernel binary, which holds the actual program code. Obviously, the program binary also has other sections such as the symbol table or static data which are, however, invalid as jump targets.

A check of the above properties on the IR is performed by computing an over-approximation of the address range the pointer may point to. That is, we assume that the pointer may address any memory cell between the maximal and minimal satisfying model determined by the constraint system for that pointer. For programs involving only statically assigned data we can directly evaluate the above properties by checking *(a)* whether the address range is assigned in the program binary and *(b)* whether it belongs to appropriate program sections for the respective use of the pointer. If dynamic memory allocation is involved, we keep track of objects and their respective locations currently allocated within the program's constraint representation. Checking the above properties is then performed as an assertion check within Yices.

Locking API usage rules. Being designed for a range of multiprocessor platforms, the Linux kernel is inherently concurrent. Hence, it employs various mechanisms implementing mutual exclusion, and primarily locking, to protect concurrently running kernel threads. The locking APIs used within the VFS are mainly spinlocks and semaphores, and each of the VFS structures contains pointers to at least one lock. In addition to these per-object locks, there exist global locks to protect access to lists of objects.

At a high level of abstraction, all locking APIs work in a similar fashion. If a kernel thread attempts to acquire a particular lock, it waits for this lock to become available, acquires it and performs its critical actions, and then releases the lock. As a result of this, a thread will wait forever if it attempts to acquire the same lock twice without releasing it in-between. Checking for the absence of this problem in single- and multi-threaded programs has recently attracted a lot of attention in the automated verification community [4, 15, 24, 23]. For software systems like the Linux kernel with its fine grained locking approach, conducting these checks is non-trivial since locks are passed by reference and due to the vast number of locks employed. A precise analysis of pointer aliasing relationships would be required to prove programs to be free of this sort of errors, which is known to be an undecidable problem in general.

In our approach, locking properties are checked by instrumenting locking related functions in their IR in such a way that a guarded jump is added to the control flow of the program, passing control to a designated "error location" whenever acquiring an already locked lock structure is attempted or an unlocked lock is released. Our symbolic analysis is then used to evaluate whether the guard may possibly be true or not, and an error message for the path is raised if the error location is reachable.

5   Applying the SOCA Verifier to the VFS

The current implementation of the SOCA Verifier is written in C, mainly for facilitating integration with the Valgrind VEX library [21]. For applying it to the VFS, we used the VFS implementation of version 2.6.18.8 of the Linux kernel, compiled with gcc 4.3.3 for the Intel Pentium-Pro architecture. All configuration options of the kernel were left as defaults. Our experiments were then carried out on an Intel Core 2 Quad machine with 2.83 GHz and 4 GBytes of RAM, typically analysing three VFS functions in parallel.

The bounds for the SOCA Verifier were set to a maximum of 1000 paths to be analysed, where a single program location may appear at most 1000 times per path, thereby effectively bounding the number of loop iterations or recursions to that depth. The Yices SMT solver was set to a timeout of 60 seconds per invocation, which was never reached in our experiments. All these bounds were chosen so that code coverage is maximised, while execution time is kept reasonably small.

Statistics and performance. Our experimental results are summarised in three tables. Table 5 provides a statistical overview of the VFS code. We report the total *number of machine instructions* that have been translated into IR by following each function's control flow. The *lines in source code* give an estimate of the checked implementation's size as the size of the C functions involved (excluding type definitions and header files, macro definitions, etc.). The next values in the table present the numbers of paths and, respectively, the lengths of the shortest and longest paths, in instructions explored by our verifier with respect to the calling context of the analysed function. The *pointer* and *locking operations* resemble the numbers of pointer de-references and lock/unlock operations encountered along the analysed paths, respectively.

Table 1. Experimental Results I: Code statistics by VFS function analysed

	creat	unlink	mkdir	rmdir	rename	totals
no. of instructions	3602	3143	3907	3419	4929	19000
lines in source code	1.4k	1.2k	1.6k	1.4k	2k	7.6k
no. of paths	279	149	212	318	431	1389
min. path length	91	41	87	72	72	41
max. path length	4138	3218	5319	3017	5910	5910
pointer operations	2537	2190	2671	2466	4387	14251
concrete	2356	2134	2458	2368	3989	13305
symbolic	181	56	213	98	398	946
locking operations	287	231	391	319	451	1679

Table 2. Experimental Results II: SOCA Verifier statistics

	creat	unlink	mkdir	rmdir	rename	totals
total time	2h27m	1h22m	2h42m	1h34m	3h45m	11h50m
max. memory (SOCA)	1.03G	752M	1.15G	743M	1.41G	1.41G
max. mem. (SOCA + Yices)	1.79G	800M	1.92G	791M	2.18G	2.18G
exec. bound exhausted	X	X	X	X	X	X
path bound exhausted	-	-	-	-	-	-
paths reaching end	154	112	165	215	182	828
assertions checked	13.4k	12.4k	15.8k	11.8k	21.9k	75.3k
ratio of failed checks	0.043	0.012	0.041	0.019	0.049	0.033

Table 3. Experimental Results III: Yices statistics

	creat	unlink	mkdir	rmdir	rename	totals
total Yices calls	27533	21067	31057	20988	44439	145k
total time spent in Yices	2h22m	1h11m	2h22m	1h24m	3h8m	10h28m
average time	311ms	192ms	271ms	198ms	376ms	248ms
standard deviation	3.7s	0.9s	5.2s	1.4s	5.9s	4.8s
max CS size in vars	450k	97k	450k	95k	450k	450k
average CS size in vars	2844	2871	2871	2862	2939	2877
standard deviation	14619	8948	14618	8898	16052	13521
max. memory consumption	766M	48M	766M	48M	766M	766M

In Table 5 we report the performance of the SOCA Verifier, showing the total time needed for analysing the kernel functions and our tool's maximum *memory consumption*. The maximum memory consumption of our tool together with the Yices solver engine is an estimate generated by summing up our tool's and Yices' maximum memory usage as given in Table 5; however, these may not necessarily hit their peak memory at the same time. The next two rows denote whether the analysis bounds were reached. We also report the number of paths reaching the end of the function analysed, the total number of assertions checked and the percentage of failed checks. Paths not reaching a return statement in the target function are terminated either due to bound exhaustion, or due to a property being violated that does not permit continuation of that path.

Finally, we outline in Table 5 the usage and behaviour of the SMT solver Yices, by reporting the number of times Yices was called when checking a particular VFS function and the total and average time spent for SMT solving. We also give the size of the checked constraint systems (CS) in boolean variables, as output by Yices and show the maximum amount of memory used by Yices.

Our analyses usually achieve a statement and condition coverage of 60% to 80% in this case study.[2] The main reason for this, at-first-sight low percentage, is that VFS functions often implement multiple different behaviours of which only a few are reachable for the given execution environment. For example, the implementation of the creat() system call resides mainly in the open_namei() function alongside different behaviours implementing the open() system call. Taking this into account, the coverage achieved by the SOCA Verifier is remarkably high when compared to testing-based approaches.

It should be noted that the above tables can only give a glimpse of the total scale of experiments that we have conducted for this case study.[2] Depending on how detailed or coarse the execution environment is specified, we experienced run times reaching from a few minutes up to several days, achieving different levels of statement and condition coverage (ranging from 20% to 80%) and different error ratios (ranging from 0 to 0.5). The discriminating value in all these experiments is the total number of "symbolic" pointers; a symbolic pointer is a pointer where the exact value cannot be determined at the point at which it is de-referenced. This usually happens when the entire pointer or some component of it (e.g., its base or offset) is retrieved from an incompletely specified component of the execution environment or directly from the input to the analysed function. While these symbolic values are generally bad for the performance of the SOCA technique since slicing is rendered inefficient and search spaces are increased, they are important for driving the analysis into paths that may be hard to reach in testing-based approaches to system validation.

Errors and false positives. As our verification technique does not include infeasible paths, all errors detected by the SOCA Verifier can actually be reproduced in the code, provided that other kernel components match the behaviour of our employed execution environment.

In advance of the experiments reported in this paper, we had tested our implementation of the SOCA technique on a variety of hand-crafted examples and also on the *Verisec* suite [18] which provides 280 examples of buffer overflow vulnerabilities taken from application programs. In all these cases we experienced low false-positive rates of less than 20%. However, as these examples represent closed systems not using external data objects, they are handled more efficiently by the SOCA Verifier than the VFS which makes heavy use of external data objects.

---

[2] A complete account of the experiments will be published in the first author's forthcoming PhD thesis and on the SOCA website located at
http://swt-bamberg.de/soca/

Our above result tables show that our analysis approach detects a number of errors of about 3% of the total number of checked assertions in each VFS function analysed. We have inspected each reported error in detail and discovered that all of them are due to an imprecisely specified execution environment. As explained in the previous section, specifying a valid but non-restrictive environment is particularly hard as all VFS functions operate on data structures that are allocated and assigned by other kernel sub-systems before the VFS functions are executed. As most of these structures form multiple lists, modelling them manually is tedious and error-prone. Therefore, our strategy was to leave many fields of those structures initially unspecified and successively add as much detail as necessary to eliminate false positives. This proved to be a good way to specify valid and at the same time non-restrictive execution environments.

Not discovering any real errors in the analysed VFS code contributes to our high confidence in the Linux kernel and is to be expected: the VFS consists of a well established and extensively used and tested code base.

6   Related Work

A survey on automated techniques for formal software verification can be found in [10]. Verification approaches employing predicate abstraction to model-check the source code of operating system components are presented in [4, 6, 15]. In theory, these are able to prove a file system implementation to be, e.g., free of deadlock, by checking the proper use of locking mechanisms. However, modern model checkers such as BLAST [15] require extensive manual preprocessing and are not able to deal with general pointer operations [20]. Recent work [22] shows further that, again in contrast to our verifier, BLAST cannot analyse programs with multiplicities of locks since its specification language does not permit the specification of observer automatons for API safety rules with respect to function parameters.

A bounded model checker for C source code based on symbolic execution and SAT solving is SATURN [24]. This tool is specialised on checking locking properties and null-pointer de-references. The authors show that their tool scales for analysing the entire Linux kernel. Unlike the SOCA Verifier, the approach in [24] computes function summaries instead of adding the respective code to the control flow, unwinds loops a fixed number of times and does not handle recursion. Hence, it can be expected to produce more unsound results but scale better than our SOCA technique.

Actual file system implementations were studied by Engler et al. in [25, 26]. In [26], model checking is used within the systematic testing of EXT3, JFS and ReiserFS. The employed verification system consists of an explicit-state model checker running the Linux kernel, a file system test driver, a permutation checker which verifies that a file system can always recover, and a recovery checker using the *fsck* recovery tool. The verification system starts with an empty file system and recursively generates successive states by executing system calls affecting the file system under analysis. After each step, the verification system is interrupted, and *fsck* is used to check whether the file system can recover to a valid state.

In contrast to this, our work focuses on checking a different class of properties, namely pointer safety and locking properties. Thanks to our memory model we can analyse these properties precisely and feed back detailed error traces together with specific initial heap state information leading to the error.

7   Conclusions and Future Work

The initial motivation for our SOCA technique to automated program verification was to explore the possibilities of using symbolic execution for analysing compiled programs. Indeed, object-code analysis is the method of choice for dealing with programs written in a combination of programming languages such as C and inlined assembly. This is particularly true for operating system code which is often highly platform specific and makes extensive use of programming constructs such as function pointers. As we show in this paper, these constructs can be dealt with efficiently in path-wise symbolic object-code analysis, while they are usually ignored by static techniques or by source-code-based approaches.

While the ideas behind the SOCA technique, namely symbolic execution, path-sensitive slicing and SMT solving, are well-known, the way in which these are integrated into the SOCA Verifier is novel. Much engineering effort went also into our SOCA implementation so that it scales to complex real-world operating system code such as the Linux VFS implementation. The SOCA Verifier is expected to scale even better for programs employing fewer external data structures than the VFS does. For example, the majority of Linux device drivers including actual file system implementations satisfies this criterion.

Regarding future work, we wish to extend the SOCA Verifier so as to be able to analyse concurrent programs. This would help for checking the VFS implementation for erroneous behaviour that is only exhibited when multiple kernel threads interact. In addition, the SOCA verifier should be integrated into widely used operating software development environments so that counterexamples found in object code can be presented in source code to the developer.

References

[1] Balakrishnan, G., Reps, T., Melski, D., Teitelbaum, T.: WYSINWYX: What You See Is Not What You eXecute. In: Meyer, B., Woodcock, J. (eds.) VSTTE 2005. LNCS, vol. 4171, pp. 202–213. Springer, Heidelberg (2008)
[2] Ball, T., Bounimova, E., Cook, B., Levin, V., Lichtenberg, J., McGarvey, C., Ondrusek, B., Rajamani, S.K., Ustuner, A.: Thorough static analysis of device drivers. In: EuroSys 2006, USA, vol. 4, pp. 73–85. ACM, New York (2006)
[3] Ball, T., Majumdar, R., Millstein, T., Rajamani, S.K.: Automatic predicate abstraction of C programs. SIGPLAN Not. 36(5), 203–213 (2001)
[4] Ball, T., Rajamani, S.K.: Automatically validating temporal safety properties of interfaces. In: Dwyer, M.B. (ed.) SPIN 2001. LNCS, vol. 2057, pp. 102–122. Springer, Heidelberg (2001)
[5] Bovet, D., Cesati, M.: Understanding the Linux Kernel. O'Reilly, Sebastopol (2005)
[6] Chaki, S., Clarke, E., Groce, A., Ouaknine, J., Strichman, O., Yorav, K.: Efficient verification of sequential and concurrent C programs. FMSD 25(2-3), 129–166 (2004)

[7] Ciardo, G., Jones, R.L., Miner, A.S., Siminiceanu, R.I.: Logic and stochastic modeling with SMART. Perform. Eval. 63(6), 578–608 (2006)

[8] Clarke, E., Kroening, D., Lerda, F.: A tool for checking ANSI-C programs. In: Jensen, K., Podelski, A. (eds.) TACAS 2004. LNCS, vol. 2988, pp. 168–176. Springer, Heidelberg (2004)

[9] Cytron, R., Ferrante, J., Rosen, B.K., Wegman, M.N., Zadeck, F.K.: Efficiently computing static single assignment form and the control dependence graph. ACM TOPLAS 13(4), 451–490 (1991)

[10] D'Silva, V., Kroening, D., Weissenbacher, G.: A survey of automated techniques for formal software verification. IEEE Transactions on Computer-Aided Design of Integrated Circuits and Systems 27(7), 1165–1178 (2008)

[11] Dutertre, B., de Moura, L.: The Yices SMT solver. Technical Report 01/2006, SRI International (2006), http://yices.csl.sri.com/tool-paper.pdf

[12] Ferdinand, C., Martin, F., Cullmann, C., Schlickling, M., Stein, I., Thesing, S., Heckmann, R.: New developments in WCET analysis. In: Reps, T., Sagiv, M., Bauer, J. (eds.) Program Analysis and Compilation, Theory and Practice. LNCS, vol. 4444, pp. 12–52. Springer, Heidelberg (2007)

[13] Galloway, A., Lüttgen, G., Mühlberg, J.T., Siminiceanu, R.: Model-checking the Linux Virtual File System. In: Jones, N.D., Müller-Olm, M. (eds.) VMCAI 2009. LNCS, vol. 5403, pp. 74–88. Springer, Heidelberg (2009)

[14] Gulavani, B.S., Rajamani, S.K.: Counterexample driven refinement for abstract interpretation. In: Hermanns, H., Palsberg, J. (eds.) TACAS 2006. LNCS, vol. 3920, pp. 474–488. Springer, Heidelberg (2006)

[15] Henzinger, T.A., Jhala, R., Majumdar, R., Necula, G.C., Sutre, G., Weimer, W.: Temporal-safety proofs for systems code. In: Brinksma, E., Larsen, K.G. (eds.) CAV 2002. LNCS, vol. 2404, p. 526. Springer, Heidelberg (2002)

[16] Hoare, T.: The verifying compiler: A grand challenge for computing research. J. ACM 50(1), 63–69 (2003)

[17] Joshi, R., Holzmann, G.J.: A mini challenge: Build a verifiable filesystem. Formal Aspects of Computing 19(2), 269–272 (2007)

[18] Ku, K., Hart, T.E., Chechik, M., Lie, D.: A buffer overflow benchmark for software model checkers. In: ASE 2007, USA, pp. 389–392. ACM, New York (2007)

[19] Leung, A., George, L.: Static single assignment form for machine code. In: PLDI 1999, USA, pp. 204–214. ACM, New York (1999)

[20] Mühlberg, J.T., Lüttgen, G.: BLASTing Linux code. In: Brim, L., Haverkort, B.R., Leucker, M., van de Pol, J. (eds.) FMICS 2006 and PDMC 2006. LNCS, vol. 4346, pp. 211–226. Springer, Heidelberg (2007)

[21] Nethercote, N., Seward, J.: Valgrind: A framework for heavyweight dynamic binary instrumentation. In: PLDI 2007, USA, vol. 42, pp. 89–100. ACM, New York (2007)

[22] Sery, O.: Enhanced property specification and verification in BLAST. In: Chechik, M., Wirsing, M. (eds.) FASE 2009. LNCS, vol. 5503, pp. 456–469. Springer, Heidelberg (2009)

[23] Witkowski, T., Blanc, N., Kroening, D., Weissenbacher, G.: Model checking concurrent Linux device drivers. In: ASE 2007, USA, pp. 501–504. ACM, New York (2007)

[24] Xie, Y., Aiken, A.: Saturn: A scalable framework for error detection using boolean satisfiability. ACM TOPLAS 29(3), 16 (2007)

[25] Yang, J., Sar, C., Twohey, P., Cadar, C., Engler, D.R.: Automatically generating malicious disks using symbolic execution. In: Security and Privacy, pp. 243–257. IEEE, Los Alamitos (2006)

[26] Yang, J., Twohey, P., Engler, D.R., Musuvathi, M.: Using model checking to find serious file system errors. In: OSDI, pp. 273–288. USENIX (2004)

Reasoning about General Quantum Programs over Mixed States

Juliana Kaizer Vizzotto[1], Giovani Rubert Librelotto[2], and Amr Sabry[3]

[1] Mestrado em Nanociências, Centro Universitário Franciscano
Santa Maria, RS/ Brazil
[2] DELC/CT, Cidade Universitária
Universidade Federal de Santa Maria, RS/ Brazil
[3] Department of Computer Science, Indiana University
Bloomington, USA

Abstract. In this work we present a functional programming language for quantum computation over mixed states. More interestingly, we develop a set of equations for the resulting programming language, proposing the first framework for *equational reasoning* about quantum computations over mixed states.

1 Introduction

Quantum computation and programming with mixed states [1,2] generalises standard quantum programming models with pure quantum states. In the pure approach of quantum computation, which allows just unitary (i.e., reversible) evolution, it is difficult or impossible to deal formally with an important class of non-unitary (i.e., non-reversible) quantum effects, including measurements, decoherence, or noise [1,3]. Summarizing, in general a quantum system is not in a pure state. Following [1] this may be attributed to the fact that we have only partial knowledge about the system, or that the system is not isolated from the rest of universe, so it does not have a well defined pure state.

A mixed quantum state is a probability distribution over pure quantum states and can be understood as an observer knowledge of the quantum system [4]. Besides to deal with the quantum effects mentioned above and to directly work with the practical information we can extract from a quantum system, the mixed approach seems to be nearer from real implementations of quantum computers. Noise and decoherence are key obstacles in implementing quantum computation devices [1]. Yet another promising approach for quantum computers architecture is based on measurements [5].

In recent work [6] we present a lambda calculus for quantum computations including measurements that builds on well-understood and familiar programming patterns and reasoning techniques. We define the calculus in three levels. We start with simply-typed lambda calculus, then we add the monadic constructions of Moggi's computational lambda calculus [7] to express pure quantum computations, and finally we add the constructions of the arrow calculus [8] to express mixed quantum computations.

M.V.M. Oliveira and J. Woodcock (Eds.): SBMF 2009, LNCS 5902, pp. 321–335, 2009.

Based on the facts discussed above about quantum computation with mixed states, and based on the idea that if we consider just the mixed state approach we can define a simpler and more elegant version of the quantum arrow calculus presented in [6], we present here a two level arrow calculus for quantum computations with mixed states. In contrast with the previous defined quantum arrow calculus, the arrow calculus for mixed states goes directly from classical states to mixed states. Going directly to mixed states turns the calculus simpler, with less constructions and, more interestingly, turns the set of equations simpler and more intuitive. Considering only mixed state computations generalises the previous language by working with the observer knowledge of the quantum system. Besides to use the equations from simply-typed lambda calculus, and arrow calculus [8], we define equations for sum of arrows (arrowplus) and scalar products for arrows. The constructors for sum and scalar product are now used to express classical probability distributions.

The essential point is that the equations of the calculus for mixed states showed as an attractive framework for equational reasoning about general quantum programs.

Moreover, we claim that our language implements the general probabilistic subroutines (functions) computed by standard quantum circuits [1]. This definition solves the problem of using subroutines in standard (or pure) quantum circuits, as the function computed by any circuit is a probabilistic one, and the standard theory of quantum circuits allows pure states only.

The remainder of this work is structured as follows. Section 2 reviews general quantum computations. Section 3 presents the quantum arrow calculus for mixed states, which is a generalisation of the calculus presented in [6]. We construct the calculus for mixed states in two levels: we start with simply-typed lambda calculus with booleans, and then we add the arrow calculus constructions to express general quantum computations. Additionally, to encompass the observer knowledge of the quantum system we add sum of arrows to represent the probability distribution generated by superpositions, and scalar product to represent the probability of each state in the mixture. In Section 4 we introduce a set of equations for the calculus. Essentially, besides to use the equations from simply-typed lambda calculus and from the arrow calculus [8], we define the equations for sum of arrows and for scalar product. We claim the soundness of the new equations using the methodology presented in [8] for defining the calculus extensions for specialised arrows. That is, soundness can be proved by showing that the laws follow in the translation of the constructions to classic arrows [9]. To illustrate the use of the equations we prove the correctness of three traditional quantum programs written with the calculus language. Section 5 remarks some related work. Section 6 concludes.

2   General Quantum Computations

Quantum computation [10] can be seen as processing of information using quantum systems. Its basic idea is to encode data using quantum bits (qubits).

In quantum theory, considering a *closed* quantum system, the qubit is a *unit* vector living in a complex inner product vector space know as *Hilbert space* [10]. We call such a vector a *ket* (from *Dirac's notation*) and denote it by $|v\rangle$ (where v stands for elements of an orthonormal basis), a column vector. Differently from the classical bit, the qubit can be in a *superposition* of the two basic states written as $\alpha|0\rangle + \beta|1\rangle$, or

$$\begin{pmatrix} \alpha \\ \beta \end{pmatrix}$$

with $|\alpha|^2 + |\beta|^2 = 1$. Intuitively, one can think that a qubit can exist as a 0, a 1, or simultaneously as both 0 and 1, with numerical coefficient (i.e., the probability amplitudes α and β) which determines the probability of each state. The quantum superposition phenomena is responsible for the so called "quantum parallelism."

Operations acting on those *isolated* or *pure* quantum states are linear operations, more specifically *unitary matrices* S. A matrix S is called *unitary* if $S^*S = I$, where S^* is the adjoint of S, and I is the identity. Essentially, those unitary transformations act on the quantum states by changing their probability amplitudes, without loss of information (i.e., they are reversible). The application of a unitary transformation to a state vector is given by usual matrix multiplication.

Unfortunately in this model of quantum computation, it is difficult or impossible to deal formally with another class of quantum effects, including measurements, decoherence, or noise.

Measurements are critical to some quantum algorithms, as they are the only way to extract *classical* information from quantum states.

A *measurement* operation projects a quantum state like $\alpha|0\rangle + \beta|1\rangle$ onto the basis $|0\rangle,|1\rangle$. The outcome of the measurement is not deterministic and it is given by the probability amplitude, i.e., the probability that the state after the measurement is $|0\rangle$ is $|\alpha|^2$ and the probability that the state is $|1\rangle$ is $|\beta|^2$. If the value of the qubit is initially unknown, than there is no way to determine α and β with that single measurement, as the measurement may *disturb* the state. But, *after* the measurement, the qubit is in a *known* state; either $|0\rangle$ or $|1\rangle$. In fact, the situation is even more complicated: measuring part of a quantum state collapses not only the measured part but any other part of the global state with which it is *entangled*. In an entangled state, two or more qubits have to be described with reference to each other, even though the individuals may be spatially separated [1].

There are several ways to deal with measurements in quantum computation, as summarized in our previous work [3]. To deal formally and elegantly with measurements, the state of the computation is represented using a *density matrix* and the operations are represented using *superoperators* [1]. Using these notions, the *projections* necessary to express measurements become expressible within the model.

---

[1] For a more detailed explanation about entanglement, see [10].

Intuitively, density matrices can be understood as a statistical perspective of the state vector. In the density matrix formalism, a quantum state that used to be modeled by a vector $|v\rangle$ is now modeled by its outer product $|v\rangle\langle v|$, where $\langle v|$ is the row vector representing the adjoint (or dual) of $|v\rangle$. For instance, the state of a quantum bit $|v\rangle = \frac{1}{\sqrt{2}}|0\rangle + \frac{1}{\sqrt{2}}|1\rangle$ is represented by the density matrix:

$$\begin{pmatrix} \frac{1}{2} & -\frac{1}{2} \\ -\frac{1}{2} & \frac{1}{2} \end{pmatrix}$$

Note that the main diagonal shows the classical probability distribution of basic quantum states, that is, these state has $\frac{1}{2}$ of probability to be $|0\rangle$ and $\frac{1}{2}$ of probability to be $|1\rangle$.

However, the appeal of density matrices is that they can represent states other than the pure ones above. In particular if we perform a measurement on the state represented above, we should get $|0\rangle$ with probability $1/2$ or $|1\rangle$ with probability $1/2$. This information, which cannot be expressed using vectors, can be represented by the following density matrix:

$$\begin{pmatrix} 1/2 & 0 \\ 0 & 0 \end{pmatrix} + \begin{pmatrix} 0 & 0 \\ 0 & 1/2 \end{pmatrix} = \begin{pmatrix} 1/2 & 0 \\ 0 & 1/2 \end{pmatrix}$$

Such a density matrix represents a *mixed state* which corresponds to the sum (and then normalization) of the density matrices for the two results of the observation.

The two kinds of quantum operations, namely unitary transformation and measurement, can both be expressed with respect to density matrices [4]. Those operations now mapping density matrices to density matrices are called *superoperators*. A unitary transformation S maps a pure quantum state $|u\rangle$ to $S|u\rangle$. Thus, it maps a pure density matrix $|u\rangle\langle u|$ to $S|u\rangle\langle u|S^*$. Moreover, a unitary transformation extends linearly to mixed states, and thus, it takes any mixed density matrix A to SAS^*.

As one can observe in the resulting matrix above, to execute a measurement corresponds to setting a certain region of the input density matrix to zero.

In next section, we present a *calculus* to express general quantum computations over mixed states.

3   The Quantum Arrow Calculus for Mixed States

In this section we present the *quantum arrow calculus for mixed states*. The calculus for mixed states is a generalisation of the calculus presented in [6], and gives a *functional programming language for general quantum computations*.

3.1   The Background

As first noted in [11] the pure model of quantum computation based on vectors and linear operators can be expressed as monads [7]. We build on that and establish in [3] that the superoperators used to express mixed quantum computations (with measurements) are an instance of the category-theoretic concept of arrows [9], a generalization of *monads* [7] and *idioms* [12]. Originally, arrows were introduced to the programming approach by extending simply-typed lambda calculus with three constants satisfying nine laws. Translating this insight to a practical programming paradigm has been difficult however. On one hand, directly using arrows is highly non-intuitive, requiring programming in the so-called "point-free" style where intermediate computations are manipulated without giving them names. Furthermore reasoning about arrow programs uses nine, somewhat idiosyncratic laws.

In recent work, Lindley *et. al.* [8] present the *arrow calculus*, which is a calculus version for the original presentation of arrows [9]. The arrow calculus augment the simply typed lambda calculus with four constructs satisfying five laws. Two of these constructs resemble function abstraction and application, and satisfy familiar beta and eta laws. The remaining two constructs resemble the unit and bind of a monad, and satisfy left unit, right unit, and associativity laws. Basically, using the arrow calculus we can understand arrows through classic well-known patterns.

Hence, in [6] we propose to express quantum computations using the arrow calculus extended with monadic constructions. We show that quantum programming can be expressed using well-understood and familiar classical patterns for programming in the presence of computational effects. We define the calculus in three levels. We start with simply-typed lambda calculus, then we add the monadic constructions of Moggi's computational lambda calculus [7] to express pure quantum computations, and finally we add the constructions of the arrow calculus [8] to express mixed quantum computations.

However, as motivated in the introduction, we consider in this work the mixed state approach and define a simpler and more elegant version of the quantum arrow calculus. In contrast with the previous defined quantum arrow calculus, the arrow calculus for mixed states goes directly from classical states to mixed states. Going directly to mixed states turns the calculus simpler, with less constructions and, more interestingly, turns the set of equations simpler and intuitive.

3.2   The Calculus

We construct the calculus for mixed states in two levels: we start with simply-typed lambda calculus with booleans, and then we add the arrow calculus constructions to express general quantum computations. Additionally, to encompass all quantum features we add sum of arrows to represent the probability distribution generated by superpositions, and scalar product to represent the probability of each state in the mixture.

The entire calculus is shown in Figure 1. Let A, B, C range over types, L, M, N range over terms, and Γ, Δ range over environments. A type judgment $\Gamma \vdash M : A$ indicates that in environment Γ term M has type A. As presented in the arrow calculus [8], we are using a Curry formulation, eliding types from terms.

Syntax for classical terms

Types $A, B, C ::= \textbf{Bool} \mid A \times B \mid A \to B$

Terms $L, M, N ::= x \mid \textsf{True} \mid \textsf{False} \mid (M, N) \mid \textsf{fst}\ L \mid \textsf{snd}\ L \mid \lambda x.N \mid L\ M$
$\qquad\qquad\quad \textsf{let}\ x = M\ \textsf{in}\ N \mid \textsf{if}\ L\ \textsf{then}\ M\ \textsf{else}\ N$

Environments $\Gamma, \Delta \quad ::= x_1 : A_1, \ldots, x_n : A_n$

Classical Types

$$\frac{}{\emptyset \vdash \textsf{False} : \textbf{Bool}} \qquad \frac{}{\emptyset \vdash \textsf{True} : \textbf{Bool}} \qquad \frac{(x : A) \in \Gamma}{\Gamma \vdash x : A}$$

$$\frac{\Gamma \vdash M : A \quad \Gamma \vdash N : B}{\Gamma \vdash (M, N) : A \times B} \qquad \frac{\Gamma \vdash L : A \times B}{\Gamma \vdash \textsf{fst}\ L : A} \qquad \frac{\Gamma \vdash L : A \times B}{\Gamma \vdash \textsf{snd}\ L : B}$$

$$\frac{\Gamma, x : A \vdash N : B}{\Gamma \vdash \lambda x.N : A \to B} \qquad \frac{\Gamma \vdash L : A \to B \quad \Gamma \vdash M : A}{\Gamma \vdash L\ M : B}$$

$$\frac{\Gamma \vdash M : A \quad \Gamma, x : A \vdash N : B}{\Gamma \vdash \textsf{let}\ x = M\ \textsf{in}\ N : B} \qquad \frac{\Gamma \vdash L : \textbf{Bool} \quad \Gamma \vdash M, N : B}{\Gamma \vdash \textsf{if}\ L\ \textsf{then}\ M\ \textsf{else}\ N : B}$$

Syntax for general quantum computations over mixed states

Probabilities $p, q \in \mathbb{R}$

Typedef $\textbf{Dens}\ A = (A, A) \to \mathbb{C} \qquad \textbf{Super}\ A\ B = (A, A) \to \textbf{Dens}\ B$

Types $A, B, C ::= \ldots \mid \textbf{Dens}\ A \mid \textbf{Super}\ A\ B$

Terms $L, M, N ::= \ldots \mid \lambda^\bullet x.Q$

Commands $P, Q, R ::= L \bullet M \mid [M] \mid \textsf{let}_A\ x = P\ \textsf{in}\ Q \mid \textsf{trL} \mid$
$\qquad\qquad\qquad P \mathbin{+\!\!+} Q \mid (p, q) * [\textsf{if}\ L\ \textsf{then}\ M\ \textsf{else}\ N] \mid \textsf{zeroarrow}$

Arrow Types

$$\frac{\Gamma; x : A \vdash Q!\ \textbf{Dens}\ B}{\Gamma \vdash \lambda^\bullet x.Q : \textbf{Super}\ A\ B} \qquad \frac{\Gamma \vdash L : \textbf{Super}\ A\ B \quad \Gamma; \Delta \vdash M : A}{\Gamma; \Delta \vdash L \bullet M!\ \textbf{Dens}\ B}$$

$$\frac{\Gamma, \Delta \vdash M : A}{\Gamma; \Delta \vdash [M]!\ \textbf{Dens}\ A} \qquad \frac{\Gamma; \Delta \vdash P!\ \textbf{Dens}\ A \quad \Gamma; \Delta, x : A \vdash Q!\ \textbf{Dens}\ B}{\Gamma; \Delta \vdash \textsf{let}_A\ x = P\ \textsf{in}\ Q!\ \textbf{Dens}\ B}$$

$$\frac{}{\Gamma; \Delta \vdash \textsf{trL} !\ \textbf{Dens}\ B} \qquad \frac{}{\Gamma; \Delta \vdash \textsf{zeroarrow} !\ \textbf{Dens}\ A}$$

$$\frac{\Gamma; \Delta \vdash P, Q !\ \textbf{Dens}\ A}{\Gamma; \Delta \vdash P \mathbin{+\!\!+} Q !\ \textbf{Dens}\ (A)} \qquad \frac{\Gamma; \Delta \vdash [\textsf{if}\ L\ \textsf{then}\ M\ \textsf{else}\ N] !\ \textbf{Dens}\ A}{\Gamma; \Delta \vdash (p, q) * [\textsf{if}\ L\ \textsf{then}\ M\ \textsf{else}\ N] !\ \textbf{Dens}\ A}$$

Fig. 1. The Quantum Arrow Calculus for Mixed States

We start the language with the constructs from simply-typed lambda calculus with booleans, products, let and if.

The presentation of the constructs for general quantum computations over mixed states begins with type definitions (i.e, type synonyms) for convenience. Type **Dens** A stands for density matrices. Type **Super** $A\ B$ means a superoperator mapping a density matrix of type A to a density matrix of type B.

As inherited from the arrow calculus [8], there are two syntactic categories. Quantum terms are ranged over by L, M, N, and commands leading to mixed states are ranged over by P, Q, R. The new term form is an arrow abstraction $\lambda^\bullet x.Q$ representing a superoperator, i.e., a probabilistic function over mixed states. There are seven command forms: superoperator application $L \bullet M$, arrow unit $[M]$, the constructor for mixed states, composition $\mathsf{let}_A\ x = P$ in Q, the partial trace superoperator trL, sum of superoperators $P \mathbin{+\!\!+} Q$, scalar product $(p,\ q) * [\mathsf{if}\ L\ \mathsf{then}\ M\ \mathsf{else}\ N]$, and the failure superoperator $\mathsf{zeroarrow}$.

In addition to the term typing judgment $\Gamma \vdash M : A$ there is also a command typing judgment $\Gamma; \Delta \vdash P!\ \mathbf{Dens}\ A$. An important feature of the arrow calculus is that the command type judgment has two environments, Γ and Δ, where variables in Γ come from ordinary lambda abstractions $\lambda x.N$, while variables in Δ come from superoperators $\lambda^\bullet x.Q$ (i.e, arrow abstraction).

The superoperator abstraction converts a mixed state into a term. This construct closely resembles function abstraction, save that the body Q is a mixed state, and the bound variable x goes into the second environment (separated from the first by a semicolon).

Application of a superoperator is given by $L \bullet M!\ \mathbf{Dens}\ B$, embedding a term (superoperator) into a command (mixed state). Arrow application closely resembles function application. The arrow to be applied is denoted by a term, not a command; this is because there is no way to apply an arrow that is itself yielded. This is why there are two different environments, Γ and Δ: variables in Γ may denote arrows that are applied to arguments, but variables in Δ may not.

Unit, $[M]!\ \mathbf{Dens}\ A$, promotes a term to a mixed state. Note that in the hypothesis there is a term judgment with one environment (i.e, there is a comma between Γ and Δ), while in the conclusion there is a command judgment with two environments (i.e, there is a semicolon between Γ and Δ).

Using the command to compose superoperators let_A, the value returned by a superoperator may be bound.

To encompass all quantum features we add sum of arrows $(+\!\!+)$, to represent the probability distribution generated by superpositions, and the composed scalar product (p, q) to represent the probability of each state in the mixture. The composed scalar product is introduced together with the if, as p is the probability of the first branch and q is the probability of the second branch. Semantically, this corresponds to the density matrix for a base value qubit (True or False). The $\mathsf{zeroarrow}$ construct represents the failure superoperator.

We have also add a partial trace superoperator, trL, which *traces out* or *projects* part of the quantum state. In the pure model, this operation is not allowed, as it requires a measurement before tracing. It is called trLeft as it traces out (or sends to trash) the left part of the quantum state.

Lastly, it is worth to comment that we do not need a specific *measurement* superoperator, as we are directly working with the observer perspective of the quantum system. Any operation in our language denotes a probabilistic function computed by quantum operations. As discussed in [1] this solves the problem of subroutines in standard (or pure) models of quantum computation, as the function computed by any pure circuit or operation is at the end a probabilistic one, and the standard theories allow pure states only.

4 Reasoning about Quantum Programs

In this section we introduce a set of equations/laws for the quantum language presented in section above. Additionally, we express three well know quantum algorithms using the quantum arrow calculus for mixed states, and show how the combined set of laws, from classical lambda calculus and arrows can be used to equational reasoning about them.

4.1 The Equations

We show the complete set of equations in Figure 2. We start with the well know equations for simply-typed lambda calculus with products, if and let.

Following, we show the laws from the arrow calculus [8]. Arrow abstraction and application satisfy beta and eta laws, $(\beta^{\leadsto})$ and $(\eta^{\leadsto})$, while arrow unit and bind satisfy left unit, right unit, and associativity laws, (left), (right), and (assoc). The beta law equates the application of an abstraction to a bind; substitution is not part of beta, but instead appears in the left unit law. The (assoc) law has the usual side condition, that x is not free in R.

Then we add our equations for sum of arrows, $+\!\!\!+$. The *arrowplus* is a generalisation of the monadic construction *monadplus* [13]. The intuition behind these laws is the same for the monadic ones, i.e., $+\!\!\!+$ is a disjunction of goals and let is a conjunction of goals. The conjunction evaluates the goals from left-to-right and is not symmetric.

Finally, we define the equations for the composed scalar product: p_1 is the simple let_A with scalar products, p_2 stands for a distributive law for composed scalar products, it just mimics the usual distributive law for products.

We claim soundness of the *arrowplus* equations using the methodology presented in [8] for defining the calculus extensions for specialised arrows. That is, soundness can be proved by showing that the equation holds for the translation of the construction in the calculus to classic arrows [9]. The translation of $+\!\!\!+$ is straightforward: $[P +\!\!\!+ Q] = [P]$ *arrowPlus* $[Q]$, where *arrowPlus* is defined in [9].

Soundness for the composed scalar products can be easily showed by using simple products.

4.2 Hadamard

To exemplify the use of the constructions, consider, for example, the hadamard quantum gate, which is the source of superpositions. For instance, hadamard applied to $|False\rangle^2$ returns $|False\rangle + |True\rangle$, and applied to $|True\rangle$ returns $|False\rangle - |True\rangle$. In our mixed calculus, is expected that the output of any quantum program is a probabilistic one. Hence hadamard applied to $|False\rangle$ would give $|False\rangle$

---

[2] Using the booleans as the basis for the vector space.

Classical Laws

(β_1^x)	fst (M, N)	$= M$
(β_2^x)	snd (M, N)	$= N$
(η^x)	(fst L, snd L)	$= L$
$(\beta^\to)$	$(\lambda x.N)M$	$= N[x := M]$
$(\eta^\to)$	$\lambda x.(L\ x)$	$= L$
(let)	let $x = M$ in N	$= N[x := M]$
(β_1^{if})	if True then M else N	$= M$
(β_2^{if})	if False then M else N	$= N$

(comm) if (if x then M else N) then L else T = if x then (if M then L else T)
else (if N then L else T)

(comm) let $x =$ (if y then M else N) in L = if y then (let $x = M$ in L)
else (let $x = N$ in L)

Arrow Laws

$(\beta^{\leadsto})$	$(\lambda^\bullet x.Q) \bullet M$	$= Q[x := M]$
$(\eta^{\leadsto})$	$\lambda^\bullet x.(L \bullet [x])$	$= L$
(left_A)	$\text{let}_A\ x = [M]$ in Q	$= Q[x := M]$
(right_A)	$\text{let}_A\ x = P$ in $[x]$	$= P$

(assoc_A) $\text{let}_A\ y = (\text{let}_A\ x = P$ in $Q)$ in $R = \text{let}_A\ x = P$ in $(\text{let}_A\ y = Q$ in $R)$

ArrowPlus Laws

(ap_1)	zeroarrow $+\!\!+\ P$	$= P$
(ap_2)	$P +\!\!+$ zeroarrow	$= P$
(ap_3)	$P +\!\!+ (Q +\!\!+ R)$	$= (P +\!\!+ Q) +\!\!+ R$
(ap_4)	$\text{let}_A\ x =$ zeroarrow in P	$=$ zeroarrow
(ap_5)	$\text{let}_A\ x = (P +\!\!+ Q)$ in $R = (\text{let}_A\ x = P$ in $R) +\!\!+ (\text{let}_A\ x = Q$ in $R)$	

Products Laws

(p_1)	$\text{let}_A\ x = (\kappa, \iota) * [M]$ in Q	$= (\kappa, \iota) * Q[x := M]$
(p_2)	$(p_1, p_2) * ((p_3, p_4) * P +\!\!+ (p_5, p_6) * Q)$	$= (p_1 * p_3, p_2 * p_4) * P +\!\!+ (p_1 * p_5, p_2 * p_6) * Q$
(p_3)	$((p_1, p_2) * P +\!\!+ (p_3, p_4) * P)$	$= (p_1 + p_3, p_2 + p_4) * P$
(p_4)	$(0, 0) * P$	$=$ zeroarrow

Fig. 2. Equations for the Quantum Arrow Calculus

with probability $1/2$ and $|\text{True}\rangle$ with probability $1/2$, and the same for hadamard applied to $|\text{True}\rangle$. Then, we define hadamard as

hadamard $= \lambda^\bullet x.\ (1/2, 1/2) * [$if x then True else False$] +\!\!+$
$(1/2, 1/2) * [$if x then False else True$]$: **Super Bool Bool**

where we have used the *arrowplus* construction, $+\!\!+$, to represent the probability distribution generated by the superpositions which hadamard generates. It is clear from the definition that if we apply hadamard to $|\text{False}\rangle$ we would get $1/2[\text{True}] + +1/2[\text{False}]$, and the same for application to $|\text{True}\rangle$, which is the right behavior for a probabilistic function computing the *output* of standard quantum gates/circuits.

Obviously, this probabilistic behavior of hadamard is not reversible. As explained in [1] the probabilistic functions solve the problem of subroutines in quantum computation affecting the state in a non-unitary manner.

For this reason, if we apply hadamard again to the output mixture, we would get the same result again. The idea is that we are going to apply hadamard to $1/2[\text{True}]$ and to $1/2[\text{False}]$. This would give $(1/4[\text{True}]+1/4[\text{False}])+(1/4[\text{True}]+1/4[\text{False}]) = 1/2[\text{True}]+1/2[\text{False}]$.

A program which applies hadamard twice is written as:

$$\lambda^{\bullet}x.\text{let}_A \; w = \text{hadamard} \bullet x \text{ in hadamard} \bullet w \; : \; \textbf{Super Bool Bool}$$

The proof goes as follows:

$\lambda^{\bullet}x.\text{let}_A \; w = \quad \text{hadamard} \bullet x \text{ in hadamard} \bullet w$
$\equiv^{\beta^{\rightsquigarrow}}$
$\lambda^{\bullet}x.\text{let}_A \; w = \quad (1/2, 1/2) * [\text{if } x \text{ then True else False}] \;+\!\!+$
$\qquad\qquad\qquad (1/2, 1/2) * [\text{if } x \text{ then False else True}]$
$\qquad\qquad\qquad \text{in hadamard} \bullet w$
$\equiv^{\text{ap}_5}$
$\lambda^{\bullet}x.(\text{let}_A \; w = \quad (1/2, 1/2) * [\text{if } x \text{ then True else False}] \text{ in hadamard} \bullet w) \;+\!\!+$
$\quad (\text{let}_A \; w = \quad (1/2, 1/2) * [\text{if } x \text{ then False else True}] \text{ in hadamard} \bullet w)$
$\equiv^{q_1}$
$\lambda^{\bullet}x.(1/2, 1/2)* \;((1/2, 1/2) * [\text{if (if } x \text{ then True else False) then True else False}])$
$\qquad\qquad\qquad\quad +\!\!+ (1/2, 1/2) * [\text{if (if } x \text{ then True else False) then False else True}])$
$+\!\!+ (1/2, 1/2)* \;((1/2, 1/2) * [\text{if (if } x \text{ then False else True) then True else False}])$
$\qquad\qquad\qquad\quad +\!\!+ (1/2, 1/2) * [\text{if (if } x \text{ then False else True) then False else True}])$
$\equiv^{\text{comm}}$
$\lambda^{\bullet}x.(1/2, 1/2)* \;((1/2, 1/2) * [\text{if } x \text{ then True else False}])$
$\qquad\qquad\qquad\quad +\!\!+ (1/2, 1/2) * [\text{if } x \text{ then False else True}])$
$+\!\!+ (1/2, 1/2)* \;((1/2, 1/2) * [\text{if } x \text{ then False else True}])$
$\qquad\qquad\qquad\quad +\!\!+ (1/2, 1/2) * [\text{if } x \text{ then True else False}])$
$\equiv^{p_2}$

$\qquad\qquad \lambda^{\bullet}x.(1/4, 1/4)* [\text{if } x \text{ then True else False}]) \;+\!\!+$
$\qquad\qquad\qquad (1/4, 1/4)* [\text{if } x \text{ then False else True}]) \;+\!\!+$
$\qquad\qquad\qquad (1/4, 1/4)* [\text{if } x \text{ then False else True}]) \;+\!\!+$
$\qquad\qquad\qquad (1/4, 1/4)* [\text{if } x \text{ then True else False}])$

$\qquad\qquad \equiv$

$\qquad\qquad \lambda^{\bullet}x.(1/2, 1/2)* [\text{if } x \text{ then True else False}]) \;+\!\!+$
$\qquad\qquad\qquad (1/2, 1/2)* [\text{if } x \text{ then False else True}])$

As one can note, the proof follows in a strikingly attractive way, very similar to the way we make proofs in classical functional programming languages. We start using the β-equation for arrows, then we use the let_A equation for *arrowplus* as a conjunction of disjunctions. Finally, we just simplify things using sums and products.

4.3   Generating Entangled Pairs

The quantum state of a system is said to be entangled when it arises from the superposition of states of identifiable correlated subsystems that cannot be factorized [14]. Entanglement is a quantum mechanical feature without a classical analogue. Essentially, if we have a pair of entangled qubits, a local interaction on one of the particle pair induces a change in the quantum state of its partner. Entanglement is an important quantum characteristic for quantum computation. Several quantum algorithms are deeply based on that, such as quantum teleportation [15], super dense coding [16], quantum cryptography [17], quantum algorithms for distributed systems [18], etc.

A traditional way for generating entangled pairs is through application of a controlled not operation to a control state in superposition. The controlled not receives two qubits as arguments and behaves as follows: if the first qubit (i.e., the control) is True then not is applied to the second one, otherwise, nothing happens. Bellow we show the implementation of Cnot in our quantum calculus.

$$\text{Cnot}: \textbf{Super}\,(\textbf{Bool}, \textbf{Bool})\,(\textbf{Bool}, \textbf{Bool})$$
$$\text{Cnot} = \lambda^\bullet(x, y).\,(1,1) * [\text{if } x \text{ then } (\text{True}, \text{not } y) \text{ else } (\text{False}, y)]$$

Then, to generate an entangled pair we just need to build a quantum program which receives two qubits, applies hadamard to the first (i.e., to the control) to make it in a superposed state, and then applies Cnot.

$$\text{epr}: \textbf{Super}\,(\textbf{Bool}, \textbf{Bool})\,(\textbf{Bool}, \textbf{Bool})$$
$$\text{epr} = \lambda^\bullet(x, y).\text{let}_A\ w = \text{hadamard} \bullet x \text{ in Cnot} \bullet (w, y)$$

The proof shows the program behaves exactly as expected, generating entangled pairs.

$$\lambda^\bullet(x, y).\text{let}_A\ w = \quad \text{hadamard} \bullet x \text{ in Cnot} \bullet (w, y)$$
$$\equiv^{\beta^\leadsto}$$
$$\lambda^\bullet(x, y).\text{let}_A\ w = \quad (1/2, 1/2) * [\text{if } x \text{ then True else False}] \ +\!\!+$$
$$(1/2, 1/2) * [\text{if } x \text{ then False else True}]$$
$$\text{in Cnot} \bullet (w, y)$$
$$\equiv^{\text{ap}_5}$$
$$\lambda^\bullet(x, y).(\text{let}_A\ w = (1/2, 1/2) * [\text{if } x \text{ then True else False}] \text{ in Cnot} \bullet (w, y)) \ +\!\!+$$
$$(\text{let}_A\ w = (1/2, 1/2) * [\text{if } x \text{ then False else True}] \text{ in Cnot} \bullet (w, y))$$
$$\equiv^{q_1}$$

$$\lambda^\bullet(x, y).(1/2, 1/2) \quad *((1,1) * [\text{if (if } x \text{ then True else False)}$$
$$\text{then } (\text{True}, \text{not } w) \text{ else } (\text{False}, w)]) \ +\!\!+$$
$$(1/2, 1/2) \quad *((1,1) * [\text{if (if } x \text{ then False else True)}$$
$$\text{then } (\text{True}, \text{not } w) \text{ else } (\text{False}, w)])$$
$$\equiv^{\text{comm}}$$
$$\lambda^\bullet(x, y).(1/2, 1/2) \quad *((1,1) * [\text{if } x \text{ then } (\text{True}, \text{not } w) \text{ else } (\text{False}, w)] \ +\!\!+$$
$$(1/2, 1/2) \quad *((1,1) * [\text{if } x \text{ then } (\text{False}, w) \text{ else } (\text{True}, \text{not } w)]$$
$$\equiv^{P_2}$$
$$\lambda^\bullet(x, y).(1/2, 1/2)* [\text{if } x \text{ then } (\text{True}, \text{not } w) \text{ else } (\text{False}, w)]) \ +\!\!+$$
$$(1/2, 1/2)* [\text{if } x \text{ then } (\text{False}, w) \text{ else } (\text{True}, \text{not } w)])$$

4.4   Teleportation

A traditional example of quantum algorithm which requires a measurement operation is the quantum teleportation [15]. It allows the transmission of a qubit to a partner with whom is shared an entangled pair. The correctness of this algorithm can showed by proving that it is equivalent to identity. This is an important result in the field of quantum computation.

We call the two partners of the teleportation algorithm, Alice and Bob. Alice has a qubit, which is going to be teleported to Bob. To realize this task it is necessary that the two partners share an *entangled* pair of qubits before the communication. The idea of the algorithm is that Alice interacts the qubit to be teleported with her part of the pair. In this way, some information about the qubit is passed via entanglement to the Bob's part of the pair. Alice then measures her two qubits and send this information to Bob, who is going to recuperate the qubit through application of some simple quantum operations. Therefore, the algorithm works with three qubits:

$$\text{Tel} : \text{Super} (\textbf{Bool}, \textbf{Bool}, \textbf{Bool}) \; \textbf{Bool}$$
$$\text{Tel} = \lambda^{\bullet}(x, y, z). \; \text{let} \; (y', z') = \text{epr} \bullet (y, z) \; \text{in}$$
$$\text{let} \; (x', y'') = \text{Alice} \bullet (x, y') \; \text{in Bob} \; (x', y'', z')$$

where y and z stand for the entangled pair: y is the Alice's part and z is the Bob's part. The qubit to be teleported is represented by x. Alice interacts the qubit x with her part of the entangled pair, y, via the following procedure:

$$\text{Alice} : \; \text{Super} (\textbf{Bool}, \textbf{Bool}) \; (\textbf{Bool}, \textbf{Bool})$$
$$\text{Alice} = \lambda^{\bullet}(x, y). \; \text{let} \; (x', y') = \text{Cnot} \bullet (x, y) \; \text{in} \; (\text{Had} \bullet x', y')$$

where Cnot and Had are the quantum controlled not operation, and the operator generating superpositions, respectively. Both implementations are showed in section above. It is interesting to note that none specific measurement operation is needed at the end of Alice's subroutine. This is because we are already working with the mixed state of the system.

Bob then interacts the result of Alice's procedure, x and y below, with his part of the entangled pair, z.

$$\text{Bob} : \textbf{Super} (\textbf{Bool}, \textbf{Bool}, \textbf{Bool}) \; \textbf{Bool}$$
$$\text{Bob} = \lambda^{\bullet}(x, y, z). \; \text{let} \; (y', z') = \text{Cnot} \bullet (y, z) \; \text{in}$$
$$\text{let} \; (x', y'') = (\text{Cz} \bullet (x, y')) \; \text{in trL} \bullet ((y'', z'), x')$$

Besides the Cnot, he also uses a controlled *phase* operation, Cz. The behavior of Cz is captured by the following program:

Cz : **Super** (**Bool**, **Bool**) (**Bool**, **Bool**)
$\text{Cz} = \lambda^{\bullet}(x, y). \; ((1, 1), (1, 1)) * [\text{if } x \; \text{then (if } y \text{ then (True, True) else (True, False))}$
$\text{else (if } y \text{ then (False, True) else (False, False))}]$

The proof of correctness about the behavior of teleportation follows the same style of the proofs presented in sections above. Lets structure the proof. We start reasoning about Alice's subroutine.

$$\lambda^\bullet(x,y).\ \mathsf{let}\ (x',y') = \mathsf{Cnot}\ \bullet(x,y)\ \mathsf{in}\ (\mathsf{Had}\bullet x',y')$$
$$\equiv^{\widetilde{\beta}}$$
$$\lambda^\bullet(x,y).\ \mathsf{let}_A\ w = (1,1)* \quad [\mathsf{if}\ x\ \mathsf{then}\ (\mathsf{True},\mathsf{not}\ y)\ \mathsf{else}\ (\mathsf{False},y)]$$
$$\mathsf{in}\ (\mathsf{Had}\bullet(\mathsf{fst}\ w),\ \mathsf{snd}\ w)$$

One can easily follow the proof and conclude that the hadamard operation is going to be applied to identity over x. Then we can do the same for Bob:

$$\lambda^\bullet(x,y,z).\ \mathsf{let}\ (y',z') = \mathsf{Cnot}\ \ \bullet(y,z)$$
$$\mathsf{in}\ \mathsf{let}\ (x',y'') = (\mathsf{Cz}\ \bullet(x,y'))\ \mathsf{in}\ \mathsf{trL}\bullet((y'',z'),x')$$
$$\equiv^{\widetilde{\beta}}$$
$$\lambda^\bullet(x,y).\ \ \mathsf{let}_A\ w = (1,1)* \quad [\mathsf{if}\ x\ \mathsf{then}\ (\mathsf{True},\mathsf{not}\ y)\ \mathsf{else}\ (\mathsf{False},y)]$$
$$\mathsf{in}\ \mathsf{let}\ (x',y'') = (\mathsf{Cz}\ \bullet(x,y'))\ \mathsf{in}\ \mathsf{trL}\bullet((y'',z'),x')$$

and substitute the results in the Tel subroutine. This is going to show that it returns identity over z.

5 Related Work

In [1] it is defined a mathematical *framework* for quantum circuits with mixed states. Aharonov *et al.* present the concept of general probabilistic subroutines (functions) computed by standard quantum circuits. This definition solves the problem of using subroutines in standard (or pure) quantum circuits, as the function computed by any circuit is a probabilistic one, and the standard theory of quantum circuits allows pure states only.

Zuliani [2] built over Aharonov *et al.*'s work and proposed a programming approach based on mixed states. The author extends the qGCL [19], which is a quantum version for Dijkstra's guarded command language, to work with mixed states. The extension is more like a mathematical specification language for quantum programs and no equational reasoning techniques are claimed.

Concerning the subject of functional quantum programming languages we can cite the following related works.

In [20] we have proposed equational reasoning techniques, however for *pure* quantum programs.

Also, in [21] the author presents a quantum lambda calculus based on linear logic, but just for pure quantum computations.

In very recent work [22] the authors set up a System F type system for the Linear Algebraic λ-Calculus. The aim of this work is to seek for a *quantum physical logic* related with probabilistic systems.

6 Conclusion

We have presented a functional programming language for quantum computation over mixed states. Every quantum construct of the language semantically denotes a probabilistic function computed by pure or general quantum operations. More interestingly, we show the first framework proposing *equational reasoning* about quantum computations over states representing the observer perspective of the quantum system.

As future work we plan to investigate the relation between arrows and comonads [23]. It seems that the side effect produced by measurements, destroying superpositions, can be expressed using the dual concept of monads. Moreover, the study about higher order, recursiveness and other quantum data types is let for future work.

References

1. Aharonov, D., Kitaev, A., Nisan, N.: Quantum circuits with mixed states. In: Proceedings of the thirtieth annual ACM symposium on Theory of computing, pp. 20–30. ACM Press, New York (1998)
2. Zuliani, P.: Quantum programming with mixed states. Electron. Notes Theor. Comput. Sci. 170, 185–199 (2007)
3. Vizzotto, J.K., Altenkirch, T., Sabry, A.: Structuring quantum effects: Superoperators as arrows. Journal of Mathematical Structures in Computer Science: special issue in quantum programming languages 16, 453–468 (2006)
4. Selinger, P.: Towards a quantum programming language. Journal of Mathematical Structures in Computer Science: special issue in quantum programming languages 16, 527–586 (2006)
5. Raussendorf, R., Browne, D.E., Briegel, H.J.: Measurement-based quantum computation with cluster states. Physical Review A 68, 022312 (2003)
6. Vizzotto, J.K., DuBois, A.R., Sabry, A.: The arrow calculus as a quantum programming language. FoLLI/LNAI Lecture Notes in Computer Science, vol. 5514, pp. 379–393. Springer, Heidelberg (2009)
7. Moggi, E.: Computational lambda-calculus and monads. In: Proceedings of the Fourth Annual Symposium on Logic in computer science, pp. 14–23. IEEE Press, Los Alamitos (1989)
8. Lindley, S., Wadler, P., Yallop, J.: The arrow calculus. Technical Report EDI-INF-RR-1258, The University of Edinburgh, School of Informatics (June 2008)
9. Hughes, J.: Generalising monads to arrows. Science of Computer Programming 37, 67–111 (2000)
10. Nielsen, M.A., Chuang, I.L.: Quantum Computation and Quantum Information. Cambridge University Press, Cambridge (2000)
11. Mu, S.C., Bird, R.: Functional quantum programming. In: Second Asian Workshop on Programming Languages and Systems, KAIST, Korea (December 2001)
12. Mcbride, C., Paterson, R.: Applicative programming with effects. J. Funct. Program. 18(1), 1–13 (2008)
13. HaskellWiki: MonadPlus (2005), http://www.haskell.org/hawiki/MonadPlus
14. Perez, R.B.: Entanglement and quantum computation: an overview. Technical Report ORNL/TM-2000/64, Oak Ridge - National Laboratory (December 2000)
15. Bennett, C.H., Brassard, G., Crepeau, C., Jozsa, R., Peres, A., Wootters, W.: Teleporting an unknown quantum state via dual classical and EPR channels. Phys. Rev. Lett., 1895–1899 (1993)
16. Bennett, C.H., Wiesner, S.J.: Communication via one- and two-particle operators on einstein–podolsky–rosen states. Phys. Rev. Lett. 69, 2881–2884 (1992)
17. Ekert, A., Palma, G.: Quantum cryptography with interferometric quantum entanglement. Journal of Modern Optics 41, 2413–2424 (1994)

18. D'Hondt, E., Panangaden, P.: The computational power of the W and GHZ states. Quantum Information and Computation 6(2), 173–183 (2006)
19. Sanders, J.W., Zuliani, P.: Quantum programming. In: Mathematics of Program Construction, pp. 80–99. Springer, Heidelberg (1999)
20. Altenkirch, T., Grattage, J., Vizzotto, J.K., Sabry, A.: An algebra of pure quantum programming. Electron. Notes Theor. Comput. Sci. 170, 23–47 (2007)
21. Tonder, A.v.: A lambda calculus for quantum computation. SIAM J. Comput. 33(5), 1109–1135 (2004)
22. Arrighi, P., Díaz-Caro, A.: Scalar system F for linear-algebraic λ-calculus: Towards a quantum physical logic. In: Proceedings of the 6th International Workshop on Quantum Physics and Logic, Oxford, UK, pp. 206–215 (2009)
23. Uustalu, T., Vene, V.: The essence of dataflow programming. In: Central European Functional Programming School, pp. 135–167 (2006)

A Simple and General Theoretical Account for Abstract Types*

Abstract. A common approach to hiding implementation details is through the use of abstract types. In this paper, we present a simple theoretical account of abstract types that make use of a recently developed notion of conditional type equality. This is in contrast to most of the existing theoretical accounts of abstract types, which rely on existential types (or similar variants). In addition, we show that this new approach to abstract types opens a promising avenue to the design and implementation of module systems that can effectively support large-scale programming.

1 Introduction

Program organization is a vital issue in the construction of large software. In general, software evolves constantly in order to accommodate emerging needs that are often difficult to foresee, and the ability to effectively localize changes made to the existing programs is of great importance during software development, maintenance and evolution. Most realistic programming languages offer some forms of module system to facilitate the task of partitioning programs into manageable components and then assembling such components into a coherent whole. As experience indicates, a fundamental problem in the design of a module system lies in properly addressing the tension between the need for hiding information about a program unit from the other program units and the need for propagating information between program units. The former need helps the construction of a program unit in relative isolation and thus restricts changes in one unit to affect other units while the latter need helps the assembly of program units into a coherent whole.

A common approach to hiding implementation details is through the use abstract types [Lis86, Wir82, CDJ+89]. In type theory, existential types [MP85] are often used to give a theoretical account of abstract types. However, there is a rather unpleasant consequence with this account of abstract types. As pointed out long ago (e.g., [Mac86]), hiding type information through existential types often result in too much type information being hidden. In particular, if an existentially quantified package is opened twice, the two abstract type variables thus introduced cannot be assumed equal. As a consequence, an opened existentially quantified package often requires a usage scope so large that most

* Partially supported by NSF grants no. CCR-0229480 and no. CCF-0702665.

M.V.M. Oliveira and J. Woodcock (Eds.): SBMF 2009, LNCS 5902, pp. 336–349, 2009.

benefits of abstract types may simply be lost. This issue is certainly of great concern and there have already been many attempts to address it. In most of such attempts, some new forms of types (e.g., dependent types [Mac86], static dependent types [SG90], abstract types via dot notation [CL90], translucent sum types [HL94], manifest types [Ler94]) are introduced to overcome certain limitations of existential types in hiding type information. However, the underlying type theories for these new forms of types are often rather complicated and can become a great deal more complicated if features such as recursive modules [CHP99] and modules as first-class values [Rus00] are to be accommodated.

The primary contribution of the paper lies in a novel theoretic account of abstract types. Instead of relying on existential quantifiers, we make use of recently introduced conditional type equality [Xi04], a seemingly simple notion that we believe is of great potential. Generally speaking, conditional type equality means that type equality is determined under the assumption that certain equations on types hold. For instance, the need for conditional type equality occurs immediately once guarded recursive datatypes are made available [XCC03]. We are to argue that conditional type equality offers an effective means to hiding type information that requires no need for introducing new and unfamiliar forms of types.

We organize the rest of the paper as follows. In Section 2, we form a language $\lambda_2^{\supset}$ that supports conditional type equality and then establish the type soundness of $\lambda_2^{\supset}$, presenting a formal account of conditional type equality. We then extend $\lambda_2^{\supset}$ to $\lambda_2^{\supset}+$ to support local binding on abstract type constructors declared at top level. In Section 3, we present some examples to illustrate how certain features of modular programming can be directly supported in $\lambda_2^{\supset}+$. Lastly, we mention some related work and then conclude. As for a proof of concept, we point out that the programming language ATS [Xi] is currently under active development and its module system, which is largely based on the abstract types presented here, is already functioning.

2   Formal Development

In this section, we first present a language $\lambda_2^{\supset}$, which is largely based upon the standard second-order polymorphically typed λ-calculus, and then extend $\lambda_2^{\supset}$ to $\lambda_2^{\supset}+$ to handle local bindings on abstract type constructors. To simplify the presentation, we only consider quantification over type variables, that is, variables ranging over types, though we also allow quantification over static terms of other sorts (e.g., *bool*, *int*) in ATS. The syntax of $\lambda_2^{\supset}$ is given as follows.

types $\tau ::= \alpha \mid TC(\tau_1, \ldots, \tau_n) \mid \{l_1 : \tau_1, \ldots, l_n : \tau_n\} \mid$
$\tau_1 \to \tau_2 \mid \forall \alpha.\tau \mid \exists \alpha.\tau$

bindings $B ::= TC(\tau_1, \ldots, \tau_n) = \tau$

exp. $e ::= x \mid f \mid \{l_1 = e_1, \ldots, l_n = e_n\} \mid e.l \mid \textbf{lam } x.e \mid \textbf{fix } f.e \mid$
$\textbf{app}(e_1, e_2) \mid \forall^+(v) \mid \forall^-(e) \mid \exists(e) \mid \textbf{let } \exists(x) = e_1 \textbf{ in } e_2$

values $v ::= x \mid \{l_1 = v_1, \ldots, l_n = v_n\} \mid \textbf{lam } x.e \mid \forall^+(v) \mid \exists(v)$

$$\frac{\alpha \in \vec{\alpha}}{\vec{\alpha} \vdash \alpha : type}$$

$$\frac{TC \text{ is } n\text{-ary} \quad \vec{\alpha} \vdash \tau_1 : type \quad \cdots \quad \vec{\alpha} \vdash \tau_n : type}{\vec{\alpha} \vdash TC(\tau_1, \ldots, \tau_n) : type}$$

$$\frac{l_1, \ldots, l_n \text{ are distinct} \quad \vec{\alpha} \vdash \tau_1 : type \quad \cdots \quad \vec{\alpha} \vdash \tau_n : type}{\vec{\alpha} \vdash \{l_1 : \tau_1, \ldots, l_n : \tau_n\} : type}$$

$$\frac{\vec{\alpha} \vdash \tau_1 : type \quad \vec{\alpha} \vdash \tau_2 : type}{\vec{\alpha} \vdash \tau_1 \rightarrow \tau_2 : type}$$

$$\frac{\vec{\alpha}, \alpha \vdash \tau : type}{\vec{\alpha} \vdash \forall \alpha.\tau : type} \qquad \frac{\vec{\alpha}, \alpha \vdash \tau : type}{\vec{\alpha} \vdash \exists \alpha.\tau : type}$$

Fig. 1. The rules for forming types

We use x for a **lam**-variable and f for a **fix**-variable, and xf for either a lam-variable or a fix-variable. A **lam**-variable is a value but a **fix**-variable is not. We use TC for a type constructor of some fixed arity. Also, we use B for a binding of the form $TC(\alpha_1, \ldots, \alpha_n) = \tau$ such that the arity of TC is n and $\alpha_1, \ldots, \alpha_n \vdash \tau : type$ is derivable, and say that B is a binding on TC. It is important to notice that for each binding $TC(\alpha_1, \ldots, \alpha_n) = \tau$, every free type variable in τ must be α_i for some $1 \leq i \leq n$. We may write TC for $TC()$ if the arity of TC is 0. Also, we write $\vec{\alpha}$ for a sequence of type variables $\alpha_1, \ldots, \alpha_n$ and $\vec{B}$ for a sequence of bindings $B_1, \ldots, B_n$, and we use $\emptyset$ for the empty sequence. The rules for forming types are given in Figure 1. In particular, given a type constructor TC of arity n and types $\tau_1, \ldots, \tau_n$, we can form a type $TC(\tau_1, \ldots, \tau_n)$. We use $\{l_1 : \tau_1, \ldots, l_n : \tau_n\}$ as a type for labeled records. All other forms of types are standard.

To assign a call-by-value dynamic semantics to expressions in $\lambda_2^{\supset}$, we make use of evaluation contexts, which are defined below:

$$\text{eval. ctx. } E ::= [] \mid E.l \mid \mathbf{app}(E, d) \mid \mathbf{app}(v, E) \mid$$
$$\forall^-(E) \mid \exists(E) \mid \mathbf{let} \; \exists(x) = E \; \mathbf{in} \; e$$

Definition 1. *We define redexes and their reductions as follows.*

- $\{l_1 = v_1, \ldots, l_n = v_n\}.l_i$ *is a redex, and its reduction is* v_i, *where* $1 \leq i \leq n$.
- $\mathbf{app}(\mathbf{lam} \; x.e, v)$ *is a redex, and its reduction is* $e[x \mapsto v]$.
- $\mathbf{fix} \; f.e$ *is redex, and its reduction is* $e[f \mapsto \mathbf{fix} \; f.e]$.
- $\forall^-(\forall^+(v))$ *is a redex, and its reduction is* v.
- $\mathbf{let} \; \exists(x) = \exists(v) \; \mathbf{in} \; e$ *is a redex, and its reduction is* $e[x \mapsto v]$.

Given two expression e_1 and e_2 such that $e_1 = E[e]$ and $e_2 = E[e']$ for some redex e and its reduction e', we write $e_1 \hookrightarrow e_2$ and say that e_1 reduces to e_2 in one step. We use $\hookrightarrow^*$ for the reflexive and transitive closure of $\hookrightarrow$.

The markers $\forall^+(\cdot)$, $\forall^-(\cdot)$ and $\exists(\cdot)$ are mainly introduced to guarantee that the last rule applied in the typing derivation of an expression e be uniquely determined by the structure of e. This in turn makes it significantly easier to establish Theorem 1

$$\frac{}{\vec{B} \models \alpha \equiv \alpha} \text{ (tyeq-var)}$$

$$\frac{\vec{B} \models \tau_1' \equiv \tau_1 \quad \vec{B} \models \tau_2 \equiv \tau_2'}{\vec{B} \models \tau_1 \to \tau_2 \equiv \tau_1' \to \tau_2'} \text{ (tyeq-}\to\text{)}$$

$$\frac{\vec{B} \models \tau \equiv \tau'}{\vec{B} \models \forall \alpha.\tau \equiv \forall \alpha.\tau'} \text{ (tyeq-}\forall\text{)}$$

$$\frac{\vec{B} \models \tau \equiv \tau'}{\vec{B} \models \exists \alpha.\tau \equiv \exists \alpha.\tau'} \text{ (tyeq-}\exists\text{)}$$

$$\frac{\vec{B} \models \vec{\tau} \equiv \vec{\tau}'}{\vec{B} \models TC(\vec{\tau}) \equiv TC(\vec{\tau}')} \text{ (tyeq-tc)}$$

$$\frac{TC(\vec{\alpha}_0) = \tau_0 \text{ is in } \vec{B}}{\vec{B} \models TC(\vec{\tau}) \equiv \tau_0[\vec{\alpha}_0 \mapsto \vec{\tau}]} \text{ (tyeq-unfold)}$$

$$\frac{TC(\vec{\alpha}_0) = \tau_0 \text{ is in } \vec{B}}{\vec{B} \models \tau_0[\vec{\alpha}_0 \mapsto \vec{\tau}] \equiv TC(\vec{\tau})} \text{ (tyeq-fold)}$$

$$\frac{\vec{B} \models \tau_1 \equiv \tau_2 \quad \vec{B} \models \tau_2 \equiv \tau_3}{\vec{B} \models \tau_1 \equiv \tau_3} \text{ (tyeq-trans)}$$

Fig. 2. The rules for conditional type equality

(subject reduction) and Theorem 2 (progress). Without these markers, it would be more involved to construct proofs by structural induction on typing derivations.

A typing judgment in $\lambda_2^{\vec{\to}}$ is of the form $\vec{\alpha}; \Gamma \vdash_{\vec{B}} e : \tau$, which basically means that e can be assigned the type τ under the context $\vec{\alpha}; \Gamma$ if the type equality is decided under $\vec{B}$ through the rules presented in Figure 2. The typing rules for $\lambda_2^{\vec{\to}}$ are listed in Figure 3, where the obvious side conditions associated with certain rules are omitted. In the following presentation, we may write $\mathcal{D} :: J$ to mean that $\mathcal{D}$ is a derivation for some form of judgment J.

Example 1. Let $\vec{B}$ be $(TC = TC \to TC)$ for some type constructor TC of arity 0. Then for every pure untyped closed λ-expression e, that is, every closed expression in $\lambda_2^{\vec{\to}}$ that can be constructed in terms of **lam**-variables and **lam** and **app** constructs, the following typing judgment is derivable:

$$\emptyset; \emptyset \vdash_{\vec{B}} e : TC$$

By Theorem 2, which is to be proven shortly, the evaluation of every pure untyped closed λ-expression either terminates or goes on forever; it can never become stuck.

Of course, it is a trivial fact that the evaluation of a pure λ-expression can never become stuck, and Example 1 presents an argument for this fact in $\lambda_2^{\vec{\to}}$. Note that $\vec{B}$ in Example 1 is cyclic (according to a definition given later). In general, conditional type equality under a cyclic binding sequence may not be decidable. On the other hand, we are to prove that conditional type equality under an acyclic binding sequence is decidable.

We first show that conditional equality is an equivalence relation.

$$\frac{\vec{\alpha}; \Gamma \vdash_{\vec{B}} e : \tau \quad \vec{B} \models \tau \equiv \tau'}{\vec{\alpha}; \Gamma \vdash_{\vec{B}} e : \tau'} \text{ (ty-eq)}$$

$$\frac{\Gamma(xf) = \tau}{\vec{\alpha}; \Gamma \vdash_{\vec{B}} xf : \tau} \text{ (ty-var)}$$

$$\frac{\vec{\alpha}; \Gamma \vdash_{\vec{B}} e_1 : \tau_1 \quad \cdots \quad \vec{\alpha}; \Gamma \vdash_{\vec{B}} e_n : \tau_n}{\vec{\alpha}; \Gamma \vdash_{\vec{B}} \{l_1 = e_1, \ldots, l_n = e_n\} : \{l_1 : \tau_1, \ldots, l_n : \tau_n\}} \text{ (ty-rec)}$$

$$\frac{\vec{\alpha}; \Gamma \vdash_{\vec{B}} e : \{l_1 : \tau_1, \ldots, l_n : \tau_n\}}{\vec{\alpha}; \Gamma \vdash_{\vec{B}} e.l_i : \tau_i} \text{ (ty-sel)}$$

$$\frac{\vec{\alpha}; \Gamma, x : \tau_1 \vdash_{\vec{B}} e : \tau_2}{\vec{\alpha}; \Gamma \vdash_{\vec{B}} \mathbf{lam}\, x.e : \tau_1 \rightarrow \tau_2} \text{ (ty-lam)}$$

$$\frac{\vec{\alpha}; \Gamma, f : \tau \vdash_{\vec{B}} e : \tau}{\vec{\alpha}; \Gamma \vdash_{\vec{B}} \mathbf{fix}\, f.e : \tau} \text{ (ty-fix)}$$

$$\frac{\vec{\alpha}; \Gamma \vdash_{\vec{B}} e_1 : \tau_1 \rightarrow \tau_2 \quad \vec{\alpha}; \Gamma \vdash_{\vec{B}} e_2 : \tau_1}{\vec{\alpha}; \Gamma \vdash_{\vec{B}} \mathbf{app}(e_1, e_2) : \tau_2} \text{ (ty-app)}$$

$$\frac{\vec{\alpha}, \alpha; \Gamma \vdash_{\vec{B}} e : \tau}{\vec{\alpha}; \Gamma \vdash_{\vec{B}} \forall^+(e) : \forall \alpha.\tau} \text{ (ty-}\forall^+\text{)}$$

$$\frac{\vec{\alpha}; \Gamma \vdash_{\vec{B}} e : \forall \alpha.\tau \quad \vec{\alpha} \vdash \tau_0 : type}{\vec{\alpha}; \Gamma \vdash_{\vec{B}} \forall^-(e) : \tau[\alpha \mapsto \tau_0]} \text{ (ty-}\forall^-\text{)}$$

$$\frac{\vec{\alpha}; \Gamma \vdash_{\vec{B}} e : \tau[\alpha \mapsto \tau_0] \quad \vec{\alpha} \vdash \tau_0 : type}{\vec{\alpha}; \Gamma \vdash_{\vec{B}} \exists(e) : \exists \alpha.\tau} \text{ (ty-}\exists^+\text{)}$$

$$\frac{\vec{\alpha}; \Gamma \vdash_{\vec{B}} e_1 : \exists \alpha.\tau_1 \quad \vec{\alpha}, \alpha; \Gamma, x : \tau_1 \vdash_{\vec{B}} e_2 : \tau_2}{\vec{\alpha}; \Gamma \vdash_{\vec{B}} \mathbf{let}\, \exists(x) = e_1 \mathbf{\ in\ } e_2 : \tau_2} \text{ (ty-}\exists^-\text{)}$$

Fig. 3. The typing rules for $\lambda_2^{\supset}$

Proposition 1. *We have the following:*

1. $\vec{B} \models \tau \equiv \tau$ *for every type* τ, *and*
2. $\vec{B} \models \tau_1 \equiv \tau_2$ *implies* $\vec{B} \models \tau_2 \equiv \tau_1$ *for every pair of types* τ_1, τ_2.

Therefore, conditional type equality is an equivalence relation by (1) and (2) plus the rule **(tyeq-trans)**.

Proof. By an inspection of the rules in Figure 2.

For every $\vec{B}$, there is a corresponding term rewriting system $\mathrm{TRS}(\vec{B})$ on types such that for each binding $TC(\vec{\alpha}) = \tau$ in $\vec{B}$, there is a corresponding rewriting rule $TC(\vec{\alpha}) \Rightarrow \tau$ in $\mathrm{TRS}(\vec{B})$, and we use $\Rightarrow_{\vec{B}}$ for the rewriting relation of $\mathrm{TRS}(\vec{B})$. Obviously, the relation $\vec{B} \models \cdot \equiv \cdot$ is the least equivalence relation containing $\Rightarrow_{\vec{B}}$.

Given a sequence $\vec{B}$ of bindings $TC_1(\vec{\alpha}_1) = \tau_1, \ldots, TC_n(\vec{\alpha}_n) = \tau_n$, we say that $\vec{B}$ is linear if $TC_1, \ldots, TC_n$ are distinct from each other.

Proposition 2. *If* $\vec{B}$ *is linear, then* $\Rightarrow_{\vec{B}}$ *is confluent.*

Proof. If $\vec{B}$ is linear, then there are no critical pairs in $\mathrm{TRS}(\vec{B})$ and thus $\Rightarrow_{\vec{B}}$ is confluent.

Given a type τ, we define $\mathbf{hd}(\tau)$ to be $\{l_1,\ldots,l_n\}$, $\rightarrow$, $\forall$ and $\exists$ if τ is of the form $\{l_1 : \tau_1,\ldots,l_n : \tau_n\}$, $\tau_1 \rightarrow \tau_2$, $\forall \alpha.\tau_0$ or $\exists \alpha.\tau$, respectively, and $\mathbf{hd}(\tau)$ is undefined otherwise. Clearly, if $\tau \Rightarrow_{\vec{B}} \tau'$ and $\mathbf{hd}(\tau)$ is defined, then $\mathbf{hd}(\tau') = \mathbf{hd}(\tau)$.

Lemma 1. *Assume $\vec{B}$ is linear and $\vec{B} \models \tau_1 \equiv \tau_2$ holds for some types τ_1 and τ_2. Then $\mathbf{hd}(\tau_1) = \mathbf{hd}(\tau_2)$ if both $\mathbf{hd}(\tau_1)$ and $\mathbf{hd}(\tau_2)$ are defined.*

Proof. By Proposition 2, we know $\tau_1 \Rightarrow_{\vec{B}} \tau$ and $\tau_2 \Rightarrow_{\vec{B}} \tau$ for some type τ. Assume $\mathbf{hd}(\tau_1) = hd_1$ and $\mathbf{hd}(\tau_2) = hd_2$ for some hd_1, hd_2. Then $\mathbf{hd}(\tau) = hd_1$ and $\mathbf{hd}(\tau) = hd_2$. Hence, $hd_1 = hd_2$.

The following lemma, which is needed for proving Theorem 2, states that the form of a well-typed closed value is uniquely determined by the type τ of the value if $\mathbf{hd}(\tau)$ is defined.

Lemma 2 (Canonical Forms). *Assume $\mathcal{D} :: \emptyset; \emptyset \vdash_{\vec{B}} v : \tau$ for some linear $\vec{B}$. Then we have the following:*

1. *If $\tau = \{l_1 : \tau_1,\ldots,l_n : \tau_n\}$, then v is of the form $\{l_1 = v_1,\ldots,l_n = v_n\}$.*
2. *If $\tau = \tau_1 \rightarrow \tau_2$, then v is of the form $\mathbf{lam}\ x.e$.*
3. *If $\tau = \forall \alpha.\tau_0$, then v is of the form $\forall^+(v_0)$.*
4. *If $\tau = \exists \alpha.\tau_0$, then v is of the form $\exists(v_0)$.*

Proof. Given that the proof is a bit nonstandard, we present some details as follows. In particular, please notice the use of Lemma 1.

We prove (2) by induction on the height of $\mathcal{D}$. If the last typing rule in $\mathcal{D}$ is **(ty-lam)**, then v is obviously of the form $\mathbf{lam}\ x.e$. Otherwise, $\mathcal{D}$ is of the following form,

$$\frac{\mathcal{D}' :: \emptyset; \emptyset \vdash_{\vec{B}} v : \tau' \quad \vec{B} \models \tau' \equiv \tau}{\emptyset; \emptyset \vdash_{\vec{B}} v : \tau} \text{ (ty-eq)}$$

and, by Lemma 1, the following two subcases are the only possibilities:

- $\tau' = \tau_1' \rightarrow \tau_2'$ such that both $\vec{B} \models \tau_1' \equiv \tau_1$ and $\vec{B} \models \tau_2 \equiv \tau_2'$ are derivable. Then by induction hypothesis on $\mathcal{D}'$, we know v is of the form $\mathbf{lam}\ x.e$.
- $\tau' = TC(\vec{\tau}')$. Then $\mathcal{D}'$ must be of the form,

$$\frac{\mathcal{D}'' :: \emptyset; \emptyset \vdash_{\vec{B}} v : \tau'' \quad \vec{B} \models \tau'' \equiv \tau'}{\emptyset; \emptyset \vdash_{\vec{B}} v : \tau'} \text{ (ty-eq)}$$

and therefore, we have the following derivation $\mathcal{D}^*$ as $\vec{B} \models \tau'' \equiv \tau$ holds:

$$\frac{\mathcal{D}'' :: \emptyset; \emptyset \vdash_{\vec{B}} v : \tau'' \quad \vec{B} \models \tau'' \equiv \tau}{\emptyset; \emptyset \vdash_{\vec{B}} v : \tau} \text{ (ty-eq)}$$

Note that $\mathbf{h}(\mathcal{D}) = 1 + \mathbf{h}(\mathcal{D}^*)$. By induction hypothesis on $\mathcal{D}^*$, we know that v is of the form $\mathbf{lam}\ x.e$.

Hence, (2) holds. (1), (3) and (4) can be proven similarly.

Lemma 3 (Substitution). *We have the following.*

1. *Assume that $\vec{\alpha}, \alpha; \Gamma \vdash_{\vec{B}} e : \tau$ and $\vec{\alpha} \vdash \tau_0 : type$ are derivable. Then $\vec{\alpha}; \Gamma[\alpha \mapsto \tau_0] \vdash_{\vec{B}} e : \tau[\alpha \mapsto \tau_0]$ is derivable.*
2. *Assume that $\vec{\alpha}; \Gamma, xf : \tau_1 \vdash_{\vec{B}} e_2 : \tau_2$ and $\vec{\alpha}; \Gamma \vdash_{\vec{B}} e_1 : \tau_1$ are derivable. Then $\vec{\alpha}; \Gamma \vdash_{\vec{B}} e_2[xf \mapsto e_1] : \tau_2$ is derivable.*

Proof. By structural induction.

We are now ready to establish the soundness of the type system of $\lambda_2^{\supset}$ by proving the following theorems:

Theorem 1 (Subject Reduction). *Assume $\mathcal{D} :: \emptyset; \emptyset \vdash_{\vec{B}} e : \tau$ in $\lambda_2^{\supset}$ and $e \hookrightarrow e'$ holds. Then $\emptyset; \emptyset \vdash_{\vec{B}} e' : \tau$ is derivable.*

Proof. Assume that $e = E[e_0]$ and $e' = E[e_0']$ for some redex e_0 and its reduction e_0'. The proof proceeds by structural induction on E. In the most interesting case where $E = []$, the proof makes use of Lemma 3.

Theorem 2 (Progress). *Assume $\mathcal{D} :: \emptyset; \emptyset \vdash_{\vec{B}} e : \tau$ in $\lambda_2^{\supset}$ and $\vec{B}$ is linear. Then e is a value or $e \hookrightarrow e'$ holds for some e'.*

Proof. The theorem follows from structural induction on $\mathcal{D}$.

We now extend $\lambda_2^{\supset}$ with a language construct to support type information hiding. We use the name $\lambda_2^{\supset}+$ for this extended language, which contains the following additional syntax for forming expressions:

$$\text{exp. } e ::= \ldots \mid \textbf{assume } B \textbf{ in } (e : \tau)$$

Note that **assume** ... **in** ... corresponds to the following concrete syntax:

```
local assume ... in ... end
```

We define two functions $|\cdot|$ and $\mathbf{B}(\cdot)$ as in Figure 4. Given an expression e in $\lambda_2^{\supset}+$,

- $|e|$ is the expression in $\lambda_2^{\supset}$ obtained from erasing in e all the local bindings on abstract type constructors, and
- $\mathbf{B}(e)$ returns a sequence consisting of all the local bindings on abstract type constructors that occur in e, from left to right.

Given a sequence of bindings $\vec{B}$, then $\mathbf{dom}(\vec{B})$ is a sequence of type constructors $\overline{TC}$ defined as follows:

$$\mathbf{dom}(\emptyset) = \emptyset$$
$$\mathbf{dom}(TC(\vec{\alpha}) = \tau, \vec{B})] = TC, \mathbf{dom}(\vec{B})$$

We say $\overline{TC}$ is linear if any TC can occur at most once in $\overline{TC}$.

$$|c| = c$$
$$|xf| = xf$$
$$|\{l_1 = e_1, \ldots, l_n = e_n\}| = \{l_1 = |e_1|, \ldots, l_n = |e_n|\}$$
$$|\mathbf{lam}\ x.e| = \mathbf{lam}\ x.|e|$$
$$|\mathbf{fix}\ f.e| = \mathbf{fix}\ f.|e|$$
$$|\mathbf{app}(e_1, e_2)| = \mathbf{app}(|e_1|, |e_2|)$$
$$|\forall^+(e)| = \forall^+(|e|)$$
$$|\forall^-(e)| = \forall^-(|e|)$$
$$|\exists(e)| = \exists(|e|)$$
$$|\mathbf{let}\ \exists(x) = e_1\ \mathbf{in}\ e_2| = \mathbf{let}\ \exists(x) = |e_1|\ \mathbf{in}\ |e_2|$$
$$|\mathbf{assume}\ B\ \mathbf{in}\ (e : \tau)| = |e|$$

$$\mathbf{B}(c) = \emptyset$$
$$\mathbf{B}(xf) = \emptyset$$
$$\mathbf{B}(\{l_1 = e_1, \ldots, l_n = e_n\}) = \mathbf{B}(e_1), \ldots, \mathbf{B}(e_n)$$
$$\mathbf{B}(\mathbf{lam}\ x.e) = \mathbf{B}(e)$$
$$\mathbf{B}(\mathbf{fix}\ f.e) = \mathbf{B}(e)$$
$$\mathbf{B}(\mathbf{app}(e_1, e_2)) = \mathbf{B}(e_1), \mathbf{B}(e_2)$$
$$\mathbf{B}(\forall^+(e)) = \mathbf{B}(e)$$
$$\mathbf{B}(\forall^-(e)) = \mathbf{B}(e)$$
$$\mathbf{B}(\exists(e)) = \mathbf{B}(e)$$
$$\mathbf{B}(\mathbf{let}\ \exists(x) = e_1\ \mathbf{in}\ e_2) = \mathbf{B}(e_1), \mathbf{B}(e_2)$$
$$\mathbf{B}(\mathbf{assume}\ B\ \mathbf{in}\ (e : \tau)) = B, \mathbf{B}(e)$$

Fig. 4. Two functions on expressions in $\lambda_2^{\supset}+$

The typing rules for $\lambda_2^{\supset}+$ are given in Figure 5, where a typing judgment is of the form $\vec{\alpha}; \vec{B}; \Gamma \vdash_{\overline{TC}} e : \tau$ such that $\mathbf{dom}(\mathbf{B}(e)) = \overline{TC}$. Note that the obvious side conditions associated with certain rules are omitted. We use $\vec{B}$ for a sequence of bindings B and $\overline{TC}$ for a sequence of type constructors TC. Please note that the occurrence of $\overline{TC}$ in a typing judgment $\vec{\alpha}; \vec{B}; \Gamma \vdash_{\overline{TC}} e : \tau$ is necessary for supporting separate type-checking as it may not be realistic to assume that (the source code of) e is always available for computing $\overline{TC}$.

Theorem 3. *Assume* $\mathcal{D} :: \vec{\alpha}; \vec{B}; \Gamma \vdash_{\overline{TC}} e : \tau$ *in* $\lambda_2^{\supset}+$ *such that* $(\mathbf{dom}(\vec{B}), \overline{TC})$ *is linear. Then* $\vec{\alpha}; \Gamma \vdash_{(\vec{B}, \mathbf{B}(e))} |e| : \tau$ *is derivable in* $\lambda_2^{\supset}$.

Proof. By structural induction on $\mathcal{D}$.

Theorem 3 is the main technical result of the paper, which provides a simple and clean theoretical account of abstract types that requires no use of existential types.[1] We emphasize that the binding sequence $\vec{B}$ in Theorem 3 is only required to be linear (so that Lemma 1 can be established). In particular, because $\vec{B}$ is

---

[1] Note that the existential types in $\lambda_2^{\supset}$ are not used to represent abstract types and they can be completely eliminated if one wants to.

$$\frac{\vec{\alpha}; \vec{B}; \Gamma \vdash_{\overline{TC}} e : \tau \quad \vec{B} \models \tau \equiv \tau'}{\vec{\alpha}; \vec{B}; \Gamma \vdash_{\overline{TC}} e : \tau'} \text{ (ty-eq)}$$

$$\frac{\Gamma(xf) = \tau}{\vec{\alpha}; \vec{B}; \Gamma \vdash_{\emptyset} xf : \tau} \text{ (ty-var)}$$

$$\frac{\vec{\alpha}; \vec{B}; \Gamma \vdash_{\overline{TC}_1} e_1 : \tau_1 \quad \cdots \quad \vec{\alpha}; \vec{B}; \Gamma \vdash_{\overline{TC}_n} e_n : \tau_n}{\overline{TC} = (\overline{TC}_1, \ldots, \overline{TC}_n) \text{ is linear}}{\vec{\alpha}; \vec{B}; \Gamma \vdash_{\overline{TC}} \{l_1 = e_1, \ldots, l_n = e_n\} : \{l_1 : \tau_1, \ldots, l_n : \tau_n\}} \text{ (ty-rec)}$$

$$\frac{\vec{\alpha}; \vec{B}; \Gamma \vdash_{\overline{TC}} e : \{l_1 : \tau_1, \ldots, l_n : \tau_n\}}{\vec{\alpha}; \vec{B}; \Gamma \vdash_{\overline{TC}} e.l_i : \tau_i} \text{ (ty-sel)}$$

$$\frac{\vec{\alpha}; \vec{B}; \Gamma, x : \tau_1 \vdash_{\overline{TC}} e : \tau_2}{\vec{\alpha}; \vec{B}; \Gamma \vdash_{\overline{TC}} \mathbf{lam}\, x.e : \tau_1 \to \tau_2} \text{ (ty-lam)}$$

$$\frac{\vec{\alpha}; \vec{B}; \Gamma, f : \tau \vdash_{\overline{TC}} e : \tau}{\vec{\alpha}; \vec{B}; \Gamma \vdash_{\overline{TC}} \mathbf{fix}\, f.e : \tau} \text{ (ty-fix)}$$

$$\frac{\vec{\alpha}; \vec{B}; \Gamma \vdash_{\overline{TC}_1} e_1 : \tau_1 \to \tau_2 \quad \vec{\alpha}; \vec{B}; \Gamma \vdash_{\overline{TC}_2} e_2 : \tau_1}{(\overline{TC}_1, \overline{TC}_2) \text{ is linear}}{\vec{\alpha}; \vec{B}; \Gamma \vdash_{\overline{TC}_1, \overline{TC}_2} \mathbf{app}(e_1, e_2) : \tau_2} \text{ (ty-app)}$$

$$\frac{\vec{\alpha}, \alpha; \vec{B}; \Gamma \vdash_{\overline{TC}} e : \tau}{\vec{\alpha}; \vec{B}; \Gamma \vdash_{\overline{TC}} \forall^+(e) : \forall \alpha.\tau} \text{ (ty-}\forall^+\text{)}$$

$$\frac{\vec{\alpha}, \alpha; \vec{B}; \Gamma \vdash_{\overline{TC}} e : \forall \alpha.\tau \quad \vec{\alpha} \vdash \tau_0 : type}{\vec{\alpha}; \vec{B}; \Gamma \vdash_{\overline{TC}} \forall^-(e) : \tau[\alpha \mapsto \tau_0]} \text{ (ty-}\forall^-\text{)}$$

$$\frac{\vec{\alpha}; \vec{B}; \Gamma \vdash_{\overline{TC}} e : \tau[\alpha \mapsto \tau_0] \quad \vec{\alpha} \vdash \tau_0 : type}{\vec{\alpha}; \vec{B}; \Gamma \vdash_{\overline{TC}} \exists(e) : \exists \alpha.\tau} \text{ (ty-}\exists^+\text{)}$$

$$\frac{\vec{\alpha}; \vec{B}; \Gamma \vdash_{\overline{TC}_1} e_1 : \exists \alpha.\tau_1 \quad \vec{\alpha}, \alpha; \vec{B}; \Gamma, x : \tau_1 \vdash_{\overline{TC}_2} e_2 : \tau_2}{(\overline{TC}_1, \overline{TC}_2) \text{ is linear}}{\vec{\alpha}; \vec{B}; \Gamma \vdash_{\overline{TC}_1, \overline{TC}_2} \mathbf{let}\, \exists(x) = e_1 \mathbf{in}\, e_2 : \tau_2} \text{ (ty-}\exists^-\text{)}$$

$$\frac{\vec{\alpha}; \vec{B}, TC(\vec{\alpha}_0) = \tau_0; \Gamma \vdash_{\overline{TC}} e : \tau \quad (TC, \overline{TC}) \text{ is linear}}{\vec{\alpha}; \vec{B}; \Gamma \vdash_{TC, \overline{TC}} \mathbf{assume}\, TC(\vec{\alpha}_0) = \tau_0 \mathbf{in}\, (e : \tau) : \tau} \text{ (ty-assume)}$$

Fig. 5. The typing rules for $\lambda_2^{\supset}+$

allowed to be cyclic, Theorem 3 cannot be proven by simply "expanding out" the bindings in $\vec{B}$.

By Theorem 3, if $\emptyset; \emptyset; \emptyset \vdash_{\overline{TC}} e : \tau$ is derivable in $\lambda_2^{\supset}+$ for some linear sequence of type constructors $\overline{TC}$, then $|e|$ can be assigned the type τ in $\lambda_2^{\supset}$ under a linear sequence of bindings $\mathbf{B}(e)$. Therefore, by Theorem 2 and Theorem 1, the evaluation of $|e|$ either terminates with a value or goes on forever; it can never become stuck.

We say that $\vec{B}$ is acyclic if $\vec{B}$ is empty or $\vec{B} = (\vec{B}', TC(\alpha) = \tau)$ such that $\vec{B}'$ is acyclic and TC has no occurrences in either τ or $\vec{B}'$; otherwise, $\vec{B}$ is cyclic. Given a binding and a type τ, the type $\tau[B]$ is defined as follows:

$$\{l_1 : \tau_1, \ldots, l_n : \tau_n\}[B] = \{l_1 : \tau_1[B], \ldots, l_n : \tau_n[B]\}$$
$$(\tau_1 \to \tau_2)[B] = \tau_1[B] \to \tau_2[B]$$
$$(\forall \alpha.\tau)[B] = \forall \alpha.\tau[B]$$
$$(\exists \alpha.\tau)[B] = \exists \alpha.\tau[B]$$
$$TC(\vec{\tau})[B] = \begin{cases} \tau'[\vec{\alpha} \mapsto \vec{\tau}[B]] & \text{if } B \text{ is } TC(\vec{\alpha}) = \tau'; \\ TC(\vec{\tau}[B]) & \text{otherwise.} \end{cases}$$

Furthermore, given a sequence of bindings $\vec{B}$ and a type τ, the type $\tau[\vec{B}]$ is defined as follows:

$$\tau[\vec{B}] = \begin{cases} \tau & \text{if } \vec{B} = \emptyset; \\ \tau[B][\vec{B}'] & \text{if } \vec{B} = \vec{B}', B. \end{cases}$$

Proposition 3. *Assume $\vec{B}$ is an acyclic sequence of bindings. Then $\vec{B} \models \tau_1 \equiv \tau_2$ if and only if $\tau_1[\vec{B}] = \tau_2[\vec{B}]$ holds.*

Proof. Straightforward.

Therefore, conditional type equality under an acyclic sequence of bindings can be readily decided. As a design choice, we may simply not allow the use cyclic binding sequences and thus guarantee the decidability of conditional type equality. Whether this choice is too restrictive to support some useful programming styles still needs to be investigated further. We have so far encountered no realistic cases where cyclic sequences of bindings are needed. An argument for this can probably be made as follows. Note that typing the code like the following does not involve cyclic binding sequences:

```
local assume TC1 = TC2 -> TC2 in ... end
local assume TC2 = TC1 -> TC1 in ... end
```

as the two bindings can never be joined together for deciding type equality. A probably more convincing argument is that we can readily handle the need for splitting mutually defined datatypes, as is to be shown in the next section, with no need for cyclic binding sequences.

Given an expression e in $\lambda_2^{\rightarrow}$, there is in general no principal type for e. For instance, in the following example:

```
abstract PairType: (type, type) -> type

local
  assume PairType (a1, a2) = a2 * a1
in
  fun makePair (x: a1, y: a2) = (y, x)
  ...
end
```

the function *makePair* can be given either the type $\forall \alpha_1.\forall \alpha_2.\alpha_1 * \alpha_2 \to \alpha_2 * \alpha_1$ or the type $\forall \alpha_1.\forall \alpha_2.\alpha_1 * \alpha_2 \to PairType(\alpha_1, \alpha_2)$, which are considered equivalent in the scope of the binding $PairType(\alpha_1, \alpha_2) = \alpha_2 * \alpha_1$; however, these two types become unrelated out of the scope. In such a case, it is the responsibility of the programmer to determine through the use of type annotation which type should be assigned to $makePair$.[2]

3   Examples

In practice, we have frequently encountered the demand for recursive modules, which are unfortunately not supported in the module system of SML [MTHM97]. When forming recursive modules, we often need to split recursively defined datatypes. For instance, we first present a definition for two datatypes $boolexp$ and $intexp$ in Figure 6 that are intended for representing boolean and integer expressions, respectively. We then show how two abstract types $boolexp\_t$ and $intexp\_t$ can be introduced to split the definition into two. In practice, we may declare $boolexp\_t$ and $intexp\_t$ in a header file and put the two new definitions

```
datatype boolexp =
  | Bool of bool | IntEq of (intexp, intexp)

and intexp =
  | Int of int | Cond of (boolexp, intexp, intexp)

// in the file exp.sats

abstype boolexp_t
abstype intexp_t

// in the file boolexp.dats

datatype boolexp =
  | Bool of bool | IntEq of (intexp_t, intexp_t)

assume boolexp_t = boolexp

// in the file intexp.dats

datatype intexp =
  | Int of int | Cond of (boolexp_t, intexp_t, intexp_t)

assume intexp_t = intexp
```

Fig. 6. A splitting of mutually defined datatypes

---

[2] In an implementation, one may use a strategy that always expands an abstract type constructor if no type annotation is given. In the case of $makePair$, this means that the type $\forall \alpha_1. \forall \alpha_2. \alpha_1 * \alpha_2 \to \alpha_2 * \alpha_1$ should be assigned to $makePair$.

in two other files. If, say, the definition of *intexp* needs to be modified later, the modification cannot affect the definition of *boolexp*. While this approach to splitting the definition of mutually defined datatypes may look exceedingly simple, it does not seem simple at all to justify the approach through the use of existential types (or similar variants). On the other hand, a justification based on conditional type equality can be given straightforwardly. Furthermore, it is probably fair to say now that the notion of conditional type equality can also significantly influence the design of module systems.

4   Related Work and Conclusion

There have been a large number of proposals for modular programming, and it is evidently impossible for us to mention even a moderate portion of these proposals here. Instead, we focus on the line of work centered around the module system of Standard ML (SML) [MTHM97], which primarily aims at setting up a theoretical foundation for modular programming based on type theories.

Type abstraction, which can be used to effectively isolate or localize changes made to existing programs, has now become one of the most widely used techniques in specifying and constructing large software systems [GHW85, Lis86]. In [MP88], a theoretical account of abstract types is given through the use of existential types. While this account is largely satisfactory in explaining the features of abstract types, it does not properly address the issue of type equality involving abstract types. Motivated by problems with existential types in modeling abstract types, MacQueen [Mac86] proposed an alternative approach in which abstract types are modeled as a form of dependent sum types, taking into account the issue of type equality involving abstract types. However, in the presence of such dependent sum types, type equality is greatly complicated, and it becomes even more complicated when features such as polymorphism, generativity, higher-order modules and modules as first-class values need to be accommodated. As a compromise between existential types and dependent sum types, translucent sum types [HL94, Lil97] and manifest types [Ler94] were proposed to better address the issue of hiding type information. There is already a considerable amount of work that studies how these new forms of types can be used to address generativity and applicativity, higher-order modules, recursive modules, modules as first-class values, etc. [Ler95, DCH03, CHP99, Rus01]. There is also work on expressing modular structures in SML and Haskell with only existential types [Rus00, SJ02].

Though the notion of conditional type equality seems surprisingly simple, it had not been recognized in clear terms until recently. We first encountered the notion of conditional type equality in a recent study on guarded recursive datatypes [XCC03].[3] This notion has since been generalized in the framework Applied Type System [Xi04].

---

[3] In Dependent ML (DML) [XP99, Xi98], the type equality may also be classified as conditional type equality. However, the conditions involved are on type indexes rather than on types as in the case of guarded recursive datatypes.

The major contribution of the paper lies in the recognition and the formalization of a simple and clean theoretic account of abstract types that is based on conditional type equality. In particular, we make no use of existentially quantified types in this account of abstract types, thus completely avoiding the well-known problems associated with the use of existentially quantified types in modeling abstract types. We claim that the presented approach to hiding type information through conditional equality is simple as well as general and it opens a promising avenue for the design and implementation of module systems in support of large-scale programming. As for a proof of concept, we point out that the module system of ATS, which is largely based on $\lambda_2^{\rightarrow}+$, is already functioning.[4]

Acknowledgments. The author acknowledges some discussion with Chiyan Chen, Assaf Kfoury, Likai Liu, Mark Sheldon and Franklyn Turbak on the subject of the paper. The research conducted in this paper has been supported in part by NSF grants no. CCR-0229480 and no. CCF-0702665.

References

[CDJ+89]   Cardelli, L., Donahue, J., Jordan, M., Kalso, B., Nelson, G.: The Modula-3 Type System. In: Proceedings of 16th Annual ACM Symposium on Principles of Programming Languages (POPL 1989), Austin, TX, January 1989, pp. 202–212 (1989)

[CHP99]   Crary, K., Harper, R., Puri, S.: What is a recursive module? In: SIGPLAN Conference on Programming Language Design and Implementation (PLDI 1999), June 1999, pp. 56–63 (1999)

[CL90]   Cardelli, L., Leroy, X.: Abstract Types and the Dot Notation. Technical Report 56, DEC SRC (1990)

[DCH03]   Dreyer, D., Crary, K., Harper, R.: A Type System for Higher-Order Modules. In: Proceedings of 30th Annual ACM SIGPLAN Symposium on Principles of Programming Languages (POPL 2003), New Orleans, LA, January 2003, pp. 236–249 (2003)

[GHW85]   Guttag, J.V., Horning, J.J., Wing, J.M.: The Larch Family of Specification Languages. IEEE Software 2(5), 24–36 (1985)

[HL94]   Harper, R.W., Lillibridge, M.: A type-theoretic approach to higher-order modules with sharing. In: Proceedings of 21st Annual ACM SIGPLAN Symposium on Principles of Programming Languages (POPL 1994), Portland, Oregon, pp. 123–137 (1994)

[Ler94]   Leroy, X.: Manifest Types, Modules, and Separate Compilation. In: Proceeding of 21st Annual ACM Conference on Principles of Programming lanugages (POPL 1994), Porland, OR (January 1994)

[Ler95]   Leroy, X.: Aplicative functors and fully transparent higher-order modules. In: Proceedings of 22nd ACM SIGPLAN Symposium on Principles of Programming Languages (POPL 1995), San Francisco, CA, January 1995, pp. 142–153 (1995)

---

[4] The current implementation of ATS is named *Anairiats*, which is documented and freely accessible to the public [Xi].

[Lil97]   Lillibridge, M.: Translucent Sums: A Foundation for Higher-Order Module Systems. Ph. D. dissertation, Carnegie Mellon University (May 1997)

[Lis86]   Liskov, B.: Abstraction and Specification in Program Development. MIT Press, Cambridge (1986)

[Mac86]   MacQueen, D.B.: Using Dependent Types to Express Modular Structure. In: Proceeding of 13th Annual ACM Symposium on Principles of Programming Languages, St. Petersburg Beach, FL, pp. 277–286 (1986)

[MP85]   Mitchell, J.C., Plotkin, G.D.: Abstract types have existential type. In: Proceedings of 12th Annual ACM Symposium on Principles of Programming Languages (POPL 1985), New Orleans, Louisiana, pp. 37–51 (1985)

[MP88]   Mitchell, J.C., Plotkin, G.D.: Abstract types have existential type. ACM Transactions on Programming Languages and Systems 10(3), 470–502 (1988)

[MTHM97]   Milner, R., Tofte, M., Harper, R.W., MacQueen, D.: The Definition of Standard ML (Revised). MIT Press, Cambridge (1997)

[Rus00]   Russo, C.V.: First-Class Structures for Standard ML. Nordic Journal of Computing 7(4), 348–374 (2000)

[Rus01]   Russo, C.V.: Recursive Structures for Standard ML. In: Proceedings of International Conference on Functional Programming, September 2001, pp. 50–61 (2001)

[SG90]   Sheldon, M.A., Gifford, D.K.: Static Dependent Types for First-Class Modules. In: Proceedings of ACM Conference on Lisp and Functional Programming, pp. 20–29 (1990)

[SJ02]   Shields, M., Jones, S.P.: First-class modules for haskell. In: Proceedings of 9th International Workshop on Foundations of ObjectOriented Languages (FOOL 9), Portland, OR (January 2002)

[Wir82]   Wirth, N.: Programming with Modula-2. Texts and Monographs in Computer Science. Springer, Heidelberg (1982)

[XCC03]   Xi, H., Chen, C., Chen, G.: Guarded Recursive Datatype Constructors. In: Proceedings of the 30th ACM SIGPLAN Symposium on Principles of Programming Languages, New Orleans, LA, pp. 224–235. ACM press, New York (2003)

[Xi]   Xi, H.: The ATS Programming Language, http://www.ats-lang.org/

[Xi98]   Xi, H.: Dependent Types in Practical Programming. PhD thesis, Carnegie Mellon University (1998), viii+181 pp. pp. viii+189, http://www.cs.cmu.edu/~hwxi/DML/thesis.ps

[Xi04]   Xi, H.: Applied Type System (extended abstract). In: Berardi, S., Coppo, M., Damiani, F. (eds.) TYPES 2003. LNCS, vol. 3085, pp. 394–408. Springer, Heidelberg (2004)

[XP99]   Xi, H., Pfenning, F.: Dependent Types in Practical Programming. In: Proceedings of 26th ACM SIGPLAN Symposium on Principles of Programming Languages, pp. 214–227. ACM Press, San Antonio (1999)

Author Index